J. EDGAR HOOVER

The Father of the Cold War

**How His Obsession with Communism Led to the Warren
Commission Coverup and Escalation of the Vietnam War**

R. Andrew Kiel

University Press of America, ® Inc.
Lanham • New York • Oxford

Copyright © 2000 by
University Press of America,® Inc.
4720 Boston Way
Lanham, Maryland 20706

12 Hid's Copse Rd.
Cumnor Hill, Oxford OX2 9JJ

Library of Congress Cataloging-in-Publication Data

Kiel, R. Andrew
J. Edgar Hoover : the father of the Cold War : how his obsession
with communism led to the Warren Commission coverup and
escalation of the Vietnam War / R. Andrew Kiel.
p.   cm.
Includes bibiographical references and index.
1.   Hoover, J. Edgar (John Edgar), 1895-1972. 2. Subversive activities—
United States—History—20th century. 3. Communism—
United States—History—20th century. 4. Cold War. 5. Kennedy, John F. (John
Fitzgerald), 1917-1963—Assassination. 6. United States. Warren Commission. 7.
Vietnamese Conflict, 1961-1975—United States. 8. United States. Federal Bureau of
Investigation—History—20th century. I. Title
E743.5.K48   2001   363.25'092—dc21   00—044331 CIP
(B)

ISBN 0-7618-1762-X (cloth: alk. ppr.)

⊖™ The paper used in this publication meets the minimum
requirements of American National Standard for Information
Sciences—Permanence of Paper for Printed Library Materials,
ANSI Z39.48—1984

Dedicated to

My wife,

Debbie

Contents

Foreword   ix

Preface   xiii

Acknowledgements and Use of Sources   xv

Introduction   xix

Part 1   **The Father of the Cold War:
                    Hoover's Obsession With
                    Communism**

  Chapter 1   **Historiographical Comparison of   3
                    Research on J. Edgar Hoover**

  Chapter 2   **Communism and Hoover: 15
                    How They Emerged Together**

  Chapter 3   **The Palmer Raids**   29

  Chapter 4   **Consolidating and Expanding   41
                    Hoover's Power at the Bureau**

  Chapter 5   **Hoover at the Peak of His Influence   61
                    on the Anti-Communist Movement**

Chapter 6   **Hoover and John Kennedy**   **73**

Part 2   **Obstruction of Justice:**
The Warren Commission Coverup

Chapter 7   **The Communists**   **127**
or the Right-Wing

Chapter 8   **Lee Harvey Oswald, the**   **143**
"Lone Communist Assassin"

Chapter 9   **The Altering of Evidence**   **179**
The Intimidation of Witnesses
And the Single Bullet Theory

Chapter 10   **Hoover and Johnson:**   **213**
Obstruction of Justice

Chapter 11   **"Those Who Were There**   **229**
Were Wrong and Confused"

Chapter 12   **Jack Ruby, the Middle Man**   **255**

Chapter 13   **The Autopsy and the Secret**   **281**
Service

Chapter 14   **Conclusion of Obstruction of**   **311**
Justice

Part 3   **Escalation of the Vietnam War**

Chapter 15   **Vietnam: A Historical Overview**   **341**

Chapter 16   **The Formation of Policy Views**   **355**
on Vietnam by Kennedy and
Johnson

Chapter 17   **"They Are the Ones Who Have to**   **369**
Win It or Lose It"

Chapter 18   **A Clean Break**   **413**

Conclusion   437

End Notes   479

Index   567

Foreword

R. Andrew Kiel's study of J. Edgar Hoover and his near half century as Director of the FBI is as exciting as a good crime novel, and one can hardly help wishing that a fiction of some kind is what it really was, happy to praise any imagination that could dream up a character as Gothically improbable as Hoover.

As it is, of course, the nightmare in question was not only an actual person but one who, alas, somehow came to be the head of our nation's most powerful police force, a position he held for nearly a half century before dying on the job.

Kiel's remarkable new book shows us that the man who for so long ran the FBI appears to have had his own private agenda. He had no use for *détente*, consistently wanting the Cold War to deepen. He favored escalation of the Vietnam War, treating those who opposed the war with hostility and contempt. He sat on strong evidence that the JFK assassination was carried out by a conspiracy rooted in the Mafia and, as Kiel shows, all too probably involving elements of the U.S. Military.

Indeed, Hoover's FBI consistently projected a reactionary image. If you were active in the cause of civil rights or in opposition to the Vietnam War, you simply learned to assume that you were under surveillance, that your meetings were attended by someone only pretending to be a friend, by

someone on assignment, there to find out how numerous you
were, what you were saying to one another, and what you
were planning to do. When you reached a little higher level of
involvement, it was safe to bet that your phone was tapped.

All thanks to Hoover.

The prevalence of such imagery in fact may be among the
more destructive effects of Hoover's long reign. Because of
him, perhaps hundreds of thousands of innocent Americans
routinely assume that the FBI keeps files on them for the
least political activity outside the framework of the two-party
system.

And yet the JFK assassination remains one of the pivotal
events of modern American history precisely because Hoover's
FBI, with its vaunted powers of investigation, refused to
respond to the many strands of evidence that pointed to
conspiracy. Indeed, Kiel's powerful reexamination of the case
makes us wonder if this failure was on purpose.

The House Select Committee on Assassinations that set
out in 1976 to rebut the Warren Commission's many critics
ended by joining them instead, concluding that JFK was
"probably" killed not by a lone nut but by a conspiracy of
unknown dimensions.

And there, since then, the case has moldered.

Kiel's book is essential reading for anyone who wants to
understand these themes as well as the Cold War as a whole,
the Vietnam War, the Red-scare era, the role played in our
national life by organized crime, military cabals, and what
has sometimes constituted virtually a secret state.

Kiel has surveyed a forbiddingly vast literature on his
subject to establish a solid foundation for his own original
research. Making use of the Freedom of Information Act and
numerous interviews with people having direct knowledge of
Hoover's career, Kiel has assembled here a compelling
narrative without the least display of sensationalism or
sacrifice of rigorous academic standards. What he shows us is
that Hoover, our nation's principal lawman, was critically
involved in the concealment of the truth about the
assassination. Indeed, Kiel shows that the Dallas Police
Department, the FBI, and the Warren Commission knew for a
fact that Kennedy was killed by a shot fired from the
celebrated grassy knoll, therefore by someone other than Lee
Harvey Oswald. Kiel shows as well that the official effort to
conceal this fact could never have succeeded without Hoover's

direct and sustained intervention. Our nation's chief lawman appears to have been an accessory after the fact of the crime of the century.

As Kiel's monumental up-date of the case makes powerfully clear, the JFK assassination is the most important single event in American history since the end of World War II. Until we know who did it and why J. Edgar Hoover killed the investigation, our belief that we are a self-governing people belongs with our faith in the tooth fairy.

Kiel's book is frightening, as I said before, but it is also exciting because it puts so clearly before us, and in such fresh and cogent detail, the reasons why we need to be concerned about the condition of our national police force. Hoover has gone, true, but the system he installed still bears the imprint of his heavy hand.

Carl Oglesby
Cambridge, Massachusetts

April 10, 2000

Preface

There have literally been thousands of books written about the Cold War, Vietnam, and the assassination of President Kennedy. Yet as one who is a product of the times that created these events, I have not been completely receptive as to the veracity of how these events have been portrayed in the history books of today. As an instructor of American History at the secondary and post-secondary level for twenty years, I believe a more accurate portrayal of how these events transpired needs to be presented and considered before the 'historical record' is etched in stone.

Ultimately, this research argues that from 1917 until his death in 1972, J. Edgar Hoover's obsession with Communism worked to shape the public and private policies of presidents, military and intelligence officials, and congressional decision-makers. The true nature of these relationships and activities are still not clear to us today. But the ramifications of Hoover's influence has been felt not only by those who held high positions of power but by all Americans. Obstruction of justice by Lyndon Johnson and J. Edgar Hoover and the escalation of the Vietnam War are but two of the "known" results of Hoover's obsession with Communism.

We, as Americans, need to face the reality of the record presented here and move on to replace the suspicions and doubts that have been allowed to fester as a result of J. Edgar

Hoover's public as well as private role as *The Father of the Cold War.*

R. Andrew Kiel

March 30, 2000

Acknowledgements and Use of Sources

The original inspiration for this research comes from the many writers, researchers and professors who have caused me to question certain aspects of our "official" historical record. Original and primary research was carried out at The National Archives in Washington and College Park, The John F. Kennedy Library in Boston, The Federal Bureau of Investigation FOIA Reading Room at Headquarters in Washington, The Assassination Archives and Research Center in Washington, The ASK Symposium held in Dallas (1993), and the COPA conference also held in Dallas (1998). This research has also brought me into contact with many of the authors and researchers mentioned below as well as numerous witnesses to the assassination who were in attendance at the COPA and ASK conferences. The list is too numerous to name all, but the following is a list (in no particular order) of those whose research, memoirs, etc. have contributed to the three parts found in this work.

Part One: The Father of the Cold War:
              Hoover's Obsession With Communism

Ovid Demaris, Curt Gentry, Fred Cook, Anthony Summers, Richard Powers, Athan Theoharis, William Turner, Hank Messick, Robert Unger, Sanford Unger, John Stuart Cox,

John Bartlow Martin, Nina Burleigh, Anthony Lewis, Arthur Schlesinger, Tip O'Neil, Larry O'Brien, Dave Powers, Ken O'Donnell and Mark North.

Part Two: Obstruction of Justice:
             The Warren Commission Coverup

David Scheim, Dick Russell, Seth Kantor, Penn Jones, Vincent Palamara, Harold Weisberg, Jim Garrison, Thomas Buchanan, Sylvia Meagher, Mark Lane, Robert Groden, Harrison Livingstone, Mark Oakes, Edward Epstein, Stewart Galanor, Richard Dudman, Anthony Summers, Phillip Melanson, Gaeton Fonzi, Oliver Stone, Fletcher Prouty, Peter Dale Scott, Jim Marrs, Bernard Fensterwald, David Lifton, James Folliard, Joachem Joesten, Gary Shaw, Jim Lesar, John Tunheim, William Sullivan, Bill Sloan, Jack White, Josiah Thompson, Gary Mack and Carl Ogelsby.

Part Three :   Escalation of the Vietnam War

David Halberstam, Ted Sorensen, Robert McNamara, Stanley Karnow, Robert Caro, John Newman, George Herring, Gary Olsen, Lee Riley Powell, Doris Kearns Goodwin, Arthur Schlesinger, George Ball, William Colby, Admiral Grant Sharp, Henry Cabot Lodge, General Maxwell Taylor, General Tran Van Don, General James Gavin, Barry Goldwater, Dean Rusk, John Kenneth Galbraith, General William Westmoreland, Jack Anderson, Walter Cronkite, Tom Wicker, General Mathew Ridgway and John Connally.

Professors who have helped to inspire and/or critique my research (Culver-Stockton College and the University of Akron):

Dr. John Sperry, Dr. Frank Edgar, Dr. Edward Sawyer, Dr. Roger Grant, Dr. David Kyvig, Dr. Sheldon Liss, Dr. Constance Bouchard, Dr. Barbara Clements and Dr. Walter Hixon.

Many thanks to friends and family who have supported me in various ways in the completion of this project over the years:

Albert and Marilyn Kiel, Debbie Kiel, Larry Atchison, Alan

Lang, Jamie Miller, Terry Angert, Dwight Boss and Brian Questel. This project could never have been completed without the hard work and patience of my typist Shirley Raymond and her husband Pete.

A special thanks to the following for help in various aspects of my research: Robert Korpus, Dr. Walter Hixon, Jim Lesar, Carl Ogelsby, Don Adams and Dan Moldea.

Sources with abbreviations:

FRUS: Foreign Relations Series of the United States State Department (documents relating to US policy in Vietnam).

WR: The Official Warren Commission Report on the Assassination of President John F. Kennedy (New York: Doubleday, 1964).

1 H 123 (ex. of) Record of the Warren Commission Hearings, Volume, and page. Report of the President's Commission on the Assassination of President John F. Kennedy, and 26 volumes of Hearings and Exhibits, U. S. Government Printing Office, Washington, D.C., 1964.

CD: (Warren) Commission Document and page.

CE: (Warren) Commission Exhibit and page.

HSCA 1 H 123 (ex. of) Volume and page. Report of the Select Committee on Assassinations (12 volumes relating to John F. Kennedy's assassination) and volumes of Hearings and Appendices, U.S. Government Printing Office, Washington, D.C. 1979.

AJ and DJ: Attorney's General files and Department of Justice files with document numbers, etc. where available (FBI FOIA Reading Room and National Archives).

ARRB: Assassination Records and Review Board Final Report. U. S. Government Printing Office, Washington, D.C., 1998.

COPA: Coalition on Political Assassinations, Dallas, Tex., 1998.

Introduction

When one stops to consider those individuals and movements that have helped to shape the course of twentieth century American history, John Edgar Hoover and the Cold War must be at the forefront. Arguably, no single person has had as much of a consistent and sustained effect on American foreign and domestic policy than J. Edgar Hoover. Hoover's Cold War was always there. It became his vehicle for power and influence over a period that covered fifty-five years and ten presidents. Communism might change but Hoover's ideas about it never would. In 1969, Hoover was still citing texts he had written in 1919 as a blueprint for the "nation's response to Communism." (1) The commonly held perception is that the Cold War began after WWII; this research argues that Hoover began his Cold War almost thirty years earlier. The introduction to Hoover's book, *On Communism* supports this belief:

> Mr. J. Edgar Hoover, the Director of the Federal Bureau of Investigation, is the nations's foremost authority on the danger of communism within the borders of the United States. Mr. Hoover, as a young attorney in 1919 for the Department of Justice, studied the earliest documents of communism to prepare legal briefs for the Attorney General. Since 1924, as head of the FBI, Mr. Hoover has followed closely the ramifications of this conspiracy. No man in

American can claim a greater knowledge of this twentieth-century conspiracy. (2)

The ways and means of how J. Edgar Hoover would wage his fifty-five year battle against Communism is of prime importance to this research. How he used the accumulation of "political information" (secret files) and its subsequent disclosure in his Cold War is documented here. Although Assistant FBI Director's Cartha DeLoach and John Mohr deny there were any secret files, the consistent recollections of many reputable insiders included in this research argues strongly against this. The immediate actions and the statements of Richard Nixon and his staff demonstrate this further. Former FBI agent and Watergate participant G. Gordon Liddy recalled that upon hearing of Hoover's death, "I called the White House at once, I said, You've got to get those files. They are a source of enormous power. You don't have much time. There's going to be a race on. Get those files." (3) Emanuel Celler was the chairman of the House Judiciary for over twenty of the forty years that he served in the House. He was a long time friend of J. Edgar Hoover but he also knew the reality of Hoover's power:

> The source of his power derived from the fact that he was the head of an agency that in turn had tremendous power, power of surveillance, power of control over the lives and destinies of every man in the nation. He had a dossier on every member of Congress and every member of the Senate. . . . He had no right to have such dossiers. But he had them, no question about it. (4)

Who ended up with the files and what ultimately happened to them is not clear and open to debate. But it is difficult to deny their existence and the fear they generated.

From the Palmer Raids, the Dies Committee, and the House Committee on Un-American Activities, Hoover's anti-communist stance was set. Through World War I, World War II, Korea, and Vietnam, "his presence and counsel" perpetuated the Cold War. His relations with Presidents Wilson, Harding, Coolidge, Hoover, Roosevelt, Truman, Eisenhower, Kennedy, Johnson, and Nixon were most often based on their stances on Communism. As the decades passed and Hoover became entrenched as head of the Federal Bureau of Investigation, he defied Presidents that he considered to be "soft on Communism." His public reputation, as the nation's foremost defender of America versus the threat of Communism, was rarely doubted. As Richard Nixon stated on the floor of the House in January 1950 following his successful prosecution of Alger Hiss, "We must give complete and unqualified support to the FBI and J. Edgar Hoover, its Chief. Mr. Hoover recognized the Communist threat long before other top officials recognized its existence." (5)

Public cracks in Hoover's armor were few and far between after the Palmer Raid investigations of the early 1920's until 1950, when Max Lowenthal published a critical book entitled, *The Federal Bureau of Investigation.* Similarly, Fred Cook's *The FBI Nobody Knows*, published in 1964, caused Hoover to be concerned about his future. Criticism of Hoover and the FBI slowly began to increase until public calls for his resignation became louder. In April 1971, House Majority Leader Hale Boggs delivered a major speech on the floor of the House which described Hoover's "Gestapo tactics" and his need to resign. (6) *Time* magazine devoted its May 10, 1971 cover story to the same theme.

One of the best examples of the power, influence, and fear generated by Hoover is found in a series of conversations involving President Nixon which were uncovered during the Watergate investigation. October 1971:

> *Richard Nixon:* For a lot of reasons he (Hoover) oughta resign.
> . . . maybe I could just call him and talk him into resigning. . .
> . There are some problems. . . . If he does go he's got to go of
> his own volition. . . . that's why we're in a hell of a problem. . .
> . I think he'll stay until he's a hundred years old.
> *John Mitchell:* He'll stay until he's buried there. Immortality
> . . .
> *Richard Nixon:* I think we've got to avoid the situation where
> he can leave with a blast. . . . We may have on our hands here
> a man who will pull down the temple with him, including me.
> . . . It's going to be a problem. (7)

The subsequent pardon that Gerald Ford gave to Richard Nixon for any crimes "he might have committed," makes Nixon's statement about "temples" open to speculation. It has never been made clear what "temples" that Nixon was concerned with but he never did force a showdown with Hoover.

Even after Hoover's death, in May of 1972, it is quite clear from the following statement, that J. Edgar Hoover had been overtly and covertly shaping American governmental policy for many years and his ability to get things done was respected by many but his methods were feared by all. February 1973: Richard Nixon: "Hoover performed. He would have fought. That was the point. He would have defied a few people. He would have scared them to death. He had a file on everybody." (8)

In reassessing J. Edgar Hoover and his role as *Father of the Cold War*, one must seriously question whether Hoover really wanted to destroy domestic Communism or did he intend to have it remain a permanent enemy in order to justify the FBI's need to investigate it? Could he not or would he not see that Communism was not monolithic and American-style capitalism and democracy were not always the best and immediate solutions for the impoverished and weak nations? It is apparent that Hoover consistently overstated the threat of domestic Communism while also refusing to seriously consider that Communism was not a centrally planned world conspiracy.

The most intriguing question in this study involves J. Edgar Hoover and the FBI's work for the Warren Commission. There is much hypothesis as well as documentation to question Hoover's role as a seeker of the truth in this investigation as Warren Commission Assistant Counsel David Slawson makes clear:

> I understood immediately that part of my assignment would be to suspect everyone. So included in that would be the . . . FBI. . . . We would sometimes speculate as to what would happen if we got firm evidence that pointed to some very high official. [deleted] Of course that would present a kind of frightening prospect because if the President [Johnson] or anyone else that high up [Hoover] was indeed involved in Kennedy's assassination, they clearly were not going to allow someone like us to bring out the truth if they could stop us. (9)

A concern that J. Edgar Hoover and/or Lyndon Johnson were taking control of the investigation and away from the Dallas Police Department on the day of the assassination is supported by Dallas Police Chief Jesse Curry:

> We got several calls insisting we send this [evidence to Washington], and nobody would tell me exactly who it was that was insisting. "[J]ust say I got a call from Washington, and they wanted this evidence up there," insinuating it was

someone in high authority that was requesting this, and we finally agreed. . . . (10)

Warren Commission Staff Counsel Melvin Eisenberg and Earl Warren were concerned with the very real possibility that some unknown forces were responsible for John Kennedy's death and Lyndon Johnson's rise to the presidency:

> . . . rumors of the most exaggerated kind were circulating in this country and overseas. . . . Some rumors went as far as attributing the assassination to a faction within the government wishing the presidency assumed by President Johnson. (11)

Richard Nixon stated to J. Edgar Hoover during a phone conversation on the day of the assassination, "What happened? Was it one of the right wing nuts?" Hoover replied, "No, it was a Communist." (12) Hoover's position never changed despite evidence compiled to the contrary by his own Bureau as well as the conclusions put forth by the House Select Committee on Assassinations. The Committee concluded in 1979, that JFK was probably killed by a conspiracy. It is not clear why the findings of the House Select Committee have been virtually ignored while the findings of the Warren Report are still considered to have the official sanction of the U. S. Government today. These opposite conclusions from two investigations sanctioned by the government have never been reconciled.

Senator Richard Schweiker, Republican member of the Church Committee and the House Select Committee investigations concluded:

> I believe that the Warren Commission was set up at the time to feed Pablum to the American people for reasons not yet known and that one of the biggest cover-ups in the history of our country occurred at that time. (13)

If Lee Harvey Oswald was really the communist-inspired assassin of an American President (as Hoover's investigation stated) and was aided by the Cubans and/or the Soviets, then why was this golden opportunity to destroy Communism once and for all, passed up? The concern of Oswald being inspired by Moscow or Havana in a Communist plot lost its importance very early in the investigation although Lyndon Johnson continued to promote this version. Johnson told Earl Warren that we could have nuclear war, "if the public became aroused against Khrushchev and Castro." (14) It appears that heading off any other investigations (which were pending by Congress and the State of Texas) and ensuring that the "public be satisfied that Oswald was the lone assassin," as Hoover directed to Assistant Attorney General Nicholas Katzenbach, became most important. (15) Assistant FBI Director William Sullivan stated that Hoover leaked the FBI report of Oswald's guilt within one week of the murder "to blunt the drive for an independent investigation of the assassination." (16) Hoover himself stated on November 29th, that "The President stated he wanted to get by with my file and my report. I told him it was very bad to have of a rash of investigations." (17)

This research analyzes the extensive political and policy influence of J. Edgar Hoover during his campaign to defeat Communism. Hoover's fanatical and obsessive fifty-five year career as the leader of the anti-communist movement, marks a period of influence and dominance seldom if ever seen in American history. There is little doubt that the communist threat to the United States was very real at various points since 1917, and it can also be argued that the times of Hoover helped to create his Cold War. But it is difficult to justify Hoover's continued assault on the Constitution and its democratic ideals in pursuit of communists, especially if it involves a very real possibility of obstruction of justice in Hoover's Warren Commission investigation.

The Warren Report was released in September, less than two months before the 1964 Presidential election. The House Select Committee on Assassinations concluded:

> that the time pressures under which the Warren Commission investigation was conducted served to compromise the work product and the conclusions of the Commission. . . . President Johnson, among others in his administration, was anxious to have the investigation completed in advance of the 1964 Presidential conventions, out of concern that the assassination could become a political issue. (18)

Wittingly or unwittingly, Hoover helped to legitimize Lyndon Johnson's election as the "peace candidate" in the 1964 election versus Barry Goldwater.

Whether J. Edgar Hoover knowingly and willfully allowed the Warren Report coverup to take place with the intention of helping Lyndon Johnson to become president and expanding

the Vietnam War is impossible to prove. Did Hoover know
that Johnson would take a stronger stance on Vietnam and
the anti-communist cause? A very strong case can be made
for this being true. It was common knowledge among those
close to Kennedy and Johnson that Johnson favored a
stronger U. S. policy in Vietnam and against Communism in
general. Secretary of Defense Robert McNamara stated:

> Johnson was convinced that the Soviet Union and China were
> bent on achieving hegemony. Johnson felt more certain than
> President Kennedy that the loss of South Vietnam had a
> higher cost than would the direct application of United States
> military force, and it was this view that shaped him and his
> policy decisions for the next five years. (19)

It would have been far easier for those, such as McNamara, to
state that John Kennedy would have continued the escalation
process and committed over 500,000 combat troops into
Vietnam. For McNamara, as well as many others, endured
tremendous criticism as a result of their decisions to escalate.
But the record presented here does not support the view that
Kennedy's course was continued by Lyndon Johnson.

This research argues that although John Kennedy held
strong anti-communist views, it is extremely doubtful that he
would have escalated the Vietnam War as Johnson did. The
combined statements and recollections of those "on the inside"
reflect the view of Clark Clifford, advisor to Presidents
Johnson and Kennedy:

> I do not believe that John Kennedy would have followed the
> same course as Lyndon Johnson in the all-important year of
> 1965, when the major decisions to escalate the ground war
> and start bombing North Vietnam were made. On the basis of
> personal intuition and a knowledge of both men, I believe that
> because of profound differences in personality and style,
> Kennedy would have taken a different path in his second
> term. (20)

This analysis differs sharply from Johnson's own assessment
on following Kennedy's Vietnam commitment "as steady on
course." Johnson stated that this meant continuing
Kennedy's unfulfilled goals for Vietnam. (21) But as Clark
Clifford has stated and as this research will show, the
escalation of the Vietnam War was not one of Kennedy's
goals. Planned or by accident, the truth in the Warren Report

was not found and the Vietnam War was escalated. Author Josiah Thompson noted that two judges considered the Report heresay: "If we are going to accept the *Warren Report* as factual then we've wasted a week of time," said Judge Bernard J. Bagert. "It is fraught with heresay and contradiction," added Judge Matthew S. Braniff. In so speaking, these judges denied a defense motion that the *Warren Report* be introduced into evidence in the pretrial hearing of alleged conspirator, Clay L. Shaw. (22)

As President, Lyndon Johnson waived the mandatory retirement for Hoover each year of his presidency. Could this have been for services rendered? No one can truly know the exact nature of their relationship and the secrets they shared. What is known is that both gained tremendous power as a result of each other's cooperation. This research does not state that Johnson and Hoover were involved in Kennedy's assassination. However, it is possible that they were involved. The arguments presented here and by other researchers, indicate that initially, both of them acted suspiciously and both obviously benefited from the assassination. Courtney Evans, the liaison between the Kennedy administration's Justice Department and the FBI, stated in a memo to FBI official Alan Belmont on November 26, 1963:

> He [Assistant Attorney General Katzenbach] noted that a tremendous responsibility had been placed on the FBI in this instance by President Johnson because this report, which is to be publicized, is for the purpose of assuring the American public and the world as to what the facts are in Kennedy's assassination and setting to rest the many, many rumors that have been circulating and speculation both in the United States and abroad. (23)

Although speculation about the possible involvement of Johnson and/or Hoover is certainly justified, concluding that they were actually involved is a serious matter and is not proveable and most likely never will be. But there can be no doubt that both obstructed justice in not searching for the truth in the investigation of John Kenney's murder.

If there was a conspiracy to kill President Kennedy, then it is, of course, possible that Johnson and/or Hoover were somehow involved. The "why" and the depth of their involvement continues to be a mystery to historians and researchers to this day. As reported in the *Dallas Morning News* on November 28, 1963, only five days after the assassination: "Most of the rumors about the case come from Europe. To Europeans, organized attempts to seize power or assassinating czars and kings are as old as history." (24) But there are many who believe that America is an exception to this rule even though assassination is a theme that runs through all of human history, not just in Europe. The events that actually took place in Dallas are still not clear today and there can be no doubt that J. Edgar Hoover's Cold War obsession played a heavy hand in obscuring the truth.

There also can be little doubt that Hoover's fifty-five year obsession with Communism helped allow these events to take place. Hoover had reached the point where his power and influence upon the leaders of American government was virtually un-questioned. Attorneys general, who were supposedly his superiors, and even presidents, were seen by him as transient officials. Dean Rusk, Secretary of State under President's Kennedy and Johnson noted: ". . . Our experiences with J. Edgar Hoover taught us that . . . he had become so institutionalized that he was virtually untouchable. No one exercising power should be untouchable in our government." (25)

Ultimately this research strongly argues that J. Edgar Hoover's main weapons in carrying out his Cold War were not used as a result of honest public debate but rather via pressure from a non-elected public official who manipulated the truth and threatened to ruin careers if he was not appeased. Hoover clearly saw himself as a protector of our basic American values but unfortunately, only as he interpreted them. Hoover violated the basic legal rights of Lee Oswald by finding him guilty on the day of the assassination without a trial and thereby partially destroying a pillar of the system he had sworn to uphold. In so doing, he helped to usher in the worst era of his Cold War, the escalation of the Vietnam War. This, unfortunately, is the legacy of J. Edgar Hoover as the *Father of the Cold War*. To Hoover, as to Niccolo Machiavelli, the ends justified the means.

Part 1

**The Father of the Cold War:
Hoover's Obsession With Communism**

Chapter 1

Historiographical Comparison of Research on J. Edgar Hoover

A comparative and objective study of the historiographical literature of J. Edgar Hoover would have been impossible twenty-five years ago. The main reason being, that during his lifetime (Hoover died in 1972), very few authors and researchers dared to criticize the FBI and its leader. There were also too few books written about Hoover at all. With his death, the number of books written about Hoover increased dramatically. Many critics had been waiting for years for the opportunity "to put the blade in." Their efforts were greatly enhanced by the disclosures and the scepticism generated as a result of the era of Vietnam and Watergate. The release of millions of pages of documents under the Freedom of Information Act, passed in 1976, gave researchers and historians access to an unprecedented amount of information. It is with this background in mind that a comparative historiographical study of the literature of J. Edgar Hoover can take place.

FBI publicist Courtney Ryley Cooper was correct when he stated in 1933, "Five years ago, J. Edgar Hoover was practically an unknown as far as the general public was concerned." (1) With the arrival of his popularity as the nation's number one G-Man came *Ten Thousand Public Enemies* (1933), written by Cooper with a foreword by Hoover. The book describes in detail how the FBI compiled a list of ten thousand of the nation's worst "public enemies." It is obviously a book that is favorable to Hoover (since he wrote the foreword) and reflects the quiet years of Hoover's war on Communism.   At the time it was written, the book was deemed to be "shocking" for the depth of its candid treatment of the fight against crime. Herschel Brickell, in the *New York Post* wrote, "It is, if you like, a shocking book, particularly in its description of the relations of the 'respectable' elements of the community to crime, but its revelations are necessary and may prove useful." (2) John Nanovic followed Cooper's lead with his gushing *Men Against Crime*, written in 1938. Nanovic is chiefly concerned with describing the training of FBI men and its anti-crime crusade. S. G. Kling, in a review published in *Books*, wrote:

> A fairly readable though highly uncritical account . . . He [Nanovic] is apparently a great admirer of Mr. Hoover and holds to the opinion that Scotland Yard and the Paris Surete have nothing on the FBI. That Hoover's organization is either as efficient or as brilliant as these world famous organizations is at least open to doubt. Mr. Nanovic rarely permits doubts to assail him. (3)

With the advent of World War II and Hoover's responsibilities and priorities affixed to espionage and counter intelligence matters, new research on Hoover's present operations was not feasible. But Max Lowenthal, in his book *Federal Bureau of Investigation* (1950), made up for lost time.   Despite the tremendous popularity and high esteem that Hoover enjoyed at this time, Lowenthal warned that the FBI and Hoover were too powerful and highly politicized. Alan Barth of the *New Republic* was so impressed with Lowenthal's "indictment" of Hoover that he wrote:

> Mr. Lowenthal's indictment is much too important to be dismissed. It ought to be brought to trial. Congress is now too torn politically to hear it an atmosphere of reason. The appropriate tribunal would be an independent commission of universally respected private citizens. There is urgent need for such a commission to make an impartial study of internal security needs and of the relationship between national security and individual freedom. (4)

Walter Trohan of the *Chicago Tribune* and Cabell Phillips from the *New York Times* voiced similar concerns. But as

Phillips warned, "This is a thoughtful and important book that too few people will take the trouble to read." (5) What is most impressive about Lowenthal's research is that most of his information was taken from congressional testimony.

In 1956, Don Whitehead wrote the first book with the cooperation of J. Edgar Hoover that would mildly criticize Hoover and the FBI. Whitehead's book, *FBI Story: A Report to the People*, was an "official" reply to the Lowenthal book. William Hogan of the *San Francisco Chronicle* wrote, "It is the work of a top reporter who was allowed complete freedom to investigate the FBI." (6) Neal Stanford of the *Christian Science Monitor* was one of the few who realized that "complete freedom to investigate," was really a relative phrase. He called the work of Whitehead:

> Fascinating—but a bit disappointing. It is disappointing in a sense, for the book makes it quite clear that the FBI files are crammed with equally gripping and documentary accounts of the FBI's war against crime that are never going to see the light of day. (7)

The work of later authors who appear in this historiographical survey would prove Stanford to be prophetic. But the research of Whitehead and others to this point, never came close to questioning Hoover's conduct of his war on Communism. Although the Cold War had begun to thaw by 1956, anti-Communism was still in vogue and Hoover was America's "father figure" in this "crusade." Mildred Comfort's 1959 book (about Hoover) entitled, *Modern Knight*, continues the "hero" vein of thought. But the words of Hoover himself would alert the world that Communism was alive and well and that the United States could never afford to let its guard down.

Masters of Deceit: The Story of Communism in American and How to Fight It* was "written" by Hoover and published through his businessman friend Clint Murchison in 1958. William Sullivan, later Assistant Director of the FBI wrote that "five or six of us at the Bureau did the writing, Hoover didn't write the book." (8) Regardless of who actually wrote the book, *Masters of Deceit* would never have been published if it did not reflect Hoover's views. This book would clearly indicate to all who read it that J. Edgar Hoover firmly believed (as he did in 1919) that Communism was the root of all evil in America. Few reviews of the book dared to suggest

that Hoover might be carrying his Cold War too far. J. B.
Oakes of the *New York Times* wrote quite insightfully (and
boldly) about the current domestic threat posed by
Communism:

> There is at times a naive and at times a slightly dated quality
> to the contents of Mr. Hoover's book, which as he himself says,
> is written "in almost primer form." It is dated because
> American Communism itself is dated. . . . If you accept his
> thesis that the American Communist Party is today "a
> powerful monster endangering us all," then this book will
> doubtless give you some sleepless nights. If, however, you
> consider that the Communist Party in this country has
> dwindled from an all-time high of eighty thousand in the early
> Forties to less than eight thousand today . . . then you may
> well wonder how justified his alarm really is. (9)

Even though the view held by Oakes was in the minority in
1958, time appears to have proven him to be correct.
Domestic Communism has not been a factor of any
consequence since that period.

Not only were cracks appearing in Hoover's war on
Communism, but the public perception of an "American Hero"
that he had so carefully cultivated was slipping away.
Masters of Deceit became a best seller but Hoover's follow-up
book, *A Study in Communism* (published in 1962) did not fare
so well. Harry Schwartz of the *New York Times* helped to
explain why. "The book gave a good description of the horrors
of the Stalinist era but failed to throw much light on the
many and important changes that have taken place in the
Soviet Union since Stalin's death." (10) The blind Cold War of
Hoover was beginning to wear thin.

The next book of major importance was one which would
help to slicken the slope towards Hoover's decline. This was
Fred Cook's *The FBI Nobody Knows*. This 1964 exposé of
Hoover was "strong stuff indeed," as W. M. Kunstler described
in a *New York Times* book review. (11) Cook continued the
charges brought forth by former FBI agent Jack Levine.
Levine charged in a September 1962 article in the *Nation,*
that Hoover had consistently and knowingly exaggerated the
communist threat. (12) "[Cook] thinks that Hoover
suffered — and continues to suffer — from an hysterical
obsession with Communism and a complete inability to
distinguish between disloyalty and dissent," observed
reviewer Allan Barth. (13) Although the allegations made by

Cook were controversial, they were not without documentation. Among the sources used were interviews by the principals involved, given to contemporary newspapers, and testimony taken from congressional hearings. Barth echoed the support of Cook's sources when he wrote:

> [Cook] charges more . . . than he actually proves. But this is not to say that the charges are unreasonable or in any sense irresponsible. On the contrary, they are supported by a prodigious amount of carefully researched and pervasive material; and they are on the whole, penetrating, illuminating and conscientiously balanced. (14)

The public criticism and pressure that Hoover was receiving was softened somewhat by President Johnson's decision to waive Hoover's "mandatory" retirement (age 70) at a public ceremony in early January 1965. Unfortunately for Hoover, the criticism would not stop. It would continue to emanate in book form from the pens of former agents of the FBI.

In 1967, former agent Norman Ollestad published *Inside the FBI*. The book portrayed the Bureau and the Director in decidedly unflattering terms and Ollestad charged that Hoover would "sometimes bug his own colleagues while at work or even at home." (15) William Turner, former ten year veteran of the Bureau, published *Hoover's FBI: The Men and the Myth* in 1970. Turner devotes much of his attention to criticizing the Bureau's personnel policies, penchant for publicity feats, and Hoover's obsessions with performance statistics and communists. As J. Edgar Hoover was fast approaching the end of the line, his "hero myth" was fading faster than he was. R. W. Schwarz wrote the following in the *Library Journal*:

> As Turner says, every story has two sides, and he sets out to depict the less savory aspects of the FBI story. . . . This is a bitter book, yet necessary as a corrective to the adulatory accounts so often purveyed by the press, TV, and motion pictures. (16)

The last major book to be published before Hoover's death was the most controversial up to that time but also the least documented of the recent works critical of Hoover. Hank Messick's charges are seen clearly in his title, *John Edgar Hoover, and his Relationship to the Continuing Partnership of*

Crime, Business, and Politics. The author argues that Hoover
refused to interfere with (and indeed protected) crime
syndicates while concentrating his investigations on bank
robbers and communists. Messick attempts to document the
web of relationships among politicians, gangsters, Hoover,
and the military industrial complex. M. S. Kingsley of the
Library Journal properly places Messick's work in the form of
a prophetically accurate summary:

> [This account] is revealing, but not as shocking as Messick
> hoped. Sparse footnoting, a loaded vocabulary and emotional,
> unsubstantiated allegations damage the author's credibility.
> Recommended with a large grain of salt; it may inspire a more
> scholarly investigation. (17)

Inspire he did, for the work of Ovid Demaris, Curt Gentry,
Athan Theoharis, Richard Powers, and Anthony Summers all
eventually combined to document many of Messick's
contentions. But the majority of these authors would not be
able to document Messick's charges until the late 1980's and
early 1990's, well after Hoover's death. Meanwhile, there
were still those who had been somewhat "close" to Hoover,
and who refused to believe or dwell on the negative
"muckraking" of "sensationalist" authors.

Apologists for Hoover would still cling tightly to the belief
that Hoover was sometimes wrong, sometimes right. He
loved America, and he fought for America. Ralph de
Toledano, (columnist of *Newsweek*) was one who believed that
for most Americans, that was enough. (18) De Toledano
published, *J. Edgar Hoover: The Man in His Time*, in 1973.
The author's main contention is that Max Lowenthal, Fred
Cook, Norman Ollestad, and William Turner were all
scurrilous authors whose arguments were weak and
unsubstantiated. De Toledano devotes six pages of his
introduction to an attempt to debunk these critical authors.
The subtitle of his book neatly summarizes the author's
methods in rationalizing Hoover's actions; "the man in his
time." This is where de Toledano makes his most important
contribution to this survey. He reminds us, that above all,
Hoover was a man who reflected his upbringing and the times
and situations in which he found himself. Unfortunately, the
author could only pass judgment on what he *knew* of Hoover's
activities and that is the point where his scholarship suffers.
It appears certain that he only "knew" J. Edgar Hoover as

well as the Director would allow him to.

Ovid Demaris makes an important contribution to this survey with the publication of *The Director* in 1975. His book is a collection of taped interviews which focus on three parts of Hoover's life; private life, public life, and secret life. Demaris spoke with former attorneys general, Hoover's friends, colleagues, those who loved him, feared him, and hated him, and many in between. Jack Forman, writing in the *Library Journal*, praises the selection of participants in the interviews held by Demaris. "[The author's] selection of people to interview is wisely made—supporters and detractors of Hoover are equally represented—and the organization and editing of the interview excerpts is very competently done." (19) Demaris seems to have not completely made up his mind, even after all the interviews, as to what he really thinks of J. Edgar Hoover. A review published in the *Christian Century* gives a realistic appraisal of where Demaris' work has taken this survey:

> Not for years can there begin to be a scholarly biography of J. Edgar Hoover, and a revealing biography of Mr. Secrets probably can never appear. In the meantime, an oral-biography portrait put together from interviews with the FBI head's friends and enemies can work some tantalizing effects. (20)

In 1979, one of the most interesting of the "insider" books was published. William Sullivan, who had risen to the number three position at the Bureau wrote, *My Thirty Years in Hoover's FBI*. The book was published posthumously after Sullivan was killed in a hunting accident in 1977. The book is ghostwritten by author Bill Brown and as a result, suffers from a lack of organization. But what the book does offer is a fascinating inside look at the upper levels of the FBI and details Hoover's "real" feelings about the Presidents that he served. The book also describes Sullivan's involvement in the infamous Cointelpro operations which smeared innocent citizens as communists. Sullivan offers evidence of the extent to which paranoia reigned supreme at the highest levels of the Bureau. The book is not an attack on the FBI but rather an attack on the Hoover legend. As a result of his untimely death, it is difficult to gauge the true intentions Sullivan had in writing this book. Frank Donner's comments in the *Nation* (Oct. 20) might accurately describe Sullivan's rationale.

"[The] memoir is best described as a plea for absolution for sins its author claims he committed under duress." (21)

Richard G. Powers is credited with writing a balanced and fascinating version of Hoover in his 1987 book *Secrecy and Power: The Life of J. Edgar Hoover.* Powers is a professor of history at City University of New York's College of Staten Island. He had previously written *G-Men: Hoover's FBI in American Popular Culture.* In this 1983 book, Powers described the emergence of the FBI as a fearless guardian of the nation's safety and security and of J. Edgar Hoover as a national hero. Joshua Freeman wrote in the *Nation*: "Powers does a first-rate job of charting the FBI's image-making before World War II." (22) This book lays the ground work for his well received 1987 work. The author's background as a historian benefits him greatly as he draws on a wealth of primary source materials—FBI files, personal documents, interviews, and presidential papers. *Secrecy and Power* covers all aspects of Hoover's career from his upbringing and the Palmer Raids through the 1960's and the anti-war movement. This book might just be the best biography yet written on J. Edgar Hoover. In the words of Scott Wright, writing in the *Library Journal*, "Overall, this is a balanced and interesting account that is likely to stand for the foreseeable future as the standard work on its subject." (23)

In 1989, two more books on Hoover appeared. The first by Athan Theoharis with help from John Stuart Cox is entitled *The Boss: J. Edgar Hoover and the Great American Inquisition.* The book, as the title implies, spares no one who would attempt to justify Hoover's activities as head of the FBI. Theoharis and Cox describe in detail how Hoover strove to expand his empire and to ensure absolute control over it. The authors rely almost exclusively on information gleaned from FBI files and therein lies their main contribution. As John T. Elliff wrote in the *Political Science Quarterly*:

> On balance, the blatant anti-Hoover bias of this attempt at biography should not discourage responsible scholars from taking advantage of its wealth of detail about a fascinating historical figure and the organization he created. (24)

William Keller's *The Liberals and J. Edgar Hoover: Rise and Fall of a Domestic Intelligence State* is the second book on Hoover published in 1989. The book is a fairly detailed and well-documented argument that the liberals needed Hoover despite the fact that they feared him. Keller argues that the liberals refused to face up to what democracies must do to survive in dangerous times. According to this argument, once the liberals had relinquished control to Hoover, the FBI became a kind of internal security state answerable only to itself. This theory has some validity but it discounts the personal motives of individual liberals as well as Hoover himself.

Curt Gentry follows the route pioneered by Theoharis and Powers in his 1991 book, *J. Edgar Hoover: The Man and the Secrets*. Gentry makes no profound judgments and fails to capture the personal side of Hoover as Powers did. Gentry relies on information derived from over three hundred personal interviews and recently de-classified FBI documents. Not being as judgmental as Theoharis is refreshing; he lays out the facts and allows the reader to judge for himself. What the reader discovers is expressed by Thomas Karel who wrote: "This is a chilling look at the darker side of American politics." (25)

Probably the most controversial of books on Hoover is Mark North's *Act of Treason*. This 1991 book argues that Hoover covered up a Mafia assassination of John Kennedy with his Warren Report investigation. Thomas Karel's review of North's research in the *Library Journal* states:

> The focus here on Hoover's activities and influence puts *Act of Treason* on a higher level than the typical conspiracy theory book. North effectively blends press reports, FBI records, and interviews to create a daily chronicle of the pertinent events of 1960-64. (26)

It is possible that the Mafia assassinated Kennedy and quite probable that Hoover was involved in a coverup of some sort. But this work fails to examine why organized crime leaders Sam Giancana, John Martino, Dave Yaras, Charles Niccoletti, John Roselli and associates, such as Jimmy Hoffa all were killed as the House Select Committee on Assassinations was beginning to hold hearings (1974-77). Was the "Mafia" killing its own or was somebody else pulling the strings? Or is it all just a series of unexplained circumstances? This book does not face these questions and leaves many others unanswered but it is a very interesting book and it whets the appetite for more. This work warrants a close examination and it will inspire more research.

Anthony Summers has also written a controversial book on Hoover. His 1993 work, *Official and Confidential: The Secret Life of J. Edgar Hoover*, focuses on two main themes; Hoover's alleged homosexuality and his protection of organized crime. Summers believes that the one, homosexuality, and the mob's knowledge of it led to the other, protection by Hoover for organized crime. Although the author does use a wealth of documentation taken from Hoover's personal files, his two main arguments cannot be proven from these sources. What Summers does accomplish is that based on the evidence collected, there is a strong inference that his contentions are correct.

Another insider's account included as a part of this survey is *Hoover's FBI* (1995) by Cartha DeLoach. The author was assistant director of the FBI in the late 1950's and 1960's and was a rival to his counterpart, William Sullivan. The purpose of the book is to destroy the charges made by Sullivan in his 1979 book; it also serves as an apologist's rebuttal to Hoover's other critics. DeLoach argues that the infamous Cointelpro operation "seemed like a good idea at the time." He insists that J. Edgar Hoover did not keep secret files to intimidate others. DeLoach devotes a complete chapter to this futile attempt to erase forty years of documented attempts at intimidation by Hoover. DeLoach's argument that there were no secret files was continued by Assistant FBI Director John Mohr at the time of Hoover's death. (27) In 1975, Helen Gandy, Hoover's secretary since 1919, testified before the staff of Congress' Government Information Sub-committee. Gandy stated that the personal files that she destroyed (by using a shredder) were small in number and merely investment records and personal correspondence. Congressman Andrew Maguire told Gandy, "I find your testimony very hard to believe." Gandy replied, "That is your privilege." (28)

One of the most recent books written about Mr. Hoover describes the "original sin" of Hoover and the FBI. Robert Unger's 1997 work, *The Union Station Massacre*, is the result of examining 89 volumes of FBI investigation files over a 14-year period and argues that Hoover lied and covered up evidence in the infamous murder of federal agents in Kansas City in 1933. Unger believes the evidence shows that Hoover needed a crusade against the criminal element of the day, kidnappers, bank robbers, ... This was needed to justify an increase in funding for more agents, new investigative powers for the agency, and ultimately more power for himself. Unger convincingly argues, "There's little doubt, that everybody in the Kansas City office knew the true story of the massacre." (29) This appears to be an early example of J. Edgar Hoover covering up the truth and obstructing justice; a forerunner of what's to come in the future.

As one studies the historiography available on J. Edgar Hoover, it is obvious that a definitive answer on the man himself is beyond our reach. For the purpose of this research on Hoover as the Father of the Cold War, probing for the deep secrets of Hoover is important but not vital. Although his means of fighting Communism were often illegal and therefore secret, his intention to "destroy" Communism was not a secret. What is needed and what will be presented is a clear and consistent pattern which demonstrates that J. Edgar Hoover, from 1917 until his death in 1972 initiated, perpetuated, and promoted his war on Communism by any means necessary.

Chapter 2

Communism and Hoover:
How They Emerged Together

The year 1917 becomes most important in a study of Hoover and Communism. If not for the Bolshevik Revolution occurring in the same year as Hoover's entry into the Justice Department, there might be no need for a study of Hoover and the Cold War. The two events were unrelated and coincidental to each other but the fact remains that J. Edgar Hoover arrived in a position to influence policy simultaneously with the threat of a "world-wide" communist revolution. What circumstances led to both Russian Communism and Mr. Hoover appearing on the world stage during the same period?

In the years after the Civil War, the United States began to change from a predominately rural nation, with little involvement by the federal government, to a largely urban nation with a strong federal government. The results of the Civil War left no doubt that the federal government would have dominion over the states and this reality has only increased with time.

The rapid growth of the railroads and factories created thousands of new jobs and towns. With little or no safeguards protecting the railroad workers, miners, or factory workers, it was inevitable that workers would find the need to be strongly organized. When looking to organize, workers in the United States looked to Europe for models that could be applied to the unique problems of American workers. As a result, groups such as the Socialist Labor Party began to build up their memberships and political influence from 1876 to 1880. During this period, the Socialist Labor Party grew to a membership of ten thousand and was supported by twenty-four newspapers. (1)

Labor groups were successful in pushing for passage of legislation that restricted Chinese immigration in order to protect "native" American railroad workers' jobs. Workers were also sympathetic to the formation of the anti-Catholic (Irish immigrants) American Protective Association which was founded in 1877. Armed miners, railroad workers, and the urban unemployed went on strike in various locales throughout the United States. Factory owners and political leaders saw the strikes as threats not only to profits but also to social stability. Aggravating the whole situation was the economic depression of 1873 - 1877 and continuing labor and political violence. President James A.Garfield was assassinated in 1881. The *New York Herald Tribune* reported that the railroad riots of 1877 "were instigated by men incapable of understanding our ideas and principles." (2) This attitude helped to further arouse nativist fears against immigrants and organized labor.

In 1880, a split occurred in the Socialist Party. By 1883, the "Black International" wing of the Party under the leadership of former German agitator, Johann Most called for the "destruction of the existing class rule by all means, i.e., by energetic, relentless, revolutionary, and international action." (3) The public call for violence by anarchists Most, Alexander Berkman, and Emma Goldman (a future adversary of Hoover) helped to galvanize public opinion against radicalism.

The Haymarket Riot and the McCormick Plant strike in 1886 increased the public's fears of violence and labor unrest. In 1888, Congressman Adams from Illinois (representing the Haymarket area) proposed the "removal of dangerous aliens from the territory of the United States." (4) This turbulent period became known as "The Great Upheaval" as a result of the frequent strikes and violence, many of which were led by the Knights of Labor. As many as five states sent out the National Guard to stop strikes in 1892 alone. Eugene V. Debs, the most well known socialist of the day, declared in 1894 during the Pullman strike that there was "a contest between the producing classes and money power of the country." (5) Deb's statement further inflamed an already volatile situation. Meanwhile, assassinations in Europe of a king, queen, prime minister, and president further shook up political and business leaders in the United States. In 1895 and 1897, Senator Chandler of New Hampshire attempted to exclude all anarchists from the United States through immigration legislation but neither bill ever reached the Senate floor.

Such was the state of the political and social climate at the time J. Edgar Hoover was born in 1895. The world was changing quickly as the twentieth century was dawning, but Hoover's upbringing in Washington, D.C. was marked more by its adherence to conservative thought rather than reflecting the complex social and political changes going on. Hoover's Capitol Hill neighborhood, Seward Square, was white, Protestant, and middle class. The only non-whites were the black servants who did not live in the neighborhood. (6) Washington was a southern city in outlook and this was reflected in its segregated treatment of blacks. Many conservatives of the day blamed immigrants for class hatred and said industrial conflict should be nonexistent. (7)

During the formative years of Hoover's life, the trend towards political violence and labor unrest would continue. On September 6, 1901, President William McKinley was assassinated by Leon Czolgosz, an anarchist. New President Theodore Roosevelt responded by announcing a war on radicalism in a speech presented to Congress on December 3, 1901; "we should war with relentless efficiency not only against anarchists but against all active and passive sympathizers with anarchists." (8)

Many of the clergy of the day held to this conservative view and the church is where J. Edgar Hoover began to mold his political and social beliefs. He hoped to move up in the world of business or government and an active church membership was looked upon favorably. Hoover was a regular attendee of the Lutheran Church of the Reformation (the current site of the Library of Congress). He was a tireless and devoted Sunday School teacher at the Presbyterian Old First Church in 1910 (at the age of fifteen). Hoover remained a member of Old First for the remainder of his life although his chauffeur and first black agent, John Crawford, stated that as time went by, Hoover rarely, if ever, attended church. (9)

In 1905, a new revolutionary group, the Industrial Workers

of the World, would organize and state boldly and publicly "that there can be no peace so long as hunger and want are found among millions of working people." (10) The I.W.W., or the Wobblies as they came to be known, set up their program in a Marxist framework and planned to organize into "one big union," industry by industry; a labor union equivalent of the Socialist Party. The constitution of the Wobblies was very extreme and quite radical. It "rejected the church and the flag as the dishonest tools of the exploiting class." (11) To add insult to injury, the I.W.W. attacked patriotism with gusto: "of all the idiotic and perverted ideas accepted by the workers from that class who live upon their misery, patriotism is the worst." (12) The words and actions of the Wobblies would produce righteous indignation from those who were of a conservative mind set. At thirteen years of age in 1908, J. Edgar Hoover would remember the I.W.W. and declare war on its leadership in the years to come.

One of the most important developments to understand when analyzing how Hoover and the FBI were able to shape policy in later years, is how its forerunner, the Bureau of Investigation came to be. In 1907, Theodore Roosevelt appealed to Congress to create a permanent detective agency under the control of the Justice Department. This new agency would be responsible for investigating western land fraud "only". (13) Roosevelt's Attorney General, Charles J. Bonaparte, was out in front debating with Congress over the need for the Bureau of Investigation. Congress, Roosevelt, and Bonaparte debated the issue back and forth.

Congressman Walter I. Smith of Iowa, a member of the House Appropriations Committee, stated: "No general system of spying upon and espionage of the people, such as has prevailed in Russia, in France, under the Empire, and at one time in Ireland, should be allowed to grow up." (14) Others in Congress claimed that detectives were compiling dossiers on the private lives of Roosevelt's enemies and opening their mail. (15) Representative John J. Fitzgerald predicted, quite accurately, that the time would come when the secret police, either to protect themselves in their own wrongdoing or for the alleged good of their service, would contend that they had to maintain secrecy, even against Congress itself. (16)

Bonaparte reasoned that the catching of criminals was all that mattered. "Anybody can shadow me as much as they please," he said. "They can watch my coming in and my going out. I do not care whether there is somebody standing at the corner and watching where I go or where I do not go." (17) Congressman J. Swager Sherley of Kentucky was enthusiastically applauded by his fellow congressman in 1908 after delivering these words:

> In my reading of history I recall no instance where a government perished because of the absence of a secret-service force, but many there are that perished as a result of the spy system. If Anglo-Saxon civilization stands for anything, it is for a government where the humblest citizen is safeguarded against the secret activities of the executive of the government . . . .
> Not in vain did our forefathers read the history of the Magna Charta and of the Bill of Rights. . . . When our Constitution was adopted, the people's restlessness under it and fear of oppression was not removed until there was embodied in it the ten Amendments constituting our American Bill of Rights.
> The Fourth Amendment declares: 'The right of the people to be secure in their persons, houses, papers, and effects, against unreasonable searches and seizures, shall not be violated. . . .
> The view of government that called it into existence is not lightly to be brushed aside. (18)

It seemed clear that Congress had intended to limit federal investigations and did not want to encourage abuse or to undermine representative self-government. In 1907 and 1908, Bonaparte formally requested Congress to establish an independent investigative division within the Justice Department and was flatly refused on both occasions. (19) Despite clear and consistent congressional opposition, Bonaparte was able to establish the Bureau of Investigation anyway as a result of an executive order signed by Roosevelt. (20) The warnings of Congressman Sherley and others went unheeded, and the investigative powers of the federal government eventually were allowed to grow unchecked.

Responding to the contemporary criticism after creating the Bureau over congressional opposition, Bonaparte announced three "safeguards" in February 1909 before he left office (as a result of the election of William H. Taft as the next President).

1. Hire quality people.
2. The Attorney General would be personally involved in all

decision making.
3. The new division would not investigate political beliefs, or personal affiliations; it would be confined to antitrust and interstate commerce violations. (21)

Almost immediately, a new development of immeasurable importance came into play, the Mann Act of 1910. This new responsibility for the Bureau led to the inevitable collection of information on prominent persons and their private lives. The Act would prove to be a valuable commodity that J. Edgar Hoover would eventually use to influence presidents, congressmen, senators, and others in positions of power and influence. The bill's sponsor, Congressman James Mann, Republican from Illinois, explained the intention of the Act; it was "intended to stop girls from being enticed from homes in the country to the city." (22)   Stanley Finch, the newly appointed Director of the Bureau (who had been reappointed by Taft's Attorney General George W. Wicker-Sham), continued the argument of Mann. He stated:

> Unless a girl was actually confined in a room and guarded, there was no girl regardless of her station in life, who was altogether safe. . . . There was need that every person be on his guard, because no one could tell when his daughter or his wife or his mother would be selected as a victim. (23)

In later years (1938), Hoover would rationalize this unchecked growth of probing into the private lives of its citizens by arguing that the Mann Act had been intended for business transactions but Congress really also intended to declare war on immorality as well. Sanford J. Unger argued that "to put a federal law enforcement service in charge of monitoring the moral behavior of the citizens was always a questionable and controversial step and it was never clear that Congress had meant to go that far." (24)   Hoover's obsession with anti-Communism would eventually merge with his capability to probe into the private lives of those that opposed his Cold War.

In the years following the passage of the Mann Act, J. Edgar Hoover became a young adult. His years in secondary school were spent at Washington's Central High from 1909 to 1913. Hoover's main interests were in competing on the debate team, reading and studying history. As a member of the Central High Brigade of Cadets he would pass the ROTC exam in 1913. All three interests would serve him well in the future. From debate, he learned to prepare well-reasoned arguments in the form of briefs. This skill would be of great use in later investigations and prosecutions for the FBI. An interest in history would benefit his knowledge of government and law. The themes of contemporary historians in that period stressed the superiority of the WASP view of the world and Hoover was no doubt influenced by these themes. Hoover would make great use of his experiences as a cadet. He would model his organization of the FBI after Company A of the Brigade of Cadets. (25) Hoover was named Captain of the company in 1913 and led his unit down Pennsylvania Avenue during Woodrow Wilson's first inauguration in 1913.

The molding and shaping of Hoover's views on radicals and immigrants was surely affected by the events taking place around him during his years at Central. From 1899 to 1907, the number of immigrants increased from three hundred thousand to almost one million per year. The level would not go below six hundred fifty thousand each year until the outbreak of World War I. (26) As Woodrow Wilson stated during his preparedness campaign, "immigrant radicals had poured the poison of disloyalty into the very arteries of our national life. America has never witnessed anything like this before . . . Such creatures of passion, disloyalty, and anarchy must be crushed out." (27) Wilson would be the first president that Hoover worked under in government service and subsequently, the first president he would attempt to shape policy under. He would soon be given the opportunity "to crush out immigrant radicals, the disloyal," and communists.

Following his graduation from Central in 1913, Hoover took a job at the Library of Congress to help support his way through the George Washington University Law School. Hoover completed his bachelor of law degree in the minimum amount of time in 1916. The nation was preoccupied with the war in Europe and whether the United States should or would enter. He continued to work at George Washington University for another year while completing the courses required for the master's degree in law. It was during this time he joined the Masons. This secret fraternal order was committed to good works and reinforced "common values," but also excluded those who did not share them. Not accepting those who did not share his values proves to be a trait that

Hoover would carry with him the rest of his life. The Masons of Washington, D.C. had among their members many congressmen and influential government employees. Attempting to document Hoover's influence with fellow Masons is difficult without records of personal correspondence, but there can be little doubt that influence was used by Hoover (and towards him) during the many years of his active membership. Lawrence Richey, a fellow Mason and an assistant to Secretary of Commerce Herbert Hoover, would later recommend that Hoover be named the permanent Director of the Bureau.

In April 1917, Woodrow Wilson delivered his war message to Congress. The draft was required of all men between the ages of twenty-one and thirty-one (Hoover was twenty-two) as of June 5. Hoover was offered a position in the Justice Department as a "clerk" or "permit officer" on July 26. (28) Along with his new position, Hoover received an indefinite deferment although he would have entered the service as a commissioned officer. (29) For one who had such a strong interest in military training only a few years earlier, it would be interesting to speculate on why he did not enlist. In later years he would be proud of his rank of major in the army reserves. As for serving in World War I, Hoover chose to remain a civilian instead.

The first official mention of Hoover's work in the Justice Department appears in a December 1917 memorandum in which Hoover is referred to as a "special agent" in the Alien Enemy Bureau. (30) This also marks the initial opportunity for him to influence policy. Hoover was assigned the responsibility for compiling lists of German aliens who might be radicals and subsequently need to be deported. (31) When Hoover first reported for work, the successful prosecutions of Emma Goldman and Alexander Berkman had just been completed by Assistant United States Attorney Harold Conant. As a result of Conant's success, he received high praise and headlines from newspapers nationwide. Hoover would remember the tactics and how the headlines were garnered (in 1919, Hoover would greet Goldman and Berkman with new successful prosecutions upon their release from prison). (32)

The timing of Hoover's entry into the world of identifying radicals and subversives, would coincide with a growth in the need to investigate radical aliens because of America's entry into the war. Spies and bombings were a legitimate concern as a result of the real threat of German subversion and sabotage. Two million pounds of dynamite were exploded on Black Tom Island in New York City's harbor in July 1916 and an explosion and fire took place at a shell assembly plant in Kingsland, New Jersey in January 1917.

President Wilson's war message in April 1917 illustrated the concern caused by the threat of internal subversion. The President's concern over the infiltration of spies and saboteurs into the United States was preceded by a news blackout of military movements in the War Department on March 25, 1917. Rumors abounded as to the whereabouts of enemy agents. (33) Congress had already begun to authorize the deportation of aliens who were "revolutionaries and anarchists" as a result of the Immigration Act, passed in February 1917. President Wilson invoked the Alien Act in March at the urging of Charles Warren, a virulent nativist who was an assistant attorney general working in the War Emergency Division. (34) In June, the Espionage Act, originally intended to prosecute those charged with treason, was amended to include political dissent. This marks another tactic that Hoover would learn early in his career and incorporate into his war on communists, silencing those who had sympathy for communists or acknowledged their right to express contrary views.

By December 1917 it appears that Hoover was not only compiling lists of alien radicals, he was also given the responsibility of summarizing cases, helping to influence and in some cases decide for himself who should be deported or jailed. One such case involved a German immigrant named Otto Mueller who had cursed and denigrated President Wilson and the United States. Hoover argued that Mueller should be imprisoned for the duration of the war because his statements were "vulgar and obscene" and carried "pro-German expressions." Hoover's immediate supervisor, Special Assistant Attorney General Charles W. Storey, disagreed. "Mueller has unquestionably overstepped the right of free speech but still his offense is no more than a failure to keep his mouth shut, and I feel that internment for the war for mere talk is rather severe. Three or four months in jail will be equally effective." (35) Hoover was developing a trait that would become familiar over the years, a desire to probe the beliefs and attitudes of those whose values were not in agreement with his. Eventually, mere probing would not suffice, and Hoover would "punish" the "subversives" and "communists" who threatened to "destroy America."

Many private citizens were convinced that they should become involved in the domestic war against subversion. The public pressure to act was demonstrated when the current Chief of the Bureau of Investigation, A. Bruce Bielaski and his boss, Attorney General Thomas W. Gregory, decided to merge forces with Albert Briggs and his quasi-legal American Protective League. In 1917 and 1918, the APL "vigilantes" grew from one hundred thousand to two hundred fifty thousand members. APL branches were set up in every major American city. The APL assisted the Bureau of Investigation in simultaneous raids on the various headquarters of the Industrial Workers of the World in September 1917. Public sentiment ran high in favor of the raids although there was a serious question as to whether the raids were justified. The case of Frank H. Little, a fiery IWW radical speaker, is but one example. Little was dragged out of his house by six masked men and hanged. United States Attorney Burton Wheeler called it "a damnable outrage" because Little had committed no crime. But Wheeler's voice was a solitary one, even Thomas R. Marshall, Woodrow Wilson's Vice President, called the hanging "a great act of patriotism." (36)

It is not clear whether Hoover was personally involved in the IWW raids. Lack of documentation during this period of his career is a major problem. (37) However, Attorney General Homer S. Cummings later stated that J. Edgar Hoover had been "since 1917 in charge of counter-radical activities as special assistant to the attorney general." (38) Whether he was personally involved cannot be proven, but there is no doubt that he was well aware of the raids and their public acceptance. A memorandum of July 1918 indicates that Hoover was in charge of a policy requiring the registration of German females. An editorial from the *New York Sun* lauded the "efficient work" of the Justice Department in the matter. (39) Hoover's presence was beginning to be felt.

The "slacker raids" on "known deserters" from the first two drafts of the war occurred from April to September 1918. Secretary of War Newton D. Baker had initiated the idea of the raids while writing a letter to Attorney General Gregory stating that there were 380,489 "known deserters." (40)

Again, because of the lack of documentation, it cannot be verified if Hoover was in anyway personally involved in the planning of the "slacker raids." What is known, is that the massive roundup (carried out by the Bureau and the APL) of "supposed deserters" proved to be misplaced despite the positive headlines it received. On September 18, 1918, the chief of the New York Bureau reported that there were 60,187 "detentions." Out of every two hundred detained, one hundred ninety-nine were mistakes. (41) Senator Hiram Johnson, the fiery progressive, was one of the few to speak out against the raids. His attempts to investigate the raids were blocked and put off until after the Palmer Raids forced Congress to take another look. (42) As the record of Homer Commings indicates, it cannot be determined if Hoover was involved in the IWW raids, or the "slacker raids," but it has been documented that Hoover has denied being intimately involved in the Palmer Raids despite documentation to the contrary. (43)

What all this means at best is that Hoover was aware of the successes and failures of the two operations. At worst, Hoover had already begun to implement policy and cover up his involvement in operations that would result in negative publicity. As 1919 and the end of the war approached, J. Edgar Hoover's role as father of the Cold War becomes clear. His "ways and means" in combating the communist threat and in maintaining his power and influence over the next fifty-three years are at the same time, undeniably documented and yet as vague as a murky maze.

The year 1919 becomes a critical year in the life of J. Edgar Hoover and the anti-communist movement. After a series of revolutions in Russia had taken place, the communist Bolsheviks were firmly in charge. As Hoover stated in his 1919 legal brief on the Communist Party,"The Red Army already exists in Russia; the Red Army soon will exist all over the world. . . In 1919 was born the Great Communist International. In 1920 will be born the Great International Soviet Republic." (44) It is worth noting that in March 1919, eight thousand five hundred United States troops were still stationed in Siberia as a result of the Russian Civil war between the "Reds and the Whites." Secretary of War Baker, argued that "to withdraw would mean to leave Siberia open to anarchy, bloodshed and Bolshevism." (45) In reality, violence committed against Russia's former ruling class was slight

until after the invasion of Russia by the Allies. (46) There
also developed a split in the worldwide communist movement
in March of 1919. The Third International was founded in
Moscow and its pronouncements that obedience to Moscow
was necessary and violent revolutions inevitable, split
Marxism around the world. As would happen many times in
the future, Hoover refused to consider that Communism
might not be the root of the problem. There were many
socialists who believed that "gradual socialism" and not
violent overthrow was the best way to achieve their goals.
Even Leon Trotsky was to declare in 1921 that, "now we see
and feel that we are not so near the goal of the conquest of
power, of the world revolution. We formerly believed in 1919,
that it was only a question of months and now we say that is
perhaps a question of years." (47) Nicholai Lenin himself
wrote in early 1920 that Western Communists should become
involved in parliamentary politics and not become involved in
conspiratorial activity. (48)

Despite the evidence indicating that Communism was
making little if any impact amongst American trade workers
in 1919 and that by 1920-21 the revolution had failed outside
of Russia, J. Edgar Hoover would continue to see Communism
as a monolithic movement. Public perception of the threat of
Communism was heightened by the media.   Over three
thousand strikes occurred in 1919, including three with major
radical overtones (Lawrence, Massachusetts; Butte, Montana;
and Seattle, Washington).   Newspaper headlines helped
inflame the situation and the new attorney general, A.
Mitchell Palmer, was appointed with the intention of dousing
the "red flame."

During this period, Mayor Ole Hanson became a national
hero after helping to crush the Seattle strike in January.
Hanson had taken control of army troops from a nearby base
and rode into the city in a flag-draped car.   Palmer (a
potential candidate for President in 1920) and Hoover
realized that rising anti-communist fervor could pay off in
political dividends. In March, the Supreme Court upheld the
convictions of Eugene Debs and Charles Schenck. Both men
were Socialist Party leaders who were denied the right to
freedom of speech under the Espionage Act. (49) Victor
Berger, the former Socialist congressman from Wisconsin,
had previously been convicted under the Espionage Act in
January. The Lusk Committee began its hearings on the

radical threat in March and this was followed by a series of bombings and bomb threats on Palmer and other anti-radical leaders in the spring of 1919. Radicalism and Communism were on the run.

Palmer now had additional ammunition "to rid the country of the Red agitators who are attempting to lay the foundation for just such trouble." (50) He related the red menace to the economic war between Communism and capitalism:

> The chief evil of the Red movement, both here and abroad, consists in the fact that it accomplishes a constant spread of a disease of evil thinking. The germs of this demoralizing sort behave very much as germs of any kind of disease do. While the body is in good condition and well nourished, the infection is fought off and neutralized, but if anything happens to lower the vitality of the body then the disease is apt to make very rapid ravage. So long as our country remains prosperous and we have abundance of employment for the masses at good pay, the condition is not alarming, so far as likelihood of revolutionary outbreaks is concerned, but given a condition of depression, bread lines, and the pressure of any wide-spread real want, then I think the 'menace' would prove grave indeed. (51)

On August 1, 1919, Attorney General Palmer created the Radical Division (General Intelligence Division). The main responsibility of this new division was to collect and assimilate intelligence information obtained by the Bureau of Investigation and other government agencies. Chosen to head the Division was J. Edgar Hoover. His power to shape policy was growing and he knew in what direction he wished to attack; the left. Hoover spent the remainder of the summer immersed in an in-depth study of the world-wide communist movement, radicals, and the writings of Marx, Engels, Lenin, and Trotsky. (52) As a result of his intensive research, Hoover had discovered:

> a conspiracy so vast, so daring, that few people at first could even grasp the sweep of the Communist vision. It was a conspiracy to destroy totally and completely the religions, governments, institutions, and thinking of the Judaic-Christian world, the Buddhist world, the Islamic world and all religious beliefs. Communism was the most evil, monstrous conspiracy against man since time began. (53)

Chapter 3

The Palmer Raids

There can be little doubt that A. Mitchell Palmer hoped to ride the popularity of his anti-communist and anti-alien radical programs towards a run at the White House in 1920. It can also be argued that the failure of the anti-radical raids from November 1919 to January of 1920 effectively ended Palmer's chances to obtain the Democratic nomination. J. Edgar Hoover's involvement in these raids did have an influence on who could have possibly become President and also how the war on Communism and radicalism was fought then and for years to come. The actions of Hoover before, during, and after the raids proved to be instrumental in shaping his role as the initiator of the war on Communism. These raids were the first major anti-communist operation carried out by the United States government. Hoover's future denials of involvement in the raids must be weighed against the body of evidence which indicts him.

The Justice Department was under heavy pressure to increase prosecutions against alien radicals. In March of 1919, Congress criticized Attorney General Thomas Gregory for not having done enough to combat radicalism. (1) After Hoover's intensive study of Communism in the summer of 1919 and the formation of the American Communist Party in August, he began to take action in preparation for the raids. The Labor Department had determined that membership in the Union of Russian Workers was a deportable offense. Hoover responded by writing to Commissioner General of the

Immigration Bureau, Anthony J. Caminetti requesting the books and records of the organization's membership records. (2) Secretary of Labor William Wilson had expanded the rights of aliens threatened with deportation by allowing them to have legal counsel at the outset of proceedings against them and to also be apprised of their warrant of arrest (Rule 22). On November 19, Hoover wrote to Caminetti suggesting a change in Rule 22 because due process was hampering deportation cases. After receiving no reply, Hoover wrote Caminetti again on December 17. He said:

> In view of the difficulty in proving the cases against persons known to be members of the Union of Russian Workers, due to the arbitrary tactics of persons employed by such members, I would appreciate an early reply to my letter of the nineteenth, in order that the same condition may not arise when future arrests are made of undesirable aliens. (3)

Caminetti sent a memo to John W. Abercrombie (in charge of deportation proceedings), explaining why a modification in Rule 22 was needed and Abercrombie agreed to the change. Copies of the change in Rule 22 were sent to all immigration agents, "Preferably at the beginning of the hearing . . . or at any rate as such hearing has proceeded sufficiently in the development of the facts to protect the Government's interests, the alien shall be . . ." (advised of his right to counsel). (4)

Hoover would later deny that he made any attempt to alter Rule 22: "now insofar as the Department of Justice is concerned in the change of Rule 22, it had no part in it whatsoever. The rule was changed at the instance of the immigration officers." (5) This change would allow Hoover (and others) much more flexibility and deniability in order to carry out their anti-communist agenda. Could Hoover have already learned to hide operations by disguising his fingerprints via layers of inter-agency involvement? A possible answer to this question can be found in various memos that indicate Hoover was issuing orders to agents in the field during the raids in the name of his superiors. (6) Another possibility is that when Palmer was taken ill from exhaustion in November (when the January raids were being planned), Hoover was able to plan the operation in the name of Palmer. (7)

The initial reaction to the November and January raids was

positive according to newspaper headlines and in Hoover's personal correspondence. (8) In a letter (January 7) to United States Attorney Stone in New Jersey, Hoover stated:

> I am endeavoring to place upon the walls of my office here a representative collection of Communists, and if you would forward to me some of the larger photographs of the world-wide Communist movement, I would greatly appreciate it, likewise any interesting banners which could be used for interior decorating would also be appreciated. (9)

The headline in the January 4, 1920, edition of the *New York Times* praised Hoover's program and demonstrated the beginning of his positive anti-communist public relations:

> Briefs had been submitted by J. Edgar Hoover, special assistant to Attorney General Palmer, demonstrating that both the Communist Party and the Communist Labor Party had as their aim the destruction of the American Government and supplanting it with Soviet Control. (10)

What "good and patriotic" American could deny that this was a cause that we should all believe in and a threat we must face up to.

Yet the "ways and means" by which Hoover was able to carry out the raids were not without criticism, but the sceptic's were drowned out by the initial roar of approval. Isaac Shorr, attorney for the National Civil Liberties Bureau, complained in a letter to Palmer that men had been beaten and property had been destroyed during the November raids. Hoover informed his supervisors that he had heard of no such violence and advised against a reply because it could be used to continue the controversy. (11)

In December, Hoover gained his most "successful" public operation to date with the sailing of the U. S. S. Buford. The ship, or "Soviet Ark" as it was dubbed, was filled with 249 aliens who were arrested as a part of the "November Raids." Each of those detained were to be deported to Russia. One hundred eighty-four of the alien radicals were members of the Union of Russian Workers. The remaining detainees were nondescript criminals except for Alexander Berkman and Emma Goldman. (12) Hoover met the radical leaders upon their release from prison, and following in the steps of Harold Conant, immediately made them the prize catch of this voyage. Front page stories in the *Washington Post* and the *New York Times* gave Hoover positive press and increased his influence in policy decision making regarding alien radicals and/or communists. (13) Hoover took pleasure in sending the Serbo-Croation Legation information on anti-Bolshevik tactics after a request was made to the Justice Department. (14)

The success and euphoria for Hoover would wear off, and rather quickly. Of the ten thousand arrested during the raids, sixty-five hundred were released without prosecution, and the vast majority were released soon afterwards. (15) In January and February 1920, Hoover was forced to defend the operation in a series of memos to Burke and Wilson:

> One of the difficulties we are facing at the present time in connection with the communists is that there is an extensive propaganda on foot that many ignorant Russians were taken in the raid who knew nothing of the organization. While this is not entirely true, yet it has proved meat for propaganda and as the deportation policy must be supported solely by public opinion, I feel that a dragnet raid would be detrimental. The [American Protective League] auxiliaries could not be restrained from venting personal animosities and local prejudices against the aliens, and this made abuses of the alien's rights inevitable. (16)

Hoover was forced to respond to the political realities going on around him. Abercrombie suddenly left the Labor Department to run for the Senate in Alabama, Caminetti had canceled warrants and reduced bail for known anarchists, and Louis F. Post became acting Secretary of Labor following the sickness of Secretary William Wilson. Post and others were not as sympathetic to the operation and Hoover was forced to tone down his rhetoric (and operations) somewhat. (17)

Hoover would still cling to his anti-communist platform in order to obtain passage of a "sedition act" in order to declare a legal "jihad" against Communism. (18) During the month of January, Secretary of Labor Wilson decided to hold hearings on whether the Communist Party came under the 1919 Immigration Act. A test case involving Engelbert Preis, who was facing deportation as a result of his membership in the Communist party, was held on January 21. Wilson decided that Preis was guilty, but he would later (in March) change Rule 22 back to its liberal interpretation (protection of the accused). (19)

This action severely hampered Hoover's deportation activities and also caused Hoover to sense from which direction favorable political winds were blowing. Despite a hesitantly favorable ruling in the Preis case, Hoover had encountered some problems with Swinburne Hale, the lawyer who represented Preis and the Communist Party. Hoover did not seem to understand how Captain Hale could defend a radical like Preis. Hoover told General Marlborough Churchill that Hale:

> is now actively engaged in the defense of radicals who find themselves in difficulty in New York State. I noted the somewhat peculiar attitude of Captain Hale upon the elements involved in the discussion and I would therefore appreciate it if you could supply me with his past history and connections. (20)

In April, Hoover declared in a public hearing that at least fifty percent of the influence behind the recent strikes could be traced to the communists. (21) Palmer and Hoover continued to attempt to stoke the fires of the Red Menace. Unfortunately, they created an unpleasant and embarrassing situation for themselves. Palmer and Hoover declared confidently to the public that on Saturday, May 1 (May Day Strike), a general uprising of violence would take place which would be led by communists. (22) But there were no bombs, riots, assassinations, or even vocal meetings. To make matters worse, on May 25, the National Popular Government League released its study of the Palmer Raids. The focus of the study is contained in its first paragraph:

> For more than six months, we the undersigned lawyers, whose sworn duty it is to uphold the Constitution and Laws of the United States, have seen with growing apprehension the continued violation of that Constitution and breaking of those Laws by the Department of Justice of the United States Government. (23)

The implication that Palmer and Hoover were involved in the breaking of laws infuriated Hoover. He reacted in characteristic fashion by opening files on all those who signed the report. (24) In 1961, Harold Arrowsmith, Jr., a researcher for the American Nazi Party, discovered a memo (February 1921) from Hoover which described the "Communist

propaganda activities" of future Supreme Court Justice Felix
Frankfurter, one of the lawyers who signed the study critical
of Palmer and Hoover. (25) Frankfurter did not hesitate to
offer his views of Hoover's culpability in the raids, "Hoover
lies when he denies responsibility for the Red Raids. He was
in it up to his ass." (26)

In 1940, Alexander Holtzoff, a close assistant and chief law
advisor to the F.B.I stated:

> Mr. J. Edgar Hoover was not in charge of and had nothing to
> do with the manner in which the arrests were made of the so-
> called radicals under the administration of Attorney General
> A. Mitchell Palmer. Mr. Hoover at that time was not
> connected with the Federal Bureau of Investigation but was a
> special assistant to the Attorney General. His function was at
> that time limited to the handling of legal matters and the
> preparation of evidence for presentation to the proper
> authorities in connection with those activities. (27)

This statement by Holtzoff was in response to one of the few
criticisms of Hoover during the 1930's and 1940's. Mrs. Mary
Beard, wife of the well-respected historian Charles A. Beard,
questioned the reestablishment of the General Intelligence
Division in 1940. In a speech in Washington, D.C., Mary
Beard refused to accept Holtzoff's explanation of Hoover's
involvement in the Palmer Raids.

Holtzoff responded by adding that the reason he was sure of
Hoover's non-involvement was because Hoover was the source
of his information:

> My statement to you that he did not direct, supervise,
> participate in, or have any connection with the manner in
> which these dragnet raids were conducted was based on Mr.
> Hoover's personal authority to me. The arrests were made
> under the direction of William J. Flynn, then head of the
> Bureau of Investigation, who together with Mr. Palmer, must
> be regarded as responsible for such excesses as took place. . . .
> He [Hoover] did not participate in ordering or carrying out the
> arrests. (28)

This statement must be compared with an order issued by
Assistant Director Frank Burke:

> On the evening of the arrests this office will be open the entire
> night, and I desire that you communicate by long distance to

Mr. Hoover any matters of vital importance or interest which may arise during the course of the arrests. . . . I desire that the morning following the arrests you should forward to this office by special delivery, marked for the "Attention of Mr. Hoover," a complete list of names of the persons arrested, with an indication of residence, or organization to which they belong, and whether they were included in the original list of warrants. . . . I desire also that the morning following the arrests that you communicate in detail by telegram "Attention Mr. Hoover," the results of the arrests made, giving the total number of persons of each organization taken into custody, together with a statement of any interesting evidence secured. (29)

It appears from this statement that Hoover was intimately involved with at least information as to how the raids were carried out and who was arrested.

Further disclosures of Hoover's involvement were made known as a result of Congressional appearances by Palmer and Hoover in 1920 and 1921. Various questions directed to Hoover and Palmer and their answers are related in the following exchanges:

> *Senator Walsh.* How many search warrants were issued?
> *Attorney General Palmer.* I cannot tell you. . . . If you would like to ask Mr. Hoover, who was in charge of this matter, he can tell you.
> *Senator Walsh.* Yes.
> *Mr. Hoover.* The search warrants were entirely a matter which the agents in charge of local offices handled. . . .
> *Senator Walsh.* And you know nothing at all about it?
> *Mr. Hoover.* No, sir.
> *Senator Walsh.* Do you know how many searches were made without a search warrant?
> *Mr. Hoover.* I do not. (30)

In relation to search warrants, Professor Zachariah Chafee, Jr. of the Harvard Law School, related to the Senate Committee investigating the raids, an example of how searches were carried out:

> *Q.* Was your room searched?
> *A.* Yes, sir.
> *Q.* . . . your presence?
> *A.* Yes, sir.
> *Q.* By whom?

A. By the men that were in there, the men in uniform, and also—
Q. Did they ask your permission to search your room?
A. They didn't. . . .
Q. Did they show a warrant?
A. They did not. (31)
Senator Borah. Do I understand that it was a practice of the department with respect to this class of arrests and all others, not to intentionally arrest any man until a warrant had been had under the regular process of the law and the Constitution?
Attorney General Palmer. Yes, sir.

Mr. Hoover was asked about his agents' affidavits in support of their applications for the issuance of warrants:

Mr. Hoover. . . . Most of the warrants issued by the Department of Labor, at the instance of the Department of Justice, were issued upon sworn affidavits.
Senator Walsh. Beforehand?
Mr. Hoover. Beforehand.
Senator Walsh. That is, all warrants that were issued were issued upon these affidavits?
Mr. Hoover. I would not say all. . . . (32)

It seems clear that Palmer believed that Hoover was responsible for these illegal searches but Hoover did not accept the responsibility.

In regards to confessions and the right to have an attorney present, Hoover had written a letter in 1920 to the Immigration Bureau (Caminetti) on the subject of confessions. He asked the Bureau to refuse to free any prisoners on bail unless he answered the questions put to him by the Bureau's detectives. "This was of vital importance. I desire to urge upon you for your earnest consideration." (33) This request appears quite similar to the arresting detectives orders during the raids, "persons taken into custody [are] not to be permitted to communicate with any outside person until after examination by this office and until permission is given by this office." (34) Was Hoover again using inter-agency confusion to deny responsibility?

Another interesting disclosure, that follows a common Cold War theme of J. Edgar Hoover, originated out of the questions raised by Judge George W. Anderson. The Judge was investigating the conduct of the raids in the New

England area and called a number of Bureau of Investigation agents to the stand. Anderson was most concerned with the activities of undercover agents and he stated that, "What does appear, beyond reasonable doubt, is that the Government owns and operates some part of the Communist Party." (35) This charge was a common one during the raids and in the decades to follow. Hoover (and others) had built up the Communist Party to be a larger threat than it was by infiltrating the Party with its own agents and helping to direct its operations. Hoover responded to Anderson's charges by stating that this was "an unjustifiable misconception of the facts, which the most perverted mind could not put upon the evidence." (36) Strong talk indeed from the youthful Hoover.

The records compiled by Senator Thomas Walsh during the Senate Judiciary Committee's investigation, the National Popular Government League, and Judge Anderson strongly indicate that J. Edgar Hoover was not telling the whole truth when denying responsibility for the Palmer Raids. In 1947, Hoover continued to deny any responsibility in a statement given to *Look* magazine. He also told the *New York Herald Tribune* in the same year, "I deplored the manner in which the raids were executed then, and my position has remained unchanged." (37) If he deplored the manner in which they were executed then a record of his views at the time have not yet been documented.

What does one make of J. Edgar Hoover and his anti-communist crusade in the spring of 1921? The Palmer Raids, the sailing of the "Soviet Ark," (and Alexander Berkman and Emma Goldman), and subsequent newspaper headlines and Congressional appearances, seemed to have whetted his appetite for power and influence in the fight against Communism. There can be no doubt that the operations of Palmer, Flynn, Burke, and Hoover severely and permanently disabled the communist movement in the United States. The problem of domestic Communism was all but eradicated in 1921; would Hoover (after becoming Director in 1924) now confine his work in the Justice Department to its original intentions? Such a suggestion was intimated in the Report compiled by the National Popular Government League. The Report stated:

> The legal functions of the Attorney General are: to advise the Government on questions of law, and to prosecute persons who have violated federal statutes. For the Attorney General

to go into the field of propaganda against radicals is a deliberate misuse of his office and a deliberate squandering of funds entrusted to him by Congress. The behavior of the Justice Department involved no question of vague and threatened menace, but a present assault upon the most sacred principles of our Constitutional liberty. (38)

According to Cartha DeLoach (later Assistant Director of the FBI), Hoover had always justified the Palmer Raids as a result of the information compiled on communists, anarchists, and agitators by Hoover and the General Intelligence Division. (39)

It seems Hoover really believed that every thought generated against "American values" had its origin in Communism. But others, in and out of government, then and now had a different view of his Cold War crusade. Emma Goldman and Alexander Berkman appear to have been quite wrong by comparing their violence to the "Sons of Liberty" in the American Revolution, but they at least admitted that they might be wrong in their beliefs and that others might be also. Berkman said, "We believe that free speech is the very foundation of liberty in this country or in any other country. We may be wrong. Maybe anarchism is all wrong. But I claim the right even to be wrong." (40) Goldman offered her own view by stating:

> I for one cannot believe that love of one's country must consist in blindness to its social faults. I know many people—I am one of them—who were not born here, and who yet love America with deeper passion and greater intensity than many natives. If America has entered the war to make the world safe for democracy, she must make democracy safe in America. (41)

Goldman is touching on a theme that is larger than the threat of Communism or any other "ism." The problems in America, from the turn of the century onward, were deeper and more complex than J. Edgar Hoover (and others) were willing to see. As Woodrow Wilson stated just before our intervention into World War I:

> Every reform we have won will be lost if we go into this war. We have been making a fight on special privilege. . . . War means autocracy. The people we have unhorsed will inevitably come into control of the country for we shall be

dependent upon the steel, ore, and financial magnates. They will run the nation. (42)

Wilson was correct, for in the upcoming battle between Capitalism and Communism, Hoover would declare war on "communist inspired" union leaders who threatened the "American way of life." In so doing, he helped to promote the industrial leadership of the United States while the centralization of the United States government continued at a quickening pace. The growth of American-style capitalism coincided with an increase in the growth of the Bureau's investigative powers and Hoover's rise to the position of Director.

Chapter 4

Consolidating and Expanding Hoover's Power at the Bureau

The election of 1920 would result in the new Republican administration of Warren G. Harding and would also mark the beginning of Hoover's reign as "the Director" (1924). Samuel Eliot Morrison described the election mood of America in 1920 in this fashion:

> Whatever may have been the reason or reasons for the 1920 vote, it is certain that World War I was the most popular war in our history while it lasted and the most hated after it was over. The Red Menace siphoned off a part of the hate, but most of it boomeranged on the administration which had led us into a futile and useless war. (1)

Hoover had played a direct role in important policy and directive decisions under the administration of Wilson and had emerged unscathed after his ill-advised and unjustified initial assault against the "Red Menace." He learned that in his zeal to defeat Communism, he must attempt to appease those who controlled his reappointment to a non-elected position. During this period, Hoover would begin the process of building the FBI into arguably the most powerful investigative force in the world.

Warren Harding took office in March of 1921, and with his new Republican administration, there would be changes. A potential problem that Hoover would have to face every four years was the prospect of a new president, attorney general, federal judges, and all with possibly new and different priorities. It wouldn't take long for Hoover to see how quickly the faces around him could and would change. Harding appointed fellow Ohio native, Harry M. Daugherty, to be the new Attorney General soon after taking office. On August 18, Daugherty fired William Flynn as Director of the Bureau and replaced him with William J. Burns. Both Burns and Flynn had formerly earned their reputations as detectives. Hoover would have little to fear in regards to Burns and his views on radicals and Communism. Questioned before the House Appropriations Committee in 1922, Burns was asked, "Do you think it[radicalism]is increasing from week to week month to month?" He replied, "I think it is. I cannot impress upon you too much how dangerous they are at the moment." (2) His views on radicalism were made even more clear in a statement made again before the House Appropriations Committee two years later:

> Radicalism is becoming stronger every day in this country. . . .
> We have absolute proof of all this; we have documentary proof
> showing that it is absolutely true. . . . I dare say that unless
> the country becomes thoroughly aroused concerning the
> danger of this radical element in this country we will have a
> very serious situation. (3)

Although Hoover undoubtedly shared the same views as Burns, as the "we" in Burns statement implies, his scars from the Palmer Raids were still fresh. He was reluctant to attack communists and radicals openly until he received a "mandate" to do so. Hoover was more concerned at this time with working his way up the ladder in the Bureau. He also had his hands full helping to carry out and cover up the schemes of the Harding administration, most notably of his superiors Attorney General Harry Daugherty and Bureau Director William Burns.

At the urging of Burns, Bureau agents in September 1922 burglarized the office of Congressman Oscar Kellar who had called for Daugherty's resignation over his stance on the rail workers strike. Agents also "spied upon" and burglarized the activities and offices of Senators Robert LaFollette and William Borah. (4) Both men were critical of the Harding administration's foreign and defense policies. According to authors Robert J. Nash and David Williams, the Bureau became "a private hole in the corner goon squad for the attorney general. Its arts were the arts of snooping, bribery, and blackmail." (5) Scholar Alpheus Mason stated:

> Included among the special agents were some with criminal records. Bureau badges and property [were] issued to persons not employed by the government and to others who posed as confidential agents and informers to frame evidence against personal enemies of the Harding administration. (6)

Hoover would eventually take charge of "cleaning" up this mess (after being named Director in 1924) but did he ever clean up the Bureau or did he just learn how not to leave tracks? There are indications that Hoover was learning his trade from none other than the "father of American intelligence," Major General Ralph H. Van Deman. Curt Gentry has written:

> What is known is that in 1922 Van Deman arranged for Hoover to receive a reserve officer's commission in the Army's Military Intelligence Division [MID]. . . . Hoover worked closely with Marlborough Churchill, Van Deman's successor as head of MID during the Palmer raids and thereafter; and that Hoover and Van Deman maintained a mutually beneficial relationship that lasted until Van Deman's death in 1952. (7)

Apparently Van Deman's knowledge of the intelligence apparatus was instrumental in Hoover setting up his Cold War operations. William Corson writes:

> In a 1971 article, the *New York Times* alleged that Van Deman was supported in his project by the army, the navy, the FBI, and various local police organizations. "Moreover, the general ran a nationwide network of informants, each identified only by a coded number, who reported great volumes of raw information to him. The files show that some information could have come only from agents who infiltrated the Communist Party, labor unions, church groups and other organizations." (8)

An example of how close their relationship was, is indicated by a reference from Van Deman to J. Edgar as:

"My dear Colonel Hoover." Also, the Van Deman file clearly bespeaks a sharing and exchange of information between himself and selected members of the intelligence services, as well as some "private" organizations and persons who have been active in combating the so-called Red menace. (9)

A further indication that Hoover was learning from the best and was covering tracks rather than cleaning up the mess is discovered when considering the activities of "special Bureau Agent," Gaston Means. Means was the most notorious of the "dollar a year" men, as the new breed of Bureau agents were called. Many of these new agents earned up to two thousand dollars a month, which is why the Bureau came to be known as the "Department of Easy Virtue." Gaston Means was a former spy for both the Germans and the British during the war. He was a former associate with William Burns in "detective work" and with "certain organized crime figures." (10) Means also had an office just down the hallway from Hoover. Although Means "officially" only collected seven dollars a day working for the Bureau, he lived in a large house with three servants, and had a chauffeur-driven limousine. (11) The implication was that Means was illegally padding his pockets as well as planning and carrying out various illegal searches and burglaries while working for the Bureau.

Means was called before a Senate Investigative Committee after revelations involving various oil and financial interests with the now deceased Harding (who died on August 3, 1923) and his administration were uncovered as a result of the oil lease scandal,Teapot Dome:

> Senator Burton Wheeler asked him this question, "You also investigated Senator LaFollette, did you not?" "Yes," replied Means. "And you went through his offices here, did you not, in the Capitol?" "I saw that it was done . . . I would just as soon investigate a tramp as anybody else. . . . The man is a number. I never ask who he is. . . . Thousands of people have been investigated. Bishops have been investigated and clergymen."
>
> The Chairman of the Senate Committee, Smith Brookhart asked, "When did this terrific spy system start in the United States, by what authority if you know?" "I never saw a candidate that loomed up. . . . that they did not go out and make an inquiry about him. . .The financial crowd finance and get investigations," replied Means. "You mean the financial

interests investigate everyone who is a candidate for office to get something on him," asked Brookhart, "so they can control him, is that the idea?" "Well, yes that would be my interpretation" . . . stated Means. "And that gang . . . said Brookhart, "is the same gang that I have denominated as the non-partisan league in Wall Street? Is that the crowd?" Means nodded, "I think President Wilson gave them the best designation, 'invisible government.'" (12)

Means was later imprisoned and died there in 1938.

Although Hoover would attempt to distance himself from Means, Hoover was the number two man at the Bureau, and Hoover was at Daugherty's side (literally and figuratively) and well aware of what was going on. The tactics used by Means would be very similar to those that Hoover would use against communists and subversives in the years to come.

According to his testimony, the contention of Gaston Means was that, "Wall Street" and an "invisible government" comprised of corporate interests, actually pushed the Bureau to destroy the careers of those that opposed them. Hoover's Seward Square and anti-union mind set, his loathing of Communism and radicalism, combined with a desire to shape minds and policy to "American values," would merge nicely with the pro-capitalist and anti-communist forces.

As a result of Means' testimony, Republican leaders asked for Daugherty's resignation, but he refused. Daugherty charged that the "Senate investigation was the work of communist agents and their tools and Senator Wheeler was no more a Democrat than Stalin, his comrade in Washington." (13) Was Hoover suggesting Daugherty's line of defense as he sat beside Daugherty's lawyers during the latter's testimony?

Wheeler stated that, "Some of our witnesses were approached to find out what testimony they would give. Others were shadowed." (14) Potential witnesses in the investigation, such as oil industry leaders, Harry Sinclair of Prairie Oil and Gas Company, Henry Blackner of Midwest Refining, and Colonel Robert W. Stewart of Standard Oil of Indiana, all left the country in January of 1924. (15) Jess Smith, a Bureau crony of Gaston Means, had recently testified before the committee; he was later found shot through the head in May of 1923, a victim of "suicide." Smith is another interesting character. He and Harry Daugherty lived in a house together on H Street in Washington thanks to the generosity of fellow agent Ned McLean who arranged for the acquisition of the house. It was believed by Theodore Roosevelt's daughter and her friend Vyla Wilson that it was "noised about Washington that the two men [Daughterty and Smith] cared for each other and that Jess was a homosexual." (16) This is a possible forerunner of the Hoover and Clyde Tolson relationship. Author Carl Anthony states, "Much of the illegal activities of Harding's administration were pinned on the late Jess Smith who was assumed to have acted with the knowledge and authority of the attorney general." (17) Evalyn McLean (Ned's wife) raises further suspicions with these comments, "He [Smith] didn't kill himself they murdered him. [Daugherty, Means, and Burns] (18) Authors Athan G. Theoharis and John Stuart Cox argue that the claim:

> that Burns shunted [Hoover] into a side office where he handled routine paper work, as one report had it, or that Hoover lay low for a time, as he himself said, simply does not square with the letters of congratulation that he received from former colleagues on the occasion of his being appointed Director in 1924 and that he carefully preserved until the end of his life. The consensus of his peers was that the title belatedly went with the job, and the warmest of the congratulations came from William J Burns. (19)

The world of J. Edgar Hoover was no doubt intertwined with the worlds of Burns, Daugherty, Smith, and Means. But only they would know the depth of those relationships

Mrs. J. B. Duckstein, former secretary to William Burns, added validity to Means' statements of an "invisible government" and that Hoover was possibly involved during her testimony before the committee in May of 1924. Hoover, who was now acting Director following the firing of Burns (August 1924), responded by dismissing Mrs. Duckstein within a week of her testimony. (20)

Whether Hoover was directly responsible for some or all of these questionable and/or illegal operations is not certain, but he was most certainly aware of all or most of them. What was of immediate importance to Hoover, was to maintain his position and to eventually ride out the storm and become the Director. The new administration of Calvin Coolidge and his new Attorney General, Harlan Stone, would most certainly have been justified in cleaning house at the Bureau after all the reports of scandal and intrigue. Stone had been a strong critic of the Palmer Raids and later recalled, "the Bureau of Investigation was . . . in an exceedingly bad odor when I became Attorney General." (21) As fate would have it, Hoover would have a friend in the right place at the right time. Lawrence Richey, Hoover's fellow Masonic Lodge member and an assistant to Secretary of Commerce Herbert Hoover, suggested to the Secretary of Commerce that J. Edgar Hoover would be a good choice to head the Bureau:

> Why should they look around when they have the man they need right over there now—a young well-educated lawyer named Hoover," said Richey. "Do you think he can do the job?" the secretary asked. "I know he can," Richey replied. "He's a good friend of mine. (22)

Secretary Hoover passed on Richey's comments to Harlan Stone and the rest is history. J. Edgar Hoover, at the age of twenty-nine, took the reins of the directorship of the Bureau of Investigation. Although the political climate was not right and despite being forced by this climate to scale back his Cold War operations, Hoover was still able to influence foreign as well as domestic policy in Communism. In January of 1924 (before Hoover became Director), Hoover was asked by Secretary of State Charles Evans Hughes to gather information for use in Hughes' argument that the Soviet Union should not be granted diplomatic recognition. Hoover's report contained almost five-hundred pages and he sat beside Hughes as he gave his testimony before a congressional committee. (23)

Upon receiving the title of Director, Hoover became concerned with reorganizing the Bureau and establishing a new image to replace that of the "Dollar a Year Men." According to future Assistant FBI Director, Cartha DeLoach, Hoover convinced Attorney General Stone, that he wanted to professionalize the Bureau and get rid of the political hacks. Promotions should be granted based on "proven ability." The reorganization that followed became known as the "great purge." (24) This is indicated in a statement Hoover made before the House Appropriations Committee in December 1926:

> During the past few months we have limited our activities, necessarily, because of the scope of our authority and also because of the volume of the work, to investigation of radical

matters only when there has been a violation of a Federal statute involved, and that is the policy we are following at present. We have many reports, practically hundreds a month, coming in to us advising us of an individual who is making communistic statements. However, there is no Federal law under which we can prosecute him at this time and there is no reason why we should waste our money in connection with that matter. The only reason we submitted that memorandum to the Secretary of State is that we have authority to submit to the Secretary of State, upon his request, information that he requires for administrative decisions. (25)

Hoover made it clear that the Bureau could still investigate communists but it should be done only on request and without publicity. (26) Further evidence of Hoover's public "holding pattern" on the investigation of communists is shown in April 1927. Two prominent anti-communists of the period, Archibald E. Stevenson (of the Lusk Committee) and Ralph Easley, visited with Hoover and Assistant Attorney General Oscar R. Luhring. The topic of the conversation was a request by Easley and Stevenson that the Bureau be turned loose on communists once again. Hoover's reply was that the "Justice Department is taking no interest whatever in the activities of the communists and other radicals in this country. It has not had a dollar to spend for that purpose." (27)

It became obvious to Hoover that he could not publicly attack an unpopular cause while establishing himself as the Director; he would have to bide his time.

Congressional interest into the probing of communist activities had waned considerably as evidenced by the failure of a joint House resolution to investigate native Bolsheviks in 1927. (28) By 1930, Congressional interest into communist activities had again increased. Publicity had been generated as a result of the disclosure of documents from a New York company, whose Soviet purchasing agent had disseminated Bolshevik propaganda. (29) Congressman Fiorello La Guardia, Republican from New York, later found the documents to be forged but it was too late to stop the establishment of the Fish committee. (30)

The committee's purpose was to investigate communist activities in the United States. Hoover appeared before the Fish committee in 1930 and reeled off numerous statistics about the current state of communist activity. He stopped short of declaring a public war on Communism unless a peacetime sedition law, similar to the one Mitchell Palmer proposed in 1919, was adopted. (31) Hoover went on to claim in closed session before the committee, that American Communists acknowledged their subservience to the Soviet Union. (32) Despite Hoover's testimony, none of the proposed legislation passed. This was another indication to Hoover, that although his zeal in carrying out his Cold War had not waned, the mandate to do so was not there.

Hoover spent much of his time investigating critics of Herbert Hoover's administration upon request and thereby ingratiating himself with those who controlled his future power and influence. One such example involved the Navy League of the United States. The Navy League was made up of a group of "super patriots" who had criticized President Hoover's lack of an increase in defense appropriations. Hoover seemed reluctant to attack this group (possibly because he was of their ilk) as evidenced by his statement to Lawrence Richey in October 1931, "information is possessed by only a few persons and seems extremely difficult to obtain confidentially." (33) During the next 30 years, Hoover would regularly socialize and vacation with wealthy and "self-described patriots" who were most often of a conservative and right-wing mindset.

Another group that J. Edgar Hoover would find difficulty in investigating during this time (and later) would be organized crime and its subsequent involvement in narcotics trafficking. Harry Anslinger, who was appointed Commissioner of the newly formed Bureau of Narcotics in September 1930, described how organized crime moved into narcotics trafficking as Prohibition was ending. He also stated that J. Edgar Hoover was one of the few public officials who was given access to a confidential book compiled by the Narcotics Bureau. (34) The book described how organized crime operated and named its leaders, and explained how many "legitimate" businessmen and public officials were involved in these illicit operations. It was during this time that Meyer Lansky and Frank Costello, two of the most powerful leaders of organized crime, helped to deliver narcotics smuggler Louis Lepke, "the most dangerous criminal in America" according to the Director into Hoover's hands. (35) According to author Hank Messick, "... Meyer Lansky made contact with a high-ranking subordinate of Hoover, and arrangements were made to surrender Lepke. . . ." (36)

Hoover was quick to see that the public was greatly impressed with his "new fixation" on bank robbers and kidnappers. Unfortunately, he became blind to the reality of organized crime activities—for whatever reasons. Many researchers and authors have attempted to document the reasons for Hoover's reluctance in this area. Hank Messick argues that Hoover's friendship with Lewis Rosentiel was an important factor. Rosentiel, a former bootlegger and current liquor baron (president of Schenley Liquor), was also a rabid anti-communist and a personal friend of mobster Meyer Lansky. Hank Messick has written:

> According to sworn statements by Rosentiel's fourth wife, her husband maintained friendly relations with such men as Meyer Lansky and Joe Linsey on the one hand, and FBI Director J. Edgar Hoover on the other. In fact, he created the J. Edgar Hoover Foundation and endowed it with Schenley stock. (37)

Three individuals who together, point towards some of the more complex and potentially suspicious relationships that Hoover enjoyed, were those of Standard Fruit board member (and Louisiana political bagman) Seymour Weiss, Hoover friend and former bootlegger Lewis Rosentiel, and New York mobster Frank Costello. As author Peter Dale Scott has noted:

> A final consequence of the Lewis Rosentiel-Frank Costello-Seymour Weiss business deals was that the influence which both Rosentiel and Costello enjoyed with Hoover was henceforth shared by Weiss as well. In 1939, amid rumors that Louisiana Governor Richard Leche and Weiss would be indicted, Leche entertained Hoover and Attorney General Frank Murphy at his governor's mansion. One week later Hoover's assistant Louis B. Nichols gave Leche and Weiss a personally guided tour of FBI headquarters in Washington. (38)

According to Curt Gentry:

> Like Hoover, Costello was a Stork Club regular, as were numerous other mob figures, and the club owner, Sherman Billingsley, who numbered J. Edgar Hoover among his closest friends, was himself a former bootlegger who had served time at Leavenworth. Billingsly's past of which Hoover was well

aware, apparently bothered the FBI director no more than did his virulent prejudice against unions, "niggers" and [with only a few exceptions, the most prominent, of course, Walter Winchell] Jews. . . . Costello didn't like Hoover and considered him a "professional blackmailer" who used the information his agency gathered for his own personal ends. (39)

Rosentiel, Lansky, and other organized crime figures were instrumental in the establishment of the J. Edgar Hoover Foundation, whose main goal was the reduction of juvenile crime. (40) Anthony Summers provides documentation that Hoover might have been blackmailed as a result of organized crime's knowledge of his alleged homosexuality. Summers argues that Billy Byars Jr. (son of the wealthy oilman) used a bungalow next to Hoover's vacation house at the Del Charro Hotel in La Jolla, California owned by Clint Murchison in the late 1960's. It is possible that organized crime was aware of his alleged homosexuality in the 1930's. (41)

Michael Milan (former FBI agent) argues that Hoover actually worked closely with organized crime on various Cold War covert operations that included assassinations. Milan's account is an interesting one when considering Meyer Lansky's role in helping to create "Operation Underworld" that helped the American effort in Sicily, Italy, and the New York port area during World War II. (42) As will be discussed in the conclusion, Hoover's FBI "alumni" had tentacles branching out in all directions. None of these possibilities (or a combination) have been proven, but it has been documented that Hoover would ignore investigating organized crime for thirty years until the administration of John Kennedy forced him to do so. It is quite possible that anti-communist organized crime figures had influence with Hoover as a result of their "political beliefs," "friendships," and "interests." Hoover would become very friendly with oilman Clint Murchison, Irving Davidson, a Washington lobbyist and lawyer for organized crime figures, hotel owner Meyer Schine, and Del Webb, a Las Vegas casino owner. Despite their relationships with organized crime figures, Hoover would stay at hotels and frequent race tracks where Murchison, Webb, Davidson, Schine, (and others), and hoodlums rubbed shoulders. (43) One certainty is that organized crime flourishes in a non-communist environment (witness Russia today). (44) As early as 1931, Al Capone, Chicago's leader of organized crime, was stating his opposition to the communist threat. "Bolshevism is knocking at our gates. We can't afford to let it in. We've got to organize ourselves against it, and put our shoulders together and hold fast." (45) Hoover himself could not have said it any better.

In June 1932, the "Bonus Army" began its march on Washington. The Army veterans were demanding the bonus that veterans had been promised after WWI. The money was not due until 1945 but because of the terrible poverty they were experiencing during the Depression, many were hoping that placing some pressure on Congress and President Herbert Hoover might help. When the Senate subsequently refused to grant them their pay, most of the 17,000 (veterans with their families) went home. Some 2,000 of the veterans remained, most because they had no place to go.

Author William Corson described how Douglas MacArthur, at the urgency of J. Edgar Hoover, labeled the remaining veterans communists and proceeded to drive them out by force:

> MacArthur had been preparing for war. He had called up reserves, tanks, and artillery from installations near Washington. In addition, he had asked J. Edgar Hoover to infiltrate the marchers' ranks and provide him with intelligence. Hoover's men reported that there were very few communists and that the marchers were remarkably well-behaved. This was not what the FBI Director nor MacArthur wanted to hear. Despite the reports of his own agents, Hoover told MacArthur that there were many dangerous communists among the Bonus Army and that they were inciting the group to violence. (46)

Hoover's report led to a clash between the veterans and the police. Several veterans and police were killed and the remaining veteran's shacks were burned to the ground. The negative publicity created by the incident led directly to the defeat of Herbert Hoover by Franklin Roosevelt in the election of 1932. J. Edgar Hoover would emerge unscarred and would witness another president come and go.

One problem that Hoover could not ignore in 1932 was another presidential election. Hoover's job security was very much at stake as a result of Herbert Hoover's "failure" to stop the Great Depression and the subsequent election of Franklin Roosevelt. On February 28, 1933, Roosevelt announced the appointment of Attorney General Thomas Walsh, Senator from Montana, who had clashed with Hoover during the

Senate investigations into the Palmer Raids. Walsh quickly announced that "he would reorganize the Department of Justice when he assumed office, probably with an almost completely new personnel." (47) Within five days of his statement to the press, Walsh was dead. He had suddenly married a wealthy Cuban girl, much to the surprise of long-time senatorial colleague Burton Wheeler. (48) The two were married in Havana and were riding a train to return to Washington for Roosevelt's inaugural, when Walsh died of a heart attack on March 3.

Burton Wheeler stated that Hoover came to see him after the death of Walsh; "Hoover got wind of this talk [that he would be replaced] and came to see me. He insisted he played no part in the reprisals against me. I had no desire to ask for Hoover's head on a platter—and I'm glad I didn't." (49) William Sullivan (later to be Assistant Director of the FBI), who knew Burton Wheeler well, claimed that Wheeler "started off distrusting Hoover and he ended up distrusting him." (50) The end result of this strange affair was that Homer Commings became the new Attorney General and he and Roosevelt decided to retain Hoover. Why he was retained is a question only they can answer, but the power and fear that Hoover generated after nearly ten years as Director, should be considered as a strong possibility why. In the words of Ray Tucker, an editorialist for *Collier's* magazine, in August of 1933:

> Under him [Hoover] the Bureau was run in a Prussian style; it became a personal and political machine. More inaccessible than Presidents, he kept his agents in fear and awe by firing and shifting them at whim; no other government office had such a turnover of personnel. . . . He always opposed Civil Service qualifications for his men. . . . He was a law and czar unto himself. (51)

As the ensuing years would show, those in positions of power (and especially Franklin Roosevelt) would be quite interested in the "political information" that Hoover generated. As Ray Tucker explained further:

> the Bureau's shadows frequently had under surveillance such dignitaries as prospective cabinet members, government officials, publishers, newspaper reporters, clerks, college professors, liberals, certain classes of the intelligentsia,

alleged communists, labor leaders and some criminals . . . the
FBI by 1933 had become a miniature America Cheka. (52)

Maybe it was miniature in 1933, but in the decades to come, it
would grow at a phenomenal rate.

In the early 1930's, the outbreaks of bank robberies and
kidnappings pushed Congress to enact legislation to give the
FBI the power to investigate these and other crimes. Richard
G. Powers described (in *G-Men: The FBI in American
Popular Culture*) how the war on crime during the 1920's and
1930's helped to perpetuate the myth of the legendary G-Men
of the FBI who were led by their fearless leader, J. Edgar
Hoover:

> By the time Roosevelt took office, the cultural materials that
> coalesced into the myth of the G-Man had all been assembled:
> popular fascination with rituals of crime and punishment,
> both in the news and in entertainment helped to create a
> hunger for mass involvement, in anti-crime action. (53)

When Franklin Roosevelt entered the White House, a pre-
defined hero role already existed for someone on the federal
level to step into. As Robert Unger argues in his book, *The
Union Station Massacre,* if the country wanted a gangbuster,
J. Edgar Hoover desperately wanted the job. (54)

Unger states that J. Edgar Hoover called the "massacre" a
turning point in the nation's fight against crime. The
massacre was actually the killing of three federal agents as
they were transferring prisoners at Kansas City's Union
Station on June 17, 1933. What caused Hoover to believe that
this incident was so important? At the time of the massacre,
Hoover's men were restricted, (with few exceptions) to
investigating white slavery [prostitution], interstate auto
theft, and federal bankruptcy violations. Demands for reform
were heard in cities and towns all over the country, but the
focus quickly settled on Hoover and his small band of federal
agents. When Hoover "screamed" that his agents needed
more power, he suddenly found sympathetic ears among the
public and in the capital. (55) Not quite one year after the
massacre, nine major anti-crime bills were signed into law; in
effect a federal criminal code which the United States had
never experienced before came into being.

Robert Unger states:

In his hands lay the seeds of unprecedented power. Hoover nurtured these seeds into fruition unmatched in American history. His FBI, his crime lab, his persona all grew to greatness. Without the *Union Station Massacre*, however, there would be no such seeds. (56)

Hoover's new fingerprint section was barely a year old in 1933. Their supposed evidence in this case helped send alleged killer Adam Richetti to his date with the executioner. But Robert Unger argues that:

> All that evidence was tainted, if not polluted beyond any legal significance. And the Bureau's experts knew it. There is little doubt that everybody in the Bureau's Kansas City office knew the true story of the massacre, but young John Edgar Hoover and his FBI needed a cause, a crusade. He needed good and evil. And he needed a victory. The truth would offer none of that. But the legend provided it all. (57)

The methods Hoover would use to cover up the truth in this investigation would be used in others in the decades to come, especially in his lifelong war against Communism.

On July 30, 1933, the President officially expanded the Bureau and renamed it the Federal Bureau of Investigation. The main responsibilities of the "new" Bureau would be centered on investigations of kidnapping and racketeering. Hoover would benefit from the expansion of the Bureau's responsibilities (as well as with the public's fascination with the G-Man myth) during the remainder of the 1930's. FBI publicists such as Courtney Ryley Cooper wrote glowing accounts of Hoover's exploits:

> Five years ago, J. Edgar Hoover was practically an unknown as far as the general public was concerned. Today he heads our best known group of man hunters—the G-men. The small boy is rare indeed who does not look upon its Director as his ideal. (58)

Not all would agree with this assessment, Senator George Norris stated:

> He's [Hoover] the greatest publicity hound on the American continent, unless we do something to stop this furor of adulation and omnipotent praise, we will have an organization of the FBI that, instead of protecting the

government from criminals, will direct the government itself.
(59)

In March of 1936, Attorney General Commings complained
personally to the publicity-seeking Hoover, "Mr. Hoover I
want you to realize I am the head of Justice, there is too much
publicity [about you] coming out from your desk." (60) This
personal and public humiliation (published in the
newspapers) by Hoover's boss, was followed by Postal
Inspector Jim Farley's criticism of Hoover, "the best
government detectives were postal inspectors, then Treasury
agents, and then G-men." (61)

These public criticisms by government officials (although
rare), combined with Hoover's dislike of many of Roosevelt's
"socialists," such as Presidential Aide Harry Hopkins and
Secretary of Agriculture Henry Wallace might have led to
rumors of Hoover's possible retirement. (62)

Anthony Summers has written that former Assistant FBI
Director William Sullivan believed:

> Hoover didn't like Roosevelt. He never passed up on a chance
> to make a snide remark when FDR's name was mentioned,
> and he never failed to express his feelings about the president
> in internal memos . . . Edgar thought Roosevelt suspiciously
> left-wing. "Hoover didn't trust liberals," said Sullivan, "and
> FDR had surrounded himself with other Liberals. (63)

Summers added:

> Edgar's attitude to the President was mild compared with his
> dislike of Eleanor Roosevelt. He had grave misgivings about
> the President's wife, about her enthusiasm for left-wing
> causes and left-wing friends, and he let the President know it.
> (64)

Former FBI agent G. Gordon Liddy agreed with Summers'
assessment about Eleanor but not about his relations with
FDR:

> During her husband's administration, he [Hoover] said, she
> had been a most dangerous enemy of the Bureau. Were it not
> for Hoover's great personal friendship and rapport with
> Franklin Roosevelt, he said, Eleanor might well have
> succeeded in interfering with the Bureau's ability to contain
> the communist menace in the United States. According to

Hoover, whenever he found that Eleanor had thrown a roadblock into the path of the FBI, he had only to speak to her husband to have it removed immediately. (65)

The problems in Asia and Europe would change any thoughts of retirement. The renewed threat of espionage, sabotage, and radicalism led Franklin Roosevelt to ask Hoover to take on these threats with a broad mandate from the President. Roosevelt, in August of 1936, directed the FBI to develop more systematic intelligence about "subversive activities in the United States, particularly Fascism and Communism." (66) Hoover responded by ordering all field offices "to obtain from all possible sources, information concerning subversive activities being conducted in the United States." (67) In the spring of 1938, Roosevelt continued the buildup of the FBI, after a request from Hoover for more funds without special legislation, "with the utmost degree of secrecy in order to avoid criticism or objections which might be raised by either ill-informed persons or individuals having some ulterior motive." (68)

In the early summer of 1939, as the threat of war escalated in Europe, President Roosevelt decided that the FBI (in cooperation with the War and Navy Departments) should take over all intelligence operations. In conjunction with these new responsibilities, Hoover set up secret "schools" to uncover "subversives." William Corson described the schools:

> On September 14, 1939, a "high administration" official revealed that for more than a year FBI agents had been receiving intensive training in the techniques of uncovering espionage, sabotage, and subversive activities. The special schools, located in Washington and the Maryland countryside, which met in units of thirty men each, were personally conducted by J. Edgar Hoover. (69)

Hoover used the possibility of dockyard and shipping sabotage during the war to set out to destroy Harry Bridges, a union leader whom he considered a communist:

> Harry Bridges, the thirty-five-year-old leader of the International Longshoremen's and Warehousemen's Union, had long been a thorn in the side of management. He was also an irritant to Edgar personally. Five years earlier, when Edgar had briefed Roosevelt on the internal threat from Communists, he had named Bridges as the man who could

paralyze the nation's shipping. Even after the union leader
came out in favor of a peace agreement with management,
Edgar pursued him relentlessly.

Bridges was vulnerable because he had been born in
Australia. Edgar claimed he was a Communist, and foreign-
born Communists could be deported for membership in "an
organization advocating the violent overthrow of the
government." Bridges said he had never joined the Party,
though he admitted being an admirer of "the Soviet workers'
state." The result of his latest deportation hearing was still
pending in the summer of 1941. (70)

The threat of sabotage during the war allowed Hoover to
operate under a cover of "national security" to carry his
investigations of Bridges and others whom Hoover believed
were of a leftist and/or communist persuasion.

After the invasion of Poland in September of 1939,
Roosevelt authorized Hoover to "temporarily" gather
information on all subversive activities in the United States.
(71) Despite the restrictions imposed by the Supreme Court
involving the Nardone and Weiss wire-tapping cases in 1939,
Roosevelt believed that the restrictions did not apply "to
grave matters involving the defense of the nation." He
therefore authorized the securing of information by listening
devices "of persons suspected of subversive activities." (72)
Hoover would use this "temporary charter" to justify
conducting domestic intelligence for the rest of his life.

Another result of this increased power were "procedures
instituted by Hoover in 1942 to ensure that FBI agents could
conduct break-ins, subject to his personal authorization,
without risk of discovery." (73) Hoover also attempted to
revive the Custodial Detention list he had first implemented
in preparation for the Palmer Raids in 1919:

> In 1943 Attorney General Biddle discovered, and reviewed,
> the Custodial Detention list, finding it "impractical, unwise,
> dangerous, illegal and inherently unreliable" and ordered
> Hoover to abolish it. He did, semantically, by changing its
> name to the Security Index and instructing his aides to keep
> its existence secret from the Justice Department. . . . (74)

From 1938 to 1945 the Dies Committee became a symbol
for the anti-communist movement in the United States. It
became a rallying point for crusading ex-communists, right-
wing interest groups, and the conservative press. When the

Dies Committee expired at the end of 1944, anti-Communism remained the peculiar prerogative of right wingers and was summarily dismissed by most Americans as conservative anti-New Deal politics. (75) At this point, J. Edgar Hoover, Franklin Roosevelt, and the rest of the nation were much more concerned with the conducting of the war. Although Hoover was never trustful of our war-time alliance with the Soviet Union, he was content with combating espionage threats and conducting counterintelligence operations. (76) Hoover was quite proud of his accomplishments during the war as this radio message from October 7, 1944 indicated:

> Today, I am happy to report that our Axis under-cover enemies have been met and completely defeated. The much vaunted Axis Fifth Column in the Western Hemisphere has been uprooted and smashed. So far, there has not been a single act of enemy-directed sabotage in our nation. Espionage has been controlled. (77)

The Dies Committee would eventually pave the way for the establishment of the House Committee on Un-American Activities in January 1945. With the war nearing its completion, Hoover would eventually give the new committee his unqualified support. A new era of extreme and fanatical anti-communist support had dawned.

Chapter 5

Hoover at the Peak of His Influence on the Anti-Communist Movement

In April 1945, Franklin Roosevelt passed into history. According to William Sullivan, Hoover had only cooperated with Roosevelt out of necessity and really did not like the President. (1)   William Donovan, Chief of the Office of Strategic Services (forerunner of the CIA) believed that, "there is only one man in political life that FDR feared. He admitted that man was Hoover." (2) Hoover had now served under five Presidents and had outlasted four attorneys general under FDR alone.   Frank Murphy, who served as attorney general in 1939, was very concerned with the conduct of Hoover. "He is almost pathological. He can get something on anybody if he starts investigating him; that is his tendency." (3) Murphy warned the next attorney general, Robert Jackson (1940-41), that the FBI spied on government officials and tapped their telephones. (4)   Francis Biddle, attorney general from 1941 to 1945, related that Hoover began "sharing some of his extraordinarily broad knowledge of the intimate details of what my associates in the cabinet did and said, of their likes and dislikes, their weaknesses and their associations." (5)   The continuing factors of fear and intimidation would soon come into play as Harry S. Truman assumed the Presidency, and with it a decision about the retention of Hoover.

President Truman made no secret of his anti-FBI feelings

and wanted to hold the FBI down because of their "Gestapo tendencies." In a memo Truman wrote to himself (one month after taking office), he stated:

> We want no Gestapo or Secret Police. FBI is tending in that direction. They are dabbling in sex life scandals and plain blackmail when they should be catching criminals. They also have a habit of sneering at local law enforcement officers. This must stop. Cooperation is what we must have. (6)

One of the first changes Truman made, was to replace Francis Biddle with Tom Clark. But Clark and Truman both realized that because of the strong public support of the anti-communist movement and the tremendous influence and prestige that Hoover enjoyed, that the administration needed J. Edgar Hoover. Curt Gentry noted:

> Before coming to the Justice Department in 1937, future Attorney General Tom Clark had acted as a lobbyist for the Texas oil interests, and he and Hoover had a number of friends in common, among them the oilmen Clint Murchison, Sid Richardson, and Billy Byers—all of whom the FBI directer "palled around with" during his annual trips to LaJolla—as well as Congressman Lyndon Baines Johnson, who had recently moved across the street from Hoover's home on Thirteenth Place NW. (7)

The problem for Truman was that Hoover did not require the support of the Truman administration. He watched as events unfolded leading to an extension of the Cold War, which was now accepted both by the American public and governmental policy makers. Hoover would watch the breakdown of the London Foreign Ministers' Conference and Stalin's speech on a permanent rivalry between Communism and capitalism in 1945. The next few years would contain many more events which would make the breech even wider in the Cold War. Winston Churchill made his Iron Curtain Speech in 1946, and in 1947 three major policy decisions were made; American aid was given to anti-communist forces in Greece, the Marshall Plan was enacted, and George Kennan's containment policy was unveiled. Hoover's status as a genuine American hero had been solidified as he graced the cover of *Newsweek* in 1947. The "Stars and Stripes" were in the background with the headline reading "How to Fight Communism." (8) One action taken to crush domestic Communism was the Taft-

Hartley Act (1947), which required all heads of local unions to take oaths swearing that they were not Communists. As a result, Hoover's confidence in his ability to influence the Truman administration to take a tougher stand against communist influence, had risen to a fever pitch.

In late 1945, Hoover went on the offensive in his anti-communist crusade. Hoover had become increasingly frustrated by the lack of response from the Truman administration in regards to the infiltration of communists in government. Hoover had sent numerous memos and reports to the President and leaders of his administration in late 1945 and on through 1946, warning them of espionage involving International Monetary Fund appointee Harry Dexter White. (9) In June of 1946, Truman disregarded Hoover's advice and White began working for the IMF. Adding to Hoover's frustration was the fact that Hoover had to approach Truman through the attorney general now, rather than on a personal basis as he had been accustomed under Roosevelt. William Sullivan explained how this situation came about. Hoover had selected Marion Chiles III, a boyhood chum of the President's, to be his personal emissary to Truman. Truman asked the agent why he was there. With a message from Mr. Hoover, Chiles said, "Mr. Hoover wants you to know that he and the FBI are at your personal disposal and will help in any way you ask." Truman replied, "Anytime I need the services of the FBI, I will ask for it through my attorney general." From that time on, Hoover's hatred of Truman knew no bounds. (10)

Hoover announced to Attorney General Clark that he was going to:

> intensify [the Bureau's] investigation of Communist Party activities and Soviet espionage cases so as to produce a list of all members of the Communist Party and any others who would be dangerous in the event of a break in diplomatic relations with the Soviet Union, or any other serious crisis involving the United States and the U.S.S.R. (11)

Hoover went on to state that "the FBI has tagged [the] 12,000 most dangerous Communists, and is ready to seize them in case of war with Russia." (12) Hoover had now reached the point where he was willing to force a showdown with Truman over his commitment to the anti-communist cause.

Hoover and the President both could see the political

realities of the day and Truman knew he was on the defensive. In June of 1946, the Republican National Committee announced the theme of the fall election campaign was the choice between Communism or Republicanism. The 1946 congressional elections gave Republicans a majority in both houses and staunch anti-Communists Joe McCarthy and Richard Nixon were elected to their first terms to the Senate and House, respectively. Truman was forced to produce his Cold War "bona fides" and he responded by announcing the Truman Doctrine of containment and Executive Order No. 9835; loyalty boards in the federal bureaucracy. Truman stated that these actions "should take the communist smear off the Democratic Party." (13) Hoover was not impressed and made a dramatic appearance before the HUAC. Hoover took a public swipe at the Truman administration:

> My feelings concerning the Communist Party of the United States are well known. I have not hesitated over the years to express my concern and apprehension. As a consequence, its professional smear brigades have conducted a relentless assault against the FBI. You who have been members of this committee also know the fury with which the party, its sympathizers and fellow travelers can launch an assault. I do not mind such attacks. What has been disillusioning is the manner in which they have been able to enlist support from apparently well-meaning but thoroughly duped persons. (14)

In a private letter to his wife in the fall of 1947, Truman indicated that despite the odds, he would not cave-in to Hoover's grandstanding attempts to increase his power and influence:

> I am sure glad the Secret Service is doing a better job. I was worried about that situation. Edgar Hoover would give his right eye to take over, and all Congressmen and senators are afraid of him. I'm not and he knows it. If I can prevent it, there'll be no NKVD or Gestapo in this country. Edgar Hoover's organization would make a good start towards a citizen spy system. Not for me. . . . (15)

One important battle that Truman did win was in the establishment of the Central Intelligence Agency (over the strong objections of Hoover). The President told aide Harry Vaughn, "One man shouldn't operate both [domestic and foreign intelligence]. He gets too big for his britches." Hoover tried to argue with the President and Truman said no. When Hoover persisted, Truman told him, "You're getting out of bounds." (16)

Despite this important setback, there were many other battles to be fought and won during Hoover's renewed Cold War. One such operation would be instituted during the Truman administration and continue into the Eisenhower presidency. Information was released to the press that stated, "During the next year (1948), the FBI expects to conduct seventy-five thousand separate investigations related to violations of the security of the atomic program and the loyalty and associations of employees having access to restricted data." (17) This would eventually lead to charges that Hoover would attempt to influence President Eisenhower to have Robert Oppenheimer "ousted from his position as a consultant to the Atomic Energy Commission and that his secret 'Q' clearance be revoked." (18) Oppenheimer's good name was eventually cleared but others were not so lucky.

From 1947-1958 (with the prodding of J. Edgar Hoover), the HUAC carried out an investigation of Hollywood actors, writers, and producers. Walt Disney served as a secret informant for the Los Angeles office of the FBI from 1940 until his death in 1966. A memo from Hoover to Disney indicates their relationship dated at least back to 1936. "I am indeed pleased that we can be of service to you in affording you a means of absolute identity throughout your lifetime." (19) During a strike of animators at his studio in 1941, Disney accused the strike leaders of "communistic agitation." (20) In 1947, when the House committee began its hearings on the Communist infiltration of the movie industry, Disney followed actors Ronald Reagan (designated as Source T-10 by the FBI) and George Murphy in warning of Communist influence in movies. During his testimony, Disney stated that he had been smeared by "Communist-front" organizations. (21) Many of these alleged communists were no more communists than Hoover. Their only sin was to be open-minded; their reward was often to be "blacklisted," and many would never work in Hollywood again.

J. Edgar Hoover's most important domestic security case during the Truman years was the 1948-49 Smith Act prosecutions. This case involved the indictment of twelve members of the National Committee of the Communist Party of the United States. The indictment of the twelve (eventually eleven, William Foster suffered from a serious illness), was drawn up under the provisions of the Alien Registration Act of 1940, which had its roots in the Sedition Act of 1798 (and which Hoover and Palmer justified their 1919-20 raids upon). (22) Professor Zachariah Chafee Jr. of the Harvard Law School, argued that the Smith act contained the most drastic restrictions on freedom of speech ever enacted in the United States during peace . . . the first Federal peacetime restrictions on speaking and writing by American citizens since the ill-fated Sedition Act of 1798. (23)

The methods used to convict the eleven involved FBI informant Herbert Philbrick, who was an FBI informer since 1940, while also serving as a middle level official of the Communist Party. This tactic was also one that Hoover had used dating back to the frame-up of Louis Fraimia, one of the founders of the American Communist Party (1920). (24) The Smith Act prosecutions were criticized by many as a violation of free speech. But in June 1951, the convictions were upheld by the Supreme Court in a 6-2 decision. Justice Hugo Black wrote a dissenting opinion and in it he stated:

> These petitioners were not charged with an attempt to overthrow the government. . . . They were not even charged with saying or writing anything designed to overthrow the government. The charge was that they agreed to assemble and to talk and to publish certain ideas at a later date. (25)

The one case that probably had the most far-reaching impact during this period on influencing a future politician's career was the Alger Hiss case in 1948 and 1949. Hiss had denied the charges brought forth by Whittaker Chambers, a former Soviet espionage agent in the 1930's. Chambers had testified before Congress and the FBI that Hiss was part of the communist underground whose purpose was the infiltration of the American government. Richard Nixon would take up the case after the first one ended in a hung jury in July 1949. Hoover had over three hundred agents working on the case in preparation for round two. (26) Was Nixon's hunch that Hiss committed perjury, just that, a hunch, or was Hoover insuring that something would be found to convict Hiss? Nixon surmised the situation in this way, "Although the committee could not determine who was lying on the issue of whether or not Hiss was a communist, we could at least determine which was lying on the issue of whether or not Chambers knew Hiss." (27)

After Hiss was convicted of perjury, Nixon would show his appreciation to Hoover during a speech on the floor of the House on January 26, 1950:

> The Hiss case meant that we must give complete and unqualified support to the FBI and J. Edgar Hoover, its chief. Mr. Hoover recognized the communist threat long before other top officials recognized its existence. The FBI, in this trial, did an amazingly effective job of running down trails over ten years old and in developing the evidence which made the prosecution successful. (28)

Alger Hiss always denied any wrongdoing. President Truman had never believed Hiss to be guilty, either. Truman said years later:

> What they were trying to do, all those birds, they were trying to get the Democrats. They were trying to get me out of the White House, and they were willing to go to any lengths to do it. [The Republicans] had been out of office a long time, and they'd done everything to get back in. They did do just about anything they could think of, all that witch-hunting . . .The Constitution has never been in such danger. (29)

Dmitri Volkogonov, military historian in post-communist Russia, called the allegations of Hiss being a Soviet agent "completely groundless." (30)   Although his complete objectivity has to be questioned, his insiders view should be taken into consideration when evaluating this period. "Not a single document substantiates the allegation that Mr. A. Hiss collaborated with the intelligence services of the Soviet Union. The fact that he was convicted in the fifties was a result of either false information or judicial error." (31)   Was this just another example of J. Edgar Hoover attempting to inflate the threat of Soviet espionage in order to continue the justification to investigate domestic Communism?

As the fall of 1948 approached, Hoover was confidently looking for a victory by the Republican candidate for President, Thomas Dewey. With the surprise reelection of Harry Truman, Hoover knew he would have to coexist with Truman for four more years. A heightening of the Cold War climate did much to make their relationship easier to maintain. In 1949 the Soviets exploded their first atomic bomb much earlier than expected and the communist revolution in mainland China had produced a new and potentially dangerous threat of world-wide Communism. The Korean War would flare up into a potential world war from 1950 to 1952 when Chinese troops became involved and General Douglas MacArthur and members of the Joint Chiefs considered using nuclear weapons. There was still plenty of ammunition left in Hoover's barrel to justify to the American people and Truman that Communism was a threat we needed to stand up to. But as Arthur Schlesinger, Jr. argued in his 1949 tract, *The Vital Center,* "there is a clear and present danger that anti-communist feeling will boil over into a vicious and unconstitutional attack on nonconformists in general and thereby the sources of our democratic strength." (32) One result of this anti-communist feeling was the passage of the McCarren Act in 1930, which forced communist party members to register with the government.

The problem was that J. Edgar Hoover had a proven track record of perpetuating the threat of Communism, even when there was none. This, combined with his desire to shape policy, and his personal vindictiveness against those who did not share his views, was proving to be counterproductive and dangerous. J. Edgar Hoover did not trust anyone else with the final say in how to feed his "anti-communist child." Only he knew best.

From 1950 to 1953, Hoover was occupied with two important cases against communist spies. The Harry Gold-Klaus Fuchs case proved to be one of Hoover's proudest moments. Klaus Fuchs was a German-born English scientist who gave Harry Gold atomic secrets from the Los Alamos laboratory. It was FBI code breakers that led British counterintelligence to Klaus Fuchs. The prosecution and eventual execution of Julius and Ethel Rosenberg was a public success but not a private one. Evidence uncovered since the death of Hoover seriously questions the contention that the information the Rosenbergs passed to the Soviets, were the secrets of the atom bomb. (33) None the less, at the time, it was viewed as another line in a string of successes.

In 1950, Joe McCarthy made his sensational claim that there were two-hundred members of the Communist Party in the Truman State Department. William Sullivan stated, "We were the ones who made the McCarthy hearings possible. We fed McCarthy all the material he was using. I knew what we were doing. I worked on it myself. At the same time, we were telling the public we had nothing to do with it." (34) "We gave McCarthy all we had, but all we had were fragments, nothing could prove his accusations. McCarthy's accusations were ridiculous." (35) Even Roy Cohn, chief counsel to the McCarthy Committee stated, "Joe McCarthy bought Communism in much the same way as other people purchase a new automobile." (36)

Hoover and McCarthy were close ideologically and socially as this quote from Hoover indicated:

> McCarthy is a former Marine. He was an amateur boxer. He's Irish. Combine those, and you're going to have a vigorous individual, who is not going to be pushed around . . .The investigating committees do a valuable job. They have subpoena rights without which some vital investigations could not be accomplished. . . . I view him as a friend and believe he so views me. (37)

Numerous memos and letters in Hoover's personal file indicate that McCarthy and Hoover were very close personal friends. (38) Despite the protestations of Cartha DeLoach that Senator Joseph McCarthy was no personal friend of J. Edgar Hoover, their friendship went beyond social and political bonds.

Hoover found McCarthy to be a useful ally to expose subjects against whom there was not enough evidence for prosecution. Hoover had recommended that McCarthy hire Donald Surine, former ten year FBI agent, as a liaison between Hoover and McCarthy. Surine was the first person that McCarthy hired on a staff that was eventually stocked with a number of ex- G-men. Among the others hired to work for the committee was David Schine. Roy Cohn, chief counsel to Joe McCarthy, was also Schine's best friend. It is interesting to note that David Schine's father, Meyer, played host to Hoover when the Director vacationed at Meyer Schine's Miami hotel, "The Gulfstream," and the nearby racetracks. (39)

With the election of Dwight Eisenhower in 1952, Hoover could no longer be intimately associated with McCarthy who attacked, not only the Truman administration, but also the administration of a man whom he wanted to win the Presidency. Faced with a choice between McCarthy and Eisenhower, there was no real choice for Hoover to make. Dwight Eisenhower's personal friends, such as oilman Syd

Richardson and Allen and Billy Byars (who helped to arrange the financing of Eisenhower's Gettysburg farm), were also personal friends of Hoovers. It was during this period that Hoover and Clyde Tolson would vacation at the expense of their friends Syd Richardson and Clint Murchison in La Jolla, California. Hoover and Tolson would frequent the Del Mar racetrack which was owned by Murchison and Richardson. Hoover defended Murchison after he was publicly criticized for a questionable racetrack foundation that was intended to help underprivileged boys. Hoover stated that Murchison was "the type of rugged individualist that made this country great." (40) William Sullivan believed Eisenhower "to have been a great general but he was a very gullible man, and Hoover soon had him wrapped around his finger. Eisenhower blindly believed everything the director told him, never questioned a word." (41)

One example of his gullibility is indicated during Eisenhower's first year in office. His oil-producer friends Byars, Richardson,and Murchison were issued sixty oil leases on government reserves compared to only sixteen in the previous fifty-five years. (42) Speaker of the House Sam Rayburn of Texas, himself from oil country, was dismayed with the number of oil leases granted by the Eisenhower administration. "This fellow Hoover helped him do it. This fellow Hoover is the worst curse that has come to government in years." (43) Hoover's friendship and support of oil producers and corporate interests was nothing new. Gaston Means had suggested as much back in the 1920's. The even larger problem was that President Eisenhower was only casting a benign look on Hoover's activities, and as a result Hoover's view of himself as an "American Hero" would continue to grow unchecked.

When Eisenhower took office, Hoover had a massive series of briefs entitled "The Role of the Communist Party USA in Soviet Intelligence" awaiting him. Despite the changes that were taking place around him in domestic and world-wide Communism, he "believed" that the threat from Communism was greater than ever. (44)

After the death of Stalin and the Korean War armistice in 1953, the Russians evacuated their troops from Austria in 1955. In the same year Eisenhower met with the leaders of France, Great Britain, and the Soviet Union in Geneva. The American Communist Party also sought to change by adopting a more compromising public platform. Hoover would have none of it:

> The Communists now [seek] . . . to divert public attention by now claiming allegiance to the United States and purporting to sever their ties with the Soviet Union. They will fool no one by this tactic. Nor will they trick this country into relaxing its vigilance. So long as Communist dictatorships threaten the peace of the world, the Communists and their agents will remain a serious threat to our internal security. It is only by continuing to expose their tactics and activities that we shall prevent the resurgence of this international conspiracy in the United States. (45)

Hoover responded with the most devastating domestic surveillance program ever uncovered in the United States. The program was called Cointelpro (Counter Intelligence Program) and was instituted in 1956 and lasted until 1971. "Its goal was to do unto others as they are doing unto you." (46)   Ironically, it overlapped with the CIA's HT-Lingual program (1954-1973) which illegally involved the interception of mail between the Soviet Union and the United States. (47) Cartha DeLoach, assistant director of the FBI when the program was first instituted, reasoned:

> The communists in the country were using a variety of techniques to destabilize large segments of American society. They were telling lies, setting one faction against another, planting incriminating evidence on innocent people, and infiltrating legitimate organizations to subvert them. Why not use the same techniques against the communists? It seemed like a good idea at the time. (48)

Ward Churchill and Jim Vander Wall document the Cointelpro operation in their book, *The Cointelpro Papers*. They relate Hoover's secret wars against the Communist Party of America, the Socialist Workers Party, the Puerto Rican Independence Movement, the Black Liberation Movement, and the American Indian Movement. Despite the argument of Cartha DeLoach, Cointelpro was not needed to combat Communism then or now. Rather its purpose was to stop dissent, perceived communist subversion, and anti-war protests.

As the 1950's were drawing to a close, a new generation was set to assume power and the Presidency. J. Edgar

Hoover was prepared for the "new generation" of leadership if it was led by his protege, Richard Nixon, but not by John Kennedy. Hoover had entered the post war period on the cover of *Time* as its "Man of the Year" in 1947. Twelve years later he was the best selling author of *Masters of Deceit* describing how communists were bringing America to its knees.

On October 18, 1960, Hoover gave an address in Miami which attacked the recent riots in San Francisco as "communist inspired." Richard G. Powers, author of *Secrecy and Power*, described Hoover's address:

> He railed against the young, holding them to be willfully susceptible to Communist blandishments: 'The diabolical influence of communism on youth was manifested in the . . . communist-inspired riots in San Francisco, where students were duped into disgraceful demonstrations against a Congressional committee. . . . (49)

The "American Hero" was going to have trouble selling his Cold War to John Kennedy but J. Edgar Hoover would not take no for an answer.

Chapter 6

Hoover and John Kennedy

Following the bitter and razor thin election victory that John Kennedy achieved over J. Edgar Hoover's Cold War protegé Richard Nixon, it appears that Hoover was not ready to accept the defeat. According to Hoover's friend, Phillip Hochstein, editor of the Newark (N.J.) *Star-Ledger*, Hoover was prepared to go ahead with an investigation of "election fraud" involving Joseph Kennedy during the election. (1) Hochstein explained that only the protests of President Eisenhower and Nixon prevented Hoover from carrying out his investigation. (2) According to Assistant FBI Director William Sullivan, Hoover was feeding damaging material to the press about Kennedy while also working behind the scenes for the election of Richard Nixon: "During the 1960 campaign, Hoover did his best to keep the press supplied with anti-Kennedy stories. . . . [Mean]while Hoover was trying to sabotage Jack Kennedy's campaign—he was quietly helping Richard Nixon." (3) As a result, despite the long-standing friendship established between Joseph Kennedy and Hoover during the 1930's, the relationships between Hoover and the Kennedy sons would be a bitter one.

When Robert Kennedy became the Attorney General, he immediately changed long-standing practices that were viewed as sacred and important to Hoover. Kennedy installed a direct line from his own office to Hoover's desk and expected the Director, and not his secretary, Helen Gandy, to answer it when the Attorney General called. (4) Robert also did not

hesitate to talk to FBI agents without speaking to Hoover
first and also dropped in on FBI meetings without notice.
These actions were viewed as a lack of respect towards
Hoover. After nearly forty years as Director, Hoover believed
that he deserved better. Hoover came to view Robert
Kennedy as a "sneaky little son of a bitch" who happened to
be the President's brother. (5) William Sullivan stated that
the two men in the world that Hoover hated most were
Martin Luther King, second, and Robert Kennedy, first. (6)

Joseph Kennedy had always been a strong supporter of the
anti-communist movement and of Joe McCarthy. The senior
Kennedy had even attempted to have his son, Robert, named
as general counsel of McCarthy's committee, but that position
would eventually go to Hoover intimate Roy Cohn. Robert
Kennedy would become a bitter rival of Cohn and his
communist-hunting friend, David Schine. The relationship
became so bitter that Robert, as Attorney General, would
indict Cohn on perjury charges. (7) Robert would only
increase the enmity between Hoover and himself (and the
President), by insisting that organized crime, which Hoover
had ignored for forty years, and not Communism, was the real
threat facing America. It is interesting to note that Jimmy
Hoffa, who (as will be presented) was known to have been
involved with organized crime, stated:

> I don't believe there is any organized crime, period. Don't
> believe it. Never believe it. I've said it for the last 40 years.
> Hoover said it! Supposed to be the greatest law enforcement
> man in America, with the means to find out. He said there
> was no Mafia, no so-called organized crime. . . That's what he
> said. That's what Hoover said. (8)

It is not clear if Robert Kennedy was aware of Roy Cohn's
close friendship with organized crime leaders such as Mo
Dalitz but such a friendship would be one that Cohn and
Hoover would not want disclosed. (9) With Kennedy's war on
organized crime of prime importance to his brother's
administration, this could have been another area where
Hoover and the Kennedys would be at odds. Dan Moldea, the
author of *The Hoffa Wars*, has written:

> The Kefauver Committee had recommended that a National
> Crime Commission be established to consolidate the federal
> effort against organized crime. But as Senator Kefauver

noted in his book, *Crime in America,* J. Edgar Hoover objected vehemently, saying such a commission might lead to establishment of a national police force. In fact, the FBI director argued that the National Crime Syndicate did not exist. The National Crime Syndicate continued to flourish right under Hoover's bulldog nose, but he was not to admit its existence until the 1960s. (10)

As will be presented in this chapter, the accusations of John Kennedy's involvement with the Mafia by Judith Exner are not substantiated. In fact, as Dan Moldea has strongly documented, the opposite is true; namely, that Robert and John Kennedy had a consistent and documented record of investigating, hounding, and prosecuting organized crime. So much so, that as will be presented in Part 2, the Mafia and/or organized crime probably had a hand in the assassination of President Kennedy.

John Kennedy and J. Edgar Hoover were from different eras and as a result each saw the world differently. The tremendous difference of opinion as to how each viewed the communist threat was most probably the deciding factor in their relationship. Kennedy had been an early supporter of much of the Cold War legislation passed by Congress but by 1960, Hoover and other conservatives could sense that he was not truly "one of them." From 1946 to 1950, Kennedy's views reflected the accepted Cold War political climate of the time. Kennedy's acceptance of the possibility of co-existence between the Communist and Capitalist worlds would be accelerated by his negative view (developed during the early 1950's) of what he perceived as a French return to colonialism in Vietnam. Upon his return from a tour of Asia in 1951, Kennedy stated, "Communism cannot be met effectively merely by force of arms." (11) In 1956, Kennedy alluded to the idea that there were other ways to defeat Communism, "What we must offer then, is a revolution—a political, economic, and social revolution far superior to anything the communists can offer." (12) By 1960, his views on how to defeat Communism differed with those of many conservatives including his father.

Two weeks before the 1961 inauguration, Hoover sent a memo to the new Attorney General, Robert Kennedy, stating that "the American Communist Party presented a greater menace to the internal security of our Nation today than it ever has since it was first founded in this country in 1919."

(13) By the end of 1961, Robert Kennedy made this comment about how the administration saw the communist threat, "It is such nonsense to have to waste time prosecuting the Communist Party. It couldn't be more feeble and less of a threat, and besides its membership consists largely of FBI agents. As far as having any real influence as a party in the United States, it's zero." (14) After forty-four years of seeing Communism as the ultimate evil, there is no doubt that Hoover was not going to go away quietly and give up his Cold War fight.

President Kennedy and Hoover appeared to be having a war of words in the press in 1961 over their views on Communism, and Hoover would not let up. In response to a speech in October of 1961 in which Kennedy stated, "we shall be neither Red nor dead, but alive and free," Hoover stated on December 7, 1961, "Fear, apologies, defeatism, and cowardice are alien to the thinking of true Americans! As for me, I would rather be Dead than Red." (15) In November of 1961, Kennedy said:

> They equate the Democratic Party with the welfare state, the welfare state with socialism, and socialism with this Communism. But you and I, and most Americans take a different view of our peril. We know that it comes from without, not within. It must be met by quick preparedness, no provocative speeches. (16)

Hoover responded by saying, "The communist threat from without must not blind us to the communist threat from within." (17) Not only would Hoover have major problems with the Kennedys on the important issue of Communism, but Robert Kennedy was Hoover's boss. With the disabling stroke to Joseph Kennedy early in JFK's Presidency there would be no close conservative buffer between Hoover and the Kennedy brothers.

In a letter to the editor of the Soviet newspaper, *Izvestia,* in 1961 Kennedy wrote:

> If the people of any country choose to follow a Communist system in a free election, after a fair opportunity for a number of views to be presented, the United States would accept that. What we find to be objectionable . . . is when a system is imposed by a small militant group by subversion. . . . (18)

As will be presented in Chapter 7, statements such as these

by President Kennedy were seen as bordering on "treason" by many conservative, right-wing, and anti-communist groups.

In the Summer of 1961, Senator J. William Fulbright sent a memo to President Kennedy and Robert McNamara criticizing and suggesting reprimands for military personnel who engaged in propaganda activities in arousing the public to the menace of the Communists during the Cold War. Fulbright came under intense criticism by members of the John Birch Society and other members of the extreme right-wing for his attack on the extreme right-wing military personnel.   Fulbright later inserted his memo into the *Congressional Record.* President Kennedy enthusiastically supported Senator Fulbright and subsequently relieved General Edwin Walker from his post in Germany. (19)

On October 18, 1962, the *New York Times* reported: "President Kennedy has signed a bill repealing the controversial non-Communist disclaimer affidavit that had been required of college students and scientists seeking Federal loans and grants. . . ." (20) This action by Kennedy could not have been pleasing to Hoover and those of the right-wing and anti-communist mindset. The belief that J. Edgar Hoover's views towards the threat of worldwide and/or domestic Communism had changed little since 1919, is supported by a review of his published 1962 anti-communist monologue, *On Communism.*

Just one day before the start of the Cuban Missile Crisis, a 10/21/62 *New York Times* review of Hoover's book *On Communism,* described the obvious weaknesses in Hoover's analysis of the Communist world:

> There is . . . disturbing internal evidence in this volume that suggests that Mr. Hoover is not entirely familiar with all these changes. . . . The worst part of the book is the discussion of the rest of the Communist bloc outside the Soviet Union. . . . Mr. Hoover owes it to his readers and himself to take energetic action to remedy these many needless faults. They prevent it from being an adequate introduction to the study of Communism, even at high-school level.

Hoover's understanding of the "true analysis" of the communist world is indicative of the vast gulf of differences between the worlds of Hoover and Kennedy.

President Kennedy believed strongly in promoting foreign and domestic programs that encouraged social and economic improvement and growth. The goals and subsequent programs envisioned by Kennedy were designed to help lead the United States to "victory" over communist nations in economic and technological "battlefields." As President, Kennedy would implement policies that reflected this view. The Alliance for Progress (1961) was instituted to improve social and economic conditions in Latin America. The Peace Corps (1961) was instituted with the intention that Americans would volunteer to serve in underdeveloped countries and help them with day-to-day problems. Kennedy's emphasis on the superiority of American technology was indicated by his backing of the space program and his pledge to place a man on the moon before the end of the decade. Writer Tom Feran related astronaut Frank Borman's view of the "Space Race" and the Cold War: "President Kennedy had promised a manned lunar landing by the end of the 1960's to overcome the humiliation of the Soviet Union's prior accomplishments in space. To [astronaut Frank] Borman, 'The Apollo program was, in its purest form, a battle in the Cold War. I felt like a Cold Warrior. I felt like we were defending freedom.'" (21)

Author Donald Gibson has written:

> President Kennedy's goal was to use government power to steer the economy and the country in certain directions. Improvements in technology, scientific advances, productive investment, educational opportunity and achievement [particularly in areas related to science and technology], a rising standard of living, challenges to people to make the country and world both more prosperous and more just, and the excitement of space exploration were all aspects of the kind of country he thought we should have. . . (22)

Many economic conservatives were highly sceptical of much of his economic programs and especially his emphasis on foreign aid. As noted previously, J. Edgar Hoover had long been associated with those of a conservative and wealthy background. His vacations were spent with his "friend," Clyde Tolson, at various plush—warm weather locations, such as the "Del Charro" and "La Jolla," in California and the "Gulfstream" in Florida. As has been noted, wealthy businessmen and oil tycoons, such as E. E. Folgelson, Bedford Wynne, Clint Murchison Sr., Meyer Schine, etc., would pay for Hoover's and Tolson's expenses during their vacations.

(23) John Kennedy's economic policies were viewed as "socialistic" by those of the Del Charro set as well as by the leading eastern banking establishment typified by David Rockefeller. (24)

Author John H. Davis described the wide variety of corporate and powerful relationships that Hoover's friend, Irving Davidson, enjoyed:

> *Davidson.* . . . was a registered lobbyist for the Teamsters and . . . a friend of Jimmy Hoffa. He was the registered lobbyist for the Somozas of Nicaragua, the Duvaliers of Haiti, the Trujillos of the Dominican Republic, and the wealthy Murchisons of Dallas, owners of the Dallas Cowboys. . . He shared his close friendship with the Murchisons and another good friend, J. Edgar Hoover, who, it has been said, relied on Davidson for inside information no one else was able to provide. . . . (25)

Author Donald Gibson has noted a number of policy proposals that would bring Kennedy into further conflict with a number of powerful corporate and business leaders:

1. Kennedy proposed the elimination of all tax breaks for companies set up by U. S. interests in the form of foreign investment companies. He also specifically targeted wealthy individuals who were transferring wealth.
2. Kennedy also proposed changes in foreign tax credits which allowed U.S.-based oil, gas, and mineral companies to avoid paying U. S. taxes abroad to avoid paying estate taxes . . .
3. Kennedy suggested the elimination of a provision which allowed wealthy people to write off up to 100 percent of their charitable contributions while a 20-to-30 percent deduction was normal for the non-wealthy. (26)

In April 1962, President Kennedy faced one of the most important crises of his presidency, a confrontation with leaders of America's steel industry. A series of negotiations involving Kennedy, Secretary of Labor Arthur Goldberg, and other Kennedy officials resulted in an agreement with the steel executives and labor on new contracts for the industry on March 31, 1962. The process of formally signing the agreements began on April 6. Under the terms of the agreement, the workers would receive no increase in wages but did gain a 2.5 percent benefits increase. (27) According to Commerce Secretary Luther Hodges and the leaders of the steel employees unions, it had been clearly understood by all involved in the negotiations, that there would be no increase in the price of steel as a result of the agreements. (28)

On April 10, Roger Blough, the president of U. S. Steel, informed President Kennedy that despite the understanding reached during the negotiations, U.S. Steel was notifying the President that effective midnight (on April 10) U.S. Steel was raising prices 3.5 percent. (29) Blough did not attempt to consult the President but merely informed him of U.S. Steel's pre-arranged decision. (30) What's more, Blough informed the President that the press had the information and was going to release it in thirty minutes. Kennedy's response was anger and the feeling of betrayal. He firmly believed that the steel industry had given no indication of their plans to raise prices and that he had been deceived. (31) During a press conference on April 11, the President denounced the actions of U.S. Steel and stated:

> The suddenness by which every [steel] company in the last few hours, one by one, as the morning went by, came in with their almost identical, if not identical price increases, which isn't really the way we expect the competitive private enterprise system to work. (32)

Donald Gibson described in *Battling Wall Street,* that on April 12, 1962, Attorney General Robert Kennedy announced that he had started a grand jury probe into the price-setting actions and that subpoenas were being issued for documents held by U.S. Steel. (33) The angry response by President Kennedy eventually led to the price increases being rescinded by the leaders of the steel industry, but Kennedy's actions left a bad taste in the mouths of business leaders who were now concerned that Kennedy was attempting to upset the status quo.

President Kennedy's confrontation with the steel executives in 1962 was a response to the extreme side of our capitalistic system. A small group of steel executives attempted to control the industry and dictate prices in a system that is supposed to be run by free choice and "fair" competition, as well as to look out for the interests of their employees. However, in the instance of the 1962 confrontation, the leaders of the industry were actually engaged in hindering competition, reneging on an agreement made with steel industry employees (who agreed to not ask for a wage increase), and with President Kennedy to not raise prices. As has been noted (and will be in more detail), Kennedy had been accused of practicing "socialistic economic policies" as well as not facing up forcefully enough to threats of communist military expansion in Laos, Vietnam, and Cuba, as well as from the Soviet Union. Kennedy's subsequent charges that the steel industry was actually engaging in "socialistic price-fixing" would not go over well with the conservative elements— although there appears to be some merit to his argument.

Donald Gibson also noted that "In March 1963, *Life* magazine criticized President Kennedy's administration for blocking mergers in the railroad and airline industries." (34) Kennedy responded to the charges that his administration was anti-business during a November 18, 1963 speech to the Florida Chamber of Commerce, just four days before his death:

> The hard facts contradict these beliefs. This administration is interested in the healthy expansion of our economy. We are interested in the steady progress of our society, and it is in this kind of program, in my opinion, that American business has the largest stake. Why is it that profits are at an all-time high in the nation today? It is because the nation as a whole is prospering. . . . I do not say that all this is due to the administration alone, but neither is it all accidental. (35)

As a result of the conflicts between the Kennedys and Hoover over their views on Communism, Robert's "brash tactics" as attorney general, President Kennedy's "liberal" economic policies, and Hoover being forced to investigate organized crime; it appears a certainty that Hoover was attempting to "pressure" President Kennedy with information on his personal life as he had done to others for decades. According to Arthur Schlesinger Jr., the true feelings of Kennedy about Hoover might best be summed up by this statement, "The three most overrated things in the world are the state of Texas, the FBI, and whatever was exasperating him at the moment." (36)

When Hoover's pressure tactics didn't work, he tried the direct approach. On March 22, 1962, the day of Kennedy's last phone call with his alleged mistress, Judith Exner, Hoover apparently confronted the President on the issue. Kennedy responded to his aide Ken O'Donnell by stating, "Get rid of that bastard. He's the biggest bore." (37) Exner's original story in her book, *My Story* states that pressure from Hoover was not the reason for the demise of their relationship. But "coincidentally," Exner does concede that the affair did end only a few months after the Hoover-Kennedy meeting. White House phone log records also document that contact between Exner and the President ended soon after the March 22 meeting between Hoover and Kennedy. (38) Exner related this version:

> If what the [House Select] committee says about the White House logs is in fact true, then it is pretty obvious that Hoover spoke to Jack about me. It is too much of a coincidence that it would happen on the same day. The only explanation I can offer is that our calls were either no longer recorded in the logs, or they have been deleted. The point is that Jack never mentioned any of this to me. I saw Jack in March and April and the calls did not stop until sometime in June. And they stopped, not because of any outside force, but because of natural attrition. The spectre of the White House killed the romance. Not J. Edgar Hoover. (39)

Kitty Kelly related in a 1988 *People* magazine article:

> To substantiate her claim, Exner wrote the 1977 book *My Story* with journalist Ovid Demaris. Part autobiography, part romantic journal, *My Story* describes her affairs with Kennedy and Giancana but makes no mention of her role as courier. . . . (40)

Kelly describes the "new" and "more complete" version that Exner began to promote in 1988:

> According to Exner, for 18 months in 1960 and 1961, she served as the President's link with the Mob. At Kennedy's request, says Exner, she regularly carried envelopes back and forth between the President and Sam Giancana, the head of the Chicago Mafia, as well as Johnny Roselli, Giancana's Los Angeles lieutenant. Furthermore, Exner says she arranged about 10 meetings between Kennedy and Giancana, one of which, she believes, took place inside the White House. Exner says she was never told what transpired between the President and the Chicago Godfather. . . .(41)

Dan Moldea believes that Exner's new story is totally false and that in reality, John and Robert Kennedy never cooperated with organized crime and in fact, caused fear and hatred against the Kennedys in return. Moldea's argument is supported by recordings made of conversations between members of organized crime in 1962.

In February 1962; this conversation was recorded by law enforcement officials and subsequent transcripts were released by the House Select Committee:

Willie Weisburg. See what Kennedy done. With Kennedy, a guy should take a knife, like all them other guys, and stab and kill the [obscenity], where he is now. Somebody should kill the [obscenity], I mean it. This is true. Honest to God. It's about time to go. But, I tell you something. I hope I get a week's notice, I'll kill. Right in the [obscenity] in the White House. Somebody's got to get rid of this [obscenity].. .
Weisburg. Do you know what this man is going to do? He ain't going to leave nobody alone.
Angelo Bruno. [Philly crime head] I know he ain't. But you see, everybody is there was bad. The other guy was good because the other guy was worse. Do you understand? Brownell came. He was no good. He was worse than the guy before.
Weisburg. Not like this one.
Bruno. Not like this one. This one is worse. Right? If something happens to this guy . . .[laughs]. (42)

On May 2, 1962, the FBI overheard Michelino Clement, of the Genovese crime family, express a similar sentiment:

Clemente. Bob Kennedy won't stop today until he puts us all in jail all over the country. Until the commission meets and puts its foot down, things will be at a standstill. When we meet, we all got to shake hands, and sit down and talk, and if there is any trouble with a particular regime, its got to be kept secret, and only the heads are to know about it, otherwise some broad finds out, and finally the newspapers.(43)

Into 1963, the pressure against certain members of the crime commission was continuing to mount, as evidenced by a conversation in which commission member Peter Maggadino bitterly cursed Attorney General Kennedy and commented on the Justice Department's increasing knowledge of the crime syndicate's inner workings, stating, "They know everything

under the sun. They know who's back of it they know there is
a commission. We got to watch right now—and stay as quiet
as possible." (44)

Just three weeks before President Kennedy's assassination,
on October 31, 1963, the FBI picked up a conversation
between two of the Maggadino brothers of Buffalo:

> *Peter Maggadino.* President Kennedy he should drop dead.
> *Stefano Maggadino.* They should kill the whole family, the
> mother and father, too. . . . When he talks he talks like a mad
> dog, he says, "my brother the Attorney General." (45)

One week after the assassination, on November 29, 1963,
Maggadino cautioned his associates not to joke openly about
the President's murder, stating, "You can be sure that the
police spies will be watching carefully to see what we think
and say about this." (46)

These accounts do not mesh with the version given by
Judith Exner. In none of the tapes that have been released is
there even a hint that Judith Exner was a courier between
John Kennedy and any purported member of organized crime.
Michael O'Brien offers a summary of Judith Exner's "new"
story of John Kennedy's involvement with Chicago organized
crime leader, Sam Giancana, in an article entitled, "Truth
and Fantasy From a President's Mistress," in the December
1999 edition of the *Washington Monthly:*

> The name Judith Campbell Exner burst into the national
> headlines on December 17, 1975. . . . [Seymour] Hersh
> produced a witness: Martin Underwood, a former political
> operative for Mayor Richard Daley, and a Kennedy campaign
> worker in 1960. According to Hersh, in April 1960 Kenny
> O'Donnell asked Underwood to take the overnight train from
> Washington to Chicago and keep an eye on Exner.
> Underwood claimed he watched her on the train and saw her
> deliver the envelope to the waiting Sam Giancana. (47)

Despite the claims of author Seymour Hersh that Marty
Underwood had an inside knowledge that Judith Exner was a
courier between JFK and Sam Giancana, Marty Underwood
denied it. According to the Assassination Records and Review
Board, "He [Underwood] . . . denied that he followed Judith
Campbell Exner on a train and that he had no knowledge
about her alleged role as a courier." (48)

O'Brien adds:

Secret Service agents who candidly testified about the President's womanizing do not confirm any of Exner's contentions about JFK's relations with Giancana. Moreover, Hersh's account of the train ride Campbell took on Kennedy's behalf in April 1960 to deliver money to Giancana has unraveled, because the key witness recanted his original story. Martin Underwood denied that he followed Judith Campbell on the train, and claims he had no knowledge about her alleged role as a courier. . . . After reading Exner's 1977 autobiography, columnist William Safire severely criticized Kennedy. But her subsequent assertions left him cold. "She's changed her story too often over the decades," Safire concluded.

. . . we should assume that the first story regarding the affair was true, because it was supported by White House logs and other evidence; but that her later claims about her role in an alleged Giancana-Roswell-Kennedy triangle, because they are not supported by other sources, are fantasy. (49)

It is interesting to note that just as researcher Vincent Palamara was conducting various Secret Service interviews and initiating correspondence with them during the months of November-December 1997, two negative accounts of President Kennedy's womanizing emerged. The first being the release of Seymour Hersh's book, *The Dark Side of Camelot* followed by the December 4, 1997 ABC Special, *Dangerous World— The Kennedy Years*. Secret Service agents Joseph Paolella, Tony Sherman, Larry Newman, and Tim McIntyre gave interviews and openly discussed and criticized President Kennedy's "incessant womanizing." (50) Newman specifically stated, ". . . you felt impotent and you couldn't do your job. It was frustrating. . . ." (51) However, these views of President Kennedy have been disputed as recently as 1993, 1994 and 1997 by agents Floyd Boring, Roy Kellerman, and Jerry Kivett. Boring stated, "President Kennedy was a very congenial man knowing most agents by their first name. He was very cooperative with the Secret Service and well liked and admired by all of us." (52) Roy Kellerman's widow June recalled, "Roy did not say that JFK was difficult to protect." (53) Agent Kivett supported the claims of Kellerman and Boring when he stated, "[JFK] was beloved by those agents on the detail and I never heard anyone say that he was difficult to protect." (54)

Regardless of which agent's accounts are more accurate, J. Edgar Hoover continued to probe the Kennedy brothers for their weaknesses. Robert Kennedy related to John Bartlow Martin, Hoover's continued attempts to pressure the Kennedys:

> I suppose every month or so he'd [Hoover] send somebody around to give information on somebody I knew or a member of my family or allegations in connection with myself. So that it would be clear—whether it was right or wrong—that he [Hoover} was on top of all of these things and received all of this information. He [Hoover] would do this also, I think, to find out what my reaction to it would be. (55)

Kennedy stated further:

> I remember on one occasion that he [Hoover] said that my brother and I had a group of girls on the twelfth floor—he didn't say it; but Senators, somebody—a group of girls on the twelfth floor of the LaSalle Hotel, and that, I think, the President used to go over there once a week and have the place surrounded by Secret Service people, and then go up and have assignations on the twelfth floor of the LaSalle. I suppose the idea was whether you'd have it investigated or what you'd do about it. (56)

Whether Robert Kennedy realized it or not, Hoover's allegations certainly had merit. If Hoover's accusations were not accurate as far as the "activities" at the LaSalle, the President certainly offered ample opportunity elsewhere.

Sam Giancana Jr. told Tom Brokaw, ". . .[organized crime was] trying to compromise Kennedy through [Frank] Sinatra." (57) This is corroborated by information from FBI files which state that, "Giancana [Sr.] says best way for Kennedy to communicate with us [is] through Sinatra." (58)

Further support that organized crime was using Frank Sinatra in an attempt to compromise President Kennedy is indicated by author Athan Theoharis:

> In a memo from FBI Assistant Director Courtney Evans to FBI Assistant Director Alan Belmont, August 11, 1962 . . . Mrs. Meyer Lansky reportedly replied, "It's all [Frank Sinatra's] fault, he is nothing but a procurer of women for those guys. [Sinatra] is the guy who gets them all together." Lansky then replied to his wife, "It's not [Sinatra's] fault and it starts with the President and goes right down the line." (59)

Organized crime expert and author of *The Hoffa Wars*, Dan Moldea, has related to this author that neither Robert or John Kennedy had any personal relationship with those associated with organized crime. Moldea has stated further that those who continue to "perpetuate this myth are engaged in a failed attempt to rewrite history." (60) As noted, there is strong evidence that organized crime attempted to influence President Kennedy through Frank Sinatra and his procuring of women for the President. Moldea states unequivocally, that these attempts failed as proved by FBI wiretaps. The wiretaps of organized crime leaders indicate "their impatience" with Sinatra "not delivering" on his apparent pledge to influence the Kennedys to ease up "their harassment" of organized crime. (61)

As previously noted, J. Edgar Hoover apparently confronted the President with proof of his relationship with Judith Exner in March 1962. It has also been documented that Kennedy immediately broke off his relationship with both Sinatra and Exner. (62)

Some current revisionist "historians," such as Seymour Hersh and Thomas Reeves, argue that John Kennedy was a reckless and out of control President and that his sexual exploits were common knowledge to Washington insiders. That he was an adulterer and used poor judgment in his personal life cannot now be questioned; but the extent of his recklessness and others' knowledge of it can be questioned. As numerous White House reporters (who are paid to keep their eyes and ears open) have noted, they did not personally know of his affairs and did not consider him reckless. Kennedy's apparent ability to obscure the affairs he was obviously engaged in does not, of course, excuse him from these behaviors. But Kennedy, as well as far too many other presidents, should not be judged solely on their private failings; even more so, as will be presented, when a more accurate portrayal of Kennedy's intentions and actual records in other areas (including his murder), have been obscured or denied. Arthur Schlesinger wrote:

Vague rumors about JFK did waft about Washington from time to time, but, as one who worked in the White House, I never saw anything untoward. Kennedy was a hard-working fellow, concentrating intently on the problems at hand. At no point in my experience did his preoccupation with women (apart from Caroline crawling around the Oval Office)

interfere with his conduct of the public business. . . . [But] It
is now accepted history [that he was having affairs]. (63)

Ben Bradlee admits in his 1995 memoir, A Good Life, "that
Kennedy jumped casually from bed to bed with a wide variety
of women.   It was not accepted history then . . . [I was]
unaware of this proclivity during his lifetime."
Hugh Sidey of Time magazine confesses:

> I can be faulted as a journalist, but on the other hand I wasn't
> sure.   He was not a man of sterling character in that
> regard—it's sad—it's a blackmark that he couldn't control
> that. I'm one of those who believes had he lived—he might
> have been forced from office—because he violated his whole
> persona. He used Jackie and the kids and the family and the
> Catholic faith—he was a hypocrite. (64)

White House reporter Helen Thomas stated:

> I've been asked many times over the years, "Why didn't you
> write about Kennedy and his girlfriends?" Let me explain
> that presidents had more privacy then and the press was not
> privy to their sexual activities—only if those liaisons ended up
> on a police blotter or, as in one infamous incident, if a
> congressman followed a fan dancer into the Tidal Basin. (65)

Walter Cronkite believed most were not aware:

> Yet it is interesting that none of the White House
> correspondents I know claimed at the time to have any
> evidence of John Kennedy's alleged bedroom escapades. Most
> will tell you today that they knew about the rumors but were
> never able to come up with enough evidence to go with the
> story. (66)

There is little or no doubt that an affair took place between
Judith Exner Campbell and John Kennedy but it appears the
affair he had with Mary Meyer is more telling of how
Kennedy operated in this private area of his life than what
has been attributed to Kennedy by Judith Exner.   Mary
Meyer was the former wife of CIA official, Cord Meyer. She
was a successful artist who traveled easily among the "artsy
world" of the Georgetown social scene. Meyer initially became
acquainted with Kennedy when he was a Senator and living
in Georgetown. Author Nina Burleigh has related in detail

the relationship between Meyer and Kennedy:

> The White House relationship between Mary Meyer and President Kennedy was first revealed by journalist James Truitt in 1976, and later corroborated by Ben Bradlee's eyewitness description of Mary's diary and by Tony Bradlee's comments to journalists. Mary apparently told the Truitts about her meetings with the president while they were happening, and Truitt kept notes with dates, times, and details. . . . Frequently a Kennedy retainer such as David F. Powers would sign in at seven-thirty with only the notation, "Powers plus one." The fact that Mary Meyer's name is so often entered means she was not hidden and was probably there more often that the logs indicate. (67)

Burleigh writes that Meyer did not believe rumors of Kennedy's other "numerous affairs." Meyer was most likely not totally objective on this subject but her account should be considered:

> Meyer told Kay Fischer about her frequent dinners with the president and observed to him that she didn't believe all the women who said they'd had flings with Kennedy. "She seemed to think that more often than not he had these women over to talk, to test out his ideas on them," Fischer said. "She felt his relations with women were exaggerated." (68)

The wife of the famous comedian, Milton Berle, concurred with Meyer:

> If all of the women who claim to have slept with Kennedy are telling the truth, he would not have strength enough to lift a teacup, let alone deal with Khrushchev. Women or not, Kennedy dealt pretty well with Khrushchev, and that may be the larger reason why Camelot will not fade away. (69)

According to Burleigh's account, Kennedy engaged in a platonic relationship with Meyer for extended periods of time before and after their sexual relationship. Apparently "his behavior" was improving towards the end of his life as some have maintained:

> Mary and Kennedy were friends before, during, and after the period during which they were romantically involved. . . .In 1963 Kennedy and Mary stayed in touch, sometimes talking on the telephone and occasionally seeing each other in the

White House residence when Jackie was out of town. . . . As his presidency wore on, Kennedy retired from some of his congressional romping way. The furtive ducking into closets and lunches with nymphets in the White House swimming pool became less frequent. But unlike the actresses and secretaries, Mary made the transition from plaything to family friend. She kept up a cordial relationship with Jackie Kennedy. (70)

Jimmy Hoffa had claimed that he had a copy of a tape that purported to have recorded the President and a girl involved in a sexual tryst. However, the tape was never produced and as Hoffa's associate, Harold Gibbons stated, "If Jimmy had something on the Kennedys, he would have used it. The pressure was on him, and he would've done just about anything to turn it off." (71) And as will be presented, there is consistent documented evidence from reputable sources, that Jimmy Hoffa fully intended to murder Robert and/or John Kennedy. One would think Hoffa would attempt to destroy them with a tape in his possession before resorting to murder.

Despite the current widespread belief that both Kennedy brothers were sexually involved with Marilyn Monroe over a period of years, even their nemesis, J. Edgar Hoover, considered this rumor dubious. Authors Athan Theoharis and John Cox have concluded after years of studying FBI files that, "as far as J. Edgar Hoover was concerned . . . there was no Kennedy [Marilyn] Monroe affair, and therefore no blackmailing the Kennedys on that score." (72) Fellow Hoover biographer, Curt Gentry, agrees with this conclusion and cautions only that the evidence is incomplete. (73)

According to Assistant FBI Director William Sullivan:

> Although Hoover was desperately trying to catch Bobby Kennedy red-handed at anything, he never did. Kennedy was almost a Puritan. . . . The stories about Bobby Kennedy and Marilyn Monroe were just stories. The original story was invented by a so-called journalist, a right-wing zealot who had a history of spinning wild yarns. It spread like wildfire, of course, and J. Edgar Hoover was right there, gleefully fanning the flames. (74)

The larger question is, why is someone continuing to fabricate evidence of an affair between Kennedy and Monroe if there is already enough so-called proof that it took place? According to an article published in the October 6, 1997 edition of *Newsweek,* there was only one sexual encounter between Marilyn Monroe and President Kennedy and none between Marilyn and Robert Kennedy:

> Probably the most responsible account by Monroe biographer, Donald Spoto, indicates that JFK and Marilyn met four times between October 1961 and August 1962. Monroe later told her closest confidante that she and the president had one sexual encounter in that period. Despite years of rumors, Spoto says there is no evidence that Robert Kennedy and Marilyn ever had a tryst.

The fact that Seymour Hersh attempted to defame the Kennedy brothers with falsified information after both were murdered, along with Marilyn Monroe who also died in a suspicious fashion, did not appear to bother him:

> "Big Deal," Hersh told *Newsweek.* Plenty of good reporters do choose promising leads that fail to pan out; Hersh says he has cut the phony story from his book and from a TV documentary scheduled to appear in November. Maybe so, but Hersh made an awful lot of money before he began entertaining serious doubts, and how he parlayed the documents into a multimillion-dollar media package reveals a great deal about the continuing fascination with the Kennedy legend and the unrelenting pressure for the big score in the worlds of both publishing and TV. (75)

In a *New York Times* review of Seymour Hersh's book, *The Dark Side of Camelot,* Thomas Powers wrote:

> What Hersh had, or thought he had . . . was a sheaf of incriminating documents . . . which proved, or purported to prove, or if true would have proved, that Marilyn Monroe changed her mind about embarrassing the President, threatened to deface the President's image as a family man with the sensational news of their sexual affair and was bribed to shut up only by the President's timely agreement to establish a substantial trust fund for the comfortable maintenance of her mother . . . But when the documents were at last examined in a serious way it was discovered . . . that the trove had been fabricated. . . . The big casualty of the Marilyn-papers fiasco is the five years of hard work Hersh put into his book. (76)

A further blow to Hersh's story is found in a May 1999

article:

> A jury yesterday found a man guilty of selling salacious forged documents claiming President Kennedy paid hush money to keep secret an affair with Marilyn Monroe. Lawrence X. Cusack III, who made a fortune selling hundreds of Kennedy-linked documents he claimed came from his father, was convicted on 13 mail and wire fraud charges. . . . (77)

In a review of Hersh's *Dark Side of Camelot*, Garry Wills writes:

> The more charges he [Hersh] adds to the score, the more I feel I should be subtracting from it. He tells us so many unbelievable things he says we never knew that we begin to doubt all the things we thought we knew. If Hersh will just write two more books about Kennedy, I could end up as starry-eyed about the man as any Sorensen or Schlesinger. (78)

Columbia University History Professor Alan Brinkley's review of the *Dark Side of Camelot* concludes:

> Hersh's account of Kennedy's policies in Vietnam is perhaps the flimsiest part of this book . . . Reading this book is a depressing experience. In part that is because of its relentless descriptions of the sordid private world of the Kennedy presidency, a world—that although long familiar—never loses its capacity to dismay. But what is even more depressing is to see such shoddy and careless arguments and such self-serving credulity coming from a celebrated investigative reporter. (79)

As will be presented in Part 3, an accurate historical portrayal of Kennedy's Vietnam and Cuban policies are sorely lacking today. Cuba would prove to be one area where elements of organized crime and anti-communist groups would align themselves together in the battle to overthrow Fidel Castro's communist regime. Organized crime had a vested interest in reclaiming the gambling casinos which were nationalized by Castro in 1960. J. Edgar Hoover became aware of CIA-Mafia plots to assassinate Castro in October 1960.

On October 18, 1960, J. Edgar Hoover stated in a memo, "[D]uring recent conversations with several friends, [Sam] Giancana stated that Fidel Castro was to be done away with very shortly." (80) When doubt was expressed regarding this statement, Giancana reportedly assured those present that Castro's assassination would occur in November. Hoover was no doubt not discouraging such a plan and, in fact, was most likely in favor of such action. There can also be little doubt that Hoover would not be accepting of President Kennedy's failure to back the CIA-Cuban-exile invasion force at the Bay of Pigs with direct American involvement.

Apparently, in 1959, J. Edgar Hoover was involved with former U.S. ambassadors to Cuba, Arthur Gardner and Earl Smith, along with then Vice-President Richard Nixon, in an effort to prop up Cuban dictator Fulgencio Batista. This effort was designed to disrupt the Cuban revolution and ensure an anti-communist leadership in Cuba. (81)

That President Eisenhower forced the hand of President Kennedy to carry out the Bay of Pigs invasion, is indicated by his readiness to invade Cuba during his "lame duck" transition period with Kennedy. According to Richard Bissell, Director of Plans for the CIA, President Eisenhower had stated on January 3, 1961, "He [Eisenhower] was prepared to 'move against Castro' before Kennedy's inauguration if a 'really good excuse' was provided by Castro." (82)

The CIA report on the Bay of Pigs invasion noted:

> on 4 November 1960 WH/4 took formal action to change the course of the project by greatly expanding the size of the Cuban paramilitary unit and redirecting its training along more conventional military lines. . . . By January 1961 the strike force strength was 644, on 3 February it was 685, by 10 March it had risen to 826, by 22 March to 973. On 6 April 1961 brigade strength was reported at 1,390. (83)

This information clearly supports the contention that the original small anti-Castro operations expanded greatly after the November election but before Kennedy took office in late January. It appears certain that Kennedy was faced with a problem not of his making.

A memo written by J. Edgar Hoover in October 1961, intimated his displeasure with Castro and the continued impact of their system on ours: "The Socialists Workers Party (SWP) has, over the past several years, been . . . strongly directing and/or supporting such causes as Castro's Cuba and integration problems arising in the south." (84)

Seymour Hersh and others have contended that President Kennedy authorized assassination plots against Fidel Castro.

The CIA's own report stated quite clearly that a full year before President Kennedy took office, the CIA had made plans to assassinate Castro. It is difficult to accept the argument that Kennedy was involved in the numerous assassination plots against Fidel Castro. It appears to be more credible to believe that the CIA-Mafia plots began before Kennedy's presidency and quite likely continued after his death.

Peter Kornbluh writes in his commentary, *The Secret CIA Report on the Invasion of Cuba:*

> . . . As early as December 1959, the head of the Agency's Western Hemisphere Division, J. C. King recommended that "thorough consideration be given to the elimination of Fidel Castro," because it "would greatly accelerate the fall of the present government." Indeed, at the first meeting of the Bay of Pigs task force, King predicted that "unless Fidel and Raul Castro and Che Guevara could be eliminated in one package . . . this operation [would] be long drawn out affair and the present government will only be overthrown by force." (85)

CIA contract agent Jacob Esterline recalled:

> . . . This plan that they had laid out with Sam Giancana, their gambling interests—Traficante was another name that comes back to my mind. They [the Mafia] were being threatened, their interests were being threatened in Cuba, and therefore they had decided they were going to do something about Castro. So all of a sudden the agency gets sucked into being a part of it, which I never could understand how this made any sense, how this added up, but in point of fact, [the CIA] had the relationship with Giancana and he needed half a million dollars to perform his part of this. (86)

In a memo, then-CIA director of security Sheffield Edwards wrote that senior agency officials approved plots to kill Castro between August 1960 and May 1961. The White House wasn't mentioned. "Knowledge of this project . . .was kept to a total of six persons," Edwards wrote. (87)

Reporter Daniel Schorr surmised:

> Had President Kennedy been pursuing a "two-track" policy of offering Castro friendship while plotting his murder? Or were the cloak and dagger people, in Senator Church's words, off like a "rouge elephant" on a singular private rampage? The mountains of testimony and documents indicate that these things could be because the CIA—proceeding on what it

claimed as previous "general authorization"—kept its incessant plotting secret, ostensibly to spare the White House embarrassment. The Kennedy administration—for ten months exploring the idea of accommodation with Castro—had kept that initiative confined to a few trusted individuals, none of them in the CIA. (88)

Richard Helms, who eventually replaced Bissell as DDP (Deputy Director of Plans), also stated that he never told CIA Director John McCone about the CIA-Mob plots to kill Castro. Helms stated, "No, it isn't my impression that I told him, at least I don't have any impression, unfortunately," (89) The Senate Report goes on to explain why Helms would not have told McCone about the plots. George McManus, Special CIA Assistant to Richard Helms, believed:

McCone had a great love for the President of the United States and he sort of looked at him as an older . . . brother, a very protective sense he had about the President, President Kennedy, and McCone would have immediately said, Jesus, this is a no win ball game. (90)

This is further corroborated by the testimony of Walter Elder, McCone's top aide:

I told Mr. Helms that Mr. McCone had expressed his feeling . . . that assassination could not be condoned and would not be approved. . . .the point is that I made Mr. Helms aware of the strength of Mr. McCone's opposition to assassination. I know that Mr. Helms could not have been under any misapprehension about Mr. McCone's feeling about this conversation. (91)

William Harvey, who was in charge of the CIA-Mafia plots concurred with Elder's testimony and stated that McCone told him the thought of trying to assassinate Castro was unacceptable. (92) Harvey went on to state that there was ". . . a very real possibility—of this government being blackmailed either by [anti-Castro] Cubans for political purposes or by figures in organized crime for their own self protection or aggrandizement. . . ." (93)

According to the Senate Intelligence Report:

McCone testified that he was not aware of the plots to assassinate Castro which took place during the years in which he was DCI, and that he did not authorize those plots. He testified that he was not briefed about the assassination plots by Dulles, Bissell, Helms, or anyone else when he succeeded Dulles as Director in November 1961. And that if he had ever been asked about the plots, he would have disapproved. (94)

Richard Bissell, Deputy Director for Plans for the CIA, testified that McCone had not been told of the plots against Castro. (95)

According to Warren Hinckle and William Turner, in their book *Deadly Secrets*, Tad Szulc, a *New York Times* correspondent reported that the President asked:

"What would you think if I ordered Castro to be assassinated?" Kennedy ordered the agency to pull out of the conspiracy. "We must not run risk of U. S. association with political assassination since the U. S. as matter of general policy cannot condone assassination." Many file copies of this cable were kept. . . . (96)

Secretary of State Dean Rusk stated:

I personally have no idea who authorized the plots to assassinate Castro and other foreign leaders. I find it hard to believe they were discussed in the 303 Committee without my knowledge, because my own representative would not have dared to withhold knowledge of such discussions from me. These plots were likely handled outside the committee. I also doubt that John Kennedy authorized the plots; things like assassinations just were not Kennedy's style. (97)

Daniel Schorr has written that attempts to kill Castro continued until 1965 and quite possibly until the mid-1970's (98)   The evidence presented argues strongly against President Kennedy's involvement in attempts to assassinate Castro.   This conclusion makes the assertion of Lyndon Johnson appear puzzling.   Jeff Shesol, author of *Mutual Contempt* has written:

LBJ's "Inner political instinct," Jack Valenti recalled, was that Castro was behind the killing. Yes, Johnson conceded, the FBI had no evidence to prove it or even to suggest it; neither did the CIA or the State Department or anybody else. But the equation had a concise, appealing logic: "President Kennedy tried to get Castro, but Castro got Kennedy first." Johnson told his aide, Joseph Califano.   Johnson said, "President Kennedy" but he knew it was Bobby who tried to "get Castro." Ever since the Bay of Pigs, LBJ had blamed Bobby for the excesses of American policy in Cuba. (99)

As will be presented in Part 2, the evidence available strongly argues against Castro's involvement in Kennedy's assassination and that Lyndon Johnson was well aware of this evidence.

Despite charges that President Kennedy initiated assassination attempts against Castro and should be blamed for the failure of the Bay of Pigs; evidence that he should be held accountable for either charge is difficult to substantiate. President Kennedy's chief consul, Ted Sorensen, noted that Kennedy very clearly stated that no "direct" American action would be involved in any effort to overthrow Fidel Castro:

> . . . The President publicly pledged at an April 12 press conference: ". . . there will not be, under any conditions, any intervention in Cuba by Untied States armed forces, and this government will do everything it possibly can—and I think it can meet its responsibilities—to make sure that there are no Americans involved in any actions inside Cuba. . . ."(100)

Dean Rusk concluded:

> . . . I am completely convinced that at no time did the president ever consider using American forces at the Bay of Pigs. Some in the CIA might have thought that if the brigade got ashore and ran into trouble, Kennedy would have to send Americans in support. The brigade itself thought so. Both completely misread the president. (101)

Some Western European leaders were concerned with the Eisenhower and Kennedy administrations' obsession with Cuba. The CIA's report on the invasion included Arthur Schlesinger's assessment of how the European's viewed the United States' obsession with Cuba in early 1963:

> . . .It was the decision to invade, not the failure, that bothered Western European political leaders," [Arthur] Schlesinger noted, "Why was Cuba such a threat to you?" they asked. "Why couldn't you live with Cuba, as the USSR lives with Turkey and Finland." U.S. allies, [President] Kennedy would later concede, "[they] think we are a little demented on Cuba." (102)

There can be little doubt that the Kennedy administration's

"Operation Mongoose" was an example of this American obsession with Cuba. Robert Kennedy was heavily involved in this anti-Castro program that appeared to center on various programs to destroy the Cuban economy. By the spring of 1963, many Cuban exiles were growing impatient with the "pin-pricks" against Castro carried out by Kennedy's "Mongoose" operations. A May 10, 1963 Associated Press article reported:

> A new all-out drive to unify Cuban refugees into a single, powerful organization to topple the Fidel Castro regime was disclosed today by exile sources. The plan calls for formation of a junta in exile to mount a three-pronged thrust consisting of sabotage, infiltration, and ultimate invasion. The exile sources said the plan had been discussed with Cuban leader by U.S. central Intelligence agents. Seeking to put together the junta was Enrique Ruiz Williams, a Bay of Pigs invasion veteran and friend of U.S. Attorney General Robert F. Kennedy. Cuban leaders said intensive sabotage and guerrilla activities inside Cuba might start in a month to spark a possible uprising. Hundreds of exiles, reported itching for action and resentful of U.S.-imposed curbs against the anti-Castro raids will be recruited to infiltrate Cuba, the sources added. (103)

Not only were the Cuban exiles prepared to up the ante but contingency plans were prepared by the Pentagon to force President Kennedy to take military action against Cuba. The Assassination Records and Review Board released documents in 1997 which clearly show to what extreme the military was prepared to go in order to create a pretext for war with Cuba. In an article published by the Scripps Howard News Service:

> The Pentagon considered shooting people on American streets to stage a pretext for overthrowing Fidel Castro. This and other bizarre schemes were seriously discussed by the Joint Chiefs of Staff in 1962 as a way of incensing the American public and faking a reason to attack Castro. . . . Cubans fleeing the Castro regime were to be the targets. The violence on U. S. soil would have been conducted by American agents but blamed on Castro's operatives. (104)

Provocative actions such as these were justified among certain elements of the military who believed "The United States cannot tolerate permanent existence of a Communist government in the Western Hemisphere." (105) The military had drawn up numerous other contingency plans to provoke attacks upon Cuba which were code-named with some of the following: "Operation Free Ride," "Operation Smasher," "Operation Break-up," "Operation Dirty Trick," and "Operation Full-Up." One of the most blatant schemes was called "Operation Bingo" and involved a fake attack on the U.S. naval base at Guantanamo Bay, Cuba. Explosive devices which would simulate actual combat were to be detonated around the base. Each step of the operation was apparently designed to force President Kennedy to launch an attack:

(1) Simulated attack on Guantanamo
(2) Word is flashed to the President
(3) President orders counterattack to include:
    (a) Immediate launch of alerted aircraft whose targets are Cuban airfields.
    (b) Immediate launch of counterattack down strategic lines in communication in Cuba.
    (c) Fleet force standing by on alert would make way toward pre-selected targets landing areas.
    (d) Immediate embarkation of airborne troops previously alerted to pre-selected targets. . . . (106)

Despite the ambitious plans formulated by those anxious to overthrow Fidel Castro by any means necessary, President Kennedy appeared to be searching for some sort of accommodation with the Castro regime. By the summer of 1963, Kennedy ordered a crackdown on exile attacks launched from and aided by the United States. A staff report from the House Select Committee stated that, "with the prospects of renewed diplomatic relations in the air and the knowledge that Kennedy possessed a more favorable attitude toward Cuba than other military or political leader, Castro would have had every reason to hope that Kennedy maintained the Presidency." (107)

Carlos Lechuga, Cuba's former ambassador to the United Nations, has written:

> McGeorge Bundy, who was closely linked to Kennedy, proposed in early 1963 that a rapprochement with the Cuban government should be considered. . . . I don't know who supported the idea and who didn't, though it is clear that the military elements and the members of the intelligence community were committed to the subversive plans that

would lead to a military invasion of Cuba. (108)

Lechuga continued to relate President Kennedy's attempts toward rapprochement via William Atwood, ambassador to Guinea, journalist Lisa Howard and French journalist, Jean Daniel. (109) Atwood recalled that he had met at the White House on November 4, 1963, with McGeorge Bundy and related that the President was possibly interested in talks with Castro leading towards some sort of understanding. Lechuga has written:

> I interpreted Daniel's visit as a gesture to try to establish communication, a bridge, a contact, because Kennedy had so much authority inside his country after the [missile] crisis that he could do things he might not have been able to do before. I think he had the courage to do it—it took courage to defy established ideas on all those things. (110)

Lechuga concluded, "As I have reported, he [Kennedy] sought a rapprochement with the revolutionary government of Cuba, which might have resulted in a normalization of relations and the end of the U.S. policy of aggression." (111) Fidel Castro stated:

> Look at the paradox, the contradictions and coincidences; on the same day and at the same hour that Jean Daniel was giving me Kennedy's message, an agent of the United States was handing over a fountain pen with a poison dart to be used in an assassination attempt against me. Look how many paradoxes and how many crazy things there are in the world! (112)

Asked in April 1964 about a deal with Castro, Robert Kennedy said, "We always discussed that as a possibility, and it was a question of trying to work it out." (113)

Revilo Oliver, a native Texan and professor at the University of Illinois, espoused the beliefs of the extreme right-wing and was a member of the John Birch Society. Oliver and J. Edgar Hoover were of the same anti-Castro mindset. Hoover was seen as a hero to the right-wing groups like the John Birch Society, Americanism Educational League, and the Cuban Anti-Communist Journalist's Association. (114) A further example of Hoover's respect among the Cuban exile community was his acceptance in 1968 as the recipient of "The Man of the Century" award.

(115) John Kennedy's softening stance on Castro and the real possibility of rapprochement between the U.S. and Cuba could not have been pleasing to the *Father of the Cold War*. Revilo Oliver wrote a scathing attack upon President Kennedy that was published in the February 1964 edition of the John Birch Society's, *American Opinion:*

> Rational men will understand that, far from sobbing over the deceased or lying to placate his vengeful ghost, it behooves us to speak of him with complete candor and historical objectivity. Jack was not sanctified by a bullet.
>
> The departed Kennedy is the John F. Kennedy who procured his election by peddling boob-bait to the suckers, including a cynical pledge to destroy the Communist base in Cuba. He is the John F. Kennedy with whose blessing and support the Central Intelligence Agency staged a fake "invasion" of Cuba designed to strengthen our mortal enemies there and to disgrace us—disgrace us not merely by ignominious failure, but by the inhuman crime of having lured brave me into a trap and sent them to suffering and death. He is the John F. Kennedy who, in close collaboration with Khrushchev, staged the phony "embargo" that was improvised both to befuddle the suckers on election day in 1962 and to provide for several months a cover for the steady and rapid transfer of Soviet troops and soviet weapons to Cuba for eventual use against us. . . . He is the John F. Kennedy who, by shameless intimidation, bribery, and blackmail, induced weaklings in Congress to approve treasonable acts designed to disarm us and to make us the helpless prey of the affiliated criminals and savages of the "United Nations."
>
> I have mentioned but a few of the hundred reasons why we shall never forget John F. Kennedy. So long as there are Americans, his memory will be cherished with distaste. If the United States is saved by the desperate exertions of patriots, we may have a future of true greatness and glory—but we shall never forget how near we were to total destruction in the year 1963. And if the international vermin succeed in completing their occupation of our country, Americans will remember Kennedy while they live, and will curse him as they face the firing squads or toil in a brutish degradation that leaves no hope for anything but a speedy death. (116)

The charges levied by Oliver and others against President Kennedy and his liberal views on Cuba and Communism in general, would soon be matched or surpassed as a result of Kennedy's changing approach to Martin Luther King and the

Civil Rights movement. In a *New York Times* story of November 18, 1962 with the headline reading, "Dr. King Critical of FBI in South," the "civil rights leader Martin Luther King, Jr. was quoted as charging that FBI agents in a small Georgia town were siding with segregationists." (117) There can be little doubt that President Kennedy was initially upset with King's attempts to quicken the pace of civil rights legislation. Kennedy did not believe he had the congressional support necessary to ensure passage. He preferred to wait until after the 1964 election. Nicholas Katzenbach concluded that "He [Kennedy] knew he couldn't get civil rights legislation through and didn't want to waste time on it. It wasn't because of his beliefs— he knew it was hopeless." (118) Ted Sorensen commented on JFK and Civil Rights, "When Congress turned out to be dominated by Southern democrats and Republicans—he [Kennedy] was slow to move." (119)

Civil rights activist and King associate Julian Bond remembered, "we had a love-hate relationship [with Kennedy]—why aren't you doing what you promised—mixed [feelings]." (120) Arthur Schlesinger stated:

> JFK underestimated the moral dynamism of civil rights—he was in favor of it—but wanted to postpone it—and move more gradually [Kennedy believed] . . . civil rights had no chance until Bull Conner unleashed the dogs on King . . . JFK took the political gamble and his popularity dropped. (121)

By the fall of 1963, it had become clear; that after the Kennedy-George Wallace showdown over the enrollment of two black students to the University of Alabama, Kennedy's foot dragging on civil rights was over. Walter Cronkite, in an interview in September 1963, asked Kennedy, "Do you think you'll lose some southern states in 1964?" Kennedy: "I'm not sure I'm the most popular political figure in the south today. But that's all right, we'll have to see a year and a half from now." Hoover's realization of eventual cooperation between Kennedy and King on civil rights caused Hoover to become intent on exposing King as a communist and an adulterer. J. Edgar Hoover, as early as 1957, had ordered his agents to begin monitoring the activities of Martin Luther King, Jr., and the Southern Christian Leadership Conference. (122) Curt Gentry described how Hoover trapped King:

"They will destroy the burrhead," commented J. Edgar

Hoover, reviewing the transcripts of tape recordings produced by a bug at the Willard Hotel. Two days after the *Times* cover story, on January 5, 1964, FBI agents in the capital had installed a microphone in the room assigned to the Reverend King. "Trespass is involved," Sullivan had admitted in a departmental memo. Trespass of another kind would follow. Fifteen reels of tape were recorded by this special MISUR, but the highlights came the first night. Two women employees of the Philadelphia Naval Yard had joined the Man of the Year and several SCLC friends for an unbuttoned fling. . . . (123)

Robert Kennedy was pressured by Hoover to authorize wiretaps of King because of the civil rights leader's alleged communist ties. Nicholas Katzenbach, assistant attorney general under Kennedy and Johnson, stated, "To say or imply that this tape was the original conception of Robert Kennedy—that he was the moving force in this situation— or that he had any doubts whatsoever as to Dr. King's integrity or loyalty is false." (124) Burke Marshall, head of the civil rights division of the justice department under Kennedy, concluded: "It's outrageous for Mr. Hoover to give characterization of selected documents concerning principally two people now dead in order to deal with adverse publicity to the Bureau." (125) Ramsey Clark, who replaced Katzenbach as attorney general in 1967 believed:

that it was deceptive for Hoover to pose as a reluctant eavesdropper of Dr. King because he repeatedly requested me to authorize FBI wiretaps on Dr. King while I was attorney general. The last of these requests, none of which was granted, came two days before the murder of Dr. King. (126)

Assistant FBI Director William Sullivan described how Hoover attempted to trap Robert Kennedy into a position where Kennedy became a party to the initiation of wiretap surveillance of Dr. King:

Hoover set a trap for Bobby Kennedy when the attorney general, accompanied by Courtney Evans, was visiting our Chicago office. The special agent in charge asked Kennedy if he would like to listen to some "sensitive" tapes which his agents had collected during the course of a criminal investigation. . . . Never a man to let an opportunity go by, Hoover insisted on and got sworn affidavits from every agent present stating that Kennedy had listened to the tapes and had not questioned their legality. Those affidavits are probably still in the files. (127)

Reporter Anthony Lewis interviewed Assistant Attorney General Burke Marshall and Robert Kennedy in 1964. Marshall and Kennedy related the following information about Hoover's attempts to wiretap King and prove that he was a communist:

> *Marshall.* . . . Mr. Hoover prepared a memorandum, classified as top secret, which was an attack on Dr. King. It went into this business about Levison [member of the Communist Party in America]. It also went into other connections with Communists or former Communists that were less dangerous than the [Stanley] Levison thing, which was undoubtedly a real effort to get some control over Dr. King. . . . He sent a copy to the President, and he sent a copy to the Attorney General, and I think he sent a copy to me.
> *Kennedy.* . . . Within all of this material that we had on the tie with Levison, there was offsetting material of conversations which Martin Luther King might have had which indicated that he didn't want to have anything to do with the communists. He wanted to make sure that the Communists stayed out of the March on Washington. There were things that gave a different side of Martin Luther King. (128)

Kennedy went on to state, ". . . But [Hoover] wrote this memorandum up in an unfair way. He started out by saying that Martin Luther King is a Marxist or something." (129)

Secretary of State Dean Rusk was of the firm belief that J. Edgar Hoover attempted to "bug" his phone. Rusk related to his son Richard: " . . . [my father] had both his home and office swept repeatedly for 'bugs;' concerned about the FBI as well as the Russians, he once told J. Edgar Hoover, in Kennedy's presence, that if the FBI ever bugged him, he would resign and publicly state his reasons." (130) The wiretapping dispute would prove to be an area of great controversy long after President Kennedy's death. J. Edgar Hoover would continue to charge Robert Kennedy with being the initiator and moving force behind the taps on King.

With Hoover's dislike of Robert Kennedy so intense—it is interesting to note that Presidential assistant, Ken O'Donnell believed, "I think Bobby perhaps got along better with Hoover than the President did." (131) This is supported by the number of meetings between President Kennedy and Hoover.

Dave Powers recalled:

> . . . I can't remember meeting him maybe seven times in the
> White House. I'd say he had three off-record dinners. October
> thirty-first, 1963, he had a long lunch with the President and
> Bobby, and, as you know, three weeks later we went to Dallas.
> Their meetings, their luncheons were all awfully long when
> they had them. (132)

Ben Bradlee recalled that in early November 1963,
President Kennedy was contemplating a more friendly
relationship with Hoover in preparation for the 1964 election:

> J. Edgar Hoover, the FBI chief, had been to lunch with
> Kennedy a few days before, and Kennedy was full of that
> meeting. He told us how FDR used to have Hoover over
> regularly, and said he felt it was wise for him to start doing
> the same thing, with rumors flying and every indication of a
> dirty campaign coming up. "Boy, the dirt he has on those
> senators," Kennedy said, shaking his head. "You wouldn't
> believe it." (133)

Dallas FBI agent James Hosty concluded:

> Early in his administration, President Kennedy had decided
> to force Hoover to retire at seventy. Kennedy had carefully
> set the stage by not granting retirement exceptions to the
> directors of the Secret Service, The Bureau of Prisons, the
> Immigration and Naturalization Service, and the Narcotics
> Bureau. Hoover was next. (134)

J. Edgar Hoover had reason for legitimate concern over his
retention as Director of the FBI. The mandatory retirement
age of 70 was fast approaching. Speculation that Hoover
would be replaced on January 1, 1965, if Kennedy was re-
elected, abounded. William Sullivan surmised, "Jack
Kennedy disliked Hoover and wanted to replace him as
director, but he had won the election by such a narrow margin
that he felt he couldn't afford to alienate Hoover's
considerable conservative following by getting rid of him."
(135) Clyde Tolson, Hoover's "closest friend" and top
assistant, felt the same way about the Kennedys in general.
He stated, "We'll be stuck with the Kennedy clan till the year
2000." (136)

James Hosty recalled Hoover's version of Kennedy's plans

for keeping him on as Director for his second term. Hosty stated, "President Kennedy told Hoover that he was going to waive the mandatory retirement requirement because, 'The President told me that the country just could not get along without me.'" (137) There are literally hundreds of letters on file in the JFK Library which document the efforts of private citizens to forestall any efforts by President Kennedy to replace J. Edgar Hoover as Director of the FBI. The majority of the letters considered Hoover the protector of America against "leftists", "liberals", and "communists." Little did most Americans know, that Hoover, in the course of protecting the nation against the threat of communist subversion, was guilty of violating and trampling on the most basic rights we have as free citizens; namely free speech, the right to privacy, and justice under the law.

William Hundley, former head of the Justice Department Organized Crime Section believed:

> I am convinced that the thing that finally destroyed their relationship was that Bobby mentioned to too many people who complained to him about Hoover that, look just wait, and we all got the message that they were going to retire him after Jack got reelected and Hoover hit seventy. And it got back to him. (138)

A graceful, but compulsory retirement by Hoover in 1965 could have solved the problem, but it was not to be. Nicholas Katzenbach described Robert Kennedy's account of his November 22, 1963 conversation with J. Edgar Hoover: "I called Bobby at his home . . . he told me the President had died . . . he said he had just heard from Mr. Hoover and Hoover told him . . . with great pleasure that the President was dead." (139) Anthony Lewis asked Robert Kennedy to expand on his conversation with Hoover, and Kennedy's belief that J. Edgar Hoover was not going to pay any attention to him after his brother was assassinated:

> *Lewis.* Now let's be concrete: Tell me some of the specific things, if you can face it, that happened with Mr. Hoover after November 22 within hours or days, that made it evident that he was not going to pay any attention to you anymore.
> *Kennedy.* First, his conversations with me on November 22 were so unpleasant. I can't go into all the details of that. Just the tone of voice and the information and what he was giving me was—I mean, it wasn't the way, under the circumstances,

I would have thought an individual would talk. . . . (140)

Kennedy aide Joe Dolan recalled that shortly after Robert Kennedy returned to work after the assassination of his brother, Kennedy remarked to Dolan, "Those people [Hoover and the FBI] don't work for us anymore." (141) Kennedy stated further to Anthony Lewis, "I think he [Hoover] is dangerous." (142) Kennedy added:

> But after November 22, 1963, he no longer had to hide his feelings. He didn't have to hide his feelings, and he no longer had to pay any attention to me. And it was in the interest, evidently, of the President of the United States—President Johnson— to have that kind of a relationship and arrangement. (143)

With the death of President Kennedy and the demise of Robert Kennedy's influence (and his subsequent murder), the historical narrative of John Kennedy's presidency would be left to others to write. Kennedy aide Arthur Schlesinger commented on the recent negative accounts of John Kennedy:

> . . . Revisionist critics see Kennedy as charming but superficial, a triumph of style over substance, a politician more concerned with image than results, who talked big but accomplished little. In the darker side of the counter myth, Kennedy becomes a faithless husband and incorrigible philanderer, a reckless risk-taker in both private and public life, a bellicose president who ordered the assassination of foreign leaders, plunged the nation into the Vietnam morass, almost provoked a nuclear war with the Soviet Union and between needless international crisis, turned the White House into a bordello. (144)

Schlesinger admits that he is not a totally objective observer but that his observations still have merit. He did, after all, know President Kennedy and does admit that certain criticisms of Kennedy are warranted:

> I make no great claim to impartiality. I served in JFK's White House, and it was the most exhilarating experience of my life. Yet close observation of a president need not be a disqualification in writing about him. I did, after all, know Kennedy, and I knew him for many years. When he was president, I saw him in the daytime as a special assistant and in evenings as a friend. I saw him in good times and in bad. I

may not be totally useless as a witness. (145)

Schlesinger offers this assessment of Kennedy's priorities for
America, the Western Hemisphere, and the world during his
second term:

> Kennedy believed that in the end America's influence in the
> world depended less on American arms than on American
> ideals.   Undertakings such as the Peace Corps and the
> Alliance for Progress were closest to his heart. The Peace
> Corps, still going strong 35 years later, sent young Americans
> to the far corners of the earth to work with local people in
> improving education, public health and agricultural
> productivity.   The Alliance for Progress was designed to
> promote economic growth and democratic institutions in Latin
> America. (146)

Former Texas Governor John Connally believed:

> Up to that very day [November 22], I had thought—and the
> polls showed—that John Kennedy's re-election was no sure
> thing. Observing him on that trip, riding with him in the car
> that morning, I knew he would get a second term. Kennedy
> would run against Barry Goldwater, who had not yet learned
> to lighten up in public, and he was going to so captivate the
> people that his record wouldn't much matter. And up to that
> point, the record was rather thin. But Kennedy would make
> Goldwater look and sound like a hardcase, pinched, and
> crabby. (147)

Connally offers this assessment of President Kennedy's
second term:

> The country would have swung neither wildly to the right nor
> to the left. The Peace Corps might have played a larger role
> in helping underdeveloped nations, and more young people
> would have been drawn into public service. Jack Kennedy's
> appeal to minorities might have spared us summers of urban
> violence. We might have become the kinder and gentler
> nation we are still looking for thirty years later. . . . He would
> have appealed to Young America's unselfishness, and just the
> absence of his terrible death would have removed a layer of
> bitterness and despair. (148)

These last words of "bitterness and despair" also accurately
describe the mood of those who have studied the record of

Kennedy's murder. For as we shall see, the truth in regards to President Kennedy's death has yet to be written.

J. Edgar Hoover, Captain of Company A of the Brigade of Cadets, in 1913. (Photograph courtesy of the National Archives.)

William Bollinger, head of the Seattle Bureau of Investigation, and Hoover in 1924. (Photograph courtesy of the National Archives.)

Left to right: Attorney General Homer Cummings, Hoover, Senator Henry Ashurst, and Assistant Attorney General Joseph P. Kennan at signing of the Crime Bill in 1934. (Photograph courtesy of the National Archives.)

Left to right: Clyde Tolson, Walter Winchell, Hoover, and Ben Bernie at the Paradise Cafe in New York, 1935. (Photograph courtesy of the National Archives.)

Clyde Tolson and J. Edgar Hoover in 1937. (Photograph courtesy of the National Archives.)

J. Edgar Hoover and Texas Rep. Lyndon Johnson with members of the Texas Boy Scout Jamboree in 1937. (Photograph courtesy of the National Archives.)

J. Edgar and former President Herbert Hoover meet in New York City during WWII in 1944. (Photograph courtesy of the National Archives.)

Hoover receiving the National Security Medal in 1955 surrounded by NY Governor Nelson Rockefeller, CIA Head Allen Dulles, President Dwight Eisenhower, Vice-President Richard Nixon and Secretary of State John Foster Dulles. (Photograph courtesy of the National Archives and Abbie Rowe.)

Director Hoover and his assistant directors pose for the unveiling of the Director's painting. (Photograph courtesy of the National Archives.)

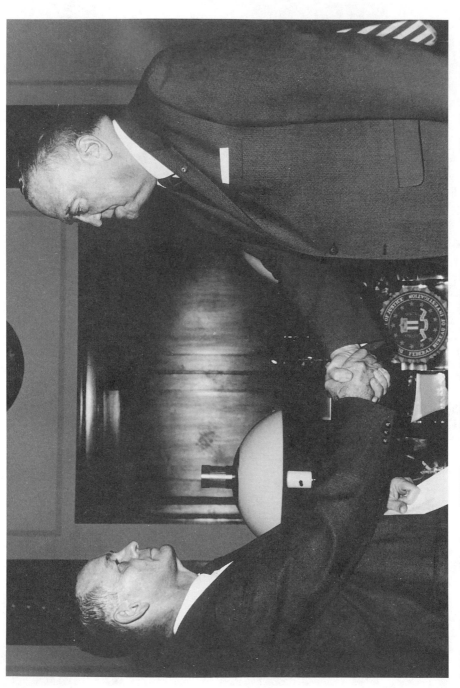

J. Edgar Hoover and Assistant FBI Director William Sullivan in 1966. (Photograph courtesy of the National Archives.)

Assistant FBI Director Louis Nichols, Lewis Rosentiel, and Hoover in 1968. (Photograph courtesy of the National Archives.)

J. Edgar Hoover and President Kennedy meet in the Oval Office in May of 1963. (Photograph courtesy of the John F. Kennedy Library.)

President Kennedy and Director Hoover in February 1961. (Photograph courtesy of the John F. Kennedy Library.)

President Kennedy, Hoover, and Attorney General Robert Kennedy
in October 1962. (Photograph courtesy of the John F. Kennedy
Library).

Part 2

**Obstruction of Justice:
The Warren Commission Coverup**

Chapter 7

The Communists or the Right-Wing?

A study of J. Edgar Hoover's role in the Warren Report investigation is relevant to Hoover, as the leader of the anti-communist cause, as well as to Lyndon Johnson's successful 1964 Presidential election victory. Lee Oswald, the accused assassin of President Kennedy, was labeled a communist by both J. Edgar Hoover and Lyndon Johnson on the day of the assassination. (1)   Yet a tape recording of a phone conversation between Lyndon Johnson and J. Edgar Hoover on November 23, the day after the murder, proves they both knew that an impostor calling himself Lee Oswald, showed up at the Soviet embassy in Mexico City two months before the assassination.   This impostor had contacted Valery Kostikov—whom the CIA had described as "a case officer in the operation which is evidently sponsored by the KGB's 13th Department responsible for assassination." (2) Documents released early in 1999 indicated that a Navy plane carried a copy of a tape and photographs that Hoover listened to and observed and then relayed to Johnson on November 23. Hoover told Johnson:

> We have up here the tape and the photograph of the man who was at the Soviet embassy using Oswald's name. That picture and the tape do not correspond to this man's voice nor to his appearance. In other words, it appears that there was a second person who was at the Soviet embassy down there. (3)

It is clear that on the day after the assassination, both
Hoover and Johnson knew that there was a distinct
possibility that Oswald was falsely tied to international
communists.   It is quite possible that Oswald was not a
bonafide communist and that he had been impersonated on
numerous occasions in the weeks leading up to the
assassination of John Kennedy.   Oswald's bonafides as a
communist lone assassin has been brought into question by
numerous researchers and will also be evaluated in depth in
Chapter 8.   The possibility that Oswald had been
impersonated has been well documented by Sylvia Meagher
in her book *Accessories After the Fact,* which was first
published in 1967. Someone resembling and using the name
Oswald, appeared at a shooting range, a gun shop, a grocery
store, and a car dealership in Dallas during the months of
September and October 1963.   The Warren Commission
admits that Oswald could not have been at these various
locations on the dates and times ascribed to him. (4) It seems
clear that J. Edgar Hoover was not truly looking for the truth
about the assassination of John Kennedy, without considering
the possibility that someone was trying to tie Oswald in with
communists in general, as well as to the Soviets and/or
Cubans.

The belief that Lyndon Johnson and J. Edgar Hoover did
not want to dig deeper into an investigation of a conspiracy is
made clear in this statement by Soviet Ambassador Anatoly
Dobrynin:

> Deputy Prime Minister Anastas Mikoyan, while in
> Washington, D.C., for President Kennedy's funeral,
> telegraphed Moscow that the U. S. Government does not want
> to involve us in this matter, but neither does it want to get
> into a fight with the extreme rightists; it clearly prefers to
> consign the whole business to oblivion as soon as possible. (5)

Ironically, after leaving Dallas on Friday morning, the day
of the assassination, Richard Nixon arrived in New York late
that afternoon. After hearing of the murder of the President,
he called J. Edgar Hoover and immediately asked Hoover "if
it was one of the right-wing nuts?" "No," Hoover replied, "it
was a communist." (6) Nixon's question seemed to be a logical
one when considering the "Wanted For Treason" handbills
passed out on the streets of Dallas the day of the murder, as
well as the "Welcome Mr. Kennedy" paid advertisement found

in the local paper the morning of the assassination. Both of these right-wing attacks depicted Kennedy as being soft on Communism as the following examples indicate:

Wanted For Treason

1. He is turning the sovereignty of the U. S. over to the communist controlled United Nations
2. He has been lax in enforcing Communist Registration laws.
3. He has given support and encouragement to the Communist inspired racial riots. (7)

Welcome Mr. Kennedy

WHY is Latin America turning either anti-American or Communistic, or both, despite increased U. S. foreign aid, State Department policy, and your own Ivy-Tower pronouncements?

WHY have you approved the sale of wheat and corn to our enemies when you know the Communist soldiers "travel on their stomachs" just as ours do? Communist soldiers are daily wounding and/or killing American soldiers in South Viet Nam.

WHY did you host, salute and entertain Tito—Moscow's Trojan Horse—just a short time after our sworn enemy, Khrushchev, embraced the Yugoslav dictator as a great hero and leader of Communism?

WHY have you banned the showing at U. S. military bases of the film "Operation Abolition"—the movie by the House Committee on Un-American Activities exposing Communism in America?

WHY have you ordered or permitted your brother Bobby, the Attorney General, to go soft on Communists, fellowtravelers and ultra-leftists in America, while permitting him to persecute loyal Americans who criticize you, your administration, and your leadership?

WHY have you scrapped the Monroe Doctrine in favor of the "Spirit of Moscow"? (8)

Richard Nixon, having been in Dallas, might have seen these right-wing and anti-Kennedy ads himself—he definitely knew the mood of the Dallas right-wing, which is surely why he immediately asked Hoover that question. Ted Dealy, publisher of the *Dallas Morning News* reflected the view of the right-wing when he stated directly to President Kennedy in 1961:

> We can annihilate Russia and should make that clear to the Soviet government. Unfortunately for America, you and your administration are weak sisters. What was needed was a man on horseback to lead this nation, and many people in Texas and the Southwest think that you are riding Caroline's tricycle. (9)

In a televised interview, General Thomas Power of the Strategic Air Command, concurred with Dealy making clear his feelings on what he believed our stance to the Soviet Union should be: "And what's more important is that Mr. Khrushchev is aware of that capability [to annihilate the Soviet Union] . . . whether you or anyone else agrees with that doesn't matter." (10)

As Dealy and Power make clear, the right-wing extremists were not at all convinced that John Kennedy was on their side in their war against Communism. And as we have seen in Part 1, these views are shared by J. Edgar Hoover.

It is interesting to take note of Deputy Prime Minister Mikoyan's view that the new American government, now led by Lyndon Johnson, did not want to "fight with the extremists." As we have seen from Richard Nixon, there was legitimate speculation as to the possibility of right-wing involvement in the assassination. It has not been made clear why Hoover did not probe into this area but it is not unreasonable to assume that he was at least sympathetic, if not a supporter of many of their views.

An interesting and possibly related piece of information that will be considered in more detail later is that in 1960, Hoover is on record as stating that an impostor was using Lee Oswald's birth certificate while Oswald was in the Soviet Union. This is made clear in a letter sent by Hoover on June 3, 1960, to the State Department's Office of Security, Hoover asks, "Since there is the possibility that an impostor is using Oswald's birth certificate—any current information the Department of State has concerning Oswald will be appreciated." (11) Dallas FBI Special Agent John W. Fain interviewed Lee Oswald's mother, Mrs. Marguerite Oswald in

April 1960. "She volunteered the information that LEE HARVEY OSWALD took his birth certificate with him when he left Fort Worth, Texas [for the Soviet Union]." (12) This adds further corroboration to the belief that Lee Oswald was being impersonated, not only in the months leading up to the assassination, but most probably almost three years earlier. When one considers that Johnson and Hoover both knew that someone was posing as Lee Oswald immediately before the assassination, and that this impostor was meeting with a KGB official responsible for assassination, it proves to be very disturbing indeed. When it's also considered that Hoover believed someone was using Oswald's birth certificate in the United States while Oswald was in the Soviet Union (three years before the assassination), one must surely wonder if Oswald was being manipulated and what Hoover's true motives in this whole affair really were. It appears quite likely that someone or some group was attempting to link Lee Oswald to the communists in an assassination attempt with Kostikov and that J. Edgar Hoover knew this and either ignored this or chose to cover it up.

The initial charge drawn up by Dallas Assistant District Attorney William Alexander on November 22 was that "Oswald was part of an international communist conspiracy." (13) "Barefoot" Sanders, a federal judge from Dallas, was puzzled as to where Alexander gained this information. Sanders said, ". . . the District Attorney's office was going to charge Oswald with being part of an international communist conspiracy. I can't really recall where that came from." (14) This research has documented J. Edgar Hoover's life-long obsession with Communism; one would surely think that he would have left no stone unturned in an investigation of a communist assassin of an American President. A question that cannot be answered at present is why Johnson and Hoover both publicly stated that a communist, Lee Harvey Oswald, killed the President but that belief was later allowed to lose its importance. An attempt to make sense of Hoover's investigation and come to a clearer understanding of this puzzle is needed.

Morris Childs, an FBI double agent and the subject of the book, *Our Man in Moscow* by John Barron was in Moscow on the day President Kennedy was killed. He personally witnessed the reaction of the Soviet leadership to Kennedy's death. (15) He reported to the FBI, in an encrypted message that was later confirmed by the Soviet defector Yuri Nosenko, that "the Soviet Union had nothing to do with the assassination of President Kennedy, and its leaders were as stunned by the tragedy as was anyone else." (16) According to Childs, Lyndon Johnson, Robert Kennedy, and the Warren Commission were personally briefed by FBI agents about this message in the weeks that followed. (17) Nosenko stated, ". . . And as far what I have seen, there wasn't a single indication that it was done by the Soviets." (18)   This view was confirmed by Under Secretary of State George Ball when he stated, ". . . Obviously our embassy in Moscow made some inquiries as well as checking the intelligence and came back with the words that the Soviets were as upset about this as we were." (19)

On November 25, 1963, Jack Childs, Morris' brother (and FBI informer), met with FBI agent Burlison who was in charge of the New York City office, to sum up the Soviet reaction to the charges that Lee Oswald was a communist sympathizer, a follower of Fidel Castro, and a former resident of the Soviet Union. The initial public perception was that Oswald must have been controlled by the communists somehow. Jack Childs told the FBI:

> The message was to the effect that the Soviets were to notify at once all world communist parties on our behalf to continue public campaign which directs fire against the ultra-right wing elements and provacateurs in the United States who are the real perpetrators of the assassination of President Kennedy, and also to strike against those commentators and others including public officials especially in the South who are falsely accusing the Communist Party of the United States of America and the USA working class. (20)

On the same day that Childs spoke to the FBI, Soviet Foreign Minister Andrei Gromyko outlined ways the Soviet press could counteract the implication and stated that the "real face of those circles who are responsible for the killing of President Kennedy, and who are now trying to cover their tracks, is more evident." (21) Was the American right-wing the "real face" that Childs was alluding to? It appears from Soviet news reports that they did believe that the American right-wing was the "real face" they were alluding to. Pravda reported, "Desperate quarters are now striving to cover up the traces of the bloody crime. . . ." (22) The Russian news agency

Tass, informed its readers that "All the circumstances of President Kennedy's tragic death allow one to assume that his murder was planned and carried out by the ultra-right-wing, fascist and racist circles." (23)

The Soviet news agency Novosti published a book written by journalists Sergei Losev and Vitaly Petruisenko in 1983. *Echo of the Shots in Dallas* argues that John Kennedy was murdered by those in the American right-wing who were against Kennedy's policies of "appeasement" towards the Russians and Castro. Was this just part of the Cold War rhetoric of the Reagan era or a continuation of Soviet fears and/or research of their own that was begun on the day of the assassination? The preponderance of evidence set forth here should cause the questioning reader to consider this subject more seriously.

The allegation by Thomas Mann, U. S. diplomat to Mexico, of communist involvement in the assassination was contained in a November 27 press release of a cablegram to the FBI. Mann apparently had no doubt that the assassination of President Kennedy and the murder of Oswald were both carried out by the communists and specifically by Castro. (24) How he "knew" this to be true, when in fact the opposite appeared more likely to be true, also needs some explaining. Mann was slated to retire, as he announced in June of 1963. His strident anti-communist views had been seen by Robert Kennedy as hindering President Kennedy's attempts at social reform in Latin America. (25) But President Johnson reappointed Mann on December 14, 1963. Ironically, it was to be Thomas Mann who helped arrange for United States recognition of the Somoza coup in Honduras. This coup reversed the perceived leftist and "communist leaning" movement attempting to take control of the United Fruit Company which was owned and operated by United States corporate interests and dominated the Honduran economy. (26)

Along with Thomas Mann, James Angleton, CIA counter-intelligence chief, and Angleton's deputy, Ray Rocca, also raised suspicions of "Soviet KGB [and] of the Cuban DGI" involvement in the assassination. (27) Angleton and Rocca served as liaisons between the CIA and the Warren Commission. Both Rocca and Angleton remained in close contact with former CIA Director Allen Dulles after President Kennedy relieved Dulles as head of the Agency after the Bay of Pigs debacle.   The Senate Intelligence Committee on Foreign Assassinations noted:

> Mr. Angleton testified he was often in contact with Dulles after he left the Agency. . . . Dulles consulted with [Angleton] before agreeing to President Johnson's request that he be on the Commission. . . . [Angleton] and Dulles informally discussed the progress of the Commission's investigation. (28)

According to a 1975 Rockefeller Commission Memo, Rocca "outlined various allegations in testimony regarding Lee Oswald's possible involvement with Cuban conspirators, particularly pro-Castro Cubans." (29) Despite being liaisons to the Commission—did Rocca and Angleton not inform the Commission of their "evidence" because they (and Hoover) knew this to be false?

The overwhelming evidence presented here strongly indicates that Hoover and others attempted to promote Oswald as an assassin tied to international communists. Hoover at one point wrote on a memo the "Red conspiracy [stories]. . . . Be sure to go over this thoroughly." (30) It appears that when Hoover realized this story would not hold up under close scrutiny, he abandoned this line in favor of Oswald, the "lone communist-inspired" assassin.

The Soviets also concluded that an Oswald letter to the Soviet embassy, dated two weeks before assassination, was a forgery and not from the Lee Oswald who lived in the Soviet Union from 1959 to 1962. "This letter was clearly a provocation," Soviet Ambassador Anatoly Dobrynin reported to Moscow:

> It gives the impression we had close ties with Oswald and were using him for some purposes of our own. It was totally unlike any other letters the embassy had previously received from Oswald. . . .The suspicion that the letter is a forgery is heightened by the fact that it was typed, whereas the other letters the embassy had received from Oswald were handwritten. One gets the definite impression that the letter was concocted by those who, judging from everything, are involved in the president's assassination. It is possible that Oswald himself wrote the letter as it was dictated to him. . . . and then . . . he was simply bumped off after his usefulness had ended. (31)

Another example of someone linking Oswald to communists

is from a letter intercepted by the U. S. Secret Service and
written by one Pedro Charles. This letter was postmarked
from Havana on November 28, 1963 and addressed to Lee
Harvey Oswald. The letter implies that Oswald had been
paid $7,000 while in Miami to carry out a mission involving
accurate shooting. However, this story did not hold up
because the FBI's chronology of Oswald's whereabouts
revealed that he had never visited Miami. (32)

The House Select Committee on Assassinations questioned
Fidel Castro on April 3, 1978:

> It was very suspicious to me, that a person who later
> appeared to be involved in the Kennedy assassination would
> have requested a visa to Cuba. Because I said to myself, what
> would have happened had by chance that man come to Cuba,
> visited Cuba, gone back to the United States and then
> appeared involved in Kennedy's death? That would have
> really been a provocation, a giant provocation. (33)

In 1963, Oswald applied for a new passport to go back to
the Soviet Union and received it with no problems within 24
hours. (34) The Passport Office at that time was run by two
fervent anti-Communists, Miss Francis Knight and Otto
Otepka. (35) It is extremely doubtful that fervent "cold
warriors" such as Knight and Otepka would have so easily
facilitated Oswald's passport to the Soviet Union if he had not
had some sort of official clearance or intelligence connections.

The Warren Commission was informed about an intent by
someone or some group to impersonate Oswald two months
before the assassination and tie him to a Cuban intent to
assassinate President Kennedy. Sylvia Odio, the daughter of
a wealthy anti-Castro Cuban exile stated, "that three men
visited her home in Dallas in late September 1963. One of
them was called "Oswald." Two days after the visit, in a
phone conversation, one of the three had described Oswald as
a potential assassin to Odio. "Well, you know, he's a Marine,
an ex-Marine, and an expert marksman. . . . He's kind of loco,
kinda nuts. . . . The American says we Cubans don't have any
guts. He says we should have shot President Kennedy after
the Bay of Pigs. He says we should do something like that."
(36) The Warren Commission considered this matter
seriously enough to direct J. Edgar Hoover that Odio's
statement must be "proved or disproved." (37) Loran Hall,
involved in training anti-Castro Cubans, was also an officer of

the Committee to Free Cuba, also known as "The Free Cuba Committee." This Committee worked in Florida in preparation for raids into Cuba. Hall stated to the Warren Commission that he was one of the three that had visited Odio and that the real Oswald was not with them. Within ten days of the Warren Commission issuing its final report, Hall recanted this story and there the matter was dropped without Hall explaining why he changed his story. (38) Sylvia Odio's account of someone impersonating Lee Oswald in an assassination attempt on President Kennedy was not properly analyzed or disproven, and has created even more suspicion as to what groups or individuals were trying to implicate Cuba in the assassination.

According to documents released through the Assassination and Records Review Board (ARRB), "An emotional and uneasy" Fidel Castro mobilized his armed forces and went on Cuban national television after President Kennedy's assassination out of fear the United States would blame him and invade in retaliation. Congress mandated in 1992 that the ARRB work for the release of files held by various government agencies that had sealed documents relating to President Kennedy's assassination. The National Security Agency, in declassified documents that were released in 1997, stated that Castro feared the United States would use the Kennedy assassination as an excuse to oust his communist government. (39) The belief that Castro was not involved in Kennedy's assassination is also supported by the recent disclosures of the Assassination Records and Review Board.

Review Board member Anna Nelson stated that the evidence she has seen eliminates Castro as a suspect in the assassination. Nelson stated, "We have done [looked at] that; Castro was not involved. Castro was not a factor. That is very important for the historical record." (40) Fellow board member and rare book archivist at Princeton, William Joyce, supports Nelson. Joyce said, "From all the evidence we have gathered about what was going on in Cuba and in the domestic leftist organizations, it is clear they were as baffled and surprised and confused as the rest of us." (41) This belief is confirmed by an Associated Press article from November 30, 1963 in which Fidel Castro said:

> In the eyes of the world it is clear that the reactionaries of the United States wanted to make our country the victim of their criminal designs even at the price of assassinating the

President of the United States . . . the authorities declared the case closed. (42)

The House Select Committee on Assassinations in 1979 also concluded that Fidel Castro and the Cuban government did not orchestrate or participate in the murder of President Kennedy. The Committee reached this conclusion based on all the available evidence they examined. The work by the Committee was the most complete of any investigation. J. Edgar Hoover surely did not adequately consider the possibility of conspiracy or attempt to pursue it. The House Select Committee's investigation differed from the Warren Commission because they pursued all possible leads prior to making their conclusion.

The initial reaction by the Soviets was to be suspicious of possible involvement in the assassination by elements of the American right-wing. This is consistent with the statement released by Moscow's radio commentator on the afternoon of the assassination — before Oswald was even arrested, the commentator told the Russian people, ". . . it is said he has been murdered by the extreme right wing elements." (43) This view was also confirmed from a UPI Press Report from November 26, 1963. It states the following:

> The deaths of President Kennedy and murder suspect Lee Harvey Oswald were presented to the Soviet Union Monday night as part of a single ultra-rightist plot to wreck Soviet American relations and world peace. The Kremlin, the Soviet Communist party and Moscow's newspapers, radio and television paid unprecedented honors to the late President. But powerful party and government organizations unleashed broadsides against what they called "influential people" in the United States who, they said, brought about Kennedy's death and the elimination of his alleged killer. . . . The government newspaper Izvestia charged that "from the moment Oswald was detained, a game was deliberately being played around him which was clearly of an anti-Soviet and anti-Communist character."

Ambassador Dobrynin and the Soviet leadership later surmised:

> What was the Soviet leadership's view of his death? The KGB on Khrushchev's orders prepared a top secret report. Its principal conclusion was that the assassination arose from a

plot hatched by ultraconservative groups and the Mafia in the United States with the goal of strengthening the reactionary and aggressive elements of American policy. (44)

A recent book by Christopher Andrew and former KGB official Vasily Mitrokhin, *The Sword and the Shield,* argues that the KGB forged documents attempting to link the CIA to the assassination of President Kennedy during the 1970's. The KGB's propaganda machine would have surely wanted to exploit this version of events.(45) It is, of course, possible that the KGB did forge these documents but even if proven to be true, this does not take away from the documented initial concerns that the Soviets faced. There were a number of well documented attempts to link Oswald to the Soviets and/or the Cubans that have proven to be false, including the previously mentioned Pedro Charles letter.

The Warren Commission had information that Gilbert Alvarado of the Nicaraguan Secret Service had reported seeing a man claiming to be Lee Oswald in the Cuban Consulate in Mexico City in September of 1963. Alvarado stated that he had seen a Negro with red hair give $6,500 to "Oswald for the expressed purpose of killing President Kennedy." (46) Apparently this was an attempt to tie Fidel Castro to the assassination of President Kennedy. But CIA Director John McCone quickly shot down the rumor and made this clear to President Johnson in a phone conversation on November 30:

> *McCone:* We got a phone call from Mexico City that this fellow Alvarado that I was telling you about this morning, signed a statement that all the statements he'd made in conjunction with that matter have been false. . . . Apparently there's no substance to it at all. (47)

Also supporting McCone's determination was Cuban Consul General Eusebio Azcue. He is on record as saying that the Oswald he recalled in the Cuban Consulate in Mexico City "in no way resembled" the Oswald later seen in film footage and press photos after the assassination. (48) Further support comes from Edwin Lopez who studied all the available photos and film footage for the House Select Committee from the United States intelligence surveillance cameras in Mexico City during the period of "Oswald's" purported visits to the Cuban and Soviet embassies during the fall of 1963. He stated that, without a doubt, the man shown in these surveillance photos was not Lee Oswald. (49) Lopez stated further, ". . . the only plausible explanation was that they were trying to set him up [as a patsy]." (50) Oswald himself "stated that he had never been in Mexico except to Tijuana on one occasion. . . ." (51)

The belief that the full story was not being told by the new leadership of the United States government was not just a Soviet or Cuban propaganda ploy as evidenced by other leaders of foreign governments. Indian leader Mr. Rajagopalachari, who was formerly close to Gandhi, stated:

> he was fearful that the "enemies of peace" might have used Oswald as a tool and then "silenced him". . . Obviously the effort . . . was to insinuate that Oswald was connected with Communism and the Soviet Union. . . .We cannot but be conscious of the fact that the man who was assassinated a few days ago was able to show men and women everywhere how to proceed along the path that will lead us to peace. (52)

The French press also made known its concerns about the truth concerning the assassination. In an article from the *Paris-Jour*, it was written, "Oswald cannot have been alone in shooting. . . . Who was really responsible for the assassination? Is there a secret organization . . . behind it all?" (53) Two German newspapers, *The Berliner Morgenpost* in West Berlin, and *Die Welt* of Hamburg, stated that ". . .Kennedy's assassination was a gang plot, it is possible that Jack Ruby silenced Oswald to cover the men behind the plot . . ." and ". . .[the case against Oswald] was a forest of question marks. . . ." (54)

The broadcast by the American-run Voice Of America also promoted the suspicions that the assassination was a product of "the extreme right-wing movement." The Voice Of America beamed this perception around the world to stations in Europe, Africa, and the Middle East. In an article printed in the *Dallas Morning News* on November 28, 1963, written by John Mashek, he writes:

> The director of the Voice of America . . . [Mr.] Loomis [stated], "It was a fact . . ." of the existence of the right-wing extremists in Dallas. Loomis also said, "Some of the commercial television media in the country were speculating on the possibility of a right-wing assassin."

In another article printed in the *News*, also on November 28, 1963, the admission that Dallas was the center of anti-communist extremism is made evident by this statement:

> Dallas Newspapers have for years warned of the Red peril. It was a Red who murdered the President. Most of the rumors [of conspiracy] about the case come from Europe. To Europeans, organized attempts to seize power by assassinating czars and kings are as old as history. To them, it is difficult to believe that there weren't people behind Oswald using him.

Was Lee Harvey Oswald really the communist-inspired, lone assassin of an American president? Why would Lyndon Johnson continue to argue that Fidel Castro and/or Nikita Khrushchev were responsible for Kennedy's death? Johnson told White House Aide Joseph Califano, "President Kennedy tried to get Castro, but Castro got Kennedy first." (55) Richard Helms answered in response to this question from the Church Committee: "Had it occurred to him in 1963 that Oswald might have shot the President on Castro's behalf if not by his direct orders?" "No, I don't recall the thought ever occurring to me at the time. The very first time I heard such a theory as that enunciated was in a very peculiar way by President Johnson." (56) The peculiar and ever-changing ruminations of Lyndon Johnson in regards to his assassination of his predecessor will be examined further in the conclusion to this research.

Certain elements of the extreme right-wing claimed immediately after the assassination that Lee Oswald's murder of President Kennedy was instigated by international communists. Revilo Oliver, a member of the John Birch Society and a featured speaker at the April 1963 Congress of Freedom meeting in New Orleans, charged that Lee Oswald, ". . . was a part of a Communist plot . . . that Lee Harvey Oswald was a Communist agent trained . . . in a school for international criminals near Minsk." (57) The Warren Commission sought to find out the source of Oliver's accusations and Oliver responded by stating that the man was Frank Capell who was "a private expert on Communism and Communistic information, who, I understand, has the cooperation of many former intelligence officers of the Army and former members of the FBI." (58) As will be discussed later, the Congress of Freedom Meeting which took place in

April 1963 in New Orleans, appears to be a key convergence of many different elements of the extreme right-wing. It very well may have set the stage for the events which culminated on November 22, 1963.

Why do those such as former Chairman of the Joint Chiefs of Staff Alexander Haig continue to push the argument of a communist conspiracy today? "Haig said that he thinks a Soviet conspiracy which will never be uncovered, led to the assassination of John Kennedy." (59) Despite consistent and documented evidence that Lee Oswald was impersonated in Mexico City, FBI agent James Hosty continued to state in 1996 that Oswald met with the Soviet vice consul in Mexico City. This "consul" was Valery Kostikov who "worked for the KGB's Department 13 which dealt in international terrorism, sabotage, and assassinations." (60) Why Hosty continues this argument when Hoover, as well as the photos and tapes prove otherwise, is baffling. The documentation, for his and Haig's argument, is simply not there.

Again, the question begs an answer—why did J. Edgar Hoover not seek to destroy the domestic leftist and/or communist movement as a result of Oswald being the "communist murderer of our President?" The man who had waged his Cold War against Communism his entire adult life did little or nothing to use this charge in his Cold War.

Chapter 8

Lee Harvey Oswald,
the "Lone Communist Assassin"

The pronouncement by J. Edgar Hoover that Lee Oswald was the lone communist assassin of President Kennedy is brought into serious question when all available evidence is closely scrutinized. In an FBI memorandum dated November 24, 1963, FBI officials Clyde Tolson and Alan Belmont outlined the case they planned to use to implicate Oswald as the lone assassin:

> to set out the evidence showing that Oswald is responsible for the shooting that killed the President. We will show that Oswald was an avowed Marxist, a former defector to the Soviet Union and an active member of the FPCC, which has been financed by Castro. . . . We will set forth the items of evidence which make it clear that Oswald is the man who killed the President. (1)

It appears that Lee Oswald suspected that his "trip" to the Soviet Union was the real reason that he was being implicated in the President's murder when he shouted to the press "They are taking me in because I have been to the Soviet Union."

David Ferrie was the commander of a local New Orleans Civil Air Patrol unit who reportedly had influenced Lee Oswald to join the Marines as a teenager. Ferrie became known as an associate of violent anti-Castro Cubans and

Louisiana crime boss Carlos Marcello. (2) In 1961, Ferrie was fired from his position as an Eastern Airlines pilot because of homosexual activity. (3)

The House Select Committee on Assassinations found a number of witnesses who confirmed that Oswald was in David Ferrie's Civil Air Patrol Unit. (4) Subsequent photos of Ferrie and Oswald together at a meeting of the New Orleans Civil Air Patrol unit further document their relationship. (5) The Committee discerned that Ferrie had "urged several boys to join the Armed Forces and Oswald had memorized the Marine Corps manual and 'knew it by heart.'" (6) As soon as Oswald turned sixteen, he attempted to lie about his age and join the Marines but was rejected until his seventeenth birthday. (7)

Edward Voebel was a high school classmate and friend of Lee Oswald and believed that Oswald's interest in Marxism was "baloney." (8) While Oswald was in high school his favorite television program, before he entered the Marines, was "I Led Three Lives" which was based on the true story of Phillip Hambrick, the famous FBI anti-communist double agent. His half-brother John Pic had joined the Marines just out of high school and Oswald would join the Marines at age seventeen. It would appear that Lee Oswald was greatly influenced by Ferrie, Pic, and his fascination with Hambrick's role in "I Led Three Lives." This apparently led him to become susceptible to the machinations of "others" into becoming their Marxist-communist patsy.

Following his return from the Soviet Union, Oswald attempted to explain his stance on whether he was a communist or a Marxist. Oswald was interviewed by a local New Orleans television station in August of 1963. He commented on the differences between Communism and Socialism and stated, "I am a Marxist, but that does not mean that I am a Communist" (9) Dallas Police Detective Jim Leavelle stated, "Captain Fritz had asked him [Oswald] if he was a Communist and he said no, but that he was a Marxist and there was a difference between the two of them." (10)

The question of whether Lee Oswald traveled to the Soviet Union as a communist bent on renouncing his U. S. citizenship and passing military secrets to the Soviets, has continually been an area of intense debate.

A United States Embassy official in Moscow, John

McVickar, stated, "He mentioned that he [Oswald] knew certain classified things in connection with having been I think a radar operator in the Marine Corps and that he was going to turn this information over to the Soviet authorities." (11)

John Donovan, a former lieutenant in the Marine Corps stated:

> shortly before I got out of the Marine Corps which was mid-December 1959, we received word that he showed up in Moscow. This necessitated a lot of change of aircraft call signs, codes, radio frequencies, radar frequencies. He had access to the location of all bases in the West Coast area, all radio frequencies for all squadrons, all tactical call signs, and the relative strength of all squadrons, number and type of aircraft in a squadron, who was the commanding officer, the authentication code of entering and exiting the ADIZ which stands for Air Defense Identification Zone. He knew the range of our radar. He knew the range of our radio. And he knew the range of the surrounding units' radio and radar. (12)

This version of how the military responded to Oswald's defection was also corroborated by U-2 Pilot Gary Francis Powers. "He [Oswald] had access to all our equipment. He knew the altitudes we flew at, how long we stayed out on any mission, and in which direction we went." (13)

Powers was of the opinion that the downing of his plane was possibly the result of information that Oswald gave to the Soviets. Amazingly, despite supposedly being in Minsk when Powers was shot down, Lee wrote his brother Robert in 1962 and stated, "[Powers] seemed to be a nice bright American type when I saw him in Moscow." (14) This information, however, does not jibe with Oswald's "official" account of being in Minsk at the time that Powers was in Moscow. Oswald's "historic" diary is the only known source that attempts to explain his whereabouts during his nearly three years in the Soviet Union.

According to handwriting experts commissioned by the House Select Committee, the "diary" was not written on a daily or even a weekly basis. In fact, the Committee's experts determined that the "diary" was written entirely on the same paper and not during periodic intervals, as would be customarily found in most journals and/or diaries. (15) Author Edward Epstein has determined that certain information contained in the diary was not placed in the proper historical and chronological order. One example being that Oswald refers to John McVickar as the head consul of the U. S. Embassy in Moscow in 1959. But the change from Richard Snyder to McVickar does not take place until 1961. The "diary" also refers to Oswald being paid in the Russian monetary exchange system of new rubles one year before the change from the ruble actually took place. (16) The historical accuracy of this "diary" must be brought into question, as well as the true activities of Lee Oswald while he was in the Soviet Union. This evidence continues to cloud up an already murky picture of Oswald's portrait as an anti-communist, a pro-communist, or the possibility that he was working for some faction of United States intelligence.

Oswald's Marine roommate at the El Torro Base in California, James Botelho, became a California judge. He stated:

> Oswald was not a Communist or a Marxist. If he was I would have taken violent action against him and so would many of the other Marines in the unit. . . . Well, when Oswald's presence in the Soviet Union was made public, it was the talk of everyone who knew him at the base. First of all, I was aware of the fact that the radio codes and other codes were not changed and that Oswald knew all of them. That made me suspicious. I knew Oswald was not a Communist and was, in fact, anti-Soviet. Then, when no real investigation about Oswald occurred at the base, I was sure that Oswald was on an intelligence assignment in Russia. . . . Oswald, it was said, was the only Marine ever to defect from his country to another country, a Communist country, during peacetime. That was a major event. When the Marine Corps and American intelligence decided not to probe the reasons for the "defection," I knew then what I know now; Oswald was on an assignment in Russia for American intelligence. (17)

Further evidence of Oswald's anti-communist beliefs following his return from the Soviet Union are found in his meetings with Pauline Bates. Bates was a Fort Worth stenographer who was asked to prepare an anti-communist manuscript dictated by Oswald:

> [Oswald] told her he intended to solicit the help of a Ft. Worth engineer in publishing a book from his notes. . . . He showed her a letter from a Ft. Worth engineer who offered to publish

the book. . . . [Oswald] hinted that he gone to the Soviet Union as a U. S. secret agent. . . . [Oswald had become] worried or scared . . . "he was fidgety, up and down, looking over my shoulder. . . ." (18)

Peter Gregory was the Ft. Worth petroleum engineer, and was also a White Russian friend of George de Mohrenschildt. Gregory later denied that he supported Oswald's anti-communist book venture and that he was simply corroborating Oswald's ability to read and speak Russian and also denied that Oswald was writing an anti-communist book. However, the following writings made by Oswald after his return from the Soviet Union, refute the claims of Gregory:

> The Communist Party of the United States has betrayed itself! It has turned itself into the traditional lever of a foreign power to overthrow the government of the United States, not in the name of freedom or high ideals, but in servile conformity to the wishes of the Soviet Union. . . . The Soviets have committed crimes unsurpassed . . . imprisonment of their own peoples . . .mass extermination . . . The Communist movement in the United States, personalized by the Communist Party, United States of America has turned itself into a "valuable gold coin" of the Kremlin. It has failed to denounce any actions of the Soviet Government when similar actions of the United States Government bring pious protest. . . .[I have] Many personal reasons to know and therefore hate and mistrust Communism. . . . (19)

George de Mohrenschildt was a former White Russian, whose father was a member of the old Russian aristocracy before the Bolshevik Revolution. Documents from the House Select Committee indicate that de Mohrenschildt was involved with American intelligence. (20) He surely was not pro-Communist and most likely would be considered a fervent anti-Communist. He befriended Lee Oswald upon his return from the Soviet Union and exerted tremendous influence over Oswald. Samuel B. Ballen, who was the chairman of the board of Highplains Natural Gas Company, believed that the friendship between Oswald and de Mohrenschildt had come about as a result "of members of the White Russian community." (21) Ballen also related that the de Mohrenschildts (George and his wife Jeanne) ". . . went out of their way to befriend the Oswalds. . . ." (22) Gary E. Taylor, de Mohrenschildt's former son-in-law stated, ". . . whatever

his [George's] suggestions were, Lee grabbed them and took
them, whether it was time to go to bed or where to stay." (23)

In a manuscript written by de Mohrenschildt, which
described his "true" relationship and understanding of Lee
Oswald, de Mohrenschildt wrote:

> Lee was not a harmful person,[but] on the contrary, a rather
> inspiring individual.   His deep desire [was] to improve
> relations between the United States and the Soviet Union. . . .
> He hoped that these two powerful countries would become
> friends and he [strived] to achieve it in a naive and maybe
> foolish, but sincere way. It is clear now that [a] war between
> these two countries would end in a holocaust.   And so, Lee
> Harvey Oswald had dreamed and hoped for a detente and for
> friendship, not so bad for a high school dropout from a New
> Orleans slum. (24)

Oswald is also on record as stating, "I have and always had
the full sanction of a U. S. embassy Moscow USSR, and hence
the U. S. government." (25)

The Warren Report disclosed that embassy consul Richard
Snyder had agreed to allow Oswald and Marina to return to
the United States. The Embassy decided on August 18, 1961,
that, "Based upon Snyder's recommendation in the
information in its files, the passport office decided Oswald
had not renounced his citizenship." (26)

Emery J. Adams who worked in the State Department's
Office of Security responded to an inquiry from J. Edgar
Hoover regarding Oswald's return to the United States.   On
May 25, 1961, Adams responded to Hoover's request when he
reported: "The Passport Office (PPT) of the Department has
advised that Mr. Oswald has been in communication with the
American Embassy at Moscow, and, at this time, there is no
information that he has renounced his nationality of the
United States." (27)

Evidently, even J. Edgar Hoover had been aware of or had
subsequently been informed, that Oswald had not renounced
his citizenship.   Even more interesting, is that the U. S.
Government loaned Oswald the money for his return (and his
new Russian family).

It is interesting to note that following Oswald's discharge
from the Marine Corps in September of 1959, he visited his
mother for a few days in Ft. Worth.   Mrs. Marguerite Oswald
stated, as quoted in a government document, that her son told

her "that he was going to New Orleans, Louisiana, to resume his employment with an export-import company at New Orleans. She stated that subject [her son] had engaged in export-import employment for a brief period of time prior to his enlistment in the U. S. Marine Corps." (28) It is quite possible that Oswald's employment with the export-import firm established a relationship between Lee Oswald and New Orleans businessman Clay Shaw. Shaw's name began to surface in relation to Oswald during the Jim Garrison investigation in the late 1960's. Information brought forth during the trial indicated that Shaw had used the alias Clay Bertrand at various times. New Orlean's attorney, Dean Andrews was asked by the Warren Commission:

> *Q.* [Y]ou finally came to the conclusion that Clay Bertrand [supposed alias of Clay Shaw] was a figment of your imagination?
> *Andrews.* That what the Feebees [FBI] put on. . . . I have been playing cops and robbers with them. You can tell when the steam is on. They are on you like the plague. They never Leave. They are like cancer. Eternal.
> *Q.* That was the description of the situation?
> *Andrews.* It was my decision if they were to stay there. If I decide yes, they stay. If I decide no, they go. So I told them, "Close your file and go someplace else." That's the real reason why it was was done. I don't know what they wrote in the report, but that's the real reason (29)

Two interesting points emerge from this information. The first one being that Clay Shaw was the manager of the International Trade Mart in New Orleans. Shaw was later implicated in the Kennedy assassination by Jim Garrison; he would surely have been knowledgeable of Lee Oswald working for an import-export firm in or near the International Trade Mart. The subsequent documented relationship between Clay Shaw and David Ferrie, who was also linked to the Garrison investigation, proves to be very interesting.

If Oswald worked for an export-import company in New Orleans, as this memo indicates, either before or after his "defection," there is no other known record of this information. Marguerite Oswald maintained after the assassination that Lee had gone to the Soviet Union on an intelligence mission. (30) Were Clay Shaw and/or others possibly involved in Lee Oswald's defection?

According to Oswald's own writings, he had changed his mind about the positive aspects of Communism. In preparing for his return to the United States from the Soviet Union, Oswald clearly showed his anti-Communist feelings, saying he was ". . . completely relieved of his illusions about the Soviet Union." (31)

The House Select Committee on Assassinations discovered that the FBI was not sure if Oswald had been involved in an intelligence mission while in the Soviet Union. "We did not know definitely whether or not he had any intelligence assignments at that time." (32)

Further corroboration for this uncertainty is indicated by Warren Commission Chief Counsel J. Lee Rankin who attempted "to find out what he [Oswald] studied at the Monterey School of the Army in the way of languages." (33) This school was designed to train U. S. Military and Intelligence personnel to learn a foreign language. (34)

Further evidence of the possibility that Oswald had worked for U.S. intelligence while in the Soviet Union is indicated by the recollections of Dennis Ofstein. Lee Oswald had worked with Ofstein after Oswald's return from the Soviet Union in 1962. Ofstein was a fellow employee of Oswald at the photographic firm, Jaggars-Chiles-Stovall that did work for the U. S. Army. Ofstein added corroboration to Oswald's knowledge of photography. He described how Oswald had explained the concept of microdotting to him during his Warren Commission testimony:

> Q: Do you know what a microdot is?
> *Ofstein*. That was explained to me by Lee Oswald.
> Q. *Tell us about that.*
> *Ofstein*. He asked me one day if I knew the term "microdot" and I told him, no, I wasn't familiar with it and he told me that that was the method of taking a large area of type or a picture and reducing it down to an extremely small size for condensing and for purposes, such as where you had a lot of type to photograph to confine them into a small area, and he said that that is the way spies sometimes sent messages and pictures of diagrams and so on, was to take a microdot photograph of it and place it under a stamp or send it. I presumed that he had either read this in a book or had some knowledge of it from somewhere, but where, I don't know. (35)

It was for this reason that Ofstein believed that Oswald had worked "with the [U.S. Government]." Apparently, Ofstein was not aware of Oswald's "defection" to the Soviet Union. (36)

Further corroboration regarding Oswald's knowledge of photography is found in a photograph published in Jesse Curry's book *JFK Assassination File*. This particular photograph shows a wide variety of cameras, lenses, and other photographic equipment, which strongly indicates that Oswald was heavily involved in advanced photographic work of some sort. (37)

Spas Raikin was the Secretary General of the American Friends of the Anti-Bolshevik Block of Nations and was the first person to meet with Lee Oswald in Hoboken, New Jersey after Oswald's return from the Soviet Union on June 13, 1962. This organization was heavily supported by General Charles Willoughby who was an extreme and fanatical proponent of various anti-Communist factions. It is interesting to note that General Willoughby was also a close friend of J. Edger Hoover and carried on a personal correspondence with him. (38) Willoughby had served as General Douglas MacArthur's Chief of Intelligence in the Pacific during and after World War II. MacArthur had described Willoughby as "my little fascist." (39) Willoughby had sung the praises of the Spanish dictator Francisco Franco as well as the Italian dictator Benito Mussolini. (40) Author Bruce Cummings described the extreme fanaticism of Willoughby in his *The Origins of the Korean War,* Vol. II:

> . . . [Willoughby] recommended all through the 1960's that various "weapons of mass destruction," unspecified, be used against the Vietnamese people. It is hard to find something nice to balance this account. Willoughby was a thoroughly loathsome person whose entire world view consisted of piles of ethnic stereotypes; he was apparently capable of anything. (41)

Raikin purportedly met with Oswald as a representative of the Traveler's Aid Society, but given the background of Raikin and his association with Willoughby, this explanation appears to be questionable.

Another clue as to the possible intelligence connections of Lee Oswald has been brought to the surface by HSCA investigator Gaeton Fonzi. Fonzi has documented that Lee Oswald was seen by anti-Castro exile leader Antonio Veciana in the company of David Phillips, a one-time head of the CIA office in Mexico City. Veciana told the HSCA that Phillips had posed as "Maurice Bishop" and was his contact with the CIA in anti-Castro activities. Veciana reportedly saw Oswald with Phillips in Dallas a month before the assassination of the President. Phillips has denied the accusation but Fonzi and Veciana have continued to state that the accusation is true. (42)

Senator Richard Schweiker stated, " . . . we do know that Oswald had intelligence connections. Everywhere you look with him, there's fingerprints of intelligence." (43) Even in the year 2000, it cannot be proven for certain who Oswald worked for from 1959 to 1963. ". . .[the Assassination Records and] the Review Board unfortunately could not open Lee Harvey Oswald's tax returns." (44)

Louis Stokes, chairman of the Select Committee on Assassinations, did not believe that Oswald was the loner portrayed by the Warren Commission. Stokes stated on *Face the Nation*, on December 31, 1978:

> The Warren Commission, you will recall, concluded that Lee Harvey Oswald was a loner. Our committee developed investigative evidence that he was in fact not a loner, and our report will reveal his association with many other people. And, so, we concluded that he was not, in fact, a loner. . . . we will be able to establish his relationship with other persons in New Orleans also.

Anti-Castro exile Carlos Bringuier was involved in training fellow Cuban exiles in preparation for guerrilla attacks aimed at deposing Fidel Castro. He had stated to the Warren Commission that Lee Oswald had offered to train Cubans in guerrilla warfare in August of 1963. On August 5, 1963, Oswald visited Bringuier at his store in New Orleans. With his Marine training handbook in hand, Oswald offered to help train Bringuier's right-wing exile group, the Cuban Student Directorate (DRE). Bringuier stated that Oswald said he "had been in the Marine Corps and was willing to train Cubans to fight Castro." (45) Bringuier had originally stated to the Commission, "I thought he [Oswald] might be an agent from the FBI or the CIA, trying to find out what we might be up to." (46) "I was suspicious of him from the start. . . . I thought he might be an agent from the FBI." (47)

Oswald was arrested in New Orleans after a scuffle with Bringuier while handing out hand bills for the Fair Play for

Cuba Committee (FPCC) of which he was the only known member. Bringuier became enraged at Oswald, believing that he had been double-crossed. A government document found in the National Archives lends credence to the notion that Oswald was not truly involved in the committee's activities:

> Confidential source fimiliar *[sic]* with Cuban activities in the New Orleans area were contacted during the month of September, 1963 and each advised he had no knowledge regarding OSWALD or any of the activities of subject organization in New Orleans, except the information regarding OSWALD's arrest and distribution of FPCC handbills. (48)

Members of the Commission were also concerned as to whether Oswald's membership in the FPCC was a charade or not:

> *Mr. Rankin.* They [the Fair Play for Cuba Committee] denied he was a member and also he wrote to them and tried to establish as one of the letters indicate, a new branch there in New Orleans, the Fair Play for Cuba.
> *Rep. Boggs.* That letter has caused me a lot of trouble. It is a much more literate and polished communication than any of his other writing. (49)

According to the House Select Committee:

> while Oswald exhibited a leftist political stance for a number of years, his activities and associations were by no means exclusively left-wing. His close friendship with George de Mohrenschildt, an oilman in Dallas with right-wing connections, is a case in point. Additionally, questions have been raised about the specific nature of Oswald's pro-Castro activities. It has been established that on at least one occasion in 1963, he offered his services for clandestine paramilitary actions against the Castro regime, though, as has been suggested, he may have merely been posing as an anti-Castro activist. That the evidence points to the possibility that Oswald was also associated in 1963 with David Ferrie, the Marcello operative who was openly and actively anti-Castro, is troubling, too. Finally, the only Cuba-related activities that have ever been established as 544 Camp Street, New Orleans, the address of an office building that Oswald stamped on some of his Fair Play for Cuba Committee handouts, were virulently anti-Castro in nature.

Thus, the committee was unable to resolve its doubts about Lee Harvey Oswald. (50)

Ron Lewis stated that he had worked with Lee Oswald in conjunction with Guy Banister's office in 1963. Banister was the former head of J. Edgar Hoover's Chicago FBI office and was heavily involved in right-wing causes; especially in anti-integration and anti-Castro operations. Lewis recalled, "He [Oswald] appeared to me to be pro-Castro when I first met him. . . before I parted company with him, he became anti-Castro. . . ." (51)

The House Select Committee also found that there was at least a possibility that Oswald and Guy Banister were acquainted. The following facts were considered:

> The 544 Camp Street address stamped on Oswald's FPCC handouts was that of the building where Banister had his office;
> Ross Banister [Guy's brother] told the committee that his brother had seen Oswald handing out FPCC literature during the summer of 1963; and
> Banister's secretary, Delphine Roberts, told the committee she saw Oswald in Banister's office on several occasions, the first being when he was interviewed for a job during the summer of 1963.
> The committee learned that Banister left extensive files when he died in 1964. Later that year, they were purchased by the Louisiana State Police from Banister's widow. According to Joseph Cambre of the State police, Oswald's name was not the subject of any file, but it was included in a file for the Fair Play for Cuba Committee. Cambre said the FPCC file contained newspaper clippings and a transcript of a radio program on which Oswald had appeared. The committee was not able to review Banister's files, since they had been destroyed pursuant to an order of the superintendent of Louisiana State Police that all files not part of the public record or pertinent to ongoing criminal investigations be burned.
> Additional evidence that Oswald may have been associated or acquainted with Ferrie and Banister was provided by the testimony of Adrian Alba, proprietor of the Crescent Garage which was next door to the Reily Coffee Co. where Oswald had worked for a couple of months in 1963. (The garage and the coffee company were both located less than a block from 544 Camp Street.) Although Alba's testimony on some points was questionable, he undoubtedly did know Oswald who

frequently visited his garage, and the committee found no reason to question his statement that he had often seen Oswald in Mancuso's Restaurant on the first floor of 544 Camp. Ferrie and Banister also were frequent customers at Mancuso's. (52)

In addition to this information obtained from the House Select Committee, the Warren Commission had earlier obtained documentation of a relationship between Sergio Archacha Smith, Ferrie, and Banister:

> A declassified CIA document has confirmed that Sergio Archacha Smith, the chief delegate of the Cuban Revolutionary Council at 544 Camp Street, "maintained extensive relations with the New Orleans FBI. . . . Two of his regular FBI contacts were [name deleted] and the deceased Guy Banister." (53)

David Ferrie and Archacha Smith also admittedly worked for Carlos Marcello, the New Orleans mob kingpin. Ferrie, in fact, stated that he was with Marcello in a New Orleans courtroom at the time John Kennedy was killed. Ironically, the case involved Robert Kennedy's continued attempts to have Marcello deported for the second time. (54) Ferrie was questioned by the FBI and the Secret Service within days of the assassination. It is obvious that both the FBI and the Secret Service were suspicious of Ferrie's activities and associations in regards to possible involvement in the assassination. Ferrie told the FBI that he had gone to Houston on the night of the assassination to "relax." (55) He and some friends drove 400 miles in the dead of night during a driving rainstorm to ice skate and goose hunt. (56) The day after the assassination, Chuck Rolland, the manager of the Winterland Skating Rink, located just outside of Galveston, remembered Ferrie making and accepting phone calls on a pay phone for over two hours. (57) They did not take any guns or skates and ended up neither skating or hunting. (58) Even more interesting is that Ferrie continually denied knowing Oswald despite photographs showing them together. (59) And according to the HSCA, a former neighbor of Oswald told the Committee that Ferrie visited her after the assassination and inquired about the whereabouts of Oswald's library card. (60)

Lou Ivon, investigator for Jim Garrison stated that in 1967, just before Ferrie "committed suicide," he received a call from Ferrie. Ivon stated that Ferrie was frantic and that "they were going to kill me." (61) Who "they" were is open to speculation but one can clearly detect a consistent theme of timely deaths running through this research. Concluding who is ultimately responsible for these deaths is nearly impossible. But to cast them aside as unfortunate and coincidental is too simplistic a solution when one considers the frequency in which they occur. One of the many examples of this is the murder of David Ferrie's close friend and anti-Castro associate, Eladio Del Valle. On February 22, 1967, the same day as the "suicide" of Ferrie, Del Valle's head was split open with a machete and he was shot through the heart. (62) Ferrie and Del Valle were to be Jim Garrison's strongest witnesses in an effort to tie the assassination plot together. With Ferrie's and Del Valle's death, Garrison's case fell apart.

Much information has been gathered which supports the view that Lee Oswald may have been working for the FBI in some capacity. Possible support for this argument is the documentation of Oswald's association with Guy Banister, who, as noted previously, had worked under J. Edgar Hoover as the head of the Chicago office of the FBI.

Researcher Anthony Summers wrote:

> Delphine Roberts worked as a secretary for former FBI agent Guy Banister. Both Roberts and Banister were heavily involved in anti-Castro activities that were center in New Orleans and were operated out of Guy Banister's office. Roberts stated that Lee Oswald entered her office in 1963 and Oswald introduced himself by name and said he was seeking an application form. "I did not think that was really why he was there. During the course of the conversation I gained the impression that he and Guy Banister already knew each other. After Oswald filled out the application form, Guy Banister called him into the office. The door was closed, and a lengthy conversation took place. . . . I presumed then, and now am certain, that the reason for Oswald being there was that he was required to act undercover." (63)

Dallas Deputy Sheriff Roger Craig believed that Oswald was upset when he was arrested in Dallas after the assassination for having had his cover blown as a result of his arrest. Craig stated that Oswald said during his interrogation at the Dallas Police Headquarters that when he said, "Now everybody will know who I am," Oswald meant that his "cover was blown" and that "it was not a boast." (64) This belief of Deputy Sheriff Craig, that Oswald believed that his cover had been blown, helps to solidify the credibility of Delphine Roberts recollections. Unfortunately, Guy Banister would not be available for the Warren Commission or future investigators to question. He died of an apparent heart attack in June 1964. (65)

A sworn affidavit is on record as stating that FBI agent James Hosty said that Lee Oswald was an FBI informant on the afternoon of the assassination. (66) Further support that Oswald was possibly an FBI informant working undercover is found in an FBI document from 12/10/63 that corroborates Oswald being approached by the FBI in regards to being an informant. "JOSEPH GOULDEN, reporter, *Philadelphia Inquirer,* interviewed and advised unnamed law enforcement officer gave him information that LEE HARVEY OSWALD approached by FBI to be informant." (67)

A January 1, 1964 article in the *Houston Post* by Lonnie Hudkins was entitled, "Oswald Rumored as Informant for U.S." A Secret Service report dated January 3, 1964, discusses an operative's interview with Lon Hudkins, and reveals at least one source for his information:

> On December 17, Mr. Hudkins advised that he had just returned from a weekend in Dallas, during which time he talked to Allan Sweatt, Chief Criminal Division, Sheriff's Office, Dallas; Chief Sweatt mentioned that it was his opinion that Lee Harvey Oswald was being paid $200 a month by the FBI as an informant in connection with their subversive investigations. He [Sweatt] furnished the alleged informant number assigned to Oswald by the FBI as "S172." (68)

Gerald Ford stated in his book, *Portrait of the Assassin:*

> The information was that Lee Oswald was actually hired by the FBI; that he was assigned the under-cover-agent number 179; that he was on the FBI payroll at two hundred dollars a month starting in September 1962 and that he was still on the payroll the day he was apprehended in the Texas Theatre. . . . (69)

Warren Commission members voiced their concerns about the possibility of Oswald being an FBI informant:

> *Rankin.* We do have a dirty rumor that is very bad for the

Commission, the problem, and it is very damaging to the
agencies that are involved in it and it must be wiped out
insofar as it is possible to do by this Commission. . . . If the
rumor was true, making the truth known might very well
result in irreparable damage to the FBI and might heighten
suspicions . . . about the assassination itself.
Dulles. . . .[Oswald being an FBI informant] a terribly hard
thing to disprove.
Boggs. [it makes] our problem utterly impossible, because you
say this rumor can't be dissipated under any circumstances.
(70)

In regards to Oswald being an informant, the Commission
members believed that Hoover would probably not tell them
the truth. The Commission also expressed concern whether
President Johnson would allow them to pursue this
possibility:

McCloy. . . . I don't think that we could recognize that any
door is closed to us, unless the President closes it to us, and in
the search for truth [deleted]. .
Dulles. . . . Hoover would say certainly he didn't have
anything to do with this fellow, [and that] we are
investigating him [Hoover]. . . . (71)

J. Edgar Hoover worked to counter the claims that Oswald
had ever been an informant for the Bureau:

Before Rankin even met with Hoover, the Director sent a
memo to the Commission denying Oswald was an informant.
He stated in part, " . . .in the event you have any further
questions concerning the activities of the Federal Bureau of
Investigation in this case, we would appreciate being
contacted directly." (72)

Senator Richard Russell indicated to his Commission
colleagues that because of Hoover's "credibility," he was
almost beyond their capabilities to question his motives:

Russell. There is no man in the employ of the Federal
Government who stands higher in the opinion of the American
people than . . . Hoover.
McCloy. If we got a statement from the Department that the
Attorney General and perhaps from . . . Hoover, or from . . .
Hoover himself, which said, "I am telling you that this man
was not in any way employed by the FBI . . ." (73)

When Hoover appeared before the Commission, he "emphatically" denied the rumor that Oswald had ever been an FBI informant. "Well, I can certainly speak for the FBI that it is false!!" (74) Hoover added: "I can most emphatically say that at no time was he ever an employee of the Bureau in any capacity, either as an agent or as a special employee, or as an informant." (75) A further example of the possibility that Oswald was involved with the FBI is indicated by the following discussion:

> *Rankin.* Why are they so eager to make . . . those conclusions [deleted].
> *Dulles.* Lee [Rankin], if this were true . . . I could see it would be in their interest to get rid of this man. . . . (76)
> *Rankin.* If that was true [that Oswald was an FBI informant] and it ever came out and could be established . . . then you would have people think that there was a conspiracy to accomplish this assassination that nothing the Commission did or anybody else could dissipate.
> *Boggs.* The implications of this are fantastic, don't you think so?
> *Warren.* Terrific.
> *Rankin.* Now it is something that would be very difficult to prove out . . . I am confident that the FBI will never admit it, and I presume their records will never show it. (77)

The *Washington Evening Star* reported on November 24, 1963:

> The FBI said its agents had interviewed Oswald only once. . . . when he got into some trouble in New Orleans. . . . FBI sources indicated Oswald came to Dallas from Forth Worth about two months ago but said the suspect's presence here was not known to them.

This statement by the FBI was denied on November 29, 1963 by Mrs. Marguerite Oswald in an article published in the *Dallas Morning News:* "The mother of accused assassin Lee Harvey Oswald says her son was questioned on three occasions by the Federal Bureau of Investigation prior to President Kennedy's death." John Fain was the FBI agent who interviewed Oswald after his "trouble" (arrest after a scuffle) in New Orleans during the summer of 1963. It is interesting to note that the Assassination Records and Review Board determined that the records pertaining to Fain's interview of Oswald have not yet been released. (78)

There appears to be strong documentation that Lee Oswald had, in fact, been an informant for the FBI. Did J. Edgar Hoover order Dallas FBI agent Hosty to not divulge the FBI's contacts with Lee Oswald? The answer to this question is not clear.

Lieutenant Jack Revill of the Dallas Police Department stated, "A Communist killed President Kennedy. . . He is in our Communist file." (79) ". . . I asked him [Hosty] why he had not told us this in the best of my recollection is that he said he couldn't. . . ." (80)

According to the House Select Committee:

> Approximately 2 or 3 weeks before the assassination of President Kennedy, Oswald allegedly delivered a note addressed to Hosty at the FBI office in Dallas. . . . Hosty recalled that the note was complaining in tone, but it contained no threats and did not suggest that Oswald was prone to violence. Hosty stated that he destroyed the note because [Gordon] Shanklin, his superior ordered him to do so.

The Committee's Report went on to conclude:

> . . .shortly after the assassination, Dallas FBI agent Hosty destroyed a note that had been delivered to his office allegedly by Oswald shortly before the Assassination. When that conduct was finally made public in 1975 it aroused great suspicions, especially since it had not been previously revealed, even to the Warren Commission. (81)

If Hoover did order Hosty to be quiet about Oswald and also order Shanklin to have Hosty destroy Oswald's alleged note, then Hoover was creating a maze of tracks. To further muddy the picture, Hoover wrote a note on December 10, 1963, which an Associated Press article described:

> After President Kennedy's assassination, an angry J. Edgar Hoover scribbled stinging remarks in the margins of an FBI memo detailing how agents had failed—sometimes for "asinine" reasons, Hoover wrote—to keep a close eye on Lee Harvey Oswald in the months before the 1963 shooting.

William Sullivan wrote about his treatment by Hoover as a result of his "alleged" responsibility in failing to identify Oswald before the assassination:

Fifteen others, including me, were given letters of censure. I had never even seen the file on Oswald and had never heard of him before the assassination, but I was head of the division and was theoretically responsible for what everyone did. Hoover was once again able to cover himself. (82)

The master of obfuscation was apparently hard at work covering his tracks. Warren Commission attorney Burt Griffin remembered: "I recall the Hosty incident . . . It established in our minds that we had to be worried about them [deleted] . . . we never forgot the incident. We were always alert, we were concerned about the problem [deleted]." (83)

The destruction of the alleged "Oswald note" brought to an end the possibility of determining the contents of the message that Oswald might have conveyed to the Bureau. Additionally damaging to J. Edgar Hoover is that according to the House Committee Report, Hoover himself ordered Gordon Shanklin to destroy the note. (84) Subsequently, J. Edgar Hoover's denial of any relationship between Lee Oswald and the FBI effectively shut down the Warren Commission's questioning in this area. Any possibility of Lee Oswald receiving a fair and objective review of where his true loyalties and associations resided were cast aside.

As a result, no meaningful legal counsel was afforded to Oswald during the weekend that he was in custody or at any time since his death. Lee Oswald protested during his press conference on the day after the assassination that ". . . I was not allowed legal representation during that short and sweet hearing [held on Friday evening]. . . . I do request that someone to come forward and give me legal assistance." Walter E. Craig, president of the American Bar Association, was appointed by the Commission to represent the interests of the slain Lee Oswald. Unfortunately, he was appointed three months after the Commission was formed. Craig himself stated, "We are not counsel for Lee Harvey Oswald." (85) It is not apparent in any official records that Craig or any of his associates named a witness of their own, or attended any of the over 20,000 interviews, or cross-examined one witness. This can hardly be construed as an example of justice in action. On December 4, 1963, Theodore Voorhees, the chancellor-elect of the Philadelphia Bar Association offered his opinion of the justice given to Lee Oswald when he stated that Oswald had been "lynched." (86) Marguerite

Oswald, mother of Lee, asked Mark Lane to represent the deceased Lee Oswald and thus was rejected:

> The Commission turned down Mark Lane's request to take part in its proceedings on behalf of Oswald's mother, who had retained him for a short while to look after her son's interests. ("He strikes me less as a truth seeker than as a tireless and somewhat demagogic advocate, and I can image the publicity circus, the confusion, the waste of time had he been given status before the Commission. . ." says Dwight Macdonald.) (87)

This did not stop Lane from searching for clues for Oswald's innocence. He was called to testify before the Commission but was not permitted to cross-examine witnesses. What Mark Lane did attempt, was to present evidence indicating Oswald was innocent. J. Edgar Hoover responded by attacking Lane's credibility before the Commission and by keeping Lane under surveillance and sending FBI reports to the Commission on the attorney. (88). Hoover stated to the Warren Commission, ". . . The first indication of [Marguerite Oswald's] emotional instability was the retaining of a lawyer [Mark Lane] that anyone would not have retained if they were really serious in trying to get down to the facts." (89)
Evidence of this FBI surveillance is shown by author Peter Dale Scott:

> In February 1964, when Mark Lane was planning to present the case for a grassy-knoll assassin before a public meeting at Town Hall in New York, the FBI tried unsuccessfully to prevent the meeting from taking place. At one stage, using what its files call "counterintelligence action," the FBI succeeded in having Town Hall (a private auditorium) cancel the meeting; when Lane's contract was later upheld in court the FBI took comfort from the fact that Lane had been required to put up a costly $25,000 performance bond. In 1966 the FBI prepared memos linking Lane and other prominent assassination critics to allegedly subversive activities; these were supplied on request to Marvin Watson, President Johnson's political trouble-shooter. (90)

After the Warren Commission's final report was completed in September 1964, Lane interviewed numerous witnesses ignored by the Commission. He published a convincing indictment of the Commission, entitled *Rush to Judgment* using these interviews, as well as evidence from the twenty-six volumes of the Commission's Report. Despite the fact that the majority of Mark Lane's material for his book came from the Warren Report itself, as well as from interviews from those who were at the scene, sixteen publishers canceled contracts before *Rush to Judgment* was published. (91) The press and the public were not ready to consider that Oswald may have been innocent. What can be determined is that Lee Oswald was deemed the sole assassin from the beginning and he would receive no legal representation in life or in death.

In attempting to make the case for Oswald's guilt in the assassination, by far the most important piece of evidence against Oswald was his ownership of the Mannlicher Carcano rifle, presumably found on the 6th floor of the Book Depository. If Oswald could not be linked to this rifle, there could be no firm proof against him. The Warren Report stated that it was "only speculation" that Deputy Constable Seymor Weitzman found a 7.65 German Mauser on the sixth floor of the Book Depository and that Weitzman was mistaken. According to the Report, "Weitzman did not handle the rifle and did not examine it at close range. He had little more than a glimpse of it and thought it was a Mauser." (92)

What is most disturbing is that the rifle linked to Lee Oswald was a 6.5 Italian rifle, which was clearly stamped on the rifle for anyone to see and determine—much less those who are trained to use and identify weapons. The affidavit signed by Weitzman on November 23, stated, "This rifle was a 7.65 Mauser bolt action equipped with a 4/18 scope, a thick leather-brownish, black sling on it." (93) This does not sound like information that was determined by a glance. Furthermore, Weitzman had more than law enforcement experience with identifying weapons, as his Warren Commission deposition makes clear: *Ball.* "Are you fairly familiar with rifles?" *Weitzman.* Fairly familiar because I was in the sporting goods business a while. (94) In fact, Weitzman received corroboration on his initial identification by the man who helped him find it, Deputy Sheriff Eugene Boone as well as Homicide Chief Will Fritz, who was also on the scene when the gun was found. In his Warren Commission testimony Boone was asked:

Ball. There is one question. Did you hear anybody refer to this rifle as a Mauser that day?
Boone. Yes, I did. And at first not knowing what it was, I

thought it was a 7.65 Mauser.
Ball. Who referred to it as a Mauser that day?
Boone. I believe Captain Fritz. (95)

Late on Friday evening, a reporter asked District Attorney
Henry Wade the make of the rifle. "It's a Mauser, I believe."
(96) Deputy Sheriff Roger Craig, who was also on the sixth
floor when the rifle was found, also stated that the rifle found
that day was a German 7.65 Mauser. . . ." Craig went on to
state, ". . . Captain Fritz held it up [the rifle]. . . . we weren't
any more than 6-8 inches from the rifle. . . . stamped right on
the barrel was 7.65 Mauser, and that's when Weitzman
pointed to the 7.65 stamp on the barrel." (97) In fact, all
known press descriptions of the rifle on November 22 stated
that the rifle found was not a 6.5 Italian rifle as evidenced by
the original and continuous UPR wire reports shown here. ". .
. A German-made Mauser . . . was found after the
assassination . . .", ". . . a Mauser rifle was found on the fifth
floor. . . .", ". . . on the fifth floor . . ., police found a German-
made Mauser. . . ." (98) What is even more compelling is that
Sheriff Boone was shown the 6.5 Italian rifle by the Warren
Commission and was unable to identify the weapon as the one
found on the sixth floor. (99) Boone reiterated this conclusion
again in 1986 during the nationally televised "Showtime"
Trial of Lee Harvey Oswald:

Q. So far as you're concerned, at the time, that gun, that you
saw, in the stacks, was a Mauser isn't that a fact?
Boone. At that point in time, yes sir.
Q. It wasn't until a certain gun in the possession of the FBI
suddenly turned out to be a Mannlicher, that it changed from
a Mauser to a Mannlicher. Isn't that true?
Boone. I would say that that is an accurate statement.
Q. And isn't it true, that you, Officer Boone, were never able
to identify the rifle you found at the Texas School Book
Depository as the one that was later shown to you as being
the gun involved in the assassination. Isn't that true?
Boone. That is correct.

Hoover elaborated further on the FBI's involvement in
establishing the guilt of Lee Oswald when he stated, "They
[the Dallas Police] really did not have a case against Oswald
until we gave them our information." (100) It is interesting to
note that the initial release of the name "A. Hidell" came from
the District Attorney's office after the FBI had released

information that Oswald had purchased the Italian Carcano rifle under that name. (101) The first indication that Oswald used the alias "A. Hidell" is shown in the "Kantor Exhibit No. 3" (Dallas reporter Seth Kantor) which states, "FBI has March 20 letter to mail order gun house in Chicago." (102)

Author Sylvia Meagher has produced strong evidence, buried in the 26 volumes of the Warren Report, that the alias "A. Hidell," supposedly used by Oswald to order the Carcano, was not known of by the Dallas Police until twenty-four hours after his arrest. It seems that all available information indicates that up until Saturday afternoon, investigators of the assassination were only aware of Oswald using the alias, "O. H. Lee." (103) Oswald apparently used the alias "Lee" to obtain a room in a boarding house on North Beckley Street while his wife, Marina, lived with Ruth Paine in Irvin.

In fact, Dallas Police Sergeant Gerald Hill stated on NBC television, on the afternoon of November 22, in response to a question, "The only way we found out what his name was to remove his billfold and check it ourselves; he wouldn't even tell us what his names was. . . . Question: What was the name on the billfold? Hill: Lee H. Oswald. O-S-W-A-L-D." (104) Despite the later claim that the identification immediately found in Oswald's wallet after his arrest was that of Alex Hidell, this information appears to be inaccurate as Hill's statement makes clear. Even more damaging to the FBI's conclusion that Oswald ordered the Carcano rifle under the Hidell alias and was carrying a card with that identification when he was arrested, is found in the following FBI document:

> Subject's wallet when it was received at the Bureau did not contain either the U.S. Marine Certificate of Service in the name of Hidell or the Selective Service card in the name of Hidell. The Selective Service card was received separately in the Lab and it was determined to be a complete forgery. (105)

Strangely enough, this is the only time that Oswald used the alias Hidell in his life. During his interrogation sessions, Oswald was asked about the Hidell card and he responded by saying, "No, I have told you all I am going to tell you about the card in my billfold-you have the card yourself and you know as much about it as I do." (106)

Marina Oswald became the star witness against her husband when she identified the assassination rifle as

belonging to her husband during her appearances before the
Warren Commission. But after examining the rifle on the day
of the assassination at the Dallas Police Station, Marina
stated that she could not identify the alleged murder rifle as
belonging to her husband. She would, later, on February 6,
1964, identify the Carcano as the rifle of Lee Oswald. (107)
But a December 1, 1963 document from the National Archives
clearly indicates that the rifle she believed belonging to her
husband did not have a scope on it, "she says till she saw the
rifle with a scope on TV the other day she not know that rifles
with scopes existed." (108)   Marina stated before the
Commission, ". . . it was a dark gun. But I don't remember
the sight on it," and ". . . she couldn't definitely recall the
sight." (109)   During Oswald's interrogation session on
Saturday, November 23, Oswald was confronted with a
photograph of him holding the alleged murder weapon:

> That is not a picture of me; it is my face, but my face has been
> superimposed—the rest of the picture is not me at all, I've
> never seen it before. No: I have never seen that picture
> before. I know all about photography, I've done a lot of
> photographic work myself. That small picture is a reduction
> of the large picture, that someone I don't know has made. I've
> been photographed repeatedly since you brought me here;
> someone took a picture of my face and faked that photograph.
> I understand photography real well and you'll see. I will
> prove that it is a fake. Now I don't wish to answer any more
> questions. (110)

Oswald had, in fact, been employed at the Dallas photo-
optics firm of Jaggars-Chiles-Stovall in Dallas. Photographs
of his possessions shown in Dallas Police Chief Jesse Curry's
book clearly show a large quantity of sophisticated
photographic equipment. (111)
The authenticity of the photographs has long since been a
point of controversy ever since Lee Oswald brought them into
question the day after the assassination. A February 1992
article from *The Houston Post* actually confirms the initial
doubts that Oswald voiced:

> recently released documents from the Dallas Police
> Department files on the assassination of President Kennedy
> [include] several photos of accused presidential killer Lee
> Harvey Oswald. . . . One photo of Oswald's backyard in the
> Oak Cliff section of Dallas shows clear evidence of darkroom

manipulation. . . . Until now, evidence of such an attempted matting has not surfaced. . . . they may represent part of the necessary steps—an empty background for example—for faking background photos of Oswald.

Even more suspicious is that Geneva White, the wife of former Dallas Policeman Roscoe White, has presented two totally different photos of Lee Oswald posing with the "guilty Carcano." (112) Yet, the Dallas Police had sworn that they initially found only two. White began work for the Dallas Police Department one month before the assassination and left in 1965. (113) Apparently White was killed as a result of burns suffered from an explosion in 1971. The brief career of Roscoe White with the Dallas Police Department and how he obtained these photographs has never been properly investigated.

Attorney William McKenzie was apparently involved in coaching the testimony of Marina, to implicate her husband in regards to ownership of the Mannlicher Carcano. "He advised her 'they will ask you if there were two guns, you tell them there was one gun that was used,' he told her." (114) This concern about the pressure placed on Marina to implicate her husband and the subsequent reliability of her testimony is indicated by an article printed in the *New York Times* on January 22, 1964: "[Attorney Mark Lane] wrote to Chief Justice Earl Warren . . . to determine the nature of [Marina Oswald's] confinement and to discover if unfair and inappropriate methods had been utilized to tamper with or influence her testimony." An FBI memo reported that Marina had, in fact, said just what McKenzie told her to say and that McKenzie had improperly coached Marina in what to tell the FBI. (115)

It is interesting to take note of the connections of William McKenzie. He was a former employee of the Great Southwest Corporation which owned the Inn of the Six Flags where Marina Oswald had been sequestered by the Secret Service after her husband was murdered. (116) McKenzie had also worked in the same law office with fellow attorney Pete White who had served as a lawyer to Jack Ruby dating back to the early 1950's. (117) Marina described on national television in 1996 how in 1963 she was convinced by the Warren Commission to testify that the rifle was her husbands:

In the middle of the table was a rifle which I identified as

Lee's rifle. And I was stupid, young girl. Right now, you show
me my husband's hunting rifle, I be smart enough to say, "I do
not know for sure," because I know up to this day, I know
nothing about the rifle. I'm not saying that was Lee's or not
rifle . . . the identify, it must be his. It was a stick with metal.
That's all rifle is to me up to this day . . . I'm not saying it
wasn't his, but that's how willingly that I wanted to help.
(118)

During the same program Marina was asked, "Do you believe
your husband had nothing to do with the killing?" She
answered, "Absolutely nothing . . . I have been lied to [by the
Warren Commission]." (119) It interesting to note that
Oswald, during his interrogation by the FBI, on Saturday,
November 23rd, ". . . denied ever owning a rifle himself." (120)
But if the Commission is somehow correct, then Oswald
ordered a weapon to kill the President with an alias and then
left the shells to be found. There is even a question as to
whether the shells found on the sixth floor were fired from the
Carcano. Two of the three shells found on the sixth floor were
marked by Lt. Carl Day but the third shell was missing. The
third shell was not marked by him. Day was asked why he
did not initially identify the third shell. Day replied, "I didn't
examine it too close at that time." (121) Day was asked, "It
appears to be flattened out here. Do you know or have you
any independent recollection as to whether or not it was
flattened out on the small end when you saw it?" Day
responded, "No, sir, I don't." (122) It is not clear why Day did
not mark the third shell after marking the first two and why
the third shell, which was missing, was a deformed shell and
how it could fit into the rifle barrel if it was bent or deformed.
After not hiding the shells, Oswald is then supposed to have
moved the boxes back that were enclosing the sniper's nest,
apparently to block the view of the shooting from anyone else
who might have been on the sixth floor. Yet, the photos of the
sniper's nest indicate there was not enough space for a man to
have slipped through, and there would have been no time to
restack them and run down four flights of stairs to arrive in
the lunch room on the second floor before he was seen by
Officer Marion Baker and Depository Superintendent Roy
Truly.
Baker was a motorcycle policeman in the motorcade and
immediately ran into the Book Depository after the last shot
was fired despite the fact that the majority of witnesses in

front of the Book Depository, along with the majority of witnesses in Dealy Plaza, ran towards the grassy knoll. Baker proceeded to ask Mr. Truly how he could get to the upper floors. Truly began to lead Baker up the stairwell to the upper floors when he noticed that the officer was no longer behind him. Baker had stopped on the second floor and amazingly enough confronted Lee Oswald with his gun drawn. Oswald was apparently in the lunch room drinking a Coke. (123) Truly was asked by the Warren Commission, "How far was the officer's gun from Lee Harvey Oswald when he [Baker] asked the question [does he work here?]. Truly: ". . . It seemed to me like it was almost touching him [on his stomach]." (124) In another amazing twist, Lee Oswald would be shot in this exact manner, two days later in the basement of the Dallas Police Station.

Even before Oswald was to have begun his flight down the stairs, he supposedly had run twenty yards across the sixth floor over books and boxes to hide the rifle. Equally amazing is that not one person reported seeing or hearing Oswald, run down the four flights of stairs. Oswald was also supposed to have used a faulty weapon with no documentation of his practicing with the rifle. He also had no extra shells and did not fire as the car was approaching which would have been a much easier shot, but instead waited until the limousine was driving away from him which would have allowed for a much easier escape for the Presidential limousine.

It is also interesting to note that the FBI supplied damning evidence about Oswald just when it is needed to incriminate him in the assassination. This appears to be what J. Edgar Hoover was referring to when he stated that "they had no case until we stepped in." Dallas Police apparently really did not have a case against Oswald until Hoover and his FBI "fortuitously" began to supply the incriminating evidence against Oswald.

Representative Thomas Downing was the Chairman of the House Select Committee in 1976. In the Congressional Record of September 17, 1976, he is quoted as stating the obvious, "Any individual, regardless of his experience in the firearms, can clearly see it is an Italian rifle because stamped clearly on the rifle are the words, 'Made in Italy' and the 'Cal. 6.5.' It is unlikely that two police officers upon close inspection would have made such a case of mistaken identification." As we have seen, there were more than two police officers at the scene who were under the impression that the gun found on the sixth floor was in fact a Mauser. Press photographer Tom Alyea stated that he was part of a group of police officers who searched the Book Depository within thirty minutes after the shooting and that they searched every floor and nothing was found. They had to search the floors again until the rifle was eventually found. (125) When this is considered along-side the evidence already presented, it allows for the speculation of the rifle being planted on the sixth floor much more feasible.

What is even more confusing is the evidence that indicates that the Mannlicher Carcano was barely a functional rifle, at best. Robert A. Frazier, a rifle expert for the FBI stated:

> When we attempted to sight this rifle at Quantico we found that the elevation adjustment in the telescopic sight was not sufficient to bring the point of impact to the aiming point. The defect in the sight was structural. . . . We left the rifle [alone] as soon as it became stabilized and fired all of our shots with the point of impact actually high and to the right . . . . apparently the scope had been taken off the rifle. (126)

Frazier's description of the inaccuracy of the Carcano is corroborated by Dial Rider, who worked at the Irving Sports Shop. Rider stated to the Commission that the ". . .[Carcano was] real cheap, common, real flimsy looking . . . [the scope was] very easily knocked out of adjustment . . . [and would] get jarred off on a high-powered rifle." (127) Rider's employer and owner of the Irving Sports Shop, Charles Greener, explained further about the unreliability of the Carcano when he stated, ". . . with this frail mount . . . the possibility of it being real accurate would be pretty small, I think . . . ." (128) Frazier also stated that the rifle fired a bullet that traveled at a rather "low velocity." This fact would make it much more difficult for a single bullet to pass through Governor Connally's rib and wrist (bones) as the Warren Report concluded. What's more, the clip did not come with the rifle and was purchased separately. There is also no evidence that Oswald had any more ammunition or that he had ever bought the clip.

In fact, the FBI had failed to prove that Lee Oswald had practiced with the Carcano at anytime, whatsoever. (129) Army rifle expert Ronald Simmons said to the Commission, that a person would need to have considerable experience with guns and "also considerable experience with this weapon because of the amount of effort required to work the bolt. . . . the pressure to open the bolt was so great that it tended to move the rifle off the target. . . ." (130) Simmons also explained that there was a problem in pulling the trigger. He stated, ". . . Our rifleman were all used to a trigger with a constant pull. When the slack was taken up, then they expected the round to fire. But actually when the slack is taken up, you tend to have a hair trigger here, which requires a bit of getting used to. . . ." (131) In an even more surprising revelation, the Warren Report stated that the Army rifle experts ". . . had not even pulled the trigger because of concern about breaking the fire pin." (132) Despite the abundance of evidence indicating the "guilty Carcano" was not even a reliable weapon, the Warren Commission determined that Lee Oswald not only fired the weapon from the sixth floor of the Book Depository on November 22, 1963, but also concluded that the bullets, fired from "his" Carcano, inflicted all the wounds to President Kennedy and Governor Connally.

Did the FBI also contribute to the placing of the prints on the rifle? This highly troubling possibility is evidenced by an article published in *The Ft. Worth Press* on November 25, 1963. The article reported that a team of FBI agents visited Miller's Funeral Home in Ft. Worth after Oswald's body was taken there in preparation for burial. The agents reportedly spent over an hour fingerprinting the deceased Oswald. Even more suspicious is that funeral director Paul Groody, told author David Lifton:

> I was not in the room . . . but I had to clean up his fingers after they got through fingerprinting him. They put black gook on his fingers, and they can't get it off. . . . It was a complete mess of his entire hand, which would leave me to believe that they did take prints of his palms. (133)

When considered in light of the Warren Commission testimony of Sebastian Latona, who was the Supervisor of the Latent Fingerprint Section of the Identification Division of the FBI, the activity by the unknown FBI agents at the Miller Funeral Home, is extremely troubling and highly suspicious. Latona was asked by the Commission, "So as of November 23, you had not found an identifiable print on Exhibit 139 [the Carcano rifle]." Latona: "That is right." (134) It wasn't until

Monday, November 25, the day after Oswald was murdered and surreptitiously fingerprinted by the FBI, that his palm print was found on the rifle. Yet it was Oswald's palm print that would later serve as the only proof that he had ever handled the Carcano rifle.

Within one hour of the assassination of President Kennedy, which occurred at 12:30 p.m., Lee Harvey Oswald became the prime suspect in the murder of Police Officer J. D. Tippit. Oswald had returned to his rooming house on North Beckley Avenue in the Dallas suburb of Oak Cliff by means which remain unclear. Deputy Sheriff Roger Craig and witness Marvin Robinson stated that they saw a man resembling Lee Oswald walk down in front of the Book Depository and enter a Rambler station wagon and was driven away. (135) The Warren Commission concluded that he took a taxi and/or a bus to his Oak Cliff rooming house. What is clear is that Oswald entered his rooming house on Beckley and was seen by his housekeeper, Earlene Roberts. What happened next is an event that remains a mystery and a key event in solving the puzzle of the murder of Officer Tippit, and most probably the assassination of President Kennedy. Roberts stated to the Warren Commission, "Now it must have been around 1:00, or maybe a little after [that Oswald arrived]." Roberts recalled that a police car stopped in front of the house and honked its horn "several times" and drove off. This was minutes before the shooting of Officer Tippit and this incident has never been explained. (136) Within ten minutes of the Dallas Police car stopping in front of Oswald's rooming house, Officer J. D. Tippit was shot and killed within one mile of the Beckley Street bus stop where Roberts had last seen Oswald.

The testimony of witnesses to the murder of Officer Tippit have proven to be contradictory and inconsistent. Mrs. Acquilla Clemons was a witness to the murder of Officer Tippit. Her testimony was not heard by the Warren Commission and she is not mentioned in the Commission's report or in its twenty-six volumes. She stated that she saw two men near the police car just before one of them shot Tippit. The two men then took off in opposite directions. (137) Author Mark Lane subsequently interviewed Clemons and she described the killer of Officer Tippit as "kind of a short guy [and] kind of chunky," a description which clearly did not resemble Lee Oswald. (138) Frank Wright who lived along the street where Tippit was murdered immediately heard the shots and ran into the street. He stated:

> I was the first person out. . . . I saw a man standing in front of
> the car. He was looking toward the man on the ground. . . .
> The man who was standing in front of him was about medium
> height. He had on a long coat. . . . He ran as fast as he could
> go, and he got into his car . . . He got into that car and drove
> away as fast as you could see. . . . After that a whole lot of
> police came up. I tried to tell two or three people what I saw.
> They didn't pay any attention. I've seen what came out on
> television and in the newspaper but I know that's not what
> happened. I know a man drove off in a gray car. Nothing in
> the world's going to change my opinion. (139)

The star witness in the case against Oswald in the murder
of Officer Tippit was witness Helen Markham. Her
identification of Oswald as the man who killed Tippit is
questionable, at best, as reflected by her Commission
testimony:

> *Ball.* Now when you went into the room you looked these
> people over, these four men?
> *Mrs. Markham:* Yes, sir.
> *Ball.* Did you recognize anyone in the line-up?
> *Mrs. Markham.* No, sir.
> *Ball.* You did not? Did you see anybody-I have asked you that
> question before-did you recognize anybody from their face?
> *Mrs. Markham.* From their face, no.
> *Ball.* Did you identify anybody in these four people?
> *Mrs. Markham.* I don't know nobody. . . I had never seen none
> of them, none of these men.
> *Ball.* No one of the four?
> *Mrs. Markham.* No one of them.
> *Ball.* No one of all four?
> *Mrs. Markham.* No, sir.
> *Ball.* Was there a number two man in there?
> *Mrs. Markham.* Number two is the one I picked. . . Number
> two was the man I saw shoot the policeman . . . I looked at
> him. When I saw this man I wasn't sure, but I had cold chills
> just run all over me. . . . (140)

Domingo Benavides was one of the closest witnesses to the
murder of Officer Tippit and he also failed to clearly identify
Lee Oswald as the killer of Officer Tippit. Benavides was
sitting in his garbage truck across the street during the
shooting of Officer Tippit. He described the killer of Tippit as

a man with curly hair. (141)   In yet another amazing
coincidence, Domingo's look-a-like brother Eddy, was shot in
the back of the head and killed, in February 1964, just as the
Warren Commission was beginning to interview witnesses.

Warren Reynolds was an eyewitness to the murder of
Officer J. D. Tippit. He had seen a man running from the
scene of the murder and chased him but lost sight of him after
one block. He was interviewed by the FBI on January 21,
1964 and stated he could not make a positive identification of
Lee Harvey Oswald as the man he saw shoot Tippit. (142)
Two days after his FBI interview on January 23, 1964,
Reynolds was shot in the head by an unknown assailant in
the basement of the used car company that he worked
for—his assailant had not broken into the building or stolen
anything. He later recovered, and evidently his memory
improved for he now stated that he could identify Oswald as
the man running from the scene. (143)   The Warren
Commission claimed that it was "wild speculation" that there
might have been a connection between the shooting of
Reynolds and his non-identification of Oswald running from
the scene of the Tippit murder. However, in an interview
with researcher Mark Lane, Reynolds hesitantly, and
understandably guarded in his comments, questioned the
Commissions conclusion. "If they would catch the man and
prove that he did do it, we could figure out from there
whether he was connected or not. Until then I don't think
anybody is smart enough to say whether it was or it isn't
[connected]." (144)

A man named Darrell Garner was later arrested in
connection with the shooting of Reynolds. On February 5,
Betty Mooney McDonald, a former stripper at Jack Ruby's
nightclub, stepped forward with an alibi for Garner. On
February 13, Betty McDonald was arrested for fighting with
her roommate. Later that same night she was found hanging,
dead in her cell—her death was ruled a suicide. In July 1964,
Reynolds had recovered from his head wound and now
positively identified Oswald as the killer of Tippit. (145)
Meanwhile, no one was ever prosecuted for the attempted
murder of Warren Reynolds and as previously mentioned,
McDonald was found hanged in her jail cell.

When the evidence available is presented in an open forum,
it is not surprising that most would not find Lee Oswald
guilty beyond a reasonable doubt. There can be little wonder

that he professed his innocence at every opportunity from the afternoon of his arrest until the morning of his murder. "I'm just a patsy, I didn't shoot anybody, no sir. I don't know what kind of dispatches you people [the reporter] have been given. I have committed no act of violence, I haven't shot anybody;" were examples of the public pronouncements of innocence that Lee Oswald conveyed to the world during the last weekend of his life. (146) The preponderance of evidence supports his belief of innocence in regards to both murders, and even more likely as will be shown, a lack of motive.

Oswald's belief in his own innocence was conveyed to the members of the Dallas Police as well. Dallas Police Detective Jim Leavelle stated [Oswald] was "Very straight forward with me. . . . denying any implication whatsoever in shooting anybody." (147) Dallas Policeman Gerald Hill stated Oswald said, "Why should I hide my face, I haven't done anything to be ashamed of." (148)

Lee Oswald's brother, Robert, stated that in July 1964, he received a phone call from Commission Counsel Wesley Liebeler. Robert was shocked that at this late date in their investigation, the Commission had turned up no evidence of his brother's motivation to carry out the assassination. "I was astonished by the question . . . here, suddenly, after taking the testimony of hundreds of witnesses, a member of the Commission staff was asking me to answer during a brief telephone conversation of one of the most import questions about the entire case." (149)

On the afternoon of November 22, Marina Oswald stated, "Lee good man. Lee not shoot anybody." (150) And she later added, ". . . [Lee] a good man," and also a good husband. (151) Her subsequent testimony before the Warren Commission would not reflect these views of her husband as a "good man" and "husband" but of course, he was not there to defend himself.

Author Sylvia Meagher has written:

> If there is one area in which all the testimony is consistent and unambiguous, it is Oswald's friendly and even admiring attitude toward President Kennedy. Witnesses of varying backgrounds and beliefs testified to Oswald's favorable feelings about the President - members of the Dallas and Fort Worth Russian-speaking community Samuel Ballen, George de Mohrenschildt, Peter Gregory, and Ilya Mamantov among others; Michael Paine; Lillian Murret and her daughter

Marilyn H. Murret (Oswald's aunt and cousin respectively, and members of a devout middle-class family) and Lieutenant Martello of the New Orleans police anti-subversive squad. No one who knew Oswald reported that he had ever said or done anything which suggested animosity toward President Kennedy. (152)

Despite the fact that the Warren Commission and the FBI were never able to establish a motive as to why Lee Oswald would have killed President Kennedy, J. Edgar Hoover's initial determination remained as the "final" conclusion.

However, the House Select Committee on Assassinations later concluded:

On conspiracy, the Commission stated,". . . if there is any . . . evidence [of it], it has been beyond the reach of all the investigative agencies and resources of the United States and has not come to the attention of this Commission." Instead of such definitive language, the Commission should have candidly acknowledged the limitations of its investigation and denoted areas where there were shortcomings.

As the committee's investigation demonstrated, substantive new information has been developed in many areas since the Warren Commission completed its work. Particular areas where the committee determined the performance of the Commission was less than complete include the following:

Oswald's activities and associations during the periods he lived in New Orleans;

The circumstances surrounding the 2 1/2 years Oswald spent in the Soviet Union. (153)

The House Select Committee also determined that the Warren Commission failed to investigate:

The full nature and extent of Oswald's visit to Mexico City 2 months prior to the assassination, including not only his contact with the Soviet and Cuban diplomatic offices there, and the CIA's monitoring of his activities there, but also his possible associations and activities outside of those offices. (154)

When one objectively considers the inadequacies of the Warren Commission investigation into the background of Lee Oswald as well as the information presented here, it is apparent that J. Edgar Hoover's early indictment of Oswald was a blatant miscarriage of justice, and most probably was known by Hoover himself to be false. Dallas Police Chief Curry's statement is a fitting summary, "We don't have any proof that Oswald fired the rifle, and never did. Nobody's yet been able to put him in that building with a gun in his hand." (155)

Chapter 9

The Altering of Evidence, the Intimidation of Witnesses, and the Single Bullet Theory

J. Edgar Hoover and the FBI assumed control of the investigation into the assassination of President Kennedy on Friday evening, November 22, despite no legal jurisdiction allowing them to do so. Dallas Police Chief Jesse Curry stated, "The evidence gathered during the assassination weekend was dispersed in many directions. The FBI had already begun to seize evidence at the scene -- Early Friday evening FBI agents were anxious to have all physical evidence released to them." (1) Press reports from the afternoon of the assassination corroborate Curry's statement:

> F-B-I Director J. Edgar Hoover immediately made all of his agents and facilities available to Dallas authorities to help apprehend those guilty of the assassination attempt on President Kennedy. Hoover telephoned city officials moments after he received word of the attempt. (2)

Further evidence of this is shown in this statement from a November 24 memo issued by Hoover, "I have ordered the evidence secured by the Police Department." (3) President Johnson gave his official sanction to the seizing of the evidence on November 26 as evidenced by this press report from the *Dallas Morning News:* "'The White House approved the decision that the FBI take charge of all evidence which officers assembled in their investigation of the murder of President Kennedy,' law enforcement sources said here Tuesday night". (4)

No autopsy was done in the city where the murder took place, which was a violation of normal police procedure in any murder case. Chief Curry stated, "Secret Service agents had seized the President's body before the required autopsy could be performed." (5)   In fact, there was a twenty-minute standoff in the hallway of Parkland Hospital pitting the Secret Service against Dallas County Medical Examiner Earl Rose.   This situation was finally settled with the Secret Service flashing their guns and pushing their way out by force.   Aubrey Rike, who worked for the O'Neal Funeral Home, recalled that it was one of the scariest periods of his life and he later became a policeman who became involved in many life and death situations. (6) The *Saturday Evening Post* of January 14, 1967, described the problem of the autopsy not being carried out in Dallas:

> . . . Secret Service men literally seized the body from local officials at Parkland Hospital, who were demanding that an autopsy be performed in accordance with Texas law. If the law had been observed, there might have been no controversy, and the Bethesda doctors, the FBI and the Secret Service would have escaped the heavy responsibility they now bear. Sadly and ironically, the report of the autopsy performed on the murdered Oswald is a model of clarity and precision alongside the sloppy, ambiguous and incomplete record of the autopsy President Kennedy received.

Dr. Rose made clear his views that the autopsy should have been performed in Dallas to researcher Vincent Palamara in 1992. Dr. Rose recalled:

> At the time of the assassination of President Kennedy, there were no federal laws on the matter of an assassination of the President or Vice President. The state laws dealt with this crime.   Therefore, the Texas laws on homicide were controlling regarding the assassination. . . . the autopsy should have been performed in Dallas. (7)

Dr. Charles Crenshaw, resident surgeon at Parkland recalled the attempts by Parkland officials to conduct the autopsy in Dallas:

I opened the door to Trauma Room 1 and stuck my head in to check on the progress of the nurses who were preparing the President's body to be transported. When I turned around, I saw, in a group of people who I believed to be Presidential aids and Secret Service agents, Vernon Stembridge, chief of surgical pathology, and Sidney Stewart, resident in pathology. The doctors were explaining, politely but forcefully that, pursuant to Texas law, they would be performing an autopsy on President Kennedy's body before it was taken from the hospital. In tones of equal forcefulness, but with greater determination, the men in suits responded that they had orders to take the President's body back to Washington D. C., just as soon as it was ready to be moved, that there would be no Texas autopsy. . . . As both sides become more entrenched in their positions, talking turned to shouting and hand waving escalated to finger pointing. Unable to prevail in their mission, Drs. Stembridge and Stewart angrily turned and stomped out of the room. Not only were they outnumbered, but the men insuits had guns. My impression was that someone, who had given explicit instructions to these men, wanted Kennedy's body out of Parkland, out of Dallas, and out of Texas in a hurry. (8)

It is true that Ken O'Donnell and others on Kennedy's staff insisted that they leave Dallas immediately after the President was pronounced dead. But this would appear understandable considering their fallen leader was murdered in Texas and the initial belief that right-wing hatred might be responsible. An illustration of the belief that the right-wing might have been involved was indicated by the recollections of Daniel Patrick Moynihan. Moynihan recalled that on the afternoon of the assassination, Minnesota Senator and future Vice-President Hubert Humphrey burst into a room in the White House after hearing of the assassination and exclaimed to Moynihan and fellow Kennedy aide Ralph Dungan, ". . .What have they done to us?" ". . . and of course by 'they' everyone understood [the right-wing] reactionaries in Texas." (9) The fact remains that the Secret Service was now under the command of Lyndon Johnson and he personally delayed Air Force One's departure so he could be sworn in. There proved to be enough time for an autopsy to be performed in Dallas.

On Sunday morning after the murder of Lee Oswald, the doctor in charge of President Kennedy's autopsy, Dr. James Humes, burned part of his original autopsy notes—most probably because there would now be no trial of Lee Oswald.

Humes' confusion over the wounds, after being told via telephone by Dr. Malcolm Perry in Dallas (the surgeon who first attended the President) that the wound in the throat was an entrance wound, could now be dismissed. Dr. Humes stated, "In the privacy of my own home, early in the morning of Sunday, November 24, I made a draft of this report which I later revised and of which this represents the revision. That draft I personally burned in the fireplace of my recreation room." (10) The 1992 Congressionally mandated Assassination Records and Review Board discovered that "Under oath . . . Dr. Humes . . . acknowledged under questioning—in testimony that appears to differ from what he told the Warren Commission—that he had destroyed his notes taken at the autopsy and the first draft of the autopsy report." (11) It is quite possible that these original notes would have corroborated the initial Dallas doctor's observations of entrance wounds from the front. The Assassination Records and Review Board determined:

> when Dr. Humes was shown some copies of autopsy photographs during his testimony before the HSCA, he made statements that were interpreted as suggesting that he had revised his original opinion significantly on the location of the entrance wound. These shortcomings should have been remedied shortly after the assassination while memories were fresh and records were more readily recoverable. (12)

An article by Richard Dudman which was published on December 18, 1963, proves to be very interesting indeed. Under the headline, "Secret Service Gets Revision On Kennedy Wounds: After Visit by Agents, Doctors Say Shot Was From Rear," Dudman wrote:

> Two Secret Service agents called last week on Dallas surgeons who attended President John F. Kennedy and obtained a reversal of their original view that the bullet in his neck entered from the front. . . . The investigators did so by showing the surgeons a document described as an autopsy report from the United States Naval Hospital at Bethesda. The surgeons changed their original view to conform with the report they were shown. (13)

Warren Commission Attorney Arlen Specter stated, "It is ridiculous to indicate that the autopsy findings were changed after November 24." (14) Despite Specter's contentions, it is also clear that the autopsy findings were tied to the conclusions reached by the Dallas surgeons. The surgeons initial view of the wound in the throat being of entrance, had to be altered to fall in line with the final autopsy report. It appears that the Dallas doctors were strongly influenced by the argument that the President had "turned to wave" and/or that ". . . [Oswald] started shooting as the President's car started coming toward him [while still on Houston Street]. . . ." as articles from the *New York Times*, November 27 and December 5 indicate. Both of these arguments are totally false as the films and photos prove. No shots were fired at the President as the limousine moved towards the Book Depository on Houston Street and the President never turned around in his seat to wave at the crowd while on Elm Street. (15) The doctors clearly changed their minds based on press reports and the persuasive efforts of the Secret Service who were armed with the autopsy report which concluded that the wounds in the President entered from the rear. According to researcher James Gouchenaur, Secret Service agent Emory Moore stated during their interview, "I did everything I was told, we all did everything we were told, or we'd get our heads cut off." (16) Moore also indicated to Gouchenaur that he felt guilty for badgering Dr. Perry into altering his testimony regarding Perry's firm belief that there was a wound of entrance in the President's throat. The Parkland Hospital doctors had little choice but to agree. J. Edgar Hoover had already concluded that Lee Oswald was the sole assassin and now the autopsy conclusions supported him.

Most importantly, with no public trial, the Warren Commission investigation would be carried out solely by the FBI. There were no public examinations of witnesses and in many cases, important eyewitnesses were not even called to testify. When one takes time to consider the information that has emanated from the Warren Report, the House Select Committee on Assassinations, and other competent researchers, one is struck by the fact that the final conclusions compiled by the Warren Report do not match what the witnesses saw.

The majority of witnesses believed shots came from the front while Oswald was in the rear, and the majority of doctors (as we shall see) who treated the President, agreed. Witnesses were portrayed by the Warren Commission as confused, disoriented, mistaken, etc. when their statements and testimony did not match the FBI version of how events transpired. Railroad workers Richard C. Dodd and James L. Simmons both watched the assassination from the railroad overpass, which was most probably the best view of the motorcade as it wound through Dealy Plaza. They and six others saw smoke from behind the fence on the knoll and believed shots came from behind the fence on the knoll. Neither Dodd nor Simmons are mentioned in the index to the Warren Commission. (17) William Newman, his wife and his two young boys were standing on Elm Street directly in front of the grassy knoll and not more than ten feet from the President's car when the fatal shot hit. William and Gayle Newman have consistently stated from the day of the assassination to the present, that shots came directly over their heads and were fired from somewhere on the grassy knoll. Their immediate reactions to the shots being fired support this. They are seen in photographs and film footage lying on the ground and ducking for cover. William Newman stated, "I was a little disappointed that I didn't get called to testify to the Warren Commission. Someone told me the reason I didn't get called to testify was that I was talking about shots from someplace other than the Depository Building." (18)

This disturbing trend runs through the findings of J. Edgar Hoover and his FBI investigation, the evidence which indicated a contrary conclusion was ignored to substantiate a preconceived conclusion that Oswald was the lone assassin. What is even more disturbing is the documented evidence of witnesses who stated that their testimony was altered, and even worse, the intimidation of some of these witnesses by the FBI because of testimony that did not match the conclusions of the FBI. The *New York Times* reported on December 5, 1963, "Most private citizens who had cooperated with newsmen reporting the crime have refused to give further help after being interviewed by agents of the Federal Bureau of Investigation." Acquila Clemmons, a witness to the murder of policeman J. D. Tippit is an example of this intimidation. She had stated that she had seen two men flee the murder scene and neither was Oswald. When interviewed by "agents of some kind," she was told "she might get hurt or killed." (19) Clemmons name is not even mentioned in the Warren Report.

Presidential Assistants Dave Powers and Ken O'Donnell

were both riding in the Secret Service car immediately behind the presidential limousine. Former Speaker of the House Tip O'Neil recounted a conversation he had with both men in 1968, "I was surprised to hear O'Donnell say that he had heard two shots that came from behind the fence." O'Donnell went on to state that, "I told the FBI what I had heard, but they said that I must have been imagining things. So I testified the way they wanted me to." Dave Powers also supported O'Donnell's recollections. (20) These statements are corroborated by Powers' Warren Commission testimony:

> My first impression was that the shots came from the right and overhead, but I also had a fleeting impression that the noise appeared to come from the front in the area of the Triple overpass. This may have resulted from my feeling, when I looked forward to the overpass, that we might have ridden into an ambush. . . . (21)

An example of outright intimidation is shown in the example of Steven Wilson. Wilson, who worked as the Vice-President of a firm working in the Book Depository, watched the assassination from the third floor of the Depository. He told the FBI that "it seemed the shots came from the west end. . . . from the colonnade (knoll). The shots really did not sound like they came from above me." (22) Wilson went on to explain to author Mark Lane that he was harassed continually by the FBI. He stated, "I couldn't get any work done at all. They were always here." (23) Lane went on to ask Wilson for a filmed interview but Wilson said if I give you the interview the FBI will be back, and my health and my work will suffer. (24)

Jean Hill was standing on the curb across from the knoll when the shots rang out right in front of her. She stated that, "4-6 shots, maybe more, came from behind the fence at the top of the knoll." (25) Hill stated that while being questioned by the FBI, she was told that only three shots were fired and that she should accept that she was wrong. (26) Author Bill Sloan writes of Hill's questioning by Arlen Specter:

> After numerous days of questioning, she encountered "around the clock FBI surveillance of her home." Hill has also stated that her Commission testimony is "heavily edited . . . completely distorted . . . a total misrepresentation of what really happened." She also clearly recalls Arlen Specter telling her frostily, however, that he knew "all about" her.

She says that he accused her of engaging in a "shabby extramarital affair," thirsting for publicity and notoriety, refusing to cooperate with federal authorities, and proving herself "totally unreliable" as a witness. Unless the Commission received her full cooperation from now on, she remembers him telling her, she would be "very, very sorry. . . ." Jean says she was warned of dire consequences if she persisted in this kind of behavior [talking of shots coming from the grassy knoll]. . . . Jean says that Specter accused her of talking "insanity" and warned that if she continued with what she was saying, she would end up looking as "crazy" as Marguerite Oswald, mother of the accused. There were long intervals, she says when at a hand signal from Specter, the stenographer stopped taking notes. In countless instances, she charges, the meaning of her remarks were altered and her actual words were changed. (27)

FBI agent James Sibert, who was present at the autopsy, also claims that Arlen Specter deliberately lied about what he had said, thus falsifying the record, "that is absolutely false there would be no way in the world that I made no notes during the autopsy. . ." (28) Parkland Nurse Margaret Hinchcliffe (Hood) also had a problem with Specter attempting to change her testimony. Hinchcliffe stated ". . . [she] resented Arlen Specter trying to get her to say it [the throat wound] might be an exit wound." (29)

This pattern of altered testimony is seen in the case of Deputy Sheriff Roger Craig who was a witness to the assassination and was also on the scene when the rifle was found on the sixth floor of the Book Depository. He told author Penn Jones that his testimony from Volume 6 of the Warren Commission report was altered. Craig stated, "Well what shocked me the most was the pattern; it was so consistent. They put all my testimony down but they altered it. . . . They changed it some fourteen times." (30) Commission Counsel David Belin stated to Craig:

Now Mr. Craig I am going to ask you this question and I want you to tell me this. And I said, Counselor, just ask me the questions, I will tell you, and he became irritated. . . . I made him mad to begin with. He started instructing me before he got a tape recorder and a stenographer there. He told her not to write anything until he instructed her to. He did not turn the recorder on and he started instructing me. (31)

Another witness, Ron Fischer, had seen a rifleman in the

sixth floor of the Book Depository before the shooting. He
stated:

> that he and Belin became engaged in an argument concerning
> the color of hair of the rifleman seen by Fischer. The witness
> said Belin tried to persuade him to say a color other than
> what he actually saw, but that he, Fischer, was unwilling to
> do so. He stated that Belin was "hard-headed on this subject;
> . . . wanted to argue" and "was going to have his way or quit."
> Belin, he said, became "enraged," told the court reporter to
> stop, and left the room for about five minutes. He returned
> "more composed" and again began questioning Fischer about
> the man's hair. When Fischer maintained his position, Belin
> finally changed the subject Fischer summed up Belin as a
> "pretty sharp character." (32)

A dancer who worked at Jack Ruby's Carousel Club, Nancy
Powell (Tami True) also reported a similar problem. Special
Agent of the Secret Service, Roger Warner, stated in a letter
to his superior, Forrest Sorrels, that Mrs. Powell complained:

> that she did not feel that her testimony had been recorded
> accurately in that deposition . . . the deposition as written was
> not acceptable to her. . . . Mrs. Powell stated that it would be
> impossible to make corrections in the deposition as written
> because to make her testimony sound right [she] would have
> to change the questions. (33)

Sam Holland, who witnessed the assassination from the
railroad overpass, related to author Josiah Thompson that he
and his lawyer:

> red marked . . .red penciled that statement [Holland's Warren
> Commission Testimony] from beginning to end . . . because
> there was a lot of errors in it. I don't know whether it was
> made with people attacking it . . . But there were a lot of
> mistakes in it and we corrected it with a red pencil . . . the
> statement that I made, as well as I remember, isn't in context
> with the Warren Commission [Hearings]. (34)

Senator Ralph Yarborough who was riding in the motorcade
with Vice-President Johnson stated:

> After I wrote them [the Warren Commission] . . . a couple of
> fellows came to see me. They walked in like they were a
> couple of deputy sheriff's and I was a bank robber. I didn't

like their attitude. As a senator I felt insulted. They went off and wrote up something and brought it back for me to sign. But I refused and let it lay there for weeks. They wanted me to sign this thing, then say this is all I know. Of course I would never have signed it. Finally, after some weeks, they began to bug me . . . demanding that I sign the report. (35)

Richard Randolph Carr witnessed the assassination from the sixth floor of the new courthouse. He stated in his Warren Commission testimony that he saw a man on the sixth floor of the Book Depository during the shooting who did not resemble Lee Oswald. (36) He later recalled his treatment at the hands of the FBI. Carr stated:

> The FBI came to my house—there were two of them--and they said they heard that I witnessed the assassination and I said that I did. They told me, "If you didn't see Lee Harvey Oswald up in the School Book Depository with a rifle, you didn't witness it." I said, "Well the man I saw on television that they tell me is Lee Harvey Oswald was not in the window of the School Book Depository. That's not the man. And [one of the agents] said I better keep my mouth shut. He did not ask me what I saw, he told me what I saw." (37)

Arnold Rowland corroborated Carr's impression that there was another man on the sixth floor just before the shooting and that he hardly resembled Oswald. Rowland and his wife were standing on Houston Street facing the corner of Houston and Elm where the Depository was located. When Rowland gave his statement to the FBI, they not only ignored his impression that shots came from the railroad yards (knoll area) but also his belief that the man on the sixth floor was not Lee Oswald. They actually deleted the portion of his statement that reflected this view. Rowland told the FBI that he had actually seen an "elderly Negro man . . . hanging out of the . . . window [alleged sniper's next] five minutes before the motorcade came by." (38) His subsequent testimony reflects the FBI's attempts at altering his Warren Commission record:

> *Question.* Was that information included in the written portion of the statement which was taken from you on Sunday?
> *Rowland.* No it wasn't . . . the agent deleted it though himself, I mean I included it in what I gave.
> *Question.* When you say deleted it, did he strike out after putting it in, or did he omit it in the transcription?

Rowland. Omitted it. (39)

Rowland went on to say, "They just didn't seem interested at all. . . . They didn't pursue the point." (40) An elderly black man in the window, five minutes before the shooting, would hardly corroborate the Warren Commission's conclusion that Oswald was laying in wait by himself preparing to kill the President. When you add the fact that the motorcade was actually five minutes late, it is no wonder that Rowland's testimony would not be accepted if J. Edgar Hoover's conclusion that Oswald was the lone assassin was "correct."

An important question that has not been clearly answered, is whether Lee Oswald ever returned to the sixth floor after 11:55 a.m. as the Warren Report states. If Rowland is correct, then someone else was at the window and Oswald was most probably not there at all. There is much evidence to indicate that Oswald was not on the sixth floor at the time of the shooting. A floor-laying crew had been working on the sixth floor until a little before noon. If Oswald had been planning to shoot the President from that window, then how could he be certain when the crew would break for lunch? Also, ten minutes before the shooting, Bonnie Ray Williams was eating lunch on the sixth floor in front of the "sniper's nest" window. Was Williams the black man Rowland saw in the window? Possibly, although Williams was not "elderly" as Rowland described. The man in the window certainly was black and Williams admits to being near the window at the time Rowland saw someone there. Williams was asked by the Warren Commission, "Did you hear anything that made you feel that there was anybody else on the sixth floor with you?" Williams replied, "[No], that is one of the reasons I left—because it was so quiet." (41) In addition, Williams stated that he saw neither Oswald or Depository employee Charles Givens, who was reportedly the last person to see Oswald on the sixth floor at 11:55. But Givens' original statement makes no mention of seeing Oswald on the sixth floor after 11:55. Givens' original affidavit, which was signed on the afternoon of November 22, states: "I worked up on the sixth floor until about 11:30 a.m. Then I went downstairs and into the bathroom. At twelve o'clock I took my lunch period. I went to the parking lot at Record and Elm . . ." (42)

In a possibly disturbing development, Givens appears to have changed his testimony after being pressured by the Dallas police. Evidence of this is indicated by a transcript from the Police radio log involving Police Inspector J. Herbert Sawyer. The radio log stated, ". . . see if we can pick this man up. Charles Douglas Givens he is a colored male . . . a porter that worked on this floor up here, he has a police record and he left." (43) Sawyer went on to tell the Warren Commission:

> he is the one that had the previous record in the narcotics, and he was supposed to have been a witness to the man being on that floor. He was supposed to have been a witness to Oswald being there . . . and he was the one employee who was missing, or that he was missing from the building. He wasn't accounted for. . . . (44)

When Givens was brought in for questioning, Oswald was already in custody. It would seem logical that Givens would make mention of seeing Oswald on the sixth floor but Givens did not mention Oswald. It is quite possible that Givens, being black, a narcotics felon, and missing from the building, was pressured into changing his story. Givens' testimony before the Commission in April 1964 reflects this view. He now remembered seeing Oswald on the sixth floor around 12:00 when his original statement mentioned he left at 11:30 and apparently saw no one. Adding credence to these suspicions is the fact that Williams, Givens, and fellow employee Harold Norman, viewed the assassination from the fifth floor window (directly below the "sniper's nest") and their actions immediately after the shooting causes one to question what really happened on the sixth floor. Instead of alerting police or running to the sixth floor to find out what happened up there, they actually ran to the window overlooking the railroad yards which is behind the grassy knoll and then down to the fourth floor. There is no record that Williams, Givens, or Norman told anyone on November 22 that they believed shots came from above them. James Altgens, Associated Press photographer, clearly expressed the belief that the three men were not behaving as if shots had just been fired from above them and that an assassin was running free in the building. Altgens stated:

> I saw a couple of Negroes [Williams, Norman and Givens] looking out of a window which I later learned was the floor below where the gun—the sniper's nest was supposed to have been, but it didn't register on me at the time that they were looking from an area that the bullet might have come from. (45)

This version of events did not emerge until weeks later.

Howard Brennan proved to be the star witness for the Warren Commission in placing Lee Oswald in the sixth floor window during the shooting. Gerald Ford, in the October 2, 1964 issue of Life magazine, stated that Howard Brennan was the most important of the witnesses. Yet Brennan's testimony to the Warren Commission was so confusing and contradictory that the Commission itself dismissed his reliability as evidenced by the following information. Just before the police line-up Brennan had seen Oswald's picture "twice on television before I [he] went down to the police station for the lineup." Brennan surely should have recognized Oswald having just seen him shoot the President and seeing his picture flashed on television. "But he declined to make a positive identification of Oswald when he first saw him in the police lineup." (46) He was also asked by a member of the Commission, "Did you see the rifle discharge, did you see the recoil or the flash?" Brennan: "No." (47) Based on Brennan's inability to identify Oswald as the man he saw in the sixth floor window, the Commission concluded, ". . .therefore, [the Commission] does not base its conclusions concerning the identify of the assassin on Brennan's subsequent certain identification." (48) In fact, Dallas Police Chief Jesse Curry makes it very clear, that neither Howard Brennan or anyone else had identified Oswald as firing from the sixth floor window of the Book Depository. In an interview on Sunday morning, November 24, Curry stated that he had not found a witness to the President's assassination, despite allegedly receiving Brennan's identification of Oswald the previous day. Q: "Chief Curry, do you have an eyewitness who saw someone shoot the President?" Curry: "No, sir; we do not." (49)

Brennan's identification of a gunman resembling Oswald on the sixth floor of the Book Depository should be considered even more questionable as a result of the following record of his testimony:

Q. Do you know a George Murray, of the National Broadcasting Co.?
Brennan. I do not . . .
Q. Did you ever state to anyone that you heard shots from opposite the Texas School Depository and saw smoke and paper wadding come out of boxes on a slope below the railroad trestle at the time of the assassination? Did you ever say that

or that, in substance, to anyone?
Brennan. I did not.
Q. . . . Is there another Howard Brennan?
Q. Well, sir; we don't know. We wanted to know whether or not you ever made this statement to anyone.
Brennan. No sir.
Warren. Thank you very much, Mr. Brennan. (50)

Amazingly, this testimony from Brennan indicates that he originally believed shots came from the front, near the grassy knoll, and not from the Book Depository.

Dallas Police Chief Jesse Curry later made clear his doubts about Oswald's presence on the sixth floor as evidenced by the following statements:

> The physical evidence and eyewitness accounts do not clearly indicate what took place on the sixth floor of the Texas School Book Depository at the time John F. Kennedy was assassinated. Speculative magazine and newspaper reports led the public to believe that numerous eyewitnesses positively identified Lee Harvey Oswald as the sniper in the sixth floor window. The testimony of the people who watched the motorcade was much more confusing that either the press or the Warren Commission seemed to indicate. (51)

A number of witnesses did claim to see Oswald on the first or second floor after 11:55. Eddie Piper testified in his affidavit of November 22, 1963 and in his appearance before counsel of the Warren Commission on April 8, 1964, that he saw and spoke to Oswald "just at twelve o'clock, down on the first floor." (52) William Shelley testified on April 7, 1964, that he saw Oswald when he "came down to eat lunch about ten to twelve." (53) It is very interesting to note that this is exactly where Oswald said he was during the shooting. "At the time the President was shot I was having my lunch on the first floor." (54) Oswald's statement of eating lunch on the first floor is also partially corroborated by Depository employee Harold Norman who was eating lunch on the first floor at noon. Norman stated, ". . . there was someone else there." . . . but he was not sure who." (55) Adding credence to this speculation is the testimony of Depository employee Carolyn Arnold. She stated that at approximately 12:15, "As she was standing in front of the building [Depository] she stated she thought she caught a fleeting glimpse of Lee Harvey Oswald standing in the hallway between the front door and the double doors leading to the warehouse, located on the first floor. She could not be sure that this was Oswald, but she said she felt it was. . . ." (56)

Despite the statements of numerous witnesses and the Chief of Police of the city where the murder occurred, the FBI report and the initial conclusions of J. Edgar Hoover would not be changed. What is worse is that testimony was altered, witnesses were "wrong" (despite being at the scene), and many were verbally and some physically intimidated. The accusations of Aubrey Rike are shocking. Rike, an assistant undertaker for the O'Neal Funeral Home, assisted in preparing President Kennedy's body for placement in his casket. His description of intimidation by the FBI dealt with much more than altered testimony. During his FBI "interview," Rike stated, "They [FBI agents] shoved me around, forced me into a chair . . . They threatened me, told me they could kick my ass. I was scared to death." (57)

It would be understandable if there were some honest mistakes made in transcribing testimony but even one example of blatant physical intimidation is too many if finding the truth was indeed the Commission's goal. Author Henry Hurt has noted that at least sixty witnesses had their Commission testimony or statements to the FBI altered. (58) There are also far too many examples of not-so-subtle verbal intimidation for these actions to be deemed innocent or accidental. Were these actions taken as a result of the direct orders of J. Edgar Hoover or just carried out in a "benign fashion" by others in order to help facilitate his conclusions? It is clear that this question merits more in-depth study and should not be dismissed as heresay. The evidence presented here should certainly create some level of suspicion as to the treatment of witnesses and evidence.

The House Select Committee on Assassinations reinvestigated the murder of John Kennedy in the late 1970's because of continued doubt as to the accuracy of the Warren Commission's findings and also because of a succession of murders involving individuals called to testify before the Church Committee and the House Select Committee. The murders involved some of the following; George DeMorenschildt, John Roselli and Sam Giancana. DeMorenschildt's death was ruled a suicide by a shotgun blast to the head. He had "befriended" Oswald in the months leading up to the assassination. Roselli and Giancana had both been linked to CIA-Mafia plots to kill Fidel Castro. The Church Committee was in the process of determining if there was a link between the assassination of President Kennedy and the CIA-Mafia plots to kill Castro when Rosseli and Giancana were both murdered. Neither killing has ever been solved. These apparent attempts to silence witnesses scheduled to appear before congressional inquiries led to the formation of the House Select Committee. Despite the formation of the House Select Committee, the attempts to intimidate witnesses and to alter testimony, as well as evidence, did not cease.

The House Select Committee was given broad investigative and subpoena problems as a result of these murders—but the Committee was criticized by some for stating that there was a conspiracy based on its acoustical study of a tape recording made in Dealy Plaza on the day of the assassination. But as we shall see, the acoustical study is partially questioned as a result of the possibility that the tape itself might have been altered. The findings by the Committee, that a fourth shot was fired from the grassy knoll, have also been brought into question by critics of the Committee's acoustical study. But if there was more than one gunman involved in the assassination, then it would be reasonable to assume that different caliber weapons might have been used. This would also cause the impulse sounds that were recorded to emit varying sounds (or volume) depending on the type of weapon fired and proximity to the recorder which was on a police motorcycle. Other possibilities then must be considered; such as a handgun fired at relatively close range, from behind the fence, as some witnesses believe was used. Dr. Charles Baxter, Parkland Hospital attending surgeon stated, "The wound in the neck was no more than a pinpoint. It was made by a small caliber weapon. And it was an entry wound. . . it might have come from a handgun." (59) Baxter's statement of the possibility that a handgun was used in the assassination is corroborated by the testimony of Secret Service agent Clint Hill, "I heard a second firecracker noise but it had a different sound—like the sound of shooting a revolver into something hard." (60) Dealy Plaza witness A. J. Millican added further corroboration when he stated, "It [the shots] sounded like a .45 automatic. . . ." (61)

There is also a possibility that a silencer could have been used during the assassination. If a silencer was used then some of the shots would obviously have not been recorded (and possibly muffled in sound), this would make even proof of four shots by virtue of the acoustical study invalid, or at least not totally accurate. Researcher Steve Barber did prove by analyzing the dictabelt recording that there is very persuasive evidence of "crosstalk" on the recording. (62)

This information indicates a number of possibilities:

1. The tapes might be dubbed or not the originals.
2. Different policeman at different times during the motorcade and from different locations had different sounds from their locations recorded — which confuses and complicates the analysis of the recording.
3. If "crosstalk" was recorded, the real sounds of gunshots could possibly be found if and when other sounds are filtered out.

House Committee researchers Robert Groden, Dr. Ernest Ashkenasy, and Dr. Mark Weiss prepared a demonstration that showed that the four impulses found on the dictabelt could very well have lined up with sequences seen on the Zapruder film of the assassination. But until the "crosstalk" confusion is solved conclusively, we can only rely on eye and ear-witness testimony. And as we shall see, the acoustic analysis was not meant to be the determining factor for the House Committee's final conclusion of conspiracy. It was only to serve as corroboration of evidence obtained from witness testimony. But it should also be noted that the Committee had also determined that there were as many as six impulses (indicating possible gunshots) found on the dictabelt recordings and that locations other than the sixth floor of the Book Depository and the grassy knoll were not considered or properly analyzed as possible shooting locations. (63) A number of witnesses testified to the fact that they heard shots from different directions and varying as to the number of shots. As stated, the House Select Committee did release evidence indicating that the dictabelt recordings did show the possibility that six shots were actually recorded. The six impulses on the recording were ten decibels above every other noise on the tape and there is a possibility they all could have been gunshots.

The statements made by former Chairman of the House Select Committee Rep. Louis Stokes on the television news program "Face the Nation" in 1978 strongly argues that the

Committee never intended to rely solely on the acoustics evidence as the basis for its findings. In response to a question about the reliability of the acoustics, Chairman Stokes was asked, "Do you have any doubts at all about the reliability of that study?" His response:

> No, but let me correct you to some extent. That's not really the basis for the Committee's conclusion. What the Committee really felt was, that the acoustical evidence was corroborative of other evidence already in the record. With reference to both the eye and ear evidence that had been received by the Warren Commission, you will recall, some 178 persons were interviewed by the Warren Commission, and they gave evidence, many of them, with reference to a shot coming from the grassy knoll. So we really felt that the acoustical evidence was corroborative of other evidence already in existence.

One of the clearest examples of eyewitness testimony which dissented from the conclusions reached by the Warren Commission was found in this statement made by witness A. J. Millican, who was standing on the north side of Elm Street about halfway between Houston and the Triple Underpass. Millican's location, facing both the Book Depository and the grassy knoll and at a point between both possible source of gunfire, makes his observations more credible. He stated:

> Just after the President's car passed, I heard three shots from up toward Elm right by the Book Depository Building, and then immediately I heard two more shots come from the arcade between the Book Store and the Underpass, then three more shots came from the same direction only sounded further back. . . . (64)

Millican was never interviewed by nor called to testify to the Warren Commission or the House Select Committee on Assassinations. Millican's statement was corroborated by his work crew supervisor Sandy Speaker. Speaker stated to author Jim Marrs:

> I was the superintendent of construction for the Republic Bank project at the time. Millican and also Howard Brennan [who stated that he saw a gunman in the 6th floor of Book Depository and will be discussed later] were working for me. We were fabricating plumbing piping for the Republic Bank Building under construction at the west end of Pacific Street

[north of Texas School Book Depository]. Millican and the whole crew had knocked off for lunch and were by the Depository building to watch the parade. I hadn't gotten there when [the motorcade] passed. I was less than a half-block away and heard the shots. I heard at least five shots and they came from different locations. I was a combat Marine with the First Marine Division in World War II, hand-to-hand combat, missions behind enemy lines, and I know what I am talking about. I've said for years there were more than three shots fired. (65)

Evidence to corroborate Millican and Speaker's (as well as others) belief that more than three shots were fired, is plentiful. Wayne Hartman and his wife Edna were standing on the corner of Record and Main Streets when the motorcade passed by. After the shooting, they ran down to the open area between Main and Elm Streets. Hartman stated, ". . . he noted a gouged-out hole in the grass—that he could stick three fingers into." Deputy Sheriff's, Buddy Walthers, Roger Craig and Al Mattox, verified the bullet had struck the ground at this point. (66) A series of photographs show police officers and bystanders searching in the grass immediately after the shooting at the location the Hartman's were referring to and that an FBI agent is seen cupping "the bullet" in his hand and placing it in his pocket. (67) Mattox, Walthers, and Police Chief Curry have verified that this man was an FBI agent. (68) But the discovery of the bullet and the true identity of the agent were never verified by J. Edgar Hoover, the FBI, or the Warren Commission. The obvious reason for allowing the discovery of this bullet to not be acknowledged, was that it would prove that there was another assassin.

Further corroboration that at least one bullet missed the President, besides the one that the Warren Commission determined had missed and wounded bystander James Tague, is found in a report published in the *Ft. Worth Star Telegram* on November 23, which printed a photo with the caption: "Assassin's bullet—One of the rifle bullets fired by the murderer of President Kennedy lies in the grass across Elm Street from the building in which the killer was hiding and from where he launched his assault." The finding of a bullet not accounted for by the Warren Commission is corroborated by an article in the November 24 edition of the *Dallas Times-Herald.* " Dallas Police Lt. Carl. Day of the crime lab estimated the distance from the sixth floor window the slayer used, to the spot where one of the bullets was recovered, at 100 yards. . . ." This is further corroborated by an article written by Richard Dudman and published in the *New Republic* of December 21, 1963 in which he states, "On the day the President was shot I happened to learn of a possible fifth [bullet]. A group of police officers were examining the area at the side of the street where the President was hit, and a police inspector told me they had just found another bullet in the grass."

Evidence of another bullet missing the limousine completely and striking the pavement in front of the Presidential limousine is shown by the testimony of motorcycle policeman Steve Ellis and Dallas Patrolman J. W. Foster. Ellis "reported seeing a bullet strike the pavement alongside the first car in the motorcade, approximately 100 to 125 feet in front of the car carrying President Kennedy." (69) Foster stated, "He found where one shot hit the turf." (70) These statements are corroborated by railroad workers Austin Miller and Royce Skelton who both witnessed a bullet strike the pavement. Skelton stated, ". . . I then heard another shot and saw the bullet hit the pavement. . . " (71) Miller recalled that "One shot apparently hit [the] street past the car." (72)

Apparently, another bullet hit the Stemmons freeway sign. Dealy Plaza witness James Hicks was standing on Elm Street with his back to the knoll. Hicks stated to the *New Orleans Times, Picayune* on January 12, 1968:

> . . . he heard four shots, and one bullet passed his head and struck a traffic caution sign, which he said was removed almost immediately after the assassination. He said as far as he knows it was never mentioned in the Warren Commission Report. Hicks said the sign was removed by men "I assumed to be members of the Dallas Police force. I assumed they would use it as evidence."

Hicks' statement is corroborated by Mrs. Donald Baker who stated, "I saw the bullet hit on down this way, I guess, right at the sign, angling out." (73) Dealy Plaza groundskeeper Emmit Hudson made an interesting comment when he stated, ". . . the Stemmons sign had been shifted from its place after the assassination. . . ." (74) A bullet hitting the sign, and its subsequent removal, was also noted by Dallas County

Surveyor Bob West and fellow surveyor Chester Breneman. Both were part of the Warren Commission re-enactments (there were two) of the assassination in Dealy Plaza. Breneman stated, ". . . right after the assassination, they were mentioning a [highway] sign which had a stress mark from a bullet on it. It's my understanding that this particular sign was quickly taken down and no one has been able to locate it." (75) Breneman concluded that as a result of these re-enactments, "I wish to state that both investigations led us to believe beyond any doubt there were two assassins." Author Jim Marrs confirmed that Bob West totally agreed with Breneman's conclusions. (76)

Those in position to describe what they had seen, heard, and experienced, were told by others who were most often not at the scene of the assassination, what they had seen and heard. Orrville Nix had filmed the assassination from the grassy area facing the knoll between Elm and Commerce Streets. He initially stated that he believed that everyone he spoke to, including the head of the Dallas office of the Secret Service Forrest Sorrels, believed that the shots came from the grassy knoll—"behind the fence." (77) He later changed his mind and stated that the shots came from the Book Depository because of what the authorities had determined "to be true." But his granddaughter, Gayle Nix Jackson, later stated that the authorities caused him to change his mind and made him "look insane."

> . . . They took him down to Dealy Plaza and said, "Mr. Nix, where did the shots come from?" He replied, "From a fence." They . . . pulled him aside [and asked], "What did the Warren Commission say? Where did they say these shots came from?" Nix replied, "The Book Depository," and they said, "That's right—that's what we want you to say." I remember riding home with him—he was so upset. I mean he would hit the . . . steering wheel and say, "Why . . . they try and make me look insane and I know that's where they [the shots] came from [the fence]—and I know that's where the shots came from." (78)

Mary Woodward, a reporter for the Dallas Morning News, was forced to change her story also. She was standing on Elm Street between the Book Depository and the knoll when she heard the shots come from behind her, which was in the direction of the fence. Her story was rewritten and reconciled with the official version of shots coming from the Book

Depository before the November 22 evening edition was published. (79)

As we shall see, the evidence does not drive the investigation towards the conclusion, but rather witness testimony that is misrepresented and/or of a questionable nature is selected to match a pre-arranged conclusion. It appears foolish to basically ignore the witnesses at the scene who believed that shots came from different directions, that there were more than three shots, and some of the shots came from the right front. Also to be considered is the evidence brought forward which brings into question the actual location and conditions of the President's and Governor Connally's wounds.

On the afternoon of the assassination the attending surgeons to President Kennedy held a press conference at Parkland Hospital to discuss the wounds. Dr. Malcolm Perry was the surgeon who performed the tracheotomy on the President's throat:

> *Question.* Where was the entrance wound?
> *Perry.* There was an entrance wound in the neck.
> *Question.* Which way was the bullet coming at the neck wound? At him?
> *Perry.* It appeared to be coming at him. (80)

This initial assumption of an entrance wound in the throat is corroborated by NBC newsman Robert MacNeil's telephone log report from the afternoon of November 22, "Dr. Malcolm Perry reported that a bullet struck him in front as he faced the assailant." At least ten other doctors and medical personnel agreed that the entrance wound in the neck is what Dr. Perry saw. (81) Dr. Perry responded to the Warren Commission's findings that he was mistaken in regards to whether the wound in the throat was an entrance wound. But later he told author Harrison Livingstone in 1979, "My whole credibility as a trauma surgeon was at stake. . . . I couldn't have made a mistake like that. It destroys my integrity if I don't know an entrance wound from an exit wound." (82) Dr. Robert McClelland, who helped Perry attend President Kennedy, told reporter Richard Dudman on December 7, 1963, that the neck wound "had the appearance of the usual entrance wound of a bullet" and that he and his colleagues at Parkland were experienced and could usually tell the difference between entry and exit wounds. (83) Dr.

Charles Carrico, another attending surgeon, recalled the visit by the Secret Service within a week of the shooting and stated, "I said that on the basis of our initial examination, this wound could have been either an entrance or an exit wound, which is what they were most concerned about." (84) As previously indicated, the intimidation of Dr. Perry is apparent from the statement of Secret Service agent Emory Moore: " . . . he [Moore] felt remorse for the way he had badgered Dr. Perry into changing his testimony to the effect that there was not, after all, an entrance wound in the front of the President's neck." (85) By stating that it was possible that the neck wound was an exit wound, the Warren Commission could eventually write in their report that there was no entrance wound in the throat and Oswald was the only assassin and fired only from behind.

The Warren Report determined that Kennedy was hit in the back, the bullet then exited his throat and proceeded to strike Governor Connally and go in and out of his ribs, chest, and end up as a fragment in his thigh. Yet, this bullet, Commission Exhibit 399, was almost pristine with no evidence of blood or clothing fabric on it. A highly improbable conclusion to say the least—if not totally impossible. But the Commission was stuck with this theory because J. Edgar Hoover's investigation stated that Oswald and he alone did the shooting with only three shots in six seconds. Yet, ironically, the Secret Service's investigation had determined that this theory was not possible and they passed this information on to the FBI as this report shows:

> Secret Service Agent J. J. Howlett advised that it had been ascertained from the movies that President Kennedy was struck with the first and third shots fired by the assassin, while Governor Connally was struck with the second shot. (86)

The Warren Report stated, "Although it is not necessary to any essential finding of the Commission to determine just which shot hit Governor Connally, there is very persuasive evidence from the experts to indicate that the same bullet which pierced the President's throat also caused Governor Connally's wounds." (87) This statement is totally inaccurate if not an outright falsehood. Determining which bullet was fired and when it struck the Governor, is crucial if the single or "magic bullet" theory stands any chance of credibility. For if any of the non-fatal bullets struck either President Kennedy or Governor Connally before or after the non-fatal wounds were inflicted, then there had to be more than three shots fired.

The "magic bullet theory," which was formulated and pushed by Warren Commission Counsel Arlen Specter, has always been a matter of controversy. Specter, a former Republican candidate for the presidency, is currently a United States Senator from Pennsylvania. He continues to argue that his theory is correct as this statement made in 1991 makes clear, "The Commissions findings have stood the test of time including the single bullet theory." (88) It would have been very interesting for him to have had to present his evidence in a court of law with an objective jury rendering a decision. Specter continues to promote his closed-door conclusion while the evidence presented in the public arena makes it clear that those more qualified than he, continue to have serious doubts.

Since the FBI investigation had determined that Lee Oswald was the lone assassin and he was only capable of firing three shots in the allotted time (one had missed), that left one bullet to inflict all seven non-fatal wounds in President Kennedy and Governor John Connally. Dr. Robert Shaw, who had operated on the governor, was asked by the Warren Commission about the possibility of one bullet causing the chest and the wrist wounds. Shaw replied, ". . . the examination of the wrist by x-ray and at the time of the surgery showed some fragments of metal that made it difficult to believe that the same missile could have caused these two wounds." (89) Note that Dr. Shaw is only referring to two of the wounds and not the other five. X-rays from the other five wounds indicated that there were still other fragments which would be indicative of at least one other bullet being fired. Dr. Shaw's testimony is corroborated by autopsy surgeon Dr. Pierre Finck as stated in Finck's Commission testimony:

> *Specter.* And could it have been the bullet which inflicted the wound on Governor Connally's right wrist?
> *Finck.* No; for the reason that there are too many fragments described in that wrist. (90)

Fellow autopsy surgeon, Dr. James Humes was asked by the Warren Commission if CE 399 (the single pristine bullet) could have caused the Governor's thigh wound.   Humes stated:

> I think that extremely unlikely. The report, again Exhibit 392 from Parkland tells of an entrance wound on the lower mid-thigh of the Governor, and X-rays taken there are described as showing metallic fragments in the bone, which apparently by this report were not removed and are still present in Governor Connally's thigh. I can't conceive of where they came from this missile. (91)

Dr. Joseph Dolce, chief consultant in wound ballistics for the U. S. Army, who supervised the ballistics test for the Warren Commission, made the following statement:

> So they gave us the original rifle—The Mannlicher Carcano, plus 100 bullets, 6.5 millimeters, and in every instance [of firing into cadavers wrists]   the front of the bullet was smashed. It's impossible for a bullet to strike a bone, even at low velocity and still come out with a perfectly normal tip. . . . under no circumstances do I believe that this bullet could hit the wrist and still not be deformed. We proved it by our experiments. (92)

Darrell Tomlinson, the senior engineer at Parkland Hospital, cast even more doubt on the single bullet theory when he described how he found the pristine bullet. He testified that he was not positive that the bullet that was found came from the Governor's stretcher. He also stated that "I made several trips [past the stretcher] before I discovered the bullet." (93) Tomlinson went on to say that "he bumped the wall, and a spent cartridge or bullet rolled out that had apparently been lodged under the edge of the mat . . . [and stated that] I believe that it was [stretcher] 'B'" which was not the stretcher that carried Governor Connally. (94)   This creates a reasonable doubt as to whether the pristine bullet was actually found on Governor Connally's stretcher. It also seems rather strange that a bullet from the Governor could somehow find itself underneath the mattress in the first place. One would think that the bullet would have been dislodged or been noticed somewhere along the line as Connally was transported from the limousine to a hospital stretcher into his hospital room for surgery. When it's considered further that Tomlinson could not be sure that this was the Governor's stretcher or how the bullet had not been noticed before is not clear and casts more doubt on the "official" story.

Tomlinson's doubts as to the authenticity of the pristine bullet is further buttressed by the Commission testimony of Parkland employee O. P. Wright. "He advised he could not positively identify [the pristine bullet] as being the same bullet which was found on November 22, 1963." (95) Wright cast further doubt on the authenticity of this bullet when he stated that the bullet [he saw] was pointed, [the one] found at Parkland [was] not CE 399 [which was rounded]." (96) In another amazing twist, Dr. David Osborne, a military doctor who was a participant during the autopsy performed on President Kennedy, "recalled seeing an intact slug roll out from clothing of President Kennedy and onto the autopsy table." (97) Osborne corroborated this statement when he told author David Lifton in 1979, that he personally handled a "reasonably clean unmarred bullet from the clothing that was around JFK's body, the bullet was not deformed in any way . . . I held the bullet in my hand, and looked at it. . . . I knew the Secret Service had it . . . the Secret Service took it." (98) This information leads to the possibility that another unaccounted for bullet was found and possibly related to the assassination. Even more troubling is the possibility that the bullet found by Osborne or CE 399 was planted, linking Oswald to the Carcano rifle.

Governor Connally cast even more doubt on the single bullet theory in his Warren Commission testimony and in other public statements. Governor Connally stated to the Warren Commission that his initial reaction was that ". . . there were either two or three people involved or more in this or someone was shooting with an automatic rifle. . . . They are going to kill us all." (99) Connally stated further:

> My recollection of that time gap, the distinct separation between the shot that hit the President and the impact of the one that hit me, is as clear today as it was then. . . . They talk about the one bullet or 2 bullet theory but as far as I'm concerned, there is no theory. There is my absolute knowledge, and Nellie's, too, that one bullet caused the President's wound, and that an entirely separate shot struck me. . . . It is a certainty. . . I'll never change my mind. (100)

Mrs. Nellie Connally corroborated her husband and stated, "No one will ever convince me otherwise." (101) Connally remained consistent in his memoirs published in 1993:

> I believe there are errors [in the Warren Report] including the so-called 'magic bullet .' My ear and my body told me I was not wounded in three places by a bullet that hit President Kennedy. I remain convinced that he was hit twice, and I once by three separate shots. . . . I certainly knew when I was hit, it was virtually impossible . . . for the bullet to exit his neck and go through my back. . . . If that encourages the conspiracy fans, so be it. I can't tailor my memories to fit someone else's diagrams. (102)

In 1998, Nellie Connally continued to reject the single bullet theory. In an Associated Press newspaper article, she argues that ". . . the Warren Commission was wrong about one bullet striking the President and her husband." (103) ". . . I will fight anybody that argues with me. . . . I do know what happened in that car. Fight me if you want to." (104)

Although Governor Connally stated that the Warren Commission was correct in stating that Oswald was the lone assassin, his own statements prove their conclusion to be incorrect . What's more, the following exchange between Commission members and the FBI's Lyndal Shaneyfelt proves that the Commission doubted the plausibility of their own theory:

> *Dulles*. But you would then have the problem you would think if Connally had been hit at the same time [he] would have reacted in the same way, and not reacted much later as these pictures show.
> *Shaneyfelt*. That is right.
> *Dulles*. Because the wounds have been inflicted.
> *McCloy*. That is what puzzles me.
> *Dulles*. That is what puzzles me. . . . (105)
> *McCloy*. This bullet business leaves me confused.
> *Warren*. It's totally inconclusive. (106)

Gerald Posner, the author of *Case Closed* (who argues that Oswald was the lone assassin), writes, "We can look at the Zapruder film, and with new enhancements and new technology, that film can answer exactly what took place on November 22nd." (107) New technology and new enhancements aside, very few photographic experts and researchers agree that the Zapruder film can tell anyone exactly what took place on November 22, 1963.

During a September 18, 1964 conversation with President Johnson, Senator Richard Russell stated, "I'm just worn out, fighting over the damned report. . . . They're trying to prove that the same bullet that hit Kennedy—hit Connally. Well, I don't believe it." (108) Senator John Sherman Cooper and Representative Hale Boggs also disagreed with the single bullet theory and joined Russell in dissent. Boggs had "strong doubts" and Cooper told author Anthony Summers in 1978, he was "unconvinced." (109)

Other evidence questioning the single bullet theory must also be considered. Dr. James Humes, the lead autopsy surgeon, had determined that the wound in the back did not even penetrate President Kennedy's body, therefore making it impossible to have exited the President's throat. Humes stated, ". . . probing determined that the distance traveled by the missile was a short distance inasmuch as the end of the opening could be felt with the finger." (110) Humes statement is corroborated by FBI agent Francis O'Neil who was present at the autopsy. O'Neil stated, ". . . absolutely no point of exit [back wound] . . . [the doctors] were totally befuddled." (111) This view is corroborated by Secret Service agent William Greer who was the driver of the Presidential limousine:

> *Specter.* Was anything said about any channel being present in the body for the bullet to have gone on through the back?
> *Greer.* No sir: I haven't heard anything like that, any trace of it going on through. (112)

J. Edgar Hoover argued that the autopsy doctor and the (James) Sibert and O'Neil Report were wrong. ". . . [T]he examining physicians' early observation that the bullet penetrated only a short distance into the President's back was probably in error." (113) Members of the Warren Commission had their own doubts that the bullet that supposedly entered the President's back had gone on to exit his throat. The following exchange makes this point clear:

> *Rankin.* There is a great range of material in regard to the wounds, and the autopsy and this point of exit or entrance of the bullet in front of the neck, and that all has to be developed much more than we have at the present time. We have an explanation there in the autopsy that probably a fragment came out the front of the neck, but with the elevation the shot must have come from, and the angle, it seems quite apparent

now, since we have the picture of where the bullet entered in the back, that the bullet entered below the shoulder blade to the right of the backbone, which is below the place where the picture shows the bullet came out in the neckband of the shirt in front, and the bullet, according to the autopsy, didn't strike any bone at all, that particular bullet, and go through -
Boggs. I thought I read that bullet just went in a finger's length -
Rankin. That is what they first said. They reached in and they could feel where it came, it didn't go further than that . . . and then they proceeded to reconstruct where they thought the bullet went, the path of it, and which is [why] we have to go into considerable items and try to find out how they could reconstruct that when they first said that they couldn't even feel the path beyond the first part of a finger. And then how it could become elevated; even so it raised rather than coming out at a sharp angle that it entered, all of that, we have to go into, too, and we are asking for help from the ballistics experts on that. We will have to probably get help from the doctors about it, and find out, we have asked for the original notes of the autopsy on that question, too. (114)

Dr. Joseph Dolce, the Warren Commission's ballistics expert, stated that this theory was impossible and Dr. Humes is now on record as admitting he destroyed his original autopsy notes. Here again, the true concerns of the members of the Warren Commission, as well as the testimony of those who were there and were experts in the field, were wrong and/or mistaken. The conclusion of J. Edgar Hoover on November 22 that Lee Oswald was the lone assassin, would not be challenged despite the obvious contradictions. But if the single bullet theory is wrong, then even the Warren Commission conceded there had to be another assassin.

Further documentation that evidence and testimony was altered or allowed to disappear, is made clear by the handling of certain photos and films taken during the assassination.

Tom Howard became the first lawyer for Jack Ruby after his murder of Lee Oswald. Howard reportedly had a copy of a photograph that showed President Kennedy at the exact moment he was shot. If this photograph exists it has never been seen by the public. The presence of this photograph is indicated by the Warren Commission testimony of Ruby's sister, Mrs. Eva Grant:

Mrs. Grant: . . .Tom Howard is trying to sell a picture of the late President Kennedy being shot and half his skull is in the

air, to Life magazine. . . and Earl [Ruby] told me to get ahold
of the Secret Service, they came out to see me . . . and we went
in the alley because I don't know if my place is bugged or not,
and the Secret Service stepped in to either squash the sale of
this particular picture or got ahold of it—the films and
everything. . .
Q. Did you ever find out whether it was true that Mr. Howard
was doing this?
Mrs. Grant: Well, since then I heard it was true. (115)

Troubling accusations that the famous Zapruder film has
been altered have been brought forward and appear to be
credible. William Greer, the driver of the Presidential
limousine, told the Warren Commission that he accelerated
after the first shot, yet Dealy Plaza witness Orrville Nix's film
clearly shows the brake lights on at the rear of the
Presidential limousine. (116) What emerges as very puzzling
and perplexing, is that the famous Zapruder film does not
show the Presidential limousine pulling to the left or coming
to a stop. Yet motorcycle policemen Howard Freeman and
Steve Ellis and over 40 witnesses believed that the limousine
had come to a halt or slowed down in front of the knoll. (117)
Could over forty witnesses be wrong?

Can one dare say that the obvious splices in the film and a
white blob on the right side of President Kennedy's head,
apparent to the naked eye when viewing the Zapruder film,
are evidence of alteration? (118) Dr. James Fetzer has
compiled an impressive list of irregularities involving people
and fixed objects in the background of the Zapruder film.
Other films and still photos, as well as consistent witness
testimony, strongly indicate that the current version of the
Zapruder film does not accurately reflect the actual events
that transpired in Dealy Plaza on November 22, 1963 (119)
What's more, when viewing the current version of the film it
appears to alternate between different zoom settings which
should not happen if the camera was set on maximum zoom
lens as Zapruder maintained. In an FBI report dated
December 4, 1963, Abraham Zapruder stated his camera ". . .
was set, manually, on maximum zoom-lens. . . . The control
buttons for the zoom lens was not touched once he started
taking photographs of the Presidential motorcade." (120)

Possible alteration has long been a point of conjecture by
assassination researchers. There were early clues from J.
Edgar Hoover that this disturbing proposition was possible.

Hoover acknowledged in a letter, dated December 14, 1965, that there was an initial "printing error" that resulted in two frames being misnumbered. (121) These two frames are frames 314 and 315, and ironically, the same frames that now show (in all the available commercial versions of the film) a white blob appearing at the exact moment of the fatal head shot. (122) Coincidence? Maybe and maybe not. The day after the assassination, a small group of reporters were shown "the film" at Abraham Zapruder's office. Dan Rather is quoted as saying, ". . . the third shot hit the President, and his head went forward." (123) A different version of the Zapruder film appears to have been viewed and is corroborated in a 12/6/63 *Life* magazine article written by Paul Mandell in which he states, ". . .the 8mm film shows the President turning his body far around to the right as he waves to someone in the crowd. His throat is exposed -- towards the sniper's nest--just before he clutches it." Further support that a totally different version of the film was viewed by others is indicated in a letter written by autopsy doctor Dr. Pierre Finck. Dr. Finck wrote to his superior officer, Brigadier General J. M. Blumberg, on February 1, 1965 and reported:

> On 16 March 1964, I also had the opportunity to examine color prints approximately 10 x 20 cm, stamped, "U.S. Secret Service, Washington D.C." on the back and made from the only color film taken at the time of the assassination of Kennedy. . . . [These] clearly show how Kennedy slumped forward from a sitting position. . . . This sequence of photographs is compatible with a bullet hitting Kennedy in the back and with another bullet hitting him in the head, both from behind. (124)

These actions of the President turning around in the seat and facing the Depository as well as his head going forward, are clearly not seen in any versions of the film available today, including the newly enhanced Zapruder film that can be bought or rented at any video store in America.

Further evidence of missing films and photos has been documented by other witnesses at the scene of the assassination. Mary Moorman told the FBI that one of the Polaroid photographs she had taken during the assassination showed the Book Depository building and the sixth floor window. (125) Deputy Sheriff John Wiseman stated in a report that he took the picture from her and agreed that the photograph did show the Book Depository building. (126) Wiseman's report of seeing the Book Depository in the picture was also supported by two deputy sheriffs who also saw the picture. (127) These accounts have been further corroborated by documents supplied to the Warren Commission from the FBI and the Dallas Sheriff's Department:

> She took this photograph with a Polaroid camera, and the photograph showed the police motorcycle escort preceding the President's car. In the background of this photograph she said, the Texas School Book Depository building was visable *[sic]*. (128) . . . Mrs. Moorman had taken a picture of the lead motorcycle officer. In the background of this picture was a picture of the Sexton Building [Book Depository Building] and the window where the gunman sat when doing the shooting. I took this picture to Chief Criminal Deputy Sheriff Allan Sweatt, who later turned it over to Secret Service Officer Patterson. (129)

Unfortunately, since Moorman's picture was taken from a Polaroid camera, there was no negative available and this picture has disappeared.

This documented evidence of a photograph showing the sixth floor window of the Book Depository during the shooting would surely have been conclusive proof of Lee Oswald's guilt or innocence. The fact that the picture had at one time existed is beyond question, the added fact that it has disappeared supports the view that it did not show Oswald at the window. The reason being, is that there is now consistent and documented evidence of too many missing and altered films and assassination-related evidence manipulated, to pass this off as another in the series of mistakes or coincidences.

Adding to the controversy regarding Mary Moorman's missing Polaroid photographs is that Moorman and her friend Jean Hill reported that she took four or five pictures, and apparently only one remains. (130) Jean Hill stated that as Mary Moorman was taking pictures of the motorcade as it traveled down Elm Street, Moorman had asked her to grab the pictures as they came out of the camera and place them in her coat pocket. Hill reported that after the assassination she ran across Elm Street, up the knoll in the direction of the fence where she believed the shots had originated. Before she reached the parking lot she was stopped by an "unidentified plain clothesman" of some sort. This plain clothesman took the pictures from her and they have apparently disappeared.

(131)

Gordon Arnold was filming the motorcade from behind the concrete wall just to the right of Abraham Zapruder and just in front of the picket fence. Immediately after the last shot (which he believed came from behind him), a policeman with a gun in hand came from behind him, apparently from behind the fence and demanded his film. Arnold stated, "the man asked me if I was taking a picture—and I told him I was . . . I gave it [the film] to him." (132) This film has also apparently disappeared and has never officially been accounted for.

Researcher Harold Weisburg determined:

> Films taken by George Phoenix and Thomas Alyea were furnished the Federal Bureau of Investigation. These films are not in the National Archives. There are no copies of records relating to pictures taken by Ron Reiland filed under his name; pictures taken by him are not in the National Archives. (133)

As previously mentioned, the film that was "shot by Beverly Oliver" across the street from the grassy knoll, has never been accounted for. Oliver stated that her film was taken for development by the FBI but was never returned and has not been publicly acknowledged by the FBI. (134) Yet numerous films and photos document that someone was filming the assassination from that location. Oliver has filed suit against the FBI for the return of her film, to no avail.

Witness Norman Similas, from Willow Dale Ontario, a suburb of Toronto, reported that he took photographs that showed the Book Depository Building during the shooting and that the pictures had subsequently disappeared. (135) Evidently somewhere between the Toronto newspaper, the *Telegram;* a Canadian magazine, *Liberty;* and J. Edgar Hoover, the negatives disappeared. (136) Hoover's involvement in this matter is indicated in an October 14 letter to J. Lee Rankin:

> I am enclosing two copies of the galley proofs for the second installment of the article furnished by you which was to appear in the August, 1964 issue of *Liberty* magazine. The galley proofs were obtained by the Royal Canadian Mounted Police and furnished to our representative in Canada on October 1, 1964. According to the Royal Canadian Mounted Police, *Liberty* magazine is no longer in business and so, unfortunately are the photographs. (137)

According to a March 11, 1964 letter from J. Lee Rankin to J. Edgar Hoover, a "newsreel film and video tape had been furnished by Mr. Eddie Barker to agents of our Bureau." (138) Apparently, there is no record that this film exists today. Dealy Plaza witness Orrville Nix stated in an interview with Mark Lane that when the FBI returned his photos to him, "frames were missing . . . here and there." The complete set of photos and films were not returned to him. (139)

One member of the Warren Commission staff, Alfred Goldberg, understood the potential importance of what the films and tapes could indicate in regards to documenting what really happened in Dallas on November 22. On May 25, 1964, Goldberg stated:

> The television tapes and films of the events in Dallas on November 22-24 are remarkable and unique documents. They are at least as important a part of the fundamental record of the events, as are the statements taken by the FBI, the hearings of the Commission, and the depositions taken by the staff. Indeed, they probably represent the most primary source for much that happened during the two days. It is the responsibility of the Commission to ensure that these tapes and films are preserved in the Archives as a part of the permanent record. (140)

But as the evidence presented here contends, not only was the preservation of the photos and films not given a priority, rather many were most probably suppressed and/or destroyed.

The evidence presented here should cause one to consider who was ultimately responsible for the altering of evidence and testimony, the intimidation of witnesses, as well as the disappearance of evidence. As stated in the beginning of this chapter, J. Edgar Hoover began to seize the evidence at the scene on the afternoon of the assassination. Ultimately, he must be held accountable for how the FBI investigation was carried out and how the evidence was handled.

Chapter 10

Hoover and Johnson: Obstruction of Justice

What was J. Edgar Hoover's true role in his investigation for the Warren Commission? We will most probably never know for sure but there can be little doubt that he and Lyndon Johnson obstructed justice in not searching for the truth in the murder of John Kennedy.

Lyndon Johnson and J. Edgar Hoover both attempted to stop Congress from mounting investigations of the assassination that were beginning to move forward. But along with LBJ's intimate, lawyer, and "Mr. Fix-it" Abe Fortas, they formulated a plan to have the Warren Commission "evaluate" a report of the assassination compiled by Hoover's FBI. Early on Friday afternoon, November 29, Johnson discussed the formation of the Warren Commission with his longtime confidante, Fortas, who had helped him through his Senate election controversy in 1948. A *New York Times* article from December 3, 1963 briefly describes their relationship:

> Abe Fortas, the Washington lawyer who has been representing (Bobby) Baker is withdrawing as counsel because of the advisory role he is playing in the Johnson Administration. Mr. Fortas is an old friend of . . . Johnson's . . . . He has been not only a friend but also a lawyer to Mr. Johnson in the past.

It is interesting to note that Edward Bennett Williams, who has represented Joe McCarthy, Jimmy Hoffa, and Frank Costello, replaced Fortas as Baker's attorney. Jimmy Hoffa was perceived as a threat to murder John and/or Robert Kennedy by Federal Agent Hawk Daniels. Daniel's, in 1962, had overheard a tape recording of Hoffa discussing these murder plots:

> *Daniels.* I learned in 1962 that Mr. Partin had been entrusted with the mission of securing plastic explosives to be used in either blowing up Mr. Bobby Kennedy, then the United States Attorney General, in his automobile or in his house.
> *Q.* Did you learn anything to back that up from your own personal experience?
> *Daniels.* Yes. There were two telephone calls monitored by me. . . . Mr. Partin discussed, as briefly as possible, being cut off by Mr. Hoffa, that he had obtained the plastic explosive that Mr. Hoffa had been seeking.
> *Q.* Do you consider that Mr. Hoffa's hatred or motive for murder was directed to the Kennedys in general?
> *Daniels.* Yes, I do.
> *Q.* And could this have also been directed against the President?
> *Daniels.* Yes, I believe that.
> *Q.* Were there close links between Hoffa and organized crime?
> *Daniels.* Those who are purportedly members of organized crime, such as Mr. Carlos Marcello of New Orleans—was closely linked to Mr. Hoffa—according to what Mr. Hoffa told me in 1964.
> *Q.* Was he [Hoffa] capable of carrying out his threats?
> *Daniels.* I think that he fully intended to carry the threats out. I really think that he had the capability. But was a question of how and when not a question of whether he had doubts as to the necessity of eliminating—at least Mr. Bobby Kennedy.
> *Q.* And possibly his brother also?
> Daniels. And possibly his brother also. (1)

Ben Bradlee of the *Washington Post* and a personal friend of the President, recalled that President Kennedy had told him that Hoffa's men had hired "some hoodlum" who was to use a silencer and come to Washington to murder Bobby Kennedy. "I found this hard to believe, but the President was obviously serious." (2) Kennedy aide Richard Goodwin added further corroboration to the belief that Hoffa and/or organized crime were viable suspects in the murder of Robert and/or

President Kennedy when he stated that Robert Kennedy told him "That if anybody else was involved it was organized crime." (3)

It is interesting to note that Hoffa related to Edwin Partin, "The ideal set-up would be to catch him somewhere in the South where it would look like some of the segregation people had done it." (4) This plan sounds similar to what eventually takes place in Dallas; only Lee Oswald and the communists replaced the segregationists.

Frank Costello was well known as a leader of organized crime while McCarthy was a notorious inquisitor of suspected and falsely accused domestic communists. J. Edgar Hoover's close relationship with Joseph McCarthy's anti-communist witch-hunt has been well documented earlier in this book as has Hoover's indifference to the existence of organized crime. These connections are very interesting and provide a web of relationships that can be perceived as powerful as well as of a possible questionable nature when viewed in light of Lyndon Johnson's and J. Edgar Hoover's subsequent obstruction of justice.

Johnson stated that he would like to have Senators Richard Russell and Sherman Cooper as well as Representatives Gerald Ford and Hale Boggs serve on the Commission. Fortas went on to facilitate the process of seeing that these and other tasks were accomplished for Johnson. Johnson stated to Fortas that anyone who dissented to serving on the Commission should be ordered to serve. "I think we ought to order them to do it and let them bellyache." (5)

The problem becomes clear when one considers that the conclusion to Hoover's FBI investigation had already been arrived at before the Warren Commission had its first meeting. According to J. Edgar Hoover's own notes, on Friday afternoon, November 22, at 4:01, he called Robert Kennedy and "told him I thought we had the man who killed the President down in Dallas at the present time." (6) A UPI wire story on November 25, 1963 reported, "FBI Director J. Edgar Hoover said today all available information indicates that Lee Harvey Oswald acted alone in the assassination of President John F. Kennedy."

Assistant FBI Director William Sullivan stated in a memo on November 26 to Hoover, "we must recognize that a matter of this magnitude cannot be fully investigated in a week's time." An obviously impatient Hoover replied, "Just how long do you estimate it will take. It seems to me we have the basic facts now." (7) Hoover continued to press for a quick resolution to the investigation as evidenced further by this quote on December 3, 1963, from the UPI wire: "An exhaustive FBI report now nearly ready for the White House will indicate that Lee Harvey Oswald was the lone and unaided assassin of President Kennedy."

The following conclusions reached by the House Select Committee indicate further Hoover's intentions to not fully investigate the assassination:

> It must be said that the FBI generally exhausted its resources in confirming the case against Lee Harvey Oswald as the lone assassin, a case that Director J. Edgar Hoover, at least, seemed determined to make within 24 hours of the assassination. . . . The Federal Bureau of Investigation failed to investigate adequately the possibility of a conspiracy to assassinate the President. . . . Rather than addressing its investigation to all significant circumstances, including all possibilities of conspiracy, the FBI investigation focused narrowly on Lee Harvey Oswald. (8)

It is also clear that Lyndon Johnson initially wanted to have the Warren Commission review Hoover's report of the assassination and to conclude its work in a few weeks, but Johnson had to settle for late September, less than two months in advance of the Presidential election. The House Select Committee determined that:

> President Johnson, among others in his administration, was anxious to have the investigation completed in advance of the 1964 Presidential conventions, out of concern that the assassination could become a political issue. The Committee made the judgment that the time pressures under which the Warren Commission investigation was conducted served to compromise the work product and the conclusions of the Commission. (9)

Johnson's quest to win the presidency on his own with no distractions was now quite apparent. He, along with Hoover, had now become without question, obstructors of justice. The question of why, remains open to debate.

A fresh look at how the Warren Commission was formed, how Hoover and the FBI became the sole investigative agency for the Commission, and most importantly, an examination of consistent eyewitness testimony that does not match the findings of the Warren Commission is needed. Even more compelling are the statements of the members of the Warren Commission and members of their staff and their doubts about the investigation run by J. Edgar Hoover and his FBI. The members of the Warren Commission were obviously fearful to question and publicly doubt Hoover.

The Church Committee report stated:

> After the Warren Commission had been established, each time Hoover received word that a particular person was being considered for the commission staff, he asked,". . . what the Bureau had on the individual." . . . On October 2, 1964, one week after the report was issued, the Director was informed that Bureau files contained derogatory information concerning the following individuals and their relatives [names deleted]. (10)

On January 21, 1975, in an article published in the Washington Post, reporter Ron Kessler wrote:

> The son of the late House Majority Leader Hale Boggs has told the Post that the FBI leaked to his father damaging material on the critics of its investigation into John F. Kennedy's assassination . . . in an apparent attempt to discredit the critics of the Warren Commission . . . includes photographs of sexual activity and reports on alleged communist affiliations of some authors of articles and books on the assassination.

The tactics and methods of J. Edgar Hoover to smear opponents with charges of communist tendencies and private indiscretions were still alive and well after five decades. It also becomes obvious that the Commission doubted the conclusions that they were "unanimously" agreeing to.

On January 19, 1970, in an article published in the Washington Post, Senator Russell finally ended his official silence relating to his doubts about the findings of the Warren Commission. "He now believes that there was a criminal conspiracy behind President Kennedy's murder." Long-time defenders of the Warren Commissioner's findings, such as Gerald Ford, Arlen Specter, and David Belin, have yet to address Russell's accusations in an objective public forum.

Chief Justice Warren explained to Staff Counsel Melvin Eisenberg how President Johnson convinced him to serve on the Commission:

> The President stated that rumors of the most exaggerated kind were circulating in this country and overseas. . . . Some rumors went as far as attributing the assassination to a faction within the government wishing the Presidency assumed by President Johnson. Others, if not quenched, could conceivably lead the country into a war which could cost 40 million lives. No one could refuse to do something which might help prevent such a possibility. He placed emphasis on the quenching of rumors, and precluding further speculation. (11)

Chief Justice Earl Warren also described to author William Manchester how Lyndon Johnson convinced him to serve on the President's Commission:

> . . . the President told me how serious the situation was. He said there had been wild rumors and that there was the international situation to think of. . . . He said that if the public became aroused against Castro and Khrushchev there might be war. "You've been in uniform before," he said, "and if I asked you, you would put on the uniform again for your country." I said, " Of course." "This is much more important than that," he said. "If you're putting it like that, I can't say no," I said. (12)

Following a phone call from Johnson on Sunday afternoon, November 24, after the murder of Oswald, Hoover wrote a memo indicating that he really did believe that there was a conspiracy of some sort. But instead of pursuing this he chose to cut off speculation about a conspiracy and implicated Oswald as the lone killer:

> [Chief] Curry I understand cannot control Captain Fritz [Dallas Homicide Chief] . . . who is giving much information to the press. Since we now think that it involves the Criminal Code on a conspiracy charge under Section 2-11, we want them to shut up. . . . The thing I am most concerned about, and so is Mr. Katzenbach, is having something issued so we can convince the public that Oswald is the real assassin. (13)

Following a discussion between Hoover and Nicholas Katzenbach, who had temporarily replaced the grief-stricken Robert Kennedy after the assassination as Acting Attorney General, Katzenbach subsequently related Hoover's instructions to Bill Moyers, assistant to President Johnson:

> The public must be satisfied that Oswald was the assassin; that he did not have confederates who are still at large; and the evidence was such that he would be convicted at a trial. Speculation about Oswald's motivation ought to be cut off, and we should have some basis for rebutting the thought that this was a communist conspiracy or a right wing conspiracy to blame it on the communists. (14)

Years later, Katzenbach attempted to rationalize this statement after a question from CBS News Anchor Dan Rather:

> *Rather.* What was your biggest mistake?
> *Katzenbach.* I certainly wrote a memo to the President -- to Bill Moyers, I guess which is not as artfully worded as I would like it to be . . . . What I meant was that if you don't put out all of the facts out and they don't have all of the facts and there are some facts concealed, you are never going to get them to get rid of—to believe that Oswald did this all alone, even if that is your conclusion. (15)

This answer does not mention or explain Katzenbach's previous discussion with J. Edgar Hoover—nor does it attempt to clearly explain an obvious attempt to not consider anyone besides Oswald as the assassin.

It appears that there was an initial concern of the possibility of a communist conspiracy or, as we have seen, a more likely attempt to blame the assassination on a communist. If at some future point there is even more documented proof of a conspiracy, then this statement must be dealt with by re-evaluating J. Edgar Hoover in even more of a questionable and possibly sinister role.

The Warren Commission (as we now know) had documented evidence of at least three plots to kill President Kennedy and then place the blame on a communist. The first of these two plots involved Army cryptographer (codebreaker) Eugene Dinkin who was stationed in Europe in 1963. He had somehow become aware of a plot to kill President Kennedy two months before the assassination, which he believed "was set in motion by high ranking members of the military" and consisted of throwing the blame onto "radical left-wing" or "communist" suspects. He was eventually placed in "detention" for leaving his post and warning that President

Kennedy would be killed. Dinkin was subsequently sent to Walter Reed Army Hospital for "psychiatric evaluations." (16)

A second plot involved Richard Nagell who was a former highly decorated Korean war hero who had also worked for the CIA as a double-agent in the war against Communism. On September 20, 1963, he walked into an El Paso, Texas bank and fired a pistol into the ceiling and then walked outside and sat in his car waiting to be arrested. Subsequent documents made available to the Warren Commission state that his purpose in being arrested was to avoid becoming involved in an impending plot to kill President Kennedy. Nagell's case came before United States District Court Judge Homer Thornberry, who had just recently been appointed to his position by his longtime friend, President Lyndon Johnson. Nagell stated that he was an "accused communist" who had been trapped into a plot formulated by "domestic forces" to kill the President. Nagell further stated that his warnings to J. Edgar Hoover and other government officials had been ignored and being arrested and placed in custody was his only way out. Judge Thornberry sentenced Nagell to ten years and "psychiatric evaluations" despite the statements of the arresting officer that Nagell had no intention of robbing the bank. (17) Dick Russell wrote:

> the intent of the conspirators, according to Nagell, was to pin the blame [for the assassination of the President] on Castro's Cuba and spark an invasion of the Island. . . he has indicated to me in the past that if he was ever subpoenaed by a government agency, he would be willing to testify. (18)

The Final Report of the Assassination Records and Review Board described its attempt to contact Nagell in 1995:

> The Assassination Record Review Board (ARRB) sent a letter to Nagell dated October 31, 1995, requesting that Nagell contact the Review Board's Executive Director to discuss any assassination records he might have in his possession. Subsequently, the Review Board was informed that Nagell had been found dead in his Los Angeles apartment the day after the ARRB's letter was mailed. (The coroner ruled that he died as a result of natural causes.) (19)

Another plot involved right-wing extremist Joseph Milteer, who was caught on tape predicting the assassination almost two weeks before it occurred and also stated that "they would pick someone up within 24 hours to throw the public off." (20) Milteer stated to an informant after the assassination, "The patriots have outsmarted the Communist group in order that the Communists would carry out the plan without the right-wing becoming involved." (21) Yet, immediately after Lee Oswald's murder and the subsequent FBI investigation, Hoover did not pursue these extremely troubling leads. In fact, Hoover and the Secret Service ordered Milteer released despite having possession of the pre-assassination prediction on tape. (22) The fascinating, yet troubling connections of Joseph Milteer might very well explain the disturbing links between factions of organized crime, the military, and right-wing extremists in the assassination. These and other leads will be considered in depth in the Conclusion of this book with a special emphasis on the information gathered in regards to the associations of Joseph Milteer.

The following are examples of Lyndon Johnson's successful attempts at manipulation in order to gain control of the investigation and to allow Hoover's report to be evaluated solely by the Warren Commission. On November 28, 1963, this telephone conversation between the President and Senator James Eastland took place:

> *LBJ.* Jim. . . on this investigation . . . this Dallas thing . . . what does your Committee plan to do on it? I didn't ask you that and I intended to and had it on my mind and I got to talking and didn't do it.
> *JE.* Well . . we plan to hold hearings and just make a record of what the proof is . . that is all. . . .
> *LBJ.* I. . .have the feeling. . .I don't know that I would. .but we've got pretty strong states' rights question here and I've had some hesitancy to have a bunch of Congressional inquiries. . and it might. . . . And, my thought would be this, if we could do it. We might get two members from each body . . . you see we're going to have three inquiries as it is . .
> *JE.* Well, I wouldn't want that. . that wouldn't do. .
> *LBJ.* Well, if it is all right with you. . . I'm not worried about your Committee. . .I know what you can handle. . .
> *JE.* Well, we can work it out. . .
> *LBJ.* You can handle your Committee. . OK. Much obliged. (23)

Lyndon Johnson's original plans to leave the investigation in the hands of a Texas inquiry was thwarted by a congressional push to sort out the early "rumors" and conflicting press reports. Johnson used the sensitive "states rights" issue with a fellow southern Senator in a successful attempt to gain Eastland's cooperation in limiting the inquiry. Evidently Johnson's argument involving "states rights" turns on congressional inquiries intruding into the local Texas (and southern) inquiry which Johnson originally wanted. The end result being, that any form of objective and open public forum is snuffed out by Johnson's creation of the Warren Commission and J. Edgar Hoover's judgment of Lee Oswald as the lone communist assassin. Similar examples but much more difficult manipulation takes place in the following series of phone conversations on November 29, 1963, at 4:05 p.m. and 8:55 p.m. between the President and Senator Richard Russell:

> *LBJ.* . . . it concerns Hoover and Secretary of State and some others. We're trying to avoid all the House Committee, Hale Boggs and a bunch has got some things started over there and Jim Eastland and Ev Dirksen and a bunch has got them started in the Senate. . .and Bobby Kennedy has got his ideas. .Hoover has got his report. . . on about a 7 man board to evaluate Hoover's report and it would be largely done by staff. . but they can work on it. . and I want to get your reaction to it. I think it would be better than the Judiciary running one investigation, the House running another investigation. . and having four or five going the opposite direction.
> *RR.* I agree with that. . but I don't think that Hoover ought to make his report too soon. .
> *LBJ.* He's ready with it now and he wants to get it off just as quick as he can. . .And he'll probably have it out today. At most, on Monday.
> *RR:* Oh-oh.
> *LBJ:* He's going to turn it over to this group and there's some things about it I can't talk about. . .I'm going to try you and Senator Cooper from the Senate.
> *RR:* Oh, no, no. get somebody else now. (24)

Johnson attempts to get Russell to agree with the concept of a commission by playing to Russell's concerns of too many congressional investigations. He even attempts to bring an investigation of the assassination by Robert Kennedy into the picture. It is unclear where this information came from or whether it is true or not. No documentation substantiating the idea that Robert Kennedy was ever promoting public hearings into his brother's death has been brought forward.

In effect, Johnson is convincing Russell to evaluate Hoover's report in private without public hearings and accountability.

8:55 P. M., November 29, (selected excerpts from the conversation between Lyndon Johnson and Senator Russell):

LBJ: I hate to bother you again but I wanted you to know that I made an announcement.

RR: Announcement of what?

LBJ: Of this special commission.

RR: Now, Mr. President, I don't have to tell you of my devotion to you but I just can't serve on that commission.

LBJ: Dick, it has already been announced. And you can serve with anybody for the good of America. And this is a question that has a good many more ramifications than on the surface. And we've got to take this out of the arena where they're testifying that Khrushchev and Castro did this and did that and kicking us into a war that can kill forty million Americans in an hour. And you would put your uniform on in a minute.

LBJ: Your future is your country and your going to do everything you can to serve America.

RR: I just can't do it. I haven't got the time.

LBJ: All right, we'll just make the time. There's not going to be any time, to begin with. All you're going to do is evaluate the Hoover report he has already made.

RR: You're taking advantage of me, . . .

LBJ: No, no, no . . . I'm going to take a hell of a lot of advantage of you, my friend because you made me and I know it and I don't ever forget. And I'll be taking advantage of you a good deal. But you're going to serve your country and do what is right. . . .

RR: I'm at your command and I'll do anything you want me to do.

LBJ: You damned sure going to be at my command! You're going to be at my command as long as I'm here.

RR: If you hadn't announced it, I would absolutely be . . .

LBJ: No you wouldn't. No you wouldn't.

RR: Yes I would. Yes I would.

LBJ: Warren told me he wouldn't do it under any circumstances. . . . And I said, Let me read you one report. And I just picked up one report and read it to him, and I said, okay forty million Americans involved here. . . . he came down here and told me no . . . twice. And I just pulled out what Hoover told me about a little incident in Mexico City and I said, now I don't want Mr. Khrushchev to be told tomorrow . . . and be testifying before a camera that he killed this fellow and that Castro killed him and all I want you to do is look at

the facts and bring in any other facts you want in here and
determine who killed the President. (25)

What Johnson did not tell Russell was that he and J. Edgar
Hoover were already aware that an impostor had been to
Mexico City impersonating Lee Oswald and that the
communists were most probably not involved at all. In fact,
he led Chief Justice Warren and Senator Russell to believe
the opposite to be true so as to convince them to serve on the
President's Commission. What's more, Johnson insinuated
that the Commission's job could involve "bringing in other
facts" and help "determine who killed the President" despite
knowing and encouraging Hoover to have his report and
findings already completed before the Commission even met.
Even more questionable is Johnson's continued threats of the
possibility of nuclear war even though he was aware that
there was little or no credence to support this argument.

Admiral Taswell Shepard related to author Noel Twyman
that there was never any crisis or threat of war of any kind,
nuclear or conventional, on November 22, 1963. (26) Shepard
was in charge of the "black box" for President Kennedy that
controlled the release of nuclear missiles, he was surely in a
position to know if the events surrounding the assassination
of President Kennedy had created a climate of crisis.

J. Edgar Hoover, John McCone, and Richard Helms had
already made clear to Johnson in conversations previously
mentioned, that the communists were not involved. Other
forces, including Thomas Mann, Ray Rocca, and James
Angleton continued to hint of communist involvement and
Johnson continues to "buy into" this theory. But J. Edgar
Hoover was content to brand Oswald as a lone killer who had
become twisted and perverted by communist thought and
indoctrination. In response to a question from Commission
member Hale Boggs, Hoover replied, "My speculation, Mr.
Boggs, is that this man was no doubt a dedicated communist.
. . . I personally believe it was . . . the twisted mentality the
man had." (27)

After a discussion with President Johnson on November 29,
Hoover wrote this memo:

> The President stated he wanted to get by with just my file and
> my report. I told him I thought it would be very bad to have a
> rash of investigations. He then indicated the only way to stop
> it is to appoint a high-level committee to evaluate my report

and tell the House and Senate to not go ahead with the investigation. (28)

There can be no doubt that LBJ and Hoover succeeded in limiting the inquiry and keeping the investigation under their control. Seven days after the assassination, President Johnson signed Executive Order 11130 creating the Commission. In the words of the Warren Report itself:

Theories and speculations mounted regarding the assassination. In many instances, the intense public demand for facts were met by partial and frequently conflicting reports from Dallas and elsewhere. After Oswald's arrest and his denial of all guilt, public attention focused both on the extent of the evidence against him and possibility of a conspiracy, domestic or foreign. His subsequent death heightened public interest and stimulated additional suspicions and rumors. After Lee Harvey Oswald was shot by Jack Ruby, it was no longer possible to arrive at the complete story of the assassination through normal judicial procedures during a trial of the alleged assassin. As speculation about the existence of a foreign or domestic conspiracy became widespread, committees in both Houses of Congress weighed the desirability of congressional hearings to discover all the facts relating to the assassination. President Johnson [and J. Edgar Hoover] sought to avoid parallel investigations [as the state of Texas and both houses of Congress were preparing to do] and to concentrate fact-finding in a body having the broadest national mandate.(29)

One week after the assassination, *Dallas Morning News* reporter Robert E. Baskin wrote: "Creation of the presidential commission appeared certain to head off several congressional inquiries into the slaying of President Kennedy in Dallas a week ago." (30)

Lyndon Johnson met with Texas Attorney General Waggoner Carr on November 24, just after the death of Oswald. Johnson's discussion with Carr made clear who would be in charge of the investigation, as this press report from November 27 indicates:

The White House approved the decision that the FBI take charge of all evidence which officers assembled in their investigation of the murder of President Kennedy. . . . Police Chief Jesse Curry announced . . . that his office would turn over its evidence to the FBI. This would place it beyond the

reach of Attorney General Waggoner Carr, who had
announced plans to convene a court of inquiry. (31)

The state of Texas had made clear its intention to conduct an
independent inquiry into the assassination. (32) A little over
a week later, on December 6, Carr met with J. Edgar Hoover
in Washington. Evidently Carr experienced a sudden change
of heart in regards to a Texas inquiry into the assassination
after meeting with Hoover. The *New York Times* stated on
December 7, "Texas Attorney General . . . Carr announced
today the indefinite postponement of a state inquiry into the
assassination." Carr explained his change of heart by stating
in the same article, "The files and the evidence . . . are in the
hands of the FBI for its use. A public inquiry in Texas at this
time might be more harmful than helpful."

As a result of these successful efforts to limit the
investigation of Kennedy's death, Johnson and Hoover were
able to control the findings of the Warren Commission. At the
Commission's first executive session, it becomes clear that the
first priority of the Commission was to dispel rumors and to
dispel the public's suspicions of a conspiracy. Mark North
noted:

> Allen Dulles said that an atmosphere of rumor and suspicion
> interferes with the functioning of the government, especially
> abroad, and one of the main tasks of the Commission was to
> dispel rumors. . . . McCloy said that it was of paramount
> importance to 'show the world, that America is not a banana
> republic where a government can be changed by conspiracy.' .
> . .Cooper said that one of the Commission's most important
> purposes was to 'lift the cloud of doubts that had been cast
> over America institutions'. . . Ford said that dispelling
> damaging rumors was a major concern of the Commission,
> and most members of the Commission agreed. (33)

In September of 1964, the twenty-six volume Warren
Report was delivered by J. Edgar Hoover to President
Johnson. The seven members of the Warren Commission
(Chief Justice Earl Warren, Richard Russell, Hale Boggs,
Gerald Ford, John Cooper, Allen Dulles, and John McCloy)
delivered a "unanimous" verdict that Lee Oswald was the lone
killer of President Kennedy.

Louis Nizer, one of America's most successful lawyers,
wrote this introduction to Doubleday's edition of the Warren
Report:

Will the report's conclusions be accepted by the Public? . . .
The reader who matches the report in dispassionate approach
and objective quest for truth will be overwhelmed by the
exhaustive scientific, and documentary evidence which
support the main theses of the report, I believe that all but a
few will bring to the report minds open to light and therefore
that the report will ultimately receive the widest acceptance.

There will be some who will resist persuasion. . . .They will
persist in theories which exploit rumors and inconsistent
statements made in the early turmoil. . . . They will insist
that the failure to explain everything perfectly taints all that
is explained. They will put the minor factors of the unknown
or unknowable against major revelations. They will not joust
fairly, by offering facts to be tested against facts, but will
utilize a question or a doubt as if it were equivalent to
disproof.

In this sense the report will not end all speculation. But in
the historic sense now that all the facts available have been
queried and justly evaluated, the report will dispose
convincingly of the major questions.

This is the incalculable service rendered by the Commission.
This is its achievement in effectuating domestic tranquility
and overcoming foreign scepticism. This is its contribution to
history. (34)

Despite the "unanimous" verdict, and the views of those like
Louis Nizer, it is most disturbing to analyze the conversations
of the Warren Commission members in regards to Hoover's
part in the investigation:

> *Mr. McCloy.* [T]he time is almost overdue for us to have a
> better perspective of the FBI investigation than we now have.
> . . . We are so dependent on them for our facts. . . .
> *Mr. Rankin (General Counsel).* Part of our difficulty in regard
> to [the investigation] is that they [the FBI] have no problem.
> They have decided that it is Oswald who committed the
> assassination, they have decided that no one else was
> involved, they have decided that -
> *Senator Russell.* They have tried the case and reached a
> verdict on every aspect.
> *Rep. Boggs.* You have put your finger on it. (35)

Boggs and Russell clearly understood that a verdict had been
reached before they had an opportunity to analyze Hoover's
report. Warren Commission Assistant Counsel David
Slawson made clear his scepticism with this statement to the
House Select Committee:

> I understood immediately that part of my assignment would
> be to suspect everyone. So included in that would be . . . FBI.
> . . . We would sometimes speculate as to what would happen if
> we got firm evidence that pointed to some very high official.
> [deleted] Of course that would present a kind of frightening
> prospect because if the President [Johnson] or anyone else
> [Hoover] that high up was indeed involved they clearly were
> not going to allow someone like us to bring out the truth if
> they could stop us. (36)

This statement should disturb anyone who desires an
objective search for the truth; for it substantiates the
argument that J. Edgar Hoover's report could very well be
false and there was nothing the Warren Commission could do
to stop him.

It is important to note that regardless of how the
assassination was actually carried out (and by whom), LBJ
and J. Edgar Hoover both stood to control two of the most
powerful positions in the world as a result of John Kennedy's
death. It is quite likely that Hoover would have been allowed
to "gracefully retire" at the age of 70 in January of 1965 as a
result of the mandatory retirement age provision which the
Kennedy administration had begun to implement as policy.
Lyndon Johnson faced the real possibility of being denied his
opportunity for the presidency if JFK had won re-election in
1964 and if Robert Kennedy or others mounted a challenge to
Johnson in 1968. As John Connally surmised:

> If Kennedy had lived, Lyndon Johnson would have run again
> in the second spot on the ticket, and he would never have
> been elected President. By 1968, his health and age—and the
> diminishing effect of eight years as Vice President—would
> have eliminated him. (37)

Both Lyndon Johnson and J. Edgar Hoover seemed
headed towards the end of the line in terms of maintaining
power, but the assassination of John Kennedy on November
22, 1963 would change that.

Chapter 11

"Those Who Were There
Were Wrong and Confused"

The closed door investigation conducted by Hoover and the FBI would receive the "distinguished" Warren Commission's dubious stamp of approval; "truth was their only client," they said. But what would the verdict have been if J. Edgar Hoover's investigation would have been evaluated in an open forum with an objective jury of peers deciding the case? Read and consider.

The Warren Commission stated:

> The shots that entered the neck and head of the President and wounded Governor Connally came from behind and above. There is no evidence that any shots were fired at the President from anywhere other than the Texas School Book Depository Building. (1)

The preponderance of evidence indicates otherwise as the following accounts from Parkland Hospital doctors and nurses, Secret Service agents, Dallas police and Sheriff's officers, and other witnesses at the scene attest.

Dr. Kemp Clark, Parkland Hospital Chief Neurosurgeon who pronounced Mr. Kennedy dead, said, ". . .one struck him at about the necktie knot, it ranged downward in his chest and did not exit." (2) This immediate conclusion by Dr. Clark totally discounts the Commission's conclusion that the shot hit Kennedy in his upper back and exited his throat.

Dr. Charles Baxter stated, "Looking at that hole, one would have to . . . and my immediate thought was that this was an entry wound because it was so small." (3) Nurse Donna Willie stated, "I saw the entry wound in the front of the President's neck. I know he was shot from the front, and I couldn't understand why that wasn't released." (4) Nurse Margaret Hinchliffe (Hood) stated, ". . . a little hole in the middle of his neck . . . About as big as the end of my little finger . . . An entrance bullet hole . . . it looked to me like . . . I have never seen an exit bullet hole. . . . I don't remember seeing one that looked like that, . . . it was just a small wound and wasn't jagged like most of the exit bullet wounds that I have seen." (5) Assistant Press Secretary Malcolm Kilduff stated during the televised press conference at Parkland Hospital on November 22, announcing the death of President Kennedy, "It is a simple matter, of a bullet right through the head," he then points to his right temple. Question: "Can you say where the bullet entered his head, Mac?" Kilduff: "It is my understanding that it entered in the temple, the right temple. They [the shots] came from the right side." (6) This is corroborated by the wire reports from November 22. "Bulletin: (Dallas) . . . President Kennedy was shot in the right temple. It was a simple matter of a bullet right through the head," said Dr. George Burkley, White House Medical Officer. (7)

Dr. Marion Jenkins, Parkland Hospital chief anesthesiologist stated in 1992, ". . . [he] saw an entry wound on JFK's neck; would let their 1963 observations stand." (8) Dr. Robert McClelland, Parkland Hospital attending surgeon stated, "This [the neck wound] did appear to be an entrance wound. . . . I think he was shot from the front." (9) Dr. Malcolm Perry, Parkland Hospital attending surgeon stated, "There was an entrance wound below his Adam's apple. . . . Mr. Kennedy was hit by a bullet in the throat, below the Adam's apple. . . . this wound had the appearance of a 'bullet entry'. . . . I thought it looked [the neck wound] like an entrance wound because it was so small." (10) Dr. Charles Crenshaw, Parkland Hospital resident surgeon stated, "I also identified a small opening about the diameter of a pencil at the midline of his throat to be an entry bullet hole. There was no doubt in my mind about that wound. . . . [was an] entrance wound in the throat." (11) Dr. Paul Peters, Parkland Hospital urologist stated, ". . . we saw the wound of entry in the throat." (12) Dr. Ronald Jones, Parkland Hospital Chief resident surgeon stated, "The hole [in the throat] was very small and relatively clean cut, as you would see in a bullet that is entering rather than exiting from a patient. (13) Jones stated in an interview, in 1983, with author David Lifton, "If you brought him in here today, I'd still say he was shot from the front. . . . . [JFK's throat wound] compatible with an entrance wound. . . . I would stand by my original impression." (14)

Parkland Hospital surgeon David Stewart stated, ". . . it was felt by all of the physicians at the time to be a wound of entry which went in the front." (15) Parkland Hospital Doctor Jody Goldstrich stated:

> It [the neck wound] was a small, almost perfectly round . . .
> somewhere between the size of a nickel and a quarter . . . and
> it was right in the middle of the front of his neck, just below
> the Adam's apple. . . . I realized how impossible it would have
> been for the neck wound I saw to have been an exit wound. . .
> . (16)

Dr. Robert McClelland stated in his report on the day of the assassination that a shot hit President Kennedy in the temple and therefore from the front. This report is very interesting because it states, "The cause of death was due to massive head and brain injury from a gunshot wound of the left temple." (17) It has been clearly established that a majority of witnesses who saw the shooting from a close proximity or viewed the President after the assassination, believed that he was hit in the right temple. McClelland's statement could mean that another bullet hit Kennedy in his left temple which could only have come from the left front. A more likely and plausible explanation is that Dr. McClelland wrote his observations after looking at the President as he faced him on the operating table. The President's right temple would then appear to be on the left side of his head as McClelland was facing him. But ultimately, which temple was struck by a bullet does not change the fact that it had to originate from the front — and this supports the witnesses who were at the scene.

If the case against Lee Oswald had ever reached an objective jury, it would have been impossible to ignore the consistent documented statements of the Parkland Hospital medical staff as the Warren Commission did. What is even more unbelievable is that the FBI Report of December 9, 1963 that was published in the December 17, 1963 edition of the *New York Times.*, supports a shot from the right front. This article stated that ". . . [a bullet] had struck his [Kennedy's] right temple." J. Edgar Hoover even had to ignore his own Bureau's conclusions in order to cling to Oswald as the sole assassin.

The following accounts taken from police officers, Secret Service agents and others in the motorcade also relate strong evidence of shots from the front.

Dallas Police Department Chief Jesse E. Curry who drove the lead car in the motorcade stated, "From the direction of the blood and the brain matter, one shot had to have come from the front." (18)   Curry's statement into the car microphone immediately after the shooting corroborates this impression, "Get a man on top of that Triple Underpass [beside the knoll] and see what happened up there." (19) Dallas Sheriff Bill Decker who rode in the lead car in the motorcade, grabbed the microphone from Curry and stated: "Have my office move all available men out of my office into the railroad yard [which was to the front and behind the grassy knoll] to try to determine what happened in there and hold everything secure until Homicide and other investigators should get there." (20)   Forrest Sorrels, head of the Dallas Office of the Secret Service was riding in the lead car with Curry and Decker, he told the Commission that he heard shots and "turned around to look up on this terrace part there [fence and concrete arcade], because the sound sounded like it came from that direction." (21)   Sorrels was even more specific when he stated, "I thought the shots came from the vicinity of the railroad or the WPA project [knoll area]." (22)   Secret Service agent Clint Hill who ran to the back of the Presidential limousine as the fatal shot was fired, was asked about the direction of the final shots. He replied, "It was right, but I cannot say for sure that it was rear, because when I mounted the car it was—it had a different sound that I heard—[it] had almost a double sound." (23)

Secret Service agent Roy Kellerman, riding in the right front seat of the Presidential limousine, stated, "And I turned my head to the right because whatever this noise was I was sure that it came from the right and perhaps into the rear, and as I turned my head to the right to view whatever it was or see whatever it was . . . a flurry of shells come into the car .

. . there have got to be more than three shots, gentlemen."
(24) Secret Service agent Sam Kinney, driver of the Secret
Service follow-up car in the motorcade stated, "I saw one shot
strike the President in the right side of the head." (25) Secret
Service agent Paul E. Landis, Jr. who rode in the follow-up
car stated:

> My reaction at this time was that the shot came from
> somewhere towards the front . . . I still was not certain from
> which direction the second shot came, but my reaction at this
> time was that the shot came from somewhere towards the
> front, right-hand side of the road. (26)

It is interesting to note the anguished comments of Secret
Service agent William Greer immediately after the shooting.
Greer, who was behind the wheel of the Presidential
limousine when the shooting occurred, told Jackie Kennedy at
Parkland Hospital, "Oh my God, Oh my God, I didn't mean to
do it, I didn't hear, I should have swerved the car. I couldn't
help it. Oh, Mrs. Kennedy, as soon as I saw it I swerved. If
only I had seen in time! Oh!" (27) What Greer meant by "as
soon as I saw it," was never pursued. But "it" was surely in
front of him as he drove towards the overpass and swerved to
the left—away from the knoll. This statement is corroborated
by FBI James Sibert, who recalled in an interview for the
HSCA, that William Greer, driver of the Presidential
limousine, stated, ". . .if I'd just been driving a little faster."
Sibert stated further that Greer was "driving so slow because
the President insisted on it." (28) The second half of this
statement was obviously false, it would have been impossible
and unrealistic to have expected President Kennedy to have
wanted to slow the vehicle down during the shooting.
Kennedy might have told Greer to drive slowly so the crowd
could see him more easily but certainly the President would
have not expected Greer to slow down and come to a stop, as
Greer's statement implies.

Numerous witnesses corroborated Greer's initial statement
that he swerved to the left, but they also consistently stated
that the limousine came to a complete stop. Greer testified to
the Warren Commission that he immediately sped up after
the first shot but that does not match his statement to Mrs.
Kennedy. He stated, "I didn't hear," and "I swerved." It is
quite possible that by the time Greer heard the shots, put on
the brakes, and swerved to the left, it was too late. There is a

strong possibility that Greer stopped to avoid a threat that he saw in front of him and to the right—just as the overwhelming evidence from the Dealy Plaza witnesses indicates.

The statements by Dealy Plaza witnesses, Roy Truly and J. W. Foster, corroborate Greer's stopping the car and pulling to the left. Dallas Policeman J. W. Foster who was located on top of the railroad overpass stated, ". . . immediately after President Kennedy was struck . . . the car in which he was riding pulled to the curb [to the left]." (29) Roy Truly, standing in front of the Book Depository stated, "I saw the President's car swerve to the left and stop. . . ." (30) Dallas motorcycle policeman Marion Baker added further corroboration to Foster and Truly with his statement to the Warren Commission. He stated that motorcycle policeman, James Chaney, who was riding to the right rear of the Presidential limousine stated, ". . . at the time, after the shooting, from the time the first shot rang out, the car stopped completely, pulled to the left and stopped. . . . Several officers said it stopped completely." (31)

Even more evidence of a shot from the front is found in the statements of motorcycle policemen Steve Ellis and Harold Freeman. Their statements of seeing a bullet hole in the windshield of the Presidential limousine corroborate Greer's stopping the car and pulling to the left. Ellis stated, ". . . there was a hole in the left front windshield [at Parkland Hospital] . . . You could put a pencil through it." (32) Freeman confirmed Ellis' statement when he said, "[I was] right beside it. I could have touched it . . . It was a bullet hole. You could tell what it was." (33) Photographs of the limousine before and after the shooting clearly show a crack in the windshield and a dent in the chrome above the rear-view mirror. (34) This is also corroborated by Secret Service agent Sam Kinney who stated that it ". . . [looked like] a bullet fragment had hit above the windshield frame above the windshield." (35) Further corroboration is given by a report in the *New York Times* on January 26, 1964 which read, ". . .[fragments or a bullet] damaged the windshield of the Presidential limousine."

How the statements by Kinney, Landis, Kellerman, and Sorrels of immediate thoughts of shots from the right and the front are not seen as credible—is actually incredible. The actions of William Greer also add strong corroboration to evidence of shots from the front. Even more amazing is that Roy Kellerman's statement, "that there had to be more than three shots," was ignored by the Commission. Kellerman was sitting directly in front of President Kennedy in the limousine, his proximity to the President and his training to detect gunshots, surely qualifies him as credible.

A number of law enforcement officers riding in the motorcade also corroborated the statements of shots from the front made by members of the Secret Service. Texas State Highway Patrolman Hurchel D. Jacks who drove LBJ's car in the motorcade stated: "Before the President's body was covered it appeared that the bullet had struck him above the right ear or near the temple." (36) James M. Chaney of the Dallas Police Department was one of two motorcycle officers in the motorcade riding along the right bumper of the Presidential limousine. He stated on television on November 22, ". . . the President was struck in the face." (37) Bobby Hargis, one of the Dallas Police Department motorcycle officers who was riding to the left rear of the Presidential limousine stated:

> it sounded like the shots were right next to me. . . they probably could have been coming from the railroad overpass, because I thought since I had got splattered, with blood . . . I was just a little back and left of . . . just a little bit back and left of Mrs. Kennedy . . . it seemed like his head exploded, and I was splattered with blood and brain, and kind of bloody water. (38)

The *New York Daily News* reported on November 24, 1963, that Hargis stated that he "thought that at first I might have been hit," because the debris of blood and brains had hit him so hard. Motorcycle Policeman B. J. Martin was riding beside Officer Hargis and corroborated his account when he stated to the Warren Commission ". . .[he saw] blood stains on the left of my helmet . . . [and] other material that looked like pieces of flesh." (39) Martin recalled further:

> I couldn't hear the shots over the noise of my cycle, but I could see what was happening. . . when that head shot hit Kennedy, I was sure it was coming from the right front because of the direction the blood flew. It looked to me like at least two people were firing from a forward position, and I thought there might be as many as six [shots] in all. (40)

Hargis also added this statement to the record in his Warren Commission testimony:

> I looked over to the Texas School Book Depository Building, and no one that was standing at the base of the building was—seemed to be looking up at the building or anything, like they knew where the shots were coming from. . . . Some people looking out of the windows up there, didn't seem like they knew what was going on. . . . About the only activity I could see was on the bridge, on the railroad bridge . . . and I thought maybe some of them had seen who did the shooting and the rifle. (41)

Dallas Sheriff Seymour Weitzman was standing at the corner of Main and Houston. Hearing the shots, he stated: "I immediately ran toward the President's car. Of course, it was speeding away and somebody said the shots or firecrackers . . . we still didn't know the President was shot . . . [the shots] came from the wall." (42) Luke Mooney was stationed in front of the Sheriff's office as were most of his fellow officers. He told the Warren Commission that ". . . [shots came from] the railroad yards" (behind the fence on the knoll). (43) Harry Weatherford, another member of the Sheriff's Office, was standing alongside Mooney and concurred with his assessment of shots emanating from the "railroad yards." (44) Harold Elkins also corroborated these observations from the same location, when he stated that the shots he heard came from the area "between the railroad yards and the Book Depository." (45) L. C. Smith was also standing in front of the Sheriff's Office. Smith reported on November 22 that he "heard a woman unknown to me say the President was shot in the head and the shots came from the fence on the north side of Elm." (46) Deputy Sheriff A. D. McCurley in his report stated:

> I rushed towards the park and saw people running towards the railroad yards beyond Elm Street and I ran over and jumped a fence and a railroad worker stated to me that he believed the smoke from the bullets came from the vicinity of a stockade fence which surrounds the park area. (47)

W. W. Mabra, then a county bailiff, later to become a police officer, was on the corner of Main and Houston and stated: "I thought it was a backfire. People ran toward the knoll. Some said they saw smoke there. I thought at first the shot may have come from there." (48) Deputy Sheriff Jack Faulkner stated:

> . . . I asked a woman if they had hit the President, and she told me that he was dead, that he had been shot through the head. I asked her where the shot came from, and she pointed toward the concrete arcade [location of the knoll and stockade fence] on the east side of Elm St., just west of Houston St. (49)

Dallas Police Department Officer H. B. McClain, one of the two forward mid-motorcade motorcycle officers stated, "I feel like that there's somebody on that railroad track shot him a second time." (50) Dallas Police Department Officer Joe Marshall Smith stated, "I was standing in the middle of Elm Street from the southeast curb of Elm and Houston Streets at the time of the shooting. I heard the shots and thought they were coming from bushes from the overpass." (51) One would think that the Secret Service and police officers could not be so consistent in their observations and yet be so wrong.

Other witnesses riding in the motorcade expressed similar views about shots originating at the street level and in front of the motorcade. Thomas Atkins, Navy White House photographer, who rode in Camera Car 1 stated:

> The shots came from below and off to the right from where I was . . . I never thought the shots came from above. They did not sound like shots coming from anything higher than street level. . . . shots sound in front of me [in front was the railroad overpass and the grassy knoll]. I didn't get the sensation that they were from up high. It sounded like they were in the crowd at my level. (52)

James Altgens, Associated Press photographer stated, "I saw a couple of Negroes looking out of a window which I later learned was the floor below where the gun—the sniper's nest was supposed to have been, but it didn't register on me at the time that they were looking from an area that the bullet might have come from." (53) Altgens also stated to the FBI, "The bullet struck President Kennedy in the right side of the head." (54) Malcolm Couch, a television reporter who was riding in the motorcade, testified: ". . . And people were pointing back around those shrubs around that west corner and—oh—you would think that there was a chase going on in that direction." (55)

Numerous witnesses stated that they smelled gunpowder

on the street level. This is hardly indicative of shots coming from the sixth floor of the Book Depository building. Senator Ralph Yarborough who was riding in President Johnson's car, ". . . I smelled gunpowder. I always thought that was strange because, being familiar with firearms, I never could see how I could smell the powder from a rifle high in that building." (56) This corroborates Yarborough's initial impressions which he gave to the press on the day of the murder. Yarborough stated, "I could smell gunpowder all the way into the hospital." (57) Secret Service agent Rufus Youngblood, who was riding in LBJ's car in the motorcade was ". . . puzzled about the number of spectators who claimed to have smelled gunpowder. So did I after the last shot." (58) Dallas Policeman Joe Marshall Smith was one of the first to run up the knoll to get behind the fence. He told reporter Ronnie Dugger in an article printed in the December 13, 1963 *Texas Observer* ". . . [I] caught the smell of gunpowder . . . I could tell it was in the air." Motorcycle Officer B. J. Martin riding to the left rear of the Presidential limousine smelled gunpowder, too. (59) Policeman Earle Brown who was stationed on the overpass, also "smelled gunpowder" behind the fence when he ran there after the shooting. (60) Mrs. Earle Cabell, wife of the mayor of Dallas, was riding in a convertible—behind the Presidential limousine. She stated during her testimony before the Warren Commission, "I was acutely aware of the odor of gunpowder." (61) She also stated that Congressman Ray Roberts, who was riding beside her also smelled gunpowder. (62) Roberts was never interviewed by the Warren Commission.

A number of railroad workers were standing on the railroad overpass with probably the best view of the motorcade as it proceeded down Elm Street and passed beneath them. Their recollections are consistent and especially damaging to the Warren Commission's conclusions of "no credible evidence" of shots coming from anywhere but the Book Depository. S. M. Holland, who worked for the Union Terminal Railroad, was asked by the policemen stationed on the railroad bridge to state which of those on the overpass were railroad workers and were therefore cleared to view the motorcade from that location. Holland stated:

> I counted four shots and about the same time all this was happening, and in this group of trees . . . there was a shot, a report, . . . And a puff of smoke came out about six or eight

feet above the ground right out from under those trees. . . . There were definitely four reports. . . . I have no doubt about it. I have no doubt about seeing that puff of smoke come out from under those trees either. . . . I definitely saw the puff of smoke and heard the report from under those trees. . . . The puff of smoke I saw definitely came from behind the arcade to the trees. . . . four or five of us saw it, the smoke . . . one of my employees even saw the muzzle flash. (63)

Austin Miller stated: "I saw something which I thought was smoke or steam coming from a group of trees north of Elm off the railroad tracks." (64) Frank Reilly stated that the shots seemed to "come out of the trees . . . on the north side of Elm Street, at the corner up there . . . where all those trees are . . . at that park where all the shrubs is up there . . . up the slope." (65) James Simmons stated to author Mark Lane that the shots, "came from the left and in from of us toward the wooden fence, and there was a puff of smoke that came underneath the trees on the embankment." (66) Standing beside Simmons was fellow railroad worker Richard Dodd. He corroborated Simmons statement, "The smoke came from behind the hedge on the north side of the plaza (knoll)" (67) Walter Winborn and Thomas Murphy, also on the overpass, concurred with these observations and stated that they saw "smoke in the trees on the knoll." (68) Clemon Johnson also concurred with his fellow workers when he told the FBI that he saw "white smoke" on the knoll. (69)

The claim of witnesses seeing smoke has been disputed by author Gerald Posner. In his book, *Case Closed,* Posner states ". . . that witnesses did not claim to see puffs of smoke from rifle fire on the knoll as Warren Commission critics claim." (70) To make such a claim when compared to statements made by witnesses, renders his argument null and void. As we shall see, Posner's argument is not objective. Much of Posner's argument that Oswald was the lone assassin is taken from the 1992 American Bar Association Mock Trial prosecution evidence against Lee Oswald. Mr. Posner, who is a lawyer, seems to have forgotten that Lee Oswald never had his day of defense in court.

Witnesses from various locations in Dealy Plaza also offered views that at least some of the shots originated from locations to the front of the President's limousine. William Newman who was standing directly in front of the knoll and was one of the closest witnesses to the President when the fatal shot hit stated:

> he [the President] was hit in the side of the head. Then he fell
> back. . . I thought the shot had come from the garden directly
> behind me [the knoll], that was on an elevation from where I
> was as I was right on the curb. I do not recall looking toward
> the Texas School Book Depository. I looked back in the
> vicinity of the garden. (71)

This is corroborated by the Tom Alyea film from 11/22/63
which was shown on national television where Newman is
shown pointing to his right temple and also by his 11/24/63
report in which he said, "The President was hit on the right
side of the head with the third shot and he heard the thud
when the bullet struck the President." (72) He stated further
to Josiah Thompson, "I thought the shot was fired from above
and behind where we were standing. And that's what scared
us, because I thought we were right in the direct path of
gunfire." (73)

Emmett J. Hudson, one of the groundskeepers of Dealy
Plaza who was standing on the steps in front of the picket
fence on the knoll stated:

> I happened to be looking right at him when that bullet hit
> him. . . . it looked like it hit him somewhere along about a
> little bit behind the ear and a little above the ear. . . . The
> shots that I heard definitely came from behind and above me.
> (74)

Jim Wilmon, an advertising salesman for the *Dallas Morning
News*, was standing on Houston Street. He recalled:

> The car turned down Elm Street. A car backfired, or so I
> thought. I said to my buddy, "The Secret Service is going to
> have a heart attack!" But it wasn't a backfire. It was shots.
> People ran toward the grassy knoll. No one seemed to look up
> at the Book Depository. (75)

Cheryl McKinnon, who became a reporter for the *San Diego
Star News* was standing on Elm Street between the Book
Depository and the knoll, she recalled:

> suddenly three shots in rapid succession rang out. Myself and
> dozens of others standing nearby turned in horror toward the
> back of the grassy knoll where it seemed the sounds had
> originated. Puffs of white smoke still hung in the air in small

patches. (76)

Dallas Morning News staff writer Mary Woodward, who was standing beside McKinnon, corroborated her account with this report published on November 23 in the *News*, ". . . and suddenly there was a horrible ear-shattering noise coming from behind us and a little to the right." (77)

Phil Willis, a witness on south side of Elm Street (across the street from the knoll and Book Depository) stated: "I'm very dead certain at least one shot came from the front. . . . No one will ever convince us that the last shot did not come from the right front, from the knoll area." (78) Willis' wife, Marilyn, further corroborated her husband's statement, when she said in a filmed interview, "The head shot seemed to come from the right front. It seemed to strike him here [indicating right temple/forehead area], his head went back, and all the brain matter went out the back of the head, it was like a red halo." (79) James Tague was standing on the curb on the south side of Elm Street near the Triple Overpass. The Warren Commission concluded that Tague was cut in the face by a bullet fragment or a piece of concrete that eventually forced the Commission to admit at least one bullet missed. This led to the necessity of creating the infamous single bullet theory. Tague indicated to the Commission that the shots he heard came from the front, on top of the knoll and behind the fence:

> *Tague.* My first impression was that up by the, whatever you call the monument, or whatever it was . . . that somebody was throwing firecrackers up there, that the police were running up there to see what was going on.
> *Leibler.* You thought the [shots] had come from . . . behind the concrete monument here. . .?
> *Tague.* Yes. (80)

Jean Hill, a Dallas school teacher, was standing on the curb across from the knoll and stated, "I saw a puff of smoke [and] a shadowy figure . . . [an] indistinct form of some kind was barely visible . . . something that seemed not to belong at that particular spot." (81) Hill also stated the first shots "were fired as though one person were firing. . . . they were rapidly fired but there was some small interval between them. . . . [then more shots which] were different . . . quicker, more automatic." (82) Later in her testimony, Hill stated in response to the following questions:

> *Mrs. Hill.* . . . I did think there was more than one person
> shooting.
> *Specter.* You did think there was more than one person
> shooting?
> *Mrs. Hill.* Yes sir.
> *Specter.* What made you think that?
> *Mrs. Hill.* The way the gun reports sounded and the difference
> in the way they were fired—the timing.
> *Specter.* What was your impression as to the source of the
> second group of shots . . .?
> *Mrs. Hill.* Well, nothing, except that I thought that they were
> fired by someone else.
> *Specter.* And did you have any idea where they were coming
> from?
> *Mrs. Hill.* No; as I said I thought they were coming from that
> general direction of that knoll. (83)

Mary Moorman was standing beside Jean Hill and had
accompanied her to Dealy Plaza to view the Presidential
motorcade. Moorman stated in a television interview, "There
was three or four [shots] real close together. . . . the shots
were still being fired after I took the picture [which shows the
impact of the fatal head shot] . . . I decided I better get on the
ground . . . I was no more than 15 feet from the car and in the
line of fire—evidently." (84)   According to Moorman's
statement, she believed that the shots were fired from directly
across the street, which was in the direction of the knoll and
the picket fence. Her photograph shows the President's head
coming backwards and to the left and is indicative of a shot
originating from the right front. (85) Moorman also indicated
that there were probably four shots and possibly more—her
statement implies that more shots were being fired even as
she snapped the photograph of the fatal head shot.

Despite the corroboration of Mary Moorman, there has been
some criticism about the inconsistency of some of Jean Hill's
statements. Some of this could be due to confusion but also to
intimidation and altering of testimony as has been
demonstrated. But Mrs. Hill has been consistent and clear
from November 22, 1963 to the present on these important
points; she believes shots came from behind the fence and
that there were more than three shots fired. These points are
documented in her televised interview on November 22, 1963,
the Warren Commission testimony, subsequent public and

private interviews, and in her book, *The Last Dissenting Witness.*

Mrs. Charles Hester told the FBI that she and her husband had been standing on the south side of Elm Street near the underpass when they heard gunshots. According to an FBI report, her husband then grabbed her and shoved her to the ground. Both Mrs. Hester and her husband believed that they had actually been in the direct line of fire. The overpass and knoll were directly behind them. (86) John A. Chism said in an FBI interview that he had been standing on the curb in front of the concrete memorial on Elm Street which is just east of the triple underpass and that he was ". . . of the opinion that the shots came from behind him." (87)

Mrs. Delores Kounas, Mr. James Crawford, and Edgar Smith were all standing on the corner of Houston and Elm and all three concurred that the shots were coming from in front of the limousine. Kounas stated that the shots came from ". . . the westerly direction . . . [the] viaduct." Crawford believed that the shots came from ". . . down the hill" (the front), and Smith stated that the shots came from ". . .the monument" (on the knoll). (88)

Robert Edwards, an employee of the Dallas County Auditor's office, was also standing on the corner of Houston and Elm when the shots rang out. He was asked by the Warren Commission where the shots appeared to be coming from. Edwards stated "They appeared to be coming from just west of the School Book Depository Building. There were some railroad tracks and there were some railroad cars back in there, . . . that area somewhere." (89)

Gordon Arnold was a young serviceman home on leave. He was in Dealy Plaza to film the Presidential motorcade on the day of the assassination:

> I walked around to the front of the fence and found a little mound of dirt to stand on to see the motorcade. . . . Just after the car turned onto Elm and started toward me, a shot went off from over my left shoulder. I felt the bullet, rather than heard it, and it went right past my left ear. . . . I had just gotten out of basic training. In my mind live ammunition was being fired. It was being fired over my head. And I hit the dirt. I buried my head in the ground and I heard several other shots. (90)

Abraham Zapruder, who filmed the assassination from just

to the left of the grassy knoll stated:

> [the shot] it came from that height. . . . Some of them were
> motorcycle cops . . . and they were running right behind me, of
> course in the line of the shooting. I guess they thought it
> came from right behind me . . . I also thought it came from
> back of me. . . . they claim it was proven it could be done by
> one man. You know there was an indication there were two.
> (91)

Marilyn Sitzman, who was standing along-side Abraham
Zapruder as he was filming, stated in an interview with
author Josiah Thompson, "And the next thing that I
remember clearly was the shot that hit directly in front of us,
or almost directly in front of us, that hit him in the side of the
face . . . above the ear and to the front . . . between the eye
and the ear." (92)

A number of workers at the Book Depository on the day of
the assassination were situated at various locations in and
out of the Book Depository as the motorcade passed by.
Steven F. Wilson was vice-president of a school textbook-
publishing company. He watched the motorcade go by from a
closed third-floor window. He stated: "At that time, it
seemed like the shots came from the west end of the building
or from the colonnade located on Elm street across from the
west end of our building [the pergola on the grassy knoll.]
The shots really did not sound like they came from above me."
(93) Dorothy Garner viewed the assassination from a fourth
floor window in the building. Oswald supposedly fired from
the sixth floor, two floors above where Garner was standing.
She stated: "I thought at the time that the shots or reports
came from a point to the west of the building [towards the
overpass in the knoll]." (94) Victoria Adams also watched the
motorcade from the fourth floor and stated, ". . . it seems as if
it came from the right below [the area of the grassy knoll]
rather than from the left above [the sixth-floor window]." (95)
Wesley Frazier, who had driven Oswald to work that
morning, was standing on the front steps of the Depository.
He stated, ". . . and from where I was standing it [the shots]
sounded like it was coming from down at the railroad tracks
there [railroad overpass and knoll]." (96) Bill Lovelady,
standing in the doorway of the Book Depository, thought that
the shots had come from ". . . right there around that concrete
little deal on that knoll . . . between the underpass and the

building right on that knoll." (97)

Roy Truly, Superintendent of the School Book Depository, testified: "I thought the shots came from the vicinity of the railroad or the WPA project, behind the WPA project west of the building [area of the knoll]. . . . There were many officers running down west of the building." (98) O. V. Campbell, Vice President of the Book Depository, was standing beside Truly and told Mrs. Robert Reid, ". . . [the shots] came from the grassy area down this way . . . in the direction . . . the parade was going, in the bottom of that direction." (99) This is corroborated in a statement he gave to the FBI, "I heard shots being fired from a point which I thought was near the railroad tracks located over the viaduct on Elm Street [knoll]." (100) William Shelley was also standing in front of the Book Depository and stated that the ". . . [shots] came from west of the building" (towards the knoll) as did Joe Molina who was standing beside Shelley and stated that the shots, ". . . sort of, kind of, [came] from the west." (101) Mrs. Peggy Hawkins, Mrs. Avery Davis, and Mrs. Donald Baker also joined the chorus of those believing the shots had originated from the front. They were also directly in front of the Book Depository when the shots rang out. Hawkins stated that the shots came from the "railroad yards," Davis stated that the shots came from the ". . . viaduct . . ." (overpass), and Baker believed that the shots came from the ". . . railroad tracks on [the] west." (102) It seems rather strange that so many witnesses, either inside of the Book Depository Building or just outside the Depository, didn't think shots came from their building. In fact, many corroborated the belief that the shots originated in front of the limousine, near the knoll and the overpass.

Various autopsy personnel including doctors, X-ray technicians, radiologists, photographers, etc. also concluded (after viewing the President's body) that shots came from the front. Jerrol F. Custer, Bethesda Naval Hospital X-ray technician stated, " . . . and that he believed he [Kennedy] had been shot from the front." (103) James E. Metzler, Bethesda Naval Hospital corpsman told author David Lifton, "It was also his impression, from the way the wound was located toward the back of the head, that President Kennedy must have been shot in the head from the front." (104) Dr. John H. Ebersole, Assistant Chief of Radiology at Bethesda stated, "The front of the body, except for a very slight bruise above the right eye on the forehead, was absolutely intact. It was

the back of the head that was blown off. . . ." (105) Major
General Philip C. Wehle, Commanding Officer of the Military
District of Washington D.C., present at the autopsy also ". . .
noticed a slight bruise over the right temple of the President."
(106) Mortician Thomas E. Robinson who helped prepare
Kennedy's body after the autopsy stated, "He also said there
was a little wound, described as a hole of about a quarter-inch
in diameter, on the right side of the forehead up near the
hairline." (107)   Paul Kelly O'Connor, Bethesda Naval
Hospital Laboratory technologist stated, "I think he was hit
four times. The first time was in the throat from the front."
(108)   James Curtis Jenkins, Bethesda Naval Hospital
Laboratory technologist stated:

> . . . from looking at the President's head, the fatal shot struck
> from the front. . . . This was a clear indication to all present of
> a shot that entered at the front of the head—which is to say, a
> shot fired by an assassin from a position in front of the
> limousine, and not from the Texas School Book Depository.
> Also noted at the time was a possible wound of entry on the
> right front side of the President's head. (109)

Edward F. Reed, Jr., Bethesda Naval Hospital X-ray
Technician also ". . . felt that the head shot came from the
front." (110)
Cheryl McKinnon, a witness to President Kennedy's
assassination who later became a reporter for the *San Diego
News,* summarized the views of many of the witnesses:

> I tried to maintain the faith with my government. I have read
> the Warren Commission Record in its entirety and dozens of
> other books as well. I am sorry to say that the only thing I am
> absolutely sure of today is that at least two of the shots fired
> that day in Dealy Plaza came from behind where I stood, on
> the knoll, not from the Book Depository. . . . I have never
> quite had the same faith and trust in those that lead us as I
> did before. (111)

The evidence compiled here by virtue of summarizing and
synthesizing the witness statements and the views of those
who studied the available evidence objectively, most certainly
leads to the inescapable conclusion of a conspiracy of some
kind to assassinate President Kennedy.
There can be no question, that based on the evidence
available to those responsible for carrying out the

investigation of the assassination, that the probability of Lee Oswald being the sole rifleman was remote to say the least. This conclusion is supported by numerous initial, as well as subsequent reports, that were released by local law enforcement officials as well as the Secret Service.

The *Houston Post* reported on November 23, 1963 " . . . there was much speculation among law enforcement officers that the murder was too well planned to have been accomplished alone."

On November 23, 1963, the *Dallas Morning News stated* [District Attorney Henry] Wade, said preliminary reports indicated more than one person was involved in the shooting which brought death to the President and left Governor John Connally wounded. . . . Wade said, "Everyone who participated in this crime—anyone who helped plan it or furnished a weapon . . . They should all go to the electric chair."

Secret Service agent Winston Lawson stated while he was at the police station Friday evening, November 22, that he was called to the phone, "they gave us some information on people that it might have been *[sic]* [involved in the assassination]—a case that wasn't Oswald" (112) Secret Service agent Sam Kinney who drove the Secret Service car immediately behind the Presidential limousine, related to Vincent Palamara, "I believe there was a conspiracy. This thing was so well set up—whoever did the shooting—he picked that area where he knew there wouldn't be any men by the car." (113) Kinney's belief in a conspiracy was supported by fellow agent Roy Kellerman in an interview with a member of the House Select Committee. (114)

As presented earlier, the initial reactions of William Greer, the driver of the Presidential limousine also implied shots emanating from the area where the overpass and the knoll joined. The previously mentioned belief of Roy Kellerman, the agent closest to the President, that "there had to be more than three shots," also substantiates shots from the area of the knoll and a conspiracy.

Strong corroborating evidence that has also been documented in this chapter, was that Dallas County Sheriff Bill Decker and Dallas Police Chief Jesse Curry immediately focused their attention on the railroad overpass and the parking lot behind the picket fence on the knoll. Dallas Policeman Joe Marshall Smith ran to the grassy knoll and

into the parking lot behind the picket fence immediately after
the shooting. He told the Warren Commission:

> *Smith.* Of course, I wasn't alone. There was some deputy
> sheriff with me, and I believe one Secret Service man when I
> got there. I got to make this statement, too. I felt awfully
> silly, but after this shot and this woman, I pulled my pistol
> from my holster, and I thought, this is silly, I don't know who
> I am looking for, and I put it back. Just as I did, he showed
> me that he was a Secret Service agent.
> *Q.* Did you accost this man?
> *Smith.* Well, he saw me coming with my pistol and right away
> he showed me who he was.
> *Q.* Do you remember who it was?
> *Smith.* No, sir, I don't. . . . (115)

Smith also reported:

> He looked like an auto mechanic. He had on a sports shirt
> and sports pants. But he had dirty fingernails, it looked like,
> and hands that looked like an auto mechanic's hands. And
> afterwards it didn't ring true for the Secret Service. At the
> time we were so pressed for time, and we were searching.
> And he had produced correct identification, and we just
> overlooked the thing. I should have checked that man closer,
> but at the time I didn't snap on it. . . . (116)

Dallas Police Chief Jesse Curry stated in 1977:

> I think he must have been bogus—certainly the suspicion
> would point to the man as being involved, someway or other,
> in the shooting, since he was in an area immediately adjacent
> to where the shots were—and the fact that he had a badge
> that purported him to be Secret Service would make it seem
> all the more suspicious. (117)

Deputy Sheriff Seymour Weitzman was standing at the
corner of Main and Houston when the shots rang out. He told
the Warren Commission:

> I immediately ran toward the President's car. Of course it
> was speeding away and somebody said the shots . . . came
> from the wall. I immediately scaled the wall [on the grass
> knoll]. . . . we noticed numerous kinds of footprints that did
> not make any sense because they were going different
> directions. . . . [searching with us were] other officers, Secret
> Service, as well. (118)

Railroad workers Richard Dodd and Sam Holland witnessed the assassination from the railroad overpass. Their statements clearly indicate the distinct possibility of gunmen behind the fence. Dodd stated "there were tracks and cigarette butts laying where someone had been standing on the bumper looking over the fence". Sam Holland told Josiah Thompson:

> And I got over to the spot where I saw the smoke come from and heard the shot; I was looking for empty shells or some indication that there was a rifleman or someone over there. Well, you know it'd been raining that morning and behind the station wagon from one end of the bumper to the other, I expect you could've counted four or five-hundred footprints down there. And on the bumper, oh about twelve or eighteen inches apart, it looked like someone had raked their shoes off; there were muddy spots up there, like someone had been standing up there . . . (119)
>
> That was the mystery to me, that they [the footprints] didn't extend further than from one end of the bumper to the other. That's as far as they would go. It looked like a lion paced a cage. (120)
>
> Just to the west of the station wagon [Holland told us], there were two sets of footprints that left . . . I noticed these two footprints leaving; now they could have stepped out between the second and third cars on the gravel or they could've got in the truck compartment of this car and pulled the lid down, which would have been very, very easy. (121)

J. C. Price witnessed the assassination from the roof of the Terminal Annex Building, which overlooked Dealy Plaza. Price recalled:

> I saw one man run towards the passenger cars on the railroad siding after the volley of shots. This man had a white dress shirt, no tie, and khaki colored trousers. His hair appeared to be long and dark and his agility running could be about 25 years of age. He had something in his hand. I couldn't be sure but it may have been a head piece (122)

Price believed that the shots came from behind the fence and never looked at the Book Depository building during the shooting. (123) He later told Mark Lane that the man "was carrying something in his right hand [that] could have been a gun." (124)

On March 28, 1966, James Simmons stated to Mark Lane

that he saw "footprints in the mud around the fence, and there were footprints on the wooden two-by-four railing on the fence." Like Dodd and Holland, Simmons also noted mud footprints "on a car bumper there, as if someone had stood up there looking over the fence." (125)

Lee Bowers worked for the Union Terminal Company in Dallas, and on November 22 he was positioned inside the railroad tower overlooking the railroad tracks and the parking lot behind the picket fence on the grassy knoll. He told the Warren Commission that at around 10:00 the police had closed off the area behind the fence, "so that anyone moving around could actually be observed." (126) Despite the fact that the parking lot behind the picket fence was supposed to have been shut off to outside traffic, he observed three automobiles enter the area in the half hour before the assassination. One of the vehicles was driven by a man who appeared to be holding a microphone to his mouth. (127) Bowers testified that he saw two men standing near the fence, "one was middle aged" [and] fairly "heavy set and the other was about mid-twenties in either a plaid shirt or a plaid coat or jacket." (128) Bowers also stated that he noticed the men standing in the same location just before the shots were fired and, "These men were the only two strangers in the area. The others were workers whom I knew." (129) Bowers stated further that "something occurred in this particular spot," and that the two men remained in that location when:

> At the time of the shooting, in the vicinity of where the two men I have described were, there was a flash of light or, as far as I am concerned, something I could not identify, but there was something which occurred which caught my eye in this immediate area on the embankment. Now, what this was, I could not state at that time and at this time I could not identify it, other than there was some unusual occurrence—a flash of light or smoke or something which caused me to feel like something out of the ordinary had occurred there. (130)

Lee Bowers amazing testimony and subsequent statements were most probably the most important corroboration to the consistently documented accounts of the shots emanating from the grassy knoll and behind the picket fence. Not only did Bowers strongly support the abundant witness testimony of shots originating from that location, but even more importantly, he was able to provide a detailed description of at least two of the men who were most likely the real assassins of President Kennedy. Despite the credible statements of Mr. Bowers, the Warren Commission was not interested in his version of how the Kennedy assassination actually transpired:

> *Lane.* In reading your testimony, Mr. Bowers, it appears that just as you were about to make that statement, you were interrupted in the middle of the sentence by the Commission counsel, who then went into another area.
> *Bowers.* Well, that's correct. I mean, I was simply trying to answer his questions, and he seemed to be satisfied with the answer to that one and did not care for me to elaborate. (131)

In what has become a truly sickening refrain, Lee Bowers was killed in a one car accident just three months after his 1966 interview with Mark Lane.

A young serviceman, Gordon Arnold, was home on leave and went to Dealy Plaza to film the motorcade. He attempted to film the motorcade from on top of the railroad overpass but was stopped by an unidentified agent of some kind. "A man came around the corner of the railroad bridge and told me I wasn't gonna be there. . . he pulled out an identification card and said I'm with the CIA." (132) Arnold then proceeded to walk halfway down behind the picket fence looking for another place to film the motorcade from and the "agent" again came up to him and stated "I told you to get out of this area." (133) Arnold then walked around to the front of the fence and a few minutes later began filming as the motorcade came by. According to Arnold the shots came "right over his left ear" and he flew to the ground. Arnold's story has been disputed because he is not seen in photographs before or after the shooting in the location he claimed to be in. However his presence was later verified by Senator Ralph Yarborough who was riding in the same car as Vice-President Johnson. Yarborough recalled:

> During the shooting, my eye was attracted to the right—I saw a movement. I saw a man jump about ten feet like an old flying tackle in football and land against the wall. I thought to myself there's a man whose been trained thoroughly in combat. The minute you hear firing you get undercover. (134)

Witness Jean Hill also reported that an "agent of some sort" had prevented her from continuing up into the parking lot behind the fence after she ran across Elm Street to where she believed the shots had originated. (135)

Witness Malcolm Summers stated, "I ran across . . . Elm Street to run up towards the knoll. We were stopped by a man in a suit and he had an overcoat over his arm. . . . I saw a gun under that over coat. . . . his comment was don't y'all come up here any further—you could get shot or get killed." (136)

Dallas Police Sergeant D. V. Harkness reported that while he was in the process of sealing off the back entrance of the Book Depository he stated, ". . . there were some secret service agents there. I didn't get them identified. They told me they were secret service." (137) Depository employee James Romack confirmed Harkness' statement about unidentified agents of some kind at the back of the Book Depository immediately after the shooting. "They were, FBI or something standing right there at the very [back] entrance and just stood there." (138)

It is also interesting to note that according to a Warren Commission document, a "U.S. Secret Service agent notified a policeman in the Oak Cliff Branch of the Dallas Public Library about a "tip" that the killer of Officer Tippit being in the Library was false. (139) This is supported by Commission Document 2003, #83 and Lt. Cunningham of the Dallas Police. Furthermore, Cunningham was instructed to go to the Texas Theatre where the "real killer," Lee Oswald had supposedly fled. (140)

The Secret Service reported to the Warren Commission that no agents were at any of these locations and the Commission and House Select Committee had no explanation of who "they" were.

Within one month of the assassination, Richard Dudman, a reporter for the *St. Louis Post-Dispatch,* and an eye-witness to the assassination, placed the conflicting evidence in its proper perspective. On December 21, 1963, Dudman's analysis of the conflicting reports was published in *The New Republic:*

> Some of the points raised here bothered me on the scene in Dallas, where I witnessed President Kennedy's assassination and the slaying of the accused assassin two days later. Three circumstances—the entry wound in the throat, the small, round hole in the windshield of the Presidential limousine, and the number of bullets found afterward—suggested that there had been a second sniper firing from a point in front of

the automobile.

The throat wound puzzled the surgeons who attended Mr. Kennedy at Parkland Memorial Hospital when they learned how the Dallas police had reconstructed the shooting. Dr. Robert McClelland, one of the three doctors who worked on the throat wound, told me afterward that they still believed it to be an entry wound, even though the shots were said to have been fired from almost directly behind the President. He explained that he and his colleagues at Parkland saw bullet wounds every day, sometimes several a day, and recognized easily the characteristically tiny holes of an entering bullet, in contrast to the larger, tearing hole that an exiting bullet would have left.

A few of us noticed the hole in the windshield when the limousine was standing at the emergency entrance after the President had been carried inside. I could not approach close enough to see on which side was the cup-shaped spot that indicates a bullet has pierced the glass from the opposite side . . . authorities repeatedly mentioned four bullets found afterward—one found in the floor of the car, a second found in the President's stretcher, a third removed from Governor Connally's left thigh, and a fourth said to have been removed from President Kennedy's body at the Naval Hospital in Bethesda. On the day the President was shot, I happened to learn of a possible fifth. A group of police officers were examining the area at the side of the street where the President was hit, and a police inspector told me they had just found another bullet in the grass. He said he did not know whether it had anything to do with the assassination.

With these circumstances in mind, I returned to the scene to see where a shot from ahead of the President's car might have originated. From the stretch traveled by the car when the shots were fired, a large sector in front is taken up by a railroad viaduct. It crosses over the triple underpass, through which the motorcade was routed. No buildings are beyond the viaduct; it forms the horizon.

Between the tracks and the near side of the viaduct is a broad gravel walkway. Along the side is a three-foot concrete balustrade, with upright slots two or three inches wide. At each end is a five-foot wooden fence that screens the approaches to the viaduct.

Normal Secret Service procedure is to have local police stationed on and under any such overpass before a Presidential motorcade approaches. The standing order also is to clear each overpass of all spectators. The Secret Service now declines all comment on the assassination, refusing to answer the specific question as to precautions taken with respect to that particular viaduct. Railroad police seem to have been assigned responsibility there. The area is marked with no-trespassing signs as private railroad property. Railroad police chased away an Associated Press photographer, [James Altgens] who tried to set up his camera there before the motorcade arrived.

Dudman's analysis is as inciteful today as it was in 1963.

There can be no rational explanation as to why all possible investigative agencies focused on the Book Depository within fifteen minutes of the assassination. Even more perplexing is that those who would argue that Lee Oswald and his location in the Book Depository were the only sources of gunfire, are virtually without foundation. The root of this blatant misrepresentation must be placed at the feet of J. Edgar Hoover, for it was he who had declared that Lee Oswald was the sole assassin on the afternoon of the assassination. Despite the determination of Lee Oswald as the lone and un-aided assassin of President Kennedy by J. Edgar Hoover, there remained the problem of convincing the public that Lee Oswald's killer, Jack Ruby, was also a lone and un-aided assassin.

Chapter 12

Jack Ruby, the Middle Man

Leon D. Hubert Jr. and Burt W. Griffin were the Warren
Commission attorneys responsible for the investigation of
Jack Ruby. On May 14, 1964, three weeks before the
Commission was set to interview Ruby, Griffin and Hubert
wrote a memorandum to general counsel J. Lee Rankin
describing the three areas that the Commission had not
adequately investigated regarding Jack Ruby. They were:
Why had Ruby killed Lee Harvey Oswald, the accused slayer
of President Kennedy? Was Ruby associated with Oswald in
any way? Did Ruby have confederates in the murder of
Oswald? Hubert stated that he and Griffin had put their
doubts on paper, ". . .to protect ourselves against any
accusation later that we had not gone far enough." (1) At this
point, six months into the Commission's investigation, Rankin
was not prepared to delve further into Ruby's activities and
intentions. Hubert was then persuaded, or was told, to resign
from his role in the investigation, but only on the condition
that he would accompany the Commission to interview Ruby
when the Commission set a date to travel to Dallas. This
agreement, of Hubert participating in the interview of Ruby,
is documented in the memorandum file that Hubert preserved
and can be found in Warren Commission documents stored at
the National Archives. (2) What is most disturbing, is that
when the Commission did go to Dallas to interview Ruby,
neither Griffin or Hubert were notified of the date of the
interview or asked to participate. (3) The end result being,

that the two men who had carried out the six-month investigation probing into the background of Jack Ruby's activities and possible motives, and who were also most qualified to ask the pointed questions that would alleviate their stated doubts, would not be permitted to do so. The Commission had already waited six months to interview the most important witness in their investigation, the murderer of the accused assassin. With no one experienced in the background investigation of Jack Ruby traveling to Dallas, no one was ever able to question Ruby in a public forum in a manner that would produce credible answers to the nagging doubts that pervaded the Commission's questionable conclusions.

Thus, it is easy to understand why the House Select Committee on Assassinations ". . . determined the performance of the Commission was less than complete [in regards to] 'the background activities of Jack Ruby particularly with regard to organized crime.'" (4) This becomes even more clear after analyzing the many statements that Ruby made before the Warren Commission. Ruby testified, "[I] also had numerous phone calls, long distance calls, all over the country." (5) Ruby was then asked, "Did any union or underworld connection have anything to do with the shooting of Oswald?" Ruby: "Very good." (6) Later in his testimony, "[Ruby asked] How about the underworld? . . . There were a lot of phone calls." (7) Later in his interrogation, Ruby was asked whether he wished to be questioned on any other topic and he replied, "Yes—whether or not I was ever mixed up with the underworld here or involved in any crime." (8) Still later in his questioning, Ruby was again asked whether he wished to be asked further questions and he replied affirmatively, "Oh, yes, sir. Has the underworld ever contributed money for me for my clubs, or was I put here as a front to the underworld or things to that effect." (9) Ruby later answered his own question when he stated, " . . . maybe I was put here as a front of the underworld and sooner or later they will get something out of me that they want done to their advantage." (10) Despite these obvious attempts to convince the Commission to ask deeper questions, the members of the Commission failed to do so. Documents available to the Warren Commission, in fact, corroborates this version of Ruby's peripheral, if not direct involvement in organized crime. "Steve Guthrie, former

Sheriff of Dallas . . . reported that shortly after his election as Sheriff in July 1946, Paul Roland Jones, representing other Chicago criminals, offered him a substantial amount of money to permit them to move in and manage illegal activities in Dallas. Although he never met Ruby, Guthrie asserted that these criminals frequently mentioned that Ruby would operate a "fabulous" restaurant as a front for gambling activities." (11) Despite this reliable source, the Commission was unable to accept this report and chose to believe others who denied Guthrie's claims.

The House Select Committee did document that Ruby had made a series of phone calls to former associates from his days in Chicago who were known members or associates of those involved in organized crime. These series of phone calls became more frequent in September and October 1963, the months leading up to the assassination of President Kennedy. Ruby at first attempted to explain these phone calls as innocent and related to business problems he was experiencing:

> Recently, I had to make so many numerous calls that I am sure you know of. Am I right? Because of trying to survive in my business. My unfair competition had been running certain shows that we were restricted to run by regulation of the union . . . and consequently I was becoming insolvent because of it. All those calls were made with only, in relation to seeing if they can help out, with the American Guild of Variety Artists. Does that confirm a lot of things you have heard? (12)

Ruby was obviously aware that the Warren Commission had a record of his phone calls and that many of these calls were to "old friends" in Chicago who had ties or were directly involved in organized crime. Despite the blatantly leading questions and comments offered by Ruby, the Commission either feigned ignorance, did not want to know, or deliberately closed the door to the possibility of these associations.

The House Select Committee "confirmed the existence of several contacts between Ruby and associates of [Teamster boss Jimmy] Hoffa during the period of October and November 1963." (13) Ruby had called Murray W. "Dusty" Miller, the head of the Southern Conference on Teamsters on November 8, 1963. The House Select Committee determined that Miller "was associated with numerous underworld figures." (14) Ruby had called noted Chicago bail bondsman, Irwin S. Weiner, on October 26, 1963. The House Select Committee documented that a list of Weiner's associates "would include a significant number of the major organized crime figures in the United States. Among them have been Jimmy Hoffa, Santo Trafficante, and Sam Giancana." (15) As has been established in other research and will be reviewed here, all three had the motive and the means to murder the President.

Not only did all three have the motive and the means, but Trafficante and Louisiana crime boss Carlos Marcello were on record as stating that Kennedy should and would be killed. (16) A prominent Cuban exile, Jose Aleman, supported this argument during his HSCA testimony. Aleman told the Committee that in 1962 Santos Trafficante was helping Aleman arrange a loan from the Teamsters and Jimmy Hoffa. Apparently Aleman had helped one of Trafficantes' relatives escape from jail in Cuba and Trafficante then arranged the loan to Aleman through Hoffa as a favor. Aleman stated that Trafficante told him "a lot of people weren't going to forget the problems Kennedy had caused them, including Hoffa." (17) Aleman stated that he was unsure of Trafficantes' meaning and Trafficante then made his message clear. "You don't understand me. Kennedy's not going to make it to the election. He is going to be hit." (18) Mr. Aleman was left with the definite impression that Trafficante "was not guessing" and that Trafficante "did in fact know that such a crime was being planned." (19) Ironically, Hoffa, Sam Giancana, and fellow west coast organized crime associate John Roselli were also involved in the original CIA-Mafia assassination plots against Fidel Castro. (20)

The relationship between Jack Ruby and John Roselli appears to have dated back to the 1930's after Ruby (then Rubenstein) left Chicago to go to California. (21) Ruby had been implicated in the murder of Leon Cooke, a Chicago union organizer and Ruby's picture had appeared on the cover of the *Chicago Tribune* in conjunction with a story describing the murder. The murder was never solved—the witness that was to identify the killer was himself murdered. Roselli and Ruby would eventually work together at the Santa Anita racetrack where Ruby sold tip sheets and performed other tasks at the racetrack. (22) Even more interesting is that Roselli,

Giancana, and Hoffa were all murdered just as the Church and House Select Committees were preparing to interview them. Hoffa is also on record as being involved in an attempt to kill Robert Kennedy. As previously noted, Federal Agent Hawk Daniels believed that, based on wire-taps he had been asked to listen to regarding Hoffa, Hoffa was also a threat to kill the President. (23) Also included in these contacts was former Chicago associate, David Yaras. Yaras had been involved in mob operations in Cuba and according to congressional investigations on organized crime, was also known to have been engaged in "extortion, mayhem, and murder" and was "a prime suspect in several gangland slayings." (24) Yaras's suspected partner in a number of these murders was another long-time Chicago "friend" of Ruby named Lenny Patrick. (25)

Barney Baker, a close associate of Jimmy Hoffa, called Jack Ruby from Chicago on November 7, and Ruby also called Baker the following day. (26) In the 1940's Baker had worked for reputed organized crime members Jake Lansky in Florida and Bugsy Siegel in Las Vegas. (27) Robert Kennedy had described Baker as one of Hoffa's "roving emissaries of violence." (28) This is corroborated by an FBI report which labeled Baker as "a reported muscle and bagman for Teamster President James Riddle Hoffa." (29) Another Ruby contact, who was identified as a top-ranking member in the world of Dallas organized crime, was Joseph Campisi. Campisi was closely associated with various Dallas crime figures as well as with various Dallas law enforcement officials and judges in the state of Texas. (30) The Warren Commission documented Campisi's visit to Ruby on November 30, 1963, where Ruby was being held in the Dallas County Jail for the murder of Lee Oswald. (31) In an interview with the FBI, Campisi had originally admitted to meeting with Ruby on the night before the assassination, only to retract this admission during his testimony before the House Select Committee in 1978. (32) Campisi inherited the leadership position in the world of Dallas organized crime from another Ruby associate, Joseph Civello. Ruby's relationship with Campisi reached back into the early 1950's and is corroborated by Civello's statements to the FBI and the subsequent statements of former Ruby employee, Bobby Gene Moore. (33)

Alexander Gruber was a long-time friend of Ruby's dating

back to his days in Chicago when Ruby and Gruber had roomed together. (34) After reportedly not being in contact with Ruby in ten years, Gruber visited Ruby in Dallas for a number of days in November 1963. (35) Gruber had a rap sheet which included six arrests and was also affiliated with Jimmy Hoffa and west coast organized crime associate, Mickey Cohen. (36)

Another interesting link between Jimmy Hoffa and Jack Ruby was found in the relationship between Ruby and Teamster official Frank Chavez. Chavez had a reputation as a thug and had been arrested for attempted murder (37) Chavez had met with Jack Ruby and other Teamster and organized crime leaders on at least two occasions in the early 1960's. (38)

Based on the preponderance of evidence available, it is apparent why Congressman Stewart McKinney asked a seemingly obvious question to a spokesman from Hoover's FBI during the House Select Committee investigation. "Wasn't it pretty well known to the FBI that Jack Ruby, No. 1, was a member of organized crime, No. 2, that he ran a strip joint and had been somewhat commonly referred to as a supplier of women and booze to political and police figures in the city of Dallas[?] Didn't you find it a little difficult to accept the Warren Commission's final output on Ruby with the knowledge that the FBI had put into the Commission?" (39) It seems reasonable to argue that Jack Ruby, like Lee Oswald before him, was much more than a "lone nut assassin."

A Warren Commission memorandum compiled by staff attorneys, Leon Hubert and Burt Griffin, who as stated previously were prevented from interrogating Jack Ruby, corroborates those who doubt that Ruby killed Oswald out of his stated love for President Kennedy. Their memo stated, "It is possible that Ruby could have been utilized by a politically motivated group either upon the promise of money or because of the influential character of the individual approaching Ruby." (40) The House Select Committee also questioned Ruby's self-proclaimed motive for his killing Lee Oswald. This doubt by the Committee was facilitated by a note that Ruby had written to his attorney, Joe Tonahill, in 1967. Ruby explained to Tonahill that his first lawyer, Tom Howard, advised him on how he should mount a defense. Ruby wrote to Tonahill, "Joe, you should know this. Tom Howard told me to say that I shot Oswald so that Caroline and Mrs. Kennedy would not have to come to Dallas to testify."Okay?" (41)

Tom Howard had visited Jack Ruby's apartment on November 24, 1963, the evening after Ruby had murdered Lee Oswald. With Howard were four other men. Two of them were reporters; Bill Hunter of the *Long Beach Press Telegram* and Jim Koethe of the *Dallas Times Herald*. Howard, Hunter, and Koethe would all be dead within a year and a half. Hunter was shot to death on April 24, 1964, Jim Koethe was killed by a karate chop to the throat, and Howard died of an apparent heart attack on March 28, 1965. (42) Little wonder that Jack Ruby's story, of why he killed Oswald, was doubted. One of Ruby's new lawyers, Melvin Belli, recalled, "Clearly [Ruby's] . . .story of trying to protect Mrs. Kennedy from a harrowing court appearance at a trial for Oswald did not add up. . . . I am sure the story was false because it didn't square with everything we knew. . . ." (43) In an article published in the *New York Times* on November 28, 1963, Dallas District Attorney Henry Wade made clear his initial impressions of Ruby's story, " . . . [Wade] said today he did not believe the story [that] . . . Ruby . . . had killed . . . Oswald to avenge the assassination of President Kennedy. 'It . . . may have involved something far deeper . . . our law enforcement agencies are still checking to determine if links exist between Oswald and Ruby. . . .'" The House Select Committee supported the scepticism of Belli and Wade when it concluded: "Based on a review of the evidence, albeit circumstantial, the Committee believed that Ruby's shooting of Oswald was not a spontaneous act, in that it involved at least some premeditation." (44)

Dallas Police Captain Frank Martin was a witness to the murder of Lee Oswald and was also acquainted with Jack Ruby. In his Warren Commission testimony he was asked, "Now Captain Martin is there anything else you would like to say concerning any aspect of this matter at all? Martin: "I . . . don't take this down! . . . " Counsel: "Well if you don't want to say it on the record, you'd better not say it at all." Martin: There's a lot to be said, but probably be better if I don't say it. (45) Captain Martin died of "apparent cancer" in June 1966.

An article written by columnist Dorothy Kilgallen and published in the *Philadelphia News* on February 22, 1964, ascribed the involvement of J. Edgar Hoover and the FBI in cutting of speculation in regards to the relationship between

Jack Ruby and Lee Oswald. Kilgallen was in Dallas covering the Ruby trial when she wrote:

> One of the best kept secrets of the Jack Ruby trial is the extent to which the Federal government is cooperating with the defense. . . . It provides Ruby's side with reams of helpful information that they never [would] have [been] able to get without the G-Men—on the condition that they do not ask for anything at all about Ruby's alleged victim, Lee Harvey Oswald. It appears that Washington knows or suspects something about Oswald that it does not want Dallas and the rest of the world to know or suspect. . . . Why is Oswald being kept in the shadows, as dim a figure as they can make him, while the defense tries to rescue his killer with the help of information with the help of the FBI? Who was Oswald anyway . . . daring defense attorney Joe H. Tonahill dashed off a letter to J. Edgar Hoover, director of the FBI, and a duplicate plea to J. Lee Rankin, chief counsel for the President's committee investigating the assassination. Tonahill asked for the world. He requested Hoover and Rankin to provide him "all the reports and minutes and evidence" in the possession of what is now known as the Warren Commission. He probably expected a rebuff. Or a polite brush off. But what he got was pure gold. On January 28, Asst. Atty. Gen. Herbert J. Miller responded to the communiques. . . The "kicker"—the punch line? Miller's sentence: "Information concerning Oswald's assassination of the President would not be available as it does not appear to be relevant." Perhaps it is dramatizing to say that there is [an] Orwellian note in that line. But it does make you think doesn't it.

Miss Kilgallen's analysis indicates that J. Edgar Hoover did not want to probe any deeper into the possible relationship between Lee Oswald and Jack Ruby. This argument is further supported by an article written by Miss Kilgallen and published in the September 30, 1964 edition of the *New York Journal American:* "I would be inclined to believe that the FBI would be more profitably employed in probing the facts of the case rather than how I get them." With the murder of Oswald, and with Ruby not taking the stand in his own defense, there would be no public questioning of either man.

Although it has never been proven that Oswald and Ruby were associated and knew each other, there has been much speculation that this, in fact, was true. Much of this speculation has originated from a number of employees of

Jack Ruby, including Rose Cheramie, Beverly Oliver, and Karen Carlin. (46) One argument as to why this has never been clearly documented is that there is such a preponderance of violent deaths associated with those close to Jack Ruby, many of them being former strippers at his clubs. These deaths include Karen Carlin, Rose Cheramie, Betty McDonald, and Marilyn "Delilah" Walle, all within three years of the assassination of President Kennedy. Coincidentally, Hank Killiam, husband of another Ruby employee, Wanda Killiam, was found bleeding to death on March 17, 1964. He apparently had slit his throat while "committing suicide," by jumping through a window. Killiam had another interesting connection—he had worked as a house painter with John Carter, who happened to live in the same rooming house as Lee Oswald at 1026 North Beckley Avenue. (49)

These deaths lend more credence to Beverly Oliver's story as to why she did not come forward with her account of knowing of a relationship between Jack Ruby and Lee Oswald before the early 1970's. Even more interesting is her account of being the "Babushka Lady" who is seen in various photographs filming the motorcade across the street from the grassy knoll. Whoever this woman was (if it was not Oliver), her vantage point across the street from the picket fence would go a long way in determining what really happened on the knoll and behind the fence. The camera model she claimed to have used was apparently not in commercial use in 1963, but the model had been developed and was possibly in limited production. One indisputable fact is that someone was filming the assassination from the location that Oliver claimed to be in and no one else has ever come forward to claim that she was the woman at the scene. It has been documented that she did live in Dallas and had also worked as a dancer at Jack Ruby's club. Although parts of Oliver's account found in her book, *Nightmare in Dallas*, appear to be questionable, no one has been able to disprove that she was filming the assassination across the street from the picket fence. In fact, her account of seeing smoke coming from behind the fence and the shots emanating from that location have been corroborated by numerous witnesses and other researchers in this work.

The statements of Karen Carlin to Secret Service agent Roger C. Warner on November 24, 1963, also makes clear a genuine fear among some of Ruby's workers of being murdered. Warner reported:

> Mrs. Carlin was highly agitated and was reluctant to make any statement to me. She stated to me that she was under the impression that Lee Harvey Oswald, Jack Ruby and other individuals unknown to her, were involved in a plot to assassinate President Kennedy and that she would be killed if she gave any information to the authorities. (50)

Warner went on to say Carlin "was reluctant to make any statement . . . [she] twisted in her chair, stammered in her speech, and seemed on the point of hysteria." Warner stated that Carlin requested "that all information she had related be kept confidential to prevent retaliation against her in case there was a plot afoot." (51)   The Warren Commission questioned Carlin further on her fears of being killed:

> *Q.* Do you recall that during the course of the Ruby trial when you were waiting to testify that there was a jail break there and some people got out of the jail, and I think they passed right near by you, I believe?
> *Mrs. Carlin.* Yes.
> *Q.* Do you remember what you screamed or said?
> *Mrs. Carlin.* Oh my God, they're after me.
> *Q.* Yes—what made you believe that "they" were after you?
> *Mrs. Carlin.* Because I was scared I was going to get killed before I even go to court. (52)

Carlin not only indicated her knowledge of a relationship between Oswald and Ruby, but she was also instrumental in the events that led to the shooting of Lee Oswald. On the morning that Lee Oswald was murdered by Jack Ruby, Carlin was the recipient of a loan that Ruby had sent to her from the Western Union office less than five minutes before the shooting occurred. After wiring the money order to Carlin, Ruby proceeded to walk less than half a block from the Western Union office and into the basement of the Dallas Police Station and shot Oswald just as he was being transferred. Ruby had stated in his Warren Commission testimony, ". . . if there was a conspiracy, then this little girl [Carlin] that called me on the phone in Ft. Worth then is part of the conspiracy." (53) Ruby went on to say, "Who else could have timed it so perfectly by seconds. If it were timed that way, then someone in the police department is guilty of giving the information as to when Lee Harvey Oswald was coming down." (54)

Ruby initially stated that on the evening of the assassination, he had carried his .38 revolver with him as he visited the police station on the floor where Oswald was being held. The implication being that Ruby was stalking Oswald, and that the subsequent murder was premeditated. It was probably for this reason that Ruby later withdrew his statement and denied that he had his gun with him on Friday night. (55) Ruby had stated to the Warren Commission that he had been "grieving" over the death of President Kennedy on Friday and Saturday before he shot Lee Oswald on Sunday morning. This is not supported by some of those that came in contact with him on Friday evening. An incident which casts doubt on Ruby's story occurred late on Friday evening and took place at a local radio station. Dallas Morning News journalist Hugh Aynsworth, related to the FBI that Ruby "feigned surprise at this announcement [the assassination of the President] and gave some show of emotion." (56) Glen Duncan also talked with Ruby at the same radio station on November 23 and stated that, " . . . [Ruby] was not grieving [and] if anything was happy that the evidence was piling up against Oswald." (57)

Ruby's known friendship with so many members of the Dallas Police makes it difficult to pinpoint who might have helped facilitate the murder of Lee Oswald. Evidence of his friendships with various members of the Dallas Police Force is found in the Commission's own report. "He is known to have brutally beaten at least 25 persons" and was never convicted or spent a night in jail. (58) "To generalize, it can be said that while living in Dallas, Ruby has carefully cultivated friendships with police officers and other public officials." (59) According to entertainer Joseph Johnson, who worked for Ruby at the Colony Club, Ruby knew over half of the twelve hundred men on the Dallas Police Department. (60) Johnson's claim is also supported by a number of Ruby's associates including Breck Wall, Robert Craven, Joseph Cavagnaro, and Reagen Thurman (61) "Ruby is also rumored to have been the tip-off man between the Dallas Police and the underworld and his primary technique in avoiding prosecution was the maintenance of friendship with police officers, public officials, and other influential persons in the Dallas community." (62) The identity of those involved might be obscure but the evidence appears to be clear, someone on "the inside," abruptly cut-short the interrogation of Lee Oswald that was taking place, just as Ruby was getting into position and Chief Curry was also called away at that precise moment to take a phone call from Dallas Mayor Earle Cabell. (63) Is this just another in a series of amazing coincidences? There appears to be too much documentation to accept the mountain of coincidences. It seems quite clear, Jack Ruby murdered Oswald with the help of others not because of his love of President Kennedy but rather to not allow Oswald to talk of who or what he knew about the assassination.

There is evidence to indicate that Jack Ruby, immediately after the assassination drove to Parkland Hospital, evidently to check on the condition of the President. This would not appear to be unusual, except for the fact that Ruby was on record as stating that he spent the morning of the assassination in the advertising office of the *Dallas Morning News*. According to Ruby and *News* entertainment director Tony Zoppi, Ruby was in his office during the assassination and for an undetermined time after the shooting. The problem with this story is that Tony Zoppi, according to Ruby's initial testimony to the Warren Commission, was not even in Dallas but had gone to New Orleans for a couple of days. (64) Zoppi later told the Warren Commission that he, indeed, had been in Dallas and Ruby had been in his office for two or three hours that morning and was there after the assassination and did not walk the two blocks to Dealy Plaza to watch the motorcade despite having such a great affection for President Kennedy. (65)

However, two separate witnesses identified Ruby as being at Parkland Hospital within one hour after the assassination. Seth Kantor, a former Dallas reporter who had become a member of the Washington press corps, reported seeing Ruby at the hospital around 1:30. Kantor was the subject of an FBI interview that was published in the Warren Report which stated:

> Kantor was pointedly told by interviewing agents that Ruby has emphatically denied he was at Parkland Hospital at any time November 22, 1963, or subsequent. Kantor was specifically asked whether he might be mistaken about seeing Ruby there . . . Kantor reiterated he is absolutely certain he saw and spoke with Ruby at the Parkland Hospital on November 22. Kantor was told that he might be called upon

to testify in this case. He was asked what he would say if under oath and on the witness stand in a court of law to the question, "Did you see and talk with Ruby at the Parkland Hospital on November 22, 1963?" Kantor stated that he would answer, "Yes," because he is absolutely certain he did. (66)

Mrs. Wilma Tice also claimed to have seen Ruby at Parkland at about the same time and was questioned by the Commission as to the accuracy of her statement:

Q. Mrs. Tice, did you know that Jack himself has denied very vehemently that he was at the hospital?
Mrs. Tice. Yes, I know he denied that, and I hated to say that I saw him out there . . . Eva Grant [Ruby's sister] told me, "Well, I asked Jack and Jack said no, he wasn't out there." And I said, "Well, anybody can make a mistake." . . . She said, "Yes, because there are many Jacks. . . and if it wasn't him it was his twin brother."
Q. Do you think you could have been mistaken about the man you saw? Mrs. Tice. It could have been somebody else that looked just like Jack, named Jack; yes. (67)

Ruby's continued denials of being at Parkland Hospital after the assassination as well as he and Zoppi's contradictory testimony cause one to doubt what Ruby was really doing on the morning of the assassination and in the hours immediately afterwards. If the answers to these contradictions are innocent ones, then there would be no need for the repeated lies. If indeed, Ruby was within two blocks of Dealy Plaza as the motorcade carrying President Kennedy came through, why did he not make an attempt to see the President as he drove by?

In yet another interesting side note, one of Jack Ruby's closest friends, Joe Goldstein had somehow been able to pass through the parking lot behind the fence and park his truck on the Elm Street extension. This is corroborated by Jean Hill and numerous other witnesses. (68) Hill stated that she "noticed an automobile circling the area. The windows were covered with cardboard and the name 'Honest Joe's Pawn Shop' was painted on the side . . . a policeman told her the driver had permission to drive in the area." (69) A. J. Millican also recalled seeing Goldstein's truck in the same area. He noticed "a truck from Uncle Joe's Pawn Shop" on the Elm Street extension just minutes before the shots rang out. (70)

Why Goldstein was parked close to the location of where many believe the shots originated from, and in an area that was supposed to be off limits, is not clear. It could be another coincidence but as we have seen, Lee Bowers noticed three vehicles and their drivers probing behind the fence towards the Elm Street extension. Goldstein's presence could mean more than has been disclosed. When this is considered in light of Ruby's other activities and claims, then one should be suspicious as to what his true intentions and activities were.

The question of whether Jack Ruby knew Officer J. D. Tippit has also brought Ruby's intentions into question. According to his Warren Commission testimony, Ruby hesitantly denied knowing "the Officer Tippit that was killed."

> *Q.* Did you know Officer Tippit?
> *Ruby.* This is off the record for a minute please.
> *Q.* Mr. Ruby, I think it would be unwise for us to go off the record on this question.
> *Ruby.* Well, all right. There were three Officer Tippit's in the police department. I only knew one.
> *Q.* Was that officer J. D. Tippit?
> *Ruby.* He's the one who was slain?
> *Q.* Yes-Officer J. D. Tippit.
> *Ruby.* No; I don't think he was the one.
> *Q.* Did you know Officer Tippit who was slain?
> *Ruby.* No: I don't know him. You see, I know so many officers and there are three Tippits, but I know one Tippit, and which one that is—if I would see him personally and see his physical features and knowing him—of course, I wouldn't have time to—I was incarcerated too soon to find out. . . ." (71)

But according to an article in the *New York Herald Tribune* of December 5, 1963, Eva Grant, who was Jack Ruby's sister stated, "Jack knew him, and I knew him . . . Jack called him buddy. . . . He was in and out of our place [Carousel Club] many times." The Warren Commission went on to deny that she made that statement. But a portion of her testimony brings that denial into question. After viewing a photograph of Officer Tippit in front of the Commission, she stated that "he looked familiar . . . and in fact recalled that Tippit was in our club sometime—a month previous to this—his killing." (72)

This documentary evidence lends credibility to the determinations and questions that the House Select

Committee, and Warren Commission attorneys Hubert and Griffin, brought to the forefront. The Commission has portrayed Jack Ruby as the lone and unaided killer of Lee Oswald and that his subsequent later testimony of his knowledge and/or involvement in a conspiracy to silence Oswald and in the assassination of President Kennedy were the ravings of a "nut," "two bit pawn," and "a loser."

There is much documented evidence that despite the Commission's conclusions, Ruby appeared not to be another "lone nut assassin." He was, in fact, closely associated with gamblers, gun-runners, policemen, elements of the right-wing, as well as certain members of organized crime. Ruby, himself, as well as the testimony and the documented statements of numerous individuals, corroborates these assertions. The Warren Commission testimony of Nancy Perrin Rich revealed in great detail the gun running activities of Jack Ruby. (73) Her testimony was not published in its report, but her statements have been documented as a result of her interview with Mark Lane in 1965. (74) Blaney Johnson, an FBI informant and a pilot who had flown cargo to Cuba, stated that Ruby "was active in arranging illegal flights of weapons from Miami to the Castro organization in Cuba." (75) According to an FBI report, an associate of Ruby named James Woodard, was also involved in gun running activities with Ruby. (76) This is corroborated by an FBI document in which Woodard admitted to have "furnished ammunition and dynamite to both Castro and Cuban exile forces." (77)

Ruby's gun running activities and smuggling activities are also given credence by the statements of Robert McKeown. McKeown told the FBI that Ruby had called him about the sale of some jeeps to Cuba in 1959. He later identified Ruby from photographs. "[McKeown believed] strongly that this individual was in fact Jack Ruby." (78) Another former associate of Ruby, James Beard, stated that Ruby had stored guns and ammunition at a location on the southern Texas coast. Beard recalled that he "personally saw many boxes of new guns, including automatic rifles and hand guns" that were eventually shipped to the followers of Fidel Castro. (79) Ruby, in a letter smuggled out of his Dallas cell, voiced concern that one of the policemen guarding him had overheard him say, "that I sent guns to Cuba that was during peace relations with Cuba, we really hadn't found out what kind of person Castro was." (80)

Just as Lee Harvey Oswald was considered to be an FBI informant, so, too, was Jack Ruby. Ruby had been in frequent contact with the FBI in 1959. The Bureau had met with him nine times from March until October. It is also possible that Ruby could have been informing the Bureau of other areas of interest to them, such as his Cuban activities. (81) The FBI indicated that Ruby's nine meetings with them had borne no fruit. But author Seth Kantor has noted that Ruby's rental of a safe deposit box coincided with his nine meetings with FBI agent Charles Flynn, and that Ruby had used the box twelve times in the year 1959. (82) Apparently, some sort of information was being passed along to the FBI, what it was is not totally clear. Warren Commission staff attorney Burt Griffin later reflected, ". . . I don't remember if it occurred to me in 1964 that such FBI contacts in 1959 might have been in connection with Cuban matters. . . . If Hoover concealed information, such a concealment would be important and serious." (83)

One of the more fascinating individuals that Jack Ruby appeared to be involved in running guns with was Thomas Eli Davis. Ruby had mentioned Davis' name in passing, as being involved in anti-Castro gun running activities during his Warren Commission testimony and the Commission took little notice. It wasn't until former Dallas reporter Seth Kantor delved into his background, that some of the activities of Davis became known. Correspondence between J. Edgar Hoover and the American State Department indicated that Davis had been taken into custody by security forces in Morroco because he had in his possession "a letter in his handwriting which referred in passing to Oswald and the Kennedy assassination." (84) What makes this even more interesting is that Davis was apparently sprung from jail as a result of the efforts of QJ/WIN, who was identified by the CIA only as a "foreign citizen with a criminal background." Jack Ruby stated to his first lawyer, Tom Howard, that bringing up the name Thomas Eli Davis would be damaging to his defense. Davis was never questioned by any investigative agency as a result of his untimely death. Davis allegedly was electrocuted while committing a "robbery" in 1973. (85)

Rose Cheramie, a former employee of Jack Ruby, who was also a heroin addict involved in narcotics smuggling, predicted that President Kennedy would be assassinated to doctors and various hospital personnel on November 20, 1963 while a patient at Louisiana State Hospital in Jackson, Louisiana. She was found by the side of the road near Eunice, Louisiana, and it was reported that she had been thrown out of a car by individuals traveling from Florida to Dallas on a narcotics run. (86) Cheramie's story has been challenged, in part because she was going through heroin withdrawal at the time she was hospitalized and because of her record as a prostitute. Louisiana State Police Lieutenant Francis Fruge was the police officer who came to Cheramie's assistance and drove her to the hospital. Cheramie related to Fruge that "the two men traveling with her from Miami were going to Dallas to kill the President" and that her role in the operation was to obtain $8,000 from an unidentified source in Dallas, and proceed to Houston and Galveston with the two men to complete a drug deal." She had also planned to pick up her son who was being watched by a friend in Dallas. (87) The House Select Committee reported that Dr. Victor Weiss, a resident physician at the Louisiana State Hospital, believed her story was credible. According to the House Select Committee:

> Dr. Victor Weiss . . . recalled that on Monday, November 25, 1963, he was asked by another physician, Dr. Bowers, to see a patient who had been committed November 20 or 21. Dr. Bowers allegedly told Weiss that the patient, Rose Cheramie, had stated before the assassination that President Kennedy was going to be killed. Weiss questioned Cheramie about her statements. She told him she had worked for Jack Ruby. She did not have any specific details of a particular assassination plot against Kennedy, but had stated the "word in the underworld" was that Kennedy would be assassinated. She further stated that she had been traveling from Florida to her home in Texas when the man traveling with her threw her from the automobile in which they were riding. (88)

Lieutenant Fruge, on November 22, on the afternoon of the assassination of President Kennedy, received authorization to proceed with an investigation in an attempt to verify Cheramie's allegations. Fruge's investigation verified that Cheramie had indeed been involved in a narcotics operation that was to involve a ship docked at the port of Galveston. (89) Lieutenant Fruge traveled to the Silver Slipper Lounge, where Cheramie and the men she had traveled with had been drinking before she was thrown out of the car. Fruge showed the owner of the bar various photographs of individuals reportedly traveling with Cheramie. Interestingly enough, the owner of the bar recognized Sergio Archacha Smith as one of the men shown to him in the photographs. (90) Smith was a known associate of Carlos Marcello and David Ferrie and possibly brings the relationship between David Ferrie, Lee Oswald, and Jack Ruby to a complete circle. Another interesting sidelight, that possibly provides further corroboration to Cheramie's account, is that Fruge recalled Cheramie laughed at the suggestion that Ruby and Oswald were not associated. Cheramie claimed that Ruby and Oswald, "had been shacking up for years" in an apparent homosexual relationship. (91) This information might easily be cast aside if it were not for other corroborating accounts. Karen Carlin had stated to the Warren Commission, "He [Ruby] was always asking the question, 'Do you think I am a queer? Do you think I look like a queer?' or 'Have you ever known a queer to look like me?' Everytime I saw him he would ask that." (92) The Commission testimony of Dean Andrews, an attorney in New Orleans, also adds credibility to Cheramie's accusations regarding a possible homosexual relationship between Oswald and Ruby:

> Andrews stated that Oswald came to his office several times in the summer of 1963 to seek advice on a less than honorable discharge from the Armed Forces, the citizenship status of his wife, and his own citizenship status. Andrews, who believed that he was contacted on November 23 to represent Oswald, testified that Oswald was always accompanied by a Mexican and was at times accompanied by apparent homosexuals. (93)

Further documentation of Rose Cheramie's allegations were brought to a sudden end by her untimely death on September 4, 1965, just one month after she had contacted the FBI in her role as an informant on criminal and narcotics activities. In another "ironic" twist of fate, Cheramie had apparently been thrown out of a car and her head was run over. (94)

Another possible corroboration of Jack Ruby being involved in gun-running, involves Marita Lorenz and her allegations that she was involved in traveling from Miami to Dallas with a number of men who were driving in separate cars on their way to Dallas to assassinate President Kennedy. Documentation for Lorenz's association with CIA plots to kill Fidel Castro have been verified by documents obtained and presented in a defamation suit brought by E. Howard Hunt (of Watergate fame) against the newspaper, *The Spotlight* and its publisher, Liberty Lobby. (95). Lorenz reported that the men she traveled with met with Jack Ruby in a Dallas hotel to complete a weapons deal the night before the assassination. (96) Author Ted Schwartz has attempted to further expand on and document Lorenz's fascinating story in a book co-written with Lorenz entitled, *One Woman's Extraordinary Tale of Love and Espionage from Castro to Kennedy.* A connection between the claims of Rose Cheramie and Marita Lorenz has never been verified but this does not mean that the possibility of Ruby being involved in these activities should be ruled out. On the contrary, the numerous examples of Jack Ruby's documented involvement with organized crime and gun-running, could lead one to see the possibilities as credible.

Authors Ray and Mary La Fontaine have offered even more documentary evidence in their book, *Oswald Talked,* of Jack Ruby's gun-running activities and that these activities linked Ruby to the world of the anti-communist activities of the John Birch Society, General Edwin Walker, and to other elements of the extreme right-wing. (97) The La Fontaine's also make a convincing case that Lee Oswald might have shared a cell with a man named John Elrod on the afternoon of the assassination and that Elrod and Oswald reportedly discussed their mutual knowledge of Jack Ruby and the gun-runners. (98)

Other areas of interest that Jack Ruby was involved in were gambling and narcotics operations. The House Select Committee concluded that Ruby "may in fact have been serving as a courier for gambling interests" while traveling to Cuba. (99) The Committee had also noted that Ruby's trips to Cuba may well have involved meeting with Santos Trafficante, the Florida mob boss, who was being held in the Trescronia prison after the Castro government had closed the casinos and temporarily imprisoned him. Ruby's relationship with other Trafficante associates, such as R. D. Mathews, Jack Todd, and James Dolan (who were all from Dallas) has also been documented by the Committee. (100) Lewis McWillie, one of Jack Ruby's closest friends, worked for Trafficante and Meyer Lansky, the reputed financial wizard of the American Mafia. Both Trafficante and Lansky owned a stake in a Havana gambling casino where McWillie served as pit boss. These associations further document Jack Ruby's

ties to organized crime and clearly establish the possibility
that Ruby was strongly influenced by certain members of
organized crime.

It is also interesting to note that Jack Ruby, during his
Warren Commission testimony, discussed his knowledge
about the death of Alfred McLane to Commission member
Earl Warren, when he stated that "Alfred was killed in a taxi
in New York." (101) It appears to have been a small world;
Warren told Ruby that he knew of Alfred McLane. McLane
was the general counsel to an oil company called Rimrock
Tidelands whose subsidiary was Rimrock International. This
company was under suspicion for being used as a cover for
international narcotics traffic. (102) Author Seth Kantor
wrote after interviewing one of McLane's law partners,
"Funny thing about McLane . . . He was was different. He
was a loner. He was driven with the obsession of getting
money, in the end he was successful. But he hung out with
promoters and there were concealed people in his life." (103)
The connections and associations of Jack Ruby appear to be
wider and more complex than the Commission publicly gave
him credit for. For in the Commission's own words, " . . .
[Ruby] became the subject of a narcotics investigation [and
was] peripherally, if not directly connected with members of
the underworld [and has] very carefully cultivated friendships
with police officers and other public officials." (104)

Further corroboration of Ruby's involvement in narcotics
traffic is evidenced by the statements of Eileen Curry. Curry,
who had been involved in narcotics and prostitution, was also
an FBI informant and told the FBI that her "husband," James
Breen, who was also known to have been involved in the
smuggling of narcotics, told her that, "In some fashion James
got the okay to operate through Jack Ruby of Dallas." (105)
Curry also stated that she witnessed James leave on a trip
with Ruby and that when he returned, James told her that
"he had been shown moving pictures of various border guards,
both Mexican and American. . . . James was enthused over
what he considered an extremely efficient operation with
narcotics traffic." (106) Despite the evidence presented here,
which was readily available to the Warren Commission, the
Final Report of the Commission dismissed the allegations
that Jack Ruby was involved in narcotics traffic. (107)

A convicted gambler named Harry Hall contacted the
Secret Service, while an inmate at the Los Angeles Federal

Prison on Terminal Island. Hall reported that he and Ruby traveled together to various cities such as Chicago, Tulsa, and Shreveport where Ruby's connections with gamblers would allow Hall to set up big-money bets on sporting events with Texas oilmen. (108) Hall also stated that Ruby was connected to the Dell Charo Resort group that included Texan Billy Byers and oilman Clint Murchison. Ironically, both Byers and Murchison were close friends of J. Edgar Hoover. (109) The Warren Commission's Preliminary Report substantiates the possibility that Ruby was involved with certain members of the "Las Vegas gambling community," who, as the report indicated, were also considered to be interested in the elimination of President Kennedy. (110) These connections were not properly considered or investigated by the Warren Commission or J. Edgar Hoover.

Another area of interest that Jack Ruby had was in the right-wing causes of H. L. Hunt, the billionaire Texas oil man. On the day before the assassination, Ruby visited the offices of Lamar Hunt, the son of H. L. Hunt. Ruby had apparently taken a young woman named Connie Trammel to a job interview with Lamar. (111) It was Lamar's brother, Nelson Bunker Hunt, who had paid for part of the full page advertisement that appeared in the *Dallas Morning News* on the morning of the assassination. (112) This ad was highly critical of John Kennedy for his perceived soft policies against Communism and was sponsored by the American Fact-Finding Committee, which in reality was a non-existent organization. (113)

Another indication of Ruby's interest and connection to the causes of the Hunts was that on the day he shot Lee Oswald, two scripts of previously aired, "Life Line" broadcasts were found in the trunk of his car. (114) The "Life Line" broadcasts were also extremely conservative in nature and highly critical of John Kennedy's perceived leftist policies. As has been discussed earlier, Dallas was the center of the extreme right-wing and Ruby's association, be it tenuous to the right-wing interests, again causes one to consider where his personal loyalties and interests were. When considered against the backdrop of Ruby's possible right-wing connections, his testimony concerning Major General Edwin Walker before the Warren Commission could be interpreted as troubling and even shocking. Walker was the acknowledged leader of the extreme right-wing in Dallas and had recently been fired by

President Kennedy as a result of his dissemination of extreme right-wing pamphlets to the troops under his command in Germany. Ruby insinuates that his life is in danger and he cannot tell the truth during this Commission hearing. It is also interesting to note that Ruby is also implying that he is not sure of where Secret Service agent Emory Moore "stands" on wanting to hear the truth in regards to Ruby's circumstances:

> *Ruby.* I want to tell the truth, and I can't tell it here. I can't tell it here, does that make sense to you? . . . Where do you stand [Emory] Moore . . . Boys, I'm in a tough spot, I tell you that. . . . Gentlemen, my life is in danger here. Not with my guilty plea of execution. Do I sound sober enough to you as I say this?
> *Chief Justice Warren.* You do. You sound entirely sober.
> *Ruby.* I tell you, gentlemen, my whole family is in jeopardy. . . . All right, there is a certain organization here—
> *Chief Justice Warren.* That I can assure you.
> *Ruby.* There is a certain organization here, Chief Justice Warren, if it takes my life at this moment to say it, and Bill Decker [Sheriff of Dallas] said be a man and say it, there is a John Birch Society right now in activity, and Edwin Walker is one of the top men of this organization—take it for what it is worth, Chief Justice Warren. Unfortunately for me, for me giving the people the opportunity to get in power, because of the act I committed, has put a lot of people in jeopardy with their lives. Don't register with you, does it?
> *Chief Justice Warren.* No, I don't understand that.
> *Ruby.* Would you rather I just delete what I said and just pretend that nothing is going on?
> *Chief Justice Warren.* I would not indeed. I am only interested in what you want to tell this Commission. That is all I am interested in.
> *Ruby.* Well, I said my life, I won't be living long now. . . . When I left my apartment that morning-
> *Chief Justice Warren.* What morning?
> *Ruby.* Sunday morning.
> *Chief Justice Warren.* Sunday morning. (115)

It appears that Ruby was attempting to explain more about his true intentions of why he killed Oswald on that "Sunday morning" to Chief Justice Warren and that Warren either did not truly understand or was not interested in what Ruby might have had to say. Ruby went on to say, "You can get more out of me, let's not break up too soon." (116) Amazingly enough, Chief Justice Warren attempted to discourage Jack Ruby from speaking about General Walker, the John Birch Society, or of his knowledge and accusations of a possible right-wing involvement in the events surrounding the assassination of President Kennedy. Within one week of the assassination, General Walker was interviewed by the right-wing German newspaper, the *National Zeitung and Soldaten Zeitung* in a UPI story, published in the November 28 edition of the *Dallas Morning News:*

> Walker: Kennedy's death did not come as such a surprise as it is now made out to be. . . . There was enough dynamite piled up, only it was covered up by false press reporting. Kennedy's policies were American policies, rich in failures and never crowned by success. . . .

Walker was then asked if the assassination was the work of "right-wing extremists" and replied, "Nonsense. . . . The murderer is a Marxist, a Communist, one of the huge mass of leftist infiltrators. . . ." When General Walker's statements are viewed in light of the evidence that indicates that Lee Oswald was most probably manipulated by right-wing elements and was most likely not the communist that J. Edgar Hoover and others made him out to be, then Jack Ruby's statements relating to the right-wing should not be dismissed lightly.

Ruby, again, attempted to make clear his concerns about his safety and divulging the truth to the Commission:

> *Ruby.* . . . Chairman Warren, if you felt your life was in danger at the moment, how would you feel? Wouldn't you be reluctant to go on speaking, even though you request me to do so?
> *Warren.* I think I might have some reluctance if I was in your position, yes; I think I would. I think I would figure it out very carefully as to whether it would endanger me or not. If you think anything that I am doing or anything that I am asking you is endangering you in any way, shape, or form, I want you to feel absolutely free to say that the interview is over.
> *Ruby.* What happens then? I didn't accomplish anything.
> *Warren.* No; nothing has been accomplished.
> *Ruby.* Well, then you won't follow up with anything further?
> *Warren.* There wouldn't be anything to follow up if you hadn't completed our statement. (117)

And even more amazing, is that this is where Jack Ruby's testimony in a public forum was allowed to end. He would continue to profess that he knew more about the assassination and the murder of Lee Oswald to those that he could occasionally pass information to. Even before Ruby's Warren Commission testimony, nationally known syndicated columnist, Dorothy Kilgallen was able to obtain an exclusive closed door interview with Ruby in the office of Judge Joe Brown during a break in his trial. After this interview with Ruby, she had reportedly told close friends that she was going to " . . . bust the whole Kennedy assassination wide open." (118) Unfortunately, Dorothy Kilgallen was found dead in her apartment on November 8, 1965, apparently a victim of a "drug overdose." (119) One of her close confidantes, Mrs. Earl Smith, also a newspaper columnist, reportedly was the recipient of Kilgallen's notes on her interview with Ruby. In another strange twist of "fate," Smith died of a cerebral hemorrhage only three days after the death of Kilgallen. (120) Whatever information that Kilgallen or Smith obtained from the interview with Jack Ruby has never been divulged.

Jack Ruby dropped other tantalizing hints as to what might have really happened, relating to the assassination and his subsequent murder of Oswald, to reporters, his prison guards, and in letters smuggled out of the Dallas jail. It is the most bizarre conspiracy in the history of the world. It'll come out at a future date." (121) In another of those amazing coincidences, Chief Justice Earl Warren came very close to finally concurring with and corroborating the claims that Warren, himself, had rejected during Ruby's Commission testimony. Warren was asked if the full report would ever be made public. He replied, "Yes,there will come a time. But it might not be in your lifetime. . . There may be some things that would involve security."(122) In a clip from a special video production program showing Ruby walking past reporters during a break in his trial, he was recorded as saying, " . . . complete conspiracy—and if you knew the true facts you'd be amazed . . . and the assassination too." (123)

Not long before he died, Ruby was granted a brief filmed interview that has now been made available to numerous television and video programs. If what he had to say is the truth, then he strongly suggests that Lyndon Johnson and J. Edgar Hoover, and possibly others high in the American government in 1966, have done more than obstruct justice:

Ruby. The only thing I can say is—everything pertaining to what's happened has never come to the surface. The world will never know the true facts of what occurred—my motive, in other words. I am the only person in the background to know the truth pertaining to everything relating to my circumstances.

Q. Will the truth ever come out, Jack?

Ruby. No. Because these people, who have so much to gain and have put me in the position I'm in, will never let the true facts come above board to the world.

Q. Are these people still in power today?

Ruby. Yes. (124)

It is clear that Ruby made contradictory statements to the Warren Commission relating to his relationship to organized crime, the murder of Oswald, and in other important areas. The important question to consider is which answers seem to be most plausible. The preceding testimony and statements, as well as the subsequent statements and testimony that Ruby gave to the Commission and to the press, clearly indicate that he was not "comfortable" telling the complete truth in regards to the events surrounding the weekend of November 22-24, 1963. Ruby makes this clear during his Commission testimony, " . . . I want to tell the truth, and I can't tell it here. I can't tell it here. Does that make sense to you? Gentlemen, my life is in danger here." (125) It has never been made clear what Ruby's true fears were. Commission member Gerald Ford was asked to comment on Ruby's fears: "He [Ruby] was an odd person . . . really a screwball. Q. Did he appear frightened? Ford: I don't think Jack Ruby's story in that regard had any credibility whatsoever." (126) It is interesting to note that although Jack Ruby lived for three years after the murders of John Kennedy and Lee Oswald, he never took the stand during his own trial. The consequence of this would be that he would never face a public cross examination. An evaluation of his statements to the Warren Commission and to the press, without the benefit of pointed questioning is all that researchers and historians have to go on at this point. In late November and early December 1966, Jack Ruby began to complain of a severe cold. As author Sylvia Meagher described, the process of Ruby's poor health advanced quite suddenly and "coincidentally:"

On December 9, 1966, Ruby was removed from the county jail

and admitted to Parkland Hospital with a diagnosis of pneumonia. The next day his illness was identified as cancer. Another day or two brought the news that the malignancy was far advanced; surgery and radiation therapy were ruled out; the prognosis was that Ruby had from two weeks to five years to live. Less than four weeks after Ruby entered Parkland Hospital, he died. (127)

There existed a reasonable possibility, that had Ruby lived, he could have become a free man by the end of 1966. On October 5, 1966, the Texas Court of Criminal Appeals had overturned his conviction and ordered a re-trial. A new trial had been set to begin on December 7, 1966 in Wichita Falls. It is quite possible that Ruby would have been credited with serving three years for murder without malice and walked away a free man. (128) With his "untimely" death, there would be no further questioning of Jack Ruby—we are left to ponder and dissect the many contradictory elements of his life.

With the death of Jack Ruby, there remained the problem of John Kennedy's autopsy further supporting Hoover's conclusions of two lone and un-aided assassins. The controversies caused by contradictory reports from the autopsy imply the involvement of others high up in the chain of command who were also involved at least in obstruction of justice and quite possibly much more.

Chapter 13

The Autopsy and the Secret Service

The Assassination Records and Review Board (ARRB) concluded in 1998, "One of the many tragedies related to the assassination of President Kennedy has been the incompleteness of the autopsy record and the suspicion caused by the shroud of secrecy that has surrounded the records that do exist." (1)

The "incompleteness" and "secrecy" surrounding the autopsy began to be noticed by some in the press as early as 1964 as *Newsweek* reported in its August 15, 1964 issue: "Autopsy photos are a mystery as to whereabouts."

Serious conflicts in the official record have been verified as the contents of a 1998 Associated Press article by Deb Reichmann indicates:

> Congress did not direct the review board to reinvestigate the assassination and the panel . . . failed to resolve discrepancies between how physicians at Parkland Hospital in Dallas described Kennedy's head injury immediately after the shooting and how it was subsequently described by pathologists at Bethesda. . . . (2)

Who was actually in charge of the autopsy has never been made clear. But it is clear that the doctor selected to "run" the autopsy, Dr. James Humes, was not as qualified as a matter of this magnitude required. Because of his inexperience and military rank, it appears to be a near

certainty that the actual direction of the autopsy was dictated
by others higher in the military chain of command. Dr.
Humes related his medical experience to the Warren
Commission:

> My type of practice, which fortunately has been in peacetime
> endeavor to a great extent, has been more extensive in the
> field of natural disease than violence. However, on several
> occasions in various places where I have been employed, I
> have had to deal with violent death, accidents, suicides, and
> so forth. (3)

Bethesda Naval Hospital photographer John Stringer's
statements before the Review Board make clear his view that
some photographs are missing and that those involved in the
autopsy proceedings were not to talk about what went on.
Stringer's ARRB deposition of July 16, 1996 noted that he
was forbidden to talk to any one about the autopsy and he
disagreed about the number of photographs taken. (4)

Ms. Saundra Spencer of the National Photographic Center
testified "that she developed post-mortem photographs of
President Kennedy in November 1963 and that these
photographs were different than those in the National
Archives since 1966." (5)

Within one week of the assassination, Chief Petty Officer
Robert Knudson, a White House photographer showed a set of
autopsy photos he had taken, to Joe O'Donnell, a government
photographer who had worked for the United States
Information Agency (USIA) in 1963. From an O'Donnell
interview, author Harrison Livingstone writes:

> O'Donnell said he remembers a photograph of a gaping wound
> in the back of the head which was big enough to put a fist
> through, in which the image clearly showed a total absence of
> hair and bone. . . . He said that another image showed a small
> round hole above the President's right eye, which he
> interpreted as an entry wound made by the same bullet which
> exited from the large wound made by the same bullet which
> exited from the large wound in the back of the head. (6)

This additional set of pictures taken at the autopsy is referred
to in an Associated Press article by Deb Reichmann on July
31, 1998:

> New testimony released . . . about the autopsy on John F.

Kennedy says a second set of pictures was taken of Kennedy's wounds—pictures never made public. The existence of additional photographs—believed taken by White House photographer Robert L. Knudson during or after the autopsy at the National Medical Center in Bethesda, Md.—raised new questions about how the autopsy was conducted. One set of autopsy photographs, now at the National Archives, has been known to exist for some years, and some of the pictures have been widely published. But the new testimony documents the existence of another set. . . . Knudson's widow, Gloria, told the review board that her husband told her he appeared before the House Select Committee on Assassination . . . and that four or five of the pictures the committee showed him did not represent what he saw or photographed that night. . . . (7)

Autopsy medical photographer Floyd Riebe believed ". . . the autopsy photographs showing the back of Kennedy's head to be intact are, forgeries . . . 'retouched to conceal a large exit wound from the bullet entering the front.'" (8) *USA Today* reported on May 29, 1992 that "Two Navy medical technicians at the autopsy of President Kennedy said government-released photos and X-rays were falsified. Bethesda X-ray technician Jerrol Custer and Floyd Riebe spoke . . . to rebut the recent reports of two Navy pathologists [James Humes and J. Thornton Boswell] who did the autopsy and who support the official findings. . . ." (9) Riebe was quoted by the ARRB as stating "that the autopsy photographs had been altered based upon his examination of photographs that had been circulating in the public domain, re-evaluated his earlier opinion when shown the actual photographs at the NARA." (10)   John Stringer corroborated Riebe in this ARRB statement, "Mr. John Stringer . . . in detailed testimony, explained the photographic procedures he followed at the autopsy and he raised some questions about whether the supplemental brain photographs that he took are those that are now in the NARA." (11)

Paul O'Conner, a Bethesda laboratory technologist was adamant that the photos were not accurate. "I don't know where those things [autopsy photos] came from but they are wrong. Totally wrong." (12) Bethesda laboratory technologist James Curtis Jenkins stated that the photos he viewed were also wrong. "That's not possible . . . there's no possible way . . . It's not possible." (13) Dr. James Humes, autopsy surgeon, was also confused by the photos: "I don't understand this great big void there. I don't understand what that's all about

. . . there's aspects of it [the X-ray] I don't understand . . . I
don't remember it." (14) FBI agent James Sibert recalled: "I
don't remember seeing anything like this photo. . . . No. I
don't recall anything like this at all during the autopsy. And
it looks like it could have been reconstructed or something, as
compared to what my recollection was and those other
photographs." (15) Dr. Robert McClelland, Parkland Hospital
surgeon recalled on the television news program, *Inside
Edition,* ". . . the X-rays do not show the same injuries to the
President's head that I saw in the emergency room . . . I think
he was shot from the front." (16) Dr. Fouad Bashour, chief
cardiologist at Parkland, in an interview with Harrison
Livingstone stated, "Why do they cover it up . . . This is not
the way it was." (17)

Dr. Crenshaw, Parkland surgeon told Vincent Palamara,
"The so-called 'official autopsy photos' I have seen do not
reflect the wounds we saw at Parkland. (18) Fellow Parkland
surgeon Dr. Richard Dulany related to *The Boston Globe* that
"The autopsy photo was shown to him. . . and he stated that it
was not accurate." (19) Parkland Hospital nurse Margaret
Hinchcliffe (Hood) told researcher Wallace Milam, ". . . the
autopsy photos were nothing like she saw." (20) Mortician
Thomas Robinson recalled "[the large rear head wound] just
doesn't show up in this photo. . . . this makes it look like the
wound was in the top of the head." (21) Parkland doctor
Marion Jenkins recalled that the autopsy photos were "No not
like that. Not like that you want to know what it really
looked like? . . . Well that picture does not look like it from the
back." (22) According to the *Boston Globe,* in a 1981
interview, Dr. Charles Carrico, another of the Parkland
doctors, made such contradictory statements to the *Globe* that
it would be inaccurate to count him as supporting the
[autopsy] picture. Dr. Kenneth Salyer, Parkland surgeon,
stated that the photos were not accurate. "You know, there's
something wrong with it. . . . something, you know, happened
to this . . . This is not right. No. . . . this has been doctored."
(23) Parkland Hospital nurse Patricia Hutton, when shown
the X-ray photos, exclaimed, "No way!" (24) Nurse Audrey
Bell concurred with Hutton denouncing the photos, the
"throat wound was an entrance wound . . . at the rear of his
head . . . Oh yes there was a big hole there." (25) Parkland
nurse Diana Bowron supported Bell in an interview with
Harrison Livingstone. He stated that "she denounced the

photos. . . . all [three photos seen] are fake completely." (26)
Dr. Kemp Clark, Parkland Hospital chief neurosurgeon,
stated in an interview: "The lower right occipital region of the
head was blown out and I saw cerebellum. In my opinion, the
wound was an exit wound. . . . a large hole in the back of the
President's head . . . blown out." (27) Dr. Clark also stated " .
. . the picture of the back of the head was inaccurate." (28)
Dr. Malcolm Perry " . . . who had been given access to copies
of the [autopsy] photos said the President's head wounds in
the pictures were not consistent with what he recalled seeing
that day 16 years ago. (29) Dr. Paul Peters, after viewing
some of the autopsy photos, stated, "I don't think its [autopsy
photo] consistent with what I saw." (30) Parkland Hospital
supervising nurse Doris Nelson related to the *Boston Globe*,
"It's not true. . . . There wasn't even hair back there. It was
blown away." (31) The closest witness to the President
corroborated the numerous accounts of a large hole in the
back of the President's head. Jackie Kennedy recalled that " .
. . from the back [I was] trying to hold his hair on, and his
skull on." (32) She stated that she was "Surprised at Warren
Commission doctor's conclusions [that the shots only came
from the rear]." (33)

Douglas Horne, ARRB's chief analyst for military records
was quoted as saying, "I am 90-95 percent certain that the
photographs in the National Archives are not of President
Kennedy's brain. If they aren't that can mean only one
thing—there has been a coverup of the medical evidence." (34)
The ARRB further elaborated on the fact that a second set of
photographs taken of President Kennedy's autopsy was
mentioned but is missing:

> The existence of additional photographs—believed taken by
> White House photographer Robert L. Knudsen during or after
> the autopsy at the National . . . of autopsy photographs, now
> at the National Archives, has been known to exist for years
> and some of the pictures have been widely published. But the
> new testimony documents the existence of another set. . . . In
> 1997, the review board located Saundra K. Spencer, who
> worked at the Naval Photographic Center in 1963. She was
> shown the archives' autopsy photos and concluded they were
> not the pictures she had helped process. . . [the] cleaned-up
> corpse and speculated that was done at the request of the
> Kennedy family in case autopsy pictures had to be made
> public." The only think I can think of is that a second set of
> autopsy pictures was shot for public release, if necessary . . .

by an agent she believed was with the FBI. . . ." She was told she said, "Process them and try not to observe too much, don't peruse. . . ." Knudsen appeared before the House Select Committee on Assassinations . . . and his widow said he later told her that four or five of the pictures the committee showed him did not represent what he saw or photographed that night and that one of them had been altered. . . . "His son Bob said that his father told him that 'hair had been drawn in' on one photo to conceal a missing portion of the top-back of President Kennedy's head." (35)

Mortician Thomas Robinson stated further that he "Disagreed with [the] autopsy photos" (36) as did autopsy technician Jerrol Custer, ". . .[the] Autopsy photos and X-rays are faked." (37)

Further conflicts in the "official" record were noted in an article by the Associated Press:

There are questions about the supplemental brain exam and the photos that were taken. "There are inconsistencies in the testimony of the autopsy doctors about when that exam took place," said Jeremy Gunn, executive director and general counsel of the board, which closed out its work in September. "These are serious issues. The records are now out there for the public to evaluate. . . ." Initially, Humes told the Warren Commission that he and Boswell and a third pathologist, Dr. Pierre Finck, were present when the brain was examined. But when he testified to the review board in 1996, Humes did not list Finck among those present. Boswell maintains Finck was not there. . . . On the other hand, Finck says the brain exam did not occur until much later. In a memo he wrote to his commanding officer 14 months after Kennedy was assassinated, Finck said Humes did not call him until Nov. 29, 1963—seven days after Kennedy's death—to say it was time to examine the brain . . . to conclude in a 32-page memo that two separate brain exams may have been conducted, "contrary to the official record as it has been presented to the American people. . . ." If true, Dr. Finck's account of a brain exam separate and distinct from the first one would . . . "two different brain exams," he writes . . . "I doubt very much that we would have called him [Finck] back over for that," Boswell said. . . . That conflicts with testimony the board obtained from Navy photographer John Stringer who said he took pictures of the brain two or three days after the autopsy. . . . Stringer also testified that official photos of the brain preserved at the archives do not match those he remembers taking. He cites discrepancies in the angles . . . In addition, former FBI Agent Francis O'Neill Jr., who watched doctors remove Kennedy's brain the night he died, told the review board that the archives' photos do not resemble what he saw, "I did not recall it [the brain] being that large," O'Neill said. . . . In contrast to observations in Dallas, Humes said there also was massive damage to the top of Kennedy's skull and right side forward of the ear." (38)

A more serious question involving what is most likely a planned deception involving elements of the Secret Service, the military team in charge of the casket, or possibly both, is indicated by Major General Philip Wehle, commanding officer of the Military District of Washington D. C.(MDW) who believed " . . . that two Navy ambulances were used and that the Navy team pursued the wrong ambulance." (39) Chief of the Day, Medical Center Command, Layton Ledbetter concurred, "I witnessed the arrival of two ambulances . . . I know there was two helicopters involved. One never did land; the other one, I think, was a decoy. . . ." (40) Hubert Clark, a Navy member of the MDW casket team, remembered ". . . it was like a decoy was set up where we were supposed to go one way and this decoy ambulance, I believe, went another way to the front. . . ." (41) Timothy Cheek, a Marine and another member of the MDW casket team, stated, "There was a lot of confusion, because . . . it was supposed to be taken in the front; we got there, and it wasn't there . . . the body wasn't there. . . ." (42) Douglas Mayfield, an Army member of the MDW casket team, stated that ". . . [the] ambulance didn't come right away." (43) Air Force Sergeant Richard Gaudreau, who was also a member of the MDW casket team, believed something was amiss because there was ". . . some confusion, and we did go off with another ambulance. . . . I can picture us being led somewhere, and finding something empty; and then being led somewhere else." (44)
Jerrol Custer recalled there being "Two caskets, one ceremonial and one regular." (45) Yet, Aubrey Rike, an employee of the O'Neal Funeral Home in Dallas, stated unequivocally, that the President was placed in a ceremonial casket and wrapped in sheets. Apparently, somewhere along the line between Dallas and Bethesda, the President was transferred to a cheap casket and then placed in a rubber body bag. Floyd Riebe, medical photographer at Bethesda, believed the President's body was in a "Body bag . . . in a shipping casket," as did Paul O'Conner, "It was a rubber body

bag." (46) Captain John Stover, the commanding officer of the National Navy Medical School recalled, ". . . I remember seeing a body bag. . . . I think I remember seeing a body bag peeled off. . . ." (47) Donald Rebentisch, a Navy Petty Officer at Bethesda, recalled that there were two ambulances involved. This is corroborated by a Bethesda staff technician Richard Muma who stated, "There were two ambulances that came in. One was lighted. It came up to the front door. The second one they kept dark, it went around to the back. That was the one that had Kennedy in it. It was common knowledge that there were two caskets." (48)

William Manchester, in his book *Death of a President*, wrote that Godfrey McHugh stated the casket was, "cheap and thin," and that the family should order another casket. (49) Donald Rebentisch remembered the casket was "Not a ceremonial casket," as did Dennis David recalling seeing the "Casket, [as a] plain shipping casket." (50) Joseph E. Hagan, chief assistant to undertaker Joseph Gawler, also believed that the casket in question was a "Shipping casket." (51)

Despite recent allegations that Robert Kennedy was responsible for the destruction of President Kennedy's ceremonial casket in 1966, this charge does not appear to be accurate. In September 1965, former Texas representative Earle Cabell wrote to then Attorney General Nicholas Katzenbach recommending that the bronze casket be discarded so it could never become a relic. . . Douglas Horne, who was the chief analyst for military records at the Congressionally-created review board, speculated that the bronze casket was destroyed to end the two coffin controversy. "I think the way to get rid of the problem is you get rid of the casket. You throw it out of an airplane", said Horne. (52)

There can be no apparent, innocent explanation for the numerous contradictions, inconsistencies, and outright falsehoods that have resulted from the events surrounding the autopsy of President Kennedy as a number of witnesses who were specifically trained to deal with gunshots and medical procedures recalled.

Dr. Ronald Jackson of Parkland Hospital related his frustrations to Vincent Palamara on September 8, 1998:

> I continue to be dissatisfied with the explanation of the Warren Commission. The reason for my skepticism is linked to discrepancies in descriptions of the Kennedy wounds between the Parkland Emergency Room and the autopsy

findings. Dr.'s McClelland, Perry, and Jenkins gave accurate descriptions of the wounds as they saw them in the Emergency Room. The descriptions in Washington were radically different. . . . Dr. McClelland and several other colleagues went to Washington and reviewed the findings with the medical authorities. . . . they then reversed themselves on the findings they had described in Dallas. . . . I am confused by this discrepancy. (53)

Dr. Jackson's views are supported by fellow Parkland Hospital surgeon David Stewart. Dr. Stewart believed that the Parkland Hospital doctors were unanimous in their view that the massive exit wound that was inflicted to President Kennedy was located to the extreme right rear of the President's head. He also made it clear that the autopsy photograph showing the back of the President's head to be intact, was not accurate and that this view was shared by all the doctors who were in attendance that day. Dr. Stewart related his doubts to author Harrison Livingstone:

there was never any controversy concerning the wounds between the doctors in attendance. I was with them either separately or in groups on many occasions over a long period of time. . . . Concerning [the official photo of the back of the head], there is no way the wound described to me by Dr. Perry and others could be the wound shown in the picture. The massive destructive wound could not remotely be pulled together well enough to give a normal contour to the head that is present in this picture. (54)

Chief of the Day Dennis David related to researcher Joanne Braun:

It is inconceivable that anyone even vaguely acquainted with gunshot wounds would conclude that the massive wound in the rear of JFK's skull could have occurred from a rear-entry projectile, unless it was from a grenade or mortar shrapnel. . . (55)

Mortician Thomas Robinson recalled that he did not agree with the official story, "The time the people moved the autopsy . . . the body was taken and the body never came . . . lots of little things like that." (56) Autopsy technician James Jenkins told author David Lifton:

I found out that supposedly he was shot from the back. I just,

you know, I just couldn't believe it, and I have never been able
to believe it. . . . I was very surprised by the conclusion, it was
really kind of shocking to me. I guess I accepted it because of
the circumstances I was in. . . . But I mean I did not accept it
as being fact. (57)

Lifton asked Jenkins, ". . .did you feel that the order not to
discuss it was related to the fact that what you saw was
different than what you were reading in the newspapers?"
Jenkins: "Yes I did." (58)

One of the most blatant and puzzling omissions involving
the investigation of the contradictions between the wounds
seen at Parkland Hospital and those seen at Bethesda Naval
Hospital, was the failure by both the Warren Commission and
the House Select Committee to question President Kennedy's
personal physician, Dr. George Burkley. Admiral Burkley
was the only medical doctor present at both the emergency
treatment at Parkland Memorial Hospital and at the autopsy
at Bethesda Naval Hospital. Burkley's testimony, as to the
discrepancies in the descriptions of the wounds, would have
been crucial in determining whether the photos taken at the
autopsy were accurate portrayals of President Kennedy's
wounds. In the late 1970's, at the time of the HSCA's
investigation, Dr. Burkley, through his attorney, suggested to
the HSCA that he might have some additional information
about the autopsy that has still never been disclosed.
Because Dr. Burkley is now deceased, the Review Board
sought additional information from both his former lawyer's
firm, and from Dr. Burkley's family.

The ARRB attempted to clear up the mystery of Dr.
Burkley's knowledge of the true nature of the President's
wounds and exactly how the autopsy was directed. "The
Burkley family . . . declined to sign a waiver of attorney-client
privilege that would have permitted the Review Board access
to the files of Mr. Illig (also now deceased) Burkley's former
attorney." (59)

"According to House Select Committee on Assassinations'
records, Burkley's personal attorney [Illig] apparently told the
HSCA that his client believed there was a conspiracy to kill
President Kennedy." (60) "In 1982 Burkley told author Henry
Hurt that he believed that President Kennedy's assassination
was the result of a conspiracy." (61) In an Oral History
interview on October 17, 1967, when questioned ". . .on the
number of bullets that entered the President's body," Burkley

replied, "I would not care to be quoted on that." (62) When Burkley's allegations of conspiracy are viewed alongside his actions during the autopsy, one must truly wonder what (or who) was the cause of his strange behavior.

Autopsy technician Jerrol Custer stated that Admiral Burkley " . . . [was] controlling everything [during the autopsy] every step of the way." (63)   James Jenkins, laboratory technician, stated that he was ". . . surprised at the conclusions the doctors' reached [autopsy]," and added ". . . what we saw that night was nothing relating to the [autopsy report]. . . .There was no relation to it." (64) Paul O'Conner stated, "We were interfered with constantly," and "Admiral Burkley interfered constantly." (65)

Autopsy photographer John Stringer recalled that Dr. Burkley instructed the doctors to not conduct a full autopsy. (66)   Secret Service agent Sam Kinney related to researcher Vincent Palamara that Dr. Burkley's controversial actions regarding the autopsy were the result of others in authority, who were present at the autopsy, attempting to control the proceedings. Kinney recalled, "Well, you have to give orders to people. . . . they were very hard on Dr. Burkley. (67) According to autopsy surgeon Dr. Thornton Boswell, Dr. Burkley was the individual who told the doctors there were only three shots fired.   But according to the Warren Commission, Burkley was waiting for the President to arrive at the Trade Mart when the assassination occurred. (68) This would mean that his view of "three shots only" had to have come from another source.   According to Dr. Boswell, Dr. Burkley gave instructions and said very early on that the police had "...captured the guy who did this, all we need is the bullet." Dr. Boswell disagreed and stated, "...we argued with him at that point...saying that the autopsy must be complete and thorough." (69)

Researcher James Folliard has described in an article entitled, *Blaming The Victims: Kennedy Family Control Over The Bethesda Autopsy,* that charges that the Kennedy family was responsible for the incomplete autopsy conducted on President Kennedy are false.   Folliard writes, "Civilian medical photographer John Stringer believed that Burkley ' . . . seemed to be acting on behalf of the Kennedy family.'" Paul O'Connor described in detail the actions of Dr. Burkley:

> Admiral Burkley was a maniac. I'd never seen anybody like that in this life. Scared the hell out of me, I'll tell you. He

was yelling and cussin' and carrying on all night. [He] kept
saying, "Don't do this because the Kennedy family won't want
that done, and don't do this and don't do that." It's just
unbelievable. . . Humes is real freaky. They were scared to
death anyway when they got down there. And then Admiral
Burkley started screaming at them. (70)

Dr. Robert Karnei, in an interview with Harrison
Livingstone in 1991, stated, "All I can say is that Jim
[Humes] and Jay [Boswell] were really handicapped that
night with regards to performing the autopsy." Livingstone
asked if it was Burkley? "No, Robert [Kennedy]," answered
Karnei. "We had to get permission all the time from Mrs.
Kennedy to proceed with the autopsy." (71)

During his 1978 House Select Committee on Assassination
testimony, Dr. Pierre Finck recalled, "There were restrictions
coming from the family and we were told at the time of the
autopsy that the autopsy should be limited to certain parts of
the body. Yes, restrictions from the family as the reason for
limiting our actions." (72)   Dr. Finck had the following
exchange with the HSCA Medical Panel in 1978:

> *Dr. Weston.* At the time this examination was done there was
> the possibility that there was going to be a criminal
> prosecution. [It is] your practice as a forensic pathologist to
> stop short of doing a short [he meant "full"] medical legal
> autopsy in face of criminal prosecution notwithstanding the
> wishes of anybody else?
> *Dr. Finck.* What you are saying, we should not have listened
> to the recommendation—
> *Dr. Weston.* No, I am not saying anything. I am asking you if
> it is not accepted medical legal practice when you anticipate a
> criminal prosecution to do a complete examination?
> *Dr. Finck.* Yes.
> *Dr. Weston.* Okay. Then the reason you did not do a complete
> examination was that you were ordered not to, is that correct?
> *Dr. Finck.* Yes, restrictions from the family as the reason for
> limiting our actions.
> *Dr. Weston.* But..is this not evidence that belongs to the state
> notwithstanding the wishes of the family when there is a
> suspected criminal prosecution?
> *Dr. Finck.* Of course it is ideal. In those circumstances you
> are told to do certain things. There are people telling you to
> do certain things. It is unfortunate.
> *Dr. Weston.* Those restrictions you mentioned were, as you
> remember now, Admiral Galloway?

Dr. Finck. Who passed them on to us as I remember so he should be consulted and asked who asked to have those restrictions.(73)

FBI agents James Sibert and Francis O'Neill reported on November 26, "Admiral Berkley *[sic]*, the President's personal physician, advised that Mrs. Kennedy had granted permission for a limited autopsy and he questioned any feasibility for a complete autopsy to obtain the bullet which had entered the President's back. . . ." (74) According to Folliard, "There's no direct, first-hand evidence that Jacqueline or Robert or McNamara said anything about how the autopsy should proceed. People consistently report that they 'had the impression,' or that 'it seemed...' or that 'they were told...' or even that 'it was all over the hospital...'" (75) Dr. Finck's 1965 report to his superior, General Blumberg, creates more doubt: "The prosectors complied with the autopsy permit and its restrictions. . . .This authority shall be limited only by the conditions expressly stated below:" (76) Folliard notes, "[Room for about four typed lines follows. The space is *completely blank.*] Mrs. Kennedy's name is typed—not signed—on the line provided for the authorizing person's signature. . . . Robert F. Kennedy's handwritten signature appears on the line provided for a witness. There are no restrictions listed. How then was Pierre Finck able to cite, 'the autopsy permit and its restrictions'?" (77) Folliard related that "in the space for an approval *signature*, the name of the Hospital Commanding Officer, R. O. Canada, is *typed* not signed." (78)

Admiral Galloway reported that Dr. Finck was in charge of the autopsy. FBI agent Francis O'Neill also recalled that "Finck seemed to take over the autopsy when he arrived." (79) Folliard comments further:

> White House Physician Admiral Burkley was not part of the Bethesda hierarchy, and had no official role at the postmortem. By rank he was clearly subordinate to Admiral Kenney, superior to everyone from Captain Canada on down. . . .FBI Agents Sibert and O'Neill . . . describe Galloway overruling Burkley. (80)

James Folliard offered this analysis of the evidence:

> Dr. Boswell recalled how he "had been concerned that they

began the autopsy without any written authorization which is
something they never do. Such authorization has to come
from the next of kin. He said that JACKIE *[sic]* finally signed
the authorization which arrived in the morgue near the end of
the autopsy." This is a very significant statement.
Unfortunately it can be interpreted in at least two ways.
Boswell can be taken literally; JBK actually signed a permit.
This would discredit the document we have, since her name
appears there typed. . . . Burkley argued strenuously for a
limited autopsy, yet the only available documentary evidence
is an authorization for a complete one. Apparently Jacqueline
and Robert Kennedy authorized a complete autopsy. This
authorization was withheld from the doctors so that Burkley,
in front of some two dozen witnesses, could appeal to "family
wishes" as the reason why only a partial postmortem should
be done. (81)

Dr. Finck stated in his autopsy report to General Blumberg:
"In my discussion with Commander Humes, I stated that we
should not check the block 'complete Autopsy' in the Autopsy
Report Form." (82) Finck again explained, "In compliance
with the wishes of the Kennedy family, the prosectors had
confined their examination to the head and chest." Despite
the determination of Finck, "Humes declared that the block
'complete Autopsy' should be checked." (83) That, in
actuality, a full autopsy was performed is supported by lab
assistant James Curtis Jenkins: "We did a full scale autopsy
on JFK. We tested for everything. We examined the testes
(they were sectioned), the adrenals, etc. There were sections
of the heart and other organs taken." (84) Creating even
more confusion is the following exchange between Dr. Robert
Karnei and Harrison E. Livingstone in 1991:

Livingstone: They couldn't find his adrenals?
Karnei: Right, there was nothing there...Jim [Humes] and Jay
[Boswell] worked long and hard in that fatty tissue in the
renal-adrenal area looking for them, and didn't find anything
that looked like adrenals...There was total atrophy as far as
we can see at the autopsy. I mean they cut that fat to a fare-
thee-well trying to find anything that looked like adrenals,
and there just wasn't. (85)

However, Dr. Boswell told the House Select Committee on
Assassination, in a report that was not released until 1993,
"Dr. Humes insisted there be a complete autopsy, saying, for
example, the adrenals were extremely important." (86) Yet,

Jim Snyder, a close friend of Dr. Humes who worked for the Washington Bureau of CBS, related yet another version of who controlled the autopsy; " . . . he [Humes] had orders from someone he refused to disclose—other than Robert Kennedy—to not do a complete autopsy." (87) There can be little question why even today, an accurate portrayal of how the autopsy was actually run, is a mystery.

Autopsy surgeon Dr. Pierre Finck's testimony during the Clay Shaw trial in 1969 strongly indicates that "someone else" in the military chain of command was directing the autopsy doctors towards the conclusion that three shots and three shots only, had been fired at President Kennedy and Governor Connally during the assassination:

> Q. Who told you that three shots were heard? Who told you that?" Finck: "As I recall, Admiral Galloway [Commanding Officer of the Naval Medical Center] heard from somebody who was present at the scene that three shots had been heard, but I cannot give the details of this. (88)

Attorney Alvin Osner asked Dr. Finck to state what individual was actually in charge of the autopsy. Finck replied, ". . . an Army General, I don't remember his name, [was] running the show." (89) Osner: "Was this Army General a qualified pathologist?" Finck: "No." Osner: "Was he a doctor?" Finck: "No." (90) Finck was then asked if he could remember the General's name and Finck replied, "No I can't I don't remember." (91)

It is clear from the analysis of James Folliard and the statements of the various autopsy personnel, especially that of Dr. Pierre Finck, that very little is actually clear in regards to the autopsy. The attempts to blame the incomplete and inept autopsy on the Kennedy family does not hold up under close scrutiny. The abundance of disturbing testimony strongly indicates that someone or some group, high in the military chain of command, was not only running the autopsy but also creating a web of secrecy and deception.

In an interview with Bill Law, James Curtis Jenkins is quoted:

> All of the doctors at the table were frustrated. . . . these people [in the gallery] were directing the doctors toward a conclusion [all the shots coming from the rear] and [the doctors] were not finding evidence for it. . . . [the doctors] were under a

tremendous amount of pressure. . . . I came out of the autopsy
expecting them to say that there were two shooters, one in the
right front, one behind . . . what we saw that night was
nothing relating to the [final] pathology report. There was no
relation to it. (92)

President Kennedy's Air Force military aide, General
Godfrey McHugh, did not agree with those who now state that
the Kennedy family directed a limited the autopsy and that
"the Kennedys" were therefore responsible for the incomplete
autopsy. That President Kennedy suffered from Addison's
disease and/or Pott's disease does not appear by itself to be
enough of a reason for the Kennedys to limit the autopsy. For
as Harold Weisberg noted: "There is no stigma attached to
Addison's disease and control over it can be maintained more
perfectly than, for example, over diabetes. It need never have
interfered with his activity as President." (93) Considering
that neither Jackie Kennedy, Robert Kennedy, Ken
O'Donnell, or Robert McNamara had any knowledge of how
an autopsy would or should be carried out, it would be foolish
to believe that they could limit or direct the autopsy. Their
concern seemed to center on completing the autopsy process.
They were grieving together on the seventeenth floor of the
Naval Hospital. It would be difficult, if not impossible, for
those untrained in medical procedures to dictate the autopsy,
much less from seventeen floors above. It would appear more
likely that Jackie Kennedy, still caked in blood and in
shock—along with the others—merely wanted the President's
body to be prepared for burial and the healing to begin.
McHugh stated, "O'Donnell and Robert Kennedy did talk of
the autopsy going slow but did not limit or direct the
autopsy." (94)

> McHugh stated to the House Select Committee that Robert
> Kennedy and Ken O'Donnell frequently telephoned him
> during the autopsy. "They inquired about the results, why
> the autopsy was consuming so much time, and the need for
> speed and efficiency, while still performing the required
> examinations." . . . McHugh said he forwarded this
> information to the pathologists, never stating or implying that
> the doctors should limit the autopsy in any manner, but
> merely reminding them to work as efficiently and quickly as
> possible. (95)

The possibility, that Bethesda Hospital Navy Lieutenant

Commander William Pitzer was filming the autopsy, is substantiated by a number of Bethesda witnesses. If true, Pitzer's film would go a long way in determining who was actually in control of the autopsy.

Jerrol Custer believed that William "Pitzer [was] taking movies." (96) There were "Lots of pictures from the gallery," stated Joseph E. Hagan. (97) Dr. Robert Karnei, who assisted with the autopsy, stated there was a ". . . second person taking photographs." (98)

In another unfortunate twist, so common in the investigation of President Kennedy's assassination, William Pitzer was found dead in his office on October 29, 1966. His death was ruled a suicide, the result of a gunshot to the head — just months before Pitzer was scheduled to retire. On November 1, three days after Pitzer's death, the autopsy personnel inventoried the autopsy photos. (99) Pitzer's death and the likely disappearance of his film is most probably one of the main problems with the reliability of the autopsy photographs today.

Dennis David, Chief of the Day at Bethesda Naval Hospital believed, "Pitzer would not — have committed suicide. . . . [And his] Family believes he was murdered." (100) In an ARRB interview, Jerrol Custer corroborates David by stating, "Pitzer [was] filming [the autopsy]." Mrs. Pitzer stated, ". . . the government wanted him to destroy the film, he refused." (101) If Pitzer was filming the autopsy from the gallery, then his films have never been found even though Dennis David recalled that he actually helped Pitzer develop some of the films. (102)

Vincent Palamara has related a conversation involving Lyndon Johnson and acting Attorney General Ramsay Clark indicate that Johnson was personally involved in the "authentification" of the autopsy photographs. Clark's written notes of the conversation were obtained from the LBJ Library and indicate Johnson's displeasure with autopsy surgeon, Dr. James Humes referring to a photograph that "does not exist." Clark's notes state:

> I think we have the three pathologists and the photographer signed up now on the autopsy review . . . we were not able to tie down the question of the missing photo entirely but we feel much better about it . . . There is this unfortunate reference to the Warren Commission report by Dr. Humes to a picture that does not exist as far as we know. (103)

The strange actions of Dr. Burkley reflect the view that he was being pressured by someone or some group to, in the final analysis, obscure the results of the autopsy. The equally strange circumstances surrounding the death of William Pitzer causes one to believe that he, most likely, had an accurate photographic record of the President's wounds and someone or some group wanted that record destroyed at any cost. As a result, as author David Lifton has argued, *The Best Evidence,* the President's body, does not reflect the true nature of his wounds—permanently obscuring the truth in the assassination.

How high up in the military chain of command did the autopsy's "obstruction of justice" go? In another disturbing trend, it appears that Lyndon Johnson was very much involved in other elements of the autopsy proceedings. Captain John Stover, commanding officer of the National Naval Medical School, was informed by Dr. Burkley on November 26, 1963, of an order from the White House to not speak to anyone about the autopsy proceedings. (104) Evidently Johnson or one of his staff also attempted to change the autopsy from Bethesda Naval Hospital to Walter Reed Army Hospital.

Johnson's direct involvement in further aspects surrounding the completion of the autopsy is indicated by a conversation that Kennedy's military aide, Ted Clifton, had regarding where the autopsy was to be performed. Clifton's instructions are taken from Air Force One radio transmissions during the flight from Dallas to Washington. "We do not want an ambulance and a ground return from Andrews to Walter Reed, and we want the regular post-mortem that has to be done by law under guard performed at Walter Reed. Is that clear?" (105) Clifton attempted to explain the contradiction: "To this day I don't know where the authority for the change came [from], because when I was on the phone telling them [we] were going to Walter Reed, that is what I had been told by Johnson or one of his staff." (106)

This is confirmed by Mrs. Andrew Chiarodo [Ms. Fehmer], who was Lyndon Johnson's personal secretary. She was shown a copy of the notes she made while aboard Air Force One which stated, "Walter Reed." She recalled, "I am sure someone told me. . . . but I have no way of remember[ing] who." (107) When one considers the reports of decoy ambulances and helicopters, different caskets, and the contradictory accounts of the wounds—the possibility of a surreptitiously run autopsy at Walter Reed Hospital (or another location before) appears to be a distinct and extremely troubling possibility.

Further investigation by the Assassination Records and Review Board has failed to clear up the controversy as their report concluded:

> the LBJ Presidential Library released edited audiocassettes of unsecured, or open voice conversation with Air Force One, Andrews Air Force Base, the White House Situation Room and the Cabinet Aircraft carrying the Secretary of State and other officials on November 22, 1963. The LBJ Library version of these tapes consists of about 110 minutes of voice transmissions, but the tapes are edited and condensed, so the Review Board staff sought access to unedited, uncondensed versions. Since the edited version of the tapes contains considerable talk about both the forthcoming autopsy on the President, as well as the reaction of a government in crisis, the tapes are of considerable interest to assassination researchers and historians. The Review Board staff could not locate any records indicating who performed the editing, or when, or where . . . The Review Board's repeated written and oral inquiries of the White House Communications Agency (WHCA) did not bear fruit. The WHCA could not produce any records that illuminated the provenance of the edited tapes.(108)

Ken O'Donnell and Robert Kennedy both disputed Lyndon Johnson's claim that they told Johnson that he should be sworn in on Air Force One. (109) They were also surprised to see Johnson on the plane in the first place. Air Force Two was an exact duplicate of Air Force One and those on the plane were expecting Johnson to fly to Washington on Air Force Two. Arthur Schlesinger adds this disturbing description:

> . . . Godfrey McHugh, President Kennedy's loyal and emotional Air Force aide, described to the Attorney General the inexplicable delay before the plane took off from Dallas and the sad confusion once they were airborne. Robert Kennedy recalled: "McHugh said that Lyndon Johnson had been —and I remember the word that he used—. . . obscene. There wasn't any other word to use and it was the worst performance he'd ever witnessed." (110)

Further evidence of a dispute involving the departure of Air Force I, the "incident" involving General McHugh, and Johnson's interest in cleaning up the "rumor" of a misunderstanding, is found in a White House memorandum from November 27, 1963:

> There are several points of misunderstanding that should be cleared up between the Attorney General and the President. Everyone's interest is involved—the President's and Bobby's, the Party's, the country's. Here are the points about which there is misunderstanding, rumor, [and] gossip, all of which has reached Bobby and the family.
>   (1) The question of the plane's departure. Is it true that LBJ said the plane couldn't take off until he was sworn in? Did Johnson hold up the departure? Why?
>   (2) What was the cause for the argument with [Air Force aide] Godfrey McHugh? Did the President curse him? . . . (111)

Evidently, the   subsequent meeting between Lyndon Johnson and Robert Kennedy did not solve the controversy. The meeting between the two lasted only twelve minutes and Kennedy and Johnson did not meet again for almost two months.

In light of the strange events that took place during the autopsy proceedings, one should take time to consider the actions of those who not only protected President Kennedy while he was alive, but were also responsible for transporting his body to the autopsy from Dallas.   Vincent Palamara stated:

> For it was the Secret Service who were responsible for the planning of the Texas trip, the implementation of security, JFK's body after death, all the major evidence in the case [CE399, the clothing, the X-rays, the photographs, the assassination films, the limousine, even Marina Oswald's captivity], LBJ taking over AF1 [Manchester, 233-35; Heymann, 403; 18 H 73; 2 H 152], and part of the actual investigation of the assassination itself, especially in the very early stages when it mattered the most to either invent stories or cover up facts [such as the December 1963 visit to Parkland to help make the doctors more 'agreeable' to the conclusions of the autopsy report. (112)

There appeared to be a number of strange coincidences involving changes in the Secret Service security during the

Dallas motorcade. The House Select Committee on Assassinations concluded that the Secret Service ". . . prevented the Dallas Police Department from inserting into the motorcade behind the Vice-Presidential car, a Dallas Police Department squad car containing homicide detectives." (113) The House Select Committee on Assassinations concluded that the Secret Service was also responsible for removing a number of motorcycle policemen who were scheduled to ride alongside the Presidential limousine. Even more interesting is that the Secret Service claimed that the removal of the motorcycles was done at the insistence of President Kennedy himself. However, the Committee determined that the motorcycle formation that was intended as extra protection for the President, had in fact been utilized by the Secret Service during the previous motorcades in San Antonio, Houston, and and even on the morning of the assassination in Ft. Worth:

> The Secret Service's alteration of the original Dallas Police Department motorcycle deployment plan prevented the use of maximum possible security precautions . . . Surprisingly, the security measure used in the prior motorcades during the same Texas visit [the day before] shows that the deployment of motorcycles in Dallas by the Secret Service may have been uniquely insecure. (114)

Why President Kennedy would have accepted the normal protection during the previous two days and on the morning of his murder, then rejected them in Dallas has not been explained. This explanation is even more questionable when viewed in light of statements, given by certain members of the Secret Service, that President Kennedy never gave the Secret Service orders on protection methods.

According to the House Select Committee, Dallas Police Captain, P. W. Lawrence stated that agent Winston Lawson was responsible for the reduction in motorcycle protection:

> Lawrence said there would be four motorcycles on either side of the motorcade immediately to the rear of the president's vehicle. Mr. Lawson stated that this was too many, that he thought two motorcycles on either side would be sufficient, about even with the rear fender of the President's car. Lawrence was instructed to disperse the other two along each side of the motorcade to the rear. (115)

Motorcycle patrolman B. J. Martin recalls a most troubling version of the reduction of motorcycle protection and the alignment of the vehicles in the motorcade:

> They also ordered us into the damnedest escort formation I've ever seen. Ordinarily, you bracket the car with four motorcycles, one on each fender. But this time, they told the four of us assigned to the president's car there'd be no forward escorts. We were to stay well to the back and not let ourselves get ahead of the car's wheels under any circumstances.
>
> "Are you sure it was Johnson's Secret Service that told you all this?" Jean [Hill] asked. "Surely, there had to be some mistake here," she thought, "it all sounded so . . . so premeditated."
>
> I guess they were the Secret Service. . . .They were sure as hell acting like they were in charge, and I know they were with Johnson, because when they got through telling us what to do, they went back to his car. Oh, and that's another thing. They changed up the order of the cars in the motorcade before we started out. (116)

Motorcycle officer Marion Baker supported Martin's claims: "When we got to the airport, our sergeant instructed me that there wouldn't be anybody riding beside the President's car." (117) Baker related to Vincent Palamara after being asked, "Are you aware of any orders not to have the motorcycles ride beside JFK's limousine?" Baker: "Yes, [and] He did not know why the press photographers were out of their usual position [in front of JFK]." (118) If Martin's and Baker's statements are correct, then either Lyndon Johnson or someone on his staff was responsible for changes in the motorcade. The possible implications have never been properly analyzed.

The Committee also supported Baker's statement that the cars were out of their normal alignment and concluded that the Presidential limousine was supposed to be seventh in line but somehow ended up being behind the lead car. (119) The change in the order of the cars is supported by Milton T. Wright, a Texas highway patrolman, and the driver of Mayor Cabell's car in the motorcade. Wright explained to author Vincent Palamara, "As I recall, prior to the President arriving at the airport, we were already staged on the tarmac. I do not recall what position I was in at the time, but it was not #1 [the number taped to his car's windshield]. At the last minute there was a lot of shuffling and I ended up in the fifth vehicle." (120)

Deputy Sheriff Roger Craig, who was assigned to stand in front of the sheriff's office on Houston Street during the motorcade stated: "We were told that we were merely spectators and not to be involved in any way in the security of the motorcade." (121) A possibly related attempt to keep individuals away from positions of importance was the experience of Maggie Barnes:

> Barnes was a secretary in the communications center of the Dallas Police Department, Radio Patrol Division. Her job consisted of receiving emergency calls and issuing information directly to the dispatcher whose office was located downtown, at headquarters, approximately one mile from Dealy Plaza. Barnes had received an unsolicited and unexpected invitation to the President's luncheon at the Dallas Trade Mart which was placed on her desk by a Dallas Policeman on the day before the assassination. She was not at her desk on the day of the assassination and would have been in a position to have heard all communications and transmissions regarding the events relating to assassination and the murder of Officer Tippit. (122)

It is also interesting to note that Chief Curry, Sheriff Decker, and Roy Kellerman all reported difficulty in radio communications during the assassination. Barnes' removal could possibly be related to these problems. (123)

Other important omissions in the motorcade planning involved the "coincidental" absence of White House Press Secretary Pierre Salinger and Special Agent in Charge Gerald Behn. Both men normally filled vital roles in security planning for President Kennedy's trips and neither was involved in the Dallas trip. Secret Service agent Robert Lilley told Vincent Palamara that Press Secretary Pierre Salinger, who normally made these trips, was "extremely knowledgeable" about motorcade planning and security concerns, because the Secret Service had "worked with Pierre on all of our advance work—except in Dallas. . . ." (124)

Gerald Behn was "conveniently" granted his first full vacation in three years during the period of the Texas trip. (125) Even more interesting is that the "number two man" responsible for protecting the President was also absent from the Dallas trip, agent Floyd Boring. (126)

President Kennedy's Air Force aide, General Godfrey McHugh, usually rode in the front seat of the limousine during motorcades and took notes. The House Select

Committee reported: "Ordinarily McHugh rode in the Presidential limousine in the front seat. This was the first time he was instructed not to ride in the car so that all attention would be focused on the President to accentuate full exposure." (127)

Another change from recent personnel protection assignments involved agent Don Lawton. Lawton had ridden on the right rear bumper of the Presidential limousine just four days before the assassination, during a motorcade in Tampa. (128) Lawton was left at Love Field on November 22 and went on to the Dallas Trade Mart where President Kennedy was scheduled to speak at 12:30. (129) Lawton was replaced by agent Glenn Bennet, who was riding protection for the first time. (130) Needless to say, President Kennedy received no protection during the assassination from agents on the right side of the follow-up car.

As was the case during the autopsy, there appears to have been an attempt to blame the victim for another inept performance. Secret Service agents were reportedly directed by President Kennedy to not ride on the rear bumper of the Presidential limousine despite strong evidence that this was, in actuality, standard practice. This attempt to blame Kennedy for his own lack of protection has also been refuted by the statements of numerous agents.

Gerald Behn recalled:

> I don't remember Kennedy ever saying that he didn't want anybody on the back of his car. I think if you watch the newsreel pictures and whatnot *[sic]* you'll find agents on there from time to time.' As just one of many examples, Behn cited the June 1963 trip to Berlin [there are many others . . .] (131)

Sam Kinney was the driver of the Secret Service follow-up car on November 23, 1963 but usually was the assigned driver of the Presidential limousine. Kinney stated:

> that is absolutely, positively false. . . . no, no, no, he had nothing to do with that [ordering agents off the rear of the limo]. . . No, never-the agents say, "o.k., men fall back on your posts.". . . President Kennedy was one of the easiest presidents to ever protect; Harry S. Truman was a jewel just like John F. Kennedy was . . . 99% of the agents would agree. . . . [JFK] was one of the best presidents ever to control-he trusted every one of us. (132)

According to author William Manchester, President Kennedy had stated, "Keep those Ivy League charlatans off the back of the car" (133) However, Agent Kinney firmly denied that charge to Vincent Palamara:

> That is false. I talked to William Manchester; he called me on the book *[sic]* . . . for the record of history that is false—Kennedy never ordered us to do anything. I asked Sam if an exception was made on 11/22/63; "Not this particular time, no. Not in this case." Sam also told me that JFK had nothing to do with the limiting of motorcycles during motorcades, and that Ken O'Donnell did not interfere with the agents: "Nobody ordered anyone around." (134)

Advance man Marty Underwood ". . .could not believe that Mr. Behn wrote his report with JFK's alleged "desires," citing Clint Hill's actions on 11/22/63 as just one of "many times" that agents were posted on the back of the JFK limousine. (135)

Agent Art Godfrey supported the belief that Kennedy never ordered the agents off the Presidential limousine, "He was 'very cooperative,' they [the other agents] told me. Kenney O'Donnell did not 'relay' any orders either. . . ." (136) Agent Godfrey recalled further, "All I can speak for is myself. When I was working [with] President Kennedy he never ask[ed] me to have my shift leave the limo when we [were] working it." (137) Dave Powers wrote, "Unless they [the Secret Service] were 'running' along beside the limo, the Secret Service rode in a car behind the President, so, no, they never had to be told to 'get off the limo.'" (138) White House photographer Cecil Stoughton recalled, "I did see a lot of the activity surrounding the various trips of the president, and in many cases I did see the agents in question riding on the rear of the President's car. In fact, I have ridden there a number of times myself during trips. . ." (139) Agents Bob Lilly and Sam Kinney also supported the argument that President Kennedy never ordered the agents off the back of the Presidential limousine. (140) Aide Dave Powers related to Palamara in 1993, "To reply to your recent inquiry about the Secret Service: No, they never had to be told to 'get off' the limousine." (141)

Agent Robert Lilly: "Oh I'm sure he didn't [order agents off the bumper]. He was very cooperative with us once he became President. He was extremely cooperative. Basically, 'whatever you guys want is the way it will be.'" Lilly recalled that on a trip with JFK in Caracas, Venezuela, he and "Roy Kellerman rode on the back of the limousine all the way to the Presidential palace" at speeds reaching "50 miles per hour [with the bubble-top on]." (142)

It is fitting, then, that Secret Service agent Clint Hill's report stated:

> I . . . never personally was requested by President John F. Kennedy not to ride on the rear of the Presidential automobile. I did receive information passed verbally from the administrative offices of the White House Detail of the Secret Service to Agents assigned to that detail that President Kennedy had made such requests. I do not know from whom I received this information . . . No written instructions regarding this were ever distributed. . . . [I] received this information after the President's return to Washington D.C. This would have been between November 19, 1963 and November 22, 1963. I do not know specifically who advised me of this request by the President. (143)

Secret Service agent Clint Hill gave his testimony to Warren Commission's Arlen Specter. "Did you have any other occasion en route from Love Field to downtown Dallas to leave the follow-up car and mount that portion of the President's car [rear portion of limousine]?" Hill: "I did the same thing approximately four times." (144) Yet, agent Hill, the only agent to react quickly enough to reach the limousine, was in Dallas only to protect Mrs. Kennedy, who was riding in her first motorcade. The Warren Commission also wondered why no agents were posted on the back of the limousine, on either side of the car, in Dallas. (145) Agent Floyd Boring told Vincent Palamara, ". . . . [JFK] was a very easy-going guy. . . . he didn't interfere with our actions at all." (146) Secret Service Chief James Rowley added his firm belief that "No President will tell the Secret Service what they can or cannot do [in regards to security measures]" (147)

One of the most disputed aspects in regards to the Secret Service protection, on November 22, 1963, is the controversial turn from Main Street to Houston, onto Elm. Interviews conducted by Vincent Palamara, as well as documentation from the Warren Report and the HSCA establish the following:

1. Agent Behn stated that the route was indeed changed.
2. Agents Kinney and Lawson stated that there were

alternate routes to the Trade Mart luncheon site.

3. Governor Connally told the New York *Herald Tribune*, 11/29/63, he was never told the the exact route.

4. The turn onto Elm violated Secret Service minimum speeds and brought the limousine by the knoll. (148)

As discussed earlier, the last point mentioned, point number 4., led to the questionable actions of limousine driver William Greer. Greer's unfortunate braking of the limousine led directly to the President's death. President Kennedy most likely would have survived the assassination attempt if not for the fatal head shot which most likely originated from the top of the knoll. Mrs. Jackie Kennedy, also questioned the actions of Agent Greer to her appointments secretary, Mary Gallagher, in December 1963. "You should get yourself a good driver. . . . so that nothing ever happens to you." (149)

Abraham Bolden, the first black member of the White House Detail of the Secret Service, made a number of serious and troubling allegations of negligence and insubordination against certain members of the Secret Service responsible for the protection of President Kennedy. (150) Bolden, a cum laude graduate from Lincoln University in Missouri, was the recipient of two commendations for breaking up counterfeit rings. (151) He was later fired by the Secret Service and imprisoned on charges that he tried to sell a government report on a counterfeiting case. (152) Three members of the Secret Service testified against him, and one, Joseph Spagnoli, later admitted that he had committed perjury. (153) Bolden claimed that he was "convicted on perjured evidence," because of his accusations of misconduct by certain members of the Secret Service. He has since attempted to have his name cleared by filing for a pardon that has continually been denied. (154) Secret Service agents Maurice Martineau and Robert Lilley have both confirmed Bolden's charges that President Kennedy's planned motorcade in Chicago on November 2, 1963 was canceled due to an assassination threat. (155) This threat was never publicly confirmed by the Secret Service, much less by the FBI or the Warren Commission.

One of the more serious charges issued by Mr. Bolden was that there was a strong anti-Kennedy backlash which had developed against the President as a result of the perceived push by Kennedy towards racial equality. (156) Bolden stated that he had heard President Kennedy referred to as a "niggar lover" by more than one agent and that one agent, in particular, Harvey Henderson, had refused to carry out the President's direct orders and was later personally fired by President Kennedy himself in the fall of 1963. (157) Support for Bolden's accusations comes from a number of fellow Secret Service agents. Secret Service agent Bert de Feese told the House Select Committee, "A threat did surface in connection with the Miami trip [11/18/63] . . . [by a] group of people." (158)

The Warren Commission was also aware of the fact that the shift responsible for protection of the President during the motorcade had been involved in an all night drinking episode on the night before the assassination.

Despite the acknowledged all night drinking party, attended by Secret Service agents the night before the assassination (which ended at 5:00 AM) at the "Cellar" in Forth Worth by members of his detail, agent Emory Roberts would later write that "there was no question in my mind as to (the agents) physical and mental capacity to function effectively in their assigned duties." (159)

Vincent Palamara described the actions of Emory Roberts as the Secret Service car was preparing to leave the airport and begin the motorcade trip through Dallas:

> Agent Roberts rose from his seat and, using his voice and several hand gestures, forced agent Henry J. Rybka to fall back from the rear area of JFK's limousine, causing a perplexed Rybka to stop and raise his arms several times in disgust . . . Although Rybka worked the follow-up in Houston the day before and was a gun-carrying protective agent, he was not allowed to do his job on November 22, 1963. (160)

Agent Rybka never publicly acknowledged or commented on this potentially important and possibly explosive incident.

Secret Service agent John Ready was actually recalled by Agent Roberts to the follow-up car when he started to react to the gunfire on 11/22/63. (161) Mr. Roberts had ordered the men not to move even after apparently recognizing the first sound during the shooting as gunfire. Kennedy aides Ken O'Donnell and Dave Powers summed up Roberts' reaction when they wrote, "Roberts, one of President Kennedy's agents . . . had decided to switch to Johnson as soon as Kennedy was shot." (162) Author William Manchester described Roberts' reaction to the President's death after viewing the President's body at Parkland Hospital:

> Powers and O'Donnell bounded toward the Lincoln. Powers
> heard Emory Roberts shouting at him to stop but disregarded
> him; a second might save Kennedy's life ...Emory Roberts
> brushed past O'Donnell, determined to make sure that
> Kennedy was dead. "Get up," he said to Jacqueline Kennedy.
> There was no reply. She was crooning faintly. From his side
> Roberts could see the President's face, so he lifted her elbow
> for a close look. He dropped it. To Kellerman, his superior, he
> said tersely, "You stay with Kennedy. I'm going to Johnson."
> (163)

Roberts' actions could very well have been the result of immediately recognizing, during the shooting, that Kennedy was dead and following confirmation of his death at the hospital, realizing that Johnson warranted immediate protection. However, this does not explain away the fact that his detail could not have been at its best after staying out all night and his later refusal to consider that there reactions might have been impaired. When this is considered alongside Roberts' apparent prevention of Agent Rybka in riding on the running board of the back-up vehicle and Roberts' questionable recall of the agents during the shooting, the role of Emory Roberts seems crucial indeed.

During recent attempts by the ARRB to gain a more accurate record of Secret Service actions during the assassination, the ARRB sought documents that pertained to the protection of President Kennedy during his three years as President. "ARRB Chairman John Tunheim stated that the Secret Service was the only agency involved in the Assassination and Records Review Board's work that destroyed records during its life; they were the most difficult of all government agencies involved." (164)

An extremely troubling report regarding the statements of Secret Service agent Elmer Moore, that were made to graduate student James Gouchenaur, was related to the HSCA and shown to Secret Service agent Floyd Boring in 1993. If this information is correct, then Moore was quoted as saying to Gouchenaur,". . . that Kennedy was a traitor for giving things away to the Russians; that it was a shame people had to die, but maybe it was a good thing: that the Secret Service personnel had to go along with the way the assassination was being investigated." (165)   If the statements by Elmer Moore, and previous accusations leveled by agent Abraham Bolden are accurate, then there is a strong implication of Secret Service negligence and possible complicity in the assassination. When the actions of Emory Roberts, as well as the changes in the motorcade protection and route are also considered, it is difficult to accept all of these circumstances as innocent or accidental coincidences. This is especially true, in light of the obstruction of justice carried out by both Lyndon Johnson and J. Edgar Hoover in the investigation of John Kennedy's death, as presented earlier. The power source responsible for both the assassination and coverup could very well have been one and the same, as Johnson's apparent complicity in the arrangement of cars in the motorcade and how the autopsy may have actually been performed indicate.

Interestingly enough, Robert Kennedy believed it to be possible that the Secret Service might have been bribed by Jimmy Hoffa in the assassination of his brother. Robert Kennedy quietly instructed Daniel Patrick Moynihan to investigate this possibility. No conclusive evidence of Hoffa's involvement was found but Moynihan's investigation did conclude that the Secret Service "in Dallas had been derelict if not corrupt." (166)

Chapter 14

Conclusion of Obstruction of Justice

The theme running through Part 2 is that J. Edgar Hoover's initial determination on November 22 of Lee Oswald's guilt is false. The House Select Committee on Assassinations determined:

> The FBI was the only Federal agency to conduct a full field investigation in the period immediately after the assassination, the period in which the evidentiary components at the crime scene for solving a homicide are assembled in the great majority of cases. Therefore, the FBI continued to assume an overwhelming share of the burden of the investigation. Since the Warren Commission did not have its own investigative staff, the Bureau was responsible for the investigative raw product including the evidence upon which the Commission's deliberations about a possible domestic conspiracy were to be based. (1)

The Committee concluded:

> the FBI's investigation into a conspiracy was deficient in the areas that the committee decided were most worthy of suspicion; organized crime, pro- and anti-Castro Cubans, and the possible associations of individuals from these areas with Lee Harvey Oswald and Jack Ruby. In those areas, in particular, the committee found that the FBI's investigation was, in all likelihood, insufficient to have uncovered a conspiracy. (2)

The mere suggestion that Hoover's conclusion of Lee Oswald's guilt could be questioned resulted in an angry response from the Director. Warren Commission Counsel Rankin stated, "I went to see Mr. Hoover before we finally put out our report. . . . He was pretty feisty when I saw him, any friendship we had in the past was not very apparent then. . . . Who could protest against what Mr. Hoover did back in those days?" (3) The House Select Committee stated " . . . Some Commission members were . . . reluctant to get involved in a confrontation with Hoover." (4)

Chief Justice Earl Warren knew from the beginning of the Commission's work that they had to rely solely on Hoover and the FBI's investigation and ultimately, their conclusions. Warren: ". . . Our job . . . is essentially one for the evaluation of evidence as distinguished from . . . gathering evidence. . . . We can start with the premise that we can rely on the report of . . . the FBI." (5)

J. Edgar Hoover's response to a direct question from J. Lee Rankin regarding the possibility of a conspiracy—is not an acceptable answer when all the evidence is considered:

> *Rankin.* From your study of this entire matter of the assassination and work in connection with it, do you know of any credible evidence that has ever come to your attention that there was a conspiracy either foreign or domestic involved in the assassination?
> *Hoover.* I know of no substantial evidence of any type that would support any contention of that character . . . I have been unable to find any scintilla of evidence showing any foreign conspiracy or any domestic conspiracy that culminated in the assassination of President Kennedy. . . . (6)

The House Select Committee also supported the view that the Commission (and therefore, the FBI and Hoover) did not adequately consider the possibility of a conspiracy:

> the Warren Report was not, in some respects, an accurate presentation of all the evidence available to the commission or a true reflection of the scope of the Commission's work, particularly on the issue of possible conspiracy in the assassination. It is a reality to be regretted that the Commission failed to live up to its promise. (7)

If the possibility of a conspiracy was not even considered, then its "main task" was compromised from the start. The

Commission had seen its task to be:

> to uncover all the facts concerning the assassination of President Kennedy and to determine if it was in any way directed or encouraged by unknown persons at home or abroad. (8)

Despite the conclusions reached in an open investigative forum by the House Select Committee that the Commission's investigation was not adequate; Warren Commission defenders continue to attempt to justify their closed-door conclusions.   Commission Attorney David Belin wrote *November 22, 1963: You Are the Jury*.   Belin strongly defended the conclusions, completeness, and integrity of the Warren Commission investigation.   He places blame "on critics, irresponsible critics who have deliberately and grossly misrepresented the [Warren Commission's] record to the American public." (9)   In an interview with reporter Daniel Schorr in 1975, this exchange took place:

> *Belin*. I don't happen to believe that Oswald was a part of any conspiracy, and as a matter of fact, the very fact that twelve years have passed and there really is no concrete evidence of any conspiracy, is in itself evidence of the fact there was no conspiracy.
> *Schorr*. Or a very good one.

Arlen Specter stated in 1988, "I think we found the real facts and certainly no one in the intervening 25 years has disproved our basic conclusions."   On December 7, 1965, in a discussion on the campus of UCLA, Commission member Allen Dulles made the following statements:

> Look, . . . there isn't a single iota of evidence indicating a conspiracy. . . . no one says there is anything like that . . . Look, there isn't one iota of evidence that the shots came from the front.   How can you say such a thing?   . . . You have nothing! Absolutely nothing! (10)

Many defenders of the Warren Commission and Hoover's investigation argue that sensationalist authors have distorted statements of the witnesses to sell books and make money and cause the public to be unnecessarily aroused.   There can be little argument that some of the authors of assassination-related books have been guilty of this.   But when it's considered that many witnesses were not called to testify, were intimidated, told not to talk, and possibly killed, then these criticisms do not hold up. The evidence seems clear that the vast majority of witnesses were just trying to tell the truth as they saw it and many of the authors and researchers were trying to write a more complete version of what really happened. As previously noted, former Warren Commission member Senator Richard Russell eventually went public and concluded that there was a conspiracy to murder President Kennedy. Russell along with Commission members Hale Boggs and John Sherman Cooper also disagreed with their Commission colleagues on the "single bullet theory." (11)

Senator Russell felt so strongly that the single bullet theory was wrong that he convinced Chief Justice Warren to hold one last Commission meeting on September 18, 1964, to formally record his dissent. (12) When Russell learned that the record of this meeting and his dissent was missing from the National Archives, he reportedly placed the blame on Lyndon Johnson. (13) The ARRB in 1997, also failed to locate the transcript. (14) Russell's biographer, Gilbert Fite, wrote: "He [Russell] frankly admitted that the debate and speculation over the circumstances of Kennedy's assassination would 'continue for a hundred years or longer.'" (15) Louisiana Senator Russell Long stated, "The possibility of conspiracy originating in New Orleans should have been investigated, and it was investigated by FBI agents. . . . Whether they found everything that was to be found is totally a different matter." (16)

Robert MacNeil ("MacNeil/Lehre News Hours," PBS) "We've seen revealed one conspiracy after another. Anybody would have to be a fool [to not believe in the possibility of a conspiracy]. . . . Perhaps we lived in a fool's paradise before the Kennedy assassination." (17)

Tom Wicker stated, "For a long time I felt quite strongly that Lee Harvey Oswald was the lone assassin. I think there is enough evidence now that there is certainly doubts about that. I'm willing to concede those doubts. I don't know what happened."(18) The statement by Tom Wicker reflects the belief shared by all of us who are interested in finding the truth; we "don't [really] know what happened." Ultimately, the assassination of President Kennedy only happened in one way. The reality being that Kennedy's murder was not the result of a theory. Too much evidence has been presented that leads one to doubt that Lee Oswald, alone and unaided, killed President Kennedy.

Since there was no public trial of Lee Oswald, the aura of secrecy that has emanated from the federal government has proven to be a hindrance to those who have proposed legitimate questions as to the veracity of J. Edgar Hoover's investigation for the Warren Commission. Following the provocative run of Oliver Stone's "JFK," the American public pushed Congress to cut down the walls of secrecy and release documents relating to the assassination that have been sealed secret by President Johnson and the Warren Commission.

It was with the goal of cutting down the walls of secrecy that the Assassination Records and Review Board (ARRB) was formed. The ARRB concluded:

> Although President Bush signed the JFK Act into law on October 26, 1992, and although the act required the President to make nominations within ninety days, President Bush made no nominations. President Clinton did not nominate the members of the Review Board until September 1993, well after he took office in January 1993, and the Board was not confirmed and sworn in until April 1994. (19)

Once the ARRB finally was able to begin reviewing documents, an important question remained to be answered; which documents and what agencies should be reviewed? Senator David Boren asked, "What is assassination material? What record regarding, for example, Cuba, Vietnam, and organized crime should be covered? This matter requires careful consideration." (20) The introduction to the ARRB Final Report states:

> The Assassination Records and Review Board was a unique solution to a unique problem. Although the tragic assassination of President John F. Kennedy was the subject of lengthy official investigations, beginning with the Warren Commission in 1964, and continuing through the House Select Committee on Assassinations, in 1978-79, the American public has continued to seek answers to nagging questions raised by the inexplicable act. These questions were compounded by the government penchant for secrecy. Fears sparked by the Cold War discouraged the release of documents, particularly those of the intelligence and security agencies. Even the records created by the investigative commissions and committees were withheld from public view

and sealed. As a result, the official record of the assassination
of President Kennedy remained shrouded in secrecy and
mystery. (21)

Then a senator, and current Secretary of Defense William
Cohen stated in 1992:

> I think today a great gulf exists between people and their
> elected officials. Doubts about this particular matter are a
> symptom of that, and so I think the purpose of this hearing is
> to ask some questions. Why does information need to be
> withheld? At this moment in time, what compelling interests
> are there for the holding back of information? Are there
> legitimate needs in this respect? Who and what is being
> protected? Which individuals, which agencies, which
> institutions are in the need of protection, and what national
> security interests still remain? (22)

There can be little doubt that the FBI and J. Edgar Hoover
as well as other government agencies have kept thousands of
files and documents from the American public. Fortunately,
we have a record from the witnesses who were there but even
their eyewitness accounts have been attempted to be
explained away by some. Despite the overwhelming and
consistent statements of those who witnessed the actual
events, the Warren Commission determined that the majority
of eye witnesses were "not credible." Gerald Posner is one of
those who believes these witnesses are not credible. Posner
writes in *Case Closed,* "Witnesses who thought the shots
came from the knoll were confused by echoes." (23) Mr.
Posner was not at the scene of the shooting, Parkland
Hospital, or the autopsy. Unless Posner is serving as the
prosecuting attorney in this case, he should allow both sides
of the evidence to speak for itself.

After reviewing the evidence at hand it is easier to
understand the doubts that the American people have
consistently held about J. Edgar Hoover's investigation for
the Warren Commission. Despite the statement by former
CIA Director and Warren Commission member Allen Dulles,
which reflected the belief that the people of America wouldn't
care or be interested in reading about the Commissions's
report—time has proven him to be wrong. Dulles stated to
his Commission colleagues on July 9, 1964, "But nobody
reads. Don't believe people read in this country. There will
be a few professors that will read the record . . . the public

will read very little." (24) The December 1991 issue of *Life* magazine stated:

> Since 1966, when the first attacks on the Warren Commission report were made, polls completed by organizations including Gallup, Harris, and the Washington Post have consistently shown that a majority of Americans believe that there was some sort of conspiracy behind the assassination.

The same could be said of the jurors in the Jim Garrison investigation of Clay Shaw. Although they easily acquitted Shaw in Garrison's charge that Shaw conspired to kill Kennedy, they did agree that there was most likely a conspiracy to assassinate the President. Edward Haggerty, the presiding judge in the Jim Garrison case against Clay Shaw stated:

> I certainly thought there was sufficient evidence to warrant bringing it to trial—there were a number of things that I believed that Shaw testified to that I did not believe. . . . I believe that Shaw was lying to the jury. (25)

In fact, an exit poll of the jurors in the case concluded that "The jurors were convinced that there was a conspiracy but not beyond a reasonable doubt that Shaw was involved." (26)

In the 1986 trial of Lee Harvey Oswald shown on national television, a jury selected from Dallas County voters, heard eyewitness testimony from those who were on the scene in Dallas in 1963—the decision rendered was "not guilty." A mock trial of the evidence against Lee Oswald held by the American Bar Association in 1992 led to a hung jury decision. The mock trial is described from the following article written by Tony Mauro and published in the *USA Today* on August 10, 1992:

> Lee Harvey Oswald gets his day in court today. A two-day mock trial, staged by the litigation section of the American Bar Association, includes computer simulations and a mock-up of President Kennedy's limousine. Jurors selected from the San Francisco area will listen to the evidence and give a verdict at the end of the trial, which will be televised on cable's Court TV. Trial organizers say they don't want to fuel conspiracy theories, so they're sticking close to the Warren Commission evidence and the testimony of actual witnesses

and experts.   A California company, Failure Analysis
Associates, has taken the 1963 evidence and the Zapruder
film of the assassination and enhanced it using computer and
video techniques.

In an affidavit signed by Roger McCarthy, the Chief
Executive Officer of Failure Analysis Associates (FAA),
McCarthy criticized the lack of objectivity shown by author
Gerald Posner.   FAA is the largest engineering firm in the
nation dedicated primarily to the analysis and prevention of
failures of an engineering or scientific nature.   McCarthy
described the process used by the FAA to render their verdict.
He was especially critical of Posner, author of *Case Closed*
whose book states unequivocally that Oswald was the lone
assassin of President Kennedy:

> Each of our teams did its best within the factual, time and
> resource constraints to assist the two eminent trial lawyer
> teams to resolve the key issues for their respective sides. . . . I
> believe the jury's inability to resolve Oswald's guilt . . . stems
> from the fact that . . . [we] did not have the time or resources
> to completely analyze the whole investigatory record and
> there are gaps in the factual record that our analysis was
> unable to bridge. . . .   Subsequent to our presentation one
> Gerald Posner contacted Dr. Robert Piziali, the leader of the
> prosecution team, and requested copies of the prosecution
> material, but not defense material, which we provided.
> Eventually Random House published a book by Mr. Posner
> entitled *Case Closed*.   [Posner] does not mention or
> acknowledge the ABA, or mention or acknowledge that there
> was additional material prepared . . . for the defense.
> Incredibly, Mr. Posner makes no mention of the fact that the
> mock jury that heard and saw the technical material that he
> believes is so persuasive and "closed" the case but which also
> saw . . . material prepared for the defense, could not reach a
> verdict.   In early televised interviews of Mr. Posner that were
> witnessed by . . . staff, Mr. Posner made no attempt to correct
> any supposition by a questioner that the . . . analytical work
> was performed at his request for him, and certainly left quite
> the opposite impression. (27)

Despite this affidavit, and the obvious slanting of Posner's
conclusions in *Case Closed*, this book was described in *U.S.
News and World Report* as "a brilliant new book [which]
finally proved who killed Kennedy." (28) It is little wonder
why a majority of the American people continue to harbor

doubts about certain segments of the mainstream media in regard to their conclusions about the assassination. When one compares the suspicions of the American public with the doubts of witnesses who were actually at the scene, the reason for continued questioning is clear. This is reflected in the previously noted 1983 written account by Cheryl McKinnon, a witness to President Kennedy's assassination:

> I tried to maintain the faith with my government. I have read the Warren Commission Record in its entirety and dozens of other books as well. . . . I have never quite had the same faith and trust in those that lead us, as I did before. (29)

The evidence compiled here by virtue of summarizing and synthesizing the witness statements and the views of those who studied the available evidence objectively, most certainly leads to the inescapable conclusion of a conspiracy of some kind to assassinate President Kennedy.

The American public has become cynical and less involved in government and politics since the 1960 Presidential election. Since the 1960 Presidential election between John Kennedy and Richard Nixon, the percentage of voter participation has shown a consistent and steady decline. The percentage of eligible voters who voted in 1960 was 62.8 percent. In 1996, the percentage of eligible voters who participated was an embarrassingly low 49 percent. Americans have not reached 60 percent voting participation since 1968 and have gone from the highest level of voting interest since the 1920's (in 1960) to the lowest level in 1996. (30) The truth in regard to the assassination has not been disclosed; a strong argument can be made that the suspicions, secrecy, and uncertainty involving the Kennedy assassination has led to the cynicism of our leaders today.

In 1999, results of an exclusive year-long survey of 36,000 people conducted by *USA Weekend* magazine also reflect the importance of the assassination of President Kennedy in the minds of many Americans. The assassination was ranked number five on a list of 100 stories of the century. Only the dropping of the atomic bomb, the Japanese attack on Pearl Harbor, the first man walking on the moon, and the Wright brothers first flight, ranked higher. (31)

The continued respect given to President Kennedy, despite the recent disclosures of his private failings, strongly indicates the public's dissatisfaction with the "official history" of his murder.   What remains to be documented is the explanation of how J. Edgar Hoover's and Lyndon Johnson's obstruction of justice led to the escalation of the Vietnam War.

The scene of the assassination; Dealy Plaza in Dallas, Texas. (Photograph courtesy of Robert Korpus.)

View from the Sniper's Nest," 6th floor of Schoolbook Depository
Building as motorcade approached on Houston Street. (Photograph
courtesy of *Sixth Floor Museum* and Robert Korpus.)

View from the "Sniper's Nest" as the motorcade proceeded down Elm Street. (Photo courtesy of the *Sixth Floor Museum* and Robert Korpus.)

View from the roof of the County Records Building—possible location of a sniper. (Photograph by the author.)

View from the railroad overpass. Grassy knoll and picket fence to the left. (Photograph courtesy of Robert Korpus.)

View of an approaching car on Elm Street from behind the corner of the fence on the knoll. (Photograph by the author.)

A more restrictive view of an approaching vehicle near the corner of the fence on the knoll. (Photograph by the author.)

Corner of the fence on the knoll from where shots most likely originated. (Photograph by the author.)

View from the fence to the railroad tower where Lee Bowers was situated. (Photograph by the author.)

The North Beckley Street rooming house of Lee Oswald. (Photograph courtesy of Robert Korpus.)

Air Force One, The plane that carried Presidents Kennedy and Johnson from Dallas to Washington, D.C. on November 22, 1963. (Photograph courtesy of Wright-Patterson Air Force Museum and Richard Wright.)

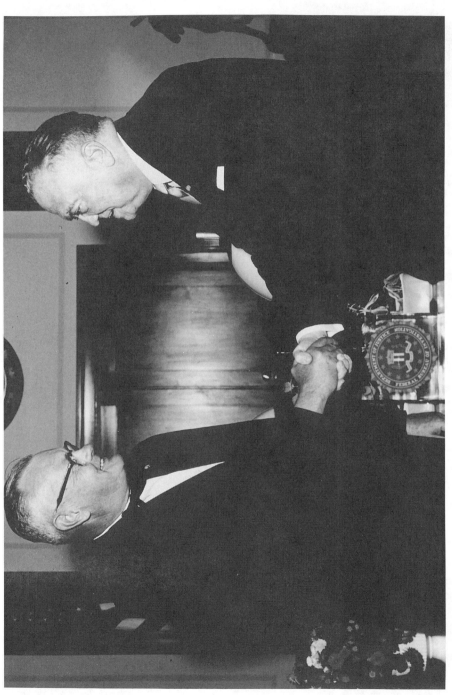

J. Edgar Hoover and Dallas Chief of Police Charles Batchelor who replaced Jesse Curry in 1966. (Photograph courtesy of the National Archives.)

J. Edgar Hoover and one of President Kennedy's autopsy surgeons, Pierre Finck, in 1966. (Photograph courtesy of the National Archives.)

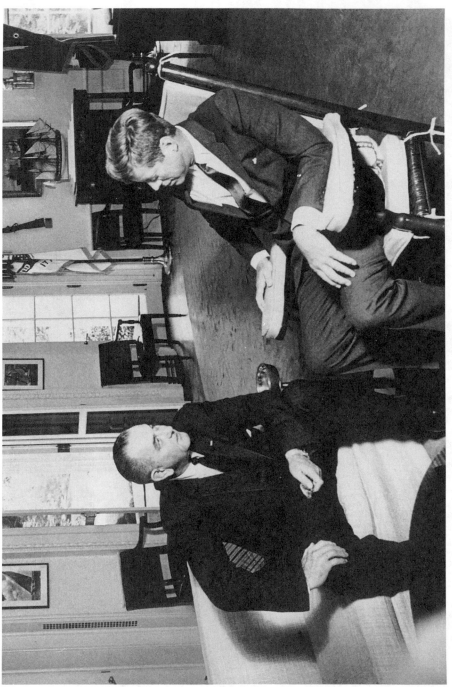

President John F. Kennedy and Vice President Lyndon B. Johnson in the Oval Office. (Photograph courtesy of the John F. Kennedy Museum.)

President Kennedy and Vice President Johnson on the White House grounds. (Photograph courtesy of the John F. Kennedy Library.)

Director Hoover expressing his appreciation to President Johnson for waiving the mandatory requirement for retirement. (Photograph courtesy of the National Archives.)

J. Edgar Hoover with Ambassador to South Vietnam Ellsworth Bunker. (Photograph courtesy of the National Archives.)

The Father of the Cold War with his book, *On Communism*.
(Photograph courtesy of the National Archives.)

Part 3

**A Clean Break:
Escalation of the Vietnam War**

Chapter 15

Vietnam: A Historical Overview

The main focus of Part 3 centers on the documentation of
research that indicates that there was a clean break rather
than continuation involving the Vietnam policies of John
Kennedy and Lyndon Johnson. As has been presented in Part
2, the subsequent escalation of the Vietnam War by Lyndon
Johnson, could not have been possible without J. Edgar
Hoover's cooperation in not allowing the assassination of John
Kennedy to develop into a   major issue during the
Presidential election of 1964.

Much has been researched and written about the Vietnam
policies of both men. Analysis of this research is crucial to
how historians will pass judgment on these men and this
particular period in history. A belief that John Kennedy
would have eventually committed the use of combat troops
and escalated the war is argued by Noam Chomsky in his
book, *Rethinking Camelot: JFK, the Vietnam War, and U.S.
Political Culture*. He states that the subsequent escalation by
Johnson was merely the result of following a continuous
policy initiated and carried out by Kennedy and his advisors.
(1)   Part 3 is a documentary reappraisal of the views of
Chomsky and others who support this argument.

This research documents the formation of United States
policy on Vietnam from its origin under the Truman and
Eisenhower administrations to the period of emphasis under
Kennedy and Johnson. The decisions and subsequent actions
of these Presidents and their advisors must be analyzed in

terms of how and why they were formed and implemented. The documentary record of French colonialism, the Geneva Accords, and the murder of Diem must be interwoven with our "losing of China," the Cuban Missile Crisis, the Nuclear Test Ban, etc. and the pressures they brought to bear must also be factored in. Vietnam policy was not developed in a vacuum. Proper analysis and judgment cannot take place without these considerations.

The period of our involvement in Vietnam (1945-75) was a unique time in United States history. The "official" war from 1965-75 was the longest in United States history and probably the most controversial. It marked a period of great social, economic, as well as military change. The power, influence, and credibility of the United States was at its peak. Many have argued that our stature in all three areas has declined as a direct result of our involvement in Vietnam. Twenty-five years have passed since the last American troops were withdrawn from Vietnam. It has been over thirty-five years since Kennedy made his last decision on Vietnam and Johnson made his first. Forty-five years have passed since the withdrawal of French troops and the beginning of United States involvement. The documentary record deserves to be scrutinized closely before this or future generations etch the current historical record of Vietnam into stone.

Lyndon Johnson described his view of "steady on course" in continuing John Kennedy's Vietnam policy in his own memoirs:

> President Kennedy believed in our nation's commitment to the Security of Southeast Asia, a commitment made in the [Southeast Asia Treaty Organization] SEATO Treaty and strengthened by his predecessor, President Eisenhower. Kennedy had explained on many occasions the reasons he took this position. By late 1963 he had sent approximately 16,000 American troops to South Vietnam to make good our SEATO pledge. Our policy would be steady on course. At a Joint Session of Congress on November 27, 1963, five days after I was sworn in, I gave my solemn pledge to the Congress and to the people of the United States: We will keep our commitments from South Vietnam to West Berlin. (2)

Johnson, as well as the majority of principals involved in decision-making on Vietnam backed a policy that failed. The subsequent memoirs and recollections should be analyzed with these considerations in mind. Would they be willing to admit that Kennedy was trying to avert what they would not?

President Kennedy was unsure and indecisive about many important problems during his Presidency (Cuba, Berlin, Civil Rights, etc.) with Vietnam being a major area of indecision. Eventually many of these decisions were made, and more of course would have been made if he would have lived. The documented record compiled indicates that Kennedy inherited a foreign policy in Vietnam that had begun the push for a military solution. The record clearly indicates that Kennedy intended to keep "a commitment to South Vietnam." However, the commitment of a large number of combat troops and the subsequent escalation was never under serious consideration by Kennedy.

Vietnam would surely be different today if left to its own initiatives. No nation, however, can remain immune from foreign contact and influence. This proved to be even more so during this period in history—the height of the Cold War. The nineteenth century saw the Southeast Asian peninsula as a battleground for competing colonial power between the British and the French. The French eventually regained control of Vietnam at the conclusion of World War II. In 1945, as the war was ending, the Japanese invaded Vietnam. The Japanese united the former French regions of Cochinchina, Tonkin, and Annam into one central government. This action rekindled the fires of independence in the Vietnamese people, as General Tran Van Don wrote:

> Following the surrender of the Japanese to Chiang Kai-shek and the nationalist Chinese (with allied approval but without their help) the victorious allies were faced with a new situation in Vietnam. Ho Chi Minh, a popular leader from the North, emerged. He had gained the respect of the Vietnamese people by standing up to the Japanese and then to the French. His Viet Minh party was well organized and his leadership amongst the people was unquestioned. The French and United States forces had to deal with him despite his communist tendencies and nationalist coalition. (3)

President Franklin Roosevelt had been sympathetic to those under colonial rule and wanted to allow them to seek independence. "In a memorandum sent to Secretary of State Cordell Hull in January 1944, Roosevelt wrote: 'France has had the country—thirty million inhabitants—for nearly one hundred years, and the people are worse off than they were at the beginning. . . France has milked it for one hundred years.

The people of Indo-China are entitled to something better than that.'" (4) But as World War II was ending, Roosevelt's priorities were elsewhere. Roosevelt and the United States had stronger obligations to Winston Churchill and Charles De Gaulle. The British and French were current allies and Western Europe was of too much importance to back the Vietnamese and their quest for independence. The United States military was pushing for bases in Southeast Asia in order to project air and sea power and also desired to protect the flow of the rich supply of raw materials that the region had to offer.

Following the death of Roosevelt in April, Harry Truman inherited Roosevelt's advisors and Truman leaned heavily upon them (James Byrnes, Dean Acheson, and George Marshall and others) for advice on Vietnam and foreign affairs. The Truman Administration initially hoped for a liberal and natural development towards independence in Vietnam. But Byrnes and Acheson stressed that there should not be a sharp break in policy from Roosevelt. (5) The Soviets were considered a threat in eastern and western Europe and the military argument of a need for bases in the Far East seemed prudent. This was the situation the United States was facing as Ho Chi Minh quoted the Declaration of Independence in September 1946, in his drive for United States recognition. Ho also sent eight urgent appeals for recognition to President Truman and no replies were given (6)

Ho Chi Minh and the Viet Minh resisted attempts at a French return to dominance in the region. Ho was willing to accept less than immediate independence for all of Vietnam. He was not willing to accept that Cochinchina, Tonkin, and Annam would not be a unified nation. The Viet Minh were most upset by the appointment of Dr. Nguyen Van Thinh as President of Cochinchina. Van Thinh was vilified by Ho and called a puppet. (7) On November 9, Van Thinh told General Tran Van Don, "France is not fair. I have not been enough of a puppet for them, so they are trying to replace me." The following day President Thinh committed suicide by hanging himself. (8) Further negotiations between the French and Ho at Dalat, Paris, and Fontainebleau resulted in a stalemate.

The French, frustrated by a lack of Vietnamese acquiesce to the negotiated agreements of 1946, ordered a naval bombardment of Haiphong which resulted in 6,000

Vietnamese deaths. The Viet Minh retreated to Hanoi and attacked the power station there on December 19, 1946. A full scale guerrilla war had now broken out and the United States backed the French. The Truman Administration continued to question French policy in Vietnam. But the year 1947 saw the issuance of the containment policy and the Marshall Plan and French support was crucial to the success of both.

A united Vietnam came into being for the first time in eighty-seven years in March 1947. (9) Despite this positive step, Ho Chi Minh and the Viet Minh were not placated and the year of 1949 would have Cold War problems of its own. The first Soviet atomic bomb was exploded much earlier than United States intelligence analysts had predicted, and under the communists, Mao took control of mainland China. The political attacks on the Truman Administration were brutal over the "loss of China." Domestic attacks led by J. Edgar Hoover and others, as presented in Part 1, also played a large part in the policies that Truman would follow. Military and economic threats to Western Europe and Japan by the Communists were to be stopped at all costs. The United States was hardening into its Cold War enclave and Vietnam became a pawn in this geo-political struggle.

Senator J. William Fulbright wrote:

> Ho Chi Minh is not a mere agent of Communist China, much less of the "international communist conspiracy" that we used to hear so much about. He is a bona-fide nationalist revolutionary, the leader of his country's rebellion against French colonialism. He is also a communist, and that is the essential reason why since at least 1950 he has been regarded as an enemy by the United States. (10)

Noted Pulitzer Prize winner and Vietnam historian Stanley Karnow has written that "Late in 1949, Secretary of State Dean Acheson persuaded President Truman to earmark $15 million in aid to the French forces in Indochina. Over the next four years, American assistance for the French war mounted to more than $2 billion." (11)

Robert McNamara wrote:

> I want to state, and I want to state it quite frankly, that if I had been a Vietnamese communist in January 1961, when the Kennedy administration came to office, I might well have believed, as I judge they did, that the United States's goal in

Southeast Asia was to destroy the Hanoi government and its
ally the NLF—that the U.S. was an implacable enemy whose
goal, in some fashion, was victory over their country.
Now why might I have believed that? Because the U.S. had:

Rejected or ignored friendly overtures to President Truman
from Ho Chi Minh in the summer and fall of 1945, following
the defeat of the Japanese.

Supported post-World War II French claims to its former
colonies in Southeast Asia and had, in addition, throughout
the early 1950s financed much of the French war against the
Vietminh insurgents, led by Ho Chi Minh.

Refused to sign the Geneva Accords of 1954, which thus
thwarted the planned Vietnamese elections for 1956 that were
mandated by the Geneva Agreement. (12)

William Blum, author of *Killing Hope: U. S. Military and
CIA Interventions Since WWII,* has written:

In 1945 and 1946, Vietminh leader Ho Chi Minh had written
at least eight letters to President Truman and the State
Department asking for America's help in winning Vietnamese
independence from the French. He wrote that world peace
was being endangered by French efforts to reconquer
Indochina and he requested that the "four powers" (US,
USSR, China, and Great Britain) intervene in order to
mediate a fair settlement and bring the Indochinese issue
before the United Nations. (This was a remarkable repeat of
history. In 1919, following the First World War, Ho Chi Minh
had appealed to US Secretary of State Robert Lansing for
America's help in achieving basic civil liberties and an
improvement in the living conditions for the colonial subjects
of French Indochina. This plea, too, was ignored.) (13)

In February 1950, the United States recognized the newly
installed Bao Dai French government in Vietnam. A 1950
National Security Council Study asked for the United States
to "scrutinize closely governments that are directly concerned
with communist aggression. Particular attention should be
paid to French IndoChina." (14) In the same year, President
Truman decided to send modest levels of military and
economic assistance to the French effort in Vietnam. (15)
June 1950 saw the eruption of the Korean War and the
United States militarily involved in Asia. Secretary of State
John Foster Dulles, Secretary of Defense Louis Johnson, and
the Joints Chief of Staff were doubtful of French or United
States military success in Vietnam in 1950. Dulles thought

that French involvement might be a hopeless military situation. (16) Secretary Johnson and the Joint Chiefs of Staff stated the United States military did not want to commit United States troops to Southeast Asia. (17) The current conflict in Korea surely had an effect on Johnson and the Joint Chief's position. However, the reality of the Vietnam situation, as espoused by Dulles, was made clear before the start of the Korean War.

By the end of the Korean War in 1952, the United States was underwriting forty percent of the French cost in the Vietnam conflict. The Eisenhower Administration not only continued the Truman policy in Vietnam, but in reality, deepened U.S. military, economic, and political support for Diem's government in Vietnam. By 1954, the U.S. military aid to the French during their war with the Vietnamese reached 1.4 billion and "constituted 78 percent of the French budget for the war." (18) As William Blum described, "'The Pentagon Papers' concluded that the decision to provide aid to France 'directly involved' the United State in Vietnam and 'set' the course for future American policy." (19) Also, in 1954, the *New York Times* reported that "The French Air Force is now almost entirely equipped with American planes." (20)

The National Security Council in an April 1954 meeting urged President Eisenhower "to inform Paris that acquiescence in a Communist take-over of Indochina would bear on its status as one of the Big Three and that U.S. aid to France would automatically cease." (21) But former Secretary of State Dean Acheson recalled it a little differently: "The U.S. came to the aid of the French in Indochina not because we approved of what they were doing, but because we needed their support for our policies in regard to NATO and Germany. The French blackmailed us. At every meeting when we asked them for greater effort in Europe they brought up Indochina. . . . They asked for our aid for Indochina but refused to tell me what they hoped to accomplish or how." (22)

The Council recommended that "It be U.S. policy to accept nothing short of a military victory in Indo-China," and stated further that "U.S. [should] actively oppose any negotiated settlements in Indo-China at Geneva" and that the U.S. should consider completing the war without French participation. (23) The realization that the United States' policy in Southeast Asia was unrealistic and was leading the country unnecessarily down the path of future involvement and escalation, as well as the subsequent introduction of combat troops, is exemplified by the statement of Secretary of State John Foster Dulles in a 1954 Cabinet meeting: "We are confronted by an unfortunate fact . . . Most of the countries of the world do not share our view that Communist control of any government anywhere is in itself a danger and a threat." (24)

In May of 1954, Admiral Arthur Radford, Chairman of the Joint Chiefs of Staff, and General Charles Willoughby, General Douglas MacArthur's director of intelligence, both contemplated the use of nuclear weapons in Indochina. Radford wrote to Defense Secretary Charles Wilson, "The employment of atomic weapons is contemplated in the event that such course appears militarily advantageous." (25) Willoughby went so far as to suggest that it was necessary "to create a belt of scorched earth across the avenues of communism to block the Asiatic hordes." (26) On July 20, 1954, the Geneva conference put an "official" end to the war in Vietnam. Only the U.S. refused to sign the Final Declaration. The U.S. refused to sign because the settlement forbid any future military efforts to defeat the Vietminh. (27) Even during the Geneva conference, the United States had begun to assemble a paramilitary team under the leadership of CIA official Edward Lansdale. Lansdale had successfully carried out a campaign of military and psychological warfare against insurgents in the Philippines. Blum described some of the various activities that Lansdale was engaged in during the remaining six months of 1954:

- Encourage the migration of Vietnamese from the North to the South through 'an extremely intensive, well-coordinated, and, in terms of its objective, very successful psychological warfare operation.
- Distributed other bogus leaflets, supposedly put out by the Vietminh, to instill trepidation in the minds of people in the North about how life would be under Communist rule. The following day, refugee registration to move south tripled.
- Created and distributed an almanac of astrological predictions carefully designed to play on Vietnamese fears and superstitions and undermine life in the North while making the future of the South appear more attractive.
- Published and circulated anti-Communist articles and "news" reports in newspapers and leaflets.
- Laid some of the foundation for the future American war in Vietnam by: sending selected Vietnamese to U.S. Pacific bases

for guerrilla training: training the armed forces of the South who had fought with the French . . . (28)

On July 16, 1955, President Diem made clear his intention of not engaging in consultations with the North as had been agreed at Geneva. Diem, of course, realized that he could not possibly win in an honest election. President Eisenhower was later to concur with this assessment when he stated, in his memoirs, "I have never talked or corresponded with a person knowledgeable in Indochinese affairs who did not agree that had elections been held as of the time of the fighting, possibly 80 percent of the population would have voted for the communist Ho Chi Minh as their leader rather than Chief of State Bao Dai." (29) As The Pentagon Papers have revealed, President Eisenhower and his administration had hoped to postpone the elections as long as possible. (30) Bowing to Western pressure, Diem conducted "free elections" in order to gain a semblance of legality. Diem was advised by the United States that a 60 percent margin of victory would appear quite sufficient "but Diem insisted on 98 percent." (31)

George Herring, former visiting professor of history at the U. S. Military Academy (West Point) and author of four books on Vietnam, including the highly acclaimed, *America's Longest War,* wrote:

> Some U.S. officials advised abandoning the area, and the administration briefly considered displacing Ngo Dinh Diem. When Diem unexpectedly prevailed over his domestic foes, however, the United States assumed from France the burden of nation building and committed itself firmly to his regime.
> Ngo Dinh Diem may well have been the "best available man," as Dulles described him, and the United States pinned its hopes exclusively on him and helped him to survive the tumultuous years 1954 and 1955. (32)

General Matthew Ridgway wrote in his memoirs which were published in 1956:

> We could have fought in Indochina. We could have won, if we had been willing to pay the tremendous cost in men and money that such intervention would have required—a cost that in my opinion would have eventually been as great as, or greater than, that we paid in Korea. In Korea, we had learned that air and naval power alone cannot win a war and that inadequate ground forces cannot win one either. It was

incredible to me that we had forgotten that bitter lesson so soon—that we were on the verge of making that same tragic error. That error, thank God, was not repeated. (33)

The French surrendered at Dien Bien Phu and negotiated a cease-fire in July 1954 in Geneva. As stated, the United States did not participate in the negotiations of the Geneva Accord that followed but did agree to adhere to the accords and issued a declaration to that effect. Two important provisions that became a part of the accords were that no foreign troops would be on Vietnamese soil and Vietnam would be divided into two zones until the 1956 elections. (34) Another reaction by the United States was the formation of the Southeast Asian Treaty Organization, also in 1954. This treaty organization was formed to protect United States and western interests as a result of the French withdrawal. However, the National Security Council meeting of July 21, 1954 concluded that the Geneva accords were a disaster due to the fact that Ho Chi Minh had captured the "hearts and minds" of the Vietnamese people. Ho had become a hero in the eyes of the Vietnamese people as a result of his leadership in repelling foreign invasion and reinstituting the goal of a united and independent Vietnam. (35)

Privately, another policy was developing. An August 3, 1954 National Security Council meeting requested an urgent program of United States economic and military aid. (36) This decision was being made at the same time that a United States intelligence estimate was prepared, also on August 3, 1954. The estimate stated, "Although it is possible that the French and Vietnamese with firm United States support and other powers may be able to establish a strong regime in South Vietnam, we believe that the chances for this development are poor and moreover, that the situation is likely to continue to deteriorate progressively over the next year." (37) It is quite obvious that the policy suggested by the National Security Council was not in concert with the intelligence information. This problem continued to plague United States policy makers from this juncture until well into the future.

In 1954, the Eisenhower Administration became a staunch ally of Ngo Dinh Diem, the new leader of South Vietnam. When Diem came to power in 1954, most participants and observers in and out of Vietnam considered him to be a strong defender of national independence and a staunch anti-communist. (38) Diem, a devout Catholic, believed that he was divinely inspired to lead Vietnam. Unfortunately, Diem immediately began to be viewed with scepticism by his own people after he chose mostly Catholics from his home sector for government positions. But the internal improvements initiated by Diem were positive and schools were opened in the countryside, rice production increased, roads were reopened. These were the best years of Diem's rule, 1954-1958. (39) However, there were those in Vietnam that distrusted Diem because he was from Central Vietnam and had been out of the country for a long time. (40) A widely held view that Ho Chi Minh ascribed to was that he could take over South Vietnam peacefully. He foresaw an internal collapse of the Saigon government followed by victory in the reunification elections of 1956. (41) Despite reservations, Diem inspired considerable respect in most foreign governments and especially from the United States. (42)

Acceptance of American foreign aid did not help Diem and his nationalist standing. The "true" nationalists belonged to Ho Chi Minh. Suppression of Buddhist sects and native chieftains by Diem's brother and second in command, Ngo Dinh Nhu, helped Ho's cause. Trying to institute a Catholic minority leadership in a country that had a majority of Buddhists proved to be a great mistake. (43) The personalities of Diem, Nhu and his family also hurt their standing with the people of Vietnam. Modesty was a trait greatly admired by the people. Diem was considered arrogant but Nhu and his wife, Madame Nhu, even more so. This was especially true in regards to intellectuals from the North who generally viewed the family with great distrust. (44) When Diem postponed the 1956 elections, the issue of independence was left to the Communists. (45)

In the countryside of South Vietnam were Ho's communist networks. Once the reunification elections were canceled, a gradual increase in network activity (guerrilla, lecturer's, recruiters, etc.) took place lasting from 1957-58. Diem's ambitious project in 1959, the "agroville" looked promising at first but it failed due in large part to the rise of the communist insurgency. (46)

January 27, 1960 marked a communist attack of a South Vietnamese regimental headquarters near the Cambodian border. This action opened up a trail that later came to be known as the Ho Chi Minh Trail by which thousands of communist insurgents entered and re-entered South Vietnam. (47) Diem's political troubles would continue. Leading civilian political figures formed a "Committee for Progress and Liberty." This group attacked the South Vietnamese government for adopting "Communist" methods of controlling the people. Diem was accused of being dictatorial, corrupt and practicing nepotism. They demanded that the government address civil rights but this petition was quickly rejected by Diem and Nhu. (48)

The stage was set for an internal United States foreign policy battle. General Sam Williams called for an invasion of North Vietnam and an increase in United States advisors (49) One section of the CIA was cooperating with a South Vietnamese coup attempt against Diem while another CIA compartment was praising the success of the "strategic hamlet" village defense program (as were Diem and Nhu). (50) A third, or possibly combined faction of the CIA, was running weapons to Burma, Thailand, Laos, and Vietnam. In exchange, the CIA helped to facilitate the opium exchange of the "Golden Triangle" with men like Laotian General Phao. (51) Bill Lair, CIA Chief of Naval Operations, believed that there were "too many people [American CIA] in Vietnam" during this period. (52) But according to Air America [covert airlines for CIA operations) Pilot Ted Moore, who flew operations into Laos, "We [Americans] weren't there." (53) Few were aware of our secret involvement in Laos and Vietnam.

The Saigon CIA mission in 1960 appeared small and to have less clout than the United States military in the region. But General Williams and Admiral Felt intended to further expand the role of CIA air missions and also pushed for a strong and quick military response. (54) The State Department, under Ambassador Eldridge Durbow and political counselor Joseph Mendenhall argued for reforms from Diem. The battle between the military and the State department would greet President Kennedy in 1961 and never leave him during the three years of his Presidency. If that was not enough, President Eisenhower upped the ante and placed tremendous pressure on the incoming President. George Herring has written that Eisenhower was "Referring to Laos as the 'cork in the bottle' whose removal could threaten all of Southeast Asia, the President, as early as September 1959, had grimly warned that it might 'develop into another Korea.'" (55)   At a meeting in late 1960, Eisenhower advised that "we cannot let Laos fall to the Communists, even if we have to fight—with our allies or without them." (56) President Kennedy inherited a policy of consistent and gradual escalation that the Truman and Eisenhower administrations had followed for over twelve years. Eisenhower's reference to Laos and Southeast Asia, in general, as the "cork in the bottle," forced Kennedy to deal with a situation in Vietnam that he did not create.

Chapter 16

The Formation of Policy Views on Vietnam by Kennedy and Johnson

How and what Johnson and Kennedy knew and learned about foreign affairs and the use of governmental power in Vietnam before they entered the White House, is very important. The forces working for and against the policies of both men and their implementation are vitally important when considering their subsequent Vietnam policies. This research attempts to describe the relationship between Kennedy's and Johnson's military experience and congressional records, as well as their personal relationship, and how these areas affected future policy views on Vietnam.

After being pushed into politics by his father Joe Sr., following the death of his older brother Joe Jr., during WWII, John Kennedy began the process of forming his own views on foreign policy. The senior Kennedy had political aspirations of his own in the 1930's. After making millions as a result of his activities in the stock market, movie industry, and the smuggling of alcohol during Prohibition, the elder Kennedy was appointed by Franklin Roosevelt to oversee Wall Street. He later persuaded Franklin Roosevelt to appoint him as ambassador to England. On December 9, 1937, this came to pass. (1) Kennedy's two goals of furthering his career and preventing war seemed possible in the spring of 1938. He saw himself as an "ambassador at large of Europe" but Roosevelt did not appreciate Kennedy's self-serving attempts at gaining important influence. (2) These power-grabbing attempts combined with the Ambassador's unpopular backing of Neville Chamberlain and neutrality in the European war towards Hitler, effectively ended Kennedy's quest for higher office. However, this did not deter his ambition for his sons to do what he could not.

John Kennedy's maternal grandfather, John "Honey" Fitzgerald, was a more conventional politician than Joe Kennedy Sr. Honey Fitz proved to be a very successful and long-time mayor of Boston. John Kennedy would learn from the counsel and practices of both men but especially from his father.

John Kennedy wrote *Why England Slept* as a Harvard thesis paper. The paper was well received and also marked a break in policy view from his father. This also marked the beginning of Kennedy's public foreign policy. In his thesis, he argued that Great Britain was slow to change from disarmament and pointed out Churchill as a hero and a prophetic figure in regards to his early warnings about Adolf Hitler.

John and Joe Jr. both entered the service and joined the Navy. Joe's untimely death in a 1944 bombing mission forced John to become the heir apparent to his father's political ambitions. Kennedy's role in the PT 109 incident helped to create a hero image for him. His judgment in this incident has since been called into question but his courage after the crash has been lauded by those involved. (3)

John Kennedy went on to win his first congressional seat in 1946. His early foreign policy views reflected the Cold War political climate of the time. They included an attack on the Truman Administration for the "loss of China," support for the McCarran Act, which included a provision that communists register with the federal government. Kennedy also supported future rival Richard Nixon, over Helen "Pink Lady" Douglas, in the California Senate Race. Kennedy later conceded to author and historian, Theodore White, that his early and strident, anti-communistic rhetoric was single-minded and wrong. Theodore White recalled:

> I remember one of my earliest meetings with Senator John F. Kennedy, when I was still trying to understand him and criticized him for an early attack he had made on two American scholars of the Far East as being part of the web of Communist conspiracy about the State Department.

This had happened in his junior years as a congressman, in the era of Joe McCarthy. He shook his head in exasperation—but not at me, at himself. "I was ignorant," he said. "I was ignorant; I was wrong; I was a kid congressman, and you know what that is—no staff, no research, nothing. I made a mistake—what else can I say?" (4)

Supreme Court Justice William O. Douglas, a friend of the Kennedy family, stated that young Kennedy "never seemed to get into the mainstream of any political thought, that he just sort of drifted." (5) Kennedy was considered offbeat by congressional standards according to Larry O'Brien, Kennedy's political strategist. O'Brien thought Kennedy was bored by the House and his frequent absences became conspicuous. In 1951, Kennedy told O'Brien that "it is up or out for me." (6) In preparing his future run for the Senate, and to break out of his somewhat "sheltered life," John Kennedy began to look to his strength in foreign relations and sharpen his views.(7)

In early 1951, Kennedy left for Europe and received a good amount of press coverage. His visits included West Germany, Spain and Yugoslavia. He visited with Tito, the Pope, and toured installations of the newly formed North Atlantic Treaty Organization. (8) During the fall, Robert Kennedy joined his older brother on a trip that would include visits to the Middle East and Asia. This would begin the crystallization of his views on Southeast Asia, and of course, Vietnam.

Robert wrote in his diary that this trip made a "very, very major impression on his brother." (9) Walt Rostow, one of Kennedy's future foreign policy advisors, called it the "formative experience" for John Kennedy. (10) Robert wrote in 1951, "Indian Prime Minister Nehru stated that communism was attractive to emerging nations because it is something worth dying for. Must give the same aura to democracy . . . We only have the status quo to offer these people. Commies can offer a change." (11)

After their arrival in Saigon, Robert wrote letters to his father criticizing the United States support for the French. An honest vote he said would give Ho seventy percent of the vote: (12)

Because of the great United States war aid to the French,

we are being closely identified with the French, the result being that we had become quite unpopular. Our mistake has been not to insist on definite political reforms by the French toward the natives as a prerequisite to any aid. As it stands now, we are becoming more and more involved to a point where we can't back out. (13)

These words would eventually prove prophetic and especially so for Lyndon Johnson.

While visiting Vietnam, John Kennedy had long conversations with the United States consular officer in Saigon, Edmund Gullion. What Kennedy learned from these discussions was that Korea should not be compared to Vietnam. The fight for Vietnam was over nationalism and not Communism. Gullion left Kennedy with the idea that in twenty years, colonies would be no more. (14) This prediction by Gullion has proven to be accurate; the era of colonialism is left to the history books for the majority of the world today. Roger Hilsman, who worked in the State Department under President Kennedy, remembers Kennedy stating, "In Indochina we have allied ourselves to the desperate effort of a French regime to hang onto the remnants of an empire." (15)

The views that Kennedy formed during this trip were quite pronounced. He had gone through quite a change from his early days of "drifting" on foreign policy. Following an interview with French commanding General Jean Marie de Lattre, the General sent a message to the State Department stating that the Kennedys were attempting to undermine French policy. The Kennedys' anti-colonial and French views were seen as harming the war effort. (16) If this experience was truly a "formative period" for John Kennedy, then this quote made upon his return from Vietnam helps to support the assertion that he believed United States combat troops would not be enough, ultimately, the solution should be left to the Vietnamese themselves. "The fires of nationalism so long dormant have been kindled and are now ablaze. Communism cannot be met effectively merely by force of arms." (17)

The next step for Kennedy in the formation of policy views was in the Senate where he continued to make statements and speeches stating his position on Vietnam. On June 30, 1953, he said, "The war can never be successful unless large numbers of Vietnamese are won over from their sullen neutrality and open hostility to it . . . [and] are assumed beyond doubt their complete independence will be theirs at the conclusion of the war." (18)   As the pressure was mounting to involve United States forces in Vietnam in the spring of 1954 as the French were under siege at Dien Bien Phu. Kennedy delivered a speech in the Senate on April 6. He explained that the British had given up India with a "civility."

> To pour money, materials, and men into the jungles of Indochina without at least a remote prospect of victory would be dangerously futile and self destructive . . . I am frankly of the belief that any amount of military assistance in Indochina cannot conquer an energy that is everywhere and at the same time nowhere. An effective native army is needed to meet Communist aggression. (19)

Kennedy had come a long way since his father had insisted that he take Joe Jr.'s position as political heir.   He had developed sharp policy differences with his conservative and isolationist father. "There were some issues which he [his father] and I don't even discuss any more," John said. (20)

Vietnam continued to be an issue that Kennedy would voice his opinions on. Speaking before the American Friends of Vietnam in Washington in June 1956, he said:

> This is our offspring. We cannot abandon it in a country where concepts of free enterprise and capitalism are meaningless, where poverty and hunger are not enemies across the 17th parallel, but enemies within our midst . . . What we must offer then, is a revolution—a political, economic, and social revolution far superior to anything the communists can offer. (21)

Kennedy's statement reflects his belief that if the South Vietnamese government is not supported by the people and reforms are not implemented, then there was little hope for success.

Despite the impression of some who believe that Kennedy had little or no experience relating to Vietnam, it is clear that he did have experience and had developed strong opinions on the subject.   These opinions were formed as a result of visiting Vietnam and speaking with French commanders who were directly involved in the reality of fighting a losing battle against the Vietnamese. In fact, one could reasonably argue that Kennedy understood the situation as well or better than most of his congressional colleagues. Kennedy also discussed and stressed the viability of defeating Communism in Southeast Asia, not merely with arms but via our superior system of freedom, technology, and capitalism. Kennedy had clearly stated that the problems in Vietnam were not merely a battle against Communism but also involved nationalism and poverty. These were ideals that he stressed consistently until November 1963. Senator Kennedy stated during an interview in 1959:

> The desire to be independent and free carries with it the desire not to become engaged as a satellite of the Soviet Union or too closely allied to the United States. We have to live with that, and if neutrality is the result of a concentration on internal problems, raising the standard of living of the people and so on, particularly in the underdeveloped countries, I would accept that. It's part of our own history for over a hundred years. I should look with friendship upon those people who want to beat the problems that almost overwhelm them, and wish to concentrate their energies on doing that, and do not want to become associated as the tail of our kite. (22)

In 1960, Kennedy observed:

> Indochina presents a clear case study in the power of anticolonial revolution sweeping Asia and Africa. What has happened also demonstrates that national independence can lead to genuine resistance to Communism. It is a long, sad story with a hopeful chapter, but the end is not in sight. On a trip to Asia in 1951 I saw firsthand that in Indochina we had allied ourselves with a colonial regime that had no real support from the people. (23)

During the 1960 Presidential campaign, Senator Kennedy attacked Vice-President Richard Nixon's pledge to help the French at Dien Bien Phu. Kennedy stated that the French and Vietnamese conflict was "a war where we would have been engaged in a hopeless struggle without allies, for an unpopular colonialist cause." (24)

By 1960, John Kennedy's views on Vietnam were well documented. He had stated his opposition to the French involvement in Vietnam as well as in Algeria. (25) He began as a Congressman, "bored" with the House, and "drifting" on the issues. Kennedy neared the threshold of the White House with a historical record on Vietnam clearly in hand.

The evidence presented here argues strongly that the historical record Kennedy accumulated before entering the White House would be implemented in actual policy and in preparation for his future policy actions. John Kennedy might indeed have continued a commitment of "some sort" to defend Vietnam against Communism. But surely not at the expense of America's escalation to the point of bombing North Vietnam or the commitment of half-a-million combat troops. The historical record presented here will clearly show that Lyndon Johnson did not continue the clearly stated intentions of John Kennedy to avoid Americanizing the war.

The formation of Lyndon Johnson's views on foreign policy were similar and yet different from John Kennedy's in crucial areas. Both men were products of the Depression, World War II, as well as the re-emergence of J. Edgar Hoover's Cold War era. Yet, Kennedy never experienced poverty while Lyndon Johnson was quite familiar with poverty. Both men had political ambition in their bloodlines. Johnson's father, Sam, was an idealist and an honest man. He won election six times to the Texas legislature and the lobbyists couldn't buy him; his colleagues called him "straight as a shingle." (26) Unfortunately, Sam Johnson lost all he had after poor real estate developments (buying back the "old Johnson ranch, etc."). (27) He remained in debt until the day he died. The Johnson family became the laughing stock of those in the "Hill country." Lyndon, the young man who his cousin, Ava Johnson, described as "someone who just had to be the leader . . . had to win, was now the son of a man who owed everybody in town." (28) His close relationship with his father quickly turned into resentment. As his brother, Sam Houston Johnson recalled, "It was most important to Lyndon not to be like Daddy." (29) The formation of Johnson's political views would not be marked by emulations of what he perceived as the root cause of his father's downfall, too much honesty and a lack of common sense. (30) Policy views that Johnson would later take hold of, would be increasingly scrutinized because of his extreme "political pragmatism" which would eventually help lead to Johnson's "credibility gap." (31) Lyndon Johnson's entrance into the world of politics officially began when he accepted the appointment as secretary to Congressman Richard Kleberg and became "Boss of the Little Congress;" the organization of Congressional assistants. While the Little Congress had no official function, it offered Johnson the opportunity to learn about the legislative process and the "real political inclinations" of many congressmen. (32)

In 1934, Johnson was appointed the state director of the National Youth Administration at the bequest of Sam Rayburn. He was the youngest director in the United States at age 26. This enabled Johnson to come into close contact with New Deal political leaders and eventually a close relationship with Franklin Roosevelt. Johnson met with the President in May 1937, when Roosevelt was visiting Texas. The President was very impressed with Johnson. Roosevelt told Tommy Corcoran, his political fixer, "I've just met the most remarkable young man, help him with anything you can." (33) Within four years, Johnson would win a seat in the House.

During his first two terms in the House, (he was unopposed in 1938 and 1940), his financial backers, George and Herman Brown, received many federal contracts to build dams and highways (34) This relationship included personal projects, such as grading work on Johnson's property, and would continue on to include millions of dollars of defense contracts in the ensuing years (which would eventually include projects in Vietnam as well) thanks to Johnson's membership in the Naval Affairs Committee (35)

Johnson announced he was a candidate for the Senate in 1941 from the steps of the White House with the blessing of President Roosevelt, the financial backing of the Brown's, and the political support of the President. Johnson was confident he would win and was flown back and forth from Texas to Washington on a "Brown and Root" plane. (36) Despite the help of Roosevelt, as well as "Brown and Root," Johnson lost the election to Governor W. Lee (Pappy) O'Daniel.

During the previous Senatorial campaign of 1941, Johnson had stated that win or lose, he would join the men in the trenches and give up his Senate seat.(37) True to his word, Johnson did resign his seat in the House and join the Navy.(38) But he later told his friend, Jonathan Daniels, that he went to the Pacific for "political reasons." (39) Johnson received the Silver Star as a result of a highly questionable thirteen minutes in battle and admitted to reporter Marshall McNeil that he didn't deserve the medal.

The reporter agreed and Johnson responded that "he would never wear the thing." (40) But eventually he would; the political tradeoff of running for office as a "war hero" would be rewarding—as he and John Kennedy would discover.

Following his time in the war, Johnson returned to the House, He was not active in presenting bills from 1939-1944. The Congressional Record makes no mention of his participation in floor proceedings. (41) He delivered a speech in 1941 on the extension of the Selective Service Act, his only Congressional speech in six years.(42) One of the reasons for his lack of action might have been his one attempt to introduce a particular bill during this period. In 1943, he introduced a bill that called for the drafting of any worker in a war factory with high absenteeism. Unfortunately, he introduced the bill in his own Naval Affairs Committee. Chairperson Mary Horton was upset with Johnson's lack of understanding how political protocol should work. As a result of his political inexperience, the bill died in the Rules Committee. (43) He would, of course, learn from that mistake and go on to become a master of political manipulation; the consummate "wheeler-dealer."

Just as John Kennedy clearly benefited from the political and monetary machinations of his father in his rise to the Presidency, so Lyndon Johnson also became involved in some highly questionable "tactics" that enabled his successful election to the Senate. The difference between Lyndon Johnson and John Kennedy in this area seems apparent in regards to their direct knowledge and understanding, as well as their personal involvement in carrying out these questionable practices. Johnson's involvement appears to be much more direct and involving more duplicity than Kennedy's but this could possibly be due to the fact that Joe Sr. had money and power of his own, and needn't have involved his son to accomplish his goals. Robert Caro has documented the controversial 1948 senatorial election results between Lyndon Johnson and Coke Stevenson. Caro's research strongly suggests that Lyndon Johnson cooperated in stealing this controversial election victory. (44)

Stevenson had actually defeated Johnson by 70,000 votes in the initial primary election but did not receive a sufficient plurality. A runoff between Johnson and Stevenson took place with Stevenson declared the winner. Within days of the election, a "correction" of votes was found (Box Thirteen) in the hamlet of Alice, in Jim Wells' county. This area was controlled by George Parr, known to his poor Mexican-American constituents as the "Duke of Duval County." (45) The "correction" included enough votes to give Johnson the victory. Governor Stevenson filed a complaint of a fraudulent vote with the federal courts. Judge T. Whitfield Davidson ruled in favor of Governor Stevenson. (46) Johnson was able to convince his attorney, Abe Fortas, to confer with Associate Supreme Court Justice Hugo Black. The Justice issued a stay in the Whitfield injunction. This decision allowed the "victory" of Johnson to stand. (47)

The Senate was persuaded to begin their own investigation into the contested election. Unfortunately, the disputed ballots from Box Thirteen were burned in a "sudden" fire. Duval County Deputy Sheriff Sam Smithwick, wrote Coke Stevenson a letter from the Texas State Penitentiary where he had been sentenced to life for murdering a newsman critical of George Parr. In the letter, Smithwick stated that he knew where Box 13 was hidden and could prove Johnson stole the election. (48) By the time Stevenson reached the Penitentiary, Smithwick had committed "suicide" by hanging himself. (49) *The Dallas News* and *The Fort Worth Telegram* reported "some guards and prisoners talked of the possibility of murder." (50) Johnson initially ignored the problem but eventually stated that this was "a continuation of a fight by a group of disgruntled and disappointed people." (51)

In a possibly related piece of information, on April 1, 1975, George Parr was found dead in his pasture, a bullet hole in his temple. The shooting was ruled a suicide. (52) Johnson had been dead for two years when the "suicide" occurred, but it is possible that Parr's death was a "fortuitous act" that helped to stem an attempt to diminish Johnson's legacy. In 1977, a Parr associate and Texas election official Louis Salas stated that he agreed to steal the election for Johnson. (53) The very real possibility that Lyndon Johnson or those who supported him were involved in blatant voter fraud, as well as possible murder, is extremely troubling indeed.

During the 1948 election campaign for the U. S. Senate, Johnson also emerged as a red-baiter in the class of Richard Nixon and Joe McCarthy. Johnson stated:

> Preparedness is the only weapon with which to halt the surging blood red tide of Communism. . . . Only the narrow straits of the Bering Sea separate Alaska from the menace

of Eurasia, and in frozen winters a man can walk those
straits. [We] must not surrender to the barbaric hordes of
godless men in Eurasia. . . . We must stand up to the war-
makers and say this far no further. (54)

Johnson responded to his opponent, Texas Governor Coke
Stevenson's counterattacks by veering even further to the
right. Robert Caro described Johnson's rhetoric:

America was in danger from the red tide of Communism.
Nobody would walk up and give Jack Dempsey a punch in
the nose. And nobody is going to give us a punch in the
nose if we're strong enough too. That is the reason why
he was for a seventy-group Air Force. Seventy groups? I
wish it were a hundred and seventy groups. We need the
best atom bomb that money can buy. And we must have a
policy of not yielding an inch to the communists. America
must draw the quarantine line and we would rather have
it on the Mediterranean than on the shore of the Gulf of
Mexico. The communists are ready to move in on Berlin if
America yields one inch. (55)

The extreme rhetoric of Johnson, as well as the information
of a documented controversy involving the probable complicity
of Johnson in the Senatorial election scandal of 1948, raises
disturbing questions about his honesty. What limits would
Johnson place on "political pragmatism?" How would this
affect political and policy decisions such as military spending
and our presence in Vietnam, or should this even be
considered when comparing the differences between the two
men? As will be presented, numerous insiders that were
intimately involved in the administrations of both men,
would agree that the personality differences between Johnson
and Kennedy did weigh in their evaluations as to why they
believe that Kennedy's policy decisions on Vietnam would
have differed from Johnson's.
Upon reaching the Senate, Johnson's first committee
assignment was the Armed Services Committee. After
United States troops were sent to Korea in 1950, Johnson
asked Senator Richard Russell to investigate the conduct of
the war. The Defense Preparedness Subcommittee was set
up. Within two months, Lyndon was criticizing the Truman
Administration for its lack of preparedness. By 1952, the
committee was arguing for sharp increases in air power. (56)
Lyndon Johnson had learned his political lessons well by

the time of his re-election to the Senate in 1954. He knew the "rules of the game" and was now the Senate Majority Leader with tremendous power and influence. The record indicates that Johnson was originally concerned with domestic policy as it related to the New Deal and the Texas economy. Johnson eventually became a vociferous proponent of increased military spending. Political correspondents and nationally known television newscasters Rowland Evans and Robert Novak, along with author Richard Kaufman, argue that Johnson, as a congressman and senator, realized that promoting government spending became most important to his political benefactors as well as to his constituents. He was able to use the international and domestic battle against Communism and turn it into a tremendous growth in the aircraft and space programs in Texas. (57) Although not totally objective on the subject of Lyndon Johnson, Barry Goldwater has earned the reputation as a "straight shooter." He summed up his view on Lyndon Johnson as a politician and a man in this blunt appraisal from his memoirs:

> Johnson was a master of manipulation. He solved tough public issues through private plotting. His answer to almost everything was a deal—an air base here a welfare project there. . . . Johnson was the epitome of the unprincipled politician . . . Johnson was a wheeler-dealer. Any campaign with him in it would involve a lot of innuendo and lies. Neither he nor anyone else could change that. That's what he was. And Johnson was treacherous to boot. . . . The last thing Lyndon Johnson wanted to do in his life was talk political principles or beliefs. He wouldn't do it. LBJ never believed in either. His only political dogma was expediency. Things were never right or wrong. Most problems in this country could be fixed with cunning and craftiness. (58)

Lyndon Johnson's record up to 1960 indicates that he was not very knowledgeable of Southeast Asia or Vietnam. He had not visited, nor had he been involved in detailed study of Vietnam before 1960. (59) It seems apparent that Johnson's beliefs on foreign policy and Vietnam were shaped as a result of a domestic and political pragmatism; with the result being Johnson's inability to see the problems in Vietnam outside of those views expressed by the fervent anti-communistic generals and advisors that he chose to listen to. Lyndon Johnson had the opportunity to veer away from those who promoted escalation in Vietnam, especially after his landslide election victory in 1964. As will be shown, Lyndon Johnson alone, made the ultimate decision to escalate the war in Vietnam.

John Kennedy surely made poor decisions on various domestic and international issues (as has been discussed), especially in his personal indiscretions and should be judged accordingly. But these mistakes should in no way lead to the conclusion that he was destined to make the poor and avoidable decisions that led to the escalation in Vietnam.

Barry Goldwater agreed with John Kennedy on few, if any domestic issues and sharply disagreed with virtually all of his foreign policy decisions relating to the Soviet Union, Berlin, and Cuba. But Goldwater knew Johnson and Kennedy well and detected a difference in the character of both men. Goldwater and Kennedy had tentatively agreed to travel together and debate the issues in the 1964 election. (60) He offered this assessment of Kennedy, "I think if Jack Kennedy had lived, he might have been just great . . . I say that because I knew him quite well." (61)

The truth in regards to Goldwater's evaluation of Kennedy and Johnson most likely lies somewhere in the middle. But as in the case of an evaluation of any decision or individual, the adage that "facts" or statistics are no substitute for good judgment fits. As has been clearly presented in this research, so called facts are not always what they appear. But clearly, in the minds of friend and foe alike—the consensus of those who knew both men, combined with the records of their actions, the evidence strongly argues against John Kennedy being held responsible for the escalation of the Vietnam War that was to follow.

Chapter 17

"They Are the Ones Who Have to Win It or Lose It"

Some scars still lingered between Johnson and Kennedy after the Democratic Presidential nomination of 1960 had been decided. Johnson and his main political strategists, Sam Rayburn, John Connally, George Reedy, and Irvin Hoff, had hoped for "convention confusion" where Johnson's record of "Mr. Fix-it" (a result of the political debts and gratitudes due him) would help save the day. (1) As the summer primary season was ending and Kennedy approached the nomination, Johnson's men went for the "jugular" in an attempt to snatch victory from defeat. Charges of "appeasement" were leveled against the Kennedys in general, due to Joseph Kennedy's neutrality during WWII, to which Robert Kennedy took great exception. Johnson also stated that Kennedy was wrong about the U-2 incident (we should never apologize) and insisted that a Catholic could not win (thus invoking bigotry as a divisive issue).(2) The possibility that Kennedy suffered from Addison's Disease was broached by Johnson supporters and also greatly angered the Kennedy camp which considered the accusation a desperate and cheap tactic. Former Speaker of the House Thomas "Tip" O'Neil recalled Johnson's attempt to convince him that Kennedy was not fit to be the Democratic nominee:

> "Now I realize you're pledged to the boy"—referring, of course, to Jack Kennedy. "But you and I both know he can't win.

> He's just a flash in the pan, and he's got no record of substance to run on. Will you be with me on the second ballot?" During the entire conversation, he [Johnson] never once mentioned Jack Kennedy by name. It was always "the boy." (3)

These scars seemed to have been healed as John Kennedy "asked" Lyndon to become his vice-president. The fact remains that the true story of the choice of Lyndon Johnson for the vice-presidency remains a secret. (4) The general feeling at the time (and currently) was that Kennedy offered Johnson the vice-presidency out of respect—with the anticipation of rejection. Seymour Hersh has suggested in his controversial book, *The Dark Side of Camelot,* that J. Edgar Hoover's knowledge of Kennedy's personal indiscretions were relayed to Lyndon Johnson. Johnson and Hoover were then able to force Kennedy to keep Johnson on the ticket. (5) Considering the number of purported indiscretions (sexual and otherwise) that have been attributed to Lyndon Johnson, this theory appears to be without substance. The indiscretions of Johnson also could have been used against him. It appears that most, if not all, of Kennedy's camp were in shock when Johnson accepted. (6) Reports had surfaced that the offer was then withdrawn. After much conversation and negotiation between a variety of individuals on both sides, Johnson emerged as the running-mate of John Kennedy. (7)

The hatchet seemed to be buried and Lyndon Johnson campaigned tirelessly for John Kennedy. There is little doubt that without Johnson, Kennedy could not have won the election in the fall. Larry O'Brien later stated that, "As far as I could see, the relationship between Kennedy and Johnson was entirely satisfactory." Not all intimates agreed with that assumption. Benjamin Bradlee, publisher of the *Washington Post*, stated, "it was not pretty to see, but Kennedy did not want Johnson around." (8)

Doris Kearns Goodwin, Johnson's self-appointed biographer, described his unprecedented attempt to rule the Senate while serving as Vice-President:

> . . . Johnson could not bear being treated as one of many advisers. Shortly after the inauguration, he sent an unusual Executive Order to the Oval Office for President Kennedy's signature. Outlining a wide range of issues over which the

new Vice President would have "general supervision," it put all the departments and agencies on notice that Lyndon Johnson was to receive all reports, information, and policy plans that were generally sent to the President himself [rejected by Kennedy]. . . . Nowhere did Johnson feel his loss of power and his uselessness more painfully than in his relations with Capitol Hill. When the Senate Democrats convened in caucus on January 3, 1961, Mike Mansfield of Montana, the new Majority Leader, proposed to change the rules and elect the new Vice President the chairman of the Democratic Conference, which would make him the presiding officer at formal meetings of the Senate's Democratic members. Mansfield's proposal, which he had discussed with no one but Johnson, met with strong opposition. Liberals and conservatives joined in arguing that such a move would surely violate the spirit of the separation of powers. . . .

Johnson interpreted the [negative] vote as a profoundly personal rejection. All the hopes he had entertained of leading the Congress from the Vice President's chair were discarded. Suddenly he felt separated forever from the institution to which he believed he had given the best part of his life. . . . From that day on he was of minimal help to Kennedy on legislation, the area in which the President desired his help. (9)

Despite these blatant attempts by Johnson to claim unwarranted and unprecedented dual power in both the executive and legislative branches, President Kennedy did offer Johnson privileges no previous Vice President had received. Arthur Schlesinger related, "Johnson was the first vice-president to have an office in the White House while most vice-presidents up until that point had offices in the Congressional building." (10) The *New York Times* announced on October 17, 1962, that ". . . Secret Service protection was extended to the Vice President under a bill signed today by President Kennedy." (11)

Robert Kennedy commented on the relationship between Johnson and his brother:

. . . the President—after [Johnson] became Vice President—was very, very pleased that he was there, rather than Majority Leader. He said he would have just been impossible. And, you know, by the time it was over, finished—by 1963—he was really irritated with him. I think [JFK} admired him—and he rather amused the President—he admired the obvious ability that he had, but [LBJ] wasn't helpful at times that he might have been helpful. He was very loyal and never spoke against the President, but he never gave any suggestions or ideas on policy. He was opposed to our policy—I mean, the two major matters; the Cuban missile crisis and the [1963] civil rights bill. He was opposed to the civil rights bill. He was opposed to the sending up any legislation. (12)

Lyndon Johnson's brother, Sam Houston, might have summed up a realistic evaluation of their relationship:

Lyndon no doubt expected a show of gratitude (for campaigning efforts) from the Kennedys and their covey of New Frontiersman. Instead, they made his stay in the vice-presidency the most miserable three years of his life. He wasn't the number two man in the administration; he was the lowest man on the totem pole. I know him well enough to know he felt humiliated time and time again, that he was openly snubbed by second-echelon White House staffers who snickered at him behind his back and called him "Uncle Cornpone." (13)

But there have been others who were close to Johnson who believed that Johnson was extremely jealous of Kennedy and Kennedy was not worthy or experienced enough to be president. Doris Kearns Goodwin, Johnson's biographer, recalled that Johnson told her that he considered Kennedy to be "a weak and indecisive politician, a nice man, a gentle man, but not a man's man." (14)

The possibility of divisive feelings should be considered when trying to understand Johnson's and Kennedy's differences over Vietnam. There can be no doubt that Robert Kennedy's relationship with Lyndon Johnson would always place a roadblock between Lyndon Johnson and John Kennedy. Johnson always blamed Robert Kennedy for the controversy created over the selection of the Vice-Presidential nominee during the 1960 election. Ken O'Donnell wrote that "Johnson blamed his fallen prestige on Bobby Kennedy." (15) Bobby Baker, Johnson's political right-hand man, during his Senate days believed that "His [Johnson's] complaints against Bobby Kennedy were frequent and may have bordered on the paranoiac." (16)

Lyndon Johnson had made a career in the House and Senate based on his Cold War support for the military as well as his political benefactors. When faced with "ostracism" by some of those on Kennedy's staff, would the hard-line generals pushing for involvement in Laos and Vietnam, be Johnson's lone supporters? As we shall see, Lyndon Johnson was much more impressed with the arguments put forth by his generals for escalation than was John Kennedy, as well as from most of the advisors who favored a more aggressive policy and were left to him from President Kennedy.

The initial Kennedy policy decisions in Southeast Asia were in Laos and not Vietnam. President Eisenhower had warned President-elect Kennedy that he might have to put combat troops in Laos in order to stop the threat of the "domino effect" overtaking Southeast Asia. (17) British Prime Minister MacMillan also stated in a private letter to former President Eisenhower on April 9:

> As I understand it, President Kennedy is under considerable pressure about appeasement in Laos . . . I should, however, be very sorry if our two countries become involved in an open-ended commitment on this dangerous and unprofitable terrain. So I would hope that in anything which you felt it necessary to say about Laos, you would not encourage these who think that a military solution in Laos is the only way of stopping the Communists in that area. (18)

Almost one week later on April 17, the ill-fated Bay of Pigs invasion began. As presented earlier, this attempt by Cuban exiles, in co-operation with the CIA, and handed to Kennedy by the Eisenhower Administration, failed miserably. Despite tremendous pressure from the Joint Chiefs and the CIA to provide American air and naval power to "save" the invasion, and to possibly invade Cuba, Kennedy declined to do so. (19)

On April 27, Admiral Arleigh Burke, Chief of Naval Operations, renewed the push for American involvement in Laos. Burke, in a cabinet meeting on Laos stated, "If we do not fight in Laos, will we fight in Thailand where the situation will be the same sometime in the future as it is now in Laos? Will we fight in Vietnam? Where will we fight? Where do we hold? And where do we draw the line?" (20) Vice-President Johnson was the only man who spoke up and agreed with Burke during this meeting; "I've always been grateful to him [Johnson] ever since," recalled Burke. (21) When considering who was ultimately responsible for the subsequent escalation of the Vietnam war, one should consider the importance of how the Joint Chiefs viewed

Kennedy's actions in Laos. Johnson voiced open support for a Joint Chiefs policy of escalation that Kennedy rejected. Admiral Burke believed, "The decision not to intervene in effect, had been made." (22)

It appears that as a result of Kennedy's perceived "failure" to intervene with combat troops into Laos, the Chiefs faced the realization that the President might follow the same course in Vietnam. Kennedy's refusal to commit troops to save the Bay of Pigs operation just weeks before, certainly played a part in the Joint Chief's assessment of Kennedy's future intentions in Vietnam. During late March 1961, British Prime Minister Harold MacMillan met with President Kennedy over the issue of Laos. MacMillan stated that Kennedy was reluctant to use force but MacMillan was sympathetic with the President's concern to not be pushed out of Laos. (23)

Kennedy's decision not to intervene in Laos did not lessen the Joint Chiefs (Earle Wheeler, Army; George Anderson, Navy; Lynman Lemnitzer, Chairman; David Shoup, Marines; and Curtis LeMay, Air Force) resolve in Vietnam. A May 10 memo from the Chiefs to Secretary of Defense Robert McNamara stated, "Assuming that the political decision is to hold Southeast Asia outside the Communist sphere, the Joint Chiefs are of the opinion that United States forces should be deployed immediately to South Vietnam." (24) The phrasing of this suggestion is important. Kennedy had just "lost" Cuba and the eventual neutralization of Laos would also be considered a "loss" to those who were keeping score in the battle against Communism. He held a strong belief that the root cause of the problems was over colonization and nationalism. Yet, publicly, he ascribed to the domino theory—he had little choice. As publisher Henry Luce had told Joseph Kennedy after the 1960 Democratic convention, "If he [John Kennedy] shows any sign of weakness toward the anti-communist cause, we'll turn on him, we'll have to tear him apart." (25) Kennedy, however, would not send combat troops to Vietnam. On May 8, General Lemnitzer sent a cable from East Asia to the Pentagon. He stated, "The unhappy sequence of events in Laos was being repeated; this can only mean the loss of Vietnam." (26) It seems clear that the military believed that Kennedy was not willing to commit combat troops to Vietnam.

President Kennedy requested that Vice-President Johnson

go to Vietnam in April of 1961. Initially, Johnson actually refused to go, as Air Force Colonel Howard Burris, Johnson's military representative, remembers, "I was listening to all this screaming. Kennedy wanting Johnson to go and Johnson just refusing." (27) The Vice-President did go as ordered, albeit, literally kicking and screaming. While in Vietnam, Johnson seemed to be working out arrangements with President Diem which were of his own making. He committed the United States to provide equipment such as helicopters and armored personnel carriers simultaneously as the South Vietnamese increased troop strength to twenty thousand. This commitment was made without the promise of Diem for "local financing" or South Vietnamese governmental support. (28) At a later meeting with Diem and Fredrik Nolting, who had replaced Ellbridge Durnbrow as Ambassador, the Vice-President suggested to Diem that he place United States combat troops on a list of recommendations to President Kennedy. (29) William Colby, head of CIA operations in Vietnam, surmised later that "LBJ might have been free wheeling out there." (30) It can reasonably be argued that Lyndon Johnson began his push for escalation, not in 1964-65, but in April 1961 as vice-president.

While visiting Vietnam as vice-president in April 1961, Johnson had offered a toast to Diem calling him the "Churchill of Southeast Asia" and also compared him favorably to George Washington and Franklin Roosevelt. (31)

In a memorandum dated May 23, 1961, to Kennedy from Johnson, about Mission to Southeast Asia, India, and Pakistan, Johnson wrote:

> American combat troop involvement is not only not required, it is not desirable. . . . This does not minimize or disregard the probability that open attack would bring calls for U.S. combat troops. But the present probability of open attack seems scant, and we might gain much needed flexibility in our policies if the spectre of combat troop commitment could be lessened domestically. . . These nations cannot be saved by United States help alone. . . . The basic decision in Southeast Asia is here. We must decide whether to help these countries to the best of our ability or throw in the towel in the area and pull back our defenses to San Francisco and a "Fortress America" concept. . . . The fundamental decision required of the United States -- and time is of the greatest importance -- is whether we are to attempt to meet the challenge of communist expansion now in Southeast Asia by a major effort

in support of the forces of freedom in the area or throw in the towel. This decision must be made in a full realization of the very heavy and continuing costs involved in terms of money, of effort and of United States prestige. It must be made with the knowledge that at some point we may be faced with the further decision of whether we commit major United States forces to the area or cut our losses and withdraw should our other efforts fail. We must remain master of this decision. (32)

Johnson added further, "I gained the impression that if communism is to be defeated, or even contained in this country, the workers must be given a feeling of belonging. . . . In other words, the voice of freedom must reach the people ahead of the voice of the Communists." (33)

One of the clear messages that Vice-President Johnson conveyed to President Kennedy was that, "American troop involvement is not . . . required." Yet documentation has also been presented that indicates Johnson "might have been freewheeling" and pushing for escalation in separate discussions with Diem.   The message conveyed by Vice President Johnson in his memorandum to Kennedy, of the need for social reform in Vietnam, would not remain a consistent belief of Lyndon Johnson. As will be presented, immediately upon assuming the Presidency, Johnson would renounce his own stated priority of the need for social reform and begin the push for a military solution. George Herring noted: "Johnson reported that the decision to negotiate in Laos had shaken Diem's confidence in the United States and warned that if a further decline in morale was to be arrested, 'deeds must follow words—soon.'" (34) Herring concluded, "In the aftermath of Johnson's visit, Diem himself requested additional aid." (35) Further support that the subsequent request by Diem for an increase in the American military presence originated with Lyndon Johnson is found in the words of Stanley Karnow:

> At Johnson's suggestion, Diem had again proposed that the size of the South Vietnamese armed forces be increased, now by one hundred thousand to a total of two hundred and seventy thousand men. This would demand an expanded American advisory group, more U.S. equipment and additional financial aid—not a package to be considered lightly. (36)

According to Admiral Grant Sharp, the Commander in Chief (Pacific) during the Vietnam War:

> Diem responded to an invitation President Kennedy had extended through the Vice President by sending an aide to Washington with a letter outlining Saigon's "essential military needs." Those needs included a large increase in U.S. financial and material support for South Vietnamese forces—large enough to raise the strength of their army from 170,000 to 270,000 men—and selected elements of the American armed forces to establish training centers for the South Vietnamese and to serve as a symbol of American commitment to South Vietnam. After some study, the United States finally agreed to support an increase of only 30,000, rather than the 100,000 requested. Interestingly enough, no answer was given to the request for elements of American armed forces. (37)

As a result of the agreement between Diem and Vice-President Johnson, the stage was now set for an increase in American involvement in Vietnam. The summer of 1961 proved to be a hot one for John Kennedy. In June, Khrushchev and Kennedy had a summit meeting in Vienna. The end result of the summit being, that West Berlin was being threatened militarily by the Soviets and the United States was forced to make a stand. Kennedy responded with increased troop deployments in Europe and an increase in military spending. (38) Unfortunately, by August, the Berlin Wall went up; a hot war versus the Soviets over Berlin was avoided, but a chilly Cold War climate remained.

In a memorandum written after President Kennedy's meeting with German ambassador William Grewe, Kennedy indicated the importance he placed on meeting the Soviet challenge in Europe, and specifically, in Berlin:

> The President stated that the situation which might develop over Berlin deserved serious thought. We wanted to convince the Soviets, in the event of a major confrontation, that the U.S. was prepared to go all out and that this deserved a last thought on their part. No one expected to fight a conventional war in Europe, which we could not do without being overwhelmed. . . . if we must face a major defeat in Europe, then nuclear weapons will be used, but we must exhaust the full battery of other possibilities before pushing the button. . . . The U.S. took this question quite seriously. We felt out survival was tied up with that of Western Europe. (39)

As evidenced by this memorandum, as well as the consistently stated priorities and intentions of President Kennedy, he would be willing to go all out over Berlin but not over Vietnam.

President Kennedy's eventual decision to increase the advisory and training role, along with an increase in the number of United States soldiers, was implemented as a result of the "arrangement" that the Vice-President had negotiated with Diem, as well as the tremendous domestic military and cabinet pressure. Kennedy was also responding to Khrushchev's attempts to intimidate him during their meeting in Vienna. Kennedy remarked: "If he thinks I'm inexperienced and have no guts . . . we won't get anywhere with him. So we have to act." (40)

There can be little doubt that the subsequent advisory buildup implemented by Kennedy was also a partial response to right-wing attacks as a result of the administration's failure during the Bay of Pigs operation. Joseph Alsop, a Kennedy confidant and an influential columnist, was writing pro-intervention articles regarding Vietnam in the fall of 1961. (41) McNamara, and advisors U. Alexis Johnson, William Bundy, Walt Rostow, Secretary of State Dean Rusk, National Security Advisor McGeorge Bundy, as well as the Joint Chiefs and the Vice-President, were in favor of intervention. (42) Advisors Chester Bowles and Roger Hilsman were known to be against intervention. The final decision was John Kennedy's and he refused. The record of the November 15,1961 National Security Council meeting makes Kennedy's point clear; "The President asked General Lemnitzer how he could justify intervention in Vietnam and not in Cuba?" Lemnitzer responded by adding, "that the Joint Chiefs were still in favor of intervention in Cuba." (43) The President was obviously still under heavy pressure to commit combat troops to Vietnam as well as to Cuba.

President Kennedy's advisory buildup in South Vietnam was based on a study prepared in July 1961 by Edward Lansdale, CIA guerrilla warfare expert. (44) This study fit with Kennedy's plan to build up indigenous strength with help from our Special Forces. William Colby's strategic hamlet programs were designed as self-defense, as well as economic and social programs, to allow the South Vietnamese to better fight the war themselves. They were initially successful and Diem and Nhu also backed them. (45)

As a result of Johnson's suggestions, Kennedy instructed General Maxwell Taylor and Rostow to make a further assessment of the situation. According to Stanley Karrow:

> Taylor's most significant message to Kennedy—for the president's "eye only"—proposed an initial commitment to Vietnam of eight thousand U.S. combat troops disguised as logistical legions to deal with a flood than ravaging the Mekong Delta. Taylor would later explain that this was a "deliberate straddle," meaning that he had merely offered Kennedy an option. His cables to the White House at the time, however, plainly indicated his preference for direct American intervention. The U.S. soldiers would "act as an advance party of such additional forces as may be introduced," and he minimized potential fighting conditions, saying that South Vietnam "is not an excessively difficult or unpleasant place to operate." (46)

In October 1961, the focus on Vietnam changed dramatically. General Taylor and National Security Advisor Walt Rostow were sent to Vietnam after Diem and Defense Minister Thuan made their request for United States combat troops. (47) Taylor cabled President Kennedy from the Philippines at the conclusion of the trip, "This message is for the purpose of presenting my reasons for recommending the introduction of a United States military force into South Vietnam. I have reached the conclusion that this is an essential action." (48)

Despite the push by Johnson and others favoring a further buildup of the U.S. military advisory force, President Kennedy turned down General Maxwell Taylor's proposal for an 8,000 man task force. The President did authorize the introduction of small helicopter units and other trainees of which many had already been authorized before Taylor's proposal of October, 1961. (49) Taylor added an assessment of the situation in Vietnam that would prove to be invalid: "North Vietnam is extremely vulnerable to conventional bombing. . . . There is no case for fearing a mass onslaught of Communist manpower into South Vietnam and its neighboring states, particularly if our air power is allowed a free hand against logistical targets." (50)

Kennedy brought Averell Harriman and George Ball (State Department) into his foreign policy inner circle as a result of the infamous "Thanksgiving Massacre," of Vietnam advisors. Both were against the introduction of combat troops.

On November 7, 1961, Ball argued against the commitment of American combat troops into Vietnam:

> I raised the question with President Kennedy. I told him that I strongly opposed the recommendations of the Rostow mission. To commit American forces to South Vietnam would, in my view, be a tragic error. Once that process started, I said, there would be no end to it. "Within five years we'll have three hundred thousand men in the paddies and jungles and never find them again. That was the French experience. Vietnam is the worst possible terrain both from a physical and political point of view." To my surprise, the President seemed quite unwilling to discuss the matter, responding with an overtone of asperity: "George, you're just crazier than hell. That just isn't going to happen." Since then, I have pondered many times as to just what President Kennedy was trying to tell me. His statement could be interpreted two ways. Either he was convinced that events would so evolve as not to require escalation, or he was determined not to permit such escalation to occur. (51)

The President was probably not expecting Taylor's request for combat troops. Kennedy turned to Robert McNamara to look after the Vietnam War as his main responsibility from this point on. (52)　McGeorge Bundy would work closely with McNamara in determining policy. This responsibility given to McNamara coincided with Diem's unhappiness at being asked by Kennedy to make reforms. The Secretary stated on November 27, the uncertainty of Diem's position and the doubts about his willingness to reform "must not prevent us from going ahead full blast on all possible actions short of large-scale introduction of United States combat forces." (53)

Operation "Beef-Up" was the direct result of this "full blast" approach. New American equipment and technology, such as an increase in helicopters, were part of this comprehensive buildup. (54)　William Colby stated that the Rostow and Taylor mission, and subsequently McNamara's "Beef-Up," changed the emphasis from Special Forces and strategic hamlet co-operation to a strictly military action. (55) Despite the start of Operation "Beef-Up", the consistent strategy emphasized by Kennedy was not to introduce combat troops. Arthur Krock wrote that in the fall of 1961:

> The President still believes, he said, in what he told the Senate several years ago—that United States troops should

not be involved [in combat] on the Asian mainland, especially in a country with the difficult terrain of Laos and inhabited by people who don't care how the East-West dispute as to freedom and self-determination was resolved. Moreover, said the President, the United States can't interfere in civil disturbances created by guerrillas, and it was hard to prove that this wasn't largely the situation in Vietnam.

I asked him what he thought of the "falling domino" theory—that is, if Laos and Vietnam go Communist, the rest of Southeast Asia will fall to them in orderly succession. The President expressed doubts that this theory has much point any more because, he remarked, the Chinese Communists are bound to get nuclear weapons in time, and from that moment on they will dominate Southeast Asia. (56)

According to William Colby, the problems in Vietnam were now in Washington's hands and not the South Vietnamese's. (57) Kennedy had not given enough personal attention to Vietnam in 1961. With Berlin, Bay of Pigs—it was not given a high priority. He delegated most of the authority on Vietnam policy to McNamara and hoped the problem would go away.

In February 1962, the Military Assistance Command Vietnam (MACV) was formed in an attempt to bring about a unity of purpose as well as in field operations. The Military Assistance Advisory Group (MAAG), the Joint Chiefs, and intelligence information all agreed that the war was going badly. (58) The different command structures of the various branches were not in agreement on policy and operations. (59) General Paul Harkins was the President's and General Taylor's choice to head MAAG, and in reality, replace General Lionel McGarr. The Air Force was in direct control of intelligence information in Vietnam and also in Washington as a result of their control of the newly established Defense Intelligence Agency, a direct recommendation from Taylor's report on the Bay of Pigs. (60)

Information on policy within the United States government about Vietnam was hard to obtain much less explain. The United States press corps was having its troubles in 1962 and 1963 as well. President Kennedy was becoming very sensitive to press accounts which depicted a widening of the war by the United States. Stories of exaggerated deaths and helicopter crashes particularly disturbed him. (61) Given Kennedy's displeasure with the small amount of casualties in 1962, it would be extremely doubtful to expect him to have accepted

the large number of casualties that took place after the
introduction of combat troops in 1965. According to the U.S.
Army Center of Military History, at the time of President
Kennedy's death in November 1963, there were 16,300
military advisors in South Vietnam and the United States
had suffered only 78 casualties. (62)

Homer Bigart, Pulitzer Prize winning correspondent for the
New York Times, was writing stories critical of United States
government representatives in South Vietnam. Bigart
charged that they were not telling the truth. (63) Vietnam
press correspondent Carl Rowan convinced Secretary Rusk
and the President to loosen press controls. (64) Charles Davis
was sent by the United States Information Agency to Vietnam
to try to establish better press relations. Davis stated that
Ambassador Fredrik Nolting and General Harkins, both
viewed him with suspicion and did not cooperate. (65) Pierre
Salinger, Kennedy's press secretary, then sent veteran
Vietnam correspondent John Mecklin back to Vietnam.
Mecklin stated that the changes did little or nothing to
liberalize the press. (66) As 1962 progressed, the relationship
between Diem and Nhu, in regards to Vietnam
correspondents Daniel Sheehan *(UPI)*, Malcolm Browne
(API), and David Halberstam *(New York Times)* became
fanatically adversarial. (67)

Kennedy was obviously receiving conflicting reports on the
progress of the war, as well as the alleged improvement in
Diem's attempts at reform. As a result of these conflicting
reports, the President began to receive and listen to a wider
range of advice on Vietnam.

An example of the advice that President Kennedy was
listening to in 1962, and the kind of advice that he would
have considered in 1964, was that which was given to him in
April 1962 by, then Ambassador to India, John Kenneth
Galbraith:

> That it be our policy to keep open the door for political
> solution. We should welcome as a solution any broadly based
> non-Communist government that is free from external
> interference. . . . We should resist all steps which commit
> American troops to combat action and impress upon all
> concerned the importance of keeping American forces out of
> actual combat commitment. (68)

Also in April, Ambassador Galbraith and President

Kennedy discussed the "possible neutralization of Vietnam, a political solution." (69) Kennedy responded with the idea, "to be prepared to seize upon any favorable moment to reduce our commitment." (70) The Joint Chiefs were concerned with this possibility and warned McNamara, "any reversal of U.S. policy would have disastrous effects." (71)

General Taylor went to Vietnam in September 1962, to report on the progress of the war. In a memo to Kennedy he stated, "the statistics—for what they are worth—indicate improvement in comparative casualties, reduced loss of weapons to the enemy and less national territory under Viet Cong control. Much progress has been accomplished since my last visit in October 1961." (72) General Harkins was also quite optimistic and was convinced that victory could be achieved in one year. (73)

In October 1962, the Cuban Missile Crisis took place. During the late summer and early fall of 1962, there had been public rumblings by Senator Kenneth Keating and quiet hints by CIA Director John McCone, that the Russians might be installing offensive weapons or missiles of some sort into Cuba. (74)

Accusations have since been levied against Kennedy for dragging his feet on the buildup of missiles in Cuba and even possibly deliberately waiting to expose his knowledge of them until just before the Congressional elections of November 1962 in order to gain a political edge. But the transcripts from Kennedy's Oval Office recording system indicate that Arthur Lundhal, of the CIA's National Photo Interpretation Center had to interpret the U-2 photos for the President. (75) Lundhal told Jack Anderson in 1982, "I had to interpret them for him[Kennedy], it's always necessary, because the layman isn't used to looking at things in the vertical. When you look down on the map, that's quite different from looking at things horizontally." (76) After Kennedy had studied the photos of the missile sites, he asked Lundhal, "Are you sure about this?" And Lundhal assured him that he was (77) Lundhal went on to state that Kennedy had never been able to clearly identify the missile sites but had relied totally on Lundhal's judgment. (78) The discussions of the photo interpretations did not begin until October 16. It would be difficult to conceive that Kennedy was using the missile crisis for political leverage, when as Lundhal reports, Kennedy could not even identify the missiles sites from the photos.

After Lundhal confirmed the existence of the missile sites, Kennedy immediately began to take action and ordered the swiftest and most-powerful assemblage of force in history. The Soviets believed that Kennedy was prepared to use force if necessary and these actions helped to defuse the crisis.

Kennedy was under tremendous pressure from the Joint Chiefs as well as Congressional leaders to bomb the missile sites and/or to launch an invasion of Cuba. White House tapes reveal Senator Richard Russell and Senator J. William Fulbright stating, "We have to take a chance, an invasion, all-out one, as quickly as possible." (79)

Ted Sorensen wrote that Lyndon Johnson strongly disagreed with President Kennedy's decision not to launch an air strike against Cuba during the missile crisis:

> Vice-President Johnson, reflecting the frustrations of the now-resurgent air strike-invasion advocates, warned us that, in the absence of stronger action achieving results, both public and congressional opinion were turning against the president: *Johnson. . . .* They want to know what we're doing. There's a great feeling of insecurity. They're going to be saying, "I told you so," tomorrow or the next day. (80)

President Kennedy was leaning more and more on the advice of his brother Robert. Just as the Cuban Missile Crisis was taking place, there were those in the military who wanted Kennedy to challenge the Soviets over its failure to act on it's Laos Treaty commitments." As Walt Rostow remembers, "They were turned down [by the President]." (81)

The concerns that Kennedy had developed in regards to the advice and intentions that the military was presenting to him, became even more pronounced (as noted in Chapter 6) after the negative performance they gave during the Bay of Pigs invasion. During the height of the Cuban Missile Crisis, General Curtis LeMay criticized President Kennedy directly on his perceived weak response towards the communist threat posed by the placement of nuclear missiles on the island:

> *LeMay.* I think that a blockade, and political talk, would be considered by a lot of our friends and neutrals as being a pretty weak response to this. And I'm sure a lot of our own citizens would feel that way, too. You're in a pretty bad fix, Mr. President.
> *Kennedy.* What did you say?
> *LeMay.* You're in a pretty bad fix. (82)

John Kenneth Galbraith recalled President Kennedy saying during the Missile Crisis, after a meeting with the Joint Chiefs in which they had advocated bombing Cuba and possibly provoking World War III, "Do these people belong to the human race?" (83) During the crisis, Nikita Khrushchev recalled what Dean Rusk had reported to Ambassador Anatoly Dobrynin:

> He [Rusk] appealed to us to do something that would avoid confrontation, but he set the condition that must remove missiles. Otherwise, a situation might develop in which the president might lose control and there would be such pressure on him that he would be forced to make a decision against his own will, with ominous consequences for both our countries. (84)

This account is corroborated by Khrushchev's son Sergi:

> Kennedy was under tremendous pressure. Father knew this, and he took it into account when he decided to withdraw the missiles from Cuba in exchange for Kennedy's promise not to invade the island—a promise he trusted. This would have been inconceivable in 1952: Trust an American president! When Father argued at a meeting of the Soviet leadership in favor of withdrawing the missiles, he made this unprecedented statement: "We have to help Kennedy withstand pressure from the hawks. They are demanding an immediate military invasion. (85)

Paul B. Fay, former assistant secretary of the Navy, recalled a conversation he had with President Kennedy concerning the possibility of a military overthrow in the United States:

> It's possible. It could happen in this country, but the conditions would have to be just right. If, for example, the country had a young President, and he had a Bay of Pigs, there would be a certain uneasiness. Maybe the military would do a little criticizing behind his back, but this would be written off as the usual military dissatisfaction with civilian control. Then, if there were another Bay of Pigs . . . the military would almost feel that it was their patriotic obligation to stand ready to preserve the integrity of the nation, and only God knows just what segment of democracy they would be defending if they overthrew the elected establishment. (86)

Presidential advisor Ted Sorensen recalled:

> Communications between the Chiefs of Staff and the Commander-in-Chief remained unsatisfactory for a large portion of his term. Enjoying a popular novel, *Seven Days in May*, about a fictional attempt by a few military brass to take over the country, the President joked, "I know a couple who wish they could." (87)

Presidential assistant Arthur Schlesinger stated that President Kennedy strongly agreed with the book, *Seven Days in May*. (88) The director of the film, John Frankenheimer, related that President Kennedy liked the book and had been involved in the decision to make it into a movie:

> Those were the days of General Walker and so on. . . . President Kennedy wanted *Seven Days in May* made. Pierre Salinger conveyed this to us. The Pentagon didn't want it done. Kennedy said that when we wanted to shoot at the White House he could conveniently go to Hyannis Port that weekend. (89)

Adding support to the extreme reactionary mindset of some of the generals under Kennedy's command is Professor William Kaufman of the Rand Corporation (1954-1970), a think tank for the military and U.S. Intelligence agencies. Kaufman described the mood and mentality of General Thomas Power of the United States Strategic Air Command (SAC):

> He [Power] demanded that I be shipped out to Omaha [SAC] to talk with him and his staff . . . come to his briefing room—and he had assembled all his generals and he said, "You academic types . . . lily-livered, all you want to do is save lives, I want to dispose of them." Kaufman went on to recall that Powers stated that "[Powers] would regard it as victory if there were two Americans and only one Russian left. . . ." He really didn't seem to be fully in control of himself it was as though I was witnessing some strange performance in which this four star general was displaying several different personalities. . . . It did lead me to wonder . . . is this the individual who really commands this enormous center of power. (90)

General Robert Huyser, a member of SAC from 1953-72 stated, ". . . towards the end he [Power] got so bad that he would not talk to anybody unless he had somebody in the room recording everything. . . . why I don't know. . . . that's some kind of a paranoia. I don't know." (91) General Horace Wade, SAC, 1949-62, recalled that "I felt he [Power] was losing his stability. . . . I think if you interview the major staff members of his command you would find that the majority of them would feel the same way." (92) CIA photo analyst from 1948-82, Dino Brugioni recalled, "During the Cuban Missile Crisis, he [LeMay] said, 'Well, the bear [the Soviet Union] has stuck his foot in the Latin American waters and we got him in a trap. Let's take his leg off right up to his testicles. . . better still let's take off his testicles too.'" (93) Those who would cast doubt on at least the possibility of a military coup ever taking place in our country, and especially during the height of the Cold War, ignore the realities of the time.

During his Farewell Address on January 17, 1961, President Eisenhower made clear his concern as to the threat that the military posed to civilian rule in the era of the Cold War:

> . . . The conjunction of an immense military establishment and a large arms industry is new in the American experience. The total influence—economic, political, even spiritual—is felt in every city, every state house, every off ice of the federal government.
>
> In the councils of government we must guard against the acquisition of unwarranted influence, whether sought or unsought, by the military industrial complex. The potential for the disastrous rise of misplaced power exists and will persist. . . .(94)

This analysis from one of the most respected generals and leaders in American history, should cause one to look more closely at the possibility that those who controlled such power might, in fact, be willing to use it if they believed it was justified.

The successful ending to the threat of nuclear war should cause us all to consider what the world might be like today if President Kennedy had not been in control of the nuclear button. Robert McNamara described the results of five conferences held between 1987-1992 on the subject of the Cuban Missile Crisis. These conferences were attended by Soviet, Cuban, and U.S. policy makers who were involved in the original 1962 crisis. Mr. McNamara concluded, "that the

crisis was more dangerous than is generally recognized. " (95)
During the course of the conferences it was learned:

> that in 1962 the Soviet forces in Cuba possessed not only
> nuclear warheads for their intermediate-range missiles
> targeted on U.S. cities but also nuclear bombs and tactical
> warheads. The tactical warheads were to be used against
> U.S. invasion forces. . . . the Central Intelligence Agency was
> reporting no warheads on the island . . . at the height of the
> missile crisis Soviet forces on Cuba possessed a total of 162
> nuclear warheads, including at least ninety tactical warheads.
> (96)

Time and again, when faced with the possibility of using
force, President Kennedy proved to be patient and resisted.
Far from reckless, as revisionist authors such as Seymour
Hersh and Thomas Reeves have argued, he was in reality
sober-minded when the chips were down. Hersh and Reeves
attempt to correlate Kennedy's sexual dalliances with
reckless policy decisions. The comparison has little validity.
Attempting to equate the personal indiscretions of particular
presidents with policy decisions can only be an inexact
science. But one must have at least a personal knowledge of a
particular president to even attempt an evaluation.
Columnist Jack Anderson knew both John Kennedy and Bill
Clinton. Both men have been severely criticized for their
sexual improprieties and rightly so, but they are of course,
different people in other areas of their lives Anderson's
analysis of the difference between the two has some
validity—only because of a personal knowledge of both men.
Anderson concluded: "Thank God we had John F. Kennedy
and not William Jefferson Clinton in October of 1962. They
are not alike." (97)

With the Cuban Missile Crisis behind him, President
Kennedy faced 1963 with a new-found confidence. But the
problem of what to do about Vietnam would not go away.
Chalmers Roberts, diplomatic correspondent for the
Washington Post, reported that President Kennedy asked
Canadian Prime Minister Lester Pearson in 1963 what to do
about Vietnam, and Pearson replied, "Get out [of Vietnam]."
Kennedy responded, "That's a stupid answer. Everybody
knows that. The question is: How do we get out?" (98)

Major General Edward Rowney was sent to South Vietnam
in January 1963, on a mission to provide new weapons and

techniques. He states he "is optimistic but has reservations; the South Vietnamese [Diem] are afraid to suffer a defeat. The Air Force does not provide adequate air support, and that there are too many [American] generals in South Vietnam." (99) An intelligence memo from January 11, 1963, states, "on balance, the war remains a slowly escalating stalemate." (100) Yet Admiral Harry Felt, Commander-in-Chief of the Pacific fleet, and General Harkins continued to plan for a defeat of the insurgency by the end of 1965 to meet the President's goal of withdrawal. (101) The summer of 1963 was fast approaching, and the intelligence information did not match the battlefield goals.

On May 8, 1963, Buddhists or South Vietnamese Communists, had begun to riot in Hue, the ancient imperial capital. South Vietnamese troops fired on the crowd and killed nine people. This was followed by the burning of Thich Quang Duc on June 11. Madame Nhu made callous remarks about monks "barbecuing themselves." Fredrik Nolting still would not abandon Diem and the Nhu's and was subsequently replaced by Henry Cabot Lodge. (102) The President pushed for reform while Lodge pushed for Diem's removal as did Dean Rusk and others in the administration. (103)

The greatest achievement of the Kennedy Administration had been secured late in the summer of 1963 with the signing of the Nuclear Test Ban Treaty. President Kennedy's earlier speech at the American University in Washington, on June 10, 1963, sung the praises of a possible early end to the Cold War:

> Both the United States and its allies, and the Soviet Union and its allies, have a mutually deep interest in a just and genuine peace and in halting the arms race. Agreements to this end are in the interests of the Soviet Union as well as ours—and even the most hostile nations can be relied on to accept and keep those treaty obligations and only those treaty obligations which are in their own interest. So let us not be blind to our differences, but let us also direct attention to our common interests and means by which these differences can be resolved. And if we cannot end our differences, at least we can help make the world safe for diversity. For, in the final analysis, our most basic common link is that we all inhabit this small planet. We all breathe the same air. We all cherish our children's future. And we are all mortal. (104)

President Kennedy addressed the U.N. General Assembly on September 20, 1963 and stated:

> Today we may have reached a pause in the Cold War—but that is not a lasting peace. A test ban treaty is a milestone—but is not a millennium. We have not been released from our obligation—we have been given an opportunity. If we fail to augment this . . . then the indictment of posterity will rightly point its finger to us all. But if we stretch this pause into a period of cooperation—if both sides can now gain new confidence and experience in concrete collaborations of peace— then, surely, this first small step can be the start of a long and fruitful journey. (105)

The Cold War had begun to thaw and the confidence of President Kennedy was never so high, but Vietnam still lingered, never far enough away. Senators Mike Mansfield, Wayne Morse, and Frank Church were speaking out against the war in September. Church entered a resolution questioning our involvement while there was no progress towards reform.

According to columnist Walter Lippmann, Kennedy had planned to appoint J. William Fulbright as secretary of state because he believed that he was best qualified but that he couldn't because of Fulbright's record on civil rights. (106) Robert Kennedy concurred with this assessment in a February 1961 memorandum. Robert explained, "Jack always wanted William Fulbright" but his appointment would be offensive to many American blacks because of his poor record on civil rights. (107)

Less than one week after President Kennedy's assassination, Senator Fulbright commented on Kennedy's ability to listen to differing opinions:

> He was the most approachable President. I never had the slightest hesitancy in saying anything I thought to him. I never thought he might take offense at any idea I might have contrary to his own. The senator was especially complimentary of Kennedy's diplomatic skills with people from other countries, saying, "I think he had a sensitiveness to foreign people that no other President had. . . . Every time I went to a White House dinner, or any kind of ceremony, I was very proud of the way he represented me and my country. (108)

Dean Rusk helps us to place Kennedy's alleged staunch anti-Communism in a different light with this statement: "President Kennedy was very practical, he was not impressed or swayed by ideology . . . either by ours or theirs [communists]." (109)

The ability of Kennedy to listen to other views would have played an important part in his future decision-making on Vietnam. His respect for Senators Church, Fulbright, Morse, and Mansfield, especially on Vietnam and foreign affairs is clear. All four senators were consistently on record as being against escalation and Americanizing the war. But all four were also sceptical about immediate withdrawal of United States troops. It seems reasonable to assume that Kennedy was contemplating a similar track; pursuing negotiations while preparing for a peace platform in 1964.

Senator Frank Church was interviewed by *Ramparts* magazine in early 1965 and explained his view on what our policy should be in Southeast Asia. Church endorsed the neutralization of Southeast Asia, opposed escalation, but did not advocate an immediate American withdrawal (which Kennedy would have been open to). He believed that if the military situation in South Vietnam drastically deteriorated, then we should accept the unpleasant consequences of a Communist Vietnam and withdraw. (110) Church and J. William Fulbright agreed that emerging Communist nations were more reflective of natural political change and limited economic progress rather than a monolithic and threatening block. (111)

Fulbright voiced an opinion that might very well have been shared by President Kennedy during the fall of 1963:

> I am opposed to unconditional withdrawal from South Vietnam because such action would betray our obligation to people we have promised to defend, because it would weaken or destroy the credibility of American guarantees to other countries. . . . (112)

In June 1962, Senator Mike Mansfield offered a mild rebuke of Kennedy's Vietnam policy, another example of the type of constructive criticism that Kennedy would have listened to. Mansfield stated during his speech:

> Support of the President, and I give him mine whole heartedly, does not preclude public discussion of the situation

in Southeast Asia. On the contrary, it presupposes it. The
President would be the last to expect a moratorium on public
participation of this kind. It is politics that needs to stop at
the water's edge, not serious consideration of the nation's
course in its relations with the rest of the world. Rather than
less, we need more public consideration of this matter. (113)

On December 18, 1962, Senator Mansfield submitted his
report on Vietnam to President Kennedy. His report was
based on his personal interviews and analysis gleaned as a
result of his own visit to Vietnam in 1962. Mansfield
proceeded to meet with President Kennedy on December 26 to
discuss the report:

> We spent about two hours going over my written report,
> which he read in detail and about which he questioned me
> minutely. He had a tremendous grasp of the situation. He
> didn't waste much time. He certainly never wasted any
> words. What effect the report had on him, I don't know, but
> he did start to raise a few points which were in disagreement
> with what I had to say, but at least he got the truth as I saw it
> and it wasn't a pleasant picture that I had depicted. (114)

According to Mansfield, Kennedy was taken aback by the
"brutally frank" assessment and Mansfield responded, "You
asked me to go out there" to which Kennedy promptly replied,
"Well I'll read it again." (115) Presidential aide Kenneth
O'Donnell recalled that President Kennedy told him later, "I
got angry with Mike for disagreeing with our policy so
completely, and I got angry with myself because I found
myself agreeing with him." O'Donnell stated further, "If I
tried to pull out completely now from Vietnam we would have
another Joe McCarthy red scare on our hands, but I can do it
after I am re-elected. So we had better make damn sure that
I am re-elected." (116) Mansfield later commented on
O'Donnell's accounting of the meeting, "The only thing
discussed at that meeting . . . was the President's desire to
bring about a withdrawal but recognizing that it could not be
done precipitantly but only over a period of months. The
election was not even mentioned . . . What conversation Mr.
O'Donnell had after my meeting I am not aware of." (117)
     Senator Mansfield believed that his debates with Kennedy
over Vietnam had borne fruit and had an effect upon the
President. Mansfield concluded that Kennedy "felt we had
made an error. He was going to order a gradual withdrawal."

(118) In 1977, Mansfield was more specific in how he believed President Kennedy felt about Vietnam in 1963:

> [Kennedy] called me down and said he had changed his mind and that he wanted to begin withdrawing troops beginning the first of the following year, that would in be in January 1964. He was very unhappy about the situation which had developed there and felt that even then with 16,000 troops we were in too deep. (119)

General Taylor and Secretary McNamara traveled to Vietnam in September and October of 1963. Two of the three recommendations made from their report, made clear the President's intentions, "to be out of Vietnam by the end of 1965" and "that the Vietnamese will be carrying out current United States functions by then." (120) It has never been made clear if the following information is related to Kennedy's possible future plans for withdrawal, to other unknown factors, or even possibly to Kennedy's death, but the implications appear disturbing. Arthur Krock, columnist for the *New York Times* wrote an article that was published in the *Times* on October 3, 1963. The title of this article "Intra-Administration War in Vietnam" was symbolic of the divisive arguments raging within the Kennedy administration over our policy in Vietnam. Krock wrote:

> according to a high United States source . . . the CIA flatly refused to carry out instructions from Ambassador Henry Cabot Lodge [and] in one instance frustrated a plan of action Mr. Lodge brought from Washington . . . because the agency disagreed with it. . . . A very high American official [stated] the CIA's growth was "likened to a malignancy. . . . [which] not even . . . the White House could control. . . . any longer."

Krock concluded his article with a sobering statement related to him by this same "very high American official:" ". . . if the United States ever experiences an attempt at a coup to overthrow the Government, it will come from the CIA." This information should be considered alongside the documented threats noted previously (in Part 2) against President Kennedy, some from elements of the extreme right. Some of these elements were on record as being violently opposed to Kennedy's policies against the communist threats posed by Cuba, the Soviet Union, and North Vietnam.

Ambassador Lodge had made clear his desire to President

Kennedy, to promote a coup against Diem, and Nhu, in particular. As previously mentioned, numerous members of Kennedy's administration believed that Diem and Nhu were incapable of making the necessary reforms to make their government more answerable to the people.

Diem's brother, Nhu, was seen by many as the problem behind Diem. As head of the security forces responsible for the brutal suppression of the Buddhist protests during the summer of 1963, Nhu was seen as the corrupter of Diem. According to Rufus Phillips, the U.S. Assistant Director of Rural Affairs in South Vietnam, "the U.S. will not support a government with Nhu in it." (121) This is supported by Air Force and CIA guerrilla expert, Edward Lansdale, who knew Diem well, "people were telling me that his brother [Nhu] had taken over in the year [1961] following [the generals coup attempt]." (122)

Two weeks before the November coup against Diem and his brother Nhu, Vice-President Johnson offered a similar, yet foreboding portend with an analogy between Diem and Nhu, and Robert Kennedy and his brother the President. Arthur Schlesinger wrote:

> [On October 16, 1963] the Vice President lunched at the *New York Post* with Dorothy Schiff, James Wechsler and Joseph Lash. To the surprise of the *Post* people, a Johnson aide set up a recording machine in the corner. Johnson, Wechsler thought, seemed in a "strange and abstracted state." He expressed great admiration for John Kennedy. When, Johnson said, the President went around the table with the question, "What would you do?" he prayed Kennedy would not turn to him first. Wechsler had the impression "a rather beaten man whose only solace was in contemplating the burdens he had escaped by failing to achieve the presidency." The talk turned to Vietnam, Johnson, explaining the degeneration of the Diem regime, said the situation was much like that in Washington—a President with a "very strong" brother. "The inescapable overtone," Wechsler thought, "was that . . . Bobby Kennedy was running things, and in view of the Vietnam analogy . . . [it] seemed to be an extremely bitter thrust." (123)

In another strange and macabre twist, Robert Kennedy had this conversation with John Bartlow Martin in 1964 relating to Lyndon Johnson and his view on the assassination of Diem and President Kennedy:

Kennedy. Lyndon Johnson said to Pierre Salinger that he wasn't sure but that the assassination of President Kennedy didn't take place in retribution for his participation in the assassination of Trujillo [Dominican Repubiic] and President Diem.

Martin. Did he mean divine retribution? Or was he suggesting conspiracy?

Kennedy. No, divine retribution . . . He said that was God's retribution for people that were bad. And this might very well be God's retribution to President Kennedy for his participation in the assassination of these two people. (124)

Since it appears quite likely that President Kennedy was not involved in either assassination, Johnson's accusations prove strange indeed.

Lodge's predecessor, Fredrik Nolting, was not positive if Kennedy wanted to back out of the coup attempt against Diem and Nhu. The President was upset by the lack of co-ordination. "I don't think that Kennedy expected the outcome that occurred." (125)

White House tape recordings from November 4, 1963, document President Kennedy's reaction to the assassination of President Diem.

I feel we must bear a good deal of responsibility for it beginning . . . In my judgment that wire was badly drafted. It should have never been sent on a Saturday. I should have never given my consent to it without round-table discussion. I was shocked by the death of Ngo Dinh Diem. He was an extraordinary character. While he became increasing difficult in the last few months, he has been able to hold his country together for the last 10 months. . . . The question is now whether the generals can stay together and build a stable government, or whether public opinion will turn on Saigon. (126)

Dean Rusk recalled: "My impression remains that after the August 24 cable we took steps to withdraw authorization for encouraging a coup d'etat, that we wanted to keep tabs on developments but not actively promote or be involved in a coup." (127) General Maxwell Taylor has written:

As a consequence of this uncoordinated and ill-advised start on a vastly important change of policy, the Kennedy team did not look its best during the critical period from August 24 to 31. . . . The President began to see that he was involved in anything but a sure thing, and that his ability to control events from Washington was going to be minimal. (128)

Taylor went on to describe the reaction of President Kennedy to the news of Diem's murder and offered his analysis of Kennedy's complicity:

> . . . shortly after we had seated ourselves around the cabinet table, a member of the White House staff entered and passed the President a flash message from the situation room. The news was the Diem and Nhu were both dead, and the coup leaders were claiming their deaths to be suicide. Kennedy leaped to his feet and rushed from the room with a look of shock and dismay on his face which I had never seen before. He had always insisted that Diem must never suffer more than exile and had been led to believe or had persuaded himself that a change in government would be carried out without bloodshed. . . . The degree of American complicity has often been raised, but here again I know of no evidence of direct American participation in carrying out the coup and certainly of none in the assassination. But there is no question but that President Kennedy and all of us who advised him bore a heavy responsibility for these happenings by having encouraged the perpetrators through the public display of our disapproval of Diem and his brother . . . That responsibility extends beyond the death of Diem—so bitterly regretted by President Kennedy. . . . (129)

U.S. Ambassador to South Vietnam, Henry Cabot Lodge, offered his view of President Kennedy's involvement in the assassination of President Diem:

> On August 30 the telegrams of August 25 and August 28 were canceled. This cancellation in effect removed the basis for the charge that the United States government, under the administration of President Kennedy had "variously authorized, sanctioned and encouraged a coup." The coup of November 1 was essentially a Vietnamese affair. Because of our lack of involvement in the intricacies of Vietnamese political life, we could not have started the coup if we had wanted to. Nor would we have stopped one once it had started. Our policy, under instructions from President Kennedy, was "not to thwart" a coup. We adhered scrupulously to that policy. I have often wondered why those who leaked the *Pentagon Papers* did not leak the whole story, notably the fact that the August 25 cable was canceled by a message dated August 30. I assume that they did not know

about it. (130)

Lodge stated further:

> Of course, we were not privy to the conspiracy to murder
> Diem. [To this day we do not know whether the murder was
> an act of private revenge or arranged by the coup plotters.]
> And we did not know until the day of the coup just what the
> precise moment would be. Being tolerably well informed is
> not the same as "authorizing, sanctioning, and encouraging"
> the coup. I well remember that I was specifically ordered by
> the president not to help in the planning, and that I
> scrupulously obeyed orders. It is hard to believe that this
> instruction is not in the files. I did offer President Diem
> safety under the aegis of the United States and was prepared
> to give him asylum in my house, to help him enter a new
> government as a ceremonial figure, or to leave the country.
> (131)

George Ball stated in regards to the August 24 cable, "In
retrospect, I think we should have waited until the question
could have been fully discussed in a well-prepared meeting,
but since Harriman and Hilsman insisted that Lodge needed
a prompt answer, I signed off on the telegram." (132) Ball
added, ". . . the President showed some misgivings that we
had acted so quickly." (133) Ball stated further, "Early in
October, we learned that a coup was on again, but in view of
the failure to move in August, the reaction was one of dubiety
and caution." (134) Ball concluded:

> I do not believe for a moment that we could have won it [the
> war] had Diem not been overthrown [and] I would have lost
> no sleep over the August 24 telegram even had it triggered
> the coup, but the evidence suggests that it had little, if
> anything, to do with it. (135)

Admiral U.S. Grant Sharp has written:

> on 23 August 1963, a group of South Vietnamese generals
> made contact with a U.S. representative to advise that a coup
> against Diem was in the offing. Ambassador Lodge was
> informed and, after consultation with Washington, notified
> the generals that the U.S. could no longer support a regime
> that included Nhu, but the decision on Diem was entirely up
> to them. For whatever reasons, however, the planned coup
> was apparently aborted, at least for the time being.

Sharp added:

> In the aftermath of the McNamara/Taylor mission, U.S.
> embassy personnel in Saigon were once again approached by
> the South Vietnamese generals with word that they were
> preparing to move against Diem.   Washington advised
> Ambassador Lodge that while the United States was
> definitely not encouraging a coup, he should nonetheless
> maintain contact with the generals so as to monitor their
> plans. By this time Lodge was convinced that Diem was
> unlikely to respond to our pressures, and although
> Washington had directed that he consider ways of delaying or
> preventing a coup if he doubted its prospect for success, it was
> his opinion that by now the matter was out of our hands. The
> generals had taken the initiative and could only be stopped at
> this point by our denouncing them to Diem. While we
> pondered our diplomatic dilemma, the generals acted out
> their plan. (136)

Kennedy's position on a coup was made known on October
5, in a message from McGeorge Bundy to Ambassador Lodge:
"President today approved recommendation that no initiative
should be taken to give any active covert encouragement to a
coup. We repeat, that this effort is not to be aimed at active
promotion of a coup but only at surveillance and readiness."
(137) Walt Rostow concluded, ". . . he [Kennedy] was against
American encouragement of a coup, and was appalled when
Diem and Nhu were killed in the coup that took place. That
the two were killed in an American-made armored troop-
carrier added to his unhappiness." (138)

The coup against Diem marked a clear change in policy.
Was Kennedy to blame? The preponderance of evidence that
has been made available from those close to the situation,
strongly indicates that President Kennedy did not initiate the
idea of a coup and especially regretted the deaths of Diem and
Nhu.   What's more, it is apparent that Kennedy, after
initially handling the August 24 cable poorly, attempted to
pull out of the coup while the South Vietnamese generals, as
well as Ambassador Lodge, continued to push for the coup.
South Vietnamese General Tran Van Don stated that CIA
Officer Lucien Conein offered his help, but Van Don decided
that it should be a total South Vietnam coup. This report, as
previously noted, is corroborated by Ambassador Lodge in a
November 4 memo. Diem was offered safe conduct if he
resigned, but Nhu persuaded him not to. (139) Ted Sorensen

added, "When it happened and Diem was killed as a result—JFK was shocked and disturbed—it surely was not his intention." (140)

It has also been rumored that the United States (CIA) had co-operated in documented coup plotting by South Vietnamese generals against Diem in 1960 that failed, and that the South Vietnamese had contemplated others before and after Kennedy's death. In fact, successful and successive coups against the South Vietnamese government were carried out in early 1964 after Kennedy, himself, was assassinated. Claims that Kennedy initiated the coup and desired the death of Diem and Nhu are dubious at best.

President Kennedy's coordination of policy and leadership in regards to his handling of the August 24 cable was clearly, poorly handled. But it is also clear that Kennedy admitted and regretted his mistakes in that matter. There, of course, is a great difference between handling the situation poorly and being responsible for murder as others have attempted to charge Kennedy with. On the Watergate tapes, Richard Nixon is overheard to say, "[Kennedy] started the damn thing. He killed Diem and he sent the first 16,000 combat troops." (141) It is interesting to note that Nixon aides, John Dean and H. R. Haldeman both reported that former CIA agent and Watergate burglar E. Howard Hunt was involved in a scheme to plant forged cables that linked John Kennedy directly to the murder of Diem. (142)

President Nixon continued to promote this falsehood despite knowing that the cable linking Kennedy to Diem's assassination was fake; as this conversation with White House Press Secretary Ron Ziegler proves:

> *Ziegler*. Specifically the Pentagon Papers break-in, but also the cable [forged by Howard Hunt] regarding the death of or the overthrow of Diem.
> *President Nixon*. Yeah, which was some sort of fake, wasn't it?
> *Ziegler*. Yes. . . . (143)

The plot thickens further when the claim of CIA Director Richard Helms is also considered. Helms heard (as had Robert Kennedy) Lyndon Johnson claim that Kennedy's murder was an act of retribution " . . . by unnamed persons seeking vengeance for the murder on November 1, 1963 of the President of South Vietnam, Ngo Dinh Diem." (144) When the documented record of altered evidence and attempts to rewrite history concerning the assassination of President Kennedy are factored in to the accusation of Kennedy's involvement in Diem's murder, the implications are extremely troubling.

The record of John Kennedy as President suggests that he repeatedly rebuffed the Joint Chiefs and other Vietnam policy advisors' requests to expand the United States war effort. The bigger question is whether Kennedy was preparing to make a complete withdrawal of United States forces if he had won the 1964 election.

Kennedy had no mandate in 1960. He wanted that with his second term. Larry O'Brien believed that Kennedy would have defeated Goldwater by a similar margin as had Johnson. (145) Kenny O'Donnell stated that Kennedy told him, "I'll be damned everywhere a Communist appeaser, but I don't care. Once I'm re-elected, I'll withdraw all troops." (146) Tip O'Neil stated that Mike Mansfield told him the same thing. (147) O'Neil added, "The Pentagon would never have exercised the power over Kennedy that it had over Johnson." (148)

Foreign policy advisor Charles E. (Chip) Bohlen commented, "By the time of his assassination, however, he was beginning to move with more confidence. I am sure he would have tried some innovations to end the dreary Cold War. I do not know what they would have been, but he could have had a fine second term." (149)

Clark Clifford described the differences between John Kennedy and Lyndon Johnson on how they viewed Vietnam:

> The two Presidents had the same advisors and would have confronted the same situation. It is safe to assume they would have gotten the same advice.
>
> But I do not believe that John Kennedy would have followed the same course as Lyndon Johnson in the all-important year of 1965, when the major decisions to escalate the ground war and start bombing North Vietnam were made. On the basis of personal intuition and a knowledge of both men, I believe that because of profound differences in personality and style, Kennedy would have taken a different path in his second term. . . .
>
> I often saw President Johnson personalize the actions of the Vietcong, interpreting them as somehow aimed personally at him. He reacted by thinking, *They can't do this to Lyndon Johnson! They can't push me around this way!* On the other hand, I believe President Kennedy would have treated the attacks strictly as an international problem—not something

aimed at him personally. In reacting to the same events, I believe he would have thought, *I don't like the looks of this. I don't like the smell of it. Sending more troops may just increase the cost—let's hold off for a while and see what happens. I'm not going to get us more deeply involved.*

Confronted with the decision either to send American ground troops to South Vietnam or risk almost certain defeat, I think President Kennedy would have looked at Vietnam with that detached eye of his, asked different questions, and reached a different conclusion. After the Bay of Pigs, he was far more sceptical of official predictions; after the Cuban Missile Crisis, he became increasingly confident in his own instincts. I believe his questioning of the military buildup would have been more intense than President Johnson's, and would have exposed the underlying fallacies of his advisers' recommendations. . . .

But once he saw that even massive American military intervention would not guarantee victory, I believe Kennedy would have initiated a search for either a negotiated settlement or a phased withdrawal—as he had done in Laos in 1961. (150)

Robert McNamara wrote a reply to Louis G. Sarris, who had written in the Op-Ed section of the *New York Times* on September 5, 1995, that Kennedy was planning to escalate in Vietnam during the fall of 1963:

I should like to respond to Louis G. Sarris' statement, referring to my book *In Retrospect,* which was printed in the Op-Ed section of the *Times,* September 5. Mr. Sarris states that just before the assassination of President Kennedy, "the groundwork was being laid for our tragic escalation of the war." I believe the record shows that far from planning an escalation, President Kennedy had decided—and publicly announced on October 2, 1963—that the United States would plan to withdraw its military forces by the end of 1965 and would start by withdrawing 1,000 (of our 16,000 men) by the end of 1963. (151)

General Maxwell Taylor, chairman of the Joint Chiefs, made clear President Kennedy's plans for withdrawal by the end of 1965 in an October 1963 meeting. He wrote, ". . . we should take the end of 1965 as the target date for the termination of the military part of American task." (152) In an October 4, 1963 memo, General Taylor gave further support to President Kennedy's intentions to withdraw from Vietnam. "All planning will be directed towards preparing

RVN [Republic of Vietnam] forces for the withdrawal of all U.S. special assistance units and personnel by the end of calendar year 1965." (153)

Henry Kissinger, former secretary of state under Richard Nixon, certainly no friend of John Kennedy, conceded that Kennedy might not have escalated the Vietnam War to the extent that Lyndon Johnson and his successor Richard Nixon did. "JFK got us involved in Vietnam although there was—is some disagreement as to whether he would have gone all the way." (154)

Paul Nitze, national security advisor to President Kennedy and later, Secretary of the Navy, described in his memoirs the pressure placed on President Kennedy by the Joint Chiefs of Staff to commit ground troops to Vietnam:

> President Kennedy was bombarded with conflicting advice from Defense, State, and the CIA. The Joint Chiefs of Staff provided the estimate that 40,000 U.S. forces would be needed to clean up the Vietcong threat and that 128,000 additional troops could cope with intervention from North Vietnam or China. (155)

According to Nitze, despite the pressure and conflicting advice placed upon him, Kennedy refused to commit the United States to the introduction of combat troops into Vietnam. (156)

Kennedy's foreign policy advisor, Director of Bureau of Research and Intelligence, and later, Assistant Secretary of State for Far Eastern Affairs Roger Hilsman recalled: ". . . President Kennedy made it abundantly clear to me on more than one occasion that what he most wanted to avoid was turning Vietnam into an American war. He was sceptical of a policy of escalation and of the effectiveness of an air attack on North Vietnam." (157)

On September 2, 1963, Walter Cronkite interviewed President Kennedy during a 30 minute program on CBS-TV. Following a question regarding Vietnam, the President replied:

> I don't think that unless a greater effort is made by the [South Vietnamese] Government to win popular support that the war can be won out there. In the final analysis, it is their war. They are the ones who have to win it or lose it. We can help them, we can give them equipment, we can send our men out there as advisers but they have to win it, the people of

Vietnam, against the Communists . . . . All we can do is help, and we are making it very clear, but I don't agree with those who say we should withdraw. That would be a great mistake. (158)

Robert McNamara has concluded that these words reflect the President's true intentions in Vietnam. (159) Walter Cronkite offered his analysis of Kennedy's statements during their interview: "It's what I would have expected him to say—the political statement—whether he was considering withdrawal or not, he would say he was not." (160) Cronkite was a close observer of both President Kennedy's statements and subsequent policies during the three years of his presidency. He had conducted a number of interviews with President Kennedy and was in a unique position to compare Kennedy's rhetoric as well as his actions. Cronkite concluded:

The evidence was clear, and is frequently forgotten today, that early on Kennedy was becoming disillusioned with the prospects of political reform in Saigon and disenchanted therefore with his own policy of support. And I have always believed that if he had lived, he would have withdrawn from Vietnam. (161)

Noted syndicated columnist Jack Anderson knew Kennedy well. They had both arrived in Washington in 1947 and Anderson had discussed foreign policy and the subject of Vietnam on numerous occasions with Kennedy. Anderson believed: "I am convinced that America would have avoided the debilitating Vietnam War . . . If Kennedy had lived to serve out a second term." (162)

Despite the consistent statements by the majority of those who knew him best and believed that he would not have escalated and Americanized the war, Kennedy publicly ascribed to the domino theory and stated he was not planning an imminent withdrawal in Vietnam on September 9, 1963. Kennedy stated to David Brinkley after being asked as to the viability of the domino theory:

No, I believe it. I believe it. I think that the struggle is close enough. China is so large, looms so high just beyond the frontiers that if South Vietnam went, it would not only give them an improved geographic position for a guerrilla assault on Malaya, but would also give the impression that the wave of the future in Southeast Asia was China and the

Communists. So I believe it. . . . What I am concerned about
is that Americans will get impatient and say because they
don't like events in Southeast Asia or they don't like the
government in Saigon, that we should withdraw. That only
makes it easy for the Communists. I think we should stay.
We should use our influence in as effective a way as we can,
but we should not withdraw. (163)

Was President Kennedy posturing in the Cold War rhetoric
of the time? Or was he attempting to deflect the criticism of
those who were pushing for the entrance of American troops
into Vietnam, while he bided time waiting for the right
opportunity—negotiations towards neutralization, or was he
waiting until after the 1964 elections to withdraw? When
Kennedy's statements are considered in light of his
consistently stated intentions to not Americanize the war, the
analysis of George Kennan appears to be accurate. Kennan,
one of America's foremost experts on foreign policy and the
Soviet Union, stated:

> one of the most consistent and incurable traits of American
> statesmanship--namely, its . . . tendency to make statements
> and take actions with regard not to their effect on the
> international scene to which they are ostensibly addressed
> but rather to their effect on those echelons of American
> opinion . . . A long series of American statesmen have behaved
> this way in various situations at various times. (164)

Again, the question begs an answer, was Kennedy
somewhere in between a possible Laos neutralization of
Vietnam or playing a waiting game until the war looked
better, or a large election mandate in 1964? Or was all this
"confusion" like the Mendenhall-Krulak trip to South
Vietnam in September? Joseph Mendenhall and General
Krulak were sent to report on military conditions in August.
Krulak reported a good chance for victory but Mendenhall
determined the opposite. He believed that there was little or
no chance for success and especially if Nhu remained in
power. Kennedy indicated his displeasure with the conflicting
conclusions when he asked the two men if they had been in
the same country. (165) Following the trip by Mendenhall
and Krulak and their subsequent report in September,
Kennedy voiced his continued support for efforts to win the
war while also stressing his desire to bring Americans home.
President Kennedy made these remarks during his

September 12, 1963 press conference:

> I think I have stated what my view is and we are for those
> things and those policies which help win the war there. That
> is why some 25,000 Americans have traveled 10,000 miles to
> participate in that struggle. What helps win the war, we
> support; what interferes with the war effort, we oppose. I
> have already made it clear that any action by either
> government which may handicap the winning of the war is
> inconsistent with our policy objectives. . . . We have a very
> simple policy in that area, I think. In some ways I think the
> Vietnamese people and ourselves agree: we want the war to
> be won, the Communists to be contained, and the Americans
> to go home. That is our policy. I am sure it is the policy of the
> people of Vietnam. But we are not there to see a war lost, and
> we will follow the policy which I have indicated today of
> advancing those causes and issues which help win the war.
> (166)

By the fall of 1963, President Kennedy was "sick of it" [our
involvement] also, and frequently told Henry Brandon of the
London Sunday Times, he "wanted to get rid of the
commitment." (167) Kennedy aide Arthur Schlesinger has
written about President Kennedy's attempts to limit
escalation despite tremendous pressure to do so. Schlesinger
recalled a conversation he had with President Kennedy in
early 1963:

> They want a force of American troops. They say it's necessary
> in order to restore confidence and maintain morale. But it
> will be just like Berlin. The troops will march in; the bands
> will play; the crowds will cheer; and in four days everyone will
> have forgotten. Then we will be told we have to send in more
> troops. It's like taking a drink. The effect wears off, and you
> have to take another. The war in Vietnam, [he added,] could
> be won only so long as it was *their war.* If it were ever
> converted into a white man's war, we would lose as the
> French had lost a decade earlier. (168)

It is quite possible that Kennedy was in the process of
considering some sort of neutralization of Vietnam. In the
summer of 1963, Charles De Gaulle "offered French
assistance in transforming the two Vietnams into a united
state, free of all foreign influences." (169) In late October,
Kennedy related to General James Gavin the prospects of a
"deal" being reached with De Gaulle during their meeting

scheduled for Washington in February 1964. "I am going to see the General [De Gaulle] in the next few months, and I think that we will be able to get something done together." (170)

At a November 12 press conference, Kennedy further elaborated on his Vietnam policy:

> Now, that is our object, to bring Americans home, permit the South Vietnamese to maintain themselves as a free and independent country, and permit democratic forces within the country to operate. (171)

Senator Wayne Morse described a conversation he had with Kennedy on the same day, November 12, 1963:

> Wayne, I want you to know you're absolutely right in your criticism of my Vietnam policy. Keep this in mind. I'm in the midst of an intensive study which substantiates your position on Vietnam. When I'm finished I want you to give me half a day and come over and analyze it point by point. (172)

During a November 14 press conference, Kennedy made clear that the situation in Vietnam had changed and that the priority given to the upcoming meeting in Honolulu (November 20-22) was to "bring Americans out of there."

> Because we do have a new situation there, and a new government, we hope, an increased effort in the war. The purpose of the meeting at Honolulu—Ambassador Lodge will be there, General Harkins will be there, Secretary McNamara and others, and then, as you know, later, Ambassador Lodge will come here—is to attempt to assess the situation: what American policy should be, and what our aid policy should be, how we can intensify the struggle, how we can bring Americans out of there. (173)

State Department official Michael Forrestal recalled what Kennedy told him on November 21:

> He asked me to stay a bit; and he said: "When you come back, I want you to come and see me, because we have to start to plan for what we are going to do now, in South Vietnam." He said: "I want to start a complete and very profound review of how we got into this country; what we thought we were doing and what we now think we can do." He said: "I even want to

think about whether or not we should be there." (174)

National Security Action Memorandum (NSAM) 273 was drawn up at the November 20, 1963 Honolulu conference. This memorandum was, of course, never seen or approved by President Kennedy and was only incorporated into policy after his death. Research completed by the Assassination Records and Review Board has determined that many documents relating to the Honolulu Conference have still not been released. (175) A more precise and clear record should emerge when the remaining records of the Honolulu Conference are released. Robert McNamara summarized President Kennedy's wishes to not commit American troops in order to win the war in Vietnam:

> President [Kennedy] did not tell me what he planned to do in the future. . . . [but] Having reviewed the record in detail, and with the advantage of hindsight, I think it highly probable that, had President Kennedy lived, he would have pulled us out of Vietnam. He would have concluded that the South Vietnamese were incapable of defending themselves, and that Saigon's grave political weaknesses made it unwise to try to offset the limitations of South Vietnamese forces by sending U.S. combat troops on a large scale. I think he would have come to that conclusion even if he reasoned, as I believe he would have, that South Vietnam and, ultimately, Southeast Asia would then be lost to communism. He would have viewed that loss as more costly than we see it now. But he would have accepted that cost because he would have sensed that the conditions he had laid down—i.e., it was a South Vietnamese war, that it could only be won by them, and to win it they needed a sound political base—could not be met. Kennedy would have agreed that withdrawal would cause a fall of the "dominoes" but that staying in would ultimately lead to the same result, while exacting a terrible price in blood. (176)

John Connally, a close personal friend and confidante of Lyndon Johnson, who later switched to the Republican party and also ran for President himself, believed that President Kennedy would have managed the Vietnam War differently than Johnson. (177) Connally wrote in his memoirs:

> If President Kennedy had not been assassinated, no one can be sure what might have happened in South Vietnam. But in any event, Lyndon Johnson became President, and the war

became his war, and the military advisors advocated sending more and more American soldiers into that Asian quagmire. (178)

Connally went on to say:

My guess is that Jack Kennedy would have withdrawn American troops from Vietnam shortly into his second term. Although he did hesitate to raise the ante, he was less charmed by the generals than Johnson and less susceptible to their pressures. I believe he had already concluded that the war was unwinnable, and had found his pitch: "we wanted to help, but in the end the sons of South Vietnam had to fight for their own country." (179)

Arthur Schlesinger further summarized his views on Kennedy's goals:

But it is difficult to suppose that Kennedy would ever have reversed himself and sent ground forces into Vietnam. Both Robert McNamara, his secretary of defense, and McGeorge Bundy, his national security adviser, have latterly said that in their judgment Kennedy would never have Americanized the war—though, ironically, they advised Johnson to do exactly that—thinking that was what Kennedy would have done. (180)

Author Jeff Shesol confirmed in 1998 during a C-SPAN television program that McGeorge Bundy had determined, and had written in his memoirs, that President Kennedy would have eventually withdrawn from Vietnam. Bundy died in 1996 and his memoirs are to be published posthumously.

Former Speaker of the House of Representatives Tip O'Neil concluded: "My last conversation with him [Kennedy said], 'as soon as I'm re-elected, I am going to get the boys out of Vietnam.' There never would have been that great destruction had he lived." (181) O'Neil also stated in his memoirs:

The other misunderstanding about Jack Kennedy is the misinformed notion that he was responsible for getting us into Vietnam. In my view, just the opposite was true. If Jack had lived to serve a second term—and there's no question that he would have creamed Goldwater—he would have pulled out all our troops within a year or two.

Certainly the Pentagon would never have exercised the kind

of power over Kennedy that it had over Johnson. Lyndon Johnson revered West Point and the military leaders who came out of there, and he believed their judgment was infallible. Kennedy, on the other hand, was an Ivy Leaguer who was always sceptical of the military. There was no way he would ever allow them to call the shots.

Kenny O'Donnell used to say—and I believe him—that as president, Jack Kennedy agreed with Mike Mansfield on the need for a complete military withdrawal from Vietnam. But because the president knew that such a move might prove wildly unpopular with the voters, he intended to wait until 1965, the beginning of his second term, to put that plan into effect. Unfortunately, he never got the chance. (182)

Dean Rusk never fully agreed with those who believe Kennedy would have not escalated the war but he does, at least, admit the possibility that Kennedy was considering it:

President Kennedy hoped that economic aid and advisory support would enable the South Vietnamese to handle North Vietnamese aggression themselves, without the direct involvement of American combat troops. He did not want to Americanize the war or send large numbers of U.S. forces to help South Vietnam deal with what was then a relatively low level of filtration from North Vietnam. When this infiltration increased and conditions in South Vietnam continued to deteriorate, we still hoped to limit our role to an advisory nature. Throughout the Kennedy years and the first year of the Johnson administration, we tried to help the South Vietnamese do this job themselves. . . . (183)

Despite Rusk's admission, that during his entire three years in the Kennedy Administration, the President's consistent goal was not to Americanize the war; Rusk was still unsure about the possibility that Kennedy might have considered withdrawal:

. . . Kennedy liked to bat the breeze and toss ideas around, and it is entirely possible that he left the impression with some that he planned on getting out of Vietnam in 1965. But that does not mean that he made a decision in 1963 to withdraw in 1965. Had he done so, I think I would have known about it. (184)

Mansfield biographer, Gregory Olsen, explained why President Kennedy might not have confided in Dean Rusk as to his plans on Vietnam:

> It seems reasonable that Kennedy would share his doubts
> with close friends like O'Donnell and Mansfield while
> concealing those doubts from Rusk. Kennedy also expected a
> sympathetic audience from Mansfield when discussing
> withdrawal, while Rusk likely would have disapproved. The
> president tended to leave Rusk out of decision making, and
> Robert Kennedy claimed that his brother planned to replace
> Rusk in his second term, which offers an independent reason
> why Rusk would have been left in the dark on the president's
> feelings about Vietnam. (185)

William Colby is convinced that John Kennedy at the very
least would have recognized the futility of a massive military
buildup as a way to fight a guerrilla war. He believed
Kennedy would have been focused on the people's war at the
village level from 1964 to 1965. "Whether we had won or lost,
we would at least not have had a half-million soldiers
involved, nor experienced the casualties they suffered and
inflicted by their operations." (186)

General James Gavin concluded: "Having discussed
military affairs with him [Kennedy] often and in detail for
fifteen years, I know he was totally opposed to the
introduction of combat troops in Southeast Asia." (187)

The *Pentagon Papers* stated that "no firm conclusion [could
be reached] on whether Kennedy would have launched a full
scale ground war in South Vietnam or an air war if he had
lived." (188) The documentation compiled for this research
strongly argues against this view. In the last pre-
assassination issue of *Business Week,* November 18, 1963, it
was reported that a military escalation was not being
considered, "The message is loud and clear a major cut in
defense spending is in the works." (189) This is further
supported by the November 22 issue of *Life* which criticized
Kennedy for considering disengagement from Vietnam, "It is
not a time to relax or schedule U.S.manpower withdrawals in
time for our 1964 elections." (190)

From 1951 until his death, November 22, 1963, John
Kennedy's policy on Vietnam occasionally wavered but the
record compiled here indicates that he never seriously
considered sending United States combat troops to Vietnam.
Ted Sorensen was often called Kennedy's alter ego—for he
quite often was able to express more clearly than the rest of
his staff, with the possible exception of Robert Kennedy, the

clearly enunciated views of President Kennedy. Sorensen stated further, ". . . Introducing American ground forces into Viet Nam and becoming involved in the 'land war in Asia' that MacArthur had warned against was one thing everybody knew Kennedy wished to avoid. . . ." (191)   Sorensen later added, "He [Kennedy] learned that you don't solve political problems with force. I don't believe he would have ever sent combat troops to S. Vietnam or bombed N. Vietnam. I believe he would have waited for some opportunity for a negotiated solution." (192)

Noted Vietnam War correspondent and author David Halberstam supported Sorenson when he wrote:

> I'm hardly a Kennedy loyalist: *The Best and the Brightest,* my book about how and why we went to war in Vietnam, was something of an early Kennedy-revisionist book, coming as it did after vastly romanticized portraits of him. But I never believed he would have sent combat troops there. (193)

Ted Sorensen makes a fitting tribute to President Kennedy and describes the growth Kennedy showed that would have enabled him to make the changes that were necessary to make the difficult decision to withdraw from Vietnam:

> John F. Kennedy's years in the White House—particularly his first eighteen months—were not wholly free from error: that he gave Vietnam too many additional military advisers and too little of his attention; that he deferred too readily to the hold-over authors of the Bay of Pigs; that he ordered too many ballistic missiles and dismissed too few inept officials; that he initially placed too much emphasis on civil defense and too little on civil rights; that he had a blind spot on Cuba and a deaf ear on China. Yet in every one of these instances he proved to be of that rare breed of political leader who could acknowledge error and change course. (194)

Sorensen summed up his memories of John Kennedy, in 1999, as someone we should miss: "JFK called himself an idealist without illusion and did what was best for the American people. . . And we just miss a wonderful human being, who could laugh and joke—interested in everything—talk about almost anything—with spirit and style—miss him very much." (195)

Chapter 18

A Clean Break

The assassination of President Kennedy dictated the ascendancy of Lyndon Johnson to the Presidency. Kennedy's death ensured his place in history as the President not responsible for what was to follow. Robert McNamara made this clear when writing his book, *In Retrospect,* by explaining his rationale for doing so: McNamara wrote: "I must explain how and why we—including Lyndon Johnson—who continued in policy-making roles after President Kennedy's death made the decisions leading to the eventual deployment to Vietnam of half-a-million U.S. combat troops." (1)

McNamara added, "Kennedy was not responsible for what happened afterwards [Vietnam escalation]." (2) President Johnson was now free to follow his own initiatives on Vietnam. The record compiled indicates as George Ball stated, "Johnson was out of his element on Vietnam. He had no experience in Far Eastern affairs." (3) Columnist Joseph Alsop concluded that in the area of foreign policy, "Johnson lacked any kind of internal compass . . . he was left, in the case of Vietnam, to pursue a policy that he neither believed in nor understood." (4) Walter Cronkite supported Ball and Alsop: "Lyndon Johnson was a superb politician and an effective administrator . . . but his weakness was foreign policy." (5) What then would his policy be based on? The record has shown that Johnson, as a member of Congress, sought the expansion of military spending and influence. As Vice-President, he had favored an earlier involvement of

United States combat troops and the escalation of our overall
military presence.

Sam Houston Johnson realistically summarized his
brother's situation on Vietnam, "As far as Vietnam is
concerned, it is important to remember that Lyndon not only
inherited an on-going war from Kennedy, but he also
inherited the men who were JFK's principal advisors." (6)
The principal advisors on Vietnam were McGeorge Bundy,
Dean Rusk, Walt Rostow, and the most influential being
Robert McNamara. All four were on record as being in favor
of the introduction of United States combat troops and
escalation early in the Kennedy Administration. But under
President Kennedy, their advice on escalation was balanced
by the counsel and advice of Galbraith, Ball, Fulbright,
Church, Morse, and Mansfield. McGeorge Bundy proved to be
very loyal to the new President and was accused of being a
sellout by some in "Kennedy's circles." (7) Bundy also proved
to be a strong advocate of escalation. Rusk was also very
loyal to the new President, and enjoyed a better relationship
with Johnson than Kennedy. Rostow was an early proponent
of the use of combat troops and proved indispensable in
formulating pro-intervention policy for Johnson. McNamara,
although the front man on Vietnam, never appeared to be
totally passionate as a hawk or a dove on Vietnam. It only
seems natural that these principal advisors and Lyndon
Johnson would eventually agree with the Joint Chiefs on the
introduction of combat troops and escalation. They only need
to have a president willing to accept their arguments for
escalation. But as at least Bundy and McNamara have since
admitted, President Kennedy was not so easily swayed by
their arguments.

Just two days after the death of President Kennedy,
Lyndon Johnson would make Vietnam a priority. Almost the
entire cabinet had been out of the country during the
weekend of the assassination. A high level meeting on
Vietnam had taken place in Honolulu on November 20.
President Johnson's initial foreign policy meeting on Vietnam
occurred on November 24 just two days after President
Kennedy's assassination. (8) Henry Cabot Lodge was of the
opinion that "the current Kennedy plans for United States
withdrawal were not adequate and we should extract more
concessions from the South Vietnamese government." (9) CIA
Director John McCone stated during Johnson's first Vietnam

meeting, that he "could not at this point or time give a particularly optimistic appraisal of the future." (10) President Johnson stated "that strong voices in Congress felt we should get out of Vietnam and that we should not have supported Diem's overthrow." (11) Johnson went on to say that "I have never been happy with our operations on Vietnam. I want no more divisions of opinions." (12) Johnson instructed Lodge to "go back and tell those generals in Saigon that Lyndon Johnson intends to stand by our word." (13) According to a memorandum describing the meeting: "President Johnson made clear on November 24 that he wanted to win the war, and that he wanted priority given to military operations." (14) Despite his 1961 letters and statements to President Kennedy promoting the concept of reform and "nation building," President Johnson definitely believed that we had placed too much emphasis on social reforms. (15)

National Security Action Memorandum (NSAM) Number 273, issued on November 26, states that the policies adopted by the Kennedy Administration at the November 20 Honolulu conference, which, as previously stated, Kennedy did not see—would be followed. (16) NSAM 273 contained new directives that resulted in escalated covert activities against North Vietnam. Kennedy might have okayed these subtle but definite escalatory actions and he might not have—we will never know for sure. But there can be little if any doubt, that the new directives stated in NSAM 273, led to the events which culminated in the Gulf of Tonkin incident. Robert McNamara noted, the "planning for covert action against North Vietnam by CIA-supported South Vietnamese forces" was first proposed and adopted as a part of NSAM 273. (17) This program became known as Operation Plan 34 A, which ultimately led to the introduction of combat troops into Vietnam.

In January 1964, a memorandum from the Joint Chiefs of Staff to Robert McNamara made clear the Chiefs' decision to escalate the war was a result of President Johnson's new and clear resolve which was based on his issuance of NSAM 273. The message clearly stated that our new goal was:

> to ensure victory . . . in South Vietnam [and] in order to achieve that victory, the Joint Chiefs of Staff are of the opinion that the United States must be prepared to put aside many of the self-imposed restrictions which now limit our efforts, and to undertake bolder actions which may embody

greater risks. (18)

This record does not appear to be one of continuity of policy. This is supported by George Ball who wrote, "Though Lyndon Johnson tried so far as possible to create the appearance of continuity with the Kennedy administration, the atmosphere perceptibly changed." (19) Drew Pearson openly questioned the "peace policies" of the new President in a November 27 editorial:

> He has a slight Texas chip on his shoulder when it comes to foreign affairs. The new President, who served on the Armed Services Committee and the Special Preparedness Committee, is close to the generals and the admirals. He is close to the Pentagon. He has the Texas right wing setting off fire crackers behind him—right wing descendants of the same Texans who galloped us into the aggressive and unwarranted war with Mexico. Will they succeed again? This is the biggest question mark facing President Johnson and the American people. (20)

General Taylor told the Pentagon on January 22, 1964, that NSAM 273, "Makes clear the resolve of the President to insure victory . . . To do this, we must prepare for whatever level activity may be required." (21) CIA Director McCone, in notes of a meeting with President Johnson, made clear the change in "emphasis" from Kennedy to Johnson:

> I received in this meeting the first "President Johnson tone" for action as contrasted with the "Kennedy tone." Johnson definitely feels that we place too much emphasis on social reforms; he has very little tolerance with our spending so much time being "do-gooders"; and he has no tolerance whatsoever with bickering and quarreling of the type that has gone on in South Vietnam. (22)

These meetings and subsequent decisions attempted to show a continuity between the two administrations. General Taylor noted that he had been encouraged with Johnson's "quick statement of intention to continue President Kennedy's Vietnam policy, which he confirmed in a National Security Council Memorandum. In this memorandum, President Johnson retained the target date of 1965 for the withdrawal of most of our military personnel. . . ." (23) However, paragraph 7 of NSAM 273 indicated that planning for different levels of possible increased activity to include resulting damage to North Vietnam had been revised. McGeorge Bundy stated that these revisions were due to Johnson holding "stronger views on the war than Kennedy did." (24)

Stanley Karnow believed:

> These ineffectual "dirty trucks" [from NSAM 273] had been conducted only intermittently before Lyndon Johnson entered office in late 1963. At that point, the Joint Chiefs of Staff conceived a more ambitious and systematic plan for covert operations against North Vietnam, typically giving it an acronym: OPLAN 34-A. (25)

President Johnson's eagerness to be elected President in his own right and to please the Joint Chiefs of Staff is apparent by his remark overheard at a 1963 Christmas Eve reception where he reportedly told the Chiefs, "Just let me get elected, and then you can have your war." (26)

McGeorge Bundy, on January 7, 1964 presented a three part plan to President Johnson that was designed to "expand" and intensify intelligence missions, psychological operations and sabotage against the North Vietnamese. (27) On the same day, Secretary McNamara commented to the President on Senator Mansfield's objections to United States policy in Vietnam and what the intended policy had been under Kennedy. "We should certainly stress that the war is essentially a Vietnamese responsibility, and this we have repeatedly done particularly in our announced policy on United States troop withdrawal." (28) Senator Mansfield had made clear that he believed that President Johnson was not following the course of not Americanizing the war which had been favored by Kennedy.

Ambassador Lodge, on January 31, met with the new coup leader, General Khanh, and outlined a program of intensified activity against the Viet Cong in South Vietnam and in North Vietnam. (29) Robert McNamara wrote:

> The chiefs recommended [early in 1964] that we broaden the war to include U.S. air attacks on North Vietnam and shift from training the south Vietnamese to carrying out the war in both South and North Vietnam with U.S. combat forces. This recommendation . . . in effect, constituted a revolutionary change in U.S. policy. (30)

This is supported by State Department advisor Roger Hilsman who wrote:

> After President Kennedy's death the pressure was renewed. General Curtis L. LeMay, Chief of Staff for the Air Force, was particularly vigorus in advocating the bombing of North Viet Nam. "We are swatting flies," LeMay said, "When we should be going after the manure pile." General Thomas S. Power said that with conventional bombs alone the Strategic Air Command, which he headed, and its B-52's could "pulverize North Viet Nam," and he made a special trip to Washington to plead the case for bombing not only North Viet Nam but the Viet Cong and their bases in South Viet Nam. (31)

On February 5, Dean Rusk sent a letter to McNamara in which he agreed wholeheartedly with every suggestion the Joint Chiefs had recommended in their memorandum of January 22, and intimated that wars of liberation by the Communists will not succeed. (32) George Herring concluded that "NSAM 288, approved March 17, did state U.S. objectives in more sweeping terms than before, emphasizing as the essential U.S. goal the preservation of an independent, non-Communist South Vietnam." (33)

In June 1964, Senator Mansfield made clear that it was President Johnson's decision and his alone on what our Vietnam policy would be. "You alone have all the available facts and considerations. You alone can make the decisions. From the Senate, we can only give you, in the last analysis, our trust, our support and such independent thoughts as may occur to us from time to time. But if our interests justify, in the last analysis, becoming fully involved on the Southeast Asia mainland then there is no issue. What must be done will be done." (34)

Admiral Sharp stated:

> On 27 July the United States announced it was sending an additional 5,000 men to South Vietnam, bringing the military mission there to a total of 21,000. It should be remembered that this was still an advisory mission and our personnel were not participating in military action at this point. (35)

Sharp noted:

> [Rostow] postulated that by applying limited, graduated military actions, as well as political and economic pressures,

on a nation [North Vietnam] providing external support for insurgency, we should be able to cause that nation to decide to reduce greatly, or eliminate altogether, its support for the insurgency. (36)

George Herring noted that after the Gulf of Tonkin "incident" in August of 1964, in which President Johnson claimed our ships were attacked by the North Vietnamese: "The captain of the *Maddox* later conceded that evidence of an attack was less than conclusive. North Vietnamese gunboats may have been operating in the area, but no evidence has ever been produced to demonstrate that they committed hostile acts." (37)

Senator Barry Goldwater believed:

The Vietnam War truly began for us on August 7, 1964, when the U. S. Congress passed the Tonkin Gulf Resolution after reported attacks on two U. S. destroyers, the *U.S.S. Maddox* and *C. Turner Joy*, by North Vietnamese patrol boats. . . . "in fact, the attack on the *Turner Joy* never took place. . . . I still question whether the *Maddox* was shot at by the North Vietnamese. . . . The *Maddox* was on a secret mission. I later learned that the operation involved U-2 spy flights over North Vietnam, kidnapping North Vietnamese for intelligence interrogation, commando raids from the sea, and parachuting psychological warfare teams into North Vietnam. . . . In this case, the facts were not revealed to the Congress. We voted on the Tonkin Gulf Resolution with critical aspects of the situation withheld from us. (38)

This "incident" eventually give Lyndon Johnson the "blank check" he needed and desired to escalate the war. According to Stanley Karnow, " Walt Rostow conceived a plan for Johnson to obtain a "blank check" from Congress to conduct the war." (39) Karnow adds, "Rostow . . . urged audacity. Send American troops to Vietnam promptly, he asserted, and the Communists would understand that 'we are prepared to face down any form of escalation' they might mount." (40)

Small wonder that Walt Rostow is one of the few who refuses to concede that President Kennedy would not have escalated the war. (41) Rostow's aggressive strategy to escalate the war appears to have been one of the leading causes of our eventual over-commitment.

The Pentagon Papers list in chronological order the gradual escalation of the war under the Johnson Administration beginning with memo #62 in January and ending with memo #67 just before the Gulf of Tonkin incident in early August 1964.

#62 - '64 memo by Joint Chiefs of Staff discussing widening of the war. January 22, 1964.

#63 - '64 McNamara report on steps to change the trend of the war. March 16, 1964.

#64 - U. S. order for preparations for some retaliatory action. March 17, 1964. NSAM 288.

#65 - Cable from President to Lodge on escalation contingencies. March 20, 1964.

#66 - Draft Resolution for Congress on Actions in Southeast Asia. May 25, 1964.

#67 - Cable from Taylor Warning on the "March North Campaign. July 25, 1964. (42)

These series of escalating actions were designed to promote retaliatory attacks by the Viet Cong against United States forces, in effect to create an incident. When the Gulf of Tonkin episode "took place" in early August 1964, Congress was ready to oblige President Johnson with the mandate he had been seeking. Johnson called in J. William Fulbright and other Congressional leaders on August 5 to describe how the North Vietnamese had flagrantly and without provocation violated the freedom of the seas and attacked two of our destroyers. "Very few thought at that time that we were being lied to." (43)

Immediately after the Gulf of Tonkin "attacks" George Ball confronted President Johnson:

> Everyone knows the De Soto Patrols have no intelligence mission that couldn't be accomplished just as well by planes or small boats at far less risk. The evidence will strongly suggest that you sent those ships up the Gulf only to provoke attack so we could retaliate. Just think what Congress and the press would do with that! They'd say you deliberately used American boys as decoy ducks and that you threw away lives just so you'd have an excuse to bomb. Mr. President, you couldn't live with that. (44)

President Johnson was trying to promote his image as a man of peace in preparation for the 1964 election. He spoke to Canadian Prime Minister Pearson on May 28, 1964, and stated, "The United States is not interested in starting wars, but in keeping peace and my administration is going to be an administration of peace." (45)   Robert Caro has written:

> during his campaign, in 1964, for election to the presidency in his own right, Lyndon Johnson had pledged not to widen the war. "Some . . . are eager to enlarge the conflict," he had said during the campaign. There are even "those who say that you ought to go north and drop bombs," he said. But not to him, he said. Or, he said, "they call upon us to supply American boys to do the job that Asian boys should do." But, he promised, over and over "we are not about to send American boys nine or ten thousand miles away from home to do what Asian boys ought to be doing for themselves." (46)

Senator J. William Fulbright wrote:

> We were also in the middle of the Presidential campaign of 1964. I thought Johnson was a peacemaker. He had spoken against sending our young men to Vietnam. If I had known it was a fraud, and a lie, I would certainly have acted differently. (47)

Stanley Karnow believed:

> Johnson had shrewdly and skillfully prevented the war from becoming a divisive political issue. He had deflected Goldwater's early attempts to rally right-wing sentiment against him, and his readiness to bomb North Vietnam had immunized him against charges of being "soft" on Communism. At the same time, he had pledged that 'we are not about to send American boys nine or ten thousand miles away from home to do what Asian boys ought to be doing for themselves. (48)

George Herring concluded that Johnson's holding pattern on an initial escalation gave him a clear but unwise mandate to further escalation after the election:

> His firm but restrained response to the alleged North Vietnamese attacks won broad popular support, his rating in the Louis Harris poll skyrocketing from 42 to 72 percent overnight. He effectively neutralized Goldwater on Vietnam, a fact that contributed to his overwhelming electoral victory in November. Moreover, this first formal congressional debate on Vietnam brought a near-unanimous endorsement of the President's policies and provided him with an apparently solid foundation on which to construct future policy. (49)

George Ball described President Johnson's reaction to the
Viet Cong attack on American planes and facilities at Bien
Hoa, an airfield near Saigon only days before the election..
This attack killed four Americans and destroyed five B-57
bombers. "The President waited to retaliate until after
election day, but he did begin to set forth 'military options' for
direct action against North Vietnam." (50)

Walt Rostow wrote:

> McNamara and Bundy wrote their famous "Fork in the Road"
> memorandum at the end of January 1965. This memorandum
> told President Johnson that he had to choose between sending
> more troops to Vietnam or "negotiations aimed at salvaging
> what little can be preserved with no further addition to our
> present military risk." Both favored the first course. (51)

There remained only the President's final okay to commit
combat troops and it was soon to be forthcoming.

Admiral Sharp added:

> Thus we moved, haltingly, toward a deeper political
> commitment in South Vietnam. At the same time, however,
> the policy objectives which had been enunciated rather firmly
> in NSAM #288 and in the Tonkin Gulf Resolution were being
> emasculated by implementing courses of action that were
> mostly weak and vacillating. Military proposals were being
> watered down or ignored. (52)

General Chester Cooper was part of the American
delegation to Saigon in February of 1965. He considered this
trip, a "fateful trip." Cooper later recalled:

> On our return trip to Washington we heard the White House
> statement over the plane's radio. "Today's joint response was
> carefully limited to military areas which are supplying men
> and arms for attacks in South Viet-Nam. As in the case of the
> North Vietnamese attacks in the Gulf of Tonkin last August,
> the response is appropriate and fitting. As the U.S.
> Government has frequently stated, we seek no wider war.
> Whether or not this course can be maintained lies with the
> North Vietnamese aggressors." (53)

Cooper believed that from that moment on, "in early
February 1965 the die was cast. The war was about to be
changed in kind rather than in degree." (54) Admiral Sharp

continued to describe the open escalation now in progress:

> The thirteenth of February, 1965, President Johnson
> approved the inauguration of an air warfare campaign against
> North Vietnam, an action we hoped might prove a decisive
> step in the right direction. Under strict limitations and
> controlled very closely by the President, these air operations
> were to be called "Rolling Thunder," a name that stayed with
> us throughout the war. As a rather unpropitious beginning,
> the JCS directive to CINCPAC on Rolling Thunder 1 indicated
> the first strike was to take place on 20 February as a one-day
> reprisal attack by U. S. and South Vietnamese forces against
> the Quang Khe naval base and the V Con barracks. (55)

In April of 1965, President Johnson and McGeorge Bundy
solicited the help of our old Cold War "father figure," J. Edgar
Hoover, as opposition to our increasing involvement began to
slowly rise. Richard Powers wrote:

> On April 27, 1965, presidential advisor McGeorge Bundy
> asked Hoover for any information he might have on the
> communist role in the antiwar demonstrations. The next day,
> the Director met with Johnson at the White House. Johnson
> told Hoover "That he was quite concerned over the anti-
> Vietnam situation that has developed in this country and he
> appreciated particularly the material that we sent him
> yesterday containing clippings from the various columnists in
> the country who had attributed the agitation in this country
> to the communists as there was no doubt in his mind but that
> they were behind the disturbances that have already
> occurred. . . ." (56)

As noted in Part 1, J. Edgar Hoover was more than willing
to adhere to a president who would allow him to be unleashed
against the perceived "communist threat" in America.
Hoover's communist obsession and the subsequent support
and cooperation given to Lyndon Johnson, were instrumental
in turning the Cold War in Vietnam into a hot one.

The previously mentioned obsession and hatred that
Hoover held for Martin Luther King Jr. would also affect
Johnson's relationship with King. Harris Wofford, President
Kennedy's Special Assistant for Civil Rights, described the
reaction of Johnson after the spring of 1965 when King began
to openly criticize our increasing involvement in Vietnam:

> There was another large political reality that gave added

support to Hoover's campaign against King: the war in Vietnam, President Johnson's determination to win it, and his fury toward anyone who opposed him. If King had not attacked Johnson's policy in Vietnam, beginning in 1965 shortly after the Selma march, the White House might well have taken action to check, if not wholly stop, Hoover's vendetta. Bill Moyers testified that by the spring of 1965 Johnson "seemed satisfied" that Hoover's "allegations about Martin Luther King were not well founded" . . . Then King started criticizing the war, and before long he was being viewed as an enemy by the new President, as well as by the Director of the FBI. (57)

By the spring of 1965, George Ball's prediction stated in 1964, that we could not stop the mass infiltration from North Vietnam to South Vietnam had come true. (58) William Colby stated that even though Johnson knew that this infiltration could not be stopped, he could not accept defeat.(59) On July 28, 1965, President Johnson outlined goals of the United States in Vietnam. He tried to explain why it was necessary to send fifty thousand more troops to Vietnam after also sending twenty-thousand troops to the Dominican Republic in an attempt to deter "communist aggression." Yet just one month before, he had attempted to convey a message of peace. As George Herring put it, "July 28, 1965 might, therefore, be called the day the United States went to war without knowing it." (60)

Stanley Karnow surmised, "But he [Johnson] alone exercised control—and with prodigious attention to detail. He made appointments, approved promotions, reviewed troop requests, determined deployments, selected bombing targets and restricted aircraft sorties." (61)

Karnow added:

> Some historians hold that events enveloped Johnson in the war. Others portray him as the victim of duplicitous aides, while still others contend that he consciously chose involvement. No single theory tells the entire story, yet each contains a grain of truth. (62)

General William Westmoreland gave his view on Johnson's duplicity regarding Vietnam:

> It was a masterpiece of obliquity, and I was unhappy about it. To my mind the American people had a right to know

forthrightly, within the actual limits of military security, what we were calling on their sons to do, and to presume that it could be concealed despite the open eyes of press and television was folly. (63)

Senator Fulbright had become convinced by the summer of 1965 that President Johnson was so blinded by anti-Communism that only secret opposition would be accepted. He believed that Johnson had been "a champion of the Eisenhower doctrine" which acted on the thesis that the Executive Branch be given unrestricted power to counter perceived Communist aggression. (64) Fulbright became even more convinced that Johnson's views on Communism had become thoroughly distorted as a result of the President's exaggerated claims of Communist infiltration into the Dominican Republic. (65)

Former Kennedy and Johnson speech writer, Richard Goodwin, adds further support to Johnson's continued exhibitions of his increasingly conservative and anti-communistic mindset in an excerpt from his June 22, 1965 diary entry:

I am not going to have anything more to do with the liberals. They won't have anything to do with me. They all just follow the communist line—liberals, intellectuals, communists. They're all the same. I detest the United Nations. They've tried to make a fool out of me. They oppose me. And I won't make any overtures to the Russians. They'll have to come to me. . . . (66)

Further support of Johnson's conservative leanings in foreign affairs is indicated by Conservative lobbyist, Dale Miller, who believed "He [Johnson] gave the impression of being much, much more liberal than he actually was." (67) Nowhere is this more evident than in the statement of his main financial backers, right-wing extremists, George and Herman Brown. George Brown concluded: "Basically, Lyndon was more conservative, more practical than people understand. You get right down to the nut-cutting, he was practical." (68) Johnson had also indicated a conservative tendency in the fall of 1963 when he strongly disagreed with President Kennedy's decision to sell wheat to the Soviet Union. Arthur Schlesinger wrote that not long after President Kennedy authorized the sale of wheat to the Soviet Union, he was confronted by

Lyndon Johnson who was unhappy with Kennedy's decision, "The Vice-President thinks that this is the worst foreign policy mistake we have made in this administration." (69)

Doris Kearns Goodwin has written that Johnson's conservative views also caused him to disagree with Kennedy on his "handling of the steel crisis" in 1962 as well as in Kennedy's perceived liberal foreign aid programs. Hugh Sidey of *Time* magazine reported:

> [Johnson aides] Richard Goodwin and Bill Moyers both believed that Johnson was exhibiting a "textbook case of paranoid disintegration" especially in relation to his fears about communism and the Kennedys. Johnson told Goodwin, "You know Dick, the Communists are taking over the country." (70)

Assistant FBI Director William Sullivan recalled that "Johnson was almost as paranoid about the Communist threat as Hoover was. . . ." (71) Further examples of Lyndon Johnson's increasingly conservative foreign policy actions were reflected in Latin America where Kennedy had made his Alliance for Progress a high priority. Author Donald Gibson has written:

> The CIA, the Johnson administration, and both U. S. and Brazilian military officials organize[d] a coup against [Joao] Goulart. . . . Goulart was an elected president with widespread support and was not a communist. . . . The Coup, code-named Operation Brother Sam in Washington, was supported by the deployment of a U.S. naval carrier task force to the Brazilian coast to provide arms and oil to the Brazilian military.(72)

According to reporter Tad Szulc:

> The Central Intelligence Agency, presumably acting with President Lyndon Johnson's authority . . . set in motion in late 1964 and 1965 a new secret plan to combine Castro's assassination with a second invasion of the island by Cuban exiles from bases located this time in Costa Rica and Nicaragua. . . . (73)

Evidently, Johnson's incursions into the Dominican Republic and South Vietnam in the summer of 1965 prevented him from launching another strike at our perceived communist enemy in Cuba. These communist threats, which appeared to Johnson in 1965 to be everywhere, apparently could only be stopped by using force.

Senator Fulbright became extremely concerned about Johnson's duplicity in justifying American intervention into the Dominican Republic as a result of the President's false statements regarding alleged atrocities that never occurred. Fulbright eventually asked Ambassador Thomas Mann to explain Johnson's wild accusations that were made during his June 17, 1965 press conference. Mann refused to believe that the President had uttered these remarks even after the Senator produced the official State Department copy of the press conference. (74) In a September 15, 1965 address to the Senate, Fulbright argued that the United States intervened in the Dominican Republic, not to save lives as President Johnson originally stated, but to prevent a revolutionary movement that he had determined to be dominated by Communists. (75) During this same speech, Fulbright went on to state:

> If we based all our policies on the mere possibility of Communism, then we would have to set ourselves against just about every progressive political movement in the world, because almost all such movements are subject to at least the theoretical danger of Communist takeover.... U.S. policy was marred by a lack of candor and by misinformation. (76)

Fulbright biographer Lee Riley Powell has written, "During the summer of 1965, Fulbright became convinced that the administration's impetuosity, duplicity, and crusading anticommunism were not confined to U.S. foreign policy in Latin America, but were fundamental characteristics of Johnson diplomacy." (77) U. N. Ambassador Adlai Stevenson believed American intervention into the Dominican Republic had destroyed the confidence that the Latin American people had in the American government and was a "massive blunder." (78) William Sullivan noted: "Johnson had taken a beating in the newspapers over his decision to send in the marines, and the president felt he could balance the bad publicity with good by ordering the FBI to join the fight against the Red Menace." (79) Athan Theoharis and John Stuart Cox have written:

> While actively involved in investigating Dominican political

leaders, [J. Edgar] Hoover also worked closely with National
Security Adviser McGeorge Bundy, screening presidential
candidates to ensure the selection of a "strong man who is
anticommunist." Agreeing to "get ourselves organized and not
to let ourselves drift," Hoover also undertook to talk to
"Dominican official [name deleted] pretty sharply and roughly
to keep him in line. . . ." (80)

Hoover again had "a friend" in the White House who would
allow him the autonomy he believed he deserved as well as a
shared concern toward the threat of Communism.

The Vietnam War would provide J. Edgar Hoover with
investigative fodder for his renewed war on subversive
activity. The anti-war and civil rights movements led by the
hated Martin Luther King would become new targets for the
FBI's Cointelpro operations. Hoover had stirred the anti-
communist pot in 1964 by declaring in statements given to
the *New York Times* and *U. S. News and World Report,* that
communists influenced and led the anti-war and civil rights
movements. (81)   Columnist Joseph Kraft took note of
Hoover's aging arguments about Communism, "There seems
to be little doubt that Hoover exaggerates both the exploits of
the Bureau, and the dangers posed by those it opposes." (82)

Hoover wrote in his book, *On Communism:*

United States involvement in the war in Vietnam was a signal
for communist propagandists to mount a huge campaign to
foster the impression that deep-seated and widespread
opposition to the war—especially non-communist
opposition—exists in the United States.   This was to
encourage the enemy to prolong the war in hope and
expectation that mounting adverse American public opinion
would eventually compel an American military withdrawal
and insure a communist victory. (83)

Cartha DeLoach to this day, continues to argue the Hoover
company line:

When the National Council of the SDS [Students for a
Democratic Society] announced that it was going to sponsor a
March on Washington in April 1965 to protest the war in
Vietnam, the FBI was put on alert to discover what we could
about the intent and strategy of the march and to report our
findings to the White House. Both the Soviets and the
Chinese communists had a strong interest in the withdrawal
of American forces from Southeast Asia. Obviously antiwar

riots at home served those ends. (84)

DeLoach's FBI antagonist, William Sullivan, disagreed:

> The majority of the students (and others) who made up the
> New Left, however were not violent. They were completely
> loyal to this country. They just wanted us to get out of
> Vietnam. (85)

There can be little doubt that Lyndon Johnson, the supreme
political pragmatist, was pushing Hoover to probe those who
believed his war was wrong and therefore, unpopular.
Sullivan argued that "Johnson used the FBI as his personal
police force right to the very end of his term." (86)

J. William Fulbright described the extent to which
President Johnson's obsession with defeating the communist
threat in Vietnam led to his duplicity during the 1964 election
and the Gulf of Tonkin incident:

> The Senate Foreign Relations Committee in 1967 conducted
> an exhaustive inquiry into the events of August 1964 in the
> Gulf of Tonkin. This investigation showed conclusively that
> the Administration had already, by the time of the Tonkin
> Resolution, determined their policy. They had already
> decided that if they had to, they were going to intervene and
> use whatever force seemed necessary to subdue Ho Chi Minh,
> prevent him from taking over all Vietnam. They were only
> looking for an opportunity to get the cooperation of Congress.
> When these alleged attacks took place in the Gulf of Tonkin,
> they found their opportunity. They misrepresented the actual
> event. They knew there had not been an unprovoked attack.
> I am sure they knew there had been provocation by the South
> Vietnamese that could lead to some kind of retaliation. And
> they knew, too, that this so-called attack was something less
> than an attack. . . . Only when we began those later hearings
> on the Tonkin Gulf in 1967 did it really begin to dawn on me
> that we had been deceived. And I have had little confidence
> in what the Government says since then. I know I should
> have been more sceptical. If I had known it was a fraud and a
> lie in the beginning, I would certainly have acted differently.
> But I think too that Lyndon Johnson would have gone ahead
> anyway, that he was just looking for the occasion to proceed
> with what he was determined to do. . . . Johnson had made it
> clear to his staff he preferred to wait until after the November
> elections before moving on Vietnam. (87)

David Halberstam, author of the *Best and the Brightest* and former Vietnam war correspondent, described the relationship between General William Westmoreland and Lyndon Johnson:

> One man was trained from the start in the art of being devious, the other in accepting and obeying commands. It was never a fair match. From the beginning, Lyndon Johnson denied publicly precisely what he was telling the General about the size of the war. In the fall of 1965, the General was promised that he would get a minimum of 500,000 men and perhaps as many as 700,000. When journalists in Saigon reported this, the President immediately and vehemently denied that the war would reach such size. (88)

Johnson related to his biographer, Doris Kearns Goodwin:

> Yet everything I knew about history told me that if I got out of Vietnam and let Ho Chi Minh run through the streets of Saigon, then I'd be doing exactly what Chamberlain did in World War II. I'd be giving a big fat reward to aggression. . . . For this time there would be Robert Kennedy out in front leading the fight against me, telling everyone that I had betrayed John Kennedy's commitment to South Vietnam. That I had let a democracy fall into the hands of the Communists. . . . (89)

Johnson gave the initial impression that "good deeds" and social reforms were not good policy in winning over the hearts and minds of people, immediately after taking office on November 24, 1963, Johnson clearly gives the exact opposite impression during this speech in 1966:

> The American people have helped generously in times past. . . . Now there must be much more massive effort to improve the life of man in that conflict-torn corner of our world. . . . I will ask the Congress to join in a billion-dollar American investment. The task is nothing less than to enrich the hopes and the existence of more than a hundred million people. And there is much to be done. The wonders of modern medicine can be spread through villages where thousands die every year from lack of care. Schools can be established to train people in the skills that are needed to manage the process of development. And these objectives are more within the reach of a cooperative and determined effort. . . . I want to leave the footprints of America in Vietnam. I want them to say when

the Americans come, this is what they leave—schools, not long cigars. We're going to turn the Mekong into a Tennessee Valley. (90)

There can be little doubt that Johnson truly wanted to eliminate poverty and hunger in America as his Great Society legacy unquestionably proves. But whether he really believed and intended to make this a reality in Vietnam is doubtful. In the end, his decision to escalate the war and bomb North Vietnam, made this goal impossible to achieve.

Doris Kearns Goodwin described Johnson's continued obsession with Robert Kennedy and Vietnam:

> All these general fears were symbolized in Johnson's image of Robert Kennedy. It is difficult to understand how anyone could have rationally believed that Kennedy might be a crusading hawk. Indeed, there is evidence that, as early as 1963, Kennedy was pressing a softer line on Vietnam. But to be fair to Johnson, it must be remembered that in 1964 Kennedy had voiced no public opposition to the war, and that before he had decided to run for the Senate he had wanted Johnson to appoint him as Ambassador to South Vietnam. Finally, however, the vivid terms in which Johnson describes the Kennedy assault—"betrayer" of John Kennedy, "unmanly"—are further evidence of what we have already observed: that whatever realistic basis there was for dislike or fear, it cannot explain the almost obsessive intensity of Johnson's feelings about Robert Kennedy. (91)

According to J. William Fulbright's summary of a 1967 Foreign Relations Committee report:

> [Congress] did not intend it to be used, as it was, as authorization for an enormous expansion of U.S. forces in Vietnam—from 16,000 military advisers to 550,000 combat troops. Securing a declaration of war and specific authorization for the introduction of combat forces in subsequent years might well have been impossible; not seeking is was clearly wrong. . . .Was the Johnson administration justified in basing its subsequent military actions in Vietnam—including an enormous expansion of force levels—on the Tonkin Gulf Resolution? Answer: Absolutely not. Although the resolution granted sufficiently broad authority to support the escalation that followed, as I have said, Congress never intended it be used as a basis for such action, and still less did the country see it so. (92)

Ray Cline of the CIA described the problem of Johnson's refusal to listen to other views; Johnson narrowed the circle of participants in the NSC to the principals, whom he began to meet at a weekly luncheon: Rusk, McNamara, Bundy (later Rostow). There were other groups; but this was the critical policy forum; intelligence did not have a place at the table. (93)

Lee Riley Powell has written:

> Johnson would arrange meetings of high-level advisors in which one of the dissenters would be present, but most of those present would be interventionists. Rather than a real consideration of distant ideas, Johnson's strategy was more an effort to make a record of having consulted all viewpoints. Cold warriors like Rusk and Rostow flourished in the Johnson administration, whereas dissenters such as Fulbright were basically considered as obstacles to be overcome, especially in restricting their dissent to private advice and memoranda. When Fulbright began publicly speaking out against the war later in the Johnson Presidency, LBJ was outraged and terminated his long friendship with the senator. (94)

This change in priority and the subsequent Vietnam escalation would continue until President Johnson had committed 500,000 United States troops to Vietnam. What does one make of Lyndon Johnson and his Vietnam policies? Was he a victim of poor advisors or was it his known love of the military and anti-Communism? Did he plunge ahead despite a fateful ignorance of Southeast Asian history?

Stanley Karnow's analysis of the Pentagon Papers concludes that the Pentagon Papers leave a false impression as to who is to blame for the escalation of the Vietnam War:

> A disservice done by the *Pentagon Papers,* the purloined collection of secret Vietnam war documents published in 1971, was to convey the idea that plans drafted by bureaucrats all reflect official policy. In fact, Washington is always awash with proposals and projects, some incredible. But they do not become policy without the president's personal approval. This was especially true under Johnson. Ultimately, Lyndon Johnson was to endorse most of the schemes for stepping up the U.S. commitment to Southeast Asia. (95)

However, the Pentagon Papers did conclude:

the introduction of even small numbers of combat troops with a specific and limited mission would violate a ground rule the United States had rigorously adhered to since the beginning of the Indochina wars. Once the first step had been taken, it would be "very difficult to hold [the] line." (96)

George Herring offers this summary: "Between November 1963 and July 1965, Lyndon Baines Johnson transformed a limited commitment to assist the South Vietnamese government into an open-ended commitment to preserve an independent, non-Communist South Vietnam." (97)

An understanding of Lyndon Johnson and Vietnam is not so easy to come by. The results of his Vietnam policy are obvious; he inherited a situation of limited commitment and escalated it beyond recognition. Despite intelligence information and congressional advice to the contrary, he continued a policy that even he believed was doomed to fail.

The real question is why? After his election mandate in 1964 (peace platform), he was free to pursue any policy he chose. Doris Kearns Goodwin concluded:

> However, at least before the escalations of 1965, it was not an American war, and a Communist victory would be viewed as a defeat for the "Free World" But probably not as the defeat—far more serious—of American military force. And, in the end, after paying a huge and bloody price, the American people seemed hardly to care when Communist forces moved into Saigon. . . . (98)

On the other hand, John Kennedy, schooled in the history of Southeast Asia, was wary of United States involvement there. He believed nationalism and colonialism had more to do with the problems in the region than Communism. But the historical reality of the time meant that a Cold War anti-communist attitude was dominant in American foreign policy. Kennedy had stumbled through a foreign policy minefield in 1961 and 1962 (Berlin, Cuba, etc.) while having no clear election mandate. By the time he gained enough confidence as a result of the Cuban Missile Crisis and Nuclear Test Ban to prepare for a second term election mandate and complete his foreign policy agenda on Vietnam, he was killed.

In his book, *Rethinking Camelot: JFK, the Vietnam War, and U.S. Political Culture* (1993), Noam Chomsky argues that Kennedy was not planning a "secret" end to the Vietnam War. (99) The record compiled indicates that Kennedy's plans were far from being secret. Kennedy's intentions to not escalate the Vietnam conflict and to not introduce a large number of United States combat troops was made clear to those involved in Vietnam decision-making.

Chomsky repeats the endorsement of Kennedy (as Senator in 1956) and the domino theory and also argues that Kennedy was a staunch anti-communist while ignoring Kennedy's criticism of French involvement in Vietnam during the same time period. Chomsky does not balance his argument by noting that Kennedy had further stated that French involvement was overly concerned with the battle against Communism rather than focusing on nationalism and/or anti-colonialism. He continues his argument with a Kennedy statement from November 1, 1963 (after the Diem coup), "the new generals regime in Saigon should concentrate on the real problems of winning the contest against the Communists and holding the confidence of it's own people." (100) This statement is consistent with Kennedy's known plans for the South Vietnamese to ultimately be responsible for winning the war and not the United States.

Robert Caro offers this assessment of Lyndon Johnson and his escalation of the Vietnam War:

> in April, 1965, the President sent American boys—40,000 of them—ten thousand miles away, into a land war in the jungles of Asia. "Lyndon Johnson told the nation "Have no fear of escalation. . . . Though it really isn't a war/We're sending 50,000 more." By July 1965, there were 175,000 men in Vietnam; by August, 219,000; by December, 1966, 385,000. By the time Lyndon Johnson left the presidency, 549,000 American troops were mired in a hopeless jungle war. By the end of 1966, more Americans had died in Vietnam than had been in Vietnam when Johnson became President. . . . (101)

The argument forwarded by Chomsky, that Johnson escalated the war only as a result of the urging of Kennedy and his advisors, is not supported by the record indicating a push by Johnson and Joint Chiefs as early as 1961. This view is called into question by Tom Wicker in his review of Chomsky's book:

> Kennedy, had he lived, would have been a different man in different circumstances from those in which Johnson found himself. Just over a year before Kennedy's death, in October 1962, he had gained great prestige and a "position of

strength" when he forced the Soviet Union to withdraw its missiles from Cuba. . . . In the fall of 1963, he had concluded the limited nuclear test ban treaty with Moscow. . . On his last swing around the country before the assassination, Kennedy had discovered that mention of the treaty never failed to evoke enthusiasm and cheers; therefore a peace theme was being planned for the 1964 campaign. Undoubtedly, JFK would have been the "peace candidate" against the hawkish Goldwater; as Johnson did, he would have found that an advantageous position. Reelection in 1964, however, would have given Kennedy a different situation—some opportunity, and a clear public endorsement, for avoiding the kind of actions that plunged Johnson and the nation into a ground war in Asia. . . . So, possibly, JFK might have seized the opportunity in 1965—not for withdrawal but for the middle course he usually sought, somewhere between quitting the war and converting it to an American enterprise. (102)

Wicker later stated, "At the very least I think I would say that President Kennedy would not have pursued that war to the extent that his successor did because they were different men. . ." (103)

Kennedy believed strongly that Communism and totalitarianism were not the waves of the future and that capitalism and freedom were superior. This belief did not necessitate a military victory by the United States in Vietnam. "Victories" achieved as a result of the Peace Corps and the "Space Race" were important aspects of Kennedy's plan to show the world that our system was better.

By the fall of 1963, it is difficult to conceive that Kennedy would have staked his battle against Communism to our military success in Vietnam. At the very least, the history of United States involvement in Vietnam should read as Robert McNamara stated: "he faults President Kennedy least of those involved in Vietnam decision making." (104) The record compiled for this research concurs with this conclusion and an invitation is made to fellow historians and researchers to further document the history of United States involvement in Vietnam.

With this goal in mind, the Assassination Records and Review Board, in 1997, attempted to look for a more complete documentary record to determine if there indeed, was continuity on Vietnam between the policies of John Kennedy and Lyndon Johnson:

> In response to the public's desire to know more about any
> shift in policy between the Kennedy and Johnson
> administrations, the Review Board extended its search at the
> LBJ Library to include Vietnam materials from the
> transitional period. Two members of the Review Board staff
> visited the LBJ Library in 1997 and reviewed a vast collection
> of National Security Files and White House Office Files. . . .
> Some of these records indicate that Vietnam, rather than
> Cuba, was quickly becoming a priority for President Johnson's
> White House. (105)

These findings lend support to the thesis that those who
were shaped by the Cold War mindset, as personified by J.
Edgar Hoover, now looked to challenge "Communism" in a hot
war in Asia. This challenge has proved to be the worst
mistake in our over 80 year battle against Communism. The
record presented here argues that without J. Edgar Hoover,
the *Father of the Cold War,* the escalation of the Vietnam War
would have never taken place.

Conclusion

From the assassination of John Kennedy in November 1963 until Lyndon Johnson left the White House in January 1969, the Cold War of J. Edgar Hoover would turn hot as a result of the escalation of the Vietnam War. Hoover and Johnson's mutual cooperation with the Warren Commission's coverup allowed Lyndon Johnson to be elected in 1964. It cannot be proven that they conspired together in this endeavor, but there can be no doubt that a coverup took place and the escalation was the result.

The close personal relationship that Hoover and Johnson enjoyed as neighbors in the same residential block from 1945 to 1963 in Washington, adds to the speculation. Johnson's last Attorney General, Ramsay Clark, believed that "the nearly two decades they spent as neighbors almost disqualified Johnson from being able to properly supervise Hoover." (1) None but they knew the depth of their relationship but Johnson did waive Hoover's mandatory retirement by executive order and therefore, had Hoover in his pocket. William Sullivan devotes twenty-one pages in his book on the Bureau to a chapter describing Hoover as "LBJ's Tool." Ironically, the previous chapter describes the negative relationship Hoover had with John Kennedy; it was entitled "Goddam the Kennedys." A further indication of how Johnson used Hoover was shown during a conversation found on the Watergate tapes. Richard Nixon stated, "Hoover was my crony. He was closer to me than Johnson, actually, although

Johnson used him more." (2). . .
    William Sullivan wrote:

> Johnson and Hoover had their mutual fear and hatred of the
> Kennedys in common—and more.   As neighbors in
> Washington since the days when Johnson was a senator from
> Texas, they had been frequent dinner guests in each other's
> homes. They remained close when Johnson served as vice-
> president, but there was a change in their relationship when
> LBJ became president. . . . Johnson began to take advantage
> of Hoover, using the bureau as his personal investigative arm.
> His never ending requests were usually political, and
> sometimes illegal. There was absolutely nothing Johnson
> wouldn't ask of the FBI, whether or not it fell within the
> bureau's jurisdiction. (3)

The autonomy that was restored to Hoover became obvious
to Robert Kennedy after returning to work six weeks after his
brother's death. "Those people [FBI] don't work for us
anymore," he said. (4) Kennedy warned Johnson that the FBI
was operating once again as an independent agency, a
warning that Johnson, no doubt, was aware of and not
concerned with. (5)   In April 1964, the Attorney General
became even more alarmed by Hoover's actions, "Hoover is
dangerous and is rather a psycho . . . the FBI is a very
dangerous organization . . . and I think he's . . .senile and
rather frightening." (6) According to Arthur Schlesinger, Jr.,
Hoover did not speak to Robert Kennedy the last six months
that Kennedy served as attorney general.
    To what extent and for what reasons did Lyndon Johnson
and J. Edgar Hoover cooperate in obstructing justice? As
argued in Chapter 9, and further supported by an article
published in the *Dallas Morning News* on November 27,1963,
"the cooperation" between J. Edgar Hoover and Lyndon
Johnson in seizing control of the evidence and the subsequent
investigation becomes clear. "The switch of the evidence from
city to federal control obviously was decided after President
Johnson ordered the FBI into the Oswald case for a full study
on the facts surrounding the Kennedy assassination." The
Assassination Records and Review Board ". . . concluded
President Johnson established the Warren Commission in an
apparent effort to prevent parallel investigations, calm
domestic fears, and defuse any potential international
repercussions of the assassination. . . ." (7) The end result of
Johnson's creation of the Warren Commission was a coverup

of a conspiracy involving the death of President Kennedy. As stated in the introduction, it can not be proven that Johnson and Hoover were involved in some sort of conspiracy, but the possibility should not be ruled out.

Noted newscaster Walter Cronkite has stated that he believes that the possibility of an elaborate conspiracy is ". . . too Machiavellian [for America]." (8) But fellow and equally noted newscaster Robert MacNeil offered this assessment: "You would have to be foolish to think there was no possibility of conspiracy . . . we lived in a fool's paradise before the Kennedy assassination." (9)

A November 29, 1963 *Time* magazine article stated, "Assassination has never been an instrument of politics in the U.S.; no plot to seize power, no palace intrigue, has ever cost an American President his life." The fact remains that murders and assassinations with the goal of seizing power have been common occurrences since the advent of government. History is full of numerous examples—from ancient times through the time of the Caesars—to the present. Are Americans immune to this "rule" of human nature that has so often presented itself in the past and continues today? Stanley Marks has noted that in the late 1950's and early 1960's:

President [Charles] DeGaulle of France was the target of five conspiracies, each a failure. Between 200 and 400 persons were involved in the conspiracies, with the leaders of those attacks being in the highest places of the French Government. Yet, outside of those persons involved, the French general public never learned of the conspiracies until the failure, capture and imprisonment of the conspirators. . . . (10)

Just six years after President Kennedy's murder, "The National Commission on Causes and Prevention of Violence stated in a 1969 report: 'the number of assassinations and acts of general violence in the United States is high, compared with other nations. . . .'" (11) Yet some will continue to argue that we as Americans are "incapable" of replacing political leaders by the bullet for we "always" replace them by the ballot.

Since it appears to be a certainty that there was a conspiracy to assassinate President Kennedy, who has had the power to conceal it for over thirty-five years? Soviet radio commentator Valentin Zorin immediately believed:

I was convinced there was some sort of conspiracy . . . so I
decided to work on the old Roman principle and I asked, I
answered my own question, Lyndon Johnson, Johnson who
will benefit . . . So the theory I wanted to put in my first
commentary was that perhaps [Johnson was involved]. . . .(12)

The Assassination Records and Review Board released this
previously edited quote from Soviet Intelligence that the FBI
had in its possession since 1966, "Our source added that in
the instructions from Moscow, it was indicated that now the
KGB was in possession of data purporting to indicate
President Johnson was responsible for the assassination of
the late President John F. Kennedy." (13) What this "data" is
has not been made clear but after all the evidence is
considered, it should not be dismissed out of hand. The roles
of both Lyndon Johnson and J. Edgar Hoover are
questionable to say the least, but this data by itself does not
prove either were involved.

As difficult as it is for Americans to have to face the
possibility that J. Edgar Hoover and/or Lyndon Johnson were
somehow involved in John Kennedy's death, the very real
possibility that they were involved must be considered. As
noted in Part 2, Warren Commission Assistant Counsel David
Slawson admitted to the House Select Committee on
Assassinations, that if President Johnson and J. Edgar
Hoover did not want us to find the truth, "they would stop
us."

The reasons to suspect Lyndon Johnson are almost too
obvious and plentiful. Johnson was responsible for the
formation of the Warren Commission and the sealing of most
of the Commission's documents until the year 2029
(subsequently changed to the year 2017). Johnson was also
personally responsible for the presidential limousine being
shipped to Detroit to be refurbished even before Kennedy was
buried. (14) This action denied the Warren Commission the
opportunity to compare the damage to the windshield, etc.,
before and after the assassination. A further example of
Johnson's personal involvement is found in a January 8, 1964,
New York Times article, "Secret Service agents are guarding
her [Marina Oswald] at the direct order of Johnson." As
noted in Chapter 8, it appears to be a certainty that Marina
Oswald's testimony was "coached" to incriminate her husband
while she was under Secret Service "protection." As was also
noted in Part 2, Warren Commission Staff Counsel Melvin

Eisenberg recalled a conversation with Chief Justice Earl Warren that was reflected in the purpose of why the Warren Commission was formed in the first place: "Some rumors went as far as attributing the assassination to a faction within the government wishing the Presidency assumed by President Johnson."

In 1966, Arthur Schlesinger cautioned William Manchester that his manuscript for *The Death of a President* contained an "unconscious argument . . . that Johnson killed Kennedy (that is, that Johnson is an expression of the forces of violence and irrationality which ran rampant through his native state and were responsible for the tragedy of Dallas)." (15) Author Arnold Bennett related Manchester "speaks of Johnson's entourage on Air Force I after the assassination as a 'tong.' He now defends his use of this word by pointing out that it merely means "group or 'association.' (16) Was this "tong" responsible for the differences between the Kennedy loyalists and Johnson's camp on the flight back to Washington aboard Air Force I? Could this "tong" have been involved in the "autopsy confusion" that was to follow? The record is not clear, but this assertion seems possible given Johnson's new role at the top of the chain of command.

Jeff Shesol writes:

> By early 1966, Manchester had already failed on one count-preventing distortion. President Johnson had some hand in this by repeatedly denying Manchester an interview. "I'm not under any obligation to Manchester," Johnson wrote Jack Valenti, in response to another series of requests for notes and documents, though Johnson did offer some written replies. Twice Johnson agreed to receive Manchester, and twice he rescinded the offer. "He could not bear to do it," Manchester wrote in his foreward, acknowledging the freshness of Johnson's wounds, but in reality Johnson thought Manchester "a fraud." The feeling was mutual. (17)

The ARRB attempted to obtain the actual recordings and/or transcripts of interviews with Robert and Jackie Kennedy by William Manchester:

> The tapes and transcripts of William Manchester's interviews of Robert F. Kennedy and Jacqueline B. Kennedy are subject to a 1967 legal agreement which states that they were not to be made public for 100 years except on the express written consent of plaintiff [Jacqueline B. Kennedy]. With Mrs.

Onassis' death, her daughter Caroline Kennedy became her
representative and is the only person with authority to give
consent to open this material. . . . Caroline Kennedy wrote to
the Review Board in late August 1998, informing the Board of
her decisions not to release the material at this time, nor
would she agree to allow one of the Review Board members to
review the material to determine whether the tapes contained
assassination-related material. . . .The Review Board was
very disappointed that Caroline Kennedy declined to even
allow the Review Board access to the material. (18)

Arnold Bennett describes Manchester as writing, "We find a
Johnson who is in constant conflict with the New Frontier.
We find a Johnson who is—in the words of the late President,
as quoted by Manchester— "in trouble." (19)

Speculation had abounded that Johnson, because of his
possible involvement in the ongoing TFX Scandal (Air Force
contract awarded to a Texas firm) and the Bobby Baker
investigation—which would involve Hoover's friend Clint
Murchison, would not be on the ticket with Kennedy in 1964.
This is corroborated by a press statement Richard Nixon
made on the morning of November 22, ironically, as he was
leaving Dallas, just before the assassination of the President
"Former Vice-President Richard Nixon says he believes
President Kennedy may find a replacement for Vice-President
Johnson next year." (20) In a statement to lobbyist Robert
Winter-Berger and Speaker of the House John McCormack,
the new President voiced his concern, "John, that son of a
bitch [Bobby Baker] is going to ruin me. If he talks, I'm
gonna land in jail, and now he's gonna make me the first
President of the United States to spend the last days of his
life behind bars." (21) Authors Victor Lasky and Peter Dale
Scott have both argued that Hoover would not cooperate with
the Justice Department investigation of Baker. Eventually
Baker would be convicted of tax evasion in 1967 but Johnson
would remain unscathed. (22)

In regards to the TFX Scandal, Fred Korth (Johnson's
fellow Texan and who was appointed Secretary of the Navy at
Johnson's suggestion), was scheduled to be the next witness
to testify before a Congressional Committee on Monday,
November 25. However, as a result of the assassination, the
hearings did not resume until 1969, after Johnson left office.
(23)

In the fall of 1963, Ben Bradlee recalled:

On the question of his vice-president, whose close ties to Baker were politically embarrassing to the Kennedy administration, the president said he felt sure Johnson had not been "on the take since he was elected." Before that, Kennedy said, "I'm not so sure." (24)

President Kennedy also related to Bradlee:

"I'm not after Bobby Baker," he [Kennedy] repeated, and then talked again about how he felt Baker was more rogue than crook. As for dumping Lyndon Johnson from the ticket in 1964, the president said, "That's preposterous on the face of it. We've got to carry Texas in '64, and maybe Georgia." (25)

It appears that President Kennedy intended to keep Johnson on the ticket but it is also possible that Kennedy was becoming more concerned that Johnson's "scandals" were now associated with him. Could Kennedy have viewed these "scandals" as unnecessary baggage as he looked towards the 1964 election? Kennedy's secretary, Evelyn Lincoln believed this to be true. Lincoln wrote:

This day, November 19, 1963, started like any other day. . . . There was no hurry, no tension, no hustle, and no bustle. Although he [Kennedy] saw many people, he would sit in my office for as long as a half an hour at a time discussing various issues and situations. . . . "I am going to Texas, because I have made a commitment. I can't patch up those waring factions. This is for them to do, but I will go because I have told them I would. And it is too early to make an announcement about another running mate—that will perhaps wait until the convention. . . ." He had talked and I had just listened, but I did venture one question. We had not seen Mr. Johnson since he left for Texas in late October. Now I asked, "Who is your choice as a running-mate?" [Kennedy replied] " . . . At this time I am thinking about Governor Terry Sanford. But it will not be Lyndon." (26)

Arthur Schlesinger has written that Robert Kennedy dismissed Lincoln's account when Kennedy stated, "Can you imagine the President was having a talk with Evelyn about a subject like this?" (27)

It does appear unlikely that the President would have this conversation with Lincoln but it is possible. President Kennedy might have viewed Lincoln as someone he could confide in with no risk of repercussion. There is no doubt that

Lincoln was aware of many aspects of Kennedy's personal life that others were not privy to. She was involved in phone communications between Judith Exner and Kennedy—and no doubt with "other women." Kennedy obviously had a great deal of trust in Lincoln but this alone does not verify Kennedy's intentions or future plans.

If Lyndon Johnson truly believed that his political career was over and that Robert Kennedy (and by association, President Kennedy) was responsible, what was his mindset? Would Johnson have been willing to listen to others who were willing to give him his only opportunity to become president? Or was he more deeply involved in certain elements of the conspiracy itself? This is a difficult question to answer with certainty.

Jack Ruby's testimony (as noted) is truly amazing, and if true, quite shocking. He claimed to be one of the few to know how the assassination really took place. The contents of a letter Ruby wrote, not long before he died, claims "Johnson and the others were involved."

Ruby described further:

> you must read Texas looks at Lyndon *[sic]*, and it may open your eyes to a lot of things. This man is a NAZI in the worst order.
>
> Here is what happened and how I am responsible for this terrible tragedy. To start with, don't believe the Warren report, that was only put out to make me look innocent, so that it would throw the Americans and all the European countries off guard. They have found a means and ways to frame me, by deception etc., and they have succeeded in same.
>
> Only one person could have had that information, and that man was Johnson who knew weeks in advance as to what was going to happen, because he is the one who was going to arrange the trip for president. This had been planned long before the president himself knew about it, so you figure that one out. The only one who gained by the shooting of the president was Johnson and he was in a car in the rear and safe when the shooting took place. (26)

It is interesting to take note of this description of Johnson from the book, *A Texan Looks at Lyndon* by J. Evetts Haley, that Ruby alluded to. Haley wrote:

> Lyndon Baines Johnson . . . is not so much a product of Texas as of the strangely deranged times that have set the stage for

his ambitious desires, his vanity, and monumental egotism, his vindictive nature and his evil genius. . . . Federal bureaucratic pressure, state demagogues, intellectually elite, labor, money, and criminal tactics combined to elevate him to high office in Texas. His special talents as a wheeler-dealer and political fixer have kept him there. (27)

Another area of concern that Haley described in relation to Johnson was the Billie Sol Estes scandal which burst onto the national scene while Johnson was vice-president. Estes was convicted in a multi-million dollar fraud operation for his part in a swindle involving cotton allotments in Texas. Estes claims that Johnson was not only involved in the cotton swindle but also ordered the murder of Henry Marshall, an employee of the Agricultural Department in 1961. (28) Marshall was responsible for overseeing the cotton allotment program and his death took place in June 1961, just as he was mounting his investigation. In 1984, a grand jury in Texas reversed the 1961 verdict that Marshall's death was a suicide. (29) The new verdict opened the door for Estes' new accusations against Johnson and two of his aides, Cliff Carter and Malcolm Wallace. A relationship between Estes and Johnson has been documented but there is no corroborating evidence to implicate Johnson or his aides in the murder of Marshall. Former Johnson aides, Walter Jenkins and Robert Hardesty, don't believe that Johnson was capable of murder. (30) But the mysterious deaths surrounding Johnson's 1948 senatorial election as well as the murder of Marshall, do cause one to speculate.

Could Johnson have really been so involved in the actual assassination or was he most likely a possible "facilitator" as Robert Morrow's description suggests? Robert Morrow was a consulting engineer who worked as a contract agent for the CIA in the early 1960's in anti-Castro operations aimed at removing the Cuban leader from power. He reported that LBJ had been making negative comments about the administration of John Kennedy with the possibility of Robert someday succeeding John Kennedy and becoming president. Morrow recalled:

The first item I removed from the folder was a memorandum handwritten on stationery headed, "Office of the Vice-President of the United States." The salutation read, "My dear Charles [Cabell, CIA official whose brother was mayor of Dallas]." It is nearly fifteen years since I read it, but I will never forget its tone and its message. After a number of critical, self-serving comments about the intention of the President and his brothers to build a Kennedy dynasty in the White House, Lyndon Johnson got to the guts of his message. The vice-president said that he had learned, "strictly by accident," that the secretary of defense had been secretly ordered to use any means at his disposal to control the activities of the CIA in order to render it powerless. (31)

Could Johnson's role have involved drawing President Kennedy to Texas? Was Johnson capable of being involved? Was his personality such that he would have considered such involvement? His first press secretary, George Ready believed, "As a human being he was a miserable person—a bully, sadist, lout, and egotist. He had no sense of loyalty (despite his protestations that it was a quality he valued above all others) and he enjoyed tormenting those who had done the most for him." (32) Robert McNamara described Johnson as "one of the most complex . . . individuals I have ever known. He possessed a kaleidoscopic personality: by turns open and devious, loving and mean, compassionate and tough, gentle and cruel." (33) Joseph Califano has written:

> The Lyndon Johnson I worked with was brave and brutal, compassionate and cruel, incredibly intelligent and infuriatingly insensitive, with a shrewd and uncanny instinct for the jugular of his allies and adversaries. He could be altruistic and petty, caring and crude, generous and petulant, bluntly honest and calculatingly devious—all within the same few minutes. (34)

It is apparent that even those who knew Johnson well and admired his qualities as a leader—also considered him to be "mean", "brutal," and "devious." The capability for Johnson's involvement seems to be there—hard, documented proof—however is not. But this should not exclude historians from ignoring the obvious suspicions that his personality and actions have presented.

As noted in Chapter 13, Johnson or some of his staff, appear to have been involved in questionable activities involving the security of the motorcade. Were local Texas officials involved in pushing Johnson to bring Kennedy to Texas and also responsible for "suggesting" certain "visibility adjustments" for the motorcade? (note "Secret Service," Chapter 13) William Manchester offered this appraisal of the need for President Kennedy's trip to Texas:

> The Lone Star State, was, after all, the Vice President's fief. . .
> . As a professional, Kennedy coolly assessed the present crisis
> and concluded that he must go after all. But he reached the
> decision grudgingly. It appeared to him that Johnson ought
> to be able to resolve this petty dispute himself. (35)

Kennedy aide Ralph Dungan concurred with Manchester's
analysis, "Absolutely, absolutely. . . . Kennedy made the trip,
I can say for all history and posterity, without a doubt, as a
favor to Lyndon Johnson [as a result of] Lyndon's strong
urging." (36) Author Jeff Shesol noted Kennedy aide Ken
O'Donnell's reticence in regards to the President's trip to
Texas. "This was hostile territory," protested Ken O'Donnell.
But to each objection Kennedy's response was reportedly the
same: "Lyndon Johnson really wants me to do it, and I've got
to do it." (37) Robert Kennedy summed up the Texas trip to
Assistant Attorney General Ramsey Clark, "[the trip was] a
strain on busy people." (38)

Ben Bradlee recalled a conversation with President
Kennedy on November 10, 1963, less than two weeks before
the trip to Dallas. Bradlee described how Kennedy viewed
the upcoming trips to Florida and Texas: ". . . Florida was
presenting no particular political problems, but the political
situation in Texas was fouled up, with Governor John
Connally feuding with Senator Ralph Yarborough, and with
Vice-President Lyndon Johnson, a less viable mediator than
he had once been. . . ." (39)

Robert Kennedy alluded to the fact that President Kennedy
was going to Texas to help fix a political situation that
Lyndon Johnson should have taken care of: "When the
President was going down to Texas, trying to get the political
situation settled in Texas, Lyndon Johnson would be no help.
That made it difficult for the President. . . ." (40) Kennedy
added later, ". . . how irritated he [President Kennedy] was
with Lyndon Johnson, who wouldn't help at all in trying to
iron out the problems in Texas,and that he was an s.o.b. . . .
[Johnson] just wouldn't lift a finger to try to assist." (41)

Johnson's personal involvement in so many areas
surrounding the assassination make it difficult to ignore his
continuing presence. Even if one does not enjoy the prospect
of what his continuing presence implies, the fact remains that
wherever one turns in this matter, Lyndon Johnson appears.

District Attorney Henry Wade later explained why he dropped his initial belief in a conspiracy when he stated:

> Cliff Carter, President Johnson's aide, called me three times from the White House that Friday night. He said that President Johnson felt any word of a conspiracy—some plot by foreign nations—to kill President Kennedy would shake our nation to its foundation. President Johnson was worried about some conspiracy on the part of the Russians. Oswald had all sorts of connections and affections toward Castro's Cuba. It might be possible to prove a conspiracy with Russia. Washington's word to me was that it would hurt foreign relations if I alleged a conspiracy—whether I could prove it or not. I would just charge Oswald with plain murder and go for the death penalty. So, I went down to the Police Department at City Hall to see Captain Fritz—to make sure the Dallas police didn't involve any foreign country in the assassination. (42)

Wade later recalled to researcher Mark Oakes, "Johnson had Cliff Carter call me three or four times that weekend" to stop the charges that Oswald was part of an international Communist conspiracy. (43)   Yet, as previously noted, Johnson would attempt to convince members of the Warren Commission (as well as others) that Castro and/or the Soviets were responsible for Kennedy's assassination. It becomes increasingly difficult to rationalize all of Johnson's "activities" as mere coincidences; but again, there is no solid evidence to implicate Lyndon Johnson as being directly involved in President Kennedy's death. But Johnson would continue to stifle public dissent in the years following the release of the Warren Report.

Jack Anderson reported in 1966, that Johnson attempted to have J. Edgar Hoover write a book to refute the claims of Warren Report critics such as Mark Lane, who had produced a well-documented critique of the Report entitled, *Rush to Judgment*.   Anderson wrote:

> Johnson wanted to re-establish the Commission's credibility and lay to rest conspiracy talk." He decided that Hoover, still a formidable figure, had the credibility to convince the American people, once and for all, that Oswald was the lone assassin.   So, LBJ, using his best behind-the-scenes technique, got his close friend, Supreme Court Justice Abe Fortas, to approach Hoover. Fortas was sceptical but made the overture through Hoover's trusted assistant, Cartha D.

DeLoach. DeLoach conferred with Hoover, who rejected the book idea as Fortas had expected. . . . Fortas then confided, states the memo, that "he had argued with the President that it was not logical for the Director to prepare this book inasmuch as the Director in doing so would necessarily have to substantiate the investigative efforts of many other agencies. (44)

Despite rejecting Johnson's efforts to write a book defending his own conclusions, the Director did issue a release which "reiterated the FBI's view that Oswald acted alone." (45)

According to an article written by Ronald Ostrow and published in the 11/5/66 edition of the *Los Angeles Times*:

President Johnson, Friday, closed the door for the present on the question of re-opening the Warren Commission's investigation of President John F. Kennedy's assassination. 'I know of no evidence that would in any way cause any reasonable person to have a doubt about the Warren Commission,' he told a news conference. (46)

This statement by Johnson is obviously in conflict with his previous claims that Castro and/or those avenging the death of President Diem were responsible for Kennedy's murder. Further support for Johnson's belief in a conspiracy is found in a conversation he had with Walter Cronkite. Johnson stated to Cronkite: "I've always thought there could have been a conspiracy." Cronkite commented on Lyndon Johnson's convincing argument to delete these comments from the broadcast of his interview. Cronkite stated, "He was so persuasive and put such pressure on Bill Pawley [President of CBS] and the . . . network that we abandoned that quote and didn't use it and [it] makes me feel it was even more important." (47)

One of the more highly questionable actions of Lyndon Johnson relating to his assassination-related activities involves the statements of Parkland Hospital Surgeon Dr. Charles Crenshaw. Crenshaw described Lyndon Johnson's personal involvement in attempting to gain a deathbed confession from Lee Oswald. Crenshaw wrote:

Had I been allowed to testify, I would have told them that there is absolutely no doubt in my mind that the bullet that killed President Kennedy was shot from the grassy knoll area. I would have also informed the Warren Commission about the call I received from Lyndon Johnson while we were operating on Lee Harvey Oswald. President Johnson told me that a man in the operating room would get a deathbed confession from Oswald. The incident confounded logic. Why the President of the United States would get personally involved in the investigation of the assassination, or why he would take the inquest out of the hands of the Texas authorities was perplexing. (48)

Dr. Crenshaw went on to describe his conversation with President Johnson:

a nurse tapped me on the shoulder and asked if I would take a telephone call in the supervisor's office. She had chosen me to take the call because I was the head of Surgical "B," the team that began the operation. I agreed to answer the call and left the operating room. "This is President Lyndon B. Johnson," the voice thundered, "Dr. Crenshaw, how is the accused assassin?" I couldn't believe what I was hearing. The very thought that I had was, "How did he know when to call?" "Mr. President, he's holding his own at the moment," I replied. "Would you mind taking a message to the operating surgeon?" he asked in a manner that sounded more like an order. . . . "Dr. Crenshaw, I want a deathbed confession from the accused assassin. There's a man in the operating room who will take the statement. I will expect full cooperation in this matter," he said firmly. (49)

Numerous attempts to destroy the credibility of Dr. Crenshaw have been made over the years. As part of an agreement in a defamation suit, Dr. Crenshaw was later paid over $200,000 and an article in the May 24/31, 1995 edition of JAMMA [Journal of American Members of Medical Association] was printed with a limited rebuttal written by Dr. Crenshaw. JAMMA charged that Crenshaw was not even in the Parkland Hospital Surgery Room where attempts at resuscitating President Kennedy were carried out, (50) The AMA [American Medical Association] and JAMMA falsely suggested that Crenshaw's observations were worthless as he was not even in JFK's trauma room. That Crenshaw was present was sworn to, by two of JAMMA's own interviewees, Drs. Baxter and McClelland, before the Warren Commission, and is also confirmed by the Warren testimonies of three other witnesses. (51)

Parkland Hospital Surgeon Dr. Phillip Williams has consistently supported the assertion of Dr. Crenshaw that

Lyndon Johnson personally called the hospital. Williams stated, "I heard the statement in the operating room . . . I have said this for years." (52) Further corroboration of Crenshaw's assertions comes from Phyllis Bartlett, chief telephone operator at Parkland Hospital. Bartlett recalled, "There very definitely was a phone call from a man with a loud voice, who identified himself as Lyndon Johnson, and he was connected to the operating room phone during Oswald's surgery." (53)

Further support of Johnson (and/or his aides') involvement in securing assassination evidence is found in the experience of Parkland nurse, Ruth Standridge. Standridge testified that she gave Governor Connally's clothes to Johnson aide Cliff Carter. (54) In Carter's statement to the Warren Commission, he makes no mention of the clothing. (55) FBI agent Robert Frazier stated:

> because of the cleaning and pressing, Frazier indicated that with the governor's clothing, because of the large size of the holes, he might have been able to indicate whether the holes were caused by mutilated bullets. (56) Because of the cleaning and pressing of the governor's clothing, Frazier was not sure if the holes in the clothing were of entrance or exit. He makes this clear by stating, "Assuming that when I first examined . . . it was in the same condition as it was at the time the hole was made. . . ." (57)

In a further effort to document the activities of Lyndon Johnson in the aftermath of President Kennedy's assassination, "The ARRB formally requested the White House Communications Agency (WHCA) for any 1963-64 records that might have pertained to the assassination [including a record of] phone logs on 11/22/63 and other information regarding the assassination." (58) Evidently the ARRB believed that the WHCA did not fully cooperate in releasing all of the relevant information. This is indicated by the fact that

> The Review Board then requested that WHCA certify, under penalty of perjury, they have no other records from the 1963-64 period that might relate to the 1964 assassination. The WHCA issued its final declaration that it had no more records of the 1963-64 period in the spring of 1998. (59)

Jack Anderson recalled, "I had watched Lyndon Johnson

long enough to learn how his mind worked. He had lined up Hoover to control the evidence that the FBI laid before the commission. . . ." (60) As a result of the record presented here, history should at least reflect that it is possible that Lyndon Johnson was involved in more than obstruction of justice with J. Edgar Hoover. Harry Blackstone Jr., the son of "The Great Blackstone," stated in a *Dallas Times Herald* article:

> I worked quite some time for Lyndon Johnson [in] broadcast personnel, and I think I learned more about the art of deception from him than I did from my father. . . . He was a man who understood the art of misdirection, of making the eye watch "a" when the dirty work was going on at "b.". . . (61)

Less than one month after the assassination, J. Edgar Hoover and Lyndon Johnson lunched together on December 16, 1963. Johnson presented Hoover with an autographed photo with the following inscription, "Than whom there is no greater from his friend of thirty years." (62)

George Ball believed that "President Johnson's odd and almost sinister relations with J. Edgar Hoover came into play. Suspicious, and sometimes vindictive, Johnson was fascinated at the thought of having at his command a man and an institution that knew so much about so many." (63)

Robert McNamara conceded the possibility that J. Edgar Hoover was possibly involved in the assassination of President Kennedy and believed it was conceivable that Lyndon Johnson might have had foreknowledge regarding the assassination although he wasn't really willing to believe it. (64) Congressman Don Edwards, a former FBI agent, stated in 1976, "There is not much question that both the FBI and CIA are somewhere behind this cover-up [John Kennedy's assassination]. I hate to think what it is they are covering up—or who it is they are covering for." (65) The concern exhibited by Congressman Edwards should be a concern to all of us who value the truth. We are still not certain what to believe about our government's involvement in the assassination of President Kennedy.

It is also not certain as to why Lyndon Johnson declared in March 1968 that he would not seek re-election, although the failure of his Vietnam policy was most probably the deciding factor. But Vietnam might not have been the only factor.

Dr. Medford Evans wrote in the June issue of the John

Birch Society *American Opinion:*

> Something stood between the President and reelection . . . as
> if the way were barred by the very sword of justice . . . neither
> the shepherd Tamburliane nor the Corsican Napoleon had
> risen further than this . . . Ichabod Crane of the Texas hill
> country . . . now he threw in his hand and a mop-headed
> juvenile delinquent from Boston took the pot. . . . There is a
> compelling reason why . . . Lyndon Johnson will not
> reconsider . . . the people who made him abdicate in the first
> place won't let him reconsider . . . it behooves Lyndon to do
> exactly what he is told. (66)

Who were "the people" that Evans was referring to? Could
Evans' scenario have been possible? Was Johnson being
"forced" aside while J. Edgar Hoover's anti-communist "son"
Richard Nixon was waiting in the wings? It is possible that
Johnson was not totally ready to give up the presidency and
that he was pressured to step down?
Walter Cronkite surmised:

> It was never established as fact, but I have always believed
> that Daley [mayor of Chicago], perhaps acting on a hint or
> more from Lyndon Johnson, was prepared to try to stampede
> the convention into drafting Johnson for another term.
> Although Johnson had said he would not run, he had Air
> Force One, the presidential plane, standing by as he watched
> the convention from his Texas ranch. Ostensibly it was there
> in case he decided to address the convention. But it could also
> have rushed him to Chicago if a draft had developed. . . .In
> the best fashion of machine politics, Daley had stacked the
> public galleries with stooges ready to follow his every
> command and prepared to demonstrate popular support for a
> Johnson draft if any speaker had brought it to the floor. . . .
> (67)

Support for the assertion that Johnson might have been
considering the possibility that he could be drafted for the
nomination is found in his earlier actions in 1960 and 1964.
As noted in Part 3, Johnson and his supporters were counting
on winning the 1960 nomination via a convention deadlock.
Johnson's strange behavior before the 1964 Democratic
convention also illustrates the possibility that he was quite
capable of fooling his own advisors in regards to his
intentions. Johnson's Press Secretary George Reedy recalled
that on August 25, 1964, just one day before the 1964

Democratic Convention in Atlantic City, Johnson had told Reedy in no uncertain terms that "he [Johnson] reiterated his intention to quit" and to not seek the nomination. (68) Reedy stated further that he and the rest of his [Johnson's] staff went to bed believing that Johnson would not accept the nomination and were not sure what Johnson was really going to do until he formally accepted the next day. (69) Reedy believed that Johnson's behavior was typical of a "manic depressive" type of person because Johnson would often have as many as 4 or 5 low to high mood swings during the course of the same day. (70)

There can be little, if any doubt that J. Edgar Hoover and Lyndon Johnson did not shed many tears upon the deaths of Robert Kennedy and Martin Luther King. Johnson might have been close to King before the escalation of the war but not afterwards. Hoover's hatred for Martin Luther King and Robert Kennedy was never more evident than when their murders took place and the news of their deaths was announced. Ramsay Clark recalled that after King was assassinated on April 4, 1968, rioting broke out in various black communities throughout the country. On Sunday, April 6, rioting broke out in the black neighborhoods in Washington and Clark attempted to contact Hoover on how to deal with the crisis but was unable to find him. Hoover had decided to go to the horse races in Baltimore instead of dealing with the problem. (71)

Just two months later, on June 6, Robert Kennedy was shot and killed in Los Angeles, just as it appeared that he might be prepared to grab the Democratic nomination. Attorney General Ramsay Clark stated that in the midst of the funeral coverage for Kennedy, Cartha DeLoach, assistant FBI director, was ordered by Hoover to inform the press that James Earl Ray had been arrested in London as the assassin of Martin Luther King. (72) This led to an interruption of the funeral coverage and diverted national attention away to the "exceptional investigative work done by Hoover and his Bureau." Even more troubling is that Clark was initially informed that Scotland Yard was responsible for the announcement during the funeral, but Clark later found this to be false. Clark recalled, "The thing I couldn't take was that I'd been lied to. . . . You can't function that way." (73)

What is certain is that both Lyndon Johnson and J. Edgar Hoover viewed the American landscape and believed that "all hell was breaking loose." Anti-war and civil rights demonstrations and riots, the assassinations of Robert Kennedy and Martin Luther King, and the subsequent major riot at the Democratic National Convention in Chicago, were signs that America was out of control. Johnson chose to flee the responsibility at hand and Hoover chose to dig in and fight; the bunker mentality. Hoover continued to see communist influence everywhere. He argued before the House Appropriations Committee in May 1968 that the Communist Party sought to unite the forces of civil rights and antiwar protest:

> to create one massive movement which they hope will ultimately change our government's policies, both foreign and domestic. At the center of the New Left movement, is an almost passionate desire to destroy, to annihilate, to tear down. If anything definite can be said about the Students for a Democratic Society, it is that it can be called anarchistic. (74)

Hoover had come full circle since the days of Emma Goldman and Alexander Berkman. He still pictured Communism in monolithic terms. There was no allowance for the possibility that the problems in American ran deeper than the evil of communistic thought. Was it not entirely possible that the American public believed that the government was out of touch with its people over the issues of the Vietnam War, civil rights, the environment, etc.?

In the 1968 presidential election, the voting public decided in a close election that Richard Nixon and "law and order" were the answers to stemming the tide of violence and turmoil across the nation. In May of 1968, Richard Nixon had voiced his public support for the retention of Hoover, although with their long-standing friendship there was no private wavering. "He's the kind of man I want to head the FBI, if I should have the opportunity to make that decision." (75) J. Edgar Hoover had waited a long time for his "anti-communist son" to be joined with the "father" of the movement. Unfortunately, the end was near for Hoover and it had long since been time to go. His relationship with President Nixon would never match the early days of cooperation. By May of 1970, Nixon was "against the wall" as a result of an "epidemic of unprecedented domestic terrorism." According to President Nixon, "Hoover had become frightened by the temper of the times [that] was turning against him and was determined not to give anyone ammunition in his last years to damage him or his organization." (76)

Hoover in 1971 refused to carry out operations that he had rationalized and sanctioned for over fifty years. Nixon and White House aides H. R. Haldeman and John Ehrlichman had become quite impatient and were in agreement that Hoover must go. As Nixon mentioned in this introduction, "We've got to avoid the situation where he could leave with a blast. . . . If he does go, he's got to go of his own volition." Ehrlichman described the situation:

> The concern with image, the cultism, has finally taken its toll. Virtually any genuine innovation or imaginative approach is stifled. . . Morale of FBI agents in the field has deteriorated badly. . . . All clandestine activities have been terminated. Liaison with the intelligence community has been disrupted and key men forced out. . . . Hoover has reportedly threatened the President. (77)

Evidently, Hoover had actually attempted to blackmail President Nixon. And if John Ehrlichman's statement is accurate, the deeper question is, with what secret would Hoover have blackmailed the President?

With J. Edgar Hoover's death in May 1972, Richard Nixon's concerns over Hoover's possible threats disappeared. One tantalizing clue as to where Hoover might have attacked Nixon is made clear from a transcript from the Watergate Tapes.

President Nixon and Haldeman, 10:04-11:39 a.m., Oval Office, June 23, 1972:

> *President Nixon.* Of course, this . . . Hunt, . . . that will uncover a lot of, a lot of—you open that scab there's a hell of a lot of things in it that we just feel that this would be very detrimental to have this thing go any further. This involves these Cubans, Hunt, and a lot of hanky-panky that we have nothing to do with ourselves. (78)

> *President Nixon.* When you get in these people . . . say: "Look, the problem is that this will open the whole, the whole Bay of Pigs thing, and the President just feels that"—without going into details—don't, don't lie to them to the extent to say there is no involvement, but just say this is sort of a comedy of errors, bizarre, without getting into it. "The President's belief

is that this is going to open the whole Bay of Pigs things up again. And because these people are plugging for, for keeps, and that they should call the FBI in and say that we wish for the country, don't go any further into this case," period. . . (79)

Later in the day, Nixon and Haldeman return to the topic of E. Howard Hunt and the "Bay of Pigs."

June 23, 1972: President Nixon and Haldeman, 1:04-1:13 p.m. Oval Office:

President Nixon. " . . . Hunt . . . knows too damn much and he was involved, we have to know that. And that it gets out . . . this is all involved in the Cuban Thing, that it's a fiasco and it's going to make the FBI—ah CIA—look bad, it's going to make Hunt look bad, and it's likely to blow the whole, uh, Bay of Pigs thing, which we think would be very unfortunate for the CIA and for the Country at this time, and for American foreign policy, and he's just gotta tell'em "lay off . . ." (80)

June 23, 1972: President Nixon and Haldeman 2:20-2:45 p.m., Oval Office:

Haldeman.   . . . it tracks back to the Bay of Pigs. It tracks back to some other—if the leads run out to people who had no involvement in this except by contact or connection, but it gets to areas that are bound to be raised . . . The whole problem of this, this fellow Hunt—so at that point [CIA Director Richard] Helms kind of got the picture. . . . and he said . . . he said, "We'll be very happy to be helpful.... and we'll handle anything, we'll do anything you want. . . ." (81)

July 1, 1972: President Nixon and White House aide Charles Colson, 8:50-9:05 a.m., Oval Office:

President Nixon. Well, I don't agree. If anything ever happens to him [Hunt], be sure that he blows the whistle, the whole Bay of Pigs. (82)

H. R. Haldeman offers an interesting commentary on President Nixon and the "original" Bay of Pigs operation that was planned before the 1960 election while Nixon was vice-president:

Apparently Nixon knew more about the genesis of the Cuban invasion that led to the Bay of Pigs than almost anyone. Recently, the man who was President of Costa Rica at that

time dealing with Nixon while the invasion was being
prepared—stated that Nixon was the man who originated the
Cuban invasion. . . .(83)

Haldeman offers this fascinating analysis of Nixon and the
Kennedy assassination: "It seems that in all of those Nixon
references to the Bay of Pigs, he was actually referring to the
Kennedy assassination." (84)

What Haldeman really meant about Nixon and his
references to the Bay of Pigs has never been made clear. Did
Richard Nixon have any inside information on the Kennedy
assassination? Why would the UPR66 Headline SR1207 PCS
(live wire ticker) from November 22 report, "Former Vice-
President Richard Nixon says he believes President Kennedy
may find a replacement for Vice-President Johnson next
year." Should any significance be given to Richard Nixon
making this statement to the press just before he flew out of
Dallas on the morning of November 22 and just prior to the
motorcade beginning its trip through Dallas?

The questionable pardoning of Richard Nixon by Gerald
Ford forever shut the door to any public questioning of Nixon
on the Bay of Pigs. As a result of his pardoning of Nixon and
numerous other questionable statements and actions, a re-
evaluation of Gerald Ford is necessary. Ford is often pictured
as the president who brought "calm" to the nation after the
trauma of civil rights, assassinations, Vietnam, and
Watergate, as his book, *A Time to Heal,* attempts to reflect.
But an argument can be made, that in reality, Gerald Ford
was a prime force in closing the door and ushering in an era of
doubt and deceit.

Author David Scheim writes:

> . . .As reported in *Time* on February 4, 1974, "After meeting
> with Nixon for nearly two hours, Vice President Gerald Ford
> declared that the White House was in possession of evidence
> that 'will exonerate the President' of complicity in the
> conspiracy to conceal the origins of the Watergate wiretap-
> burglary. When asked what the evidence was, Ford replied
> that the President had offered to show it to him, but he had
> 'not had time' to look at it." (85)

William Sullivan concluded:

> Hoover was delighted when Ford was named to the Warren
> Commission. The Director wrote in one of his internal memos

that the bureau could expect Ford to "look after FBI interests: and he did, keeping us fully advised of what was going on behind closed doors. He was our . . . informant on the Warren Commission. (86)

Ford has since denied these charges and Sullivan was unable to be interviewed by the House Select Committee on Assassinations to verify his statements. Sullivan was mistaken for a deer and shot during a "hunting accident" in 1978. (87) Future Assistant FBI Director Cartha DeLoach supported Sullivan's claims in the following memo written on December 12, 1963: "Ford indicated he would keep me thoroughly advised as to the activities of the Commission on a confidential basis." (88)

William Sullivan had also believed that Ford had been close to Hoover since his early days in the House:

Gerald Ford was a friend of Hoover's and he first proved it when he made a speech not long after he came to Congress recommending a pay raise for J. Edgar Hoover, the great director of the FBI. He proved it again when he tried to impeach Supreme Court Justice William O. Douglas, a Hoover enemy. (89)

Robert Oswald, brother of Lee, stated, "Gerry Ford struck me as a very ambitious young man who saw his assignment on the Commission as an opportunity to get some public attention. The way he walked, the way he talked, his entire manner seemed to bear out this interpretation." (90) Edward Epstein, author of *Inquest*, described how Ford attempted to insert a more definite conclusion of the veracity of the single bullet theory in the Warren Commission's final conclusions. "Ford wanted to state that there was 'compelling' evidence. John McCloy finally suggested that the adjective 'persuasive' be used and this word was agreed upon." (91) As recently as 1993, Ford stated, "The staff report said that there was no conspiracy . . . the commission found no evidence of conspiracy, foreign or domestic . . . I have seen no evidence since then—that would indicate to me that there was a conspiracy." (92)

Author Sylvia Meagher explained how Ford was able to exert more influence on the Commission's conclusions than any other member. "During the Warren Commission hearings, Ford served as House Minority Leader. He had been the single most active Warren Commission member. He attended the questioning of more commission witnesses than any other member." (93)

This research has clearly documented that a number of federal agencies, not the least being Hoover's FBI, failed to fully cooperate with the Warren Commission, the House Select Committee, and the Assassination Records and Review Board. Yet while Gerald Ford was president, the Washington *Post* reported on May 30, 1976, that Ford had stated on May 29, that he not only still firmly believed the Warren Commission conclusions, but also believed the Commission "got full cooperation of all Federal Agencies at the time." Ford indicated that he saw no reason to question the performance of either agency (FBI or CIA) in investigating the Kennedy murder.

The December 1994 issue of *Vanity Fair* offers a description of Ford that would have reflected J. Edgar Hoover's conclusions on November 22, 1963: "Warren Commission member and future President Gerald Ford declared early on, the 'monumental record of the President's Commission will stand like a Gibraltar of factual literature through the ages to come.'" (94) It is doubtful if any statement regarding the assassination of President Kennedy could be disputed any more than Ford's "Gibraltar" declaration. Gerald Ford could do himself and the nation a service by at least admitting the obvious, he and others involved in the investigation of the assassination were not attempting to find the truth, but rather to calm the public.

The Associated Press on July 2, 1997, published an article which stated,

> Mr. Ford, who was a member of the commission, wanted a change to show that the bullet entered Kennedy 'at the back of his neck' rather than in his uppermost back, as the commission originally wrote. Mr. Ford said today that the change was intended to clarify meaning, not alter history. (95)

The record presented here differs greatly from Gerald Ford's rationalization for moving the location of the wound. Any student of the investigation realizes that the location of the back wound is crucial evidence in determining whether the single bullet theory was plausible. Mr. Ford's attempts to move the location of the wound, do in fact, represent an attempt to rewrite history in an attempt to confirm J. Edgar Hoover's lone assassin conclusion. Again, it would do all

Americans a service, for Mr. Ford to admit that J. Edgar Hoover might have influenced or taken advantage of him. It seems clear that this is most probably what happened, otherwise, Ford was knowingly involved in a coverup. If this is true, one has to truly wonder where all this really ends.

When analyzing the information compiled for this study, two main themes have emerged. The first was the obvious public impact that J. Edgar Hoover had on the anti-communist movement and the second, his incredible ability to maintain power and influence for over fifty years. If one has to choose the single most important figure in the history of anti-Communism, it would arguably be J. Edgar Hoover. He was certainly the most durable and the one with the furthest reach. Although the public impact he created was always there, the private web of relationships that created the public view has not been made clear. That being said, one still cannot accept the assumption that secrecy was the sole basis for the success he achieved.

Many of Hoover's successful operations were not fully exposed to public scrutiny but they were widely known and accepted within certain government circles. From 1940 until his death, there were more references to Hoover (almost all were laudatory) in the "Congressional Record" than to any other person. (96) It appears that the majority of Hoover's activities were conducted in full view of the entire nation. The public was truly frightened (although the threat was exaggerated) by the spread of Communism across Europe and in the United States after 1919. Citizens were legitimately concerned as a result of the Depression and the threat of Nazi sabotage during World War II. The rise of the Soviet Union, communist China, and North Korea led to the real fear of nuclear war. Hoover's Cold War on these fronts were all known, understood, and generally accepted by the American people. He was greatly aided over the years in promoting these publicly accepted battles by his ability to understand the right political and media levers to manipulate. Over the years, journalists such as Rex Collier, George Sokolsky, Drew Pearson, Walter Winchell, and Ralph De Toledano were privy to information that Hoover would want dispensed. Hoover's ability to maintain a positive public persona with key members of the military, Congress, various Presidents, and other branches of government often by discreet applications of "sensitive information" was also very important. Herein lies the key; invariably J. Edgar Hoover controlled the dissemination of information. Disclosing the successful operations for public consumption was all well and good, but the evidence is overwhelming that Hoover would not face up and be accountable for his operations that failed and/or were contrary to the best interests of a democracy.

From this research, we learn of his questionable and/or illegal activities during the Palmer Raids, associations with and protection of organized crime figures, ruining careers during the McCarthy period, and obstruction of justice during his work for the Warren Commission. The claims of Cartha DeLoach not withstanding, there is too much accumulated evidence to believe that he was not, in fact, keeping secret derogatory files on individuals and groups with the intention of destroying those that questioned him. His friendships and associations with wealthy, reactionary, and often shady figures makes one wonder where his true interests, associations, and priorities were.

A major problem one confronts when trying to analyze Hoover's operations and associations was his ability to deny responsibility via inter-agency involvement or outright deniability. William W. Turner, former FBI agent of ten years, documents the vast number of ex-agents who worked for other intelligence agencies, various police forces, the corporate world, or entered politics. (97)

When the CIA was formed in the late forties, many FBI agents moved to the rival agency, including some who would prove important to the Warren Report and House Select Committee investigations such as Winston Scott, William Harvey, and Guy Bannister. According to William Corson, author of *Armies of Ignorance,* Hoover did not bemoan these losses; in some cases he secretly arranged them. Even those who were not witting spies for the Director usually maintained their fraternal old-boy-network ties with the Bureau and, if the need arose, could be called upon for assistance. (98) This corroborates William Sullivan's claim that "Hoover continued the FBI office in Mexico as usual (pre-1947)." (99)

The ability of J. Edgar Hoover to cloud his associations and operations combined with his vindictiveness to destroy those who opposed him, makes one wonder how far the tentacles of his power truly spread. Michael Milan claimed to be a member of a super secret group personally hired by J. Edgar

Hoover to carry out assassinations in conjunction with the Mafia and the Office of Strategic Service (OSS) (WWII forerunner of the CIA). This group operated from 1947 until 1971 and died with the death of Hoover himself. According to Milan, Hoover believed that the courts of the United States did not administer justice as they should. (100) These charges are difficult to substantiate, but even if true, they would be almost impossible to prove. However, Milan's accusations do have some credible support. U. S. Navy Captain Anthony J. Marsloe, of the Office of Naval Intelligence, has described the relationship between organized crime and the U.S. military during World War II. Marsloe recounted his description of how "Operation Underworld" worked. This operation involved using American Mafia as well as Sicilian Mafia during the invasions of Sicily and Italy during World War II. Marsloe also described how the head of the New York Bureau of Investigation, Frank Hogan, proved that the U. S. military and other U. S. intelligence services employed the mob in assassinations and therefore cooperated with them and strengthened the Mafia. (101)

Much evidence has been presented that casts a deep shadow of suspicion on the involvement of organized crime in Kennedy's death. There can be little doubt that elements of organized crime were somehow involved in the assassination; but as stated in Chapter 7 and throughout this research, there appears to have been other elements at work. The House Select Committee concluded:

> The conspiratorial and potentially violent climate created by the Cuban issue in the early 1960's, in particular the possible consequences of the CIA-Mafia assassination plots against Castro, and their concealment from officials of the Kennedy administration, [The Committee also noted] . . .
> The potential significance of specific threats identified by the Secret Service during 1963, and their possible relationship to the ultimate assassination of the President. (102)

The House Select Committee adds further support to the possibility that the Secret Service had uncovered the strong likelihood of an anti-Castro-organized crime partnership in the assassination of the President.

the Acting Special Agent-in-Charge of the Chicago field office to write an urgent memorandum indicating he had received reliable information of "a group in the Chicago area who *[sic]* may have a connection with the J.F.K. assassination." The memorandum was based on a tip from an informant who reported a conversation on November 21, 1963, with a Cuban activist names Homer S. Echevarria. They were discussing an illegal arms sale, and Echevarria was quoted as saying his group now had "plenty of money" and that his backers would proceed "as soon as we take care of Kennedy." . . .Following the initial memorandum, the Secret Service instructed its informant to continue his association with Echevarria and notified the Chicago FBI office. It learned that Echevarria might have been a member of the 30th of November anti-Castro organization, that he was associated with Juan Francisco Blanco-Fernandez, military director of the DRE, and that the arms deal was being financed through one Paulino Sierra Martinez by hoodlum elements in Chicago and elsewhere. . . . Although the Secret Service recommended further investigation, the FBI initially took the position that the Echevarria case "was primarily a protection matter and that the continued investigation would be left to the U.S. Secret Service," and that the Cuban group in question was probably not involved in illegal activities. The Secret Service initially was reluctant to accept this position, since it had developed evidence that illegal acts were, in fact, involved. Then, on November 29, 1963, President Johnson created the Warren Commission and gave the FBI primary investigative responsibility in the assassination. Based on its initial understanding that the President's order meant primary, not exclusive, investigative responsibility, the Secret Service continued its efforts; but when the FBI made clear that it wanted the Secret Service to terminate its investigation, it did so, turning over its files to the FBI. The FBI, in turn, did not pursue the Echevarria case. (103)

Agents Joseph Noonan, and fellow Chicago agent Maurice Martineau, added their personal involvement in the anti-Castro link to the assassination in this account described by Vincent Palamara:

[Noonan] participated directly in surveillance involving Tom Mosely and Homer Echevarria. . . . he and [the] other agents were uneasy that the Cubans might have some ties to the CIA. . . . a little later they received a call from Headquarters to drop everything on Mosely and Echevarria and send all memos, files, and their notebooks to Washington and not to discuss the case with anyone. (104)

The House Select Committee did go on and conclude that anti-Castro Cubans did have the motive and means to assassinate President Kennedy. (105)   What is also interesting is that Warren Commission Staff Attorneys W. P. David Slawson and William Coleman wrote a memo reflecting the very real possibility that anti-Castro groups might have set-up Oswald as a patsy to justify an invasion of Cuba. (106) This possibility was ignored in the final Warren Commission Report, strongly indicating that this part of the investigation should have been given a high priority.

The belief, that only through the assassination of President Kennedy could a free Cuba be again restored, was not just idle speculation. In April 1963, a bitter anti-Kennedy flyer was delivered to the Cuban community in Miami. The flyer stated:

> Only through one development will you Cuban patriots ever live again in your homeland as freeman. . . . [only] if an inspired Act of God should place in the White House within weeks a Texan known to be a friend of all Latin Americans . . . though he must under present conditions bow to the Zionists who since 1905 came into control of the United States, and for whom Jack Kennedy and Nelson Rockefeller and other members of the Council of Foreign Relations and allied agencies are only stooges and pawns. Though Johnson must now bow to these craft and cunning Communist-hatching Jews, yet, did an Act of God suddenly elevate him into the top position [he] would revert to what his beloved father and grandfather were, and to their values and principles, and loyalties. (107)

Other possible links to Homer Echevarria, Thomas Mosely, and the 30th of November anti-Castro group were also ignored. The record strongly indicates that Echevarria and Mosely were involved in gun-running and narcotics trafficking with organized crime associates from Chicago. It is quite possible that these associations might have linked the world of Jack Ruby, Rose Cheramie, Marita Lorenz and/or Thomas Eli Davis. All of these individuals have documented ties with narcotics and drug smuggling as well as ties to organized crime.

One of the most troubling aspects of the Echevarria information is that J. Edgar Hoover and Lyndon Johnson were responsible for limiting and eventually shutting down the Secret Service investigation into the activities and relationships of Echevarria, Mosely and their associates. This refusal to investigate promising leads only adds to the suspicions directed towards Johnson and Hoover.

Further support of anti-Castro involvement in the assassination comes from FBI informant Garrett Trapnell. Trapnell was heavily involved in anti-Castro Cuban exile activity in Texas and Louisiana in the early 1960's. Trapnell supports the belief that anti-Castro groups should have been properly investigated before and after the assassination of President Kennedy. According to Warren Commission Document 196, and other documents in the National Archives, Trapnell told the FBI that a kidnap/assassination attempt that was scheduled against Robert Kennedy for August 19, 1963, was switched in September to a 1963 assassination plot against John F. Kennedy. (108) On August 29, 1963, Trapnell was interviewed by the FBI who reiterated his previous statements of a plot to kidnap and/or kill Robert Kennedy. He "protested that he was telling the truth and that he really cared for the life of the Kennedy family." (109) Trapnell went on to say, "I think the FBI had their hand and glove in what happened to Kennedy. The fact that they knew about it, and didn't stop it. That's what I believe." (110)

Groups such as the World Anti-Communist League, the China Anti-Communist Liberty Lobby, the United States Anti-Communist Lobby, etc. were made up of members who were of the same mindset as Hoover. One man who worked for many of these groups was Major General Charles Willoboughy, who was a long-standing personal friend of J. Edgar Hoover. (111) The extreme and fanatical views and operations of Willoboughy and these groups has been documented in the books *Inside the League* by Scott and John Lee Anderson and Dick Russell's *The Man Who Knew Too Much*.

One of the more interesting groups that J. Edgar Hoover was undoubtedly aware of, was the Congress of Freedom (COF). There is strong evidence to support the belief that within this organization were powerful and wealthy groups and individuals who believed that President Kennedy was a "traitor" in his dealing with Communism and the communist world. Information obtained from informants who attended the April 1963 Congress of Freedom meetings in New Orleans indicate that certain members of the Congress of Freedom were planning to use the "criminal element" to carry out political assassinations.

A notarized statement dated April 10, 1963, was dictated to a court reporter by Detective Lochart F. Gracey, Jr. and addressed to Detective Sergeant C. H. Sapp of the Intelligence Unit of the Miami police department and to Richard E. Gerstein, State Attorney, Dade County, Florida. This statement describes Gracey's information about a group of right-wing extremists who at least talked a great deal about political assassinations:

On April 4, 5, and 6 of 1963, the Congress of Freedom, Inc., held an annual meeting at the Fontainebleau Motel-Hotel in New Orleans, Louisiana. This was different in that for the past twelve years the same organization, under the same and different leaderships, had met somewhere within the United States for their annual conference.

The second phase of this program was the setting up of a criminal activity to assassinate particular persons and groups of persons throughout the United States which are or have been in the process of formulating the policy of these United States through various governmental agencies, in particular the Council on Foreign Relations.

. . . in a generalized feeling, there was indicated the overthrow of the present government of the United States in that, as members of the Congress of Freedom, Inc., they did not and do not believe in the policies of the United States as they have been formulated between the administrations of Dwight Eisenhower and John F. Kennedy.

At this meeting of the Congress of Freedom there were in attendance high ranking industrialists, bankers, insurance executives, men and women generally that have access to great amounts of money. . .

. . . The informer states that for practically fifteen to twenty years he has been involved in outfits such as this and it is his considered opinion that for assassinations through rifles, dynamite and other types of devices, this is the worst outfit that he has ever come across. Membership within the Congress of Freedom, Inc. contain high ranking members of the Armed Forces that secretly belong to the organization. . . . although there is nothing definite in actual words that have been spoken, it is the feeling of the informer that this group believes that under President Kennedy, the government of the United States this year will be placed under the United Nations in some capacity and such sponsorship will rest in the Council of Foreign Relations, and it is at that time that this so-called inner circle will begin the assassination. . . . (112)

FBI documents (MM 157-739) obtained under the Freedom of Information Act (FOIA No. 381480) relating to the Congress of Freedom relay the informant's further descriptions of the Congress of Freedom meetings in New Orleans April 4, 5, and 6, 1963. These FBI documents support the notarized statement offered by Detective Gracey:

> For approximately fifteen to twenty years, he has attended a number of conventions and meetings of different organizations and the COF and groups which have allied themselves with this organization are the most dedicated group of individuals he has ever come across. The source noted that at many of the conventions and meetings of other groups which he has attended in the past, there was always a great amount of drinking and "raising hell" but this was not the case at this convention in New Orleans. He noted that most of the individuals attending the convention stayed at the Fontainebleau Motel-Hotel in New Orleans and that he did not observe any of these individuals sitting around bars or "raising hell" and it appeared to him that these individuals were attending the convention strictly on business. . . .
>
> The source noted that in his opinion, approximately 75% of the COF members are also members of the John Birch Society and that any action by the COF regarding assassinations would have the sanction of the John Birch Society. (113)

The mention of possible involvement with the John Birch Society causes one to remember the Warren Commission testimony of Jack Ruby. During his testimony, Ruby implicated both the John Birch Society and General Edwin Walker in the assassination of President Kennedy. The statements by Detective Gracey add more credibility to Ruby's assertions. Further support of the Congress of Freedom's dislike of President Kennedy and his policies is found on pages 72-82 of the FBI documents which detail interviews with various COF members. The consensus indicated their personal beliefs that President Kennedy was turning the United States over to the Communists. As noted in Chapter 7, the prediction of Kennedy's assassination by Congress of Freedom participant Joseph Milteer on November 9, 1963, was ignored by both the FBI and the Secret Service in Dallas.

Willie Sommerset was a childhood friend of Joseph Milteer and also an FBI informant who convinced Detective Sergeant C. H. Sapp and Miami Police Detective Everrett Kay to tape-record a meeting between Milteer and Sommerset on November 9, 1963. Sommerset, in early 1962, told Circuit Judge Seymour Gelber, later the mayor of Miami Beach that, "Those people [Congress of Freedom] are people of means, financially, and educationally . . . I will bet my head on a chopping block there will be some people killed by this time next year and it will be in high places." (114) Miami Police Detective Everrett Kay was in charge of the surveillance program involving informant Willie Sommerset and Joseph Milteer. Kay was responsible for installing a recording device in Sommerset's apartment. Detective Kay stated, "No particular city [was] mentioned" on the tape in regards to where the assassination was to take place. For this reason Kay and his men were concerned that an assassination attempt against President Kennedy was a real possibility with the President's impending visit to Miami on November 18. Kay recalled:

> . . . the close proximity of a tape being made in his [Kennedy's] visit made [for] quite a few changes in the security. They changed the motorcade and I believe he was helicoptered rather than have a motorcade. . . . There was a drastic change in the procedure. He wasn't as accessible in this city as he might have been in the past. (115)

Not only did the Dallas motorcade take place despite the concerns noted by Detective Kay, but as noted in Chapter 13 there appears to have been a form of "security stripping"—in Dallas despite the knowledge and possession of Joseph Milteer's recording. Miami Detective Kay made clear that "no specific city was mentioned;" security should have been strengthened in Dallas and not lessened. There appears to have been a deliberate and successful attempt to limit the flow of information on the possibility of threats to the President in Dallas. Despite evidence of canceled motorcades in Chicago and Miami, as well as the recorded threat of Joseph Milteer, no known threats were passed on to the Secret Service in Dallas. (116) According to Secret Service Agent Roy Kellerman it was "unusual" for the Secret Service to not have any reports of possible threats before a presidential visit to a particular city. (117)

The November 9, 1963 recording of Milteer and Sommerset revealed that there was a plot to kill President Kennedy, "from an office building with a high powered rifle . . . it is in the works. . . . They wouldn't leave any stone unturned there, no way. They will pick up somebody within hours afterwards. . . . just to throw the public off . . . somebody is going to have to go to jail." (118) On Saturday, November 23, the day after the assassination, Milteer called Sommerset and stated, "Everything ran true to form. I guess you thought I was kidding. . . . The patriots have outsmarted the Communist group in order that the Communists would carry out the plan without the right-wing becoming involved." (119)

Former FBI agent Don Adams related to writer Bob Dyer (and to this author) his surveillance and subsequent arrest of Joseph Milteer after the assassination of President Kennedy:

> On November 14, 1963, while serving in an FBI office in southern Georgia, he began to track a wealthy white supremacist named Joseph A Milteer. Milteer, a ringleader of the White Citizens Council had been distributing vitriolic anti-Kennedy literature for months. Don Adams followed Milteer, interviewed him, put together a profile and turned it in to his superiors.
>
> Only days later, JFK was gunned down. Within an hour of the assassination, Adams was summoned by his bosses and told to track down and detain Milteer. In a guilt-ridden frenzy, Don Adams checked all of Milteer's usual haunts and couldn't find him. He feared he had let an assassin slip through his grip. When Oswald was arrested a short time later, Adams let out a sigh of relief.
>
> Finally, five days after the assassination, Milteer returned to the area. Adams immediately nabbed him and turned him over to the Secret Service for questioning. The Secret Service quickly released him. . . .
>
> The tape, made by an FBI informant, resulted in the cancellation of a Kennedy motorcade scheduled for Nov. 18 in Miami. "When I read about that tape recording, I was devastated," Adams says. "I said, 'Why didn't people let us know?'"
>
> It was the FBI's ironclad policy to funnel all information about a suspect to the office in the suspect's home district. But nobody in Miami sent word of the incident to Atlanta. As a result, Adams' supposedly definitive work-up on Milteer was sadly lacking. "Had I known that, I would have never ever recommended the president go there [to Dallas]," Adams says. "My whole investigation would have been completely different." He also can't understand why an FBI colleague in Atlanta would later say Milteer was in Georgia on the day of the assassination. Adams was the agent charged with trying to find Milteer; he couldn't. (120)

Adams related to this author that the FBI report stating Milteer was at his home in Quitman, Georgia during the assassination is totally false. Adams was in charge of the surveillance program of Milteer's home and confirmed that Milteer could not be accounted for until his return to Quitman four days after Kennedy's assassination.

Agent Adams concluded, "'I love the FBI,' he says. 'My life has been the FBI. When we put a package together to do a job, we did a job. . . Why the hell this one can't be solved is beyond me. My question is, do they want to solve it? Here we are 35 years later and we're no farther than we were in 1963.'" (121)

Unfortunately for Don Adams and other loyal members of the FBI, they were not privy to the machinations of their boss, J. Edgar Hoover. A Teletype sent from the Special Agent in charge of the FBI office in Atlanta to FBI Director J. Edgar Hoover states the contents of an interview with Joseph Milteer on 11/28/63:

> Joseph Adams Milteer, Quitman, GA. Interviewed tonight at Valdosta, GA, RA. advised during April sixty three he attended national meeting of 'Congress of Freedom' at New Orleans, LA. Milteer denies he or anyone in his presence at New Orleans discussed the elimination of President Kennedy by assassination. (122)

J. Edgar Hoover had possession of Joseph Milteer's tape recorded prediction of President Kennedy's assassination. He also knew that Milteer's description "dovetailed" nicely with the actual events in Dealy Plaza; why would he accept Milteer's denials? It is entirely possible that the role of J. Edgar Hoover, in the assassination, was to direct the flow of information before, during, and after the murder. He most probably found a willing ally in Lyndon Johnson. Despite the preponderance of circumstantial evidence, it appears highly doubtful that Johnson and Hoover were the prime movers in the plot, although it is possible. There can be little doubt that in their positions at the top of the chain of command on November 22 and during the Warren Commission investigation, they facilitated a successful coverup of the assassination. However, it appears to have been too risky for either to have initiated the assassination themselves. One would believe there was little need to do so. There appears to have been a number of other powerful forces willing to carry out the assassination. But this does not lessen charges of their possible involvement. It would be reasonable to assume that the real assassins of President Kennedy would have not been successful, as well as remain undetected, without the cooperation of Lyndon Johnson and J. Edgar Hoover.

It is interesting to note the connection between Detective Gracey's statements and those of Private Eugene Dinkin. Dinkin was a U. S. Army cryptographer stationed in Metz, France. As previously presented in Chapter 7, Dinkin had predicted that President Kennedy would be killed by leading elements of the American military. Gracey's notarized statement described how certain "high-ranking members of the U.S. military" were "secretly" involved with the assassination plans of the Congress of Freedom.

The Congress of Freedom also provided a link to the anti-Castro exiles, violent anti-Kennedy racists, and to organized crime. Gracey's statement made clear the goal of the COF to hire "criminal elements" to carry out the assassination. COF members in New Orleans were well aware of Carlos Marcello's hatred of the Kennedys. The New Orleans nexus of Marcello and Guy Bannister's anti-Castro activities would have been a natural fit for the COF.

If Lyndon Johnson and/or J. Edgar Hoover were aware of these relationships, their role as "obstructors of justice" might well have been the extent of their involvement. But as a result of the evidence presented in this research, any definite conclusion seems presumptuous.

A document supporting Private Dinkin's claims was sent to Warren Commission General Counsel J. Lee Rankin on May 19, 1964. The subject of the memorandum was Allegations of Pfc-U.S. Army Relative to Assassination Plot Against President Kennedy as Translated. (123) The documents confirm that Dinkin was absent without leave from his unit in Metz, France on November 6 and 7, 1963, and went to Geneva, Switzerland. Dinkin related his prediction of the impending assassination to a Time-Life stringer named Alex Fontaines.

Page 4 of a report entitled, Re: Eugene B. Dinkin contained the following information:

> [Dinkin] had declined to furnish this information to persons of authority in the United States Army since he believed that the plot against President Kennedy was being set in motion by high ranking members of the military. . . . Since he

believed that the plot consisted in part of throwing blame for the assassination onto "radical left-wing" or "communist" suspects, he stated that the religious tie-in would lead the average citizen to accept more readily the theory that a "communist" committed the crime since "they were an atheistic group anyway.". . . On October 25, 1963, Dinkin went to the United States Embassy at Luxembourg where he stated, he attempted for several hours to see a Mr. Cunningham, the Charge d'Affairs at the Embassy. He stated that he sent word to Mr. Cunningham that he had information concerning a plot to assassinate President Kennedy, and at one point spoke to Mr. Cunningham by phone. . . . Following this incident, Dinkin was notified by his superiors that he was to undergo psychiatric evaluation on November 5, 1963. Due to this pending development, Dinkin said he went absent without leave to Geneva Switzerland where he attempted to present his theory to the editor of the Geneva Diplomat, a newspaper published in Geneva Switzerland. . . . Dinkin advised that on his return to the custody of the United States Army in November 1963, he was held in detention. Mr. Dinkin advised that he had undergone numerous psychiatric tests at Walter Reed Army Hospital in Washington, D.C. He stated that he was aware that the Army psychiatrist had declared him to be "psychotic" and "paranoid." Dinkin advised that he first became aware of this "plot" to assassinate President Kennedy in September 1963. (124)

Could the strange death of intelligence agent and arms expert J. Gary Underhill be related to his knowledge of a military-CIA plot to assassinate President Kennedy? *Ramparts* reported in June 1967 that Underhill reportedly told friends and family:

. . . A small clique within the CIA was responsible for the assassination, he [Gary Underhill] confided, and he was afraid for his life and probably would have to leave the country. Less than six months later Underhill was found shot to death in his Washington apartment. The coroner ruled it suicide. J. Garret Underhill had been an intelligence agent during World War II and was a recognized authority on limited warfare and small arms. A researcher and writer on military affairs, he was on a first-name basis with many of the top brass in the Pentagon. He was also on intimate terms with a number of high-ranking CIA officials. . . . The verdict of suicide in Underhill's death is by no means convincing. His body was found by a writing collaborator, Asher Brynes of the

New Republic.

The death of Underhill has never been properly analyzed. It is possible that his personal knowledge of those involved in Kennedy's murder led to his death—we most probably will never know for sure.

There can be little doubt that J. Edgar Hoover was aware of the predictions of President Kennedy's assassination by Eugene Dinkin and Joseph Milteer. Hoover was also well aware of the documented warnings noted by Richard Nagell (Chapter 7) and Garrett Trapnell. In fact, in each of the four predictions mentioned here, the FBI was directly involved in investigating the threats. The evidence presented here is clear, J. Edgar Hoover at the very least was negligent in not helping to prevent the assassination. On the other hand, it is quite possible that Hoover was actively involved in "facilitating" the assassination. Historians today should note that it is difficult to prove Hoover's involvement but that a strong possibility exists that he may have been. Because of the power and fear generated by Hoover while alive and the lack of documentation since his death, this, unfortunately, is all that can be said for sure.

House Majority leader Hale Boggs told Jack Anderson:

> No one would dare question J. Edgar Hoover's fitness for duty, Boggs said . . . because the FBI had files on everybody. Hoover could open up Washington's most exalted closets, with a great rattling of skeletons. "Anyone who takes him on will be destroyed," Boggs said, knowingly. He described how Hoover engaged in delicate blackmail to hold the nations' leaders in his sway. The venerable lawman would place a friendly call to a high muck-a-muck, learning that enemies had gotten wind of some deep, dark transgression but that the FBI could be counted on to make sure the secret stayed safely buried. It wouldn't be necessary to ask that Hoover might occasionally need a favor in return. What Hale Boggs told me was hardly a surprise. But here was the House majority leader confessing that the nations elected leaders, including himself, were afraid to offend Hoover. (126)

Former FBI agent William Turner wrote:

> Few would question J. Edgar Hoover's status as the father figure of theological anticommunism. . . . In recognition of this role, he has been showered with honors. In 1961, the Valley

Forge Freedom Foundation gave him its annual award for "writings alerting the American people to the dangers of Communism." In 1964 he was named "American of the Year" by the Americanism Educational League, a right-wing organization based in Southern California. The ultimate accolade came in 1968 from the Cuban Anticommunist Journalist Association in Miami, an exile group that is violently anti-Castro. It named him "The Man of the Century." The list goes on and on. (127)

Turner added this description of Hoover's right-wing ties:

Invoking Hoover's magic name was standard procedure with right-wing propagandists. In his tract *None Dare Call It Treason,* widely distributed by the hard-core elements behind Barry Goldwater, author John A. Stormer reverently quoted the Director on Communism no less than seventeen times, and on the jacket is his summons to arms: "We are at war with Communism and the sooner every red-blooded American realizes this, the safer we will be." *Fin-Pro News,* the periodical of a reactionary group within the Los Angeles police department, likewise called on Hoover's authority. "FBI Chief J. Edgar Hoover's warnings that this nation's youth is the number one target of the Communist Party have been confirmed by accelerated Party activity." (128)

Hoover's extreme right-wing ties have resulted in further charges against the Director. A number of recent books have been written that attempt to document the FBI's questionable role in Martin Luther King's death. *Orders to Kill,* by William Pepper, charges the FBI with accessory to murder in the King assassination. Earl Hutchinson wrote in the December 14, 1999 edition of the *Cleveland Plain Dealer* that Hoover's FBI files are still the place to look for clues to the King assassination:

The King family and those who sincerely want to get to the truth about the King murder would be better served by publicly campaigning for the FBI to open its files, which were ordered sealed for 50 years by a federal court in 1977. If the court refuses, then public pressure should be put on Attorney General Janet Reno to increase the scope of the limited investigation that she ordered at the bequest of the family and appoint an independent counsel. (129)

In a further attempt to find out more about "Mr. Secrets,"

the Assassination Records and Review Board, in 1996, attempted to locate more of Hoover's FBI files:

> Public speculation regarding the alleged secret files of FBI Director J. Edgar Hoover is widespread. Of course, following Hoover's death, his personal secretary, Helen Gandy, destroyed many of his "Personal and Confidential" files, so that the full extent of Hoover's Personal files will never be known. . . . The Review Board also requested and received from the FBI access to the files of Clyde Tolson, which consisted solely of original memoranda from Director Hoover. Unfortunately, the chronological file started with January 1965, and the FBI could not account for any 1963-64 files that Tolson may have maintained. (130)

The description of Hoover as given by Senator James Buckley summarizes the apologist view of Ralph de Toledano:

> I am convinced that the criticism made of J. Edgar Hoover during recent years tells us more about the intellectual and moral values of the critics and of the current level of public debate in America than it does about Mr. Hoover. . . . What will remain and what will continue to shape the FBI for years to come is his vision of public service as one of the highest vocations. (131)

This view is echoed from the words of Hoover during his last appearance before the House Appropriations subcommittee in 1972. "Mr. Chairman [old friend Representative John Rooney], I have a philosophy: You are honored by your friends and you are distinguished by your enemies. I have been very distinguished." (132) Ovid Demaris concurred when he wrote: "Yes, indeed, distinguished and honored, in a career that spanned nearly one-third of our history as a nation. He was, whatever his failings, an extraordinary man, truly one of a kind." (133)

The critics of Hoover would not rest on Demaris' conclusion. Hank Messick wrote:

> Hoover used his power to enhance his reputation and that of the FBI. Sworn to defend the country, he was unable to distinguish its true enemies. Posing as a moral leader, he helped to create a generation of cynics. Under the guise of fighting subversion, he encouraged those on the right who distrusted democracy. (134)

Fred Cook echoed the sentiments of Messick with these words:

> The pattern makes it clear that, behind the scenes, loftily above the battle and unsmudged by the battle smoke, Hoover has been the heart and soul of the witch-hunt era. His persistent overestimation of the threat of domestic Communism has been a major factor in creating a national mood of hysteria and unreason. (135)

A final commentary, written by Richard Powers, might be the most enlightening and objective analysis on Hoover:

> The very qualities that made for Hoover's success and popularity encouraged his assaults on political freedom. Those actions, open as well as secret, will permanently stain his record in American history. Hoover's historic legacy is profoundly ambiguous. He achieved his life's goal by destroying American Communism and was a powerful support for traditional values; his covert attack on personal and public enemies violated principles of constitutional limits on government power. (136)

The legacy of J. Edgar Hoover as the *Father of the Cold War* lies in the understanding that even in times of a presumed national emergency, such as the communist threat to our nation's security, the government must obey the law and conduct its duties in a manner open to public scrutiny. As a result of the lack of public scrutiny in regards to J. Edgar Hoover's investigation for the Warren Commission, the American public accepted Lyndon Johnson as the continuance of John Kennedy's legacy. This, in turn, led to a lack of Congressional and public scrutiny into Johnson's Vietnam policies. A nation torn at the seams by the escalation of the Vietnam War was the result.

At the bitter end, *The Father of the Cold War* ended his career with two ironic twists; he kept his position as Director by attempting to intimidate his anti-communist protegé and his last day alive was spent on May Day, the "holy day" for communists throughout the world. As of this writing, Fidel Castro still reigns in Cuba, North and South Korea are still separated over the issue of Communism, Russia has withstood a challenge to return to Communism, and mainland communist China continues to be an economic and military threat. The threat of Communism continues to generate possible threats to American security to this day. The important question to consider is how would the United States respond to a new Cold War. We have a record of how Hoover responded to "his Cold War" for over fifty years. Only time will tell if these methods will be used again. But it is quite doubtful that anyone would influence a new Cold War as did J. Edgar Hoover.

End Notes

Introduction

1. James. D. Bales, ed., memo brief in *J. Edgar Hoover Speaks Concerning Communism* (Washington: Capital Hill Press, 1970), 266-88.

2. *J. Edgar Hoover on Communism* (New York: Random House, 1969), 4.

3. Anthony Summers, *Official and Confidential: The Secret Life of J. Edgar Hoover* (New York: G. P. Putnam and Sons, 1993), 423.

4. Ovid Demaris, *The Director* (New York: Harper's Magazine Press, 1975), 164.

5. Richard Nixon, January 26, 1950 Congressional Record, 81st Cong., 2nd sess., 999-1000.

6. Hale Boggs, April 22, 1971, Congressional Record.

7. Summers, *Official and Confidential,* 9.

8. The White House Transcripts Submission of Recorded Presidential Conversations to the Committee on the Judiciary of the House of Representatives, February 26, 1973 (New York: Bantam Books, 1973), 77-78.

9. House Select Committee on Assassinations, Vol. 2, 1979, 43-53.

10. Jim Marrs, *Crossfire* (New York: Carroll and Graf Publishing, Inc., 1989), 357.

11. Melvin Eisenberg, Warren Commission Internal Memorandum,

February 17, 1964 cited in Bernard Fensterwald and Michael Ewing, *Assassination of JFK: By Coincidence or Conspiracy* (New York: Zebra Books, 1977), 73.

12. *The Memoirs of Richard Nixon* (New York: Warner Books, 1978), 1: 312.

13. BBC Panorama Special: "The Kennedy Assassination: What We Know Now That We Didn't Know Then," 1978, adapted in America to "The Plot To Kill the President."

14. William Manchester, *Death of a President* (New York: Harper and Row, 1967), 717.

15. House Select Committee on Assassinations, Vol. 3, 1979, 471-73.

16. Senate Intelligence Committee Report on the Kennedy Assassination, 1975, 33-35.

17. Ibid., 35.

18. *The Final Assassination Report: Report of the Select Committee on Assassinations,* (New York: Bantam Books, Inc., 1979), 322.

19. Robert S. McNamara, *In Retrospect: The Tragedy and Lessons of Vietnam* (New York: Random House, Inc., 1996), 102.

20. Clark Clifford with Richard Holbrooke, *Council to the President: A Memoir* (New York: Random House, 1991), 381.

21. Lyndon Baines Johnson, *The Vantage Point* (New York: Popular Library, 1971), 42-43.

22. Josiah Thompson, *Six Seconds in Dallas* (New York: Bernard Geis Associates, 1967), 209.

23. FBI document DL-105-18766, cited in *Oswald, the Secret Files,* 94.

24. *Dallas Morning News,* 28 November 1963.

25. Dean Rusk, *As I Saw It* (Middlesex: Penguin Books, 1990), 564.

Chapter 1

1. Albert E. Kahan, *High Treason: The Plot Against the People* (New York: Hour Books, 1950), 127.

2. *New York Post*, 9 March 1935.

3. *Books*, 25 September 1938.

4. *New Republic*, 4 December 1950.

5. *New York Times*, 26 November 1950.

6. *San Francisco Chronicle*, 12 December 1956.

7. *Christian Science Monitor*, 13 December 1956.

8. William Sullivan, *The Bureau: My Thirty Years in Hoover's FBI* (New York: W. W. Norton and Company, 1979), 33-34.

9. *New York Times*, 9 March 1958.

10. Fred J. Cook, *The FBI Nobody Knows* (New York: Pyramid Books, 1964), 53.

11. *New York Times*, 11 October 1964.

12. Cook, *The FBI Nobody Knows*, 36.

13. *Bookweek*, 4 October 1964.

14. Ibid.

15. Norman Ollestad, *Inside the FBI* (New York: Lyle Stuart, 1967), 68, 105.

16. *Library Journal*, 15 May 1970.

17. Ibid., 15 April 1972.

18. Ralph de Toledano, *J. Edgar Hoover: The Man in His Time* (New Rochelle, N.Y.: Arlington House, 1973), 377.

19. *Library Journal*, 1 March 1976.

20. *Christian Century*, 10 December 1975.

21. *Nation*, 20 October 1979.

22. Ibid., 14 January 1984.

23. *Library Journal*, 1 February 1987.

24. *Political Science Quarterly*, (winter, 1989).

25. *Library Journal*, 19 August 1991.

26. Ibid., 1 November 1991.

27. Summers, *Official and Confidential,* 424, 426.

28. Ibid.

29. Robert Unger, *The Union Station Massacre: The Original Sin of J. Edgar Hoover's FBI* (Kansas City, Mo.: Andrews McNeal Publishing Co., 1997), 233.

Chapter 2

1. William Preston, *Aliens and Dissenters, 1903-1933,* (Cambridge, Mass.: Harvard University Press, 1963), 25.

2. Ibid.

3. Ibid.

4. Ibid., 27.

5. Ibid.

6. Richard G. Powers, *Secrecy and Power* (New York: The Free Press, 1987), 9.

7. Ibid., 17.

8. Ibid., 16.

9. Ibid., 31.

10. Ibid., 39.

11. Ibid., 41.

12. Ibid.

13. Cook, *The FBI Nobody Knows*, 53.

14. Ibid., 54.

15. Ibid., 55.

16. Ibid., 57.

17. Ibid.

18. Cited in Ibid.

19. Athan G. Theoharis and John Stuart Cox, *The Boss: J. Edgar Hoover and the Great American Inquisition* (New York: Bantam Books, 1988), 47.

20. Ibid.

21. Ibid.

22. Ibid., 48.

23. Cook, *The FBI Nobody Knows*, 59.

24. Sanford J. Unger, *FBI: An Un-Censored Look Behind the Walls* (Boston: Little, Brown and Company, 1975), 41.

25. Curt Gentry, *J. Edgar Hoover: The Man and the Secrets* (New York: W. W. Norton and Company, 1991), 66.

26. Powers, *Secrecy and Power*, 33.

27. John Higham, *Strangers in the Land: Patterns of American Nativism, 1860-1925* (New York: Atheneum, 1973), 59, 110.

28. Theoharis and Cox, *The Boss*, 46.

29. Powers, *Secrecy and Power*, 68.

30. Hoover Personnel File, FBI 67-561, FOIA Reading Rm; Kidd to Appointment Clerk, July 20, 1917, R G 60, NA.

31. Powers, *Secrecy and Power*, 51.

32. Gentry, *J. Edgar Hoover*, 69.

33. Joan M. Jensen, *The Price of Vigilance* (Chicago: Rand McNally, 1968), 15, 26-27.

34. Department of Justice Memo, O'Brian to Attorney General, October 7, 1918, D J File 190470.

35. Department of Justice Memo, Hoover to O'Brian, December 18, 1917, File 9-16-12-1400, D J Control Files.

36. Cook, *The FBI Nobody Knows*, 66.

37. Gentry, *J. Edgar Hoover*, 73.

38. Ibid.

39. Department of Justice Memo, Hoover to O'Brian, July 3, 1918, D J File 9-16-19-51-290.

40. Cook, *The FBI Nobody Knows,* 66.

41. Ibid., 69.

42. Ibid., 67.

43. Summers, *Official and Confidential*, 39, 103-4.

44. Powers, *Secrecy and Power*, 56.

45. Theoharis and Cox, *The Boss*, 62.

46. Joel Kovel, *Red Hunting in the Promised Land* (New York: Basic Books, 1994), 251.

47. Powers, *Secrecy and Power*, 93.

48. Ibid., 124.

49. Ibid., 61.

50. Preston, *Aliens and Dissenters*, 193-94.

51. Cited in Ibid., 193.

52. Stanley Coben, *A. Mitchell Palmer* (New York: Columbia Univ. Press, 1963), 207.

53. Ibid.

Chapter 3

1. Jensen, *The Price of Vigilance*, 267 and Powers, *Secrecy and Power*, 69.

2. Department of Justice Memo, Creighton to Caminetti, Aug. 7, 1919, D J File 203557-2 and August 20, 1919, D J File 203557-3, R G 60, NA.

3. Cited in Coben, *A. Mitchell Palmer*, 223.

4. Ibid.

5. Ibid.

6. Department of Justice Memo, Creighton to Hoover, December 20, 1919, D J File 203557-63, R G 60, NA.

7. Coben, *A. Mitchell Palmer*, 222.

8. Department of Justice Memo, Hoover to Stone, January 17, 1920, D J File 205492-226, R G 60, NA.

9. Ibid.

10. Cited in Powers, *Secrecy and Power*, 106.

11. Department of Justice File, Shorr to Palmer, November 13, 1919, D J File (Unnumbered) and Hoover to Creighton, December 4, 1917, D J File (Unnumbered).

12. Powers, *Secrecy and Power*, 86.

13. Ibid., 88-89.

14. Department of Justice Memo, Palmer to Grouitch (initialed JEH), April 30, 1920, D J File 202600-59-37, R G 60, NA.

15. Max Lowenthal, *The Federal Bureau of Investigation* (New York: William Sloane Associates, 1950), 172.

16. Department of Justice Memo, Hoover to Burke, February 21, 1920, D J File 186701-14, R G 60, NA and Hoover to Wilson (JEH initialed) January 2, 1920, D J Files 205492-243, R G NA.

17. Department of Justice Memo, Hoover to Caminetti, April 19, 22, 30, 1920, D J Files 2026-00.

18. Department of Justice Memo, Hoover to Palmer, May 25, 1920, D J File 209264.

19. Powers, *Secrecy and Power*, 114.

20. Department of Justice Memo, Hoover to Churchill, January 23, 1920, D J File 205492-294, R G 60, NA.

21. Coben, *A. Mitchell Palmer*, 188.

22. Powers, *Secrecy and Power*, 235.

23. Cited in Gentry, *J. Edgar Hoover*, 98.

24. Ibid., 99.

25. Theoharis and Cox, *The Boss*, 76-77.

26. Summers, *Official and Confidential*, 37.

27. Cited in Cook, *The FBI Nobody Knows*, 103.

28. Cited in Ibid.

29. Cited in Ibid., 104.

30. Cited in Lowenthal, *The Federal Bureau of Investigation*, 191.

31. Ibid., 190.

32. Cited in Ibid., 185-86.

33. Kovel, *Red Hunting in the Promised Land*, 173.

34. Lowenthal, *The Federal Bureau of Investigation*, 210.

35. Ibid., 211.

36. Gentry, *J. Edgar Hoover*, 101.

37. Powers, *Secrecy and Power*, 117.

38. Cited in Cook, *The FBI Nobody Knows*, 103.

39. Powers, *Secrecy and Power*, 120.

40. Cartha DeLoach, *Hoover's FBI* (New York: Regenery Publishing, 1995), 14-15.

41. Cited in *Scholastic Update*, 8 December 1995, 17.

42. Cited in Robert K. Murray, *Red Scare: A Study of National Hysteria, 1919-20* (New York: McGraw Hill Book Company, 1955), 9.

Chapter 4

1. Samuel E. Morrison, *The Oxford History of the American People*

(New York: Oxford University Press, 1965), 886.

2. Cook, *The FBI Nobody Knows*, 119.

3. Cited in Ibid.

4. Theoharis and Cox, *The Boss*, 86.

5. Ibid.

6. Cited in Ibid.

7. Gentry, *J. Edgar Hoover*, 110.

8. William Corson, *The Armies of Ignorance* (New York: Dial Press, 1977), 104.

9. Ibid., 105.

10. Gentry, *J. Edgar Hoover*, 117-18.

11. Ibid., 118.

12. Cited in Kahan, *High Treason*, 75.

13. Cited in Ibid., 74.

14. Gentry, *J. Edgar Hoover*, 120.

15. Kahan, *High Treason*, 72.

16. Cook, *The FBI Nobody Knows*, 126.

17. Carl Anthony, *Florence Harding: The First Lady, The Jazz Age, And the Death of America's Most Scandalous President* (New York: William Morrow and Co., 1998), 293.

18. Ibid., 503.

19. Theoharis and Cox, *The Boss*, 87.

20. Gentry, *J. Edgar Hoover*, 128.

21. Ibid., 124.

22. Cited in Ibid., 125.

23. Powers, *Secrecy and Power*, 164.

24. DeLoach, *Hoover's FBI*, 15.

25. Cited in Powers, *Secrecy and Power*, 165.

26. Ibid.

27. Ibid., 166.

28. Kenneth O'Reilly, *Hoover and the Un-Americans* (Philadelphia: Temple University Press, 1983), 14-15.

29. Ibid., 15.

30. Ibid.

31. Powers, *Secrecy and Power*, 167.

32. O'Reilly, *Hoover and the Un-Americans,* 15.

33. Ibid., 20.

34. Harry Anslinger, *The Protectors* (New York: Farrar, Straus and Company, 1964), 82.

35. Hank Messick, *Lansky* (New York: Berkley Medallion Books, 1971), 101.

36. Ibid.

37. Ibid., 69.

38. Peter Dale Scott, *Deep Politics and the Death of JFK* (Berkeley: Univ. of Cal. Press, 1993), 99.

39. Gentry, *J. Edgar Hoover*, 329.

40. Hank Messick, *John Edgar Hoover* (New York: David McCay, 1972), 50, 104.

41. Summers, *Official and Confidential*, 240-42, 377.

42. Michael Milan, *The Squad* (New York: Berkley Books, 1989), 1-2 and Scott, *Deep Politics*, 145.

43. Summers, *Official and Confidential*, 230-36 and Scott, *Deep Politics,* 206 and Powers, *Secrecy and Power,* 315.

44. *Cleveland Plain Dealer,* 13 February 1993.

45. Messick, *John Edgar Hoover,* 35.

46. Corson, *The Armies of Ignorance,* 70.

47. Gentry, *J. Edgar Hoover,* 153.

48. Ibid., 154.

49. Ibid., 157.

50. Ibid.

51. Kahan, *High Treason,* 128.

52. Ibid.

53. Powers, *G-Men: The FBI in American Popular Culture* (Carbondale, Ill.: South Illinois University Press, 1983), 32.

54. Robert Unger, *The Union Station Massacre,* 233.

55. Ibid., 232.

56. Ibid., 2.

57. Ibid., 2, 231.

58. Powers, *G-Men,* 127.

59. Cited in Ibid.

60. Hoover Personnel File, FBI 67-561, FOIA Reading Rm., *San Francisco Chronicle*, March 3, 1936, R G 60, NA.

61. Hoover Personnel File, FBI 67-561, FOIA Reading Rm., May 28, 1936, R G 60, NA.

62. Hoover Personnel File, FBI 67-561, FOIA Reading Rm., Special Agent John Little to Hoover, July 29, 1935, R G 60, NA.

63. Summers, *Official and Confidential,* 104.

64. Ibid., 104-5.

65. G. Gordon Liddy, *Will* (New York: St. Martin's Paperbacks, 1980), 116.

66. O'Reilly, *Hoover and the Un-Americans,* 22.

67. Ibid.

68. Summers, *Official and Confidential,* 107.

69. *New York Times,* 15 September 1993, cited in Corson, *The Armies of Ignorance,* 94.

70. Cited in Summers, *Official and Confidential,* 113.

71. Ibid., 109.

72. William Keller, *The Liberals and J. Edgar Hoover* (Princeton, N.J.: Princeton University Press, 1989), 9.

73. Theoharis, *Secret Files,* 113.

74. Cited in Gentry, *J. Edgar Hoover,* 244.

75. O'Reilly, *Hoover and the Un-Americans,* 74.

76. Powers, *Secrecy and Power,* 267 and Sullivan, *The Bureau,* 33-34.

77. Cited in Gentry, *J. Edgar Hoover,* 228.

Chapter 5

1. Sullivan, *The Bureau,* 35.

2. Summers, *Official and Confidential,* 104.

3. Ibid., 109.

4. Ibid., 110.

5. Ibid., 110-11.

6. Cited in Powers, *Secrecy and Power,* 276 and Summers, *Official and Confidential,* 152.

7. Gentry, *J. Edgar Hoover,* 244.

8. Summers, *Official and Confidential,* 160.

9. Powers, *Secrecy and Power,* 280-81.

10. Sullivan, *The Bureau,* 38.

11. Cited in Powers, *Secrecy and Power*, 282.

12. *Washington Post*, 8 September 1950.

13. Kovel, *Red Hunting in the Promised Land*, 129.

14. Record of the House of Representatives Investigation of Un-American Propaganda Activities in the United States, March 26, 1947, 34. Copy courtesty of the National Archives.

15. Cited in Summers, *Official and Confidential*, 165.

16. Ibid., 155.

17. Hoover Personnel File, FBI 67-561 Volume 4, FOIA Reading Rm., United Press Correspondent Fred Mullen; July 26, 1947, NA.

18. Philip M. Stern, *The Oppenheimer Case* (New York: Harper and Row, 1969), 222.

19. "Disney, FBI Drew On One Another," *Cleveland Plain Dealer*, 7 May 1993.

20. Ibid.

21. Ibid.

22. Kahan, *High Treason*, 333.

23. Ibid.

24. Powers, *Secrecy and Power*, 295.

25. "1950's Witch Hunt Still Haunts Many," Cited in *Cleveland Plain Dealer*, 26 February 1996.

26. Powers, *Secrecy and Power*, 299.

27. Ibid.

28. Ibid., 301.

29. Cited in Summers, *Official and Confidential*, 168.

30. Ibid.

31. Ibid.

32. Kovel, *Red Hunting in the Promised Land*, 143.

33. Powers, *Secrecy and Power*, 302.

34. Summers, *Official and Confidential*, 179.

35. Sullivan, *The Bureau*, 45-46.

36. Messick, *John Edgar Hoover*, 120.

37. Cited in Powers, *Secrecy and Power*, 321.

38. Hoover Personal File, FOIA Reading Rm., FBI File No's 9-31071, October 22, 1956, 121-23278, July 16, 1950, and 94-37708, February 3, 1948.

39. Powers, *Secrecy and Power*, 320-21.

40. Summers, *Official and Confidential*, 182-83.

41. Sullivan, *The Bureau*, 45.

42. Summers, *Official and Confidential*, 183.

43. Ibid.

44. Powers, *Secrecy and Power*, 336-37.

45. Cited in Ibid., 342-43.

46. DeLoach, *Hoover's FBI*, 270.

47. Kovel, *Red Hunting in the Promised Land*, 173.

48. DeLoach, *Hoover's FBI*, 270.

49. Hoover's Speech to the American Legion Convention in Miami, FL, 18 October 1960, cited in Powers, *Secrecy and Power*, 350-51.

Chapter 6

1. Victor Lasky, *It Didn't Start With Watergate* (New York: Dell Publishing, 1977), 59.

2. Ibid.

3. Sullivan, *The Bureau,* 48.

4. Cited in Arthur M. Schlesinger, Jr., *Robert Kennedy and His Times* (New York: Ballantine Books, 1978), 276.

5. Ibid., 279.

6. Ibid., 280.

7. Messick, *John Edgar Hoover,* 177.

8. James R. Hoffa, interview in *Playboy*, December 1975.

9. Messick, *Lansky,* 38.

10. Dan E. Moldea, *The Hoffa Wars: Teamsters, Rebels, Politicians, and the Mob* (New York: Charter, 1978), 85.

11. Peter Collier and David Horowitz, *The Kennedys: An American Drama* (New York: Warner Books, 1984), 22.

12. Collier and Horowitz, *The Kennedys,* 247.

13. Schlesinger, *Robert Kennedy and His Times,* 280-81.

14. Ibid., 274.

15. Cited in Mark North, *Act of Treason* (New York: Carroll & Graf Publishing, Inc., 1991), 116.

16. Cited in Ibid., 113.

17. Ibid., 116.

18. Cited in Theodore C. Sorensen, *Kennedy 25 Years* (New York: Harper & Row, 1965), 515.

19. Lee Riley Powell, *J. William Fulbright and His Time* (Memphis: Guild Bindery Press, 1996), 193-94.

20. *New York Times,* 18 October 1962.

21. Tom Feran, *Cleveland Plain Dealer*, 21 November 1996.

22. Don Gibson, *Battling Wall Street* (New York: Sheridan Square Press, 1994), 199.

23. Scott, *Deep Politics,* 206.

24. Gibson, *Battling Wall Street,* 65.

25. John H. Davis, *Mafia Kingfish: Carlos Marcello and the Assassination of John F. Kennedy* (New York: New American Library, 1989), 474-75.

26. Gibson, *Battling Wall Street*, 63.

27. Ibid., 10.

28. Ibid.

29. Ibid.

30. Ibid.

31. Ibid., 10-11.

32. Ibid., 12.

33. Ibid., 11.

34. Ibid., 63.

35. Cited in Ibid., 54.

36. Schlesinger, Jr., *Robert Kennedy and His Times*, 274.

37. Anthony Summers, *Goddess* (New York: New American Library, 1986), 294.

38. David Scheim, *Contract on America* (New York: Zebra Books, 1988), 89.

39. Judith Exner, *My Story* (New York: Grove Press, Inc., 1977), 251-52.

40. Kitty Kelly, "The Dark Side of Camelot," *People,* 29 February 1988.

41. Ibid.

42. *The Final Assassination Report*, 202-3.

43. Davis, *Mafia Kingfish,* 314-16.

44. *The Final Assassination Report,* 201-2.

45. Ibid., 203.

46. Ibid., 204.

47. Michael O'Brien,"The Exner File: Truth and Fantasy From a President's Mistress," *The Washington Monthly,* December 1999.

48. Ibid., 36. (Marty Underwood told the ARRB).

49. Ibid., 40.

50. Vincent Palamara, "The Secret Service in Their Own Words," 8, copy courtesy of John F. Kennedy Library.

51. Ibid., 7.

52. Ibid., 1.

53. Ibid., 1.

54. Ibid., 2.

55. *Robert Kennedy in His Own Words* (London: Bantam Press, 1988), 128.

56. Ibid., 128-29.

57. "Entertainment Tonight" TV Program, 8 December 1998, commenting on release of FBI files.

58. "CBS Evening News" with Tom Brokaw, 8 December 1998.

59. Athan Theoharis, *From the Secret Files of J. Edgar Hoover* (Chicago: Ivan R. Dee, 1991), 48.

60. Dan E. Moldea, interview with author, 5 March 2000.

61. Ibid.

62. David Scheim, *Contract on America* (New York: Zebra Books, 1988), 89.

63. Arthur Schlesinger, Jr., "JFK Revisited," *Cigar Aficionado,* Vol. 7, No. 1, (New York: M. Shankean Communications, Inc., December 1998).

64. "JFK: A New Look," History Channel, 23 December 1999.

65. Helen Thomas, *Front Row at the White House* (New York:

Scribner, 1999), 298.

66. Walter Cronkite, *A Reporter's Life* (New York: Ballantine Books, 1996), 220.

67. Nina Burleigh, *A Very Private Woman* (New York: Bantam Books, 1998), 199.

68. Ibid., 203.

69. Hugh Sidey, "Busy in Bed, But Also in Berlin," *Time,* 17 November 1997.

70. Burleigh, *A Very Private Woman,* 205, 218.

71. Moldea, *The Hoffa Wars,* 137.

72. Theoharis and Cox, *The Boss,* 336, 338.

73. Gentry, *J. Edgar Hoover*, 493-94.

74. Sullivan, *The Bureau,* 56.

75. Evan Thomas,"The JFK-Marilyn Hoax," *Newsweek,* 6 October 1997.

76. Thomas Powers, review of *The Dark Side of Camelot,* by Seymour Hersh, *New York Times Book Review,* 30 November 1997.

77. "Jury Says Documents on JFK Forged," *Cleveland Plain Dealer,* 1 May 1999.

78. Garry Wills, review of *The Dark Side of Camelot, by Seymour Hersh,* "A Second Assassination," *New York Review of Books,* 18 December, 1997.

79. Ibid and Alan Brinkley, review of *The Dark Side of Camelot, by Seymour Hersh,* "One Historians' View: Shoddy Work," *Time,* 17 November 1997.

80. Memo, Hoover to DCI (Att. DDP, 10/18/60 cited in Newman, "Oswald and the CIA", 203.

81. Carlos Lechuga, *In the Eye of the Storm: Castro, Khrushchev, Kennedy and the Missile Crisis* (Melbourne: Ocean Press, 1995), 13.

82. Associated Press article, 21 April 1996.

83. Peter Kornbluh, *Bay of Pigs Declassified: The Secret CIA Report on the Invasion of Cuba* (New York: The New Press, 1998), 32.

84. FBI Director memo of October 12, 1961, to Special Agent in Charge (SAC) New York cited in Scott, *Deep Politics*, 266.

85. Kornbluh, *Bay of Pigs Declassified*, 9.

86. Ibid., 264.

87. Laura Myers, Associated Press article, 3 July 1997.

88. Schorr, *Clearing the Air* (New York: Berkley Publishing Corp., 1978), 168-69.

89. Ibid., 100.

90. Ibid., 101, and Senate Intelligence Committee Report on Foreign Assassinations, cited in Fensterwald and Ewing, *Coincidence or Conspiracy*, 200.

91. Ibid., 105.

92. Ibid.

93. Ibid., 102.

94. Senate Intelligence Committee Report on Foreign Assassination, 107-8, cited in Fensterwald and Ewing, *Coincidence or Conspiracy*.

95. Ibid., 100.

96. Warren Hinckle and William Turner, *Deadly Secrets: The CIA-Mafia War Against Castro and the Assassination of JFK* (New York: Thunder's Mouth Press, 1981), 112-13.

97. Rusk, *As I Saw It*, 556.

98. Schorr, *Clearing the Air*, 169.

99. Jeff Shesol, *Mutual Contempt: Lyndon Johnson, Robert Kennedy and the Feud That Defined a Decade* (New York: W. W. Norton and Company, 1997), 132.

100. Sorensen, *Kennedy 25 Years*, 298.

101. Rusk, *As I Saw it*, 213.

102. Kornbluh, *Bay of Pigs Declassified*, 2.

103. Paris Flammonde, *The Kennedy Conspiracy: An Uncommissioned Report on the Jim Garrison Investigation* (New York: Meredith Press, 1969), 252.

104. John Lang, Scripps Howard News Service article cited in *Wooster (Ohio) Daily Record*, 21 November 1997.

105. Ibid.

106. Ibid.

107. HSCA 10, 165-66, 182.

108. Ibid., 195-96.

109. Ibid., 197-208.

110. Ibid., 208-9.

111. Ibid., 209.

112. Ibid., 208.

113. Cited in Schlesinger, *Robert Kennedy and His Times*, 593.

114. William W. Turner, *Hoover's FBI* (New York: Thunder's Mouth Press, 1993), 171.

115. Ibid.

116. 20 H 724-726.

117. Gentry, *J. Edgar Hoover*, 497.

118. "JFK: A New Look," video.

119. Ibid.

120. Ibid.

121. Ibid.

122. Gentry, *J. Edgar Hoover*, 500.

123. Ibid., 568.

124. Turner, *Hoover's FBI,* 101.

125. Ibid.

126. Turner, *Hoover's FBI,* 101.

127. Sullivan, *The Bureau,* 56.

128. *Robert Kennedy in His Own Words,* 145-46.

129. Ibid.

130. Rusk, *As I Saw It,* 197.

131. Ibid., 191.

132. Cited in Demaris, *The Director,* 170.

133. Benjamin C. Bradlee, *Conversations with Kennedy* (New York: W. W. Norton and Company, 1975), 225.

134. James Hosty, *Assignment Oswald* (New York: Arcade Publishing, 1996).

135. Sullivan, *The Bureau,* 49.

136. Schlesinger, *Robert Kennedy and His Times,* 273.

137. Hosty, *Assignment Oswald,* 154.

138. Cited in Demaris, *The Director,* 147.

139. "The End of Camelot," Discovery Channel, 1992.

140. *Robert Kennedy in His Own Words,* 127.

141. Cited in Schlesinger, *Robert Kennedy and His Times,* 678.

142. *Robert Kennedy in His Own Words,* 134.

143. Ibid., 127.

144. Schlesinger, *Cigar Aficionado.*

145. Ibid., 153.

146. Ibid., 175.

147. John Connally and Mickey Herskowitz, *In History's Shadow: An American Odyssey* (New York: Hyperion, 1993), 11.

148. Ibid., 357-58.

Chapter 7

1. *The Memoirs of Richard Nixon* (New York: Warner Books, 1978), 1:312.

2. AP Wire Story, 22 November 1999.

3. Ibid.

4. Sylvia Meagher, *Accessories After The Fact* (New York: Vintage Books, 1967), 351-56, 364-71.

5. *American History* (magazine), December 1999.

6. *Nixon Memoirs*, 1:312.

7. From handbill passed out on the street in Dallas, November 22, 1963.

8. *Dallas Morning News,* 22 November 1963.

9. William Manchester, *Death of a President* (New York: Harper and Row, 1967), 72-73.

10. History Channel, 1998.

11. Newman, *Oswald and the CIA* (New York: Carroll and Graf Publishing, Inc., 1995), 144.

12. Ibid., 160.

13. Manchester, *Death of a President*, 326.

14. "The End of Camelot,"Discovery Channel, 1992.

15. John Barron, *Operation Solo: The FBI's Man in the Kremlin* (Washington, D.C.: Regenery Publishing, Inc. 1996), 97-98.

16. Ibid., 102.

17. Ibid.

18. Burrell's Transcripts, *Who Killed JFK: The Final Chapter*, 19 November, 1993.

19. "The End of Camelot, "Discovery Channel, 1992.

20. Barron, *Operation Solo,* 103.

21. *American History Illustrated*, December 1999.

22. *New York Times,* 28 November 1963.

23. Ibid., 26 November 1963.

24. Scott, *Deep Politics,* 124.

25. Ibid., 94.

26. Ibid.,124.

27. Ibid., 54, 67, 124.

28. Fensterwald and Ewing, *Coincidence or Conspiracy,* 186.

29. Ibid., 183.

30. Scott, *Deep Politics,* 54.

31. *American History Illustrated*, December 1999.

32. Sid Blumenthal and Harvey Yazijian, eds., *Government by Gunplay: Assassination Conspiracy Theories from Dallas to Today* (New York: New American Library, 1996), 116.

33. Carl Francis Tagg, *Fidel Castro and The Kennedy Assassination* (Ann Arbor: University Microfilms International, 1983).

34. Warren Report (WR), 667.

35. 22 H 12; 24 H 509.

36. Summers, *Conspiracy* (New York: Paragon House, 1989), 414.

37. HSCA, H 26, 595.

38. Meagher, *Accessories After the Fact,* 387.

39. *Akron Beacon Journal*, 20 August 1997.

40. John Wallach, *Penthouse,* December 1996.

41. Ibid.

42. *Dallas Morning News*, 30 November 1963.

43. UPE 105 A 154 PCD 11/22 live wire ticker, copy courtesy of Alan Lang.

44. Anatoly Dobrynin, *In Confidence* (New York: Times Books, 1995), 115.

45. James Risen, *New York Times*, reprint, *Cleveland Plain Dealer*, 12 September 1999.

46. Scott, *Deep Politics*, 121.

47. Michael Beschloss, ed., *Taking Charge: The Johnson White House Tapes* (New York: Simon and Schuster Publishing, 1997), 78.

48. Scott, *Deep Politics*, 43.

49. Ibid. and 3 AH 136.

50. "On Trial: Lee Harvey Oswald," video, 1986.

51. FBI File DL 89-43, cited in *Oswald, The Secret Files; Controversial Documents From the Secret Censored Archives of the FBI, CIA, and More,* (Las Vegas: Goldstein & Associates, Inc., 1992).

52. *New York Times,* 28 November 1963.

53. *Boston Record American,* 27 November 1963.

54. *Dallas Morning News*, 28 November 1963.

55. Joseph Califano, *The Triumph and Tragedy of Lyndon Johnson: The White House Years,* (New York: Simon and Schuster, 1991), 295.

56. Shesol, *Mutual Contempt,* 131.

57. 15 H 710.

58. 15 H 718, 714, 742-743.

59. Victor Dix, "Off The Record," *Wooster (Ohio) Daily Record,* 12 November 1992.

60. Hosty, *Assignment Oswald,* 152-53.

Chapter 8

1. *Oswald, the Secret Files*, 95.

2. Phillip Melanson, *Spy Saga: Lee Harvey Oswald and U. S. Intelligence* (New York, Prager, 1990), 39.

3. Ibid., 40.

4. HSCA 10, 102-4, 108-9; 8, 14.

5. Robert Groden, *The Search For Lee Harvey Oswald* (New York: Penguin Group, 1995).

6. 15 HSCA 140.

7. Ibid.

8. Summers, *Conspiracy*, 143.

9. "End of Camelot," Discovery Channel, 1992.

10. Ibid.

11. 5 H 301.

12. 8 H 298.

13. *New York Times,* 20 April 1971.

14. Epstein, *Legend,* 121.

15. HSCA 12, 391.

16. Epstein, *Legend,* 109, 198.

17. Marrs, *Crossfire,* 110-11.

18. *New York Herald Tribune,* 30 November 1963.

19. 16 H 422-423.

20. HSCA, 12, 57.

21. FBI document DL-105-18766, cited in *Oswald, the Secret Files* , 114.

22. Ibid.

23. 9 HSCA 96.

24. 12 HSCA 306.

25. Harold Weisberg, *Selections From Whitewash* (New York: Carroll and Graf Publishing, Inc., 1994), 231.

26. Ibid., 235.

27. Cited in Newman, *Oswald and the CIA,* 218.

28. Government document DL 100-10461, cited in *Oswald, The Secret Files,* 6.

29. 11 H 334.

30. Jack Anderson, "Plot to Kill Kennedy," video.

31. 18 H 137.

32. Senate Select Committee, Investigation Into the Assassination of JFK, 54, cited in Hurt, *Reasonable Doubt*, 242.

33. Warren Commission Executive Session transcript, January 27, 1964, cited in Melanson, *Spy Saga,* 12.

34. Ibid.

35. Melanson, *Spy Saga,* 85.

36. Ibid.

37. Jesse Curry, *JFK Assassination File* (Dallas: American Poster and Printing Co., Inc., 1969), 113.

38. Dick Russell, *The Man Who Knew Too Much* (New York: Carroll and Graf Publishing, 1992), 690.

39. Bruce Cummings, *The Origins of the Korean War,* Vol. II, *The Roaring of the Cataract, 1947-1950* (Princeton: Princeton University Press, 1990), 104.

40. Noel Twyman, *Bloody Treason* (Rancho Santa Fe, Calif.: Laurel Publishing, 1997), 572.

41. Cummings, *Origin of the Korean War,* 104-5.

42. Gaeton Fonzi, *The Last Investigation* (New York: Thunder's Mouth Press, 1993), 261, 336, 408.

43. *Village Voice*, 15 December 1975.

44. *Final Report of the Assassination Records and Review Board,* 1998, Washington D.C., 83.

45. Thomas Buchanan, *Who Killed Kennedy?* (New York: McFadden-Bartell & Sons, 1965), 127.

46. *Washington Post*, 23 November 1963, and 10 H 35.

47. *Washington Post,* 23 November 1963.

48. Government Document No. 97-74, courtesy of Jim Lesar, Assassination Archives and Research Center, Washington, D.C. and Ibid., 11.

49. Weisberg, *Whitewash IV,* 53, from Warren Commission Session transcript 12764, 144.

50. *The Final Assassination Report,* 223-24.

51. "Beyond JFK: The Question of Conspiracy," video, Embassy Productions, 1992.

52. *The Final Assassination Report,* 175-76.

53. 11 H 348, 357.

54. Melanson, *Spy Saga,* 39.

55. 10 HSCA 123-27.

56. Hurt, *Reasonable Doubt,* 289.

57. Melanson, *Spy Saga,* 42.

58. Summers, *Conspiracy*, 321.

59. Groden, *Oswald,* 18-19.

60. HSCA 10, 114.

61. "Beyond JFK," video.

62. Craig Roberts and John Armstrong, *JFK: The Dead Witnesses,* (Tulsa, OK: Consolidated Press International, 1995), 50.

63. Summers, *Conspiracy,* 295.

64. "Two Men in Dallas," video, Alpa Productions, 1977, Stewart Galanor interview with Roger Craig.

65. Roberts and Armstrong, *JFK: The Dead Witnesses,* 17.

66. Coalition on Political Assassinations (COPA), Dallas, statement by John Newman, 1998.

67. FBI Document 105-9958, cited in *Oswald, The Secret Files.*

68. Warren Commission Document No. 320 cited in Flammonde, *The Kennedy Conspiracy.*

69. Gerald R. Ford, *Portrait of the Assassin* (New York: Simon and Schuster, 1964), 13-14.

70. Epstein, *Inquest,* 48-49.

71. HSCA 11, 36-40.

72. HSCA 11, 41 and G. Robert Blakey and Richard N. Billings, *Fatal Hour: The Assassination of President Kennedy By Organized Crime* (New York: Berkley Books, 1981), 27.

73. Epstein, *Inquest,* 49-50.

74. 5 H 97-120.

75. Epstein, *Inquest,* 48-49.

76. HSCA 11, 34-36.

77. La Fontaine, *Oswald Talked,* 435.

78. Statement by John Newman 1998 COPA Conference, Dallas.

79. 5 H 34.

80. 5 H 37.

81. *The Final Assassination Report,* 231.

82. Sullivan, *The Bureau,* 53.

83. HSCA 11, 43-53.

84. HSCA Report, 195-96.

85. Cited in Mark Lane, *Rush to Judgment* (New York: Thunder's Mouth Press, 1992), 378.

86. *New York Times*, 5 December 1963.

87. Dwight Macdonald, "A Critique of the Warren Report," *Esquire*, cited in Weaver, *Warren,* 323.

88. Warren Commission Memorandum, February 24, 1968, Willens to General Counsel J. Lee Rankin cited in Fensterwald and Ewing, *Coincidence or Conspiracy,* 101-2.

89. 5 H 97-120.

90. Scott, *Deep Politics,* 45.

91. COPA, Dallas, 1998.

92. Meagher, *Accessories After the Fact,* 95.

93. Ibid and CE 2003, 63.

94. 7 H 108.

95. 3 H 295.

96. Meagher, *Accessories After the Fact,* 95 and CE2169.

97. "Two Men in Dallas," video.

98. UPR 142 K&FK 442 11/22; UPR 172 11/22; UPR 202 SR 104 PCS 11/22 live wire ticker reports, copies courtesy of Alan Lang.

99. WR 3 294.

100. HSCA 3, 471-73.

101. 2 H 46.

102. Meagher, *Accessories After the Fact,* 188.

103. Ibid.

104. CE 2160.

105. Airtel to SAC, from Director, FBI (105-82555), 12/18/63, cited in *Oswald, The Secret Files*.

106. Meagher, *Accessories After the Fact* , 182.

107. 1 H 164-65; 4 H 211; 24 H 219.

108. Lane, *Rush to Judgment*, 310.

109. 24 H 219; 3 H 82.

110. Meagher, *Accessories After the Fact*, 235.

111. Curry, *JFK Assassination File*, 46.

112. La Fontaine, *Oswald Talked*, 335.

113. Ibid.

114. 2 H 321; 336-337.

115. 2 H 321, 22 H 785.

116. Scott, *Deep Politics*, 288.

117. Ibid., 289.

118. Burrell's Transcripts, Harpo Productions, Inc. from the Oprah Winfrey Show, 22 November 1996.

119. Ibid.

120. FBI File DL 89-43, cited in *Oswald, The Secret Files*.

121. 4 H 253-255.

122. Ibid.

123. CE3076.

124. H 224-225.

125. C-Span. 26 November 1996.

126. 3 H 405, 411.

127. 11 H 203, 233.

128. 11 H 252-253.

129. CE 2694 cited in Meagher, *Accessories After the Fact*, 103.

130. 3 H 449.

131. 3 H 450-451.

132. WR 193-194 cited in Meagher, *Accessories After the Fact*, 102.

133. David Lifton, *Best Evidence: Disguise and Deception in the Assassination of John F. Kennedy* (New York: Carroll and Graf Publishing, Inc., 1980), 356.

134. 4 H 23.

135. "Two Men in Dallas," video.

136. 7 H 439.

137. 2 H 32, 51; 1 H 330; 21 H 139; 24 H 7.

138. Emile de Antonio and Mark Lane, "Plot to Kill JFK: Rush to Judgment," video, 1967.

139. Nash interview, "New Leader," October 12, 1964.

140. 3 H 310-311.

141. 6 H 452.

142. 11 H 435 and CE 2523.

143. Bob Considine, *New York Journal-American*, 23 February 1964.

144. Mark Lane interview with Warren Reynolds, "Rush to Judgment," video.

145. Bob Considine, *New York Journal-American*, 23 February 1964.

146. Lifton, *Best Evidence*, 27.

147. "End of Camelot," Discovery Channel, 1992.

148. 7 H 59.

149. Robert Oswald, *Lee* (New York: Coward-McCann, Inc., 1967), 228.

150. Fensterwald and Ewing, *Coincidence or Conspiracy,* 44.

151. 1 H 32.

152. Meagher, *Accessories After the Fact,* 234.

153. *The Final Assassination Report,* 314.

154. Ibid., 336.

155. Groden & Livingstone, *High Treason,* 203.

Chapter 9

1. Curry, *JFK Assassination File* , 81.

2. UPR107, A156PCD 11/22 live wire ticker reports, copies courtesy of Alan Lang.

3. HSCA 3, 471-473.

4. *Dallas Morning News,* 27 November 1963.

5. Curry, *JFK Assassination File,* 81.

6. "The Men Who Killed Kennedy," video, 1988.

7. Vincent Palamara, *JFK: The Medical Evidence Reference: Who's Who in the Medical Evidence — The Principal Witnesses from November 22, 1963* (1998), 56.

8. Charles Crenshaw, *JFK: Conspiracy of Silence* (New York: Signet Books, 1992), 98-99.

9. *JFK Legacy,* History Channel, 1998 and Carl Solbert, *Hubert Humphrey, A Biography* (New York: W. W. Norton and Company, 1984), 240.

10. Meagher, *Accessories After the Fact,* 137.

11. Assassination Records and Review Board, 122.

12. *ARRB Final Report,* 121-22.

13. *St. Louis Post Dispatch,* 18 December 1963.

14. *Look*, 12 July 1966.

15. "Image of An Assassination: A New Look At the Zapruder Film," 1998, MPI Media Group, video.

16. Palamara, *JFK: The Medical Evidence Reference*, 62.

17. Lane, *Rush to Judgment*, 40.

18. Marrs, *Crossfire*, 70.

19. Lane, *Rush to Judgment*, 194.

20. Tip O'Neil with William Novak, *Man of the House: The Life and Political Memoirs of Speaker Tip O'Neil*, (New York: St. Martin's Press, 1987), 211.

21. 7 H 472-474.

22. 22 H 684.

23. Lane, *Rush to Judgment*, 112.

24. Ibid.

25. Bill Sloan and Jean Hill, *The Last Dissenting Witness*(Gretna, La.: Pelican Publishing, 1992), 30.

26. Ibid., 55-72.

27. Sloan and Hill, *The Last Dissenting Witness*, 72, 101-2.

28. Statement given to the ARRB, cited in Palamara, *JFK: The Medical Evidence Reference*, 121.

29. Margaret Hinchcliffe (Hood) interview by Wallace Milam, 25 June 1993, in Palamara,*The Medical Evidence Reference*, 43.

30. Penn Jones interview with Roger Craig for "Forgive My Grief," 1968.

31. Gary Shaw, "Cover-up: The Governmental Conspiracy to Conceal the Facts About the Public Execution of John Kennedy", Austin, TX, 1976, 28.

32. Ibid.

33. CD 1542.

34. Thompson, *Six Seconds in Dallas*, 112.

35. Marrs, *Crossfire,* 482.

36. CD 329, 28-31.

37. Marrs, *Crossfire,* 318.

38. 2 H 175-176, 188; 24 H 224; 26 H 166.

39. 2 H 184.

40. 2 H 185.

41. 3 H 178.

42. CE 2993, 26 cited in Meagher, *Accessories After the Fact,* 67.

43. CE 1974, 83.

44. 6 H 321-322.

45. 7 H 518-519.

46. 3 H 147-148.

47. 3 H 154.

48. Ibid.

49. 24 H 781.

50. 3 H 211.

51. Curry, *JFK Assassination File,* 61.

52. 6 H 383.

53. 6 H 328.

54. WR 598-636 cited in Meagher, *Accessories After the Fact,* 225.

55. CD 5, 41.

56. CD 5, 41 cited in Meagher, *Accessories After the Fact,* 225.

57. Joel Wagoner interview, 28 August 1991, cited in *The Third Decade,* Jan.-March 1992 edition.

58. Bill Sloan, *Breaking the Silence,* (Dallas: Taylor Publishing, 1993), 92 .

59. Henry Hurt, *Reasonable Doubt,* 29.

60. 18 H 742.

61. 19 H 486.

62. Groden and Livingstone, *High Treason,* 216-17.

63. Ibid., 207-10.

64. 19 H 486.

65. Jim Marrs, *Crossfire* (New York: Carroll and Graf Publishing, Inc., 1989), 29.

66. "Two Men in Dallas," video and Mark Oakes, "Eyewitness Three," video, 1998.

67. Ibid.

68. Ibid.

69. 12 HSCA 23.

70. 6 H 248-253 and Mark Oakes, "Eyewitness Three," video.

71. Marrs, *Crossfire,* 59.

72. Ibid.

73. 7 H 508-509.

74. 7 H 562-563.

75. Marrs, *Crossfire,* 456.

76. Ibid., 454-56.

77. Lane, *Rush to Judgment,* 1966.

78. "The JFK Assassination: The Jim Garrison Tapes," Vestron Video, 1992.

79. "The Men Who Killed Kennedy," video, 1988.

80. Lifton, *Best Evidence,* 62.

81. Meagher, *Accessories After the Fact,* 150-54.

82. Livingstone, *High Treason Two* (New York: Carroll and Graf Publishing, Inc. 1992), 121.

83. Meagher, *Accessories After the Fact,* 153.

84. Ibid., 154.

85. Gouchenaur interview with Agent Moore and taken from HSCA 6, 177 interview transcript and cited in Palamara, *JFK: The Medical Evidence Reference,* 62.

86. FBI Report November 29, 1963, CD 5 and Thompson, *Six Seconds in Dallas,* 95.

87. WR 19.

88. *People* (magazine), 13 May 1991.

89. 4 H 113.

90. 2 H 382.

91. 2 H 376.

92. "Reasonable Doubt, the Single Bullet Theory," shown on Arts & Entertainment TV network, 1988.

93. 6 H 132-34.

94. 6 H 130.

95. 24 H 412.

96. Palamara, *JFK: The Medical Evidence Reference,* 54.

97. 7 HSCA 15-16.

98. Lifton, *Best Evidence,* 645-47.

99. 4 H 133.

100. Thompson, *Six Seconds in Dallas,* 69.

101. Ibid.

102. Connally and Herskowitz, *In History's Shadow,* 186, 188.

103. *USA Today*, Associated Press article, 17 November 1998.

104. Ibid., 23 November 1999.

105. 5 H 155.

106. Cited in Lifton, *Best Evidence*, 85.

107. Burrell's Transcripts, *Who Killed JFK; The Final Chapter*, November 18, 1993.

108. Beschloss, *Taking Charge,* 560.

109. Summers, *Conspiracy,* 36.

110. From Sibert and O'Neil Report, 26 November 1963, cited in Weisberg, *Post Mortem: JFK Assassination Smashed!* Frederick, Md.: self-published, 1975, 533-36.

111. "Research vs. Witness: Questioning the Facts," video, 1992, interview conducted by George Michael Evica, cited in Palamara, *JFK: The Medical Evidence Reference,* 120.

112. 2 H 127.

113. John Weaver, *Warren*, 318.

114. Hurt, *Reasonable Doubt*, 43.

115. 14 H 479-80.

116. "JFK: The Case For Conspiracy," video, New Frontier Productions, 1993; Robert Groden, *The Killing of a President: The Complete Photographic Record of the JFK Assassination, The Conspiracy, and the Coverup* (New York: Viking Studio Books, 1993) and Richard Trask, *That Day In Dallas* (Danvers, Mass.: Yeoman Press, 1998).

117. Vincent Palamara, *The Third Alternative,* 72.

118. "Image of An Assassination," video.

119. Fetzer, "Assassination Science," 2.

120. FBI report interview with Abraham Zapruder, File DL 89-43, cited in "Assassination Science," edited by James Fetzer,

Catfeet Press, Chicago, 1998, 233.

121. Meagher, *Accessories After the Fact*, 22.

122. "Image of an Assassination," video.

123. Fetzer, *Assassination Science*, 216.

124. Ibid., 299-300.

125. 22 H 838-839.

126. 19 H 487.

127. 19 H 533-536.

128. Federal Bureau of Investigation report, File DL, 89-43, November 22, 1963, cited in Lane, *Rush to Judgment*, 344.

129. Supplementary Investigation Report, Dallas Sheriff's Department, November 23, 1963, cited in Lane, *Rush to Judgment*, 344.

130. Sloan and Hill, *The Last Dissenting Witness*, 21, 26-27.

131. Ibid.

132. "The Men Who Killed Kennedy," video, 1988.

133. Harold Weisberg, *Selections From Whitewash* (New York: Caroll and Graf Publishers, 1994), 156.

134. Beverly Oliver and Coke Buchanan, *Nightmare in Dallas,* (Lancaster, PA: Starburst Inc., 1994).

135. Weisberg, *Selections From Whitewash,* 169.

136. Ibid., 169-70.

137. Ibid., 170.

138. Weisberg, *Selections From Whitewash,* 175.

139. de Antonio and Lane, "Rush to Judgment," video.

140. Ibid., 179.

Chapter 10

1. Originally shown by the BBC in a program entitled, "The Kennedy Assassination: What Do We Know Now That We Didn't Know Then? (1978) and later adapted into a United States television special entitled, "The Plot To Kill President Kennedy," also available on home video.

2. Bradlee, *Conversations with Kennedy,* 125-26.

3. "Beyond JFK," video.

4. Edward Partin, "An Insider's Chilling Story of Hoffa's Savage Kingdom," *Life,* 15 May 1964.

5. Beschloss, *Taking Charge,* 51.

6. *Newsweek,* 2 November 1993.

7. *The Final Assassination Report,* 313.

8. Ibid., 150, 306, 313.

9. Ibid., 332.

10. Senate Intelligence Committee Report on the Kennedy Assassination, 47, 53, cited in Fensterwald and Ewing, *Coincidence or Conspiracy,* 252-53.

11. Warren Commission Internal Memorandum by Melvin Eisenberg, February 17, 1964 cited in Fensterwald and Ewing, *Coincidence or Conspiracy,* 73.

12. Manchester, *Death of a President,* 717.

13. 3 HSCA 471-473.

14. Senate Intelligence Committee Report on the Kennedy Assassination, 33.

15. Burrell's Transcripts, *Who Killed JFK: The Final Chapter?* 19 November 1993

16. Twyman, *Bloody Treason,* 539 and CD 1107, Vol. 2, 361, copy courtesy of Jim Lesar and Assassination Archives Research Center, Washington, D.C.

17. Dick Russell, *The Man Who Knew Too Much,* 45, 52, 56, 618,

622.

18. *ARRB Final Report,* 133, Dick Russell, March 24 1995.

19. Ibid.

20. "The Men Who Killed Kennedy," video, 1988.

21. Cited in Scott Van Wynsbeghe, "Dead Suspects, Part V," *The Third Decade,* January 1988, 4.

22. Inverview with Don Adams, March 19, 2000.

23. Copy of transcripts 28 November 1963 from LBJ Library, obtained from Jim Lesar and Assassination Archives and Research Center, Washington, D.C.

24. Ibid.

25. Beschloss, *Taking Charge,* 58-59, 66-72.

26. Twyman, *Bloody Treason,* 499.

27. H 5 97-120.

28. HSCA 3, 476.

29. The Warren Report, M.S.A.: The Associated Press, vii, 1964.

30. *Dallas Morning News*, 29 November 1963.

31. Ibid.

32. *New York Times*, 27 November 1963.

33. Edward Epstein, *Inquest; The Warren Commission and the Establishment of Truth,* (New York: Viking Press, 1966), 46-47.

34. Louis Nizer, *An Analysis and Commentary,* introduction, The Official Warren Commission Report on the Assassination of President John F. Kennedy, New York: Doubleday, 1964. .

35. Warren Commission Session Transcript, 1/27/64, 171-72, 180, copy courtesy of James Lesar, Assassination Archives and Research Center, Washington, D.C.

36. HSCA 11, 43-53.

37. Connally and Herskowitz, *In History's Shadow,* 358.

Chapter 11

1. Warren Commission Final Report Appendix xii, 271, 1964.

2. John Herbers, *New York Times*, 27 November 1963.

3. Harrison Livingstone, *Killing the Truth* (New York: Carroll and Graf Publishing, Inc., 1993), 172, 177-78, 718.

4. Livingstone & Groden, *High Treason,* 456, reprinted from article by Nicole Lelicoff, *Jenkintown (Penn.) Times Chronicle.*

5. 6 H 141; 143.

6. Copy courtesy of Jim Lesar, Assassination Archives and Research Center, Washington D.C. , from transcript of Kilduff Press Conference, 22 November 1963, 1327 B - LBJ Library.

7. UPR 101, 11/22; A14 SPCD 11/22 live wire ticker reports, copies courtesy of Alan Lang.

8. Livingstone, *Killing the Truth*, 41, 118, 172-78.

9. *St. Louis Post Dispatch*, 1 December 1963.

10. 7 HSCA 292-93, 302, 312.

11. Charles Crenshaw, *Conspiracy of Silence*, (New York: Penguin Books, 1992), 86.

12. 6 H 70-71.

13. 6 H 53-54, 56.

14. Lifton, *Best Evidence*, 705.

15. "The Joe Dolan Show," 10 April 1967, KNEW Radio, Oakland, CA., cited in Palamara, *JFK: The Medical Evidence Reference,* 48-49.

16. Bill Sloan, *JFK: Breaking the Silence*, 84-97.

17. *Dallas Times Herald,* 22 November 1963.

18. "The Killing of President Kennedy Declassified: The Plot to Kill President Kennedy, 1978-1988," video, cited in Palamara, *JFK:*

The Medical Evidence Reference, 213.

19. 17 H 461.

20. 23 H 913.

21. 7 H 345.

22. 3 H 227.

23. 2 H 144.

24. 2 H 73-74, 78-82.

25. 18 H 732.

26. 18 H 751-757.

27. Manchester, *Death of a President,* 290.

28. 7 HSCA 19 cited in Palamara, *JFK: The Medical Evidence Reference,* 119.

29. CD 897, 20, 21.

30. 3 H 266; 3 H 220.

31. 2 H 44-45; 3 H 266.

32. Lifton, *Best Evidence,* 370, from interviews by Gill Toff, 21 April 1971 and 22 April 1971.

33. Ibid.

34. "JFK: The Case For Conspiracy," video; Groden, *The Killing of a President* and Trask, *That Day In Dallas.*

35. From HSCA interview and cited in Palamara, *JFK: The Medical Evidence Reference,* 66.

36. 18 H 801.

37. WFAA (Dallas Radio Station) 22 November 1963 and cited in Thompson, *Six Seconds in Dallas,* 103.

38. 6 H 294.

39. 6 H 290.

40. Sloan and Hill, *The Last Dissenting Witness,* 56.

41. 6 H 295.

42. 7 H 105-109, 24 H 228, CD 5.

43. 3 H 281-296.

44. 19 H 502-504.

45. 19 H 540.

46. 19 H 516.

47. 19 H 514.

48. 19 H 541.

49. 19 H 511.

50. Oakes, *Eyewitness Video Tape III*, 1993.

51. Statement given to Chief Curry from *JFK Assassination File*, 105.

52. Richard Trask, *Pictures of the Pain,* cited in Palamara, from *JFK: The Medical Evidence Reference,* 226.

53. 7 H 518-19.

54. Weisberg, *Photographic Whitewash: Suppressed Kennedy Assassination Pictures* (Frederick, Md.: self-published, 1976), 202-6.

55. 6 H 160.

56. Marrs, *Crossfire,* 16.

57. *Houston Post,* 23 November 1963.

58. 6 H 165.

59. From *Murder From Within* by Fred Newcomb and Perry Adams, cited in Palamara, *JFK: The Medical Evidence Reference,* 211.

60. 6 H 231-236; 22 H 600.

61. 7 H 476-485.

62. Ibid.

63. 6 H 243-245 and *New York Times*, 23 November 1966.

64. 24 H 217.

65. 6 H 230.

66. Lane, *Rush to Judgment,* 40.

67. Ibid.

68. Lane, *Rush to Judgment,* from interview with Stewart Galanor, 40.

69. 22 H 836.

70. Gerald Posner, *Case Closed* (New York: Random House, 1993), 256.

71. 19 H 490; 24 H 219.

72. 22 H 842-843.

73. Thompson, *Six Seconds in Dallas*, 103.

74. CD 5, 30-31; 7 H 558-565; 19 H 481.

75. Marrs, *Crossfire,* 23

76. Ibid., 71.

77. Mary Woodward, *Dallas Morning News,* 23 November 1963.

78. "The Men Who Killed Kennedy," video, 1988.

79. Ibid.

80. 7 H 557.

81. Sloan and Hill, *The Last Dissenting Witness,* 22, 33.

82. 6 H 207.

83. 6 H 213.

84. de Antonio and Lane, "Rush to Judgment," video.

85. Groden, *The Killing of a President,* 34.

86. 24 H 523; 19 H 478; 22 H 841.

87. 19 H 471; 24 H 525.

88. (22 H 659-846), (CD 329, 22; 6 H 171-174); (7 H 565-569; 22 H 604).

89. CD 205, 19-22; 6 H 200-205; 19 H 473; 647.

90. Marrs, *Crossfire,* 78.

91. 7 H 569-576.

92. Thompson, *Six Seconds in Dallas,* 102.

93. 22 H 685.

94. 22 H 648.

95. CD 5, 39; 6 H 388; 22 H 632.

96. 22 H 210-245; 7 H 581; 22 H 647; 24 H 209.

97. 6 H 338.

98. 3 H 227, 241.

99. 3 H 274.

100. 22 H 638, 845.

101. 6 H 368-373; 6 H 327-334; 24 H 226.

102. CD 837, 35-36, (CD 593, 232-234; 22 H 642) and CD 5, 66-67; 7 H 507; 22 H 615.

103. Lifton, *Best Evidence,* 619, 621, 696.

104. Ibid., 631-34.

105. Ibid., 543.

106. HSCA Record No. 10010042, File No. 002086, 2, cited in Palamara, *JFK: The Medical Evidence Reference,* 142.

107. HSCA RIF No. 189-10089, cited in Ibid., 123.

108. Bill Law interview, 1997, cited in Ibid., 128.

109. Bill Law interview, 1998, cited in Ibid., 129-31.

110. Lifton, *Best Evidence,* 619, 696.

111. Marrs, *Crossfire,* 71.

112. 4 H 356.

113. Palamara, *The Third Alternative,* 4.

114. *Vanity Fair,* December 1994.

115. 7 H 538.

116. Summers, *Conspiracy,* 50.

117. Ibid., 51.

118. 7 H 107.

119. Taped interview, 30 November 1966, cited in Thompson, *Six Seconds in Dallas.*

120. Thompson, *Six Seconds in Dallas,* 122.

121. Taped interview, 30 November 1966, cited in Thompson, *Six Seconds in Dallas,* 123.

122. 19 H 492 and Thompson, *Six Seconds in Dallas,* 123.

123. de Antonio and Lane, "Rush to Judgment," video.

124. Ibid.

125. Lane, op. cit. 34 and Thompson, *Six Seconds in Dallas,* 138.

126. 6 H 285.

127. 6 H 286.

128. 6 H 287 and interview with Lee Bowers, cited in *Rush to Judgment,* 31.

129. Interview with Lee Bowers by Mark Lane, cited in *Rush to*

Judgment, 31.

130. Ibid., 32.

131. Ibid.

132. "The Men Who Killed Kennedy," video, 1988.

133. Ibid.

134. Ibid.

135. Sloan and Hill, *The Last Dissenting Witness,* 21, 26-27.

136. *Who Murdered JFK: American Exposé* narrated by Jack Anderson. Shown on VH1, 1992.

137. 6 H 308.

138. 6 H 277.

139. Stanley Marks, *Coup d'etat: November 22, 1963; The Conspiracies That Murdered President John F. Kennedy, the Rev. Martin Luther King, and Senator Robert F. Kennedy* (Los Angeles: Bureau of International Affairs, 1970), 79.

140. Ibid.

Chapter 12

1. Seth Kantor, Interview with Leon Hubert, 9 August 1976, cited in Seth Kantor, *The Ruby Cover-up* (New York: Kensington Publishing Company, 1978), 18.

2. Ibid., 18.

3. Ibid., 18-19.

4. *The Final Assassination Report,* 335-36.

5. 14 H 543.

6. Ibid.

7. 14 H 548.

8. 14 H 565.

9. 14 H 566.

10. Ibid.

11. WR 793.

12. 5 H 200.

13. *The Final Assassination Report*, 219.

14. Twyman, *Bloody Treason,* 255.

15. Ibid.

16. *The Final Assassination Report,* 208-17.

17. James P. Duffy, *Conspiracy: Who Killed JFK* (New York: Shapolsky Publishers, 1992), 214-15.

18. Ibid.

19. Ibid.

20. Robert Maheu and Richard Hack, *Next to Hughes,* (New York: Harper, 1992), 43 and Scott, *Deep Politics,* 171.

21. Scott, *Deep Politics,* 157.

22. Ibid.

23. Ibid., 217-21 and Daniels interview from BBC program "The Kennedy Assassination: What Do We Know Now That We Didn't Know Then?" This program was adapted in the United States into the "Plot to Kill Kennedy."

24. Scheim, *Contract on America*, 135.

25. Twyman, *Bloody Treason*, 256.

26. CE 2303.

27. U.S. Senate, McClellan Labor Hearings, 14052-53 and Walter Sheridan, *The Rise and Fall of Jimmy Hoffa,* 21.

28. Robert Kennedy, *The Enemy Within* (New York: Harper, 1960), 91.

29. CE 2331.

30. HSCA 9, 335-336, 412.

31. CE 2259; CD 86, 138-39.

32. CE 2259; HSCA 9, 363-64, 374.

33. CD 84, 91 and CD 302, 30.

34. CE 2243, 2284.

35. 5 H 185-86.

36. CD 1144, 5-6 and Seth Kantor, *Who Was Jack Ruby?* (New York: Everest House, 1978), 22.

37. Scheim, *Contract on America*, 125.

38. CD 86, 558, and Dan Moldea, *The Hoffa Wars,* 163.

39. HSCA, 3 H 494.

40. 26 H 450.

41. HSCA Report, 158.

42. Roberts and Armstrong, *The Dead Witnesses*, 10.

43. Ibid., 25.

44. Ibid., 27.

45. Blakey and Billings, *Fatal Hour,* 358.

46. Duffy, *Conspiracy: Who Killed Kennedy*, 231.

47. Marks, *Coup d état*, 137.

48. HSCA 384, 52; Oliver and Buchanan, *Nightmare in Dallas,* 94 and 15 H 620.

49. Roberts and Armstrong, *The Dead Witnesses*, 9.

50. 15 H 620.

51. 15 H 619-20.

52. 15 H 660.

53. 14 H 567.

54. 5 H 206.

55. Summers, *Conspiracy,* 457.

56. Ibid., 456.

57. 15 H 487-88.

58. 26 H 468.

59. 26 H 469.

60. de Antonio and Lane, "Rush to Judgment," video.

61. CE 1535, 14 H 603, CE 1592, and CE 1467.

62. 26 H 470.

63. Curry, *JFK Assassination File,* 127, 133.

64. Scott, *Deep Politics,* 198-99.

65. Ibid.

66. Kantor, Exhibit 8, cited in Meagher, *Accessories After the Fact,* 395.

67. 15 H 391.

68. Palamara, *The Third Alternative,* 42.

69. Weisberg, *Selections From Whitewash,* 148.

70. Marrs, *Crossfire,* 28.

71. 14 H 559.

72. 14 H 485-86.

73. Ibid., 286, 296-97.

74. Lane, *Rush to Judgment,* 287-96.

75. CE 3063.

76. WR 788.

77. CE 3065.

78. CE 1689.

79. Summers, *Conspiracy ,*436.

80. *Ramparts,* February 1967, Copy of letter written by Jack Ruby.

81. Kantor, *Who Was Jack Ruby?* 88.

82. Ibid., 128.

83. Ibid.

84. Hurt, *Reasonable Doubt,* 2.

85. Kantor, *Who Was Jack Ruby?* 14, 29, 137 and Summers, *Conspiracy,* 470-71.

86. 10 HSCA 199-205.

87. Ibid., 201-2.

88. Ibid., 200-201.

89. HSCA Report, 202.

90. Ibid., 202-3.

91. Ibid., 199, 202.

92. John D. Weaver, *Warren, The Man, The Court, The Era* (Boston: Little, Brown, and Company, 1967), 310.

93. WR 325.

94. HSCA Report, 204.

95. Mark Lane, *Plausible Denial: Was the CIA Involved in the Assassination of JFK?* (New York: Thunder's Mouth Press, 1991), 291-303.

96. Ibid.

97. Ray La Fontaine and Mary La Fontaine, *Oswald Talked* (Gretna, La.: Pelican Publishing, 1996), 282, 284.

98. La Fontaine and La Fontaine, *Oswald Talked,* 2.

99. *The Final Assassination's Report*, 214.

100. Ibid.

101. 5 H 206.

102. Scott, *Deep Politics*, 202-3.

103. Kantor, *Who Was Jack Ruby?*, 12.

104. CE 2980.

105. 23 H 369.

106. 23 H 370.

107. Ibid.

108. 23 H 363.

109. Ibid.

110. 26 H 470.

111. Kantor, *Who Was Jack Ruby?* 35.

112. Ibid.

113. Ibid.

114. Ibid.

115. 5 H 196-198.

116. 5 H 208.

117. 5 H 196.

118. Roberts and Armstrong, *JFK: The Dead Witnesses,* 31-33.

119. Ibid.

120. Ibid.

121. Jack Ruby statement to former aide to Lyndon Johnson, cited in Groden and Livingstone, *High Treason,* 203.

122. Epstein, *Inquest*, 50.

123. "Beyond JFK," video.

124. "The Garrison Tapes," video.

125. 5 H 194, 196.

126. "Who Murdered JFK," video.

127. Meagher, *Accessories After the Fact,* 452.

128. Ibid.

Chapter 13

1. *ARRB Final Report,* 122.

2. Deb Reichmann, AP, 19 November 1998.

3. 2 H 348.

4. Cited in Palamara, *JFK: The Medical Evidence Reference,* 117.

5. *ARRB Final Report,* 122.

6. Robert's interview with ARRB's Jeremy Gunn and Douglas Horne, 28 February 1997, cited in Robert Groden and Harrison Livingstone, *High Treason 1998,* 420.

7. Deb Reichmann, Associated Press article, 31 July 1998.

8. Scott Hatfield,"RT Disputes X-ray Photos in JFK Case," 31 August 1992, cited in Palamara, *JFK: The Medical Evidence Reference,* 146.

9. *USA Today,* 29 May 1992.

10. *ARRB Final Report,* 123.

11. Ibid.

12. "The Men Who Killed Kennedy," video, 1988.

13. Lifton, *Best Evidence,* 608-14, 615-19, 696.

14. ARRB deposition 13 February 1996, cited in Groden and Livingstone, *High Treason, 1998,* 446-55.

15. ARRB interview 11 September 1997, cited in Groden and Livingstone, *High Treason, 1998,* 404-7.

16. *Inside Edition*, June 1989.

17. Groden and Livingstone, *High Treason,* 45.

18. Related to Livingstone, 1992, cited in Palamara, *JFK: The Medical Evidence Reference,* 31.

19. *Boston Globe,* 21 June 1981.

20. Interview with Wallace Milam, cited in Palamara, *JFK: The Medical Evidence Reference,* 43.

21. ARRB interview, June 1996, cited in Palamara, *JFK: The Medical Evidence Reference,* 123.

22. Groden and Livingstone, *High Treason,* 46.

23. "JFK: Case For Conspiracy," video, 1993, New Frontier Productions, Robert Groden.

24. Lifton, *Best Evidence,* 706.

25. "JFK: Case For Conspiracy," video.

26. Livingstone, *Killing The Truth,* 187.

27. David Naro interviews from 5, 20 and 28 January 1994, from COPA abstract, cited in Palamara, *JFK: The Medical Evidence Reference,* 13.

28. Livingstone, *Killing the Truth,* 702.

29. Ibid.

30. *Boston Globe,* 21 June 1981.

31. Ibid.

32. 5 H 180.

33. Ibid.

34. George Lardner, *Washington Post*, October 1998.

35. Deb Reichmann, AP, 1 August 1998.

36. Cited in Palamara, *JFK: The Medical Evidence Reference,* 124-25.

37. Ibid., 133-34.

38. Deb Reichmann, AP, 19 November 1998.

39. Lifton, *Best Evidence,* 396-97.

40. Interview with David Lifton, cited in Summers, *Conspiracy,* 250.

41. Ibid., 483.

42. Interview with David Lifton, cited in Lifton, *Best Evidence,* 398-99.

43. Ibid., 398, 408.

44. Ibid., 414.

45. Cited in Palamara, *JFK: The Medical Evidence Reference,* 133-34.

46. Ibid., 126, 145-46.

47. Lifton, *Best Evidence,* 630, 651.

48. UPI, 25 January 1981.

49. Manchester, *Death of a President,* 644.

50. Cited in Palamara, *JFK The Medical Evidence Reference,* 147.

51. Ibid., 126.

52. Karen Gullo and Deb Riechmann, AP, 30 May 1999.

53. Cited in Palamara, *JFK: The Medical Evidence Reference,* 84.

54. Livingstone, *High Treason Two,* 107.

55. Related to Joanne Braun, cited in Palamara, *JFK: The Medical Evidence Reference,* 147.

56. HSCA interview with Andrew Purdy and Jim Conzelman, cited in Palamara, *JFK: The Medical Evidence Reference,* 123.

57. Lifton, *Best Evidence,* 610.

58. Ibid.

59. *ARRB Final Report,* 123.

60. Ibid., 131.

61. Hurt, *Reasonable Doubt,* 49.

62. Ibid.

63. Interview with Bill Law and Vincent Palamara, cited in Palamara, *JFK: The Medical Evidence Reference,* 136.

64. Interview with Bill Law, cited in Palamara, *JFK: The Medical Evidence Reference,* 131.

65. "On Trial: Lee Harvey Oswald," video, 1986.

66. HSCA interview with Andrew Purdy, cited in Palamara, *JFK: The Medical Evidence Reference,* 116.

67. Palamara, *JFK: The Medical Evidence Reference,* 68.

68. Manchester, *Death of a President,* 174.

69. James Folliard, *Blaming the Victims: Kennedy Family Control Over the Bethesda Autopsy,* The Fourth Decade, Vol. 2, No. 4, 7.

70. Folliard, *Blaming the Victims,* 6-7.

71. Ibid., 7.

72. Ibid.

73. Cited in Ibid., 5-7.

74. Ibid., 6.

75. Ibid., 8.

76. Ibid.

77. Ibid.

78. Ibid.

79. Ibid., 10.

80. Ibid.

81. Ibid., 10-11.

82. Ibid.

83. Ibid., 11.

84. Livingstone, *Killing The Truth,* 716.

85. Livingstone, *High Treason Two,* 179-80.

86. Folliard, *Blaming the Victims,* 12.

87. Ibid., 11.

88. Weisberg, *Post Mortem*, 236.

89. From Finck's testimony, 24 and 25 February 1969, 48, cited in Weisberg, *Selections From Whitewash,* 428.

90. Ibid., 429.

91. Ibid.

92. *Lancer/Line,* 5 October 1998,interview with Bill Law.

93. Folliard, *Blaming the Victims,* The Fourth Decade, Vol. 2, No. 4, p 5.

94. 7 HSCA 14.

95. Ibid.

96. Cited in Palamara, *JFK: The Medical Evidence Reference*, 133-34.

97. Ibid., 126.

98. Ibid., 125.

99. The Third Decade, Vol. IV, No. 2, January 1988, 21.

100. Cited in Palamara, *JFK: The Medical Evidence Reference,* 146-49.

101. Cited in Ibid., 148.

102. Ibid., 187.

103. LBJ Notes, 26 January 1997, LBJ Library, cited in Ibid., 167-68.

104. Twyman, *Bloody Treason*, 201.

105. *Air Force One* radio transmissions, cited in Lifton, *Best Evidence*, 681, 686-89.

106. Ibid., 688-89, interview with General Clifton.

107. Lifton, *Best Evidence*, 690.

108. *ARRB Final Report*, 116.

109. *Robert Kennedy In His Own Words*, 411.

110. Schlesinger, *Robert Kennedy and His Times*, 675.

111. Jeff Shesol, *Mutual Contempt*, 122.

112. Palamara, *The Third Alternative*, 84.

113. 11 HSCA 530.

114. 11 HSCA 527, 529.

115. 11 HSCA 527.

116. Sloan and Hill, *The Last Dissenting Witness*, 113-14.

117. 3 H 241-70.

118. Palamara, *JFK: The Medical Evidence Reference*, 209 and 6 H 163.

119. 11 HSCA.

120. Palamara, *JFK: The Medical Evidence Reference*, 70.

121. Stuart Galanor interview, 1974.

122. *Los Angeles Free Press* reprint from *Press West, Inc.*, 1978,. 35.

123. Ibid.

124. Palamara, *The Third Alternative,* 3.

125. Jerry ter Horst, *The Flying White House: The Story of Air Force One* (New York, Bantam Books, 1979), 214.

126. 4 H 342.

127. 7 HSCA 14.

128. "JFK/Deep Politics Quarterly," Vol. 2, No. 1, October 1996,. 16.

129. Ibid., 17.

130. "JFK/Deep Politics Quarterly," Vol. 2, No. 3, April 1997, 35.

131. Ibid., 6.

132. Ibid.

133. Manchester, *Death of a President,* 37.

134. Ibid., 4.

135. Palamara, *The Third Alternative,* 8.

136. Ibid., 18.

137. Vincent Palamara, "The Secret Service in Their Own Words," 2, copy courtesy of John F. Kennedy Library.

138. Ibid., 3.

139. Ibid.

140. Ibid., 4.

141. Ibid., 6.

142. Ibid.

143. Ibid.

144. Ibid.

145. 18 H 803-809.

146. Palamara, *The Third Alternative,* 9.

147. 5 H 470.

148. Palamara, *The Third Alternative,* 79.

149. Mary Barelli Gallagher, *My Life With Jacqueline Kennedy* (New York: D. McKay Co., 1969), 351

150. Palamara, *The Third Alternative,* 59-66.

151. *Washington News,* 21 May 1964.

152. Palamara, *The Third Alternative,* 61.

153. Ibid., 62.

154. Ibid., 60, 62.

155. Ibid., 65-66.

156. Ibid., 61, 65.

157. Ibid.

158. "JFK/Deep Politics Quarterly," Vol. 2 No. 3, article by Vincent Palamara, April 1997, 35.

159. Palamara, *The Third Alternative,* 17)

160. "JFK/Deep Politics Quarterly," Vol. 2, No. 1, October 1996, 17, "The Strange Actions (and Inaction) of Agent Emory Roberts" by Vincent Palamara.

161. 18 H 749-750; 18 H 734-735.

162. Kenneth O'Donnell and David Powers, *Johnny, We Hardly Knew Ye,* (Boston: Little, Brown & Co., 1970), 32.

163. Ibid., 19.

164. COPA, Dallas, 1998.

165. Gouchenaur statements from Agent Moore are from his HSCA 6/77 interview transcript along with Boring's examination of the transcript, cited in Palamara, *JFK: The Medical Evidence Reference, 62.*

166. Hinckle and Turner, *Deadly Secrets,* 259.

Chapter 14

1. *The Final Assassination Report,* 309.

2. Ibid., 310.

3. HSCA Vol. 11, 49.

4. Ibid., 41.

5. Blakey and Billings, *Fatal Hour*, 25 and HSCA, Vol. 11, 32.

6. 5 H 97-120.

7. *The Final Assassination Report,* 336.

8. Ibid., 331.

9. "Face the Nation," CBS interview with David Belin, 23 November 1975.

10. Lifton, *Best Evidence,* 34, 36.

11. "The Warren Commission," History Channel, 1999.

12. Ibid.

13. Ibid.

14. Ibid.

15. Gilbert C. Fite, *Senator Richard B. Russell: Senator From Georgia* (Chapel Hill & London: University of North Carolina Press, 1991), 423.

16. "Beyond JFK," video.

17. Ibid.

18. Ibid.

19. Ibid., 13.

20. Cited in *ARRB Final Report*, 17, Senator David L. Boren, May 12, 1992.

21. *ARRB Final Report,*. xxiii.

22. Ibid., 46, Senator William S. Cohen, May 2, 1992, cited in *ARRB Final Report.*

23. Posner, *Case Closed,* 128.

24. Lane, *Plausible Denial,* 53.

25. "Beyond JFK," video.

26. Statement by former FBI agent William Turner, Ibid.

27. From The National Conference; Coalition on Political Assassinations, Washington D.C., October 7-10, 1994, Conference Abstracts Presentation Summaries.

28. *U. S. News and World Report,* 30 August 1993, 6 September 1993.

29. Marrs, *Crossfire,* 71.

30. *1999 World Almanac,* Federal Election Commission for Study of American Electorate, Congressional Quarterly.

31. *USA Weekend,* 24-25 December 1999.

Chapter 15

1. Noam Chomsky, *Rethinking Camelot: JFK, the Vietnam War, and U.S. Political Culture* (Boston: South End Press, 1993).

2. Lyndon Baines Johnson, *The Vantage Point* (New York: Holt Rinehart, and Winston of Canada, 1971), 42-43.

3. Van Don, *Our Endless War: Inside Vietnam,* 18, 22, 28.

4. Cited in J. William Fulbright, *The Arrogance of Power* (New York: Random House, 1966), 115.

5. David L. Anderson, *Shadow on the White House: Presidents and the Vietnam War, 1956-75* (Lawrence: University Press of Kansas, 1993), 28.

6. Neil Sheehan, ed., *Pentagon Papers* as published by *New York Times* (Chicago: Bantam Books, 1971), 4.

7. Anderson, *Shadow on the White House,* 28.

8. Van Don, *Our Endless War,* 33.

9. Ibid., 40.

10. J. William Fulbright, *The Arrogance of Power*, 112.

11. Stanley Karnow, *Vietnam: A History* (New York: Penguin Books, 1984), legend following page 175.

12. Robert S. McNamara, James G. Blight, and Robert K. Brigham, *Argument Without End: In Search of Answers To The Vietnam Tragedy* (New York: Public Affairs, 1999), 40.

13. William Blum, *Killing Hope: U.S. Military and CIA Intervention Since World War II* (Monroe, Maine: Common Courage Press, 1995), 123.

14. *Pentagon Papers*, 4.

15. Anderson, *Shadow on the White House*, 19.

16. Ibid., 40.

17. Department of State, *Foreign Relations of the United States, 1950*: Volume Six: Washington D.C.: U.S. Government Printing Office, 1988-91, 780-85.

18. Blum, *Killing Hope*, 123.

19. Cited in Ibid., 123.

20. Cited in Ibid., 124.

21. Ibid.

22. Cited in McNamara, Blight, and Brigham, *Argument Without End*, 64.

23. Blum, *Killing Hope,* 124.

24. Ibid.

25. Ibid.

26. Ibid.

27. Ibid., 125.

28. Ibid., 125-26.

29. Ibid., 126.

30. Ibid., 127.

31. Ibid.

32. Dulles news conference, March 1, 1955, Dulles Papers, Princeton, N. J., Box 99, cited in George W. Herring, *America's Longest War: The United States and Vietnam, 1950-1975,* 3rd. Ed. (New York: McGraw-Hill, Inc., 1979), 78-79.

33. General Matthew B. Ridgway, U.S.A. (Ret.), *Soldier: The Memoirs of Matthew B. Ridgway* (New York: Harper & Brothers, 1956), 277.

34. *Pentagon Papers,* 1.

35. Ibid.

36. Ibid.

37. *Pentagon Papers,* 6.

38. Van Don, *Our Endless War,* 48.

39. Ibid., 49.

40. William Colby, *Honorable Men* (New York: Simon and Schuster, 1978), 158.

41. Ibid., 144.

42. Van Don, *Our Endless War,* 48.

43. Colby, *Honorable Men,* 146.

44. Ibid., 50, 52.

45. Ibid., 67.

46. Ibid., 158.

47. Ibid.

48. Ibid., 159.

49. Ibid., 160.

50. Ibid., 164.

51. Alfred McCoy, *The Politics of Heroin* (New York: Harper and Row, 1972).

52. History Channel, 21 November 1999.

53. Ibid.

54. Colby, *Honorable Men*, 159.

55. Gordon Gray memorandum, 14 September 1959, Eisenhower Papers, "Cleanup" File, Box 5, and cited in Herring, *America's Longest War*, 78.

56. Herring, *America's Longest War*, 78

Chapter 16

1. Collier and Horowitz, *The Kennedys*, 87.

2. Ibid.

3. Ibid., 94-95.

4. Theodore H. White, *The Making of the President, 1964* (New York: New American Library, 1966), 33.

5. Collier and Horowitz, *The Kennedys*, 110.

6. Lawrence F. O'Brien, *No Final Victories* (New York: Ballantine, 1974), 17.

7. Ibid., 21.

8. Collier and Horowitz, *The Kennedys*, 216.

9. Ibid., 221.

10. Ibid.

11. Ibid., 220.

12. Ibid., 221.

13. Cited in Ibid., 221.

14. Ibid., 221.

15. Roger Hilsman, *To Move a Nation* (New York: Doubleday, 1967), 99.

16. Collier and Horowitz, *The Kennedys,* 221.

17. Ibid., 222.

18. Cited in Ibid., 245.

19. Cited in Ibid., 246.

20. Cited in Ibid.

21. Cited in Ibid., 247.

22. Cited in Gibson, *Battling Wall Street,* 39.

23. Cited in Gibson, *Battling Wall Street,* 48.

24. Gregory Allen Olsen, *Mansfield and Vietnam: A Study in Rhetorical Adaptation* (East Lansing: Michigan State University Press, 1995), 96.

25. Sorensen, *Kennedy 25 Years,* 547.

26. Robert A. Caro, *The Years of Lyndon Johnson: Means of Ascent* (New York: Alfred A. Knopf, Inc., 1990), 6.

27. Ibid.

28. Ibid., 7.

29. Sam Houston Johnson, *My Brother Lyndon* (New York: Cowles Book Company, 1969), 6.

30. Caro, *The Years of Lyndon Johnson,* 7.

31. S. H. Johnson, *My Brother Lyndon,* 6.

32. Caro, *The Years of Lyndon Johnson,* 10.

33. Ibid., xxv.

34. Ibid., 16.

35. Ibid.

36. Ibid., 18.

37. Ibid., 19.

38. Ibid., 51.

39. Ibid.

40. Ibid., 48, 51.

41. Ibid., 71.

42. Ibid., 77.

43. Ibid., 78-79.

44. Ibid.

45. Ibid.

46. Ibid.

47. Ibid., 78-79.

48. Ibid., 358.

49. Ibid.

50. Ibid.

51. Ibid., 386.

52. Victor Lasky, *It Didn't Start With Watergate* (New York: Dell Publishing, 1977), 132.

53. Caro, *The Years of Lyndon Johnson,* 388.

54. Cited in Ibid., 196.

55. Ibid., 152-53.

56. Richard F. Kaufman, *The War Profiteers* (Garden City, NY: Anchor Books, 1972), 34-35.

57. Rowland Evans and Robert Novak, *Lyndon B. Johnson: The Exercise of Power* (New York: New American Library, 1966), 16-17.

58. *Barry Goldwater* with Jack Casserly, (New York: St. Martin's Press, 1988), 190-92.

59. George Ball, *The Past Has Another Pattern: Memoirs* (New York: W. W. Norton and Company, 1982), 350.

60. Dotson Rader, "This Country Has to Make a Decided Change," *Parade*, 28 November 1993.

61. Ibid.

Chapter 17

1. Theodore H. White, *The Making of the President: 1960* (New York: Atheneum House, 1961), 53.

2. Ibid., 160-61.

3. O'Neil and Novak, *Man of the House,* 215.

4. White, *The Making of the President: 1960,* 206.

5. Seymour Hersh, *The Dark Side of Camelot* (Boston: Little, Brown, and Co., 1997), 129.

6. White, *The Making of the President: 1960,* 206.

7. Ibid., 211-12.

8. Bradlee, *Conversations with Kennedy,* 184.

9. Doris Kearns Goodwin, *Lyndon Johnson and the American Dream* (New York: Harper and Row, 1976), 164-65.

10. C-Span, Arthur Schlesinger, May 15, 1994.

11. *New York Times,* 17 October 1962.

12. *Robert Kennedy in His Own Words* (London: Bantam Press, 1988), 23.

13. S. H. Johnson, *My Brother Lyndon,* 108.

14. Twyman, *Bloody Treason,* 804.

15. Schlesinger, *Robert Kennedy and His Times,* 671.

16. Ibid.

17. Ibid., 113.

18. Cited in Ibid.

19. Sorensen, *Kennedy 25 Years,* 299.

20. John M. Newman, *JFK and Vietnam* (New York: Warner Books, 1992), 18.

21. Ibid.

22. Ibid.

23. Schlesinger, *Robert Kennedy and His Times,* 757.

24. *Pentagon Papers,* 125.

25. David Halberstam, *The Best and the Brightest* (New York: Penguin Books, 1972), 27.

26. Newman, *JFK and Vietnam,* 57.

27. Ibid., 67.

28. Ibid.

29. Ibid., 76.

30. Ibid., 67.

31. Olsen, *Mansfield and Vietnam,* 125.

32. Declassified Memorandum from the *Pentagon Papers* December 13, 1977, Courtesy of John F. Kennedy Library, 4-6, 9.

33. Comments and Observations Relative to the May 9-24, 1961 Southeast Asia, Middle East, Round-the-World Trip with Vice President Johnson, James A. Suffridge, 3.

34. Johnson to Kennedy, May 23, 1961, Kennedy Papers, Office File, Box 30., cited in Herring, *America's Longest War,* 86-87.

35. Ibid.

36. Karnow, *Vietnam,* 268.

37. Admiral U.S.G. Sharp, USN (Ret.), *Strategy for Defeat: Vietnam in Retrospect* (Novato, Calif.: Presidio Press, 1978), 17.

38. Sorensen, *Kennedy 25 Years,* 592.

39. Ernest May and Philip Zelkow, eds., *The Kennedy Tapes,* (Cambridge, Mass.: Belknap Press, Div. of Harvard University Press, 1997), 34.

40. Michael R. Beschloss, *The Crisis Years* (New York: Burlingame Books, 1991), 87, 225.

41. Halberstam, *The Best and the Brightest,* 204.

42. Newman, *JFK and Vietnam*, 118-20.

43. Cited in Newman, *JFK and Vietnam*, 138-39.

44. *Pentagon Papers*, 130.

45. Colby, *Honorable Men,* 168.

46. Karnow, *Vietnam,* 269.

47. *Pentagon Papers*, 140.

48. Ibid., 141.

49. Newman, *JFK and Vietnam,* 147, 160-61.

50. Cited in Karnow, *Vietnam,* 269.

51. Ball, *The Past Has Another Pattern,* 366-67.

52. Newman, *JFK and Vietnam,* 147.

53. Cited in Ibid., 155.

54. Ibid., 156.

55. Colby, *Honorable Men,* 169.

56. Arthur Krock, *Memoirs* (New York: Popular Library, 1968), 333.

57. Colby, *Honorable Men,* 170.

58. Newman, *JFK and Vietnam,* 173.

59. Ibid.

60. Ibid., 187.

61. Pierre Salinger, *With Kennedy* (New York: Doubleday. 1966), 315.

62. Robert S. McNamara, *In Retrospect: The Tragedy and Lessons of Vietnam* (New York: Random House, Inc., 1996), 321.

63. Salinger, *With Kennedy*, 315.

64. Ibid., 318.

65. Ibid.

66. Ibid., 322.

67. Ibid.

68. John Kenneth Galbraith, James Goodman, ed., *Letters To Kennedy* (Cambridge, Mass.: Harvard University Press, 1998), 101-3.
69. Cited in Newman, *JFK and Vietnam*, 236.

70. Cited in Ibid.

71. Cited in Ibid.

72. Cited in Ibid., 294.

73. Ibid., 292.

74. May and Zelkow, *The Kennedy Tapes*, 36-38, 45.

75. Ibid., 47-54.

76. Jack Anderson interview with Arthur Lundhal, cited in the *Cleveland Plain Dealer,* 21 November 1982.

77. Ibid.

78. Ibid.

79. May and Zelkow, *The Kennedy Tapes,* 27.

80. "From the Eye of the Storm," *Washington Monthly,* November 1997.

81. Cited in McNamara, *In Retrospect,* 436.

82. May and Zelkow, *The Kennedy Tapes.*

83. "History Undercover: General Curtis LeMay," History Channel, 1998.

84. *Khrushchev Remembers: The Glasnost Tapes,* (Boston: Little, Brown and Company, 1990), 175.

85. "Inside the Evil Empire: The Memoirs of Sergi Krushchev," *Dayton Daily News,* 27 February 2000.

86. Paul B. Fay, Jr., *The Pleasure of His Company* (New York: Harper and Row, 1966), 174-75.

87. Sorensen, *Kennedy 25 Years,* 684.

88. Arthur M. Schlesinger, Jr., *The Imperial Presidency* (New York: Popular Library Edition, 1974), 198, 417.

89. Charles Higham and Joel Greenbert, *The Celluloid Muse: Hollywood Directors Speak* (New York: Signet Books, 1972), 92.

90. "History Undercover: General Curtis LeMay," History Channel, 1998.

91. Ibid.

92. Ibid.

93. Ibid.

94. From the "Farewell Address of President Dwight D. Eisenhower," 17 January 1961.

95. McNamara, Blight, and Brigham, *Argument Without End,* 9.

96. Ibid., 10.

97. C-Span, 7 January 1999.

98. Schlesinger, *Robert Kennedy and His Times,* 676.

99. FRUS, Vietnam, August-December 1963, Vol. IV, 11.

100. Ibid., 22.

101. Ibid., 36, 122.

102. Colby, *Honorable Men,* 207.

103. Newman, *JFK and Vietnam,* 369.

104. Cited in Paris Flammonde, *The Kennedy Conspiracy,* 247.

105. Andre Fontaine, *History of the Cold War from the Korean War to the Present,* trans. Renaud Bruce, (New York: Pantheon Books, 1969), 474-75.

106. Powell, *J. William Fulbright and His Time,* 188.

107. Ibid., 190.

108. Ibid., 204.

109. "Remembering John Kennedy, "Arts & Entertainment Interview, November 1988.

110. Powell, *J. William Fulbright and His Time,* 225.

111. Ibid.

112. Cited in Ibid., 249.

113. Cited in Olsen, *Mansfield and Vietnam,* 99.

114. Ibid., 111.

115. Ibid.

116. Cited in Ibid., 112.

117. Ibid.

118. Cited in Ibid., 117.

119. Ibid.

120. Cited in Newman, *JFK and Vietnam,* 402.

121. Ibid., 372.

122. Interview with Dennis O'Brien, 119, July 11, 1970, courtesy of John F. Kennedy Library.

123. From Jeffery Potter, *Men, Money, and Magic: The Story of Dorothy Schiff,* cited in Schlesinger, *Robert Kennedy and His Times,* 674.

124. *Robert Kennedy in His Own Words*, 326-27.

125. Fredrik Nolting, *From Trust to Tragedy* (New York: Praeger, 1988), 125, 131, 133.

126. Brian Macquarrie, *New York Times,* cited in *Cleveland Plain Dealer,* 25 November 1998.

127. Rusk, *As I Saw It,* 439.

128. Maxwell Taylor, *Swords and Plowshares* (New York: Da Capo Press, Inc., 1972), 294-95.

129. Ibid., 301-2.

130. Henry Cabot Lodge, *The Storm Has Many Eyes: A Personal Narrative* (New York: W. W. Norton and Company, 1973), 209.

131. Ibid., 210.

132. Ball, *The Past Has Another Pattern,* 372.

133. Ibid.

134. Ibid., 373.

135. Ibid., 374.

136. Sharp, *Strategy for Defeat,* 21, 23.

137. Cited in Newman, *JFK and Vietnam*, 412.

138. Appendix to the Vintage Edition of McNamara, *In Retrospect,* "The Case for the War" by W. W. Rostow, *Times Literary Supplement (*London), June 9, 1995, 429.

139. Nolting, *From Trust to Tragedy,* 250.

140. "JFK: A New Look," video.

141. John Farrell, *Boston Globe,* reprinted in the *Cleveland Plain Dealer,* 15 October 1999.

142. H. R. Haldeman, *The Ends of Power* (New York, Dell Publishing, 1978), 217, and John Dean, *Blind Ambition* (New York: Pocket Books, 1976), 110.

143. Stanley I. Kutler, *Abuse of Power* (New York: Simon &

Schuster, 1997), 366.

144. Powers, *The Man Who Kept the Secrets* (New York: Knopf, 1979), 121.

145. O'Brien, *No Final Victories,* 147.

146. O'Donnell and Powers, *Johnny, We Hardly Knew Ye,* 16.

147. O'Neil and Novak, *Man of the House,* 208.

148. Ibid.

149. Charles E. Bohlen, *Witness to History, 1929-1969* (New York: W. W. Norton and Company, 1973), 504.

150. Clark Clifford and Richard Holbrook, *Counsel to the President: A Memoir,* (New York: Random House, 1991), 381-82.

151. McNamara, *In Retrospect,* 399.

152. Taylor, *Swords and Plowshares,* 298.

153. Mike Feinsilber, Associated Press article, 23 December 1997.

154. "Hardball," CNBC, 20 July 1999 with Chris Matthews.

155. Paul Nitze, *From Hiroshima to Glasnost: At the Center of Decision, A Memoir* (New York: Grove Weidenfeld, 1989), 256.

156. Ibid., 257.

157. Roger Hilsman, *To Move A Nation* (New York: Doubleday and Company, Inc., 1964), 536.

158. Cited in McNamara, *In Retrospect,* 62.

159. Ibid.

160. "JFK: A New Look," video.

161. Cronkite, *A Reporter's Life,* 243.

162. Jack Anderson with Daryl Gibson, *Peace, War, and Politics: An Eyewitness Account,* (New York: A Tom Doherty Associates Book, 1999), 103.

163. Cited in John M. Newman, *JFK and Vietnam* (New York:

Warner Books, Inc., 1992), 387.

164. *George F. Kennan: Memoirs, 1925-1950* (Boston: Bantam Books, 1969), 54-55.

165. Newman, *JFK and Vietnam*, 372.

166. Cited in Ibid., 387-88.

167. Schlesinger, *Robert Kennedy and His Times,* 772.

168. Ibid., 538.

169. Ibid., 776.

170. Ibid., 778.

171. Cited in Newman, *JFK and Vietnam,* 426.

172. Cited in Ibid., 423-24.

173. Cited in Ibid., 425-26.

174. Cited in Ibid., 427.

175. Statement from Professor John Newman at COPA Conference, Dallas, 1998.

176. Ibid., *In Retrospect,* 95, 96.

177. Connally and Herskowitz, *In History's Shadow,* 358.

178. Ibid., 204.

179. Ibid., 358.

180. Schlesinger, *Cigar Aficionado.*

181. "Beyond JFK," video.

182. O'Neil and Novak, *Man of the House,* 208.

183. Rusk, *As I Saw It,* 435.

184. Ibid., 442.

185. Olsen, *Mansfield and Vietnam,* 57.

186. Colby, *Honorable Men,* 221.

187. James M. Gavin, "We Can Get Out of Vietnam," *Saturday Evening Post,* 24 February 1968.

188. *Pentagon Papers*, xxiii.

189. *Business Week*, 18 November 1963.

190. Cited in Gibson, "Wall Street", *Moody's Investor Service,* 1964.

191. Sorensen, *Kennedy 25 Years*, 504.

192. "JFK: A New Look," video.

193. David Halberstam, "The Vietnam War is Finally Over. . . What a Shame," *George*, April, 2000.

194. Sorensen, *Kennedy 25 Years,* xi.

195. "JFK: A New Look", video.

Chapter 18

1. McNamara, *In Retrospect,* 97.

2. "Straight Forward," CNBC, 22 April 1995.

3. Ball, *The Past Has Another Pattern,* 375.

4. Olsen, *Mansfield and Vietnam,* 126.

5. Cronkite, *A Reporter's Life*, 248.

6. S. H. Johnson, *My Brother Lyndon,* 198.

7. Ibid., 196, 199.

8. FRUS, Vietnam, 1964, 631.

9. Ibid., 633.

10. Ibid.

11. Ibid.

12. Ibid.

13. Herring, *America's Longest War*, 122.

14. Memorandum for the Record of a Meeting, Executive Office Building, November 24, 1963, FRUS, 1961-1963, Vol 4, 635-637.

15. FRUS, Vietnam, 1964., 637.

16. Ibid., 638.

17. McNamara, *In Retrospect*, 103.

18. Ibid., 108.

19. George Ball, *The Past Has Another Pattern*, 318.

20. Drew Pearson, *Wooster (Ohio) Daily Record*, 27 November 1963.

21. Memorandum of January, 1964; cited in *Pentagon Papers*, 274-75.

22. Cited in Newman, *JFK and Vietnam*, 443.

23. Taylor, *Swords and Plowshares*, 304.

24. FRUS, Vietnam, 1964, 445.

25. Karnow, *Vietnam*, 379.

26. Olsen, *Mansfield and Vietnam*, 127.

27. FRUS, Vietnam, 1964, 4.

28. Ibid., 12.

29. Ibid.

30. McNamara, *In Retrospect*, 109.

31. Hilsman, *To Move a Nation*, 527.

32. FRUS, Vietnam, 1964, 63.

33. Cited in Herring, *America's Longest War*, 130.

34. Ibid., 133; Cited in Powell, *J. William Fulbright and His Time*.

35. Sharp, *Strategy for Defeat,* 39.

36. Ibid., 47.

37. Herring, *America's Longest War,* 134.

38. Jack Casserly, *Goldwater,* (New York: St. Martin's Press, 1988), 295-96.

39. Legend following 363, cited in Karnow, *Vietnam.*

40. Ibid., 421.

41. W. W. Rostow, *The Case for the War* (London: Times Literary Supplement, 1995), cited in McNamara, *In Retrospect,* 425-42.

42. *Pentagon Papers,* 274-89.

43. J. William Fulbright, "They Found Their Opportunity," *Memories* (magazine), August-September 1989.

44. Ball, *The Past Has Another Pattern,* 380.

45. FRUS; Vietnam, 1964, 13.

46. Caro, *The Years of Lyndon Johnson*, xxiii.

47. Fulbright, *Memories* , 1989.

48. Karnow, *Vietnam,* 411.

49. Herring, *America's Longest War,* 137.

50. Ball, *The Past Has Another Pattern,* 388.

51. McNamara, *In Retrospect,* 432.

52. Sharp, *Strategy for Defeat,* 62.

53. Cited in McNamara, Blight, and Brigham, *Argument Without End,* 172.

54. Ibid.

55. Sharp, *Strategy for Defeat,* 63.

56. Powers, *Secrecy and Power,* 427-28.

57. Harris Wofford, *Of Kennedys and Kings: Making Sense of the Sixties* (Pittsburgh: University of Pittsburgh Press, 1980), 220-21.

58. Ball, *The Past Has Another Pattern,* 375.

59. Colby, *Honorable Men,* 225.

60. Herring, *America's Longest War,* 3.

61. Karnow, *Vietnam,* 358.

62. Ibid.

63. Ibid., 433.

64. Powell, *J. William Fulbright and His Time,* 193.

65. Ibid., 234.

66. Lyndon Johnson in personal conversation [excerpt from Goodwin's diary entry of June 22, 1965], Richard N. Goodwin, *Remembering America: A Voice From the Sixties,* (New York: Little, Brown, and Company), 392.

67. Caro, *The Years of Lyndon Johnson,* 15.

68. Ibid.

69. Schlesinger, *Robert Kennedy and His Times,* 623.

70. Hugh Sidey, *Time,* 6 September 1988.

71. Sullivan, *The Bureau,* 64.

72. Gibson, *Battling Wall Street,* 79-80.

73. Cited in *Khrushchev Remembers: The Last Testament* (New York: Little, Brown and Company, 1974), 510.

74. Powell, *J. William Fulbright and His Time,* 253, 258.

75. Ibid., 259.

76. Ibid., 261.

77. Ibid., 265.

78. Ibid., 256.

79. Sullivan, *The Bureau,* 70.

80. Theoharis and Cox, *The Boss,* 446.

81. *New York Times,* 22 April 1964 and *U. S. News and World Report,* 4 May 1964.

82. Joseph Kraft, *J. Edgar Hoover: The Complete Bureaucrat,* "Commentary," February 1965, 60.

83. *J. Edgar Hoover on Communism,* (New York: Random House, 1969), 114-15.

84. DeLoach, *Hoover's FBI,* 282-84.

85. Sullivan, *The Bureau,* 152-56.

86. Ibid., 77.

87. Fulbright, *Memories* .

88. *Parade* Magazine, 7 July 1985.

89. Goodwin, *Lyndon Johnson,* 253.

90. Ibid., 267.

91. Goodwin, *Lyndon Johnson,* 258-59.

92. Powell, *J. William Fulbright and His Time,* 218.

93. John Ranelagh, *The Rise and Decline of the Agency* (New York: Simon and Schuster, 1986), 422.

94. Powell, *J. William Fulbright and His Time,* 203.

95. Karnow, *Vietnam,* 414.

96. *Pentagon Papers (Gravel),* III, 418 cited in Herring, *America's Longest War,* 145.

97. Herring, *America's Longest War,* 121.

98. Goodwin, *Lyndon Johnson,* 259.

99. Tom Wicker, "Committed to a Quagmire," Diplomatic History,

Vol. 19, No. 1, (winter 1995), 167.

100. Ibid., 168-70.

101. Caro, *The Years of Lyndon Johnson*, xxiv.

102. Tom Wicker, "Committed to a Quagmire," Diplomatic History, Vol. 19, No. 1, (winter 1995),170-71.

103. Beyond JFK," video.

104. *Newsweek,* 17 April 1995.

105. *ARRB Final Report,* 94.

Conclusion

1. Powers, *Secrecy and Power,* 394.

2. *The White House Transcripts Submission of Recorded Presidential Conversations to the Committee on the Judiciary of the House of Representatives* (New York: Bantam Books, ed., 1973), 77.

3. Sullivan, *The Bureau,* 60.

4. Schlesinger, *Robert Kennedy and His Times,* 678.

5. Ibid., 679.

6. Schlesinger, *Robert Kennedy and His Times,* 679-80.

7. *ARRB Final Report,* 4.

8. "Beyond JFK," video.

9. Ibid.

10. Marks, *Coup d état,* 145.

11. William C. Spragens, "Political Impact of Presidential Assassinations and Attempted Assassinations," *Presidential Studies Quarterly,* Vol. X, (summer 1980), 336.

12. "End of Camelot," Discovery Channel, 1992.

13. Janet Gilmore, AP, *Los Angeles Daily News,* 9 September 1996.

14. Craig Zirbel, *The Texas Connection: The Assassination of John F. Kennedy,* (Scottsdale Ariz.: Texas Connection Publishers, 1991), 254.

15. Shesol, *Mutual Contempt,* 135.

16. Arnold Bennett, *Jackie, Bobby, and Manchester* (New York: Bee-hive Books, Inc. 1967), 49.

17. Shesol, *Mutual Contempt,* 354.

18. *ARRB Final Report,* 117-18.

19. Bennett, *Jackie, Bobby, and Manchester,* 151.

20. United Press International, 22 November 1963.

21. Scheim, *Contract on America,* 250.

22. Scott, *Deep Politics,* 217-21, and Lasky, *It Didn't Start With Watergate,* 154.

23. Scott, *Deep Politics,* 221.

24. Bradlee, *Conversations with Kennedy,* 213.

25. Ibid., 214-15.

26. "The Letter," *Ramparts* magazine, February 1967.

27. J. Evetts Haley, *A Texan Looks at Lyndon: A Study in Illegitimate Power* (Canyon, Tex.: PaloDuro Press, 1964), 7.

28. *Dallas Times Herald* article cited in *Cleveland Plain Dealer,* 24 March 1984.

29. Ibid.

30. Ibid.

31. Robert Morrow, *Betrayal* (Chicago: Henry Regenery Company, 1976), 22.

32. George Ready, *Lyndon B. Johnson: A Memoir,* (Fairway, Kans.: Universal Press Syndicate Co., 1982).

33. McNamara, In Retrospect, 98.

34. Califano, *The Triumph and Tragedy of Lyndon Johnson,* 10.

35. Manchester, *Death of a President,* 3.

36. Shesol, *Mutual Contempt,* 137.

37. Ibid.

38. Cited in Ibid., 138.

39. Bradlee, *Conversations with Kennedy,* 236.

40. *Robert Kennedy in His Own Words,* 411.

41. Shesol, *Mutual Contempt,* 113.

42. Marrs, *Crossfire,* 356.

43. Wade Interview with researcher Mark Oakes, "Eyewitness Video," 1992.

44. *Washington Post,* 1 April 1985.

45. Ibid.

46. Ronald J. Ostrow, *Los Angeles Times,* 5 November 1966.

47. "Beyond JFK," video.

48. Crenshaw, *Conspiracy of Silence,* 5.

49. Ibid., 186-87.

50. COPA, Washington, D.C. 20-22 October 1995 Conference Abstracts, Phi-Slamma Jamma, The Settlement.

51. 6 H 32, 40, 60, 80, 131; COPA, Washington, D.C. 7-10 October 1994 Conference Abstracts by D. Bradley Kizzia, J.D.

52. Cited in "Assassination Science," *New York Times,* 27 May 1992.

53. Cited in "Assassination Science," *Dallas Morning News,* 15 July 1992.

54. 6 H 118.

55. 7 H 474-75.

56. 5 H 63-66.

57. 5 H 60.

58. *ARRB Final Report,* 159.

59. Ibid.

60. Anderson with Gibson, *Peace, War, and Politics,* 118.

61. *Dallas Times Herald,* 20 May 1989.

62. North, *Act of Treason,* 483.

63. Ball, *The Past Has Another Pattern,* 321.

64. Twyman, *Bloody Treason,* 500.

65. Fensterwald and Ewing, *Coincidence or Conspiracy,* 89-90.

66. Cited in Flammonde, *The Kennedy Conspiracy,* 275.

67. Cronkite, *A Reporter's Life,* 189.

68. "The Johnson Tapes," video, 1999.

69. Ibid.

70. Ibid.

71. Gentry, *J. Edgar Hoover,* 606.

72. Ibid.

73. Cited in Gentry, *J. Edgar Hoover,* 607.

74. Hoover's testimony quoted, cited in *New York Times,* 19 May 1968.

75. *New York Times,* 27 May 1968.

76. Powers, *Secrecy and Power,* 450-51.

77. Cited in Summers, *Official and Confidential,* 402.

78. Kutler, *Abuse of Power,* 68.

79. Ibid., 69.

80. Ibid.

81. Ibid., 70.

82. Ibid., 91.

83. H. R. Haldeman and Joseph DiMona, *The Ends of Power* (New York: A Dell Book, 1978), 54, 68.

84. Ibid.

85. Cited in Scheim, *Contract on America,* 235.

86. Sullivan, *The Bureau,* 53.

87. Roberts and Armstrong, *The Dead Witnesses,* 155-56.

88. Russell, *The Man Who Knew Too Much,* 709.

89. Sullivan, *The Bureau,* 53.

90. Oswald, *Lee,* 198.

91. Epstein, *Inquest,* 152.

92. Burrell's Transcripts, *Who Killed JFK,* 19 November 1993.

93. Meagher, *Accessories After the Fact,* 30.

94. Quoted in "The Ghosts of November," *Vanity Fair,* December 1994.

95. *New York Times,* 3 July 1997.

96. Kovel, *Red Hunting in the Promised Land,* 88.

97. Turner, *Hoover's FBI,* 290-300.

98. Corson, *The Armies of Ignorance,* 286.

99. Sullivan, *The Bureau,* 40.

100. Milan, *The Squad,* 1-2.

101. "U. S. Military and the Mafia: Operation Underworld," History Channel, September 20, 1999.

102. *The Final Assassination Report,* 335-36.

103. Ibid.

104. Ibid., 33; "JFK/Deep Politics Quarterly," Vol. II No. 3, by Vincent Palamara, April 1997.

105. *The Final Assassination Report,* 153-59.

106. Ibid.

107. Manchester, *Death of a President,* 46.

108. Russell, *The Man Who Knew Too Much,* 410-11.

109. Cited in Ibid., 412.

110. Ibid., 416.

111. Ibid., 690.

112. *The Third Decade:* "A Journal of Research on the John F. Kennedy Assassination," Vol. 2, #2, January 1986, 6-10.

113. MM157-739 10, 15, 17, Copy courtesy of Jim Lesar, Assassination Archives and Research Center, Washington, D.C.

114. Russell, *The Man Who Knew Too Much,* 548.

115. "The Men Who Killed Kennedy," video, 1988.

116. Palamara, *Third Alternative,* 53.

117. 11 HSCA 523.

118. "The Men Who Killed Kennedy," video, 1988.

119. Henry Hurt, *Reasonable Doubt,* 411; Summers, *Conspiracy,* 607; 1 HSCA 115 and CD 137, 120 and CD 1347, 121; *The Third Decade,* "Dead Suspects Part V" by Scott Van Wynsbeghe, January 1988, 3.

120. Bob Dyer, "New Clues on the JFK Assassination," *Akron (Ohio) Beacon Journal,* 22 November 1998.

121. Ibid.

122. Copy obtained courtesy of James Lesar, Assassination Archives and Research Center, Washington D.C.

123. Warren Commission Document, 305, copy courtesy of James Lesar, Assassination Archives and Research Center, Washington, D.C.

124. Ibid., 358-61.

125. *Ramparts,* June 1967.

126. Anderson with Gibson, *Peace, War and Politics,* 155-56.

127. Turner, *Hoover's FBI,* 177.

128. Ibid., 200.

129. Earl Ofari Hutchinson, "Questions for FBI in King Investigation Won't Go Away," *Cleveland Plain Dealer,* 1 4 December 1999.

130. *ARRB Final Report,* 96-97.

131. de Toledano, *J. Edgar Hoover,* 376.

132. Demaris, *The Director,* 323.

133. Ibid.

134. Messick, *John Edgar Hoover,* 254-55.

135. Cook, *The FBI Nobody Knows,* 402.

136. Powers, *Secrecy and Power,* 491-92.

Index

Abercrombie, John W., 30
Acheson, Dean, 344, 345, 347
Adams, Congressman, 16
Adams, Don, 470, 471
Adams, Emery, 148
Adams, Victoria, 244
Alba, Adrian, 154, 155
Aleman, Jose, 238
Alexander, William, 131
Alsop, Joseph, 378, 413
Altgens, James, 190, 237, 254
Alvarado, Gilbert, 138
Alyea, Tom, 170, 211, 240
Anderson, Admiral George, 374
Anderson, George, 36, 37
Anderson, Jack, 383, 388, 403,
  448, 451, 474
Anderson, John Lee, 466
Anderson, Scott, 466
Andrew, Christopher, 138
Andrews, Dean, 149, 272
Angleton, James, 133,134, 224
Anslinger, Harry, 49
Anthony, Carl, 45
Arnold, Carolyn, 192
Arnold, Gordon, 210, 211, 243,
  251
Arrowsmith, Harold, 33
Ashkenasy, Ernest, 195
Atkins, Thomas, 237
Atwood, William, 100
Aynsworth, Hugh, 265
Azcue, Eusebio, 138

Bagert, Bernard, xxiv
Baker, Barney, 259
Baker, Bobby, 214, 373, 442, 443
Baker, Marion, 168, 169, 234,
  302
Baker, Mrs. Donald, 198, 245
Baker, Newton, 24, 25
Ball, George, 132, 379, 397, 413,
  414, 416, 420, 422, 424, 452
Ball, Joseph, 163, 164, 173
Ballen, Samuel, 147, 175
Bannister, Guy, 154, 155, 156,
  461, 471
Bannister, Ross, 154
Barber, Steve, 195
Barker, Mrs. Eddie, 212
Barnes, Margie, 303
Barron, John, 131
Barth, Alan, 4, 6
Bartlett, Phyllis, 449
Bashour, Foad, 284
Baskin, Robert, 225
Bates, Pauline, 146
Batista, Fulgencio, 93
Baxter, Charles, 194, 230, 450
Beard, Charles, 34
Beard, James, 269
Beard, Mary, 34
Behn, Gerald, 303, 304, 305, 306
Belin, David, 186, 217, 313
Bell, Audrey, 284
Belli, Melvin, 261
Belmont, Alan, xxiv, 86, 143

567

Benavides, Domingo, 173
Benavides, Eddy, 174
Bennet, Glen, 304
Bennett, Arnold, 442
Berger, Victor, 26
Berkman, Alexander, 16, 22, 31, 37, 38, 454
Berle, Milton, 89
Biddle, Francis, 58, 61, 62
Bielaski, Bruce, 24
Bigart, Homer, 382
Billingsley, Sherman, 50
Bissell, Richard, 93, 95, 96
Black, Hugo, 66, 364
Blackner, Henry, 45
Blackstone, Harry Jr., 560
Blanco-Fernandez, Juan, 462
Blough, Roger, 80
Blum, William, 346, 347, 348
Blumberg, J. M., 209, 293, 294
Boggs, Hale, xix, 153, 159, 206, 207, 215, 217, 222, 224, 226, 227, 472
Bohlen, Charles, 400
Bolden, Abraham, 307, 308, 310
Bonaparte, Charles, 18, 19
Bond, Julian, 102
Boone, Eugene, 163, 164
Borah, William, 36, 42
Boren, David, 315
Boring, Floyd, 85, 303, 306, 309
Borman, Frank, 78
Boswell, J. Thornton, 283, 286, 291, 292, 293, 294
Botello, James, 146
Bowers, Dr., 271
Bowers, Lee, 250, 251, 268
Bowles, Chester, 378
Bowron, Diana, 284
Bradlee, Ben, 88, 89, 105, 214, 443, 447
Bradlee, Tony, 89
Brandon, Henry, 405
Braniff, Matthew, xxiv
Braun, Joanne, 289
Breen, James, 274
Breneman, Chester, 199
Brennan, Howard, 191, 192

Brickell, Herschel, 4
Bridges, Harry, 57, 58
Briggs, Albert, 24
Bringuier, Carlos, 152, 153
Brinkley, Alan, 92
Brinkley, David, 404
Brokaw, Tom, 86
Brookhart, Smith, 44
Brown, Bill, 9
Brown, Earl, 238
Brown, George, 362, 425
Brown, Herman, 362, 425
Browne, Malcolm, 382
Brugioni, Dino, 387
Bruno, Angelo, 83
Brynes, Asher, 473
Buckley, James, 476
Bundy, McGeorge, 99, 100, 378, 380, 398, 408, 414, 417, 422, 423, 428, 432
Bundy, William, 378
Burke, Arleigh, 373, 374
Burke, Frank, 30, 32, 34, 37
Burkley, George, 290, 291, 292, 293, 294, 298
Burleigh, Nina, 88, 89
Burns, William, 42, 44, 46
Burris, Howard, 375
Bush, George, 315
Byars, Billy Jr., 51
Byars, Billy Sr., 62, 70, 275
Byrnes, James, 344
Cabell, Charles, 445
Cabell, Earle, 266, 288, 302
Cabell, Mrs. Earle, 238
Califano, Joseph, 96, 140, 446
Cambre, Joseph, 154
Caminetti, Anthony, 30, 32, 36
Campbell, O. V., 245
Campisi, Joseph, 259
Canada, Robert, 293
Capell, Frank, 140
Capone, Al, 51
Carlin, Karen, 263, 264, 272
Caro, Robert, 363, 365, 421, 434
Carr, Richard, 188
Carr, Waggoner, 225, 226
Carrico, Charles, 201, 284

Carter, Cliff, 445, 448, 451
Carter, John, 263
Castro, Fidel, xxii, 92, 93, 94, 95,
   96, 97, 98, 99, 100, 132, 133,
   135, 136, 137, 138, 140, 143,
   152, 194, 218, 223, 258, 269,
   272, 426, 448, 449, 463, 464,
   475, 477
Castro, Raul, 94
Cavagnaro, Joseph, 265
Celler, Emmanuel, xviii
Chafee, Zachariah, 35, 66
Chamberlain, Neville, 356
Chambers, Whittaker, 66
Chandler, Senator, 17
Chaney, James, 234, 235
Charles, Pedro, 135
Chavez, Frank, 208
Cheek, Timothy, 287
Cheramie, Rose, 263, 270, 271,
   272, 465
Chiarodo, Mrs. Andrew, 298
Childs, Jack, 132
Childs, Morris, 131, 132
Chiles, Marion III, 63
Chism, John, 243
Chomsky, Noam, 341, 433, 434
Church, Frank, 94, 390, 391, 414
Churchill, Marlborough, 33, 43
Churchill, Ward, 71
Churchill, Winston, 62, 344, 356,
   375
Civello, Joe, 259
Clark, Hubert, 287
Clark, Kemp, 229, 285
Clark, Ramsay, 103, 297, 437,
   446, 454
Clark, Tom, 62, 63
Clement, Michelino, 83
Clemons, Acquilla, 172, 184
Clifford, Clark, xxiii, 400
Clifton, Ted, 298
Cline, Ray, 432
Clinton, Bill, 315, 388
Cohen, Mickey, 208
Cohen, William, 316
Cohn, Roy, 69, 74
Colby, William, 375, 378, 380,

381, 410, 424
Coleman, William, 465
Collier, Rex, 461
Comfort, Mildred, 5
Commings, Homer, 24, 53, 55
Conant, Harold, 22, 31
Connally, John, 108, 170, 171,
   200, 201, 202, 203, 204, 205,
   206, 228, 229, 253, 295, 307,
   369, 408, 447, 451
Connally, Nellie, 204, 205
Cook, Fred, xix, 6, 7, 8, 477
Cooke, Leon, 258
Coolidge, Calvin, xviii, 46
Cooper, Chester, 422
Cooper, Courtney Riley, 3, 55
Cooper, John Sherman, 206, 215,
   226
Corcoran, Tommy, 362
Corson, William, 43, 52, 57, 462
Costello, Frank, 49, 50, 214, 215
Couch, Malcolm, 237
Cox, John Stewart, 10, 46, 90,
   427
Craig, Roger, 156, 157, 164, 172,
   186, 197, 303
Craig, Walter, 161,
Craven, Robert, 265
Crawford, James, 243
Crawford, John, 17
Crenshaw, Charles, 180, 230,
   284, 448, 450, 451
Cronkite, Walter, 88, 102, 402,
   403, 413, 439, 449
Cummings, Bruce, 151
Cunningham, Lt., 252
Curry, Eileen, 274
Curry, Jesse, xx, 151, 166, 177,
   179, 180, 191, 192, 197, 218,
   225, 232, 247, 248, 266, 303
Cusack, Lawrence, 92
Custer, Jerrol, 245, 283, 286,
   287, 291, 297
Czolgosz, Leon, 17
Dai, Bo, 349
Daley, Richard, 84, 453
Dalitz, Mo, 74
Daniel, Jean, 100

Daniel, W. Lee, 362
Daniels, Hawk, 214, 259
Daniels, Jonathan, 362
Daugherty, Harry, 42, 45
David, Dennis, 288, 289, 297
Davidson, Irving, 51, 79
Davidson, T. Whitfield, 364
Davis, Charles, 382
Davis, John, 79
Davis, Mrs. Avery, 245
Davis, Thomas Eli, 270, 465
Day, Carl, 168, 197
Dealy, Ted, 130
Dean, John, 399
Debs, Eugene, 16, 17, 26
Decker, Bill, 232, 247, 276, 303
deFeese, Bert, 308
deGaulle, Charles, 344, 405, 406,
    439
Del Valle, Eladio, 156
deLattre, Jean Marie, 358
DeLoach, Cartha, xviii, 12, 38,
    47, 69, 71, 428, 449, 454, 459,
    462
Demaris, Ovid, 8, 9, 82, 476
deMohrenschildt, George, 147,
    148, 153, 175, 193
Dempsey, Jack, 365
deToledano, Ralph, 8, 461, 476
Dewey, Thomas, 67
Diem, Ngo Dinh, 349, 350, 351,
    352, 375, 376, 377, 378, 379,
    382, 389, 394, 395, 396, 397,
    398, 399, 400, 415, 434, 449
Dinkin, Eugene, 219, 220, 472,
    473, 474
Dirksen, Everett, 222
Disney, Walt, 65
Dobrynin, Anatoly, 134, 137, 385
Dodd, Richard, 184, 239, 249,
    250
Dolan, James, 273
Dolan, Joe, 107
Dolce, Joseph, 203, 207
Donner, Frank, 9
Donovan, John, 145
Donovan, William, 61
Douglas, Helen, 356

Douglas, William 357, 459
Downing, Thomas, 169
Duckstein, Mrs. J. B., 46
Dudman, Richard, 182, 198, 200,
    252
Dugger, Ronnie, 238
Dulany, Richard, 284
Dulles, Allen, 96, 133, 134, 158,
    159, 205, 226, 313, 316
Dulles, John Foster, 346, 347,
    348, 349
Duncan, Glen, 276
Dungan, Ralph, 181, 447
Durnbrow, Eldridge, 352, 375
Dyer, Bob, 468
Easley, Ralph, 48
Eastland, James, 221, 222
Ebersole, John, 245
Echevarria, Homer, 464, 465,
    466
Edwards, Don, 451
Edwards, Robert, 243
Edwards, Sheffield, 94
Ehrlichman, John, 454, 455
Eisenberg, Melvin, xxi, 217, 441
Eisenhower, Dwight, xviii, 65,
    69, 70, 93, 97, 341, 342, 347,
    349, 350, 352, 353, 373, 387,
    425, 467
Elder, Walter, 95
Eliff, John, 10
Elkins, Harold, 236
Ellis, Steve, 198, 208, 234
Elrod, John, 273
Engels, Friedrich, 27
Epstein, Edward, 145, 459
Esterline, Jacob, 94
Estes, Billy Sol, 444
Evans, Courtney, xxiv, 103
Evans, Medford, 452
Evans, Rowland, 366
Exner, Judith, 75, 81, 82, 84, 87,
    88, 444
Fain, John, 130, 159, 160
Farley, Jim, 55
Faulkner, Jack, 237
Fay, Paul, 385
Felt, Harry, 389

Feran, Tom, 78
Ferrie, David, 143, 144, 149, 153, 154, 155, 156
Fetzer, James, 208
Finch, Stanley, 20
Finck, Pierre, 202, 209, 286, 287, 292, 293, 294, 295
Fischer, Kay, 89
Fischer, Ron, 186, 187
Fite, Gilbert, 314
Fitzgerald, John, 18, 356
Flynn, Charles, 270
Flynn, William, 30, 34, 37, 42
Fogelson, E. E., 78
Folliard, James, 291, 292, 293, 294, 295
Fontaines, Alex, 471
Fonzi, Gaeton, 151
Ford, Gerald, xix, 157, 191, 217, 226, 279, 458, 459, 460, 461
Forman, Jack, 9
Forrestal, Michael, 406
Fortas, Abe, 214, 215, 364, 448, 449
Foster, J. W., 198, 234
Foster, William, 66
Framia, Louis, 66
Franco, Francisco, 151
Frankenheimer, John, 386
Frankfurter, Felix, 34
Frazier, Buell Wesley, 244
Frazier, Robert, 170, 451
Freeman, Howard, 208, 234
Freeman, Joshua, 10
Fritz, Will, 144, 163, 164, 218, 446
Fruge, Francis, 271
Fuchs, Klaus, 68
Fulbright, J. William, 77, 345, 384, 390, 391, 414, 420, 421, 425, 427, 429, 431
Galbraith, John Kenneth, 382, 385
Gallagher, Mary, 307
Galloway, Calvin, 292, 293, 295
Gandy, Helen, 12, 73, 476
Gardner, Arthur, 93
Garfield, James, 16

Garner, Darrell, 174
Garner, Dorothy, 244
Garrison, Jim, 149, 155, 156, 317
Gaudreau, Richard, 287
Gavin, James, 410
Gawler, Joseph, 288
Gelber, Seymour, 467
Gentry, Curt, 8, 11, 43, 50, 62, 90
Gerstein, Richard, 467
Giancana, Sam Jr., 86
Giancana, Sam Sr., 11, 82, 84, 85, 92, 93, 193, 194, 258, 259
Gibbons, Harold, 90
Gibson, Donald, 78, 79, 80, 81, 426
Givens, Charles, 189, 190
Godfrey, Art, 305
Gold, Harry, 68
Goldberg, Alfred, 212
Goldberg, Arthur, 79
Goldman, Emma, 16, 22, 31, 37, 38, 455
Goldstein, Joe, 267, 268
Goldstrich, Jody, 231
Goldwater, Barry, xxii, 106, 366, 367, 400, 408, 419, 421, 435, 475
Goodwin, Doris Kearns, 370, 372, 426, 430, 431, 433
Goodwin, Richard, 214, 425, 426
Gouchenaur, James, 183, 309
Goulart, Joao, 426
Goulden, James, 157
Gracey, Lochart, 467, 468, 472
Grant, Eva, 207, 208, 267, 268
Greener, Charles, 170
Greer, William, 206, 208, 233, 234, 247, 307, 308
Gregory, Peter, 147, 175
Gregory, Thomas, 24, 29
Grewe, William, 377
Griffin, Burt, 161, 255, 260, 269, 270
Groden, Robert, 195
Gromyko, Andrei, 132
Groody, Paul, 171
Gruber, Alexander, 259, 260

Guerva, Che, 94
Gullion, Edmund, 358
Gunn, Jeremy, 286
Guthrie, Steve, 256, 257
Hagan, Joseph, 288, 297
Haggerty, Edward, 317
Haig, Alexander, 141
Halberstam, David, 382, 430, 411
Haldeman, H. R., 399, 456, 457,458
Hale, Swinburn, 330
Haley, J. Evetts, 444
Hall, Harry, 274, 275
Hall, Loran, 135, 136
Hambrick, Phillip, 144
Hanson, Ole, 26
Hardesty, Robert, 444
Harding, Warren, xviii, 41, 43, 44
Hargis, Bobby, 235, 236
Harkins, Paul, 381, 382, 383, 389, 406
Harkness, D. V., 252
Harriman, Averell, 379, 397
Harris, Louis, 421
Hartman, Edna, 197
Hartman, Wayne, 197
Harvey, William, 95, 461
Hawkins, Mrs. Peggy, 245
Helms, Richard, 95, 96, 140, 224, 399, 457
Henderson, Harvey, 308
Herring, George, 349, 352, 376, 418, 419, 421, 424, 433
Hersh, Seymour, 84, 87, 91, 92, 93, 388
Hester, Charles, 243
Hester, Mrs. Charles, 243
Hicks, James, 198
Hidell, Alex, 164, 165
Hill, Clint, 194, 232, 305, 306
Hill, Gerald, 165, 175
Hill, Jean, 185, 186, 210, 241, 242, 302
Hilsman, Roger, 358, 378, 397, 402, 418
Hinchcliffe, Margaret, 186, 230,

284
Hinckle, Warren, 96
Hiss, Alger, 66, 67
Hitler, Adolf, 356
Hochstein, Phillip, 73
Hodges, Luther, 80
Hoff, Irvin, 369
Hoffa, Jimmy, 11, 74, 79, 90, 214, 215, 257, 258, 259, 260, 310
Hogan, Frank, 463
Holland, Sam, 187, 238, 249, 250
Holtzoff, Alexander, 34
Hoover, Herbert, 46, 47, 49, 52
Hoover, J. Edgar, xvii, xviii, xix, xx, xxi, xxii, xxiv, xxv, 3, 4, 5, 6, 7, 8, 9, 10, 11,12, 13, 15, 16, 17, 18, 20, 21, 22, 23, 24, 25, 26, 27, 29, 30, 31, 32, 33, 34, 35, 36, 37, 38, 39, 41, 42, 43, 44, 45, 46, 47, 48, 49, 50, 51, 52, 53, 54, 55, 56, 57, 58, 59, 61, 62, 63, 64, 65, 66, 67, 68, 69, 70, 71, 72, 73, 74, 75, 76, 77, 78, 79, 81, 82, 85, 86, 87, 90, 92, 93, 100, 102, 103, 104, 105, 106, 127, 128, 130, 131, 132, 134, 135, 137, 141, 143, 148, 151, 154, 156, 158, 159, 160, 161, 162, 164, 169, 176, 177, 179, 183, 184, 189, 193, 197, 201, 206, 207, 208, 209, 211, 212, 213, 215, 216, 217, 218, 219, 220, 221, 222, 223, 224, 225, 226, 227, 228, 229, 232, 254, 262, 270, 275, 278, 280, 310, 311, 312, 313, 316, 320, 341, 345, 361, 370, 423, 426, 428, 436, 437, 438, 440, 447, 450, 451, 452, 453, 454, 455, 457, 458, 459, 460, 461, 464, 465, 469, 470, 471, 472, 473, 474, 475, 476, 477, 478
Hopkins, Harry, 56
Horne, Douglas, 285, 288
Horton, Mary, 363
Hosty, James, 105, 106, 141, 157, 160

Howard, Lisa, 100
Howard, Tom, 207, 208, 260, 261, 270
Howlett, J. J., 201
Hubert, Leon, 255, 260, 269
Hudkins, Lonnie, 157
Hudson, Emmit, 198, 240
Hughes, Charles Evans, 47
Hull, Cordell, 343
Humes, James, 181, 182, 202, 203, 206, 207, 281, 282, 283, 284, 286, 287, 292, 294, 295, 297, 298
Humphrey, Hubert, 181
Hundley, William, 106
Hunt, E. Howard, 272, 399, 456, 457
Hunt, H. L., 275
Hunt, Lamar, 275
Hunt, Nelson Bunker, 275
Hunter, Bill, 261
Hurt, Henry, 193, 290
Hutchinson, Earl, 475
Hutton, Patricia, 284, 285
Huyser, Robert, 386
Illig, Mr., 290
Ivon, Lou, 155, 156
Jacks, Hurchel, 235
Jackson, Gail Nix, 199
Jackson, Robert, 61
Jackson, Ronald, 288, 289
Jenkins, James, 246, 283, 289, 290, 294, 295
Jenkins, Marion, 230, 284, 289
Jenkins, Walter, 445
Johnson, Alexis, 378
Johnson, Ava, 361
Johnson, Blaney, 269
Johnson, Hiram, 25
Johnson, Joseph, 265
Johnson, Louis, 346, 347
Johnson, Lyndon, xviii, xx, xxi, xxii, xxiii, xxiv, xxv, 7, 62, 96, 97, 127, 128, 130, 131, 132, 133, 138, 140, 158, 162, 179, 181, 187, 206, 214, 215, 216, 217, 218, 219, 220, 221, 222, 223, 224, 225, 226, 228, 235,

238, 251, 278, 297, 298, 299, 300, 302, 309, 310, 320, 341, 342, 355, 358, 361, 362, 363, 364, 365, 366, 367, 369, 370, 371, 372, 373, 374, 375, 376, 377, 384, 394, 395, 400, 401, 402, 408, 409, 413, 414, 415, 416, 417, 418, 419, 420, 421, 422, 423, 424, 425, 426, 427, 429, 430, 431, 432, 433, 434, 435, 436, 437, 438, 439, 440, 441, 442, 443, 444, 445, 446, 447, 448, 449, 450, 451, 452, 453, 464, 470, 471, 475, 477
Johnson, Sam Early, 361
Johnson, Sam Houston, 361, 372, 414
Jones, Paul Roland, 256
Jones, Ronald, 230
Joyce, William, 136
Kantor, Seth, 165, 266, 267, 270, 274
Karel, Thomas, 11
Karnei, Robert, 292, 294, 297
Karnow, Stanley, 345, 376, 379, 417, 419, 421, 424, 432
Katzenbach, Nicholas, xxii, xxiv, 102, 106, 218, 219, 288
Kaufman, Richard, 366
Kaufman, William, 386
Kay, Everrett, 468, 469
Keating, Kenneth, 383
Kefauver, Estes, 74
Kellar, Oscar, 42
Keller, William, 10, 11
Kellerman, June, 85
Kellerman, Roy, 85, 232, 234, 235, 247, 303, 306, 309
Kelly, Kitty, 82
Kennan, George, 62, 404
Kennedy, Caroline, 261, 442
Kennedy, Jackie, 90, 233, 235, 261, 285, 292, 293, 294, 296, 306, 307, 309, 442
Kennedy, John, xviii, xxi, xxiii, xxiv, xxv, 11, 72, 73, 75, 76, 77, 78, 79, 80, 81, 82, 83, 84, 85, 86, 87, 88, 89, 90, 91, 92, 93,

94, 95, 96, 97, 98, 99, 101, 102,
103, 104, 105, 106, 107, 108,
109, 127, 128, 129, 130, 131,
132, 133, 135, 136, 137, 138,
140, 141, 143, 149, 155, 159,
160, 161, 166, 171, 172, 175,
176, 180, 182, 192, 193, 198,
200, 201, 202, 206, 207, 208,
209, 214, 215, 216, 220, 226,
228, 229, 230, 231, 233, 235,
246, 251, 253, 254, 255, 257,
258, 260, 264, 265, 266, 271,
272, 275, 276, 280, 281, 282,
283, 285, 286, 288, 289, 290,
291, 292, 295, 296, 297, 301,
305, 306, 307, 308, 309, 310,
313, 314, 315, 316, 318, 319,
341, 342, 343, 345, 352, 353,
355, 356, 357, 358, 359, 360,
361, 363, 365, 367, 369, 370,
371, 372, 373, 374, 375, 376,
377, 378, 379, 380, 381, 382,
383, 384, 385, 386, 387, 388,
389, 390, 391, 392, 393, 394,
395, 396, 397, 398, 399, 400,
401, 402, 403, 404, 405, 406,
407, 408, 409, 410, 411, 413,
414, 415, 416, 419, 425, 426,
430, 431, 433, 434, 435, 436,
437, 438, 439, 440, 441, 442,
443, 445, 446, 447, 450, 451,
459, 462, 463, 464, 465, 466,
467, 468, 469, 470, 471, 472,
473, 477
Kennedy, Joseph Jr., 355, 356,
359
Kennedy, Joseph Sr., 73, 74,
355, 356, 363, 369, 374
Kennedy, Robert, 73, 74, 75, 80,
81, 83, 85, 86, 87, 90, 91, 96,
98, 100, 103, 104, 105, 106,
107, 129, 132, 155, 214, 215,
218, 222, 228, 259, 288, 292,
293, 294, 295, 296, 299, 300,
310, 357, 369, 371, 372, 384,
394, 395, 400, 410, 430, 431,
438, 441, 443, 444, 445, 447,
454, 455, 466

Kenney, Edward, 294
Kessler, Ron, 217
Khanh, General, 417
Khrushchev, Nikita, xxii, 89,
129, 130, 137, 140, 218, 223,
377, 378, 385
Khrushchev, Sergi, 385
Kilduff, Malcolm, 230
Kilgallen, Dorothy, 261, 262, 278
Killiam, Hank, 263
Killiam, Wanda, 263
King, J. C., 94
King, Martin Luther Jr., 74, 101,
102, 103, 104, 423, 424, 428,
454, 455, 475
Kingsley, M. S., 8
Kinney, Sam, 233, 234, 247, 291,
304, 305, 306
Kissinger, Henry, 402
Kivett, Jerry, 85
Kleberg, Richard, 361
Kling, S. G., 4
Knight, Francis, 135
Knudson, Gloria, 283
Knudson, Robert Jr., 286
Knudson, Robert Sr., 282, 283,
285, 286,
Koethe, Jim, 261
Kornbluh, Peter, 94
Korth, Fred, 442
Kostikov, Valery, 127, 131, 141
Kounas, Delores, 243
Kraft, Joseph, 428
Krock, Arthur, 380, 393
Krulak, Victor, 405
Kuntsler, W. M., 6
La Fontaine, Mary, 273
La Fontaine, Ray, 273
La Guardia, Fiorello, 48
LaFollette, Robert, 42, 44
Lair, Bill, 352
Landis, Paul, 233
Lane, Mark, 162, 163, 167, 172,
174, 185, 212, 239, 249, 251,
269, 448
Lansdale, Edward, 348, 378, 394
Lansing, Robert, 346
Lansky, Jake, 259

Lansky, Meyer, 49, 51, 86, 273
Lash, Joseph, 394
Latona, Sebastian, 171
Law, Bill, 295
Lawrence, P. W., 301
Lawson, Winston, 247, 301, 306
Lawton, Don, 304
Leavelle, Jim, 144, 175
Leche, Richard, 50
Lechuga, Carlos, 99, 100
Ledbetter, Layton, 287
LeMay, Curtis, 384, 387, 418
Lemnitzer, Lyman, 374, 378
Lenin, Nicholai, 26, 27
Lepke, Louis, 49
Levine, Jack, 6
Levison, Stanley, 104
Lewis, Anthony, 106, 107
Lewis, Ron, 154
Liddy, Gordon, xviii, 56
Liebler, Wesley, 175, 241
Lifton, David, 204, 231, 245, 289,
    290
Lilley, Robert, 305
Lincoln, Evelyn, 443, 444
Linsey, Joe, 50
Lippmann, Walter, 390
Livingstone, Harrison, 200, 282,
    284, 289, 292, 294
Lodge, Henry Cabot, 389, 393,
    395, 396, 397, 398, 406, 414,
    417, 420
Long, Russell, 314
Loomis, Mr., 139
Lopez, Edwin, 138
Lorenz, Marita, 272, 273, 465
Losev, Sergei, 133
Lovelady, Billy, 244
Lowenthal, Max, xix, 4, 5, 8
Luce, Henry, 374
Luhring, Oscar, 48
Lundhal, Arthur, 383, 384
Mabra, W. W., 236
MacArthur, Douglas, 52, 68, 151,
    348, 411
Machiavelli, Niccolo, xxv
MacNeil, Robert, 200, 314, 439
Maggadino, Peter, 83, 84

Maggadino, Stefano, 84
Maguire, Andrew, 12
Mamantov, Ilya, 175
Manchester, William, 218, 288,
    300, 305, 308, 441, 442, 446,
    447
Mandell, Paul, 209
Mann, James, 20
Mann, Thomas, 133, 224, 427
Mansfield, Mike, 371, 390, 391,
    392, 393, 400, 409, 410, 414,
    417, 418
Marcello, Carlos, 144, 155, 214,
    258, 472
Markham, Helen, 175
Marrs, Jim, 196, 199
Marshall, Burke, 103, 104
Marshall, George, 344
Marshall, Henry, 445
Marslowe, Anthony, 463
Martello, Francis, 176
Martin, B. J., 235, 238, 302
Martin, Frank, 261
Martin, John Bartlow, 86, 394,
    395
Martineau, Maurice, 307, 464
Martinez, Paulino, 462
Martino, John, 11
Marx, Karl, 27
Mashek, John, 139
Mason, Alpheus, 43
Mathews, R. D., 273
Mattox, Al, 197
Mauro, Tony, 317
Mayfield, Douglas, 287
McCarthy, Joe, 64, 68, 69, 74,
    214, 215, 357, 364, 392
McCarthy, Roger, 318
McClain, H. B., 237
McClelland, Robert, 200, 230,
    231, 253, 284, 289, 449
McCloy, John, 158, 159, 205,
    226, 227, 458
McCone, John, 95, 96, 138, 224,
    383, 414, 416
McCormack, John, 442
McCurley, A. D., 236
McDonald, Betty, 174, 263

McGarr, Lionel, 381
McHugh, Godfrey, 288, 296, 299, 300, 303, 304
McIntire, Tim, 85
McKenzie, William, 167
McKeown, Robert, 269
McKinley, William, 17
McKinney, Stewart, 260
McKinnon, Cheryl, 240, 246, 319
McLane, Alfred, 274
McLean, Evalyn, 46
McLean, Ned, 45
McManus, George, 95
McMillan, Harold, 373, 374
McNamara, Robert, xxiii, 77, 296, 345, 374, 378, 380, 383, 387, 393, 398, 401, 403, 406, 407, 408, 413, 414, 415, 417, 418, 422, 432, 435, 446, 451
McNeil, Marshall, 362
McVickar, John, 145, 146
McWillie, Lewis, 273
Meagher, Sylvia, 128, 165, 175, 279, 458
Means, Gaston, 44, 45, 46
Mecklin, John, 382
Mendenhall, Joseph, 352, 404,
Messick, Hank, 7, 8, 49, 50, 476, 477
Metzler, James, 245
Meyer, Cord, 88, 89
Meyer, Mary, 88, 89
Mikoyan, Anastas, 128, 130
Milam, Wallace, 284
Milan, Michael, 51, 462, 463
Miller, Austin, 198, 239
Miller, Dale, 425
Miller, Herbert, 262
Miller, Murray, 257, 258
Millican, A. J., 194, 196, 197, 267
Milteer, Joseph, 220, 221, 468, 469, 470, 471
Minh, Ho Chi, 343, 344, 345, 346, 349, 350, 351, 429, 430
Mitchell, John, xix
Mitrokhin, Vasily, 138
Mohr, John, xviii, 12

Moldea, Dan, 74, 75, 82, 83, 87
Molina, Joe, 245
Monroe, Marilyn, 90, 91, 92
Mooney, Luke, 236
Moore, Bobby Gene, 259
Moore, Elmer, 183, 201, 276, 309, 310
Moore, Ted, 352
Moorman, Mary, 209, 210, 242
Morrison, Samuel E., 41
Morrow, Robert, 444, 445
Morse, Wayne, 390, 391, 406, 414
Mosely Thomas, 464, 465
Most, Johann, 16
Moyers, Bill, 219, 424, 426
Moynihan, Daniel, 181, 310
Mueller, Otto, 23
Muma, Richard, 288
Murchison, Clint, 5, 51, 62, 70, 78, 79, 275, 442
Murphy, Frank, 61, 65
Murphy, George, 56
Murphy, Thomas, 239
Murray, George, 191
Murret, Lillian, 175
Murret, Marilyn, 176
Mussolini, Benito, 151
Nagell, Richard, 220, 472
Nanovic, John, 4
Nash, Robert, 42
Nehru, Jawaharlal, 357
Nelson, Anna, 136
Nelson, Doris, 285
Newman, Gayle, 184
Newman, Larry, 85
Newman, William, 184, 239, 240
Nhu, Madame, 389
Nhu, Ngo Dinh 351, 352, 379, 382, 389, 394, 395, 396, 397, 398, 399, 404
Nichols, Louis, 50
Nicolletti, Charles, 11
Nitze, Paul, 402
Nix, Orrville, 199, 208, 212
Nixon, Richard, xviii, xix, xx, xxi, 64, 66, 67, 72, 73, 93, 128, 129, 130, 319, 356, 360, 364,

399, 402, 437, 442, 453, 455,
456, 457, 458
Nizer, Louis, 226, 227
Nolting, Fredrick, 375, 382, 389,
395
Noonan, Joseph, 463
Norman, Harold, 190, 192
Norris, George, 55
North, Mark, 11, 226
Nosenko, Yuri, 132
Novak, Robert, 366
O'Brien, Larry, 357, 370, 400
O'Brien, Michael, 84
O'Conner, Paul, 246, 283, 287,
291, 292
O'Donnell, Joe, 282
O'Donnell, Kenneth, 82, 104,
181, 184, 185, 296, 299, 305,
308, 309, 372, 392, 400, 409,
410, 445
O'Neil, Francis, 206, 287, 293,
294
O'Neil, Tip, 185, 369, 400
Oakes, J. B., 6
Oakes, Mark, 447
Odio, Sylvia, 135, 136
Ofstein, Dennis, 150, 151
Oliver, Beverly, 211, 265
Oliver, Revilo, 100, 101, 140
Ollestad, Norman, 7, 8
Olsen, Gregory, 410
Oppenheimer, Robert, 65
Osborne, David, 204
Osner, Alvin, 295
Ostrow, Ronald, 447
Oswald, Lee, xxi, xxii, xxv, 127,
128, 130, 131, 133, 134, 135,
136, 137, 138, 139, 140, 141,
143, 144, 145, 146, 147, 148,
149, 150, 151, 152, 153, 154,
155, 156, 157, 158, 159, 160,
161, 162, 163, 164, 165, 166,
167, 168, 169, 170, 171, 172,
173, 174, 175, 176, 177, 181,
183, 187, 189, 190, 191, 192,
201, 202, 204, 207, 210, 215,
216, 219, 221, 224, 225, 231,
239, 247, 252, 254, 255, 256,

259, 260, 261, 262, 263, 264,
265, 266, 270, 272, 278, 279,
311, 312, 313, 314, 315, 317,
318, 448, 449, 450, 451
Oswald, Marguerite, 130, 148,
149, 159, 161, 162, 186
Oswald, Marina, 148, 165, 167,
168, 175, 300
Oswald, Robert, 145, 175, 459
Otepka, Otto, 135
Paine, Michael, 175
Paine, Ruth, 165
Palamara, Vincent, 85, 180, 247,
284, 288, 291, 297, 300, 302,
303, 305, 306, 308, 464
Palmer, Mitchell, 26, 27, 29, 30,
31, 33, 35, 36, 37, 48, 66
Paolella, Joseph, 85
Parr, George, 364
Partin, Edward, 214, 215
Patrick, Lenny, 259
Pawley, Bill, 449
Pearson, Drew, 416, 461
Pearson, Lester, 388, 420
Pepper, William, 473
Perry, Malcolm, 182, 183, 200,
201, 230, 285, 289
Peters, Paul, 230, 285
Petruisenko, Vitaly, 133
Phao, General, 352
Philbrick, Herbert, 66
Phillips, Cabell, 4
Phillips, David, 151, 152
Phillips, Rufus, 394
Phoenix, George, 211
Pic, John, 144
Piper, Eddie, 192
Pitzer, Mrs. William, 297
Pitzer, William, 297, 298
Piziali, Robert, 318
Posner, Gerald, 205, 239, 316,
318
Post, Louis, 32
Powell, Lee Riley, 427, 432
Powell, Nancy, 187
Power, General Thomas, 130,
386, 387, 418
Power, Thomas, 91

Powers, Dave, 89, 105, 184, 185, 305, 308, 309
Powers, Gary, 145
Powers, Richard, 8, 10, 11, 54, 72, 423, 477
Preis, Engelbert, 32
Price, J. C., 249
Radford, Arthur, 348
Raikan, Spas, 151
Rajagopalachari, Mr., 139
Rankin, J. Lee, 150, 153, 157, 158, 159, 206, 207, 211, 227, 255, 262, 312, 472
Rather, Dan, 209, 219
Ray, James Earl, 454
Rayburn, Sam, 70, 369
Ready, John, 308
Reagen, Ronald, 65, 133
Rebentisch, Donald, 288
Reed, Edward, 246
Reedy, George, 369, 446, 453
Reeves, Thomas, 87, 388
Reichmann, Deb, 281, 282
Reid, Mrs. Robert, 245
Reiland, Ron, 211
Reily, Frank, 239
Reno, Janet, 475
Revill, Jack, 160
Reynolds, Warren, 174
Rich, Nancy Perrin, 268
Richardson, Sid, 62, 70
Richetti, Adam, 54
Richey, Lawrence, 22, 46, 47, 49
Ridgway, Matthew, 349
Riebe, Floyd, 283, 287
Rike, Aubrey, 193, 287
Roberts, Delphine, 154, 156
Roberts, Earlene, 172
Roberts, Emory, 308, 309
Roberts, Ray, 238
Robinson, Marvin, 172
Robinson, Thomas, 246, 284, 286, 289
Rocca, Ray, 133, 134, 224
Rockefeller, David, 79
Rockefeller, Nelson, 465
Rolland, Chuck, 155
Romack, James, 252

Rooney, John, 476
Roosevelt, Eleanor, 56
Roosevelt, Franklin, xviii, 52, 53, 54, 56, 57, 58, 59, 61, 63, 343, 355, 362, 375
Roosevelt, Theodore, 17, 18, 19
Rose, Earl, 180
Roselli, John, 11, 82, 193, 194, 258
Rosenberg, Ethel, 68
Rosenberg, Julius, 68
Rosentiel, Lewis, 50, 51
Rostow, Walt, 378, 379, 380, 384, 398, 414, 418, 419, 422, 432
Rowan, Carl, 382
Rowland, Arnold, 188, 189
Rowley, James, 306
Rowney, Edward, 389
Ruby, Earl, 208
Ruby, Jack, 139, 167, 174, 187, 207, 225, 254, 255, 256, 257, 258, 259, 260, 261, 262, 263, 264, 265, 266, 267, 268, 270, 271, 272, 273, 274, 275, 276, 277, 278, 279, 280, 311, 444, 465, 468
Rusk, Dean, xxv, 96, 97, 104, 378, 382, 385, 389, 391, 395, 409, 410, 414, 418, 432
Rusk, Richard, 104
Russell, Dick, 220, 466
Russell, Richard, 158, 206, 215, 217, 222, 223, 224, 226, 227, 314, 365, 384,
Rybka, Henry, 308, 309
Ryder, Dial, 170
Safire, William, 85
Salas, Louis, 364
Sallinger, Pierre, 303, 382, 386, 395
Salyer, Kenneth, 284
Sanders, "Barefoot," 131
Sapp,.C. H., 467, 468
Sarris, Louis, 401
Sawyer, Herbert, 190
Scheim, David, 457
Schenck, Charles, 26
Schiff, Dorothy, 394

Schine, David, 69, 74
Schine, Meyer, 51, 69, 78
Schlesinger, Arthur Jr., 68, 81, 87, 97, 102, 107, 108, 299, 371, 386, 394, 405, 408, 425, 438, 441
Schorr, Daniel, 313
Schorr, David, 94, 96
Schwartz, Harry, 6
Schwartz, R. W., 7
Schwartz, Ted, 273
Schweiker, Richard, xxi, 152
Scott, Peter Dale, 50, 162, 442
Scott, Winston, 462
Shaneyfelt, Lyndal, 205
Shanklin, Gordon, 160, 161
Sharp, Grant, 377, 397, 418, 422
Shaw, Clay, 149, 150, 295, 317
Shaw, Robert, 202
Sheehan, Daniel, 382
Shelley, William, 192, 245
Shepard, Tazwell, 224
Sherley, J. Swager, 19
Sherman, Tony, 85
Shesol, Jeff, 96, 408, 447
Shorr, Isaac, 31
Shoup, David, 374
Sibert, James, 186, 233, 284, 293, 294
Sidey, Hugh, 88, 426
Siegel, Bugsy, 259
Similas, Norman, 211
Simmons, James L. 184, 239, 249, 250
Simmons, Ronald, 170
Sinatra, Frank, 86, 87
Sinclair, Harry, 45
Sitzman, Marilyn, 244
Skelton, Royce, 198
Slawson, David, xx, 227, 465
Sloan, Bill, 185
Smith, Earl, 93
Smith, Edgar, 243
Smith, Jess, 45, 46
Smith, Joe Marshall, 237, 238, 247, 248
Smith, L. C., 236
Smith, Mrs. Earl, 278

Smith, Sergio Archacha, 155, 272
Smith, Walter, 18
Smithwick, Sam, 364
Snyder, Jim, 295
Snyder, Richard, 146, 148
Sokolsky, George, 460
Sommerset, Willie, 467
Sorensen, Ted, 97, 102, 384, 386, 398, 410, 411
Sorrels, Forrest, 187, 199, 232
Spagnoli, Joseph, 307
Speaker, Sandy, 196, 197
Specter, Arlen, 182, 185, 186, 202, 206, 217, 242, 306
Spencer, Saundra, 282, 285
Stalin, Joseph, 6, 45, 62, 70
Standridge, Ruth, 451
Stanford, Neal, 5
Stembridge, Vernon, 181
Stevenson, Adlai, 427
Stevenson, Archibald, 48
Stevenson, Coke, 363, 364, 365
Stewart, David, 231, 289
Stewart, Robert W., 45
Stewart, Sidney, 181
Stokes, Louis, 152, 195, 196
Stone, Harlan, 46, 47
Stone, Oliver, 315
Stone, U. S. Attorney, 31
Storey, Charles, 23
Stormer, John, 473
Stoughton, Cecil, 305
Stover, John, 288, 298
Stringer, John, 282, 283, 286, 291
Sullivan, William, xxii, 5, 9, 12, 53, 56, 61, 63, 68, 70, 73, 74, 90, 103, 105, 160, 215, 426, 427, 429, 437, 438, 458, 462
Summers, Anthony, 8, 12, 51, 56, 156, 206
Summers, Malcolm, 252
Surine, Donald, 69
Sweatt, Alan, 157, 210
Szulc, Tad, 96, 426
Taft, William H., 19
Tague, James, 197, 241

Taylor, Gary, 147
Taylor, Maxwell, 379, 380, 381, 383, 393, 396, 398, 401, 416, 420
Theoharis, Athan, 8, 10, 11, 46, 86, 90, 427
Thomas, Helen, 88
Thompson, Josiah, xxiv, 239, 249
Thornberry, Homer, 220
Thuan, Nguyen Dinh, 379
Thurman, Reagen, 265
Tice, Wilma, 267
Tippit, J. D., 172, 173, 174, 184, 252, 268
Tito, Marshall, 357
Todd, Jack, 273
Tolson, Clyde, 45, 78, 105, 143, 476
Tomlinson, Darrell, 203
Tonahill, Joe, 260, 262
Traficante, Santos, 258, 273
Trammel, Connie, 275
Trapnell, Garrett, 466, 474
Trohan, Walter, 4
Trotsky, Leon, 27
Truitt, James, 89
Trujillo, Rafael, 395
Truly, Roy, 168, 169, 234, 245
Truman, Harry, xviii, 61, 62, 63, 64, 65, 67, 304, 341, 344, 345, 346, 347, 353, 356, 365
Tse-tung, Mao, 345
Tucker, Ray, 53
Tunheim, John, 309
Turner, William, 7, 8, 96, 462, 474
Twyman, Noel, 224
Underhill, Gary, 473, 474
Underwood, Martin, 84, 85, 307
Unger, Robert, 12, 13, 54
Unger, Sanford, 20
Valenti, Jack, 96, 441
Van Deman, Ralph H., 43
Van Don, Tran, 343, 398
Van Thinh, Nguyen, 344
Vanderwall, Jim, 71
Vaughn, Harry, 64
Veciana, Antonio, 151, 152

Voebel, Edward, 144
Volkogonov, Dmitri, 67
Voorhees, Theodore, 161
Wade, Henry, 164, 247, 261, 448
Wade, Horace, 387
Walker, Edwin, 77, 273, 275, 276, 277, 386, 468
Wall, Breck, 265
Wallace, George, 102
Wallace, Henry, 56
Wallace, Malcolm, 445
Walle, Marilyn, 263
Walsh, Thomas, 35, 36, 52
Walthers, Buddy, 197
Warner, Roger, 187, 263, 264
Warren, Charles, 23
Warren, Earl, xxi, 159, 167, 205, 217, 218, 224, 226, 274, 276, 277, 278, 312, 314, 441
Washington, George, 375
Watson, Marvin, 162
Weatherford, Harry, 236
Webb, Del, 51
Wechsler, James, 394
Wehle, Philip, 246, 287
Weiner, Irwin, 258
Weisberg, Harold, 211, 296
Weisburg, Willie, 83
Weiss, Mark, 195
Weiss, Seymour, 50
Weiss, Victor, 271
Weitzman, Seymour, 163, 236, 248
West, Bob, 199
Westmoreland, William, 424, 430
Weston, Dr., 292, 293
Wheeler, Burton, 24, 44, 45, 53
Wheeler, Earle, 374
White, Geneva, 167
White, Harry Dexter, 63
White, Pete, 167
White, Roscoe, 167
White, Theodore, 356
Whitehead, Don, 5
Wicker, Tom, 314, 434, 435
Wicker-Sham, George, 20
Williams, Bonnie Ray, 189, 190

Williams, David, 42
Williams, Edward Bennett, 214
Williams, Enrique, 98
Williams, Phillip, 450, 451
Williams, Sam, 352
Willie, Donna, 230
Willis, Gary, 92
Willis, Marilyn, 241
Willis, Phil, 241
Willoughby, Charles, 151, 348, 466
Wilmon, Jim, 240
Wilson, Charles, 348
Wilson, Steven, 185, 244
Wilson, Vyla, 45
Wilson, William, 30, 32, 38, 39
Wilson, Woodrow, xviii, 21, 22, 23, 24, 41
Winborn, Walter, 241
Winchell, Walter, 50, 461
Winter-Berger, Robert, 442
Wiseman, John, 209, 210
Wofford, Harris, 423
Woodard, James, 269
Woodward, Mary, 199, 241
Wright, Frank, 173
Wright, Milton, 302
Wright, O. P., 204
Wright, Scott, 10
Wynne,Bedford, 78
Yaras, Dave, 11, 259
Yarborough, Ralph, 187, 238, 251, 447
Youngblood, Rufus, 238
Zapruder, Abraham, 208, 209, 211, 243, 244
Ziegler, Ron, 399
Zoppi, Tony, 266, 267
Zorin, Valentin, 439